Frommer's

NXV

S0-BZP-558

Denmark

4th Edition

by Darwin Porter & Danforth Prince

Here's what the critics say about Frommer's:

"Amazingly easy to use. Very portable, very complete."

—*Booklist*

"Detailed, accurate, and easy-to-read information for all price ranges."
—*Glamour Magazine*

"Hotel information is close to encyclopedic."

—*Des Moines Sunday Register*

"Frommer's Guides have a way of giving you a real feel for a place."
—*Knight Ridder Newspapers*

WILEY

Wiley Publishing, Inc.

About the Authors

As a team of veteran travel writers, **Darwin Porter** and **Danforth Prince** have produced numerous titles for Frommer's, including best-selling guides to Italy, France, the Caribbean, England, and Germany. Porter, a former bureau chief of *The Miami Herald*, is also a Hollywood biographer, his most recent releases entitled *Katharine the Great*, the latter a close-up of the private life of the late Katharine Hepburn, and *Howard Hughes: Hell's Angel*. Prince was formerly employed by the Paris bureau of the *New York Times*, and is today the president of Blood Moon Productions and other media-related firms.

Published by:

Wiley Publishing, Inc.

111 River St.
Hoboken, NJ 07030-5774

ISBN-13: 978-0-7645-7824-3
ISBN-10: 0-7645-7824-3

Editor: Kathleen Warnock
Production Editor: Ian Skinnari
Cartographer: Nicholas Trotter
Photo Editor: Richard Fox
Production by Wiley Indianapolis Composition Services

Front cover photo: Copenhagen, Nyhavn: View from a boat
Back cover photo: Egeskov Castle in Kværndrup

For information on our other products and services or to obtain technical support, please contact our Customer Care Department within the U.S. at 800/762-2974, outside the U.S. at 317/572-3993 or fax 317/572-4002.

Wiley also publishes its books in a variety of electronic formats. Some content that appears in print may not be available in electronic formats.

Manufactured in the United States of America

5   4   3   2   1

Contents

List of Maps

An Invitation to the Reader

In researching this book, we discovered many wonderful places—hotels, restaurants, shops, and more. We're sure you'll find others. Please tell us about them, so we can share the information with your fellow travelers in upcoming editions. If you were disappointed with a recommendation, we'd love to know that, too. Please write to:

Frommer's Denmark, 4th Edition
Wiley Publishing, Inc.• 111 River St. • Hoboken, NJ 07030-5774

An Additional Note

Please be advised that travel information is subject to change at any time—and this is especially true of prices. We therefore suggest that you write or call ahead for confirmation when making your travel plans. The authors, editors, and publisher cannot be held responsible for the experiences of readers while traveling. Your safety is important to us, however, so we encourage you to stay alert and be aware of your surroundings. Keep a close eye on cameras, purses, and wallets, all favorite targets of thieves and pickpockets.

Frommer's Star Ratings, Icons & Abbreviations

Every hotel, restaurant, and attraction listing in this guide has been ranked for quality, value, service, amenities, and special features using a **star-rating system.** In country, state, and regional guides, we also rate towns and regions to help you narrow down your choices and budget your time accordingly. Hotels and restaurants are rated on a scale of zero (recommended) to three stars (exceptional). Attractions, shopping, nightlife, towns, and regions are rated according to the following scale: zero stars (recommended), one star (highly recommended), two stars (very highly recommended), and three stars (must-see).

In addition to the star-rating system, we also use **seven feature icons** that point you to the great deals, in-the-know advice, and unique experiences that separate travelers from tourists. Throughout the book, look for:

Finds	Special finds—those places only insiders know about
Fun Fact	Fun facts—details that make travelers more informed and their trips more fun
Kids	Best bets for kids and advice for the whole family
Moments	Special moments—those experiences that memories are made of
Overrated	Places or experiences not worth your time or money
Tips	Insider tips—great ways to save time and money
Value	Great values—where to get the best deals

The following **abbreviations** are used for credit cards:

AE	American Express	DISC	Discover	V	Visa
DC	Diners Club	MC	MasterCard		

Frommers.com

Now that you have the guidebook to a great trip, visit our website at **www.frommers.com** for travel information on more than 3,000 destinations. With features updated regularly, we give you instant access to the most current trip-planning information available. At Frommers.com, you'll also find the best prices on airfares, accommodations, and car rentals—and you can even book travel online through our travel booking partners. At Frommers.com, you'll also find the following:

- Online updates to our most popular guidebooks
- Vacation sweepstakes and contest giveaways
- Newsletter highlighting the hottest travel trends
- Online travel message boards with featured travel discussions

What's New in Denmark

Many of the old towns and villages remain relatively the same year after year, but we've noted some updates and changes below. Of course, in cosmopolitan Copenhagen the pulse always beats faster, so there's lots to report. Here are some of the newest developments in various categories.

The biggest cultural news in all Scandinavia in 2004 was the opening of the **Copenhagen Opera House** at Ekuipagemesteruej 10 (℃ **33-69-69-33**). A private foundation donated $441 million to create this dramatic, modern, 1,700-seat house, which immediately became the new home of the Royal Danish Opera. Verdi's *Aida* opened the season. See p 122.

COPENHAGEN Accommodations The big news in '04 was the opening of **Hotel Skt. Petri** (℃ **33-45-91-00;** p. 59), a converted department store that's been reincarnated as a hotel. Today, it's one of Copenhagen's grandest, with a stunning design of Danish modern (of course). Musicians, artists, and designers flock here, and its bar is one of the most fashionable in the city.

Another addition to the hotel scene is **DGI-byen's Hotel** (℃ **33-29-80-00;** p. 66), behind the main train station in the center of town. It's Valhalla for the sports lover, with a bowling alley, swim center, spa, and even a climbing wall.

Dining A host of new challengers has risen to give competition to old favorites on Copenhagen's hectic restaurant scene. Among these is the French restaurant, **Le Sommelier** (℃ **33-11-45-15;** p. 75), which evokes a Left Bank bistro. Winner of several culinary awards, it boasts one of Copenhagen's finest wine cellars.

Café Ketchup (℃ **33-32-30-30;** p. 81) (don't you just love the name?) is not only one of the coolest bars in town but serves a savory international cuisine to a beautiful crowd of people, including many models. If you're into Cosmopolitans and that minty rum drink, *mojitos,* this bar serves the best ones in town. Any place that features mango salsa and artichoke salads is after our culinary heart.

Fashionable and trendy, **Sult** (℃ **33-74-34-17;** p. 82) is in the Danish Film Institute. Its menu offers a combination of fusion and Southern European cuisine, which it does exceedingly well. Market-fresh ingredients are used to create innovative, engaging dishes.

No longer the most famous brothel in Copenhagen, **TyvenKokkenHans Koneog-HendesElsker** (℃ **33-16-12-92;** p. 83) has blossomed into an international restaurant in a restored 18th-century town house in the center of Copenhagen. The chefs are inspired, and their "Lobstermenu" with champagne is the most divine in town. You can invite the Queen or at least the new Crown Princess.

The Paul (℃ **33-75-07-75;** p. 89) has emerged as the finest dining choice in the Tivoli Gardens. Chef Paul Cunningham is a media darling, bringing innovative, exciting ideas to his cuisine. Every winter when the gardens close, he travels the world looking for more inspiration.

In the district of Frederiksberg in western Copenhagen, **Formel B.** (✆ **33-25-10-66;** p. 89) attracts serious foodies. Ultrastylish, it's a Danish/French marriage of cuisines that, in the words of its chef, "speaks to all the senses."

Attractions The big addition at the **Tivoli Gardens** (p. 93) for 2004 was "The Demon," the biggest roller coaster in Denmark. Passengers whiz through a trio of loops, reaching a top speed of 80kmph (50 mph).

Funky and eclectic, the Copenhagen district of **Vesterbro** is attracting the Danish version of young people who flock to New York's Williamsburg for entertainment and dining. Its main street, Istedgade, is now the center of late-night action in cafes and bars. The district is filled with ethnic restaurants, especially around its main square, Halmtorvet. See p. 54.

After Dark Currently, one of the most fashionable places to be in Copenhagen around midnight is **Cavi** (✆ **33-11-20-20;** p. 122), where the city's best DJs entertain you with R & B, funk, soul, or hip-hop music. In summer, the big panoramic roof terrace here is the place to be if you're young and gorgeous.

BORNHOLM In the town of Nexø, on the Danish holiday island of Bornholm, east of Copenhagen, **Tre Søstre** (✆ **56-49-33-93;** p. 212) has been installed at the harborfront in a former storage warehouse. "The Three Sisters" (its English name) serves one of the island's finest seafood cuisines, with plenty of other well-crafted Danish specialties. Expect an appropriate nautical decor as you feast on "fruits of the sea."

HELSINGØR In the city where Shakespeare's *Hamlet* lived and died,

the **Danmarks Tekniske Museet** (✆ **49-22-26-11;** p. 145) has moved into better headquarters and has improved its exhibits considerably. Among its offerings is a large collection of everything from steam engines to airplanes, the latter ranging from gyrocopters to helicopters, even a complete Caravella airplane.

KOLDING The city of Kolding, in South Jutland, appeared in the headlines around the world and on TV on November 4, 2004. A mammoth explosion occurred in a fireworks factory, damaging 350 buildings. Actually, the blast occurred in the residential suburb of Seest, 3 kilometers (1.9 miles) from the historic core of Kolding. Kolding's attractions, including hotels and restaurants, were not affected by the blast. See p. 261.

KØGE Accommodations Better known in the Middle Ages than it is today, the city of Køge lies only 40km (25 miles) south of Copenhagen. Like the rest of South Zealand, it's been sleepy post-Millennium. However, its best hotel, **Best Western Hotel Niels Juel** (Køge; ✆ **56-63-18-00**), has redecorated both its public and private rooms in a Feng Shui style. See p. 171.

NYBORG After crossing the bridge from Zealand, the island on which Copenhagen sits, you land on the island of Funen, Denmark's second largest island. To celebrate your arrival, we recommend **Central Cafeen** (✆ **65-31-01-83**), a new restaurant in an 18th-century house. Four dining rooms await, serving modern Danish cuisine, with fixed-price menus of two or three courses. The "cafe" is actually a full-fledged restaurant, and a lovely introduction the charms of Funen. See p. 223.

The Best of Denmark

Denmark presents visitors with everything from a world-class city in Copenhagen to historic castles, wind-swept offshore islands, quaint villages, and more. To help you decide how best to spend your time in Denmark, we compiled a list of our favorite experiences and discoveries. In the following pages you'll find the kind of candid advice we'd give our close friends.

1 The Best Danish Experiences

- **A Day (and Night) at Tivoli Gardens:** These 150-year-old pleasure gardens are almost worth the trip to Copenhagen by themselves. They offer a little bit of everything: open-air dancing, restaurants, theaters, concert halls, an amusement park . . . and, oh yes, gardens. From the first bloom of spring until the autumn leaves start to fall (*note:* Tivoli's closed in the winter!), they're devoted to lighthearted fun. The gardens are worth a visit any time but are especially pleasant at twilight when the lights begin to glint among the trees. See p. 93.

- **A Week Down on the Farm:** The best way to see the heart of Denmark and meet the Danes is to spend a week on one of their farms. Nearly 400 farms, all over the country, take in paying guests. Stick a pin anywhere on a map of Denmark away from the cities and seacoast, and you'll find a thatched and timbered farm, or perhaps a more modern homestead. Almost anyplace makes a good base from which to explore the rest of the country on day trips. You join the host family and other guests for meals. You can learn about the farm, and help

with the chores if you like. Activities range from bonfires and folk dancing to riding lessons or horse-and-buggy rides. Although there's no official agency to arrange such holidays, many visitors seeking this kind of accommodation surf the Internet for farms that advertise their willingness to receive guests. Another way to hook up is to decide what part of Denmark you'd like to visit, then contact the tourist office for a list of farms willing to accept paying guests.

- **On the Trail of the Vikings:** Renowned for centuries of fantastic exploits, the Vikings explored Greenland to the north, North America to the west, and the Caspian Sea to the south and east from roughly A.D. 750 to 1050 Their legacy lives on in Denmark. Relive the age of Vikings at the **Nationalmuseet** in Copenhagen, which displays burial grounds of the Viking period, along with the largest and richest hoards of treasure, including relics from the "Silver Age." Even Viking costumes are exhibited. See p. 102. At Roskilde, explore the **Viking Ship Museum,** containing five vessels found in a fjord nearby, the largest of which was built in Ireland around 1060 and manned by 60 to 100 warriors. See p. 159. If you're in Ribe, check out the **Museum of the Viking Age,** where a multimedia room, "Odin's Eye," introduces the visitor to the world of the Vikings through a vivid sound and vision experience. See p. 281. And, at Jelling, see two **enormous mounds** (the largest in Denmark), one of which was the burial ground of King Gorm. See "Jelling," in chapter 10.

- **In the Footsteps of H. C. Andersen:** To some visitors, this storyteller is the symbol of Denmark itself. The fairy tale lives on in Odense, on the island of Funen, where Andersen was born the son of a shoemaker in 1805. His childhood home, a small half-timbered house on Munkemøllestraede, where he lived from 1807 to 1817, has been turned into a museum. You can also visit **H. C. Andersen's Hus,** where much of his memorabilia is stored (including his walking stick and top hat), and take a few moments to listen to his tales on tape. But mostly

you can wander the cobblestone streets that he knew, marveling at the life of this man—and his works—that, in the words of his obituary, struck "chords that reverberated in every human heart," as they still do today. See "Odense: Birthplace of Hans Christian Andersen," in chapter 8.

- **Cycling Around Ærø:** Regardless of how busy our schedule, we always like to devote at least one sunny day to what we view as the greatest cycling trip in Denmark: a slow, scenic ride around the island of Ærø, lying off the coast of Funen. Relatively flat, its countryside dotted with windmills, the island evokes the fields of Holland, but is unique unto itself. Country roads will take you across fertile fields and into villages of cobbled streets and half-timbered houses. This is small-town Denmark at its best. Yes, you'll even pass a whistling postman in red jacket and gold-and-black cap looking like an extra in one of those Technicolor MGM movies from the '40s.

2 The Best Hotels

- **Phoenix Copenhagen** (Copenhagen; © **33-95-95-00**): The Danish Communist Party used to have its headquarters here, but the "Reds" of the Cold War era wouldn't recognize this pocket of posh today. It reeks of capitalistic excess and splendor, from its dazzling public rooms with French antiques to its rooms with Louis XVI styling. See p. 59.
- **Hotel d'Angleterre** (Copenhagen; © **800/44-UTELL** in the U.S., or 33-12-00-95): Some critics rate this as the finest hotel in Denmark. As it drifted toward mediocrity a few years back, a massive investment was made to save it. Now the hotel is better than

ever—housing a swimming pool and a nightclub. Behind its Georgian facade, much of the ambience is in the traditional English mode. Service is perhaps the finest in Copenhagen. See p. 58.
- **Falsled Kro** (Falsled; © **62-68-11-11**): Not only is this Funen Island's finest accommodation, but it's the quintessential Danish inn, with origins going back to the 1400s. This Relais & Châteaux property is now a stellar inn with elegant furnishings as well as a top-quality restaurant, rivaling the best in Copenhagen. See p. 244.
- **Hotel Hesselet** (Nyborg; © **65-31-30-29**): This stylish modern hotel on Funen Island occupies a

woodland setting in a beech forest. The spacious rooms are artfully decorated, often with traditional furnishings. A library, Oriental carpets, and an open fireplace add graceful touches to the public areas. Many Copenhagen residents come here for a retreat, patronizing the hotel's gourmet restaurant at night. See p. 222.

- **Hotel Dagmar** (Ribe; ✆ **75-42-00-33**): Jutland's most glamorous hotel was converted from a private home in 1850, although the building itself dates back to 1581. This half-timbered hotel encapsulates the charm of the 16th century, with such adornments as carved chairs, sloping wooden floors, and stained-glass windows. Many bedrooms are furnished with antique canopy beds. A fine restaurant, serving both Danish and international dishes, completes the picture. See p. 283.

3 The Best Restaurants

- **Era Ora** (Copenhagen; ✆ **32-54-06-93**): This is the best Italian restaurant in Denmark. This 20-year-old restaurant is the domain of two Tuscan-born partners who have delighted some of the most discerning palates in Copenhagen. Denmark's superb array of fresh seafood, among other produce, is given a decidedly Mediterranean twist at this citadel of refined cuisine. See p. 74.

- **Godt** (Copenhagen; ✆ **33-15-21-22**): Even the Queen of Denmark dines at this superb restaurant, celebrated for its international cuisine. The best and freshest produce and various ingredients at the market are fashioned into the most pleasing and quintessential dishes. See p. 74.

- **The Paul** (Copenhagen; ✆ **33-75-07-75**): Winning a coveted Michelin star, this is the best restaurant among the deluxe dining rooms of the Tivoli Gardens. Drawing gourmet diners with its carefully crafted international menu, it offers an inspired cuisine in these pleasure gardens. There is a daring and innovation here found in no other Tivoli restaurant. See p. 89.

- **Marie Louise** (Odense; ✆ **66-17-92-95**): Glittering with crystal and silver, this dining room on a pedestrian street is one of the finest on the island of Funen. In an antique house, this Danish/Franco alliance offers a cuisine that's the epitome of taste, preparation, and service. Seafood and fish are the favored dishes. See p. 233.

- **Falsled Kro** (Falsled; ✆ **62-68-11-11**): Even if you don't stay at the hotel, consider stopping for a meal. A favorite among well-heeled Europeans, this restaurant produces a stellar French-inspired cuisine and uses seasonal produce from its own gardens. The succulent salmon is smoked in one of the outbuildings, and the owners breed quail locally. Such care and attention to detail make this one of Denmark's top restaurants. See p. 244.

4 The Best Buys

- **Danish Design:** It's worth making a shopping trip to Denmark. The simple but elegant style that became fashionable in the 1950s has made a comeback. Danish modern chairs, glassware, and even buildings have returned. Collectors celebrate "old masters" such as Arne Jacobsen, Hans Wegner, and Poul Kjærholm, whose designs from the 1940s and 1950s are sold in antiques stores. Wegner, noted for his sculptured teak chairs, for example, is now viewed as the grand old man of Danish design. Younger designers have followed in the old masters' footsteps, producing carefully crafted items for the home—everything from chairs, desks, and furnishings to table settings and silverware. For the best display of Danish design today, walk along the pedestrians-only Strøget, the major shopping street in Copenhagen. The best single showcase for modern Danish design may be **Illums Bolighus,** Amagertorv 10 (© 33-14-19-41). See p. 120.

- **Crystal & Porcelain:** Holmegaard crystal and Royal Copenhagen porcelain are household names, known for their beauty and craftsmanship. These items cost less in Denmark than in the United States, although signed art glass is costly everywhere. To avoid high prices, you can shop for seconds, which are discounted by 20% to 50% (sometimes the imperfection can be detected only by an expert). The best centers for these collectors' items in Copenhagen are **Royal Copenhagen Porcelain,** Amagertorv 6 (© 33-13-71-81), and **Holmegaards Glasværker,** Amagertorv 6 (© 33-12-44-77). See p. 119.

- **Silver:** Danish designers have made a name for themselves in this field. Even with taxes and shipping charges, you can still save about 50% when purchasing silver in Denmark as compared with in the United States. If you're willing to consider "used" silver, you can get some remarkable discounts. The big name in international silver—and you can buy it at the source—is **Georg Jensen,** Amagertorv 6, Copenhagen (© 33-11-40-80). See p. 121.

5 The Most Scenic Towns & Villages

- **Dragør:** At the doorstep of Copenhagen, this old seafaring town once flourished as a bustling herring port on the Baltic. Time, however, has passed it by, and for that we can be grateful, because it looks much as it used to, with half-timbered ocher and pink 18th-century cottages topped with thatch or red-tile roofs. The entire village is under the protection of the National Trust of Denmark. A 35-minute ride from the Danish capital will take you back 2 centuries. See "Side Trips from Copenhagen," in chapter 4.

- **Ærøskøbing:** This little village on the country's most charming island (Ærø) is storybook Denmark. A 13th-century market town, Ærøskøbing is a Lilliputian souvenir of the past, complete with gingerbread houses. You expect Hansel and Gretel to arrive at any moment. See "Ærø," in chapter 8.

- **Odense:** The birthplace of Hans Christian Andersen is Denmark's third-largest city, and still has a medieval core. You can walk its cobblestone streets and admire its half-timbered houses. Other than its associations with the writer, Odense is a worthwhile destination in its own right, filled with attractions (including **St. Canute's Cathedral**). On the outskirts, you can explore the 1554 Renaissance castle, Egeskov, as well as a 10th-century Viking ship at Ladby. See "Odense: Birthplace of Hans Christian Andersen," in chapter 8.

- **Ribe:** On the Jutland peninsula (the European mainland), this is the best-preserved medieval town in Denmark, and is known for its narrow cobblestone lanes and crooked, half-timbered houses. An important trading center during the Viking era, today it's known as the town where the endangered stork—the subject of European myth and legend—nests every April. The National Trust protects the medieval center. From April to mid-September a night watchman circles Ribe, spinning tales of the town's legendary days and singing traditional songs. See "Ribe" in chapter 9.

- **Ebeltoft:** On Jutland, this well-preserved town of half-timbered buildings is the capital of the Mols hill country. It's a town of sloping row houses, crooked streets, and local handicraft shops. The Town Hall looks as if it had been erected for kindergarten children; in Ebeltoft you can also visit the 1860 frigate *Jylland*, the oldest man-of-war in Denmark. See "Ebeltoft" in chapter 10.

6 The Best Active Vacations

- **Fishing:** For centuries, much of Denmark relied on the sea and whatever the country's fishermen could pull out of it for its diet. Since then, no *smørrebrød* buffet has been complete without a selection of shrimp, herring, and salmon. The preparations of plaice, cod, eel, perch, and trout are culinary art forms. The seas off Funen, especially within the Great Belt, have yielded countless tons of seafood, and that tradition has encouraged anglers and sport enthusiasts to test their luck in the rich waters of the Baltic. Many outfitters can introduce you to the mysteries of fresh- and salt-water fishing. One of the most reliable is **Ole Dehn,** Søndergard 22, Lohals, DK-5953 Tranekær (© **62-55-17-00**), on the island of Langeland, south of Funen. Its most popular offering involves half-day deep-sea fishing tours on the Great Sound, which cost 220DKK ($37) per person. See p. 19.

- **Biking:** A nation of bikers, Denmark has organized the roads to suit the national sport. A network of bike routes and paths is protected from heavy traffic, and much of the terrain is flat. Bicycling vacations are available as inclusive tours that cover bike rental, ferry tickets, and accommodations en route. Some deluxe tours transport your luggage from one hotel to the next. For more information, contact the **Danish Cycling Federation,** Rømersgade 7, DK-1362 Copenhagen (© **33-32-31-21;** www.dcf.dk).

- **Camping:** With about 550 officially sanctioned campgrounds, Denmark has one of the highest numbers, per capita, of campgrounds of any nation in the world, and living in a tent or a pop-up trailer in the great outdoors is something of a national obsession. There are plenty of campsites near the city limits of Copenhagen, and many more are located around the country in areas of scenic or historic interest, some near the sea. The official website and address of the **Danish Camping Federation** is www.campingraadet.dk. Either via their website, or by calling or writing them at Campingrådet, Mosedalsvej 15, DK-2500 Valby (© **39-27-88-44**), you can request that the staff send you information about the nation's campsites. Other sources of information about camping are available at www.visitdenmark.com (the official website of the Danish Tourist Board), or an equivalent site, www.dk-camp.dk, which lists more than 300 campsites that are privately owned. You can obtain a free *DK Camping Danmark* catalog at all DK-CAMPing grounds, tourist offices, and many service stations.

- **Golf:** There are about 130 golf courses scattered across the flat, sandy, and sometimes windy landscapes of Denmark, many of them landscaped around the sand dunes, ponds, forests, and rocky outcroppings for which the country is well-known. Most clubs welcome visitors, although in some cases you might be asked to present a membership card from your club at home. Local tourism offices are usually well versed in steering golfers to worthwhile courses, but for some insight into

what's available, click on any of the following websites for information about the sport: www.golfonline.dk or www.golf-in-europe.com/denmark/denmark.htm.

- **Horseback Riding:** Riding schools throughout Denmark rent horses, and local tourist offices can hook you up with a stable, if available in their area. Our favorite place for riding is **Kursus & Feriecenter Krogbækgaard,** Læsø, DK-9940 (✆ **98-49-15-05;** www.rideferie.dk). It is on Langeland, a long and narrow tidal barrier off the southern coast of Funen. The stable houses 120 Icelandic ponies, a sturdy breed that survives well in the harsh climate and scrub-covered landscape of this wind-swept island. A 2-hour horseback-riding trek costs 250DKK ($42), with a 5- to 6-hour tour a better value at 600DKK ($100), including lunch. See "Laesø," in chapter 11.

7 The Best Castles & Palaces

- **Christiansborg Palace** (Copenhagen): The queen receives official guests here in the Royal Reception Chamber, where you must don slippers to protect the floors. The complex also holds the Parliament House and the Supreme Court. From 1441 until the fire of 1795, this was the official residence of Denmark's monarchy. You can tour the richly decorated rooms, including the Throne Room and banqueting hall. Below you can see the well-preserved ruins of the 1167 castle of Bishop Absalon, founder of Copenhagen. See p. 132.

- **Rosenborg Castle** (Copenhagen): Built by Christian IV in the 17th century, this red-brick Renaissance castle remained a royal residence until the early 19th century, when the building was converted

into a museum. It still houses the crown jewels, and its collection of costumes and royal memorabilia is unequaled in Denmark. See p. 101.

- **Kronborg Slot** (Helsingør): Shakespeare never saw this castle, and Hamlet (if he existed at all) lived centuries before it was built. But Shakespeare did set his immortal play here. Intriguing secret passages fill its cannon-studded bastions, and it often serves as the backdrop for modern productions of *Hamlet*. The brooding statue of Holger Danske sleeps in the dungeon, but according to legend, this Viking chief will rise again to defend Denmark if the country is endangered. See p. 144.

- **Frederiksborg Castle** (Hillerød): Known as the Danish Versailles, this moated *slot* (castle) is the most elaborate in Scandinavia. It was built in the Dutch Renaissance style of red brick with a copper roof, and its oldest parts date from 1560. Much of the castle was constructed under the direction of the "master builder," Christian IV, from 1600 to 1620. Fire ravaged the castle in 1859, and the structure had to be completely restored. It is now a national history museum. See p. 134.

• **Egeskov Castle** (Kværndrup): On the island of Funen, this 1554 Renaissance "water castle" is set amid splendid gardens. The most romantic example of Denmark's fortified manors, the castle was built in the middle of a moat, surrounded by a park. The best-preserved Renaissance castle of its type in Europe, it has many attractions on its grounds, including airplane and vintage-automobile museums. See p. 229.

8 The Best Offbeat Experiences

• **Journeying Back to the 1960s:** If you're nostalgic for the counterculture of the 1960s, it lives on in Christiania, a Copenhagen community located at the corner of Prinsessegade and Badsmandsstræde on Christianshavn. Founded in 1972, this anarchists' commune occupies former army barracks; its current residents preach a gospel of drugs and peace. Christiania's residents have even organized their own government and passed laws, for example, to legalize drugs. They're not complete anarchists, however, since they venture into the city at least once a month to pick up their social welfare checks. Today you can wander about their community, which is complete with a theater, cafes, grocery stores, and even a local radio station. See chapter 4.

• **Exploring Erotica:** Denmark was the first country to "liberate" pornography, in 1968, and today there's a museum in Copenhagen devoted to the subject. In the **Erotica Museum** (at Købmagergade 24; ✆ **33-12-03-11**), you can learn about the sex lives of such famous figures as Nietzsche, Freud, and even Duke Ellington. Founded by a photographer of nudes, the museum has exhibits ranging from the tame to the tempestuous—starting from Etruscan drawings and progressing to the further reaches of the erotic and sexual. See p. 102.

• **Calling on Artists & Craftspeople:** West Jutland has many open workshops where you can see craftspeople in action; you can meet the potter, the glassblower, the painter, the textile designer, and even the candlestick maker. Local tourist offices can tell you which studios are open to receive guests in such centers as Tønder, Ribe, Esbjerg, Varde, Billund, Herning, Struer, and Skive. The island of **Langeland** seems to have more artists and artisan studios than most. For some of the best craftspeople practicing there, refer to "Visiting Working Artists." See p. 259.

2

Planning Your Trip to Denmark

In the following pages, we've compiled all of the practical information you'll need to plan your trip in advance—airline information, what things cost, a calendar of events, and more.

1 The Regions in Brief

ZEALAND

Home to Denmark's capital, **Copenhagen,** the island of Zealand draws more visitors than any other region. The largest island in Denmark, Zealand is also the wealthiest and most densely populated. Other cities include **Roskilde,** 32km (20 miles) west of Copenhagen, which is home to a landmark cathedral (burial place of many kings) and a collection of Viking vessels discovered in a fjord. In the medieval town of **Køge,** witches were burned in the Middle Ages. One of the most popular attractions on the island is **Helsingør** ("Elsinore" in English), about 40km (25 miles) north of Copenhagen, where visitors flock to see "Hamlet's castle." Off the southeast corner of the island lies the island of **Møn,** home to Møns Klint, an expanse of white cliffs that rises sharply out of the Baltic.

JUTLAND

The peninsula of Jutland links the mostly island nation of Denmark with Germany. It is the only part of Denmark on the European continent. Jutland has miles of coastline, with some of northern Europe's finest sandy beaches. Giant dunes and moors abound on the west coast, whereas the interior has rolling pastures and beech forests. Jutland's more interesting towns and villages include **Jelling,** heralded as the birthplace of Denmark

and the ancient seat of the Danish kings; here you can see an extensive collection of Viking artifacts excavated from ancient burial mounds. The Viking port of **Ribe** is the oldest town in Denmark. It's known throughout the world as the preferred nesting ground for numerous endangered storks. The resort of **Fanø,** with its giant dunes, heather-covered moors, and forests, is an excellent place to bird-watch or view Denmark's varied wildlife. The university city of **Århus** is Jutland's capital and second only to Copenhagen in size. **Aalborg,** founded by Vikings more than 1,000 years ago, is a thriving commercial center in northern Jutland. It lies close to Rebild National Park and the Rold Forest.

FUNEN

With an area of 2,980 sq. km (1,150 sq. miles), Funen is Denmark's second-largest island. Called the "garden of Denmark," Funen is known to the world as the birthplace of Hans Christian Andersen. Orchards, stately manors, and castles dot its rolling countryside. **Odense,** Andersen's birthplace, is a mecca for fairy-tale writers and fans from around the world. Nearby stands Egeskov Castle, resting on oak columns in the middle of a small lake. It's Europe's best-preserved Renaissance castle. Funen has a number of bustling ports, including **Nyborg** in the east and

Denmark

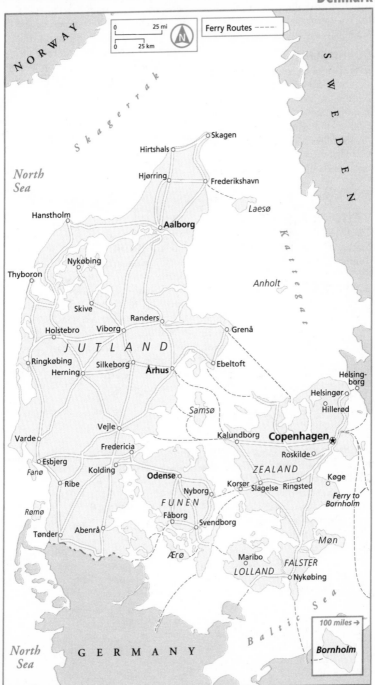

NORWAY

SWEDEN

0   25 mi
0   25 km

Ferry Routes - - - - -

North
Sea

Skagerrak

Skagen

Hirtshals

Hjørring

Frederikshavn

Laesø

Hanstholm

Aalborg

Kattegat

Nykøbing

Anholt

Thyboron

Skive

Randers

Grenå

Holstebro   Viborg

JUTLAND

Ringkøbing

Silkeborg

Ebeltoft

Helsing-
borg

Herning

Århus

Helsingør

Hillerød

Samsø

Vejle

Kalundborg   **Copenhagen** ✪

Varde

Fredericia

Roskilde

ZEALAND

Esbjerg

Kolding

Fanø

Odense

Køge

Ribe

Nyborg   Korsør

FUNEN   Slagelse Ringsted

Ferry to
Bornholm

Rømø

Fåborg

Tønder   Abenrå

Svendborg

Møn

Ærø

Maribo

FALSTER

LOLLAND   Nykøbing

North
Sea

GERMANY

Baltic Sea

100 miles →

Bornholm

Svendborg at the southern end of the island. **Ærøskøbing** is a medieval market town that's a showplace of Scandinavian heritage.

BORNHOLM

In the Baltic Sea, southeast of Zealand and close to Sweden, lies the island of Bornholm. Prehistoric monuments and runic stones pepper the countryside, and numerous fishing villages dot the shoreline. On the northern coast, near **Hammerhus,** the Bornholm Animal and Nature Park is home to many native species as well as some that have been introduced from other parts of Scandinavia. Some of Europe's largest castle ruins dot this region of the island. The town of **Rønne** is the site of Denmark's oldest regional theater; it stages numerous concerts and shows year-round. The island of **Christiansø,** off the coast of Bornholm, was the site of Denmark's penal colony. Criminals sentenced to life imprisonment were deported to the island, where they spent their lives in slavery.

2 Visitor Information

VISITOR INFORMATION

TOURIST OFFICES In the **United States,** contact the **Scandinavian Tourist Board,** 655 Third Ave., 18th Floor, New York, NY 10017 (② 212/ 885-9700; www.goscandinavia.com), for maps, sightseeing information, ferry schedules, or whatever other travel information you need. You can also try the **Danish Tourist Board,** 655 Third Ave., 18th Floor, New York, NY 10017 (② 212/885-9700).

In the **United Kingdom,** contact the **Danish Tourist Board,** 55 Sloane St., London SW1X 9SY (② 020/ 7259-5959).

WEBSITES To begin your exploration of Denmark, visit the **Scandinavian Tourist Board** (www.go scandinavia.com), the **Danish Tourist Board** (www.visitdenmark.com), and **Wonderful Copenhagen** (www. woco.dk), all of which offer extensive links to other organizations, accommodations, attractions, and other information. Get information on Danish culture, tour suggestions, and events at **CultureNet Denmark** (www.kulturnet.dk).

3 Entry Requirements & Customs

ENTRY REQUIREMENTS

U.S., Canadian, U.K., Irish, Australian, and New Zealand citizens with a **valid passport** don't need a visa to enter Denmark if they don't expect to stay more than 90 days and don't expect to work there. If after entering Denmark you want to stay more than 90 days, you can apply for a permit for an extra 90 days at your home country's consulate, which as a rule is granted immediately. If your passport is lost or stolen, head to your consulate as soon as possible for a replacement.

CUSTOMS
WHAT YOU CAN BRING INTO DENMARK

Foreign visitors can bring along most items for personal use duty-free, including fishing tackle, a pair of skis, two tennis rackets, a baby carriage, two hand cameras with 10 rolls of film, and 400 cigarettes or a quantity of cigars or pipe tobacco not exceeding 500 grams (1.1 lb.). There are strict limits on importing alcoholic beverages. However, for alcohol bought tax-paid, limits are much more liberal than in other countries of the European Union.

WHAT YOU CAN TAKE HOME

Returning **U.S. citizens** who have been away for at least 48 hours are allowed to bring back, once every 30 days, $800 worth of merchandise duty-free. You'll be charged a flat rate of duty on the next $1,000 worth of purchases. Any dollar amount beyond that is dutiable at whatever rates apply. On mailed gifts, the duty-free limit is $200. Be sure to have your receipts or purchases handy to expedite the declaration process. ***Note:*** If you owe duty, you are required to pay on arrival in the U.S., by cash, personal check, government or traveler's check, or money order, and in some locations, a Visa or MasterCard.

To avoid having to pay duty on foreign-made personal items you owned before you left on your trip, bring along a bill of sale, insurance policy, jeweler's appraisal, or receipts of purchase. Or you can register items that can be readily identified by a permanently affixed serial number or marking—think laptop computers, cameras, and CD players—with Customs before you leave. Take the items to the nearest Customs office or register them with Customs at the airport from which you're departing. You'll receive, at no cost, a Certificate of Registration, which allows duty-free entry for the life of the item.

With some exceptions, you cannot bring fresh fruits and vegetables into the United States. For specifics on what you can bring back, download the invaluable free pamphlet *Know Before You Go* online at **www.cbp.gov**. (Click on "Travel" and then click on "Know Before You Go") Or contact the **U.S. Customs & Border Protection (CBP),** 1300 Pennsylvania Ave., NW, Washington, DC 20229 (© 877/287-8667), and request the pamphlet.

For a clear summary of **Canadian** rules, write for the booklet *I Declare,* issued by the **Canada Border Services Agency (© 800/461-9999** in Canada, or 204/983-3500; www.cbsa-asfc.gc.ca). Canada allows its citizens a C$750 exemption, and you're allowed to bring back duty-free one carton of cigarettes, 1 can of tobacco, 40 imperial ounces of liquor, and 50 cigars. In addition, you're allowed to mail gifts to Canada valued at less than C$60 a day, if they're unsolicited and don't contain alcohol or tobacco (write on the package UNSOLICITED GIFT, UNDER $60 VALUE). All valuables should be declared on the Y-38 form before departure from Canada, including serial numbers of valuables you own, such as foreign cameras. ***Note:*** The $750 exemption can be used only once a year and only after an absence of 7 days.

Citizens of the U.K. who are **returning from a European Union (EU) country** will go through a separate Customs Exit (called the "Blue Exit") for EU travelers. In essence, there is no limit on what you can bring back from an EU country, as long as the items are for personal use (this includes gifts), and you have already paid the necessary duty and tax. However, customs law sets out guidance levels. If you bring in more than these levels, you may be asked to prove that the goods are for your own use. Guidance levels on goods bought in the EU for your own use are 3,200 cigarettes, 200 cigars, 400 cigarillos, 3 kilograms of smoking tobacco, 10 liters of spirits, 90 liters of wine, 20 liters of fortified wine (such as port or sherry), and 110 liters of beer.

The duty-free allowance in **Australia** is A$400 or, for those under 18, A$200. Citizens can bring in 250 cigarettes or 250 grams of loose tobacco, and 1,125 milliliters of alcohol. If you're returning with valuables you already own, such as foreign-made cameras, you should file form B263. A helpful brochure available from Australian consulates or Customs offices is

Know Before You Go. For more information, call the **Australian Customs** **Service** at ℂ **1300/363-263,** or log on to www.customs.gov.au.

4 Money

CURRENCY

Although a member of the European Union, the Danes rejected the euro as their form of currency. They continue to use the **krone** (crown), which breaks down into 100 **øre.** The plural is **kroner.** The international monetary designation for the Danish kroner is "DKK." (The Swedish currency is the kronor, but note the different spelling.)

It's a good idea to exchange at least some money—just enough to cover airport incidentals and transportation to your hotel—before you leave home (though don't expect the exchange rate to be ideal), so you can avoid lines at airport ATMs. You can exchange money at your local American Express or Thomas Cook office or your bank. If your bank doesn't offer

---

The Danish Krone

For American Readers At this writing, $1 = approximately 6 kroner (or 1 krone = approximately 16.7 US¢); this was the rate of exchange used to calculate the dollar values given throughout this edition. Bear in mind that throughout the context of this book, dollar amounts less than $10 are rounded to the nearest nickel, and dollar amounts greater than $10 are rounded to the nearest dollar.

For British Readers At this writing, £1 = approximately 11.1 kroner (or 1 krone = approximately 9 pence). This was the rate of exchange used to calculate the pound values in the table below.

Regarding the Euro At the time of this writing, one Danish kroner = .134 Euros. Or, stated differently, 1 Euro = 7.43 DKK. These ratios can and probably will change during the lifetime of this edition. For updates on these currency conversions, check an up-to-date source at the time of your trip to Denmark.

DKK	US$	UK£	Euro €	DKK	US$	UK£	Euro €
1.00	0.17	0.09	0.13	75.00	12.53	6.75	10.05
2.00	0.33	0.18	0.27	100.00	16.70	9.00	13.40
3.00	0.50	0.27	0.40	125.00	20.88	11.25	16.75
4.00	0.67	0.36	0.54	150.00	25.05	13.50	20.10
5.00	0.84	0.45	0.67	175.00	29.23	15.75	23.45
6.00	1.00	0.54	0.80	200.00	33.40	18.00	26.80
7.00	1.17	0.63	0.94	225.00	37.58	20.25	30.15
8.00	1.34	0.72	1.07	250.00	41.75	22.50	33.50
9.00	1.50	0.81	1.21	275.00	45.93	24.75	36.85
10.00	1.67	0.90	1.34	300.00	50.10	27.00	40.20
15.00	2.51	1.35	2.01	350.00	58.45	31.50	46.90
20.00	3.34	1.80	2.68	400.00	66.80	36.00	53.60
25.00	4.18	2.25	3.35	500.00	83.50	45.00	67.00
50.00	8.35	4.50	6.70	1000.00	167.00	90.00	134.00

currency-exchange services, American Express offers traveler's checks and foreign currency, though with a $15 order fee and additional shipping costs, at www.americanexpress.com or ℂ **800/807-6233.**

ATMs

Plus, Cirrus, and other networks connecting automated-teller machines operate throughout Denmark. If your credit card has a PIN (personal identification number), you can probably use your card at Danish ATMs to withdraw money from your bank account and credit card. Always determine the frequency limits for withdrawals, and check to see if your PIN must be reprogrammed for use abroad. Discover cards are not accepted in Denmark.

For **Cirrus** locations abroad, call ℂ **800/424-7787.** For **PLUS** usage abroad, check www.visa.com or call ℂ **800/843-7587.**

Also keep in mind that many banks impose a fee every time a card is used at a different bank's ATM, and that fee can be higher for international transactions (up to $5 or more). On top of this, the bank from which you withdraw cash may charge its own fee. For international withdrawal fees, ask your bank.

You can also get cash advances on your **credit card** at an ATM. Keep in mind that credit card companies try to protect themselves from theft by limiting the funds someone can withdraw outside their home country, so call your credit card company before you leave home. And keep in mind that you'll pay interest from the moment of your withdrawal, even if you pay your monthly bills on time.

CURRENCY EXCHANGE

Many hotels in Denmark will not accept a dollar- or pound-denominated personal check; those that do will certainly charge for making the conversion. In some cases, a hotel may accept countersigned traveler's checks or a credit or charge card.

If you're making a deposit on a hotel reservation that doesn't take credit cards, it's cheaper and easier to pay with a check drawn on a Norwegian bank. This can be arranged by a large commercial bank or by a specialist like **Ruesch International,** 700 11th St. NW, 4th Floor, Washington, DC 20001 (ℂ **800/424-2923** or 202/408-1200; www.ruesch.com). It performs a wide variety of conversion-related tasks, usually for about $15 per transaction.

If you need a check payable in a Danish currency, call Ruesch's toll-free number, describe what you need, and write down the transaction number. Mail your dollar-denominated personal check (payable to Ruesch International) to the Washington, D.C., office. When it's received, the company will mail you a check denominated in the requested currency for the specified amount, minus the $3 charge. The company can also help you with wire transfers, as well as the conversion of VAT (value-added tax) refund checks. Information is mailed upon request.

In England, contact Ruesch International Ltd., Marble Arch Tower, 14th Floor, 55-Bryanston St., London W1H 7AA (ℂ **0207/563-3300;** fax 0207/563-3390).

TRAVELER'S CHECKS

Traveler's checks are something of an anachronism from the days before the ATM made cash accessible at any time. Traveler's checks used to be the only sound alternative to traveling with dangerously large amounts of cash. They were as reliable as currency but, unlike cash, could be replaced if lost or stolen.

These days, traveler's checks are less necessary because most cities have 24-hour ATMs that allow you to withdraw small amounts of cash as needed.

What Things Cost in Copenhagen	US$	UK£	DKK
Taxi from the airport to the city center	25.00	13.56	150.00
Subway from Central Station to outlying suburbs	2.85	1.54	17.10
Local telephone call	0.13	0.07	0.78
Double room at the Hotel d'Angleterre (very expensive)	412.00	223.57	2,472.00
Double room, with bathroom, at the Hotel Kong Arthur (moderate)	234.00	126.00	1,404.00
Double room, without bathroom, at the Hotel Valberg (inexpensive)	125.00	67.87	750.00
Lunch for one at Restaurant Els (moderate)	33.00	17.91	198.00
Lunch for one at Ida Davidsen (inexpensive)	18.00	9.77	108.00
Dinner for one, without wine, at Kommandanten (very expensive)	100.00	54.30	600.00
Dinner for one, without wine, at Copenhagen Corner (moderate)	42.00	22.80	252.00
Dinner for one, without wine, at Nyhavns Færgekro (inexpensive)	28.00	15.20	168.00
Pint of beer (draft Pilsner)	5.30	2.87	31.80
Coca-Cola	3.35	1.81	20.10
Cup of coffee	2.60	1.41	15.60
Admission to the Tivoli Gardens	11.00	5.97	66.00
Movie ticket	8.00	4.34	48.00
Roll of ASA 100 color film, 36 exposures	11.50	6.24	69.00
Ticket to the Royal Theater	12.00–103.00	6.51–55.91	72.00–618.00

However, keep in mind that you will likely be charged an ATM withdrawal fee if the bank is not your own, so if you're withdrawing money every day, you might be better off with traveler's checks—provided that you don't mind showing identification every time you want to cash one.

You can get traveler's checks at almost any bank. **American Express** offers denominations of $20, $50, $100, $500, and (for cardholders only) $1,000. You'll pay a service charge ranging from 1% to 4%. You can also get American Express traveler's checks over the phone by calling

✆ **800/221-7282;** Amex gold and platinum cardholders who use this number are exempt from the 1% fee.

Visa offers traveler's checks at Citibank locations nationwide, as well as at several other banks. The service charge ranges between 1.5% and 2%; checks come in denominations of $20, $50, $100, $500, and $1,000. Call ✆ **800/732-1322** for information. AAA members can obtain Visa checks without a fee at most AAA offices or by calling ✆ 866/339-3378. **MasterCard** also offers traveler's checks. Call ✆ **800/223-9920** for a location near you.

Foreign currency traveler's checks are useful if you're traveling to one country, or to the Euro zone; they're accepted at locations such as bed-and-breakfasts where dollar checks may not be, and they minimize the amount of math you have to do at your destination. **American Express, Thomas Cook, Visa,** and **MasterCard** offer foreign currency traveler's checks. You'll pay the rate of exchange at the time of your purchase (so it's a good idea to monitor the rate before you take the plunge), and most companies charge a transaction fee per order (and a shipping fee if you order online).

If you choose to carry traveler's checks, be sure to keep a record of their serial numbers separate from your checks in the event that they are stolen or lost. You'll get a refund faster if you know the numbers.

5 When to Go

CLIMATE
Denmark's climate is mild for a Scandinavian country—New England farmers experience harsher winters. Summer temperatures average between 61°F and 77°F (16°C–25°C).

Winter temperatures seldom go below 30°F (–1°C), thanks to the warming waters of the Gulf Stream. From the weather perspective, mid-April to November is a good time to visit.

Denmark's Average Daytime Temperatures

	Jan	Feb	Mar	Apr	May	June	July	Aug	Sept	Oct	Nov	Dec
°F	32	32	35	44	53	60	64	63	57	49	42	37
°C	0	0	2	7	12	16	18	17	14	9	6	3

HOLIDAYS
Danish public holidays are January 1 (New Year's Day), Maundy Thursday, Good Friday, Easter Sunday, Easter Monday, May 1 (Labor Day), Common Prayers Day (4th Fri after Easter), Ascension Day (mid-May), Whitsunday (late May), Whitmonday, June 5 (Constitution Day), December 25 (Christmas Day), and December 26 (Boxing Day).

DENMARK CALENDAR OF EVENTS
Note: Exact dates below apply for 2005. Should you be using this guide in 2006, check with local tourist boards for exact dates.

May

Carnival in Copenhagen. A great citywide event. There's also a children's carnival. For information, call ℂ **33-38-85-04;** www.karneval.dk. May 13 to 15.

Ballet and Opera Festival (Copenhagen). Classical and modern dance and two operatic masterpieces are presented at the Old Stage of the Royal Theater in Copenhagen. For tickets, contact the Royal Theater, Box 2185, DK-1017 Copenhagen (ℂ **33-69-69-69;** www.kgl-teater. dk). Mid-May to June.

Aalborg Carnival. This is one of the country's great spring events. The streets fill with people in colorful costumes. Thousands take part in the celebration, which honors the victory of spring over winter. For information, call ℂ **98-13-72-11;** www.karnevalaalborg.dk. Late May.

June

Viking Festival (Frederikssund, 8 miles southwest of Hillerød). For almost a month every summer, "bearded Vikings" present old

Nordic sagas in an open-air setting. After each performance, a traditional Viking meal is served. Call © **47-31-06-85;** www.vikingespil. dk for more information. Mid-June to early July.

Midsummer's Night (throughout the country). This age-old event is celebrated throughout Denmark. It is the longest day of the year. Festivities throughout the nation begin at around 10pm with bonfires and celebrations along the myriad coasts. June 21.

Roskilde Festival. Europe's biggest rock festival has been going strong for more than 30 years, now bringing about 90,000 revelers each year to the central Zealand town. Besides major rock concerts, which often draw big names, scheduled activities include theater and film presentations. For more information, call © **46-36-66-13;** www. roskilde-festival.dk. June 30 to July 3.

July

Copenhagen Jazz Festival. International jazz musicians play in the streets, squares, and theaters. Pick up a copy of *Copenhagen This Week* to find the venues. For information, call © **33-93-20-13;** www.jazz festival.dk. July 1 to 10.

July 4th (Rebild). Rebild National Park, near Aalborg, is one of the few places outside the United States to honor American Independence Day. For more information, contact the Aalborg Tourist Office, Østerågade 8, DK-9000 Aalborg (© **98-12-60-22**). July 4th.

Funen Festival. This annual musical extravaganza draws big, international headliners. The festival's music is often hard-core rock, but gentler, classical melodies are presented as well. It takes place in the city of Odense, on the island of Funen. For more information, call

the Odense tourist bureau (© **66-12-75-20**). July 7 to 11.

Sønderborg Tilting Festival. Dating from the Middle Ages, the "tilting at the ring" tradition has survived in the town of Sønderborg on the island of Als in southern Jutland. While riding at a gallop, a horseman uses his lance to see how many times (in 24 attempts) he can take the ring. Parades, music, and entertainment are included. For more information, contact the Turistbureau, Rådhustorvet 7, DK-6400 Sønderborg (© **74-42-35-55**). Early July.

August

Fire Festival Regatta (Silkeborg). Denmark's oldest and biggest festival features nightly cruises on the lakes, with thousands of candles illuminating the shores. The fireworks display on the last night is the largest and most spectacular in northern Europe. Popular Danish artists provide entertainment at a large fun fair. For more information, contact the Turistbureau, Godthåbsuej 4, DK-8600 Silkeborg (© **86-82-19-11**). Early August.

Fall Ballet Festival (Copenhagen). The internationally acclaimed Royal Danish Ballet returns home to perform at the Old Stage of the Royal Theater just before the tourist season ends. For tickets, contact the Royal Theater, Box 2185, DK-1017 Copenhagen (© **33-69-69-69;** www.kgl-teater. dk). Mid-August to September.

Århus Festival Week. A wide range of cultural activities—including opera, jazz, classical and folk music, ballet, and theater—is presented. It's the largest cultural festival in Scandinavia. Sporting activities and street parties abound as well. For more information, contact © **89-40-91-85;** www.aarhusfestival.dk. August 26 to September 4.

6 The Active Vacation Planner

BEACHES

With some 8,000km (5,000 miles) of coastline, Denmark has many long strips of sandy beaches. In many cases, dunes protect the beaches from sea winds. Most of these beaches are relatively unspoiled, and the Danes like to keep them that way (any polluted beaches are clearly marked). Many Danes like to go nude at the beach. Nudist beaches aren't clearly identified; often you'll see bathers with and without clothing using the same beach. The best beach resorts are those on the north coast of Zealand and the southern tip of the island of Bornholm. Beaches on the east coast of Jutland are also good, often attracting Germans from the south. Funen also has a number of good beaches, especially in the south.

BIKING

A nation of bikers, the Danes have organized their roads to suit this national sport. Bikers can pedal along a network of biking routes and paths protected from heavy traffic. The Danish landscape is made for this type of vacation. Most tourist offices publish biking tour suggestions for their own district; it's a great way to see the sights and get in shape at the same time. The **Dansk Cyklist Forbund** (Danish Cycling Federation), Rømersgade 7, DK-1362 Copenhagen (© **33-32-31-21;** www.dcf.dk), also publishes excellent guides covering the whole country. They can also provide information about a number of prepackaged biking vacations that are available.

FISHING

Since no place in Denmark is more than 56km (35 miles) from the sea, fishing is a major pastime. Denmark also has well-stocked rivers and lakes, including fjord waters around the Limfjord. Anglers between the ages of 18 and 67 must obtain a fishing permit from the Danish Ministry of Fisheries for 140DKK ($23); these are available at any post office. Jutland is known for its good trout fishing; salmon is also available, but it is found more readily in Norway. Anglers who fish from the beach can catch eel, mackerel, turbot, sea trout, plaice, and flounder. For more information about fishing in Denmark, contact **Sportfiskerforbund,** Worsåesgade 1, DK-7100 Vejle (© **75-82-06-99**).

GOLF

In recent years, this has become a very popular sport. Denmark's undulating landscape is ideal for the construction of golf courses. Prospective golfers should bring with them a valid golf club membership card from home. For information on the best courses near where you're staying, contact local tourist offices.

HANG GLIDING & PARAGLIDING

Although Denmark is a relatively flat country, good possibilities for paragliding do exist. **The Danish Union of Windgliders** provides information about suitable locations. As a rule, the union has arranged with local landowners that a slope or some other suitable place may be used. Since equipment cannot be rented in Denmark, clients must bring their own. More information is available from **Dansk Drageflyver Union** (© **75-24-51-10;** www.danskdrageflyverunion. dk).

SAILING

Denmark has about 600 harbors, both large and small, including the island of Bornholm. Those who like to sail have many opportunities to do so, especially in the open waters of the Baltic or in the more sheltered waters of the South Funen Sea between

Lolland/Falster and Zealand. The Lim-fjord in North Jutland is also ideal for sailing. Many sailing boats are available for rent, as are cruisers. For information, contact the tourist offices.

WALKING

About 20 pamphlets describing walks of short or long duration in Danish forests are printed in English and are available from local tourist offices.

7 Travel Insurance

Check your existing insurance policies and credit card coverage before you buy travel insurance. You may already be covered for lost luggage, cancelled tickets, or medical expenses.

The cost of travel insurance varies widely, depending on the cost and length of your trip, your age and health, and the type of trip you're taking, but expect to pay between 5% and 8% of the vacation itself.

TRIP-CANCELLATION INSURANCE Trip-cancellation insurance helps you get your money back if you have to back out of a trip, if you have to go home early, or if your travel supplier goes bankrupt. Allowed reasons for cancellation can range from sickness to natural disasters to the State Department declaring your destination unsafe for travel. (Insurers usually won't cover vague fears, though, as many travelers discovered who tried to cancel their trips in October 2001 because they were wary of flying.) In this unstable world, trip-cancellation insurance is a good buy if you're getting tickets well in advance—who knows what the state of the world, or of your airline, will be in 9 months? Insurance policy details vary, so read the fine print—and make sure that your airline or cruise line is on the list of carriers covered in case of bankruptcy. A good resource is **"Travel Guard Alerts,"** a list of companies considered high-risk by Travel Guard International (see website below). Protect yourself further by paying for the insurance with a credit card—by law, consumers can get their money back on goods and services not received if they report the loss within 60 days

after the charge is listed on their credit card statement.

Note: Many tour operators, particularly those offering trips to remote or high-risk areas, include insurance in the cost of the trip or can arrange insurance policies through a partnering provider, a convenient and often cost-effective way for the traveler to obtain insurance. Make sure the tour company is a reputable one, however: Some experts suggest you avoid buying insurance from the tour or cruise company you're traveling with, saying it's better to buy from a "third party" insurer than to put all your money in one place.

For more information, contact one of the following recommended insurers: **Access America** (© 866/807-3982; www.accessamerica.com); **Travel Guard International** (© 800/826-4919; www.travelguard.com); **Travel Insured International** (© 800/243-3174; www.travelinsured.com); and **Travelex Insurance Services** (© 888/457-4602; www.travelex-insurance.com).

MEDICAL INSURANCE For travel overseas, most health plans (including Medicare and Medicaid) do not provide coverage, and the ones that do often require you to pay for services upfront and reimburse you only after you return home. Even if your plan does cover overseas treatment, most out-of-country hospitals make you pay your bills upfront, and send you a refund only after you've returned home and filed the necessary paperwork with your insurance company. As a safety net, you may want to buy travel medical insurance, particularly

Tips **Quick ID**

Tie a colorful ribbon or piece of yarn around your luggage handle, or slap a distinctive sticker on the side of your bag. This makes it less likely that someone will mistakenly appropriate it. And if your luggage gets lost, it will be easier to find.

if you're traveling to a remote or high-risk area where emergency evacuation is a possible scenario. If you require additional medical insurance, try **MEDEX Assistance** (© 410/453-6300; www.medexassist.com) or **Travel Assistance International** (© 800/821-2828; www.travelassistance.com; for general information on services, call the company's Worldwide Assistance Services, Inc., at © **800/777-8710**).

LOST-LUGGAGE INSURANCE
On domestic flights, checked baggage is covered up to $2,500 per ticketed passenger. On international flights (including U.S. portions of international trips), baggage coverage is limited to approximately $9.07 per pound, up to approximately $635 per checked bag. If you plan to check items more valuable than the standard liability, see if your valuables are covered by your homeowner's policy, get baggage insurance as part of your comprehensive travel-insurance package, or buy Travel Guard's "BagTrak" product. Don't buy insurance at the airport, as it's usually overpriced. Be sure to take any valuables or irreplaceable items with you in your carry-on luggage, as many valuables (including books, money, and electronics) aren't covered by airline policies.

If your luggage is lost, immediately file a lost-luggage claim at the airport, detailing the luggage contents. For most airlines, you must report delayed, damaged, or lost baggage within 4 hours of arrival. The airlines are required to deliver luggage, once found, directly to your house or destination free of charge.

CAR-RENTAL INSURANCE (LOSS/DAMAGE WAIVER OR COLLISION DAMAGE WAIVER)
If you hold a U.S. auto insurance policy, you probably are covered in the United States but not abroad for loss or damage to the car and liability in case a passenger is injured. The credit card you used to rent the card also might provide some coverage.

Car-rental insurance probably does not cover liability if you caused the accident. Check your own auto insurance policy, the rental company policy, and your credit card coverage for the extent of coverage. Is your destination covered? Are other drivers covered? How much liability is covered if a passenger is injured? (If you rely on your credit card for coverage, you might want to bring a second credit card with you: Damages might be charged to your card, and you could find yourself stranded with no money.)

Car-rental insurance costs from $20 a day.

8 Health & Safety

STAYING HEALTHY
Denmark is viewed as a "safe" destination, although problems, of course, can and do occur anywhere. You don't need to get shots, most foodstuff is safe, and the water in cities and towns potable.

If you're concerned, order bottled water. It is easy to get a prescription filled in towns and cities, and nearly all places throughout Denmark contain hospitals with English-speaking doctors and well-trained medical staffs.

Denmark is part of the civilized world. In fact, it's one of the most advanced countries on the planet.

WHAT TO DO IF YOU GET SICK AWAY FROM HOME

Any foreign consulate can provide a list of area doctors who speak English. If you get sick, consider asking your hotel concierge to recommend a local doctor—even his or her own. You can also try the emergency room at a local hospital. Many hospitals also have walk-in clinics for emergency cases that are not life-threatening; you may not get immediate attention, but you won't pay the high price of an emergency room visit. We list hospitals and emergency numbers under "Fast Facts," p. 47.

If you worry about getting sick away from home, consider purchasing **medical travel insurance** and carry your ID card in your purse or wallet. In most cases, your existing health plan will provide the coverage you need. See the section on insurance earlier in this chapter for more information.

If you suffer from a chronic illness, consult your doctor before your departure. For conditions like epilepsy, diabetes, or heart problems, wear a **MedicAlert identification tag** (© **888/633-4298;** www.medicalert. org), which will immediately alert doctors to your condition and give them access to your records through MedicAlert's 24-hour hot line.

Pack **prescription medications** in your carry-on luggage, and carry prescription medications in their original containers. Also bring along copies of your prescriptions in case you lose or run out of your pills. Carry the generic name of prescription medicines, in case a local pharmacist is unfamiliar with the brand name.

And don't forget sunglasses and an extra pair of contact lenses or prescription glasses.

Contact the **International Association for Medical Assistance to Travellers (IAMAT)** (© **716/754-4883** or in Canada 416/652-0137; www.iamat.org) for tips on travel and health concerns in Scandinavia and lists of local, English-speaking doctors. The United States **Centers for Disease Control and Prevention** (© **800/311-3435;** www.cdc.gov) provides up-to-date information on necessary vaccines and health hazards by region or country.

STAYING SAFE

Denmark has a relatively low crime rate with rare, but increasing, instances of violent crime. Most crimes involve the theft of personal property from cars or residences or in public areas. Pickpockets and purse snatchers often work in pairs or groups with one distracting the victim while another grabs valuables. Often they operate in or near the major rail stations in Copenhagen. Hotel breakfast rooms and lobbies attract professional, well-dressed thieves who blend in with guests and target purses and briefcases left unguarded by unsuspecting tourists and business travelers. Valuables should not be left unguarded in parked vehicles.

The loss or theft abroad of a U.S. passport should be reported immediately to the local police and the nearest U.S. Embassy or Consulate. If you are the victim of a crime while overseas, in addition to reporting to local police, contact the nearest U.S. Embassy or Consulate for assistance. The Embassy/Consulate staff can, for example, assist you in finding appropriate medical care and contacting family members or friends, and explain how funds could be transferred. Although the investigation and prosecution of the crime is solely the responsibility of local authorities, consular officers can help you to understand the local criminal justice process and to find an attorney if needed.

U.S. citizens may refer to the Department of State's pamphlet *A Safe*

Trip Abroad for ways to promote a trouble-free journey. The pamphlet is available by mail from the **Superintendent of Documents, U.S. Government Printing Office,** Washington, DC 20402; via the Internet at www.gpoaccess.gov; or via the Bureau of Consular Affairs home page at http://travel.state.gov.

9 Specialized Travel Resources

TRAVELERS WITH DISABILITIES

Most disabilities shouldn't stop anyone from traveling. There are more options and resources out there than ever before.

In general, Denmark's trains, airlines, ferries, department stores, and malls are accessible. For information about wheelchair access, ferry and air travel, parking, and other matters, contact the **Danish Tourist Board** (see "Visitor Information," earlier in this chapter).

Useful information for people with disabilities is provided by *De Samvirkende Invalideorganisationer* (**Danish Disability Council,** abbreviated in Denmark as DSI), Kløverprisvej 10 B, DK-2650 Hvidovre, Denmark (© 36-75-17-77). Established in 1934, it organizes 29 smaller organizations, each involved with issues of concern to physically challenged people, into one coherent grouping that represents the estimated 300,000 persons with disabilities living in Denmark today. For the best overview of what this organization does, click on their website at www.handicap.dk.

Many travel agencies offer customized tours and itineraries for travelers with disabilities. **Flying Wheels Travel** (© 507/451-5005; www.flyingwheelstravel.com) offers escorted tours and cruises that emphasize sports, and private tours in minivans with lifts. **Access-Able Travel Source** (© 303/232-2979; www.access-able.com) offers extensive access information and advice for traveling around the world with disabilities. **Accessible Journeys** (© 800/846-4537 or 610/521-0339; www.disabilitytravel.com) caters specifically to slow walkers and wheelchair travelers and their families and friends.

Organizations that offer assistance to travelers with disabilities include **MossRehab** (www.mossresourcenet.org), which provides a library of accessible-travel resources online; **SATH** (Society for Accessible Travel & Hospitality) (© 212/447-7284; www.sath.org; annual membership fees: $45 adults, $30 seniors and students), which offers a wealth of travel resources for all types of disabilities and informed recommendations on destinations, access guides, travel agents, tour operators, vehicle rentals, and companion services; and the **American Foundation for the Blind (AFB)** (© 800/232-5463; www.afb.org), a referral resource for those who are blind or visually impaired that includes information on traveling with Seeing Eye dogs.

For more information specifically targeted to travelers with disabilities, the community website **iCan** (www.icanonline.net) has destination guides and several regular columns on accessible travel. Also check out the quarterly magazine *Emerging Horizons* ($14.95 per year, $19.95 outside the U.S.; www.emerginghorizons.com) and *Open World* magazine, published by SATH (see above; subscription: $13 per year, $21 outside the U.S.).

FOR BRITISH TRAVELERS

The **Royal Association for Disability and Rehabilitation (RADAR),** Unit 12, City Forum, 250 City Rd., London EC1V 8AF (© 020/7250-3222; www.radar.org.uk), publishes three holiday "fact packs" for £2 ($3.30) each or £5 ($8.25) for all three. The first provides general information, including tips for planning and booking a holiday, obtaining insurance, and handling finances; the second outlines transportation available when going abroad and equipment for rent; and the third deals with specialized accommodations. Another good resource is **Holiday Care Service,** 7th floor, Sunley House, 4 Bedford Park, Croydon, Surrey CR0 2AP (© **0845/124-9971;** www.holidaycare.org.uk), a national charity advising on accessible accommodations for the elderly and persons with disabilities. Annual membership is £37 ($61).

GAY & LESBIAN TRAVELERS

In general, Denmark is one of the most gay-friendly countries in Europe and was one of the first to embrace same-sex marriages. Antidiscrimination laws have been in effect since 1987. Most Danes are exceptionally friendly and tolerant of lifestyles of either sexual preference. Obviously, an urban center such as Copenhagen will have a more openly gay life than rural areas. In many ways, the Erotic Museum in Copenhagen illustrates the city's attitudes toward sex—both heterosexual and homosexual. The history of both forms of sexual pleasure is presented in an unprejudiced manner.

The **Danish National Association for Gays and Lesbians** (Landsforeningen for Bøsser og Lesbiske, abbreviated as LBL), maintains its headquarters at Teglgaardstræde 13, 1007 Copenhagen (© **33-13-19-48;** www.lbl.dk), with branches in at least four of the larger cities of Denmark. You might find it hard to reach a live person on their telephone line (their hours of operation are limited), but they maintain one of the most informative and user-friendly websites of any gay organization in Europe, complete with maps on how to reach the gay and lesbian venues they describe on their site.

The International Gay and Lesbian Travel Association (IGLTA) (© **800/448-8550** or 954/776-2626; www.iglta.org) is the trade association for the gay and lesbian travel industry, and offers an online directory of gay- and lesbian-friendly travel businesses; go to their website and click on "Members."

Many agencies offer tours and travel itineraries specifically for gay and lesbian travelers. **Above and Beyond Tours** (© **800/397-2681;** www.abovebeyondtours.com) is the exclusive gay and lesbian tour operator for United Airlines. **Now, Voyager** (© **800/255-6951;** www.nowvoyager. com) is a well-known San Francisco–based gay-owned and -operated travel service.

The following travel guides are available at most travel bookstores and gay and lesbian bookstores: *Frommer's Gay & Lesbian Europe,* an excellent travel resource, which includes a chapter on Copenhagen.

Gay.com Travel (© **800/929-2268** or 415/644-8044; www.gay.com/ travel or www.outandabout.com) is an online resource that's a successor to the popular *Out & About* print magazine.

It provides regularly updated information about gay-owned, gay-oriented, and gay-friendly lodging, dining, sightseeing, nightlife, and shopping establishments, in every important destination worldwide, and trip-planning information for gay and lesbian travelers for more than 50 destinations and along different themes ranging from Sex & Travel to Vacations for Couples.

Spartacus International Gay Guide (Bruno Gmünder Verlag; www. spartacusworld.com/gayguide/) and *Odysseus: The International Gay Travel Planner* (Odysseus Enterprises Ltd.), are both good, annual English-language guidebooks focused on gay men; also look for the *Damron* guides (www.damron.com), with separate, annual books for gay men and lesbians; and *Gay Travel A to Z: The World of Gay & Lesbian Travel Options at Your Fingertips,* by Marianne Ferrari (Ferrari International; Box 35575, Phoenix, AZ 85069), is a good gay and lesbian guidebook series.

SENIOR TRAVEL

Mention the fact that you're a senior citizen when you make your travel reservations. Although all of the major U.S. airlines except America West have cancelled their senior discount and coupon book programs, many hotels in Scandinavia still offer discounts for seniors. In most cities, people over the age of 60 may qualify for reduced admission to theaters, museums, and other attractions, as well as discounted fares on public transportation.

Members of **AARP** (formerly known as the American Association of Retired Persons), 601 E St. NW, Washington, DC 20049 (© **888/ 687-2277**; www.aarp.org), get discounts on hotels, airfares, and car rentals. AARP offers members a wide range of benefits, including *AARP: The Magazine* and a monthly newsletter. Anyone over 50 can join.

Many reliable agencies and organizations target the 50-plus market. **Elderhostel** (© **877/426-8056;** www. elderhostel.org) arranges study programs for those age 55 and over (and a spouse or companion of any age) in the U.S. and in more than 80 countries around the world. Most courses last 5 to 7 days in the U.S. (2–4 weeks abroad), and many include airfare, accommodations in university dormitories or modest inns, meals, and tuition. **ElderTreks** (© **800/741- 7956;** www.eldertreks.com) offers small-group tours to off-the-beaten-path or adventure-travel locations, restricted to travelers 50 and older.

INTRAV (© **800/456-8100;** www. intrav.com) is a high-end tour operator that caters to the mature, discerning traveler, not specifically seniors, with trips around the world that include guided safaris, polar expeditions, private-jet adventures, and small-boat cruises down jungle rivers.

Recommended publications offering travel resources and discounts for seniors include the quarterly magazine *Travel 50 & Beyond* (www.travel50 andbeyond.com); *Travel Unlimited: Uncommon Adventures for the Mature Traveler* (Avalon); *101 Tips*

Traveling with Minors

It's always wise to have plenty of documentation when traveling in today's world with children. For changing details on entry requirements for children traveling abroad, keep up-to-date by going to the U.S. State Department website: http://travel.state.gov. To prevent international child abduction, EU governments have initiated procedures at entry and exit points. These often (but not always) include requiring documentary evidence of relationship and permission for the child's travel from the parent or legal guardian not present. Having such documentation on hand, even if not required, facilitates entries and exits. All children must have their own passport. To obtain a passport, the child *must* be present—that is, in person—at the center issuing the passport. Both parents must be present as well. If not, then a notarized statement from the parents is required. Any questions parents or guardians might have can be answered by calling the **National Passport Information Center** at © **877/487-2778** Monday to Friday 8am to 8pm Eastern Standard Time.

for Mature Travelers, available from Grand Circle Travel (© **800/221-2610** or 617/350-7500; www.gct.com); and *Unbelievably Good Deals and Great Adventures That You Absolutely Can't Get Unless You're Over 50* (McGraw-Hill), by Joann Rattner Heilman.

FAMILY TRAVEL

The family vacation is a rite of passage for many households, one that in a split second can devolve into a *National Lampoon* farce. But as any veteran family vacationer will assure you, a family trip can be among the most pleasurable and rewarding times of your life.

Most Danish hoteliers let children 12 and under stay in a room with their parents for free; others do not. Sometimes this requires a little negotiation at the reception desk.

Danes like kids but don't offer a lot of special amenities for them. For example, a kiddies' menu in a restaurant is a rarity. You can, however, order a half portion, and most waiters will oblige.

At attractions—even if it isn't specifically posted—inquire if a kids' discount is available. European Community citizens under 18 are admitted free to all state-run museums.

To locate those accommodations, restaurants, and attractions that are particularly kid-friendly, refer to the "Kids" icon throughout this guide.

Familyhostel (© **800/733-9753;** www.learn.unh.edu/familyhostel) takes the whole family, including kids ages 8 to 15, on moderately priced domestic and international learning vacations. Lectures, field trips, and sightseeing are guided by a team of academics.

Recommended family travel Internet sites include **Family Travel Forum** (www.familytravelforum.com), a comprehensive site that offers customized trip planning; **Family Travel Network** (www.familytravelnetwork.com), an

award-winning site that offers travel features, deals, and tips; **Traveling Internationally with Your Kids** (www.travelwithyourkids.com), a comprehensive site offering sound advice for long-distance and international travel with children; and **Family Travel Files** (www.thefamilytravelfiles.com), which offers an online magazine and a directory of off-the-beaten-path tours and tour operators for families.

STUDENT TRAVEL

If you're planning to travel outside the U.S., you'd be wise to arm yourself with an **International Student Identity Card (ISIC),** which offers substantial savings on rail passes, plane tickets, and entrance fees. It also provides you with basic health and life insurance and a 24-hour help line. The card is available for $22 from **STA Travel** (© **800/781-4040** in North America; www.sta.com), the biggest student travel agency in the world. If you're no longer a student but are still under 26, you can get an **International Youth Travel Card (IYTC)** for the same price from the same people, which entitles you to some discounts (but not on museum admissions). (*Note:* In 2002, STA Travel bought competitors **Council Travel** and **USIT Campus** after it went bankrupt. It's still operating some offices under the Council name, but it's owned by STA.) **Travel CUTS** (© **800/667-2887** or 416/614-2887; www.travelcuts.com) offers similar services for both Canadians and U.S. residents. Irish students may prefer to turn to **USIT** (© **01/602-1600;** www.usitnow.ie), an Ireland-based specialist in student, youth, and independent travel.

SINGLE TRAVELERS

Single travelers are often hit with a "single supplement" to the base price. To avoid it, you can agree to room with other single travelers on the trip, or you can find a compatible roommate before you go from one of the many roommate locator agencies.

Travel Buddies Singles Travel Club (℃ **800/998-9099;** www.travel buddiesworldwide.com), based in Canada, runs small, intimate, single-friendly group trips and will match you with a roommate free of charge. **TravelChums** (℃ **212/787-2621;** www.travelchums.com) is an Internet-only travel-companion matching service with elements of an online personals-type site, hosted by the respected New York–based Shaw Guides travel service. **The Single Gourmet Club** (www.singlegourmet.com/chapters.php) is an international social, dining, and travel club for singles of all ages, with club chapters in 21 cities in the U.S. and Canada. Annual membership fees vary from city to city.

Many reputable tour companies offer singles-only trips. **Singles Travel International** (℃ **877/765-6874;** www.singlestravelintl.com)offers singles-only trips to places like London, Fiji, and the Greek Islands.

For more information, check out Eleanor Berman's latest edition of *Traveling Solo: Advice and Ideas for More Than 250 Great Vacations* (Globe Pequot), a guide with advice on traveling alone, whether on your own or on a group tour.

10 Planning Your Trip Online

SURFING FOR AIRFARES

The "big three" online travel agencies, **Expedia.com, Travelocity.com,** and **Orbitz.com,** sell most of the air tickets bought on the Internet. (Canadian travelers should try expedia.ca and Travelocity.ca; U.K. residents can go for expedia.co.uk and opodo.co.uk.) Each has different business deals with the airlines and may offer different fares on the same flights, so it's wise to shop around. Expedia and Travelocity will also send you **e-mail notification** when a cheap fare becomes available to your favorite destination. Of the smaller travel agency websites, **Side-Step** (www.sidestep.com) has gotten the best reviews from Frommer's authors. It's a browser add-on that purports to "search 140 sites at once," but in reality beats competitors' fares only as often as other sites do.

Also remember to check **airline websites,** especially those for low-fare carriers such as Southwest, JetBlue, AirTran, WestJet, or Ryanair, whose fares are often misreported or simply missing from travel agency websites. Even with major airlines, you can often shave a few bucks from a fare by booking directly through the airline and avoiding a travel agency's transaction fee. But you'll get these discounts only by **booking online:** Most airlines now offer online-only fares that even their phone agents know nothing about. For the websites of airlines that fly to and from your destination, go to "Getting There," p. 33.

Great **last-minute deals** are available through free weekly e-mail services provided directly by the airlines. Most of these are announced on Tuesday or Wednesday and must be purchased online. Most are valid only for travel that weekend, but some (such as Southwest's) can be booked weeks or months in advance. Sign up for weekly e-mail alerts at airline websites or check megasites that compile comprehensive lists of last-minute specials, such as **SmarterTravel.com.** For last-minute trips, **site59.com** and **last-minutetravel.com** in the U.S. and **lastminute.com** in Europe often have better air-and-hotel package deals than the major-label sites. A website listing numerous bargain sites and airlines around the world is **www.itravel net.com**.

If you're willing to give up some control over your flight details, use what is called an **"opaque" fare service** like **Priceline** (www.priceline.com; www.priceline.co.uk for Europeans) or its smaller competitor **Hotwire** (www.hotwire.com). Both offer rock-bottom prices in exchange for travel on a "mystery airline" at a mysterious time of day, often with a mysterious change of planes en route. The mystery airlines are all major, well-known carriers—and the possibility of being sent from Philadelphia to Chicago via Tampa is remote; the airlines' routing computers have gotten a lot better than they used to be. But your chances of getting a 6am or 11pm flight are pretty high. Hotwire tells you flight prices before you buy; Priceline usually has better deals than Hotwire, but you have to play their "name our price" game. If you're new at this, the helpful folks at **BiddingForTravel** (www.biddingfortravel.com) do a good job of demystifying Priceline's prices and strategies. Priceline and Hotwire are great for flights within North America and between the U.S. and Europe. *Note:* In 2004 Priceline added non-opaque service to its roster. You now have the option to pick exact flights, times, and airlines from a list of offers—or opt to bid on opaque fares as before.

For much more about airfares and savvy air-travel tips and advice, pick up a copy of *Frommer's Fly Safe, Fly Smart* (Wiley Publishing, Inc.).

SURFING FOR HOTELS

Shopping online for hotels is generally done one of two ways: by booking through the hotel's own website or through an independent booking agency (or a fare-service agency like Priceline; see below). These Internet hotel agencies have multiplied in mind-boggling numbers of late, competing for the business of millions of consumers surfing for accommodations around the world. This competitiveness can be a boon to consumers

who have the patience and time to shop and compare the online sites for good deals—but shop they must, for prices can vary considerably from site to site. And keep in mind that hotels at the top of a site's listing may be there for no other reason than that they paid money to get the placement.

Of the "big three" sites, **Expedia** offers a long list of special deals and "virtual tours" or photos of available rooms so you can see what you're paying for (a feature that helps counter the claims that the best rooms are often held back from bargain booking websites). **Travelocity** posts unvarnished customer reviews and ranks its properties according to the AAA rating system. Also reliable are **Hotels.com** and **Quikbook.com.** An excellent free program, **Travelaxe** (www.travelaxe.net), can help you search multiple hotel sites at once, even ones you may never have heard of—and conveniently lists the total price of the room, including the taxes and service charges. Another booking site, **Travelweb** (www.travelweb.com), is partly owned by the hotels it represents (including the Hilton, Hyatt, and Starwood chains) and is therefore plugged directly into the hotels' reservations systems—unlike independent online agencies, which have to fax or e-mail reservation requests to the hotel, a good portion of which get misplaced in the shuffle. More than once, travelers have arrived at the hotel only to be told that they have no reservation. To be fair, many of the major sites are undergoing improvements in service and ease of use, and Expedia will soon be able to plug directly into the reservations systems of many hotel chains—none of which can be bad news for consumers. In the meantime, it's a good idea to **get a confirmation number** and **make a printout** of any online booking transaction.

In the opaque website category, **Priceline** and **Hotwire** are even better

Frommers.com: The Complete Travel Resource

For an excellent travel-planning resource, we highly recommend **Frommers.com** (www.frommers.com), voted Best Travel Site by *PC Magazine*. We're a little biased, of course, but we guarantee that you'll find the travel tips, reviews, monthly vacation giveaways, bookstore, and online-booking capabilities thoroughly indispensable. Among the special features are our popular **Destinations** section, where you'll get expert travel tips, hotel and dining recommendations, and advice on the sights to see for more than 3,500 destinations around the globe; the **Frommers.com Newsletter,** with the latest deals, travel trends, and money-saving secrets; our **Community** area featuring **Message Boards,** where Frommer's readers post queries and share advice (sometimes even our authors show up to answer questions); and our **Photo Center,** where you can post and share vacation tips. When your research is done, the **Online Reservations System** (www.frommers.com/book_a_trip) takes you to Frommer's preferred online partners for booking your vacation at affordable prices.

for hotels than for airfares; with both, you're allowed to pick the neighborhood and quality level of your hotel before offering up your money. Priceline's hotel product even covers Europe and Asia, though it's much better at getting five-star lodging for three-star prices than at finding anything at the bottom of the scale. On the downside, many hotels stick Priceline guests in their least desirable rooms. Be sure to go to the Bidding-ForTravel website (see above) before bidding on a hotel room on Priceline; it features a fairly up-to-date list of hotels that Priceline uses in major cities. For both Priceline and Hotwire, you pay upfront, and the fee is nonrefundable. *Note:* Some hotels do not provide loyalty program credits or points or other frequent-stay amenities when you book a room through opaque online services.

SURFING FOR RENTAL CARS

For booking rental cars online, the best deals are usually found at rental-car company websites, although all the major online travel agencies also offer rental-car reservations services. Priceline and Hotwire work well for rental cars, too; the only "mystery" is which major rental company you get, and for most travelers the difference between Hertz, Avis, and Budget is negligible.

11 The 21st-Century Traveler

INTERNET ACCESS AWAY FROM HOME

Travelers have any number of ways to check their e-mail and access the Internet on the road. Of course, using your own laptop—or even a PDA (personal digital assistant) or electronic organizer with a modem—gives you the most flexibility. But even if you don't have a computer, you can still access your e-mail and even your office computer from cybercafes.

WITHOUT YOUR OWN COMPUTER

It's hard nowadays to find a city that *doesn't* have a few cybercafes. Although there's no definitive directory for cybercafes—these are independent businesses, after all—three places to start looking are at **www.cyber captive.com**, **netcafes.com**, and **www.cybercafe.com**. See "Fast Facts" in each chapter for cybercafes.

Aside from formal cybercafes, most **youth hostels** nowadays have at least one computer you can get to the Internet on. And most **public libraries** across the world offer Internet access free or for a small charge. Avoid **hotel business centers,** unless you're willing to pay exorbitant rates.

Most major airports now have **Internet kiosks** scattered throughout their gates. These kiosks, which you'll also see in shopping malls, hotel lobbies, and tourist information offices around the world, give you basic Web access for a per-minute fee that's usually higher than cybercafe prices. The kiosks' clunkiness and high price means they should be avoided whenever possible.

To retrieve your e-mail, ask your **Internet Service Provider (ISP)** if it has a Web-based interface tied to your existing e-mail account. If your ISP doesn't have such an interface, you can use the free **mail2web** service (www. mail2web.com) to view and reply to your home e-mail. For more flexibility, you may want to open a free, Web-based e-mail account with **Yahoo! Mail** (http://mail.yahoo.com). (Microsoft's Hotmail is another popular option, but Hotmail has severe spam problems.) Your home ISP may be able to forward your e-mail to the Web-based account automatically.

If you need to access files on your office computer, look into a service called **GoToMyPC** (www.gotomypc. com). The service provides a Web-based interface for you to access and manipulate a distant PC from anywhere—even a cybercafe—provided your "target" PC is on and has an always-on connection to the Internet (such as with Road Runner cable). The service offers top-quality security, but if you're worried about hackers, use your own laptop rather than a cybercafe to access the GoToMyPC system.

WITH YOUR OWN COMPUTER

Wi-fi (wireless fidelity) is the buzzword in computer access, and more and more hotels, cafes, and retailers are signing on as wireless "hot spots" from where you can get high-speed connection without cable wires, networking hardware, or a phone line (see below). You can get wi-fi connection one of several ways. Many laptops sold in the past year have built-in wi-fi capability (an 802.11b wireless Ethernet connection). Mac owners have their own networking technology, Apple AirPort. For those with older computers, an 802.11b/**Wi-Fi card** (around $50) can be plugged into your laptop. You sign up for wireless access service much as you do cellphone service, through a plan offered by one of several commercial companies that have made wireless service available in airports, hotel lobbies, and coffee shops, primarily in the U.S. (followed by the U.K. and Japan). **T-Mobile HotSpot** (www. t-mobile.com/hotspot) serves up wireless connections at more than 1,000 Starbucks coffee shops nationwide. **Boingo** (www.boingo.com) and **Wayport** (www.wayport.com) have set up networks in airports and high-class hotel lobbies. IPass providers (see below) also give you access to a few hundred wireless hotel-lobby setups. Best of all, you don't need to be staying at the Four Seasons to use the hotel's network; just set yourself up on a nice couch in the lobby. The companies' pricing policies can be Byzantine, with a variety of monthly, per-connection, and per-minute plans, but in general you pay around $30 a month for limited access—and as more and more companies jump on the wireless bandwagon, prices are likely to get even more competitive.

There are also places that provide **free wireless networks** in cities around the world. To locate these free hot spots, go to **www.personaltelco. net/index.cgi/WirelessCommunities**.

If wi-fi is not available at your destination, most business-class hotels throughout the world offer dataports for laptop modems, and a few thousand hotels in the U.S. and Europe now offer free high-speed Internet access using an Ethernet network cable. You can bring your own cables, but most hotels rent them for around $10. **Call your hotel in advance** to see what your options are.

In addition, major ISPs have **local access numbers** around the world, allowing you to go online by simply placing a local call. Check your ISP's website or call its toll-free number and ask how you can use your current account away from home, and how much it will cost.

If you're traveling outside the reach of your ISP, the **iPass** network has dial-up numbers in most of the world's countries. You'll have to sign up with an iPass provider, who will then tell you how to set up your computer for your destination(s). For a list of iPass providers, go to www.ipass. com and click on "Individual Purchase." One solid provider is **i2roam** (www.i2roam.com; ☎ **866/811-6209** or 920/235-0475).

Wherever you go, bring a **connection kit** of the right power and phone adapters, a spare phone cord, and a spare Ethernet network cable—or find out whether your hotel supplies them to guests.

USING A CELLPHONE
OUTSIDE THE U.S.

The three letters that define much of the world's **wireless capabilities** are GSM (Global System for Mobiles), a big, seamless network that makes for easy cross-border cellphone use throughout Europe and dozens of other countries worldwide. In the U.S., T-Mobile, AT&T Wireless, and Cingular use this quasi-universal system; in Canada, Microcell and some Rogers customers are GSM, and all Europeans and most Australians use GSM.

If your cellphone is on a GSM system, and you have a world-capable multiband phone such as many (but not all) Sony Ericsson, Motorola, or Samsung models, you can make and receive calls across civilized areas on much of the globe. Just call your wireless operator and ask for "international roaming" to be activated on your account. Unfortunately, per-minute charges can be high—usually $1 to $1.50 in Western Europe.

That's why it's important to buy an "unlocked" world phone from the get-go. Many cellphone operators sell "locked" phones that restrict you from using any other removable computer memory phone chip (called a **SIM card**) other than the ones they supply. Having an unlocked phone allows you to install a cheap, prepaid SIM card (found at a local retailer) in your destination country. (Show your phone to the salesperson; not all phones work on all networks.) You'll get a local phone number—and much, much lower calling rates. Getting an already locked phone unlocked can be a complicated process, but it can be done— just call your cellular operator and say you'll be going abroad for several months and want to use the phone with a local provider.

For many, **renting** a phone is a good idea. While you can rent a phone from any number of overseas sites, including kiosks at airports and at car-rental agencies, we suggest renting the phone before you leave home. That way you can give loved ones and business associates your new number, make sure the phone works, and take the phone wherever you go—especially helpful for overseas trips through several countries, where local phone-rental agencies often bill in local currency and may not let you take the phone to another country.

Phone rental isn't cheap. You'll usually pay $40 to $50 per week, plus airtime fees of at least a dollar a minute. If you're traveling to Europe, though, local rental companies often offer free incoming calls within their home country, which can save you big bucks. The bottom line: Shop around.

Two good wireless-rental companies are **InTouch USA** (© **800/ 872-7626;** www.intouchglobal.com) and **Roadpost** (© **888/290-1606** or 905/272-5665; www.roadpost.com). Give them your itinerary, and they'll tell you what wireless products you need. InTouch will also, for free, advise you on whether your existing phone will work overseas; simply call © **703/222-7161** between 9am and 4pm EST, or go to http://intouch global.com/travel.htm.

For trips of more than a few weeks spent in one country, **buying a phone** becomes economically attractive, as many nations have cheap,

---

Online Traveler's Toolbox

Veteran travelers usually carry some essential items to make their trips easier. Following is a selection of handy online tools to bookmark and use.

- **Airplane Seating and Food.** Find out which seats to reserve and which to avoid (and more) on all major domestic airlines at www.seatguru. com. And check out the type of meal (with photos) you'll likely be served on airlines around the world at www.airlinemeals.com.
- **Foreign Languages for Travelers** (www.travlang.com). Learn basic terms in more than 70 languages and click on any underlined phrase to hear what it sounds like.
- **Intellicast** (www.intellicast.com) and **Weather.com** (www.weather. com). Gives weather forecasts for all 50 states and for cities around the world.
- **Mapquest** (www.mapquest.com). This best of the mapping sites lets you choose a specific address or destination, and in seconds, it will return a map and detailed directions.
- **Subway Navigator** (www.subwaynavigator.com). Download subway maps and get savvy advice on using subway systems in dozens of major cities around the world.
- **Time and Date** (www.timeanddate.com). See what time (and day) it is anywhere in the world.
- **Universal Currency Converter** (www.xe.com/ucc). See what your dollar or pound is worth in more than 100 other countries.
- **Visa ATM Locator** (www.visa.com), for locations of PLUS ATMs worldwide, or **MasterCard ATM Locator** (www.mastercard.com), for locations of Cirrus ATMs worldwide.

no-questions-asked prepaid phone systems. Once you arrive at your destination, stop by a local cellphone shop and get the cheapest package; you'll probably pay less than $100 for a phone and a starter calling card. Local calls may be as low as 10¢ per minute, and in many countries incoming calls are free.

12 Getting There

BY PLANE

Flying in winter—Scandinavia's off season—is cheapest; summer is the most expensive. Spring and fall are in between. In any season, midweek fares (Mon–Thurs) are the lowest.

THE MAJOR AIRLINES
FROM NORTH AMERICA SAS (Scandinavian Airlines Systems; © **800/221-2350** in the U.S. or 0870/6072-7727 in the U.K.; www.Scandinavian.net) has more nonstop flights to Scandinavia from more North American cities than any other airline, and it has more flights to and from Denmark and within Scandinavia than any other airline in the world. From Seattle and Chicago, SAS offers nonstop flights to Copenhagen daily in midsummer and almost every day in winter; from Newark, New Jersey, there are daily flights year-round to Copenhagen. SAS's agreement with United Airlines, the "Star Alliance," connects other U.S. cities (such as Dallas/Fort Worth, Denver, Houston, Los Angeles, Minneapolis/St. Paul, New York, San Francisco, and Washington, D.C.) to the three U.S. gateway cities.

SAS offers one of the lowest fares to Copenhagen from New York. With restrictions, and flying during specific off-peak seasons, round-trip economy tickets can cost as little as $362 for those who pay for their tickets within 2 days after booking and stay abroad between 7 and 30 days. No refunds or changes in flight dates are permitted. A similar round-trip ticket from Chicago to Copenhagen costs $403. Both tickets cost more for travel on Friday, Saturday, or Sunday. These prices can—and almost certainly will—change during the lifetime of this edition. Always confirm prices before booking your ticket.

Nonstop flights to Copenhagen from the greater New York area take about 7½ hours; from Chicago, around 8½ hours; from Seattle, 9½ hours.

FROM THE U.K.   British Airways (© **800/AIRWAYS,** or 0870/850-9850 in the U.K.; www.ba.com) offers convenient connections through Heathrow and Gatwick to Copenhagen. The price structure (and discounted prices on hotel packages) sometimes makes a stopover in Britain less expensive than you might have thought. **SAS** offers five daily nonstop flights to Copenhagen from Heathrow (1¾ hr.), two daily nonstops from Glasgow (2 hr.), and three daily nonstops from Manchester (2 hr., 20 min.). Other European airlines with connections through their home countries to Copenhagen include **Icelandair** (© **800/223-5500** in the U.S., or 020/78-74-10-00 in the U.K.; www.icelandair.com), **KLM** (© **800/374-7747** in the U.S., or 0870/507-4074 in the U.K.; www.klm.com), and **Lufthansa** (© **800/645-3880** in the U.S., or 0870/8377-747 in the U.K.; www.lufthansa.com). Be aware, however, that unless you make all your flight arrangements in North America before you go, you might find some of these flights prohibitively expensive.

A NOTE FOR BRITISH TRAVELERS   British newspapers are always full of classified ads touting "slashed" fares from London to other destinations. One good source is *Time Out,* a magazine filled with cultural information about London. The *Evening Standard* maintains a daily travel section, and the Sunday editions of virtually any newspaper in the British Isles will run ads.

Although competition among airline consolidators is fierce, one well-recommended company is **Trailfinders** (© **0845/05-05-891** in London; www.trailfinder.com). Buying blocks of tickets from such carriers as British Airways, SAS, and KLM, it offers cost-conscious fares from London's Heathrow or Gatwick airports to Stockholm.

In London, many bucket shops around Victoria and Earl's Court offer low fares. Make sure that the company you deal with is a member of the IATA, ABTA, or ATOL. These umbrella organizations will help you if anything goes wrong.

CEEFAX, a British television information service, airs on many home and hotel TVs and runs details of package holidays and flights to Stockholm and beyond. Just switch to your CEEFAX channel, and you'll find a menu of listings that includes travel information.

Make sure that you understand the bottom line on any special deal. Ask if all surcharges, including airport taxes and other hidden costs, are included before committing. Upon investigation, some of these "deals" are not as attractive as advertised. Also, find out about any penalties incurred if you're forced to cancel at the last minute.

GETTING THROUGH THE AIRPORT

With the federalization of airport security, procedures at U.S. airports are more stable and consistent than ever. Generally, you'll be fine if you arrive **1 hour** before a domestic flight and **2 hours** before an international flight; if you show up late, tell an airline employee and she'll probably whisk you to the front of the line.

Bring a **current, government-issued photo ID** such as a driver's license or passport. Keep your ID at the ready to show at check-in, the security checkpoint, and sometimes even the gate. (Children under 18 do not need government-issued photo IDs for domestic flights, but they do for international flights to most countries.)

In 2003, the TSA phased out **gate check-in** at all U.S. airports. And **e-tickets** have made paper tickets nearly obsolete. Passengers with e-tickets can beat the ticket-counter lines by using airport **electronic kiosks** or even **online check-in** from your home computer. Online check-in involves logging on to your airlines' website, accessing your reservation, and printing out your boarding pass—and the airline may even offer you bonus miles to do so! If you're using a kiosk at the airport, bring the credit card you used to book the ticket or your frequent-flier card. Print out your boarding pass from the kiosk and simply proceed to the security checkpoint with your pass and a photo ID. If you're checking bags or looking to snag an exit-row seat, you will be able to do so using most airline kiosks. Even the smaller airlines are employing the kiosk system, but always call your airline to make sure these alternatives are available. **Curbside check-in** is also a good way to avoid lines, although a few airlines still ban curbside check-in; call before you go.

Security checkpoint lines are mostly shorter than they were during 2001 and 2002, but some doozies remain. If you have trouble standing for long periods of time, tell an airline employee; the airline will provide a wheelchair. Speed up security by **not wearing metal objects** such as big belt buckles. If you've got metallic body parts, a note from your doctor can prevent a long chat with the security screeners. Keep in mind that only **ticketed passengers** are allowed past security, except for folks escorting passengers with disabilities or children.

Federalization has stabilized **what you can carry on** and **what you can't.** The general rule is that sharp things are out, nail clippers are okay, and food and beverages must be passed through the X-ray machine—but that security screeners can't make you drink from your coffee cup. Bring food in your carry-on rather than checking it, as explosive-detection machines used on checked luggage have been known to mistake food (especially chocolate, for some reason) for bombs. Travelers in the U.S. are allowed one carry-on bag, plus a "personal item" such as a purse, briefcase, or laptop bag. Carry-on hoarders can stuff all sorts of things into a laptop bag; as long as it has a laptop in it, it's still considered a personal item. The Transportation Security Administration (TSA) has issued a list of restricted items; check its website (www.tsa.gov/public/index.jsp) for details.

Airport screeners may decide that your checked luggage needs to be searched by hand. You can now purchase luggage locks that allow screeners to open and relock a checked bag if hand-searching is necessary. Look for Travel Sentry certified locks at luggage or travel shops and Brookstone stores (you can buy them online at www.brookstone.com). These locks, approved by the TSA, can be opened by luggage inspectors with a special code or key. For more information on the locks, visit www.travelsentry.org. If you use something other than TSA-approved locks, your lock will be cut off your suitcase if a TSA agent needs to hand-search your luggage.

FLYING FOR LESS: TIPS FOR GETTING THE BEST AIRFARE

Passengers sharing the same airplane cabin rarely pay the same fare. Travelers who need to purchase tickets at the last minute, change their itinerary at a moment's notice, or fly one-way often get stuck paying the premium rate. Here are some ways to keep your airfare costs down.

- Passengers who can book their ticket **long in advance,** who can **stay over Saturday night,** or who **fly midweek** or **at less-trafficked hours** may pay a fraction of the full fare. If your schedule is flexible, say so, and ask if you can secure a cheaper fare by changing your flight plans.

- You can also save on airfares by keeping an eye out in local newspapers for **promotional specials** or **fare wars,** when airlines lower prices on their most popular routes. You rarely see fare wars offered for peak travel times, but if you can travel in the off months, you may snag a bargain.

- Search **the Internet** for cheap fares (see "Planning Your Trip Online").

- **Consolidators,** also known as bucket shops, are great sources for international tickets, although they usually can't beat the Internet on fares within North America. Start by looking in Sunday newspaper travel sections; U.S. travelers should focus on the *New York Times, Los Angeles Times,* and *Miami Herald.* For less-developed destinations, small travel agents who cater to immigrant communities in large cities often have the best deals. *Beware:* Bucket shop tickets are usually nonrefundable or rigged with stiff cancellation penalties, often as high as 50% to 75% of the ticket price, and some put you on charter airlines, which may leave at inconvenient times and experience delays.

Several reliable consolidators are worldwide and available on the Net. **STA Travel** is now the world's leader in student travel, thanks to its purchase of Council Travel. It also offers good fares for travelers of all ages. **ELTExpress (Flights. com)** (✆ 800/TRAV-800; www. eltexpress.com) started in Europe and has excellent fares worldwide, but particularly to that continent. It also has "local" websites in 12 countries. **FlyCheap** (✆ 800/ FLY-CHEAP; www.1800flycheap. com) is owned by package-holiday megalith MyTravel and so has especially good access to fares for sunny destinations. **Air Tickets Direct** (✆ 800/778-3447; www. airticketsdirect.com) is based in Montreal and leverages the currently weak Canadian dollar for low fares.

- Join **frequent-flier clubs.** Accrue enough miles, and you'll be rewarded with free flights and elite status. It's free, and you'll get the best choice of seats, faster response to phone inquiries, and prompter service if your luggage is stolen, if your flight is canceled or delayed, or if you want to change your seat. You don't need to fly to build frequent-flier miles—**frequent-flier credit cards** can provide thousands of miles for doing your everyday shopping.

- For many more tips about air travel, including a rundown of the major frequent-flier credit cards, pick up a copy of *Frommer's Fly Safe, Fly Smart* (Wiley Publishing, Inc.).

BY CAR

You can easily drive to Denmark from Germany. Many people drive to Jutland from Hamburg, Bremerhaven, and Lübeck. A bridge links Jutland and the central island of Funen. In 1998 a bridge opened that goes across the Great Belt from Funen to the island of Zealand, site of the city of Copenhagen. The bridge lies near Nyborg, Denmark. Once in West Zealand, you'll still have to drive east across the island to Copenhagen.

Car-ferry service to Denmark from the United Kingdom generally leaves passengers at Esbjerg, where they must cross from Jutland to Copenhagen. From Germany, it's possible to take a car ferry from Travemünde, northeast of Lübeck, which will deposit you at Gedser, Denmark. From here, connect with E55, an express highway north to Copenhagen.

BY TRAIN

If you're in Europe, it's easy to get to Denmark by train. Copenhagen is the main rail hub between Scandinavia and the rest of Europe. For example, the London–Copenhagen train— through Ostende, Belgium, or Hook, Holland—leaves four times daily and takes 22 hours. About 10 daily express trains run from Hamburg to Copenhagen (5½ hr.). There are also intercity trains on the Merkur route from Karlsruhe, Germany, to Cologne to Hamburg to Copenhagen. The Berlin-Ostbahnhof-Copenhagen train (8½ hr.) connects with Eastern European trains. Two daily express trains make this run.

Thousands of trains run from Britain to the Continent, and at least some of them go directly across or under the Channel, through France or Belgium and Germany into Denmark. For example, a train leaves London's Victoria Station daily at 9am and arrives in Copenhagen the next day at 8:25am. Another train leaves London's Victoria Station at 8:45pm and arrives in Copenhagen the next day at 8:20pm. Both go through Dover–Ostende, or with a connection at Brussels. Once you're in Copenhagen, you can make rail connections to Norway, Finland, and Sweden. Because of the time and distances involved, many passengers rent a couchette (sleeping berth), which costs around £18 per person. Designed like padded benches stacked bunk-style, they're usually clustered six to a compartment.

If you plan to travel extensively on European and/or British railroads, it would be worthwhile for you to get a copy of the latest edition of the *Thomas Cook European Timetable of Railroads*. It's available online at www.thomascooktimetables.com, at a cost of $27.95, plus $4.95 priority shipping in the States and US$6.95 for airmail shipments to Canada.

RAIL PASSES FOR NORTH AMERICAN TRAVELERS

EURAILPASS If you plan to travel extensively in Europe, the **Eurailpass** may be a good bet. It's valid for first-class rail travel in 17 European countries. With one ticket, you travel whenever and wherever you please; more than 100,000 rail miles are at your disposal. Here's how it works: The pass is sold only in North America. A Eurailpass good for 15 days costs $588, a pass for 21 days is $762, a 1-month pass costs $946, a 2-month pass is $1,338, and a 3-month pass goes for $1,654. Children under 4 travel free if they don't occupy a seat; all children under 12 who take up a seat are charged half-price. If you're under 26, you can buy a **Eurail Youthpass,** which entitles you to unlimited second-class travel for 15 days for $414, 21 days for $534, 1 month for $664, 2 months for $938 or 3 months for $1,160. Travelers considering buying a 15-day or 1-month pass should estimate rail distance before deciding whether a pass is worthwhile. To take full advantage of the tickets for 15 days

or a month, you'd have to spend a great deal of time on the train. Eurailpass holders are entitled to substantial discounts on certain buses and ferries as well. Travel agents in all towns and railway agents in such major cities as New York, Montreal, and Los Angeles, sell these tickets. For information on Eurailpasses, and other European train data, call RailEurope at © **800/438-7245,** or visit them on the Web at **www.raileurope.com**.

Eurail Saverpass offers 15% discounts to groups of three or more people traveling together between April and September, or two people traveling together between October and March. The price of a Saverpass, valid all over Europe for first class only, is $498 for 15 days, $648 for 21 days, $804 for 1 month, $1,138 for 2 months, and $1,408 for 3 months. Even more freedom is offered by the **Saver Flexipass,** similar to the Eurail Saverpass, except that you are not confined to consecutive-day travel. For travel over any 10 days within 2 months, the fare is $592; for any 15 days over 2 months, the fare is $778.

Eurail Flexipass allows even greater flexibility. It's valid in first class and offers the same privileges as the Eurailpass. However, it provides a number of individual travel days over a much longer period of consecutive days. Using this pass makes it possible to stay longer in one city and not lose a single day of travel. There are two Flexipasses: 10 days of travel within 2 months for $694, and 15 days of travel within 2 months for $914.

With many of the same qualifications and restrictions as the Eurail Flexipass, the **Eurail Youth Flexipass** is sold only to travelers under age 25. It allows 10 days of travel within 2 months for $488 and 15 days of travel within 2 months for $642.

SCANRAIL PASS If your visit to Europe will be primarily in Scandinavia, the Scanrail pass may be better and cheaper than the Eurailpass. This pass allows its owner a designated number of days of free rail travel within a larger time block. (Presumably, this allows for days devoted to sightseeing scattered among days of rail transfers between cities or sites of interest.) You can choose a total of any 5 days of unlimited rail travel during a 2-month period, 10 days of rail travel within a 2-month period, or 21 days of unlimited rail travel. The pass, which is valid on all lines of the state railways of Denmark, Finland, Norway, and Sweden, offers discounts or free travel on some (but not all) of the region's ferry lines as well. The pass can be purchased only in North America. It's available from any office of **RailEurope** (© **800/848-7245** in U.S., or 800/361-RAIL in Canada) or **ScanAm World Tours,** 108 N. Main St., Cranbury, NJ 08512 (© **800/545-2204;** www.scandinaviantravel.com).

Depending on whether you choose first- or second-class rail transport, 5 days out of 2 months costs $291, 10 days out of 2 months costs $390, and 21 consecutive days of unlimited travel costs $453. Seniors get an 11% discount; students, a 30% discount.

RAIL PASSES FOR BRITISH TRAVELERS

If you plan to do a lot of exploring, you may prefer one of the three rail passes designed for unlimited train travel within a designated region during a predetermined number of days. These passes are sold in Britain and several other European countries.

An **InterRail Pass** is available to passengers of any nationality, with some restrictions—they must be under age 26 and able to prove residency in a European or North African country (Morocco, Algeria, and Tunisia) for at least 6 months before buying the pass. It allows unlimited travel through Europe, except Albania and the republics of the former Soviet Union. Prices are complicated and

vary depending on the countries you want to include. For pricing purposes, Europe is divided into eight zones; the cost depends on the number of zones you include. The most expensive option £295 ($487) allows 1 month of unlimited travel in all eight zones and is known to BritRail staff as a "global." The least expensive option £119 ($196) allows 12 days of travel within only one zone.

Passengers age 26 and older can buy an **InterRail 26-Plus Pass** that, unfortunately, is severely limited geographically. It is, however, accepted for travel throughout Denmark, Finland, Norway, and Sweden. Second-class travel with the pass costs £223 ($368) for 12 days or £415 ($685) for 22 days. Passengers must meet the same residency requirements that apply to the InterRail Pass (described above).

For information on buying individual rail tickets or any of the just-mentioned passes, contact **National Rail Inquiries,** Victoria Station, London (© **08705/848-848** or 0845/748-4950). Tickets and passes also are available at any of the larger railway stations as well as selected travel agencies throughout Britain and the rest of Europe.

BY SHIP & FERRY

It's easy to travel by water from several ports to Denmark. Liners carrying cars and passengers operate from England, Germany, Poland, Norway, and Sweden. Check with your travel agent about these cruises.

FROM BRITAIN DFDS Seaways (© 0870/458-5120; www.dfds seaways.com) runs vessels year-round between Harwich, England, and Esbjerg in West Jutland. The crossing takes 16 to 20 hours. The same line also sails from Newcastle upon Tyne to Esbjerg, but only in the summer, as part of a 22-hour passage. Overnight cabins and space for cars are available on both routes.

FROM NORWAY & SWEDEN
The **Norwegian Coastal Voyage/Bergen Line Services** (℃ **800/323-7436** or 212/319-1300 in the U.S.; www.coastalvoyage.com) operates vessels from Oslo to Hirtshals in North Jutland.

Stena Line (www.stenaline.com) runs popular sea links from Oslo to Frederikshavn, North Jutland (11½ hr.), and from Gothenburg, Sweden, to Frederikshavn (3 hr.). For information, schedules, and fares, contact **Stena Line UK, Ltd.,** Charter House Park St., Ashford, Kent TN24 8EX (℃ **01233/647-047;** www.stenaline. co.uk). For 24-hour updates on sailing, call ℃ **08705/755-755.**

FROM GERMANY From the Baltic coast, ferries operate between Kiel and Bagenkop on the Danish island of Langeland. Reserve tickets at **Langeland–Kiel Touristik,** Oslokai 3, Kiel (℃ **0431/97415-0).**

13 Packages & Specialty Vacations

PACKAGE TOURS
For travelers who feel more comfortable if everything is prearranged—hotels, transportation, sightseeing excursions, luggage handling, tips, taxes, and even meals—a package tour is the obvious choice, and it may even help save money.

Reliable tour operators include **Olson Travelworld,** 1145 Clark St., Stevens Point, WI 54481 (℃ **800/826-4026**), and **Scantours, Inc.,** 3439 Wade St., Los Angeles, CA 90006 (℃ **800/223-7226** or 310/636-4656; www.scantours.com).

BUS TOURS   ScanAm World Tours (℃ **800/545-2204;** www.scanamtours.com) offers a tour through the "Heart of Fairy Tale Denmark." You can choose a 5-day, 4-night trip through Hans Christian Andersen country, including a visit to Odense (his birthplace) and an excursion to Legoland. Tours begin at $535 per person.

SELF-DRIVE   TOURS Several companies offer self-drive tours, which usually include accommodations, rental cars, and customized itineraries. **Scantours, Inc.** (℃ **800/223-7226;** www.scantours.com) features the 5-day "A Taste of Danish Castles," which is available year-round. Prices begin at $1,075 per person. The company also sponsors a tour of Danish inns. The 4-day self-drive tour includes accommodations, breakfast, car rental, and an itinerary. Prices start at $350 per person.

BICYCLE TOURS An excellent way to explore the flat, rolling Danish countryside is on a bicycle. Numerous organizations (including Scantours, Inc. and ScanAm Tours) sponsor bike tours through various regions of the country. You can choose one that covers the castles, beaches, and fjords of northern Denmark; the southern Funen islands; the beaches and marshland of western Jutland; or the lake country in eastern Jutland. **Blue Marble Travel** (℃ **800/258-8689;** www. bluemarble.org) offers 7-day excursions to Hans Christian Andersen country and several small islands in the Baltic for $1,545 per person. **Dansk Cyklist Forbund,** Rømersgade 7, DK-1362 Copenhagen K (℃ **33-32-31-21;** www.dcf.dk), can provide the latest information on cycling tours in Denmark.

ADVENTURE TRAVEL OPERATORS
In North America, a few companies offer adventure trips to Denmark. **Crossing Latitudes,** 420 W. Koch St., Bozeman, MT 59715 (℃ **800/572-8747** or fax 406/585-5356; www. crossinglatitudes.com), offers sea kayaking and backpacking expeditions throughout the region; and **Blue Marble Travel,** 222A Race St.,

Philadelphia, PA 19106 (© **800/ 258-8689** or 215/923-3788; www. bluemarble.org), features reasonably priced biking and hiking trips in Denmark and Norway.

IN THE U.K.

The oldest travel agency in Britain, **Cox & Kings,** Gordon House 10, Greencoat Place, London SW1P 1PH (© **020/7873-5000;** www.coxand kings.co.uk), was established in 1758. Today the company specializes in unusual, if pricey, holidays. Its offerings in Scandinavia include cruises through the spectacular fjords and waterways, bus and rail tours through sites of historic and aesthetic interest, and visits to the region's best-known handicraft centers, Viking burial sites, and historic churches. The company's staff is noted for its focus on tours of ecological and environmental interest.

To cycle through the splendors of Scandinavia, you can join Britain's oldest and largest association of bicycle riders, the **Cyclists' Touring Club,** Cotterell House, 69 Meadrow, Godalming, Surrey GU7 3HS (© **0870/873-0060;** www.ctc.org.uk). Founded in 1878, it charges £30.50 ($50) a year for membership, which includes information, maps, a subscription to a newsletter packed with practical information and morale boosters, plus recommended cycling routes through virtually every country in Europe. The organization's information bank on scenic routes through Scandinavia is especially comprehensive. Membership can be arranged over the phone with a credit card (such as MasterCard, Visa, Access, or Barclaycard).

LEARNING VACATIONS

Danish Cultural Institute (Det Danske Kultur Institutu), Kultorvet 2, DK-1175 Copenhagen (© **33-13-54-48;** fax 33-15-10-91; www.dankultur. dk), offers summer seminars in English, including a course in Danish culture. Credit programs are available, but many courses are geared toward professional groups from abroad. An especially interesting course for those with some knowledge of Danish is "Danmark, Danskerne, Dansk," which includes language instruction.

An international series of programs for persons over 50 who are interested in combining travel and learning is offered by **Interhostel,** developed by the University of New Hampshire. Each program lasts 2 weeks, is led by a university faculty or staff member, and is arranged in conjunction with a host college, university, or cultural institution. Participants may stay longer if they want. Interhostel offers programs consisting of cultural and intellectual activities, with field trips to museums and other centers of interest. For information, contact the University of New Hampshire, Division of Continuing Education, 6 Garrison Ave., Durham, NH 03824 (© **800/313-5327** or 603/862-2015; www.learn.unh.edu).

Another good source of information about courses in Denmark is the **American Institute for Foreign Study (AIFS),** River Plaza, 9 W. Broad St., Stamford, CT 06902 (© **800/ 727-2437** or 203/399-5000; www. aifs.org). This organization can set up transportation and arrange for summer courses, with bed and board included.

The largest organization dealing with higher education in Europe is the **Institute of International Education (IIE),** 809 United Nations Plaza, New York, NY 10017 (© **800/445-0443** or 212/883-8200; www.iie.org). A few of its booklets are free; for $46.95, plus $6 for postage, you can buy the more definitive *Vacation Study Abroad.* The Information Center in New York is open to the public Tuesday through Thursday from 11am to 4pm. The institute is closed on major holidays.

One well-recommended clearinghouse for academic programs throughout the world is the **National Registration Center for Study**

Heritage—The Search for Roots

More than 12 million North Americans have Scandinavian roots, many in Denmark. To help you trace your ancestry, Danish consulates can furnish fact sheets. Many original Danish records are available on microfilm from **The Family History Museum,** 35 N. West Temple, Salt Lake City, UT 84150 (© **801/240-2331**).

Established in 1992, the **Danish Immigrant Museum,** Elk Horn, Iowa (© **712/764-7001;** www.dkmuseum.org), is devoted to telling the story of Scandinavian migration to the United States. It also collects and preserves a vital chapter in Danish-American history.

In Denmark itself, the major archives concerning immigration are held at **Det Danske Udvandrerarkiv** (Danes' Worldwide Archives), Arkivstraede 1, P.O. Box 1731, DK-9100 Aalborg (© **99-31-42-20;** fax 98-10-22-48; www.emiarch.dk).

Abroad (NRCSA), 823 N. 2nd St., P.O. Box 1393, Milwaukee, WI 53203 (© **414/278-0631;** www.nrcsa.com). The organization maintains language study programs throughout Europe.

HOME STAYS

Friendship Force International (FFI), 34 Peachtree St. NW, Suite 900, Atlanta, GA 30303 (© **404/522-9490;** www.friendshipforce.org), is a nonprofit organization that encourages friendship among people worldwide. Dozens of branch offices throughout North America arrange visits, usually once a year. Because of group bookings, the airfare to the host country is usually less than the cost of individual APEX tickets. Each participant spends 2 weeks in the host country, one as a guest in the home of a family and the second traveling in the host country.

Servas, 11 St. John St., Suite 505, New York, NY 10038 (© **212/267-0252;** www.usservas.org), is an international nonprofit, nongovernmental, interfaith network of travelers and hosts whose goal is to help promote world peace, goodwill, and understanding. (Its name means "to serve" in Esperanto.) Servas hosts offer travelers hospitality for 2 days. Travelers pay an

$85 annual fee and a $25 list deposit after filling out an application and being approved by an interviewer (interviewers are located across the United States). They then receive Servas directories listing the names and addresses of Servas hosts.

HOME EXCHANGES

One of the most exciting breakthroughs in modern tourism is the home exchange. Sometimes the family automobile is included. Of course, you must be comfortable with the idea of having strangers in your home, and you must be content to spend your vacation in one place.

Home exchanges cut costs. You don't pay hotel bills, and you can also save money by shopping in markets and eating in. One potential problem, though, is that you may not get a home in the area you request.

Intervac, U.S., 30 Corte San Fernando, Tiburon, CA 94920 (© **800/756-HOME** or 415/435-3497; www.intervacus.com), is part of the largest worldwide exchange network. It publishes four catalogs a year, containing more than 10,000 homes in more than 36 countries. Members contact each other directly. The cost is $65 plus postage, which includes the purchase of three of the company's catalogs (which will be mailed to you), plus the inclusion of your own listing in whichever one of the three catalogs you select.

The Invented City, 41 Sutter St., Suite 1090, San Francisco, CA 94104 (© **415/252-1141;** www.invented-city.com), publishes home-exchange listings three times a year. For the $50 membership fee, you can list your home with your own written descriptive summary.

HomeLink (© **800/638-3841;** www.homelink.org) will send you five directories a year—in one of which you're listed—for $75.

14 Getting Around Denmark

BY PLANE

The best way to get around Scandinavia is to take advantage of air passes that apply to the whole region. If you're traveling extensively in Europe, special European passes are also available.

SAS'S VISIT SCANDINAVIA FARE

The vast distances encourage air travel between Scandinavia's far-flung points. One of the most worthwhile promotions is SAS's **Visit Scandinavia Pass.** Available only to travelers who fly SAS across the Atlantic, it includes up to six coupons, each of which is valid for any SAS flight within or between Denmark, Norway, and Sweden. Each coupon costs $69, a price that's especially appealing when you consider that an economy-class ticket between Stockholm and Copenhagen can cost as much as $250 each way. The pass is especially valuable if you plan to travel to the northern frontiers of Sweden or Norway; in that case, the savings over the price of an economy-class ticket can be substantial. For information on buying the pass, call **SAS** (© **800/221-2350**).

WITHIN DENMARK   For those in a hurry, **SAS** (© **70-10-20-00** in Copenhagen) operates daily service between Copenhagen and points on Jutland's mainland. From Copenhagen it takes about 40 minutes to fly to Aalborg, 35 minutes to Århus, and 30 minutes to Odense's Beldringe Airport.

Fares to other Danish cities are sometimes included in a transatlantic ticket at no extra charge, as long as the additional cities are specified when the ticket is written.

BY TRAIN

Flat, low-lying Denmark, with its hundreds of bridges and absence of mountains, has a large network of railway lines that connect virtually every hamlet with the largest city, Copenhagen. For **information, schedules, and fares** anywhere in Denmark, call © **70-13-14-15.** Waiting times for a live person on this telephone line range from long to very long. Alternatively, you can check the Danish National Railways website, **www.dsb.dk**, for schedules and prices, and to reserve seats.

A word you're likely to see and hear frequently is *Lyntog* ("Express Trains"), which are the fastest trains presently operational in Denmark. Be warned in advance that the most crowded times on Danish trains are Fridays, Sundays, and national holidays, so plan your reservations accordingly.

On any train in Denmark, children between the ages of 4 and 15 are charged half-price if they're accompanied by an adult, and up to two children under 4 can travel for free with an adult on any train in Denmark. Seniors (age 65 or older) receive a discount of 20% for travel on Fridays, Sundays, and holidays, and a discount of 45% every other day of the week. No identification is needed when you buy your ticket, but the conductor who checks your ticket might ask for proof of age.

The Danish government offers dozens of discounts on the country's rail networks—depending on the type of traveler, days or hours traveled, and destination. Because discounts change often, it's best to ask for a discount based on your age and the number of days (or hours) you intend to travel.

BY BUS

By far the best way to visit rural Denmark is by car, but if you want or need to travel by bus, be aware that you'll probably get your bus at the railway station. (In much of Scandinavia, buses take passengers to destinations not served by the train; therefore, the bus route often originates at the railway station.) The arrival of trains and departure of buses are usually closely timed.

For seniors (ages 65 and over), round-trip bus tickets are sometimes offered at one-way prices (excluding Sat, Sun, and peak travel periods around Christmas and Easter). Most discounts are granted only to seniors who are traveling beyond the city limits of their point of origin.

BY CAR

RENTALS Avis, Budget, and Hertz offer well-serviced, well-maintained fleets of cars. You may have to reserve and pay for your rental car in advance (usually 2 weeks, but occasionally as little as 48 hr.) to get the lowest rates. Unfortunately, if your trip is canceled or your arrival date changes, you might have to fill out a lot of forms for a refund. All three companies may charge slightly higher rates to clients who reserve less than 48 hours in advance and pay at pickup. The highest rates are charged to walk-in customers who arrange their rentals after they arrive in Denmark.

Before you rent, you should know that the Danish government imposes a whopping **25% tax** on **all car rentals.** Agencies that encourage prepaid rates almost never collect this tax in advance—instead, it's imposed as part of a separate transaction when you pick up the car. Furthermore, any car retrieved at a Danish airport is subject to a one-time supplemental tax of 150DKK ($25); you might prefer to pick up your car at a downtown location. Membership in certain travel clubs or organizations (such as AAA or AARP) might qualify you for a modest discount.

Note: The following rates are for 1 week's rental of a Volkswagen Polo (the smallest car available). They include unlimited mileage and are subject to change.

Avis (© **800/331-1212** in the U.S.; www.avis.com) maintains three offices in Copenhagen: two at the arrivals hall of the airport and another at Kampmannsgade 1 (© **32-51-20-99**). The rate is $258—if you pay 2 weeks before your departure. "Walk-in" customers who don't reserve from North America pay double that rate.

Budget (© **800/472-3325** in the U.S.; www.budget.com) has two rental locations in Copenhagen. Budget's rate is $136 if you pay in North America. The price is considerably higher for walk-in customers. Budget has a large branch at the Copenhagen airport (© **32-52-39-00**).

Hertz (© **800/654-3131** in the U.S.; www.hertz.com) charges a prepaid rate of $181. Hertz's office in central Copenhagen is at Ved Vesterport 3 (© **33-17-90-20**); another office is at the airport (© **32-50-93-00**).

Also consider using a small company. **Kemwel** (© **800/678-0678** in the U.S.; www.kemwel.com) is the North American representative for two Denmark-based car companies, Van Wijk and Hertz. It may be able to offer attractive rental prices to North Americans who pay in full at least 10 days before their departure. Seniors and members of AAA get a 5% discount.

15 Tips on Accommodations

There are other alternatives, but, chances are, most visitors to Denmark will check into a hotel. Accommodations range from the most basic, perhaps lacking private bathrooms, to the most deluxe. Outside of Copenhagen, you are likely to encounter first class in the top category instead of *luxe* accommodations. The one thing you'll not find is a truly cheap hotel. Even the most inexpensive hotels might be considered a bit pricey in some parts of the world. To compensate, many hotels, especially chain members, offer discounted rates on weekends when hotels lose their most reliable client—the commercial traveler.

Our accommodation listings include service charges and taxes so you won't be shocked when the time comes to pay the bill and a lot of extras are added on, as is the situation in many European countries.

Denmark classifies its hotels by stars ranging from one (the most basic) to five (deluxe). A hotel without a restaurant is called Hotel *Garni*. One-star hotel rooms have a hand basin with hot and cold running water and at least one bathroom per 10 rooms for communal use; two-star hotels have at least 30% of the units with private bathrooms; three-star hotels offer rooms with their own private bathroom (such hotels also have an elevator if there are more than two floors). Moving up, four-star hotels offer round-the-clock reception, an a la carte restaurant, room service, minibars, laundry service, and a bar. The best hotels in Denmark are five-stars, with luxuriously appointed rooms, often indoor pools, professionally staffed fitness centers, air conditioning, safes in the rooms, and round-the-clock room service among other luxuries.

In one star hotels, expect rooms to cost up to $75 a night; two stars, $76 to $120; three stars, $121 to $150;

four stars, $151 to $210, and five stars, $211 to $250, or beyond.

If you have not booked a room prior to your arrival in Copenhagen, you may call personally at **Wonderful Copenhagen Tourist Information** at Bernstorffsgade 1, opposite the Central Station next to Tivoli. A handling fee of $9 is charged. There is also a booking desk, charging the same handling fee, at the **Copenhagen Airport Arrival Hall**.

Advance booking online is possible through **Wonderful Copenhagen Tourist Information & Booking Center**, Gammel Kongevej 1, DK 1610 Copenhagen (© **70-22-24-42;** www.visitcopenhagen.dk). Outside Copenhagen, bookings can be made online at www.danishhotels.dk and www.visitdenmark.com, through local tourist offices, or directly with the hotel.

ALTERNATIVE ACCOMMODATIONS

If you'd like to avoid a stay in a hotel, consider these other options:

Bed & Breakfast: Dansk Bed & Breakfast (see below) publishes a catalogue of guest houses throughout Denmark that receive visitors for overnight stays, fortifying them the next morning with a hearty Danish breakfast. A typical B&B, of several possibilities, might be a century-old farmhouse built of granite and half-timbering and dating from the 18th century, standing on 8 acres (3.2 hectares) of land, with a small lake and an ecological vegetable garden. Contact **Dansk Bed & Breakfast** at Bernstorffsvej 71A, DK-2900 Hellerup/ Copenhagen (© **39-61-04-05;** www. bedandbreakfast.dk).

The best and densest concentration of B&Bs is found on the Hans Christian Andersen island of Funen. There is a separate organization handling these bookings: **Nyborg Tourist Office,** Torvey 9, DK-5800 Nyborg (© **65-31-02-80;** www.bed-breakfast-fyn.dk). The typical overnight price for a double room in a B&B is 160DKK ($27).

Castles & Manor Houses: Denmark is riddled with old manor houses and even a few small castles that received paying guests all year. In our view, this type of lodging is the most exciting way to live in Denmark, because of the grandeur of the buildings. You get to feel like a king (or queen), or at least a prince and princess for the night. Some of the establishments in this category are more like country homes than castles or manors. By taking in boarders, many of the owners of these privately owned estates are preserving Denmark's cultural heritage. For more information, contact **Danish Castles & Manor Houses,** Sankt Leonis Straede 1A, DK-8800 Viborg (© **86-60-38-44;** www.slotte-herregaarde.dk).

Danish Inns: Nearly 100 atmospheric and often old world accommodations spread across the country have formed an association, offering accommodations in old inns (called *kros*) and hotels that often date back hundreds of years. The bedrooms, however, are mostly renovated in the modern style. You get atmosphere and comfort, and most often good, solid food, both regional dishes but in many cases French specialties as well. For this type of accommodation, book through **Danska Kroer og Hoteller,** Vejlevej 16, DK- 8700 Horsens (© **75-64-87-00;** www.krohotel.dk).

Farm Holidays: Some 110 farms all over Denmark receive paying guests. To get close to the heart of the country and to meet the Danes, there is no better way than spending a week on one of these farms. In addition to an atmospheric stay, you can enjoy good country cooking with fresh vegetables, newly laid eggs, and rich butter. You stay on a farm as the guest of the family, joining members and other guests for meals. Often lodgings are in a small apartment on the grounds or even a cottage near the main building. In many cases you do your own housekeeping. Prices average around $30 per person, including a full Danish breakfast. You can book with the farm directly or else go through **Landsforeningen for Landboturisme,** Lerbakken 7, DK-8410 Rønde. (© **87-37-39-00;** www.bondegaardsferie.dk).

Holiday Homes: Yes, it's possible to rent your own house—most often a seaside cottage—throughout Denmark. The houses may be a snug retreat for two or else spacious enough to accommodate 10 to 12 guests. Some of these holiday homes are within a 30-minute drive of Copenhagen. They are available all year, and prices begin at around $500 per week, the rates depending on the season, size, and location. Naturally, seaside holiday homes are the most sought after and most expensive in July and August. Many of the best homes are found on the west coast of Jutland, often with an indoor swimming pool and sauna. To book one of these homes contact one of the following organizations: **DanCenter** (© **70-13-16-16;** www.dancenter.com); **Dansommer** (© **86-17-61-22;** www.dansommer.com); **Novasol AS** (© **70-42-44-24;** www.novasol.com); and **Sol og Strand** (© **99-44-44-44;** www.sologstrand.com).

Chain Hotels & Discounts: The most prevalent chain hotel in Denmark is **Best Western.** (© **800/WESTERN**). It offers a Best Western Advance Card that allows you to take advantage of special "summer low" or "winter special promotion" rates, and grants such privileges as allowing one child under the age of 12 to stay free in a room shared with parents.

16 Suggested Itineraries

If You Have 1 Week

Days 1–3 Spend your first 3 days in Copenhagen. After recovering from the flight, have dinner at the Tivoli Gardens (in the summer) or Nyhavn (in the winter). If you're arriving from nearby and will not have jet lag on your first day, explore Copenhagen by walking along Strøget—the world's largest pedestrian street—then visiting Kongens Nytorv (King's New Square). Spend the morning of the second day taking one of our walking tours (see chapter 4, "Exploring Copenhagen"); then (in summer) spend the afternoon wandering through the Tivoli and listening to the free music. Devote Day 3 to more serious sightseeing, including visits to Christiansborg Palace and the Ny Carlsberg Glyptotek.

Day 4 Leave Copenhagen and head north, stopping over at the modern art museum, Louisiana, before heading to Helsingør, site of Kronborg Castle of *Hamlet* fame. Spend the night in Helsingør, or return to Copenhagen.

Day 5 Journey to Odense on the island of Funen, birthplace of Hans Christian Andersen. Spend the rest of the day and evening exploring its many attractions.

Day 6 Stop in Roskilde to see its cathedral and the Viking Ship Museum. Return to Copenhagen and spend the night.

Day 7 Try another walking tour, and schedule interior visits to Rosenborg Castle and, if you have time, the National Museum. Return to the Tivoli for a farewell drink.

If You Have 2 Weeks

Day 1 Recover from jet lag and have dinner at the Tivoli (in the summer) or at Scala, a restaurant complex across from the Tivoli (in the off season).

Day 2 In the morning, take our first walking tour (see chapter 4). Spend the afternoon wandering around the Tivoli Gardens (in the summer).

Day 3 Take another walking tour and visit Christiansborg Palace and the Ny Carlsberg Glyptotek.

Day 4 Head north from Copenhagen. Visit the modern art museum, Louisiana, and have lunch at Helsingør, site of Kronborg Castle of *Hamlet* fame. Spend the night in Helsingør.

Day 5 Explore North Zealand, with visits to the royal palace at Fredensborg and the 17th-century Frederiksberg Castle at Hillerød. Spend the night in Helsingør.

Day 6 Return to Copenhagen and visit Rosenborg Castle and the National Museum.

Day 7 In Copenhagen, explore the other attractions of Zealand, journeying outside the capital to the open-air museum, Frilandsmuseet. Head to Roskilde for lunch, and visit the cathedral, the Viking Ship Museum, and the Iron Age Village at Lejre.

Day 8 Head south from Copenhagen to explore South Zealand. Visit the old market town of Køge, Vallø Castle, and Selso Slot. Spend the night in a typical inn on Zealand.

Day 9 Go west, crossing mid-Zealand. At Korsør, cross the bridge to Nyborg. Visit Nyborg Castle before driving to Odense to explore the city of Hans Christian Andersen. Stop overnight in Odense.

Day 10 Spend time exploring more of Odense, and then visit the Viking ship at Ladby and Egeskov Castle, outside Odense.

Day 11 Drive south from Odense to Svendborg. Explore the nearby islands of Thurø and Tåsinge.

Day 12   From Svendborg, board a ferry (make a reservation) and head for the island of Ærø. Spend the night in the capital, Ærøskøbing, or at an island inn.

Day 13   Leave Ærø and return to Svendborg by ferry. Drive north toward Odense along Route 9 until you connect with E20 west, the highway into Jutland. In Jutland, take Route 32 at the junction with E20 to Ribe. Spend the night in Ribe.

Day 14   Leave Ribe and drive to Silkeborg to view Sky Mountain. Ride on a paddle-wheel steamer on the Silkeborg Lakes. Visit the Silkeborg Museum. From Silkeborg, drive to Århus, where you can explore the Old Town. Have fun at Århus's Tivoli amusement park. Spend the night.

17 Recommended Books

HISTORY & PHILOSOPHY *A Kierkegaard Anthology,* edited by Robert Bretall (Princeton University Press), explores the work of the Copenhagen-born philosopher who developed an almost-pathological sense of involvement in theology. A representative selection of some of his more significant works is included.

Copenhagen, A Historical Guide, by Torben Ejlersen (published by Høst & Søn in Denmark, and available at most bookstores there), an 88-page guide, takes you on a brief tour of the city that began as a ferry landing and became one of the most important capitals of Europe.

Of Danish Ways, written by two Danish-Americans, Ingeborg S. MacHiffic and Margaret A. Nielsen (Harper & Row, 1984), a delightful account of a land and its people, has a little bit of everything: history, social consciousness, customs, food, handicrafts, art, music, and theater.

BIOGRAPHY & LITERATURE *Andersen's Fairy Tales,* by H. C. Andersen (New American Library), and *The Complete Hans Christian Andersen Fairy Tales* (Crown) are anthologies that include all of his most important works, such as *The Little Mermaid, The Tinderbox,* and *The Princess and the Pea.*

Danish Literature: A Short Critical Guide, by Paul Borum (Nordic Books), is a well-written review that explores Danish literature from the Middle Ages to the 1970s.

Out of Africa (Modern Library), *Letters from Africa* (University of Chicago Press), and *Seven Gothic Tales* (Random House) are all by Karen Blixen (who wrote under the name Isak Dinesen), one of the major authors of the 20th century who gained renewed fame with the release of the 1985 movie *Out of Africa,* with Meryl Streep and Robert Redford. *Isak Dinesen,* by Judith Thurman (St. Martin's Press) chronicles Blixen's amazing life from an unhappy childhood in Denmark to marriage to Baron Blixen to immigration to Kenya to her passionate love affair with Denys Finch Hatton.

FAST FACTS: Denmark

Business Hours Most **banks** are open Monday through Friday from 9:30am to 4pm (Thurs to 6pm), but outside Copenhagen, banking hours vary. **Stores** are generally open Monday through Thursday from 9am to 5:30pm, Friday 9am to 7 or 8pm, and Saturday noon to 2pm; most are closed Sunday.

Drug Laws Penalties for the possession, use, purchase, sale, or manufacturing of drugs are severe. The quantity of the controlled substance is more important than the type of substance. Danish police are particularly strict with cases involving the sale of drugs to children.

Electricity Voltage is generally 220 volts AC, 50 to 60 cycles. In many camping sites, 110-volt power plugs are also available. Adapters and transformers may be purchased in Denmark. It's always best to check at your hotel desk before using an electrical outlet.

Embassies All embassies are in Copenhagen. The embassy of the **United States** is at Dag Hammärskjölds Allé 24, DK-2100 Copenhagen (② 35-55-31-44). Other embassies are the **United Kingdom,** Kastelsvej 40, DK-2100 Copenhagen (② 35-44-52-00); **Canada,** Kristen Berniskows Gade 1, DK-1105 Copenhagen K (② 33-48-32-00); **Australia,** Dampfaergeveg 26, DK-2100 Copenhagen (② 70-26-36-76); and **Ireland,** Østbanegade 21, DK-2100 Copenhagen (② 35-42-32-33).

Emergencies Dial ② **112** for the fire department, the police, or an ambulance, or to report a sea or an air accident. Emergency calls from public telephone kiosks are free (no coins needed).

Holidays See "When to Go," earlier in this chapter.

Language Danish is the national tongue. English is commonly spoken, especially among young people. You should have few, if any, language barriers. The best phrase book is *Danish for Travellers* (Berlitz).

Liquor Laws To consume alcohol in Danish bars, restaurants, or cafes, customers must be 18 or older. There are no restrictions on children under 18 who drink at home or, for example, from a bottle in a public park. Danish police tend to be lenient unless drinkers become raucous or uncontrollable. There is no leniency, however, in the matter of driving while intoxicated. It's illegal to drive with a blood-alcohol level of 0.8 or more, which could be produced by two drinks. If the level is 1.5, motorists pay a serious fine. If it's more than 1.5, drivers can lose their license. If the level is 2.0 or more (usually produced by six or seven drinks), a prison term of at least 14 days might follow. Liquor stores in Denmark are closed on Sunday.

Mail Most post offices are open Monday through Friday from 9 or 10am to 5 or 6pm and Saturday from 9am to noon; they're closed Sunday. All mail to North America is sent airmail without extra charge. The cost for mail weighing 20 grams (.175 oz.) is 6DKK ($1). Mailboxes are painted red and display the embossed crown and trumpet of the Danish Postal Society.

Maps The best map for touring Denmark is part of the series published by Hallwag. It's for sale at all major bookstores in Copenhagen, including the most centrally located one, **Boghallen,** Rådhuspladsen 37 (② **33-47-25-60**), in the Town Hall Square.

Newspapers & Magazines English-language newspapers are sold at all major news kiosks in Copenhagen but are much harder to find in the provinces. London papers are flown in for early-morning delivery, but you may find the *International Herald Tribune* or *USA Today* more interesting. Pick up a copy of *Copenhagen This Week,* printed in English, which contains useful information.

Passports **For Residents of the United States:** Whether you're applying in person or by mail, you can download passport applications from the U.S. State Department website at **http://travel.state.gov**. For general information, call the **National Passport Agency** (✆ **202/647-0518**). To find your regional passport office, either check the U.S. State Department website or call the **National Passport Information Center** toll-free number (✆ **877/ 487-2778**) for automated information.

For Residents of Canada: Passport applications are available at travel agencies throughout Canada or from the central **Passport Office,** Department of Foreign Affairs and International Trade, Ottawa, ON K1A 0G3 (✆ **800/567-6868**; www.ppt.gc.ca).

For Residents of the United Kingdom: To pick up an application for a standard 10-year passport (5-yr. passport for children under 16), visit your nearest passport office, major post office, or travel agency or contact the **United Kingdom Passport Service** at ✆ **0870/521-0410** or search its website at www.ukpa.gov.uk.

For Residents of Ireland: You can apply for a 10-year passport at the **Passport Office,** Setanta Centre, Molesworth Street, Dublin 2 (✆ **01/671- 1633**; www.irlgov.ie/iveagh). Those under age 18 and over 65 must apply for a €12 3-year passport. You can also apply at 1A South Mall, Cork (✆ **021/272-525**), or at most main post offices.

For Residents of Australia: You can pick up an application from your local post office or any branch of Passports Australia, but you must schedule an interview at the passport office to present your application materials. Call the **Australian Passport Information Service** at ✆ **131-232,** or visit the government website at www.passports.gov.au.

For Residents of New Zealand: You can pick up a passport application at any New Zealand Passports Office or download it from their website. Contact the **Passports Office** at ✆ **0800/225-050** in New Zealand or 04/ 474-8100, or log on to www.passports.govt.nz.

Pharmacies They're known as *apoteker* in Danish and are open Monday through Thursday from 9am to 5:30pm, Friday 9am to 7pm, and Saturday 9am to 1pm.

Police Dial ✆ **112** for police assistance.

Radio & TV No English-language radio or TV stations broadcast from Denmark. Only radios and TVs with satellite reception can receive signals from countries such as Britain. News programs in English are broadcast Monday through Saturday at 8:30am on Radio Denmark, 93.85 MHz. Radio 1 (90.8 MHz VHF) features news and classical music. Channels 2 and 3 (96.5/93.9 MHz) include some entertainment, broadcast light news items, and offer light music. Most TV stations transmit from 7:30am to 11:30pm. Most films (many of which are American) are shown in their original languages, with Danish subtitles.

Restrooms All big plazas, such as Town Hall Square in Copenhagen, have public lavatories. In small towns and villages, head for the marketplace. Hygienic standards are usually adequate. Sometimes men and women patronize the same toilets (signs read TOILETTER or WC). Otherwise, men's rooms are marked HERRER or H, and women's rooms are marked DAMER or D.

Safety Denmark is one of the safest European countries for travelers. Copenhagen, the major population center, naturally experiences the most crime. Muggings have been reported in the vicinity of the railway station, especially late at night, but crimes of extreme violence are exceedingly rare. Exercise the usual precautions you would when traveling anywhere.

Taxes The 25% VAT (value-added tax) on goods and services is known in Denmark as *moms* (pronounced "mumps"). Special tax-free exports are possible, and many stores will mail goods home to you, circumventing moms. If you want to take your purchases with you, look for shops displaying Danish tax-free shopping notices. Such shops offer tourists tax refunds for personal export. This refund applies to purchases of at least 300DKK ($50) for U.S. and Canadian visitors. Danish Customs must stamp your tax-free invoice when you leave the country. You can receive your refund at Copenhagen's Kastrup International Airport when you depart. If you go by land or sea, you can receive your refund by mail. Mail requests for refunds to Danish Tax-Free Shopping A/S, H. J. Holstvej 5A, DK-2605 Brøndby, Denmark. You'll be reimbursed by check, cash, or credit- or charge-card credit in the currency you want.

For the refund to apply, the 300 DKK must be spent in one store, but not necessarily at the same time. Some major department stores allow purchases to be made over several days or even weeks, at the end of which receipts will be tallied. Service and handling fees are deducted from the total, so actual refunds come up to about 19%. Information on this program is available from the Danish Tourist Board (see "Visitor Information," earlier in this chapter).

A 25% moms is included in hotel and restaurant bills, service charges, entrance fees, and repair bills for foreign-registered cars. No refunds are possible on these items.

Telephone The country code for Denmark is **45**. It should precede any call made to Denmark from another country.

Danish phones are fully automatic. Dial the eight-digit number; there are no city area codes. Don't insert any coins until your party answers. At public telephone booths, use two 50-øre coins or a 1-krone or 5-krone coin only. You can make more than one call on the same payment if your time hasn't run out. Emergency calls are free.

Time Denmark operates on Central European Time—1 hour ahead of Greenwich Mean Time and 6 hours ahead of Eastern Standard Time. Daylight saving time is from the end of March to the end of September.

Tipping Tips are seldom expected, but when they are, you should give only 1 or 2DKK (15¢ to 35¢). Porters charge fixed prices, and tipping is not customary for hairdressers or barbers. Service is built into the system, and hotels, restaurants, and even taxis include a 15% service charge in their rates. Because of the service charge, plus the 25% moms, you'll probably have to pay an additional 40% for some services!

Consider tipping only for special services—some Danes would feel insulted if you offered them a tip.

Water Tap water is safe to drink throughout Denmark.

3

Settling into Copenhagen

Copenhagen, the capital of Denmark, got its name from the word *køben-havn,* which means "merchants' harbor." It grew in size and importance because of its position on the Øresund (the Sound), the body of water between Denmark and Sweden, guarding the entrance to the Baltic.

From its humble beginnings, Copenhagen has become the largest city in Scandinavia, home to 1.5 million people. It's the seat of one of the oldest kingdoms in the world.

Over the centuries Copenhagen has suffered more than its share of invasions and disasters. In the 17th century, the Swedes repeatedly besieged it, and in the 18th century, it endured the plague and two devastating fires. The British attacked twice during the Napoleonic wars in the early 1800s. In 1940, the Nazis invaded Denmark and held the city until 1945, when the British army moved in again, this time as liberators.

Copenhagen is a city with much charm, as reflected in its canals, narrow streets, and old houses. Its most famous resident was Hans Christian Andersen, whose memory lives on. Another of Copenhagen's world-renowned inhabitants was Søren Kierkegaard, who used to take long morning strolls in the city, planning his next addition to the collection of essays that eventually earned him the title "father of existentialism."

In 2000, the Øresund Bridge was officially opened, linking Sweden and Denmark physically for the first time. Today there's a 16km (9.9-mile) car and train link between Zealand (the eastern part of Denmark) and Skån, the southern part of Sweden. If you'd like to tie in a visit with Copenhagen with the château country of Sweden, just drive across the bridge.

Copenhagen still retains some of the characteristics of a village. If you forget the suburbs, you can cover most of the central belt on foot. It's almost as if the city was designed for strolling, as reflected by its Strøget, the longest and oldest pedestrians-only street in Europe.

1 Orientation

GETTING THERE

BY PLANE You arrive at **Kastrup Airport** (② 32-31-32-31; www.cph.dk), 12km (7½ miles) from the center of Copenhagen. Air-rail trains link the airport with the Central Railway Station in the center of Copenhagen. The ride takes 11 minutes, and costs 25.50DKK ($4.25). Located right under the airport's arrivals and departures halls, the Air Rail Terminal is a short escalator ride from the gates. You can also take an SAS bus to the city terminal; the fare is 25.50DKK ($4.25). A taxi to the city center costs around 150DKK ($25).

BY TRAIN Trains arrive at the **Hoved Banegård** (Central Railroad Station; ② 70-13-14-15 for rail information), in the center of Copenhagen, near Tivoli Gardens and the Rådhuspladsen. The station operates a luggage-checking service, but room bookings are available only at the tourist office (see "Visitor

Information," below). You can exchange money at **Den Danske Bank** (© **33-12-04-11**), open daily 7am to 8pm.

From the Central Railroad Station, you can connect with the **S-tog,** a local train; trains depart from platforms in the terminal itself. The information desk is near tracks 5 and 6.

BY BUS   Buses from Zealand and elsewhere pull into the Central Railroad Station. For bus information, call © **36-13-14-15** daily 7am to 9:30pm.

BY CAR   If you're driving from Germany, a car ferry will take you from Travemünde to Gedser in southern Denmark. From Gedser, get on E55 north, an express highway that will deliver you to the southern outskirts of Copenhagen. If you're coming from Sweden and crossing at Helsingborg, you'll land on the Danish side of Helsingør. From there, take express highway E55 south to the northern outskirts of Copenhagen.

BY FERRY   Most ferryboats land at Havnegade, at the southern tip of Nyhavn, a short walk from the center of Copenhagen. Taxis also wait here for ferry arrivals. Most arrivals are from Malmö, Sweden; ferries from continental Europe usually land in South Zealand.

VISITOR INFORMATION
The **Copenhagen Tourist Information Center,** Vesterbrogade 4A (© **70-22-24-42;** www.woco.dk), across from Tivoli's main entrance, dispenses information. It's open in July and August Monday to Saturday 9am to 8pm; May and June Monday to Saturday 9am to 6pm; September to April Monday to Friday 9am to 4pm and Saturday 9am to 2pm.

CITY LAYOUT
MAIN ARTERIES & STREETS   The heart of Old Copenhagen is a warren of pedestrian streets, bounded by Nørreport Station to the north, Rådhuspladsen (Town Hall Square) to the west, and Kongens Nytorv to the east. **Strøget,** the longest continuous pedestrians-only route in Europe, goes east from Town Hall Square to Kongens Nytorv, and is made up of five streets: Frederiksberggade, Nygade, Vimmelskaftet, Amagertorv, and Østergade. Strøget is lined with shops, bars, restaurants, and, in summer, sidewalk cafes. **Pistolstræde** is a maze of galleries, restaurants, and boutiques, housed in restored 18th-century buildings.

Fiolstræde (Violet St.), a dignified street with antiques shops and bookshops, cuts through the university (Latin Quarter). If you turn into Rosengaarden at the top of Fiolstræde, you'll come to **Kultorvet** (Coal Square), just before you reach Nørreport Station. Here you join the third main pedestrian street, **Købmagergade** (Butcher St.), which winds around and finally meets Strøget at Amagertorv.

At the end of Strøget you approach **Kongens Nytorv** (King's Square). This is the site of the Royal Theater and Magasin, the largest department store in Copenhagen. This will put you at the beginning of **Nyhavn,** the former seamen's quarter that has been gentrified into an upmarket area of expensive restaurants, apartments, cafes, and boutiques.

The government of Denmark is centered on the small island of **Slotsholmen,** which is connected to the center by eight different bridges. You'll find several museums, notably Christiansborg Castle, on the island.

The center of Copenhagen is **Rådhuspladsen** (Town Hall Square). From here it's a short walk to the Tivoli Gardens, the major attraction of Copenhagen, and the Central Railroad Station, S-tog, and bus terminus. **Vesterbrogade,** a wide boulevard, passes by Tivoli en route to the Central Railroad Station. **H. C. Andersens Boulevard,** another major avenue named after Denmark's most famous writer, runs along Rådhuspladsen and Tivoli Gardens.

FINDING AN ADDRESS All even numbers are on one side of the street, all odd numbers on the other. Buildings are listed in numerical order. A, B, or C is often inserted after the street number.

NEIGHBORHOODS IN BRIEF

Tivoli Gardens These amusement gardens were built on the site of former fortifications in the heart of Copenhagen, on the south side of Rådhuspladsen. Some 160,000 flowers and 110,000 electric lights set the scene. A collection of restaurants, dance halls, theaters, beer gardens, and lakes make up Tivoli, built in 1843.

Strøget This pedestrians-only street begins at Rådhuspladsen. Lying on either side of Strøget are its most interesting features, Gammeltorv and Nytorv, "old" and "new" squares. They're the sites of fruit and vegetable markets, as well as stalls selling bric-a-brac and handmade jewelry. The word "Strøget" doesn't appear on any maps. Instead, Strøget encompasses five streets: Frederiksberggade, Nygade, Villelskaftet, Amagertorv, and Østergade.

Nyhavn This is the harbor area, which was for years the haunt of sailors looking for tattoos and other diversions. Nowadays it's one of the most elegant sections of the city, site of the deluxe Hotel d'Angleterre and many prestigious restaurants. The Royal Theater stands on Kongens Nytorv.

Indre By This is the Old Town, the heart of Copenhagen. Once filled with monasteries, it's a maze of streets, alleyways, and squares. If you cross Gammeltorv and Nørregade, you'll be in the university area, nicknamed the Latin Quarter. The **Vor Frue Kirke** (cathedral of Copenhagen) is here, and the **Rundetårn** (Round Tower).

Slotsholmen This island, site of Christiansborg Palace, was where Bishop Absalon built the first fortress in the city in 1167. Today it's the seat of the Danish parliament and home of Thorvaldsen's Museum. Bridges link Slotsholmen to Indre. You can also visit the Royal Library, the Theater Museum, and the Royal Stables. The 17th-century Børsen (stock exchange) is also here.

Christianshavn This was the "new town" ordered by master builder King Christian IV in the early 1500s. The town was originally constructed to house workers in the shipbuilding industry. Visitors come today mainly to see the Danish Film Museum on Store Søndervoldstræde, and **Vors Frelsers Kirke,** on the corner of Prinsessegade and Skt. Annægade. Sightseers can climb the spire of the old church for a panoramic view.

Christiania This offbeat district, once a barracks for soldiers, is within walking distance of Vor Frelsers Kirke at Christianshavn. You can enter the area on Prinsessegade. The craft shops and restaurants here are fairly cheap because the residents refuse to pay Denmark's crippling 25% tax. In 1971 many young and homeless people moved in, without the city's permission, proclaiming Christiania a "free city." It has been a controversial place ever since.

Vesterbro Funky and eclectic, Vesterbro would be comparable to the East Village or Williamsburg in New York City. Its main street, **Istedgade,** the center of the action, runs west from the rail depot in the center of town. Don't come here for monuments or museums, but for hip cafes, bars, music, and ethnic restaurants. No longer a slum, Vesterbro centers on Halmtorvet. Cafes and trendy young people dominate the night around Halmtorvet, Vesterbro's main square, not drug dealers and prostitutes. Expect gentrification but also cultural diversity such as Turkish-Kurdish gift shops, Manila food markets, Thai video stars, and Istanbul barbers.

Nørrebro Adjacent to Vesterbro (see above), Nørrebro takes the immigrant overflow, and is also rich in artisan shops and ethnic restaurants, especially Turkish and Pakistani. This area has been a blue-collar neighborhood since the middle of the 19th century. The original Danish settlers have long since departed, replaced by immigrants who are not always greeted with a friendly reception in Copenhagen. The area also abounds with artists, students, and musicians who can't afford the high rents elsewhere.

Numerous secondhand clothing stores—especially around Sankt Hans Torv—give Nørrebro the flavor of a Middle Eastern bazaar. Antiques shops (believe us, many of the furnishings and objets d'art aren't authentic) also fill the area. Most of these "antiques" stores lie along Ravnsborgade. On Saturday morning a flea market is in full swing along the wall of Assistens Kirkegård, to the west of Nørrebrogade.

Frederiksberg Heading west of the inner city along Vesterbrogade, you will reach the residential and business district of Frederiksberg. It grew up around **Frederiksberg Palace,** constructed in the Italianate style with an ocher facade. A park, Frederiksberg Have, surrounds the palace. To the west of the palace is the Zoologisk Have, one of the largest zoos in Europe.

Dragør Dragør is a fishing village south of the city that dates from the 16th century. Along with Tivoli, this seems to be everybody's favorite leisure spot. It's especially recommended if you only have time to see the Copenhagen area. Walk its cobblestone streets and enjoy its 65 old red-roofed houses, designated as national landmarks.

2 Getting Around

Copenhagen is a walker's paradise, neat and compact. Many of the major sightseeing attractions are close to one another.

BY PUBLIC TRANSPORTATION

A joint zone fare system includes Copenhagen Transport buses; State Railway, Metro, and S-tog trains in Copenhagen and North Zealand; plus some private railway routes within a 40km (25-mile) radius of the capital, enabling you to transfer from train to bus and vice versa with the same ticket.

BASIC FARES A *grundbillet* (basic ticket) for both buses and trains costs 17DKK ($2.85). You can buy 10 tickets for 10DKK ($1.65). Children 11 and under ride for half fare; those 4 and under go free on local trains; and those 6 and under go free on buses. For 100DKK ($17) you can purchase a ticket allowing 24-hour bus and train travel through nearly half of Zealand; it's half-price for children 7 to 11, and free for children 6 and under.

DISCOUNT PASSES   The **Copenhagen Card** entitles you to free and unlimited travel by bus and rail throughout the metropolitan area (including North Zealand), 25% to 50% discounts on crossings to and from Sweden, and free admission to many sights and museums. The card is available for 1 or 3 days and costs 199DKK ($33) and 399DKK ($67), respectively. Up to 2 children under the age of 10 are allowed to go free with each adult card. If you have 3 or more children, a 50% discount is granted. Buy the card at tourist offices, at the airport, at train stations, and at most hotels. For more information, contact the Copenhagen Tourist Information Center (see the previous section, "Orientation").

Students who have an **International Student Identity Card (ISIC)** are entitled to a number of travel breaks in Copenhagen. A card can be purchased in the United States at any **Council Travel office** (for the office nearest you, call ✆ **800/GET-AN-ID**).

For information about low-cost train, ferry, and plane trips, go to **Wasteels,** Skoubogade 6 (✆ **33-14-46-33**), in Copenhagen. It's open Monday to Friday 9am to 7pm and Saturday 10am to 3pm.

Eurailpasses (which must be purchased in the U.S.) and **Nordturist Pass** tickets (which can be purchased at any train station in Scandinavia) can be used on local trains in Copenhagen. (For a more complete discussion of the cost/use of these passes, see p. 37.)

BY BUS   Copenhagen's well-maintained buses are the least expensive method of getting around. Most buses leave from Rådhuspladsen. A basic ticket allows 1 hour of travel and unlimited transfers within the zone where you started your trip. For information, call ✆ **36-13-14-15.**

BY METRO   In 2002, Copenhagen launched its first Metro line, taking passengers from east to west across the city or vice versa. Operating 24 hours, the Metro runs as far west as Vanlose or as far south as Vestmager. Nørreport is the transfer station to the **S-tog** system, the commuter rail link to the suburbs. Metro trains run every 2 minutes during rush hours and every 15 minutes at night. Fares are integrated into the existing zonal systems (see "Basic Fares," above).

BY S-TOG   The S-tog connects the heart of Copenhagen with its suburbs. Use of the tickets is the same as on buses (see "Basic Fares," above). You can transfer from a bus line to an S-tog train on the same ticket. Eurailpass holders generally ride free. For more information, call ✆ **33-14-17-01.**

BY CAR

Because of the widespread availability of traffic-free walkways in Copenhagen, and because of its many parks, gardens, and canalside promenades, the Danish capital is well suited to pedestrian promenades. It's best to park your car in any of the dozens of city parking lots, then retrieve it when you're ready to explore the suburbs or countryside. Many parking lots are open 24 hours, but a few close between 1 and 7am; some close on Saturday afternoon and on Sunday when traffic is generally lighter. The cost ranges from 23DKK to 25DKK ($3.85–$4.20) per hour or 240DKK ($40) for 24 hours. Two centrally located parking lots are **Industriens Hus,** H. C. Andersens Blvd. 18 (✆ **33-91-21-75**), open Monday to Friday 7am to 1:30am, and Saturday and Sunday 9am to 12:45am; and **Park City,** Israels Plads (✆ **70-22-92-20**), open daily from 6am to midnight.

BY TAXI

Watch for the FRI (free) sign or green light to hail a taxi. Be sure the taxis are metered. **Taxa 4x35** (𝒞 **35-35-35-35**) operates the largest fleet of cabs. Tips are included in the meter price: 23DKK ($3.85) at the drop of the flag and 11.25DKK ($1.90) per kilometer thereafter, Monday to Friday 7am to 4pm. From 6pm to 6am, and all day Saturday and Sunday, the cost is 15DKK ($2.50) per kilometer. Many drivers speak English.

BY BICYCLE

To reduce pollution from cars (among other reasons), many Copenhageners ride bicycles. You can rent a bike at **Københavns Cyklebors,** Gothersgade 157 (𝒞 **33-14-07-17**). Depending on the bike, daily rates range from 60DKK to 150DKK ($10–$25), with deposits from 200DKK to 500DKK ($33–$84). Hours are Monday to Friday 8:30am to 5:30pm and Saturday 10am to 1:30pm.

FAST FACTS: Copenhagen

American Express Amex is represented throughout Denmark by **Nyman & Schultz,** Nørregade 7A (𝒞 **33-13-11-81;** bus: 34 or 35), with a branch in Terminal 3 of the Copenhagen Airport. Fulfilling all the functions of American Express except for foreign exchange services, the main office is open Monday to Thursday 8:30am to 4:30pm, and Friday 8:30am to 4pm. The airport office remains open until 8:30pm Monday to Friday. On weekends, and overnight on weekdays, a recorded message, in English, will deliver the phone number of a 24-hour AMEX service in Stockholm. This is useful for anyone who has lost a card or traveler's checks.

Bookstores One of the best and most centrally located is **Politikens Boghallen,** Rådhuspladsen 37 (𝒞 **33-47-25-60;** bus: 2, 8, or 30), offering more English titles than its competitors. Hours are Monday to Friday 10am to 7pm, and Saturday 10am to 4pm.

Business Hours Most **banks** are open Monday to Friday 10am to 4pm (to 6pm Thurs). **Stores** are generally open Monday to Thursday 9am to 6pm, Friday 9am to 7 or 8pm, and Saturday 9am to 2pm; most are closed Sunday. **Offices** are open Monday to Friday 9 or 10am to 4 or 5pm.

Currency Exchange Banks are generally your best bet. The main branch of Den Danske Bank (The Danish Bank), Holmens Kanal, 2-12 (𝒞 **33-44-00-00**), is open Monday to Friday from 10am to 4pm (to 6pm Thurs). When banks are closed, you can exchange money at **Forex** (𝒞 **33-11-29-05**) in the Central Railroad Station, daily 8am to 9pm, or at the **Change Group,** Østergade 61 (𝒞 **33-93-04-55;** bus: 9 or 10), daily 8am to 8pm.

Dentists During regular business hours, ask your hotel to call the nearest English-speaking dentist. For emergencies, go to **Tandlægevagten,** Oslo Plads 14 (𝒞 **35-38-02-51;** bus: 6 or 9), near Østerport Station and the U.S. Embassy. It's open Monday to Friday 8am to 9:30pm and Saturday, Sunday, and holidays 10am to noon. Be prepared to pay in cash.

Doctors To reach a doctor, dial 𝒞 **70-27-57-57.** The doctor's fee is payable in cash, with most visits costing 250DKK ($42) if you're from a non-EU country. Virtually every doctor speaks English.

Emergencies Dial ✆ **112** to report a fire or to call the police or an ambulance. State your phone number and address. Emergency calls from public telephones are free (no coins needed).

Hospitals In cases of illness or accident, even foreigners are entitled to free medical treatment in Denmark. One of the most centrally located hospitals is **Rigshospitalet,** Blegdamsvej 9 (✆ **35-45-35-45**; bus: 10).

Internet Access To check your e-mail or to send messages, go to **Copenhagen Hovebibliotek,** Krystalgade 15 (✆ **33-73-60-60**; bus: 5, 14, or 16), open Monday to Friday 10am to 7pm, Saturday 10am to 2pm.

Lost Property The Lost and Found Property office at Slotsherrensvej 113, 2720 Vanløse (✆ **38-74-88-22**; bus: 12 or 22), is open Monday, Wednesday, and Friday 9am to 2pm, Tuesday and Thursday 9am to 5:30pm.

Luggage Storage & Lockers Luggage can be stored in lockers at Central Railroad Station. Lockers are available Monday to Saturday 5:30am to 1am and Sunday 6am to 1am. The cost is 35DKK ($5.85) for 24 hours.

Newspapers Foreign newspapers, particularly the *International Herald Tribune* and *USA Today,* are available at the Central Railroad Station in front of the Palladium movie theater on Vesterbrogade, on Strøget, and at the newsstands of big hotels.

Pharmacies An *apotek* (pharmacy) open 24 hours a day is **Steno Apotek,** Vesterbrogade 6C (✆ **33-14-82-66**), lying opposite the central rail station. Bus: 6.

Police In an emergency, dial ✆ **112**. For other matters, go to the police station at Halmtorvet 20 (✆ **33-25-14-48**).

Post Office For information about the Copenhagen post office, phone ✆ **80-20-70-30**. The main post office, where your *poste restante* (general delivery) letters can be picked up, is located at Tietgensgade 37, DK-1704 København (✆ **80-20-70-30**; bus: 10 or 46). It's open Monday to Friday 11am to 6pm and Saturday 10am to 1pm. The post office at the Central Railroad Station is open Monday to Friday 8am to 9pm, Saturday 9am to 4pm, and Sunday 10am to 4pm.

Restrooms Public toilets are at Rådhuspladsen (Town Hall Square), the Central Railroad Station, and at all terminals. Look for the signs TOILETTER, WC, DAMER (women), or HERRER (men). There is no charge.

Safety Compared with other European capital cities, Copenhagen is relatively safe. However, since the early 1990s, with the increase of homelessness and unemployment, crime has risen. Guard your wallet, purse, and other valuables as you would when traveling in any big city.

Taxes Throughout Denmark you'll come across MOMS on your bills, a government-imposed value-added tax of 25%. It's included in hotel and restaurant bills, service charges, entrance fees, and repair of foreign-registered cars. No refunds are given on these items. For more information, see "Shopping," in chapter 4.

Transit Information Day or night, phone ✆ **70-13-14-15** for bus and Metro information or ✆ **33-14-17-01** for S-tog information.

3 Where to Stay

High season in Denmark is May to September, which pretty much coincides with the schedule at Tivoli Gardens. Once Tivoli closes for the winter, lots of rooms become available. Make sure to ask about winter discounts. And ask if breakfast is included (usually it isn't).

Nearly all doubles come with a private bathroom. Find out, though, whether this means a shower or a tub. At moderate and inexpensive hotels, you can save money by requesting a room without a bathroom. Keep in mind that in most moderate and nearly all of the inexpensive hotels, bathrooms are cramped, and there's never enough room to spread out all of your stuff. Many were added to older buildings that weren't designed for bathrooms. Also, get used to towels that are much thinner than you might like—not the thick, fluffy types.

Several inexpensive hotels in Copenhagen are known as **mission hotels;** they were originally founded by a temperance society, but now about half of them are fully licensed to serve alcohol. They tend to cater to middle-class families.

RESERVATIONS SERVICE   At Bernstorffsgade 1, across from the Tivoli's main entrance, the Tourist Information Center maintains a useful hotel-booking service, **Værelsænvisningen** (© **70-22-24-42**). The charge, whether you book into a private home, a hostel, or a luxury hotel, is 60DKK ($10) per person. A deposit, about 8.6% of the accommodation cost, must be paid, but it will later be deducted from your room rent. You'll also be given a city map and bus directions. This particular office doesn't accept advance reservations; it can arrange private accommodations if the hotels in your price range are already full. The office is open April 19 to September 30, daily 9am to 9pm, and October to April 18, Monday to Friday 9am to 5pm and Saturday 9am to 2pm.

In the same building is another service—the **Hotel Booking Service** (© **33-25-38-44**)—that will reserve hotel rooms in advance.

NEAR KONGENS NYTORV & NYHAVN

Once the home of sailor bars and tattoo parlors, Nyhavn is now a chic, up-and-coming section of Copenhagen. The central canal, filled with 19th-century boats and the 18th-century facades of the buildings around it, contributes to the area's special ambience.

VERY EXPENSIVE

Hotel d'Angleterre ★★★ _Kids_   At the top of Nyhavn, this is the premier hotel choice in Denmark. Although a bit staid and stodgy, the hotel is the best address in Copenhagen. The seven-story property, a Leading Hotels of the World member, was built in 1755. Guests have included Hans Christian Andersen and almost every celebrity who has ever visited Denmark. It's a medley of styles: Empire, Louis XVI, and modern. The guest rooms are beautifully furnished with art objects and occasional antiques. Room sizes and views vary, but room each has a high ceiling and marble bathroom, complete with robes, phone, and tub/shower combination. The deluxe rooms are in front, but those facing the courtyard are more tranquil and also receive a fair amount of sunlight—when the sun is shining, that is.

Kongens Nytorv 34, DK-1050 København. © **800/44-UTELL** in the U.S., or 33-12-00-95. Fax 33-12-11-18. www.remmen.dk. 123 units. 2,470DKK–3,470DKK ($412–$579) double; from 4,470DKK ($746) suite. AE, DC, MC, V. Parking 175DKK ($29). Bus: 1, 6, or 9. **Amenities:** Restaurant; bar; indoor heated pool; fitness center; spa; sauna; 24-hr. room service; babysitting; laundry service; dry cleaning; nonsmoking rooms. _In room:_ A/C, TV, dataport, minibar, hair dryer, safe.

Phoenix Copenhagen ★★ More than any other hotel in Copenhagen, this top-of-the-line lodging poses a serious challenge to the discreet grandeur of the nearby Hotel d'Angleterre. The Phoenix was a royal guesthouse, originally built in the 1700s to accommodate the aristocratic courtiers of Amalienborg Palace. When it was converted into a hotel in 1991, tons of white and colored marble were imported to create the elegant Louis XVI–style decor that has impressed guests ever since. Beds are large, and wool carpeting and chandeliers add graceful notes to the guest rooms. The Italian marble bathrooms are sufficiently large and contain tub/shower combinations, and robes. The best accommodations also have faxes, trouser presses, and phones in the bathrooms.

Bredgade 37, DK-1260 København. ✆ 33-95-95-00. Fax 33-33-98-33. www.phoenixcopenhagen.dk. 213 units. 1,990DKK–2,890DKK ($332–$483) double; from 3,500DKK ($585) suite. AE, DC, MC, V. Parking 113DKK ($19). Bus: 1, 6, 9, or 10. **Amenities:** Restaurant; bar; car rental; 24-hr. room service; babysitting; laundry service; dry cleaning; nonsmoking rooms. *In room:* A/C, TV, dataport, minibar, hair dryer, iron/ironing board, safe.

EXPENSIVE
Clarion Neptune Hotel ★ Updated in 2002, the interior of this 1854 hotel resembles an upper-crust living room, with English-style furniture and even a chess table. Some rooms overlook two quiet, covered interior courtyards. On the hotel's outdoor terrace on the 6th floor, you can order drinks in the summer. The rooms are tastefully furnished in modern style. Closets are small, and the tiled bathrooms with tub/shower combinations are modest in size. Only some units are air-conditioned (which is rarely a consideration, even in summer). Ask for a room that opens onto the courtyard—they are the brightest during the day and the most tranquil in the evening. Suites, most often booked by businesspeople, have dataports and faxes.

Skt. Annæ Plads 18–20, DK-1250 København. ✆ 800/654-6200 in the U.S., or 33-96-20-00. Fax 33-96-20-66. www.choicehotels.dk. 133 units. 1,695DKK ($283) double; 2,495DKK ($417) suite. Rates include buffet breakfast. AE, DC, MC, V. Free parking. Bus: 1, 6, 9, or 19. **Amenities:** Restaurant; bar; room service (noon–9pm); babysitting; laundry service; dry cleaning; nonsmoking rooms. *In room:* A/C, TV, dataport (in some), minibar, hair dryer, safe.

Hotel Skt. Petri ★★★ Since the 1930s the site of this hotel was the much loved department store, Dalle Valle. Today, in an amazing reincarnation, it's become one of the grandest hotels in Copenhagen. Modern Danish design, as interpreted by interior designer Per Arnoldi, is showcased here. Rooms are individually done in a minimalist yet elegant style, with bright, cheerful colors and such touches as Mondrian-inspired headboards. The beds are among the most comfortable we've encountered in the Danish capital, with down mattress pads, soft pillows, Angora blankets, and comfy duvets. Opt for a double with terrace on the fifth or sixth floors. The ceilings are a bit low, but the lobby rises three floors, embracing an atrium garden. Musicians, artists, and designers are among those who frequent the fashionable **Bar Rouge,** or dine at **Brasserie Bleu.**

Krystalgade 22, DK-1172 Copenhagen. ✆ 33-45-91-00. Fax 33-45-91-10. 270 units. 998DKK–2,695DKK ($167–$450) double; from 3,095DKK ($517) suite. AE, DC, MC, V. Parking 150DKK ($25). S-tog: Nørreport. **Amenities:** Restaurant; bar; fitness room; 24-hr. room service; laundry service; dry cleaning; nonsmoking rooms; rooms for those with limited mobility. *In room:* A/C, TV, dataport, minibar, hair dryer, safe.

71 Nyhavn ★★ On the corner between Copenhagen harbor and Nyhavn Canal, this red-brick hotel is in a restored warehouse that dates from 1804—one of the few buildings in the area spared by an 1807 British bombardment. The warehouse was converted into a hotel in 1971, with its fine Pomeranian pine beams left intact.

Copenhagen Accommodations

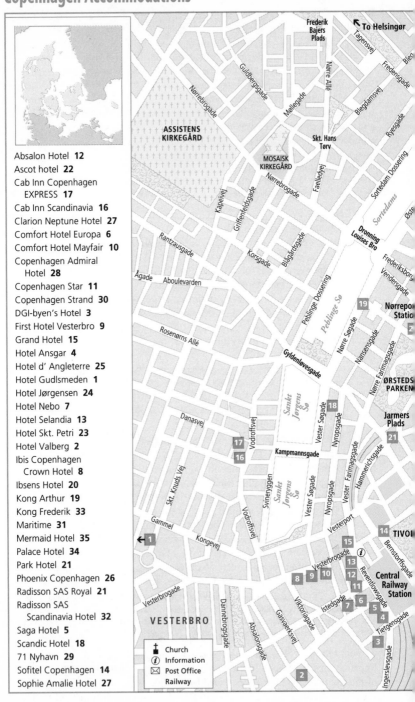

Absalon Hotel **12**
Ascot hotel **22**
Cab Inn Copenhagen
  EXPRESS **17**
Cab Inn Scandinavia **16**
Clarion Neptune Hotel **27**
Comfort Hotel Europa **6**
Comfort Hotel Mayfair **10**
Copenhagen Admiral
  Hotel **28**
Copenhagen Star **11**
Copenhagen Strand **30**
DGI-byen's Hotel **3**
First Hotel Vesterbro **9**
Grand Hotel **15**
Hotel Ansgar **4**
Hotel d' Angleterre **25**
Hotel Gudlsmeden **1**
Hotel Jørgensen **24**
Hotel Nebo **7**
Hotel Selandia **13**
Hotel Skt. Petri **23**
Hotel Valberg **2**
Ibis Copenhagen
  Crown Hotel **8**
Ibsens Hotel **20**
Kong Arthur **19**
Kong Frederik **33**
Maritime **31**
Mermaid Hotel **35**
Palace Hotel **34**
Park Hotel **21**
Phoenix Copenhagen **26**
Radisson SAS Royal **21**
Radisson SAS
  Scandinavia Hotel **32**
Saga Hotel **5**
Scandic Hotel **18**
71 Nyhavn **29**
Sofitel Copenhagen **14**
Sophie Amalie Hotel **27**

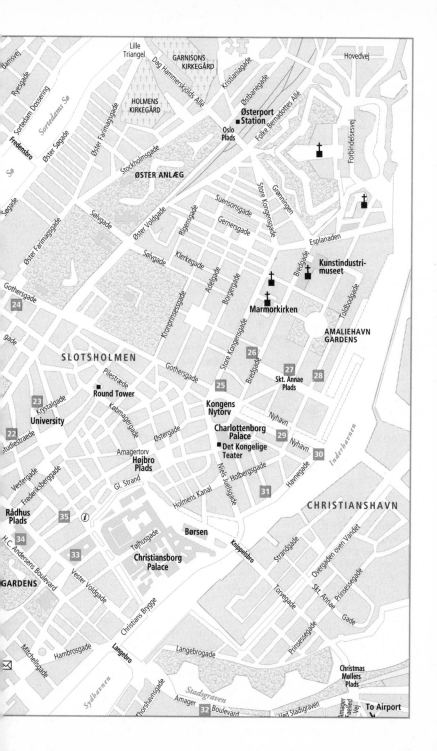

Most rooms have a view of the harbor and canal. Nice touches include trouser presses and double-glazed windows. The best units also have ironing boards, faxes, and robes, and computer plugs are available at the reception desk. Non-smoking accommodations are available. Bathrooms are rather small, but are tiled and contain mostly tub/shower combinations.

Nyhavn 71, DK-1051 København. ⓒ 33-43-62-00. Fax 33-43-62-01. www.71nyhavnhotelcopenhagen.dk. 150 units. Mon–Thurs 1,650DKK–2,350DKK ($276–$392) double, 3,000DKK–5,000DKK ($501–$835) suite; Fri–Sun 1,290DKK–1,790DKK ($215–$299) double, 2,190DKK–3,800DKK ($366–$635) suite. Rates include breakfast (weekends only). AE, DC, MC, V. Free parking. S-tog: Kongensnytorv. **Amenities:** Restaurant; bar; car rental; room service (7am–10:30pm); babysitting; laundry service; dry cleaning; nonsmoking rooms. *In room:* A/C, TV, dataport, minibar, hair dryer, trouser press, iron/ironing board, safe.

MODERATE

Copenhagen Admiral Hotel   Only 2 blocks from the Nyhavn Canal, this hotel was built as a granary in 1787 but was turned into a hotel in 1988 and last renovated in 2003. Although rooms lack a certain coziness and charm, they're well maintained, and some have harbor views. Some are smoke free, and some open onto French balconies. The split-level sixth-floor suites (actually studios) are the best, with large sitting areas, upgraded furnishings, and views of the water. Bathrooms are small but have bidets and tub/shower combinations.

A popular lunch buffet is served in the hotel restaurant. At night, guests enjoy formal service and an international cuisine.

Toldbodgade 24–28, DK-1253 København. ⓒ 33-74-14-14. Fax 33-74-14-16. www.admiralhotel.dk. 366 units. 1,335DKK–1,470DKK ($223–$245) double; 2,100DKK ($351) suite. AE, MC, V. Free parking. Bus: 1, 9, 10, 28, or 41. **Amenities:** Restaurant; bar; nightclub; sauna; 24-hr. room service; laundry service; dry cleaning; nonsmoking rooms; solarium. *In room:* TV, dataport, minibar, hair dryer.

Copenhagen Strand ⭐ (Value)   This hotel opened in 2000 in what were once two 18th-century brick-and-timber factories. The architects retained as many of the old-fashioned details as they could, adding a nautical gloss to the lobby— lots of varnished wood, brass hardware, and paintings of ships and the nearby piers that used to service them. There's a bar in the lobby, and a reception staff that works double time mixing drinks and pulling pints. The medium-size bed-rooms are less richly decorated than the lobby, but filled with comfortable, con-temporary furnishings. All units contain well-kept bathrooms with tub/shower combinations. The hotel is rated three stars by the Danish government, but frankly, all that it lacks for four-star status is a restaurant.

Havnegade 37, DK-1058 København K. ⓒ 33-48-99-00. Fax 33-48-99-01. www.copenhagenstrand.dk. 174 units. Mon–Thurs 1,560DKK–2,260DKK ($261–$377) double, 2,760DKK–3,160DKK ($461–$528) suite; Fri–Sun 1,260DKK–1,760DKK ($210–$294) double, 1,960DKK–2,960DKK ($327–$494) suite. Rates include buffet breakfast. AE, DC, MC, V. Parking 113DKK ($19). Tram: 1 or 6. **Amenities:** Breakfast room; bar; car rental; business center; 24-hr. room service; babysitting; laundry service; dry cleaning; nonsmoking rooms. *In room:* TV, dataport (in most units), minibar, hair dryer, trouser press, iron/ironing board.

Maritime   Although the guest rooms are comfortable and tastefully conserva-tive in style in this building that's more than a century old, you might be put off by the pretentious and somewhat rigid staff. Ignore them, and relish your hotel's enviable location near hotels that cost a lot more. The neighborhood lies between high glamour (Kongens Nytorv, site of the Hotel d'Angleterre) and the Nyhavn Canal, a reminder of seafaring Copenhagen. Each unit is well kept with a bathroom containing a shower unit.

Peder Skrams Gade 19, DK-1054 København. ⓒ 33-13-48-82. Fax 33-15-03-45. www.hotel-maritime.dk. 64 units. 1,100DKK–1,600DKK ($184–$267) double; 1,200DKK–2,000DKK ($200–$334) triple. AE, DC, DISC, MC,

V. Bus: 1, 6, or 9. **Amenities:** Restaurant; bar; lounge; laundry service; dry cleaning; nonsmoking rooms. *In room:* TV, dataport, hair dryer.

Sophie Amalie Hotel ⚜   Sophie Amalie is a first-class hotel on the harbor-front, close to Amalienborg Castle. From the rooms facing north, you can see the castle, where Queen Margrethe II lives. Within walking distance of Nyhavn, it's convenient for exploring the business and shopping districts. Dating from 1948, the hotel has been vastly improved and upgraded over the years. Its guest rooms are furnished with the best of Scandinavian modern design. Double-glazing on the windows cuts down on street noise. Closets are large, but bathrooms are small, with mosaic tiles and tub/shower combinations. In the sixth-floor suites, curved staircases connect the two levels. The hotel is named for Sophie Amalie (1628–85), a duke's daughter who married King Frederik III at the age of 15.

Skt. Annæ Plads 21, DK-1021 København. © **33-13-34-00.** Fax 33-11-77-07. www.remmen.dk. 134 units. 1,275DKK–1,475DKK ($213–$246) double; 1,775DKK–2,075DKK ($296–$347) suite. Winter discounts available. AE, DC, MC, V. Free parking. Bus: 650-S. **Amenities:** Restaurant; bar; sauna; 24-hr. room service; babysitting; laundry service; dry cleaning. *In room:* TV, dataport (in most units), minibar, hair dryer.

NEAR RÅDHUSPLADSEN & TIVOLI GARDENS

Some of the most expensive hotels in Copenhagen are here. In the heart of the city, around Rådhuspladsen (Town Hall Square), Tivoli Gardens, and the Central Railroad Station, you'll be near all public transportation and many attractions.

VERY EXPENSIVE

Palace Hotel ⚜   Opened in 1910 and declared a historic landmark in 1985, the Palace Hotel has been a respite for countless camera-shy celebrities. Although the hotel has tried to keep abreast of the times, it's no longer the front-runner it once was (that distinction now belongs to other recommended hotels, including the Kong Frederik). The modern rooms are attractively furnished in an English country style—conservative furniture, floral chintz curtains. Most bathrooms are cramped, but they do have tub/shower combinations. The best rooms are on the top floor, away from street noises. If you're assigned a room on floors 2 and 3, you are still in luck—they have high ceilings and tasteful furnishings and appointments. The reception desk staff is especially helpful in arranging for theater tickets, tours, and transportation. There's also a roof terrace.

Rådhuspladsen 57, DK-1550 København. © **800/448-8355** in the U.S., or 33-14-40-50. Fax 33-14-52- 79. www.palace-hotel.dk. 162 units. 2,175DKK ($363) double; 3,525DKK ($589) suite. 25% discount may be available on weekends and in midwinter, depending on occupancy. AE, DC, MC, V. Parking 150DKK ($25). Bus: 2, 30, 32, 33, 34, or 35. **Amenities:** Restaurant; bar; room service (7am–10pm); massage; babysitting; laundry service; dry cleaning; nonsmoking rooms. *In room:* TV, minibar, hair dryer, trouser press, safe.

Radisson SAS Royal   Long favored by business travelers, this international deluxe hotel, filled with facilities and conveniences, is in the city center, near Tivoli and the Town Hall Square. The hotel has an aura of modern Danish style. Rooms are beautifully furnished and well maintained with nice extras. Bathrooms have tub/shower combinations and are spacious, except for those in the single rooms, which are small and often lack tubs. At the Business Club on the top floors, guests can take advantage of a lounge with complimentary refreshments, speedier check-ins, and such amenities as free cable and Internet connections.

The hotel has the prestigious Italian restaurant **Alberto K** on the top floor. There's also the **Café Royal,** a lobby bar, and the **Royal Bar.**

Hammerichsgade 1, DK-1611 København. ✆ **800/333-3333** in the U.S., or 33-42-60-00. Fax 33-42-61-00. www.radissonsas.com. 265 units. 2,490DKK–2,645DKK ($416–$442) double; 2,695DKK–2,895DKK ($450–$483) suite. Business Club from 3,095DKK ($517) suite. AE, DC, MC, V. Parking 180DKK ($30). Bus: 14 or 16. **Amenities:** Restaurant; bar; fitness room; sauna; 24-hr. room service; massage; babysitting; laundry service; dry cleaning; nonsmoking rooms; solarium. *In room:* A/C, TV, dataport, minibar, coffeemaker, hair dryer, iron/ironing board, safe.

EXPENSIVE

First Hotel Vesterbro ★★   When this hotel opened in 1999, it was the first newly built hotel in the center of Copenhagen in more than 15 years. Just a 5-minute walk from the Tivoli Gardens, this luxury hotel is the third largest in Denmark. Rooms are midsize to spacious and as modern as tomorrow. In the so-called "Lady Rooms," we were impressed with the robes laid out, the makeup mirror, the beauty products from Clarins, the dress hangers, even an assortment of women's magazines. We would have thought Martha Stewart had just checked out if we didn't know otherwise. The sun-flooded lobby sets the high sense of style and fashion, with windows going from floor to ceiling. The furnishings are like a showcase of Danish design with much use of blond wood. We loved the style, comfort, and taste of the bedrooms, with their pastel-colored walls that brighten a dull gray day in Copenhagen, along with the Spanish cherrywood furniture and the modern lithographs. Our favorite spot here is the atrium garden, lined in brick, and a suntrap on a fair day, ideal for its hanging baskets. You sit at marble tables on wicker chairs. No need to leave the hotel at night for dinner. On-site is the highly professional **Alex Vinbar & Kokken Restaurant,** offering a superb contemporary Danish cuisine with a selection of international specialties as well. Since it's just a short walk to the Central Station, the hotel is convenient to most buses. Guests can use for free a fitness center nearby.

Vesterbrogade 23–29, DK-1620 Copenhagen. ✆ **33-78-80-00.** Fax 33-78-80-80. www.firsthotels.com. 403 units. 1,400DKK–2,050DKK ($234–$342) double. AE, DC, MC, V. Parking 200DKK ($33). **Amenities:** Restaurant; bar; room service (7am–1am); laundry service; dry cleaning; nonsmoking rooms; rooms for those with limited mobility. *In room:* A/C, TV, dataport, minibar, hair dryer, trouser press, iron/ironing board, safe.

Grand Hotel ★   Originally built in 1880, this surprisingly elegant landmark hotel near the Central Railroad Station underwent a 1998 renovation that gave it a new life. The charm of the old building was preserved, while the rooms and bathrooms were updated—each tastefully furnished and well maintained. Bathrooms are quite superior, generous in size, and furnished with tub/shower combinations. Singles opening onto the courtyard are more tranquil but don't have views. The corner rooms are the best and most expensive because they have been the most recently renovated and are larger.

The **Grand Bar** overflows in summer onto a sidewalk cafe, and the **Restaurant Frascati** serves freshly prepared Italian specialties.

Vesterbrogade 9A, DK-1620 København. ✆ **33-27-69-00.** Fax 33-27-69-01. www.grandhotelcopenhagen.dk. 161 units. 1,590DKK–1,990DKK ($266–$332) double; 3,000DKK ($501) suite. Rates include buffet breakfast. AE, DC, MC, V. Bus: 1, 6, 16, 27, 28, or 29. **Amenities:** Restaurant; bar; car rental; business center; room service (7am–9pm); laundry service; dry cleaning; nonsmoking rooms. *In room:* A/C, TV, dataport, minibar, hair dryer, trouser press, ironing board, safe.

Kong Frederik ★★ *(Finds)*   The smallest of the ultrachic hotels in Copenhagen, the Kong Frederik has the feeling of an unpretentious but elegant private club thanks to discreet service, dark paneling, and a labyrinth of antiques-filled lounges. Many guests feel that it's much cozier than the Hotel d'Angleterre. Originally built around 1850 as two separate hotels, and then combined around a central courtyard about 1990, it has always appealed to glamorous showbiz types. The rooms are conservatively decorated in a wide array of styles with striped fabrics, overstuffed chairs, and antique prints. The hotel has some of the best bathrooms in town, with good lighting, top-brand toiletries, and tub/shower combinations. The accommodations in the front are brighter.

Restaurant Frederik is recognized for its fine cuisine and excellent service. A sliding-glass roof lets in the sun and breezes, creating a Mediterranean-style atmosphere. Surrounded by the mellow panels of the **Queen's Pub,** you can order both food and drink.

Vester Voldgade 25, DK-1552 København. ℂ 800/44-UTELL in the U.S., or 33-12-59-02. Fax 33-93-59-01. www.remmen.dk. 110 units. 1,240DKK–1,840DKK ($207–$307) double; from 3,240DKK ($541) suite. AE, DC, MC, V. Parking 150DKK ($25). Bus: 1, 6, or 28. **Amenities:** Restaurant; bar; fitness center; spa; room service (7am–10pm); laundry service; dry cleaning; nonsmoking rooms. *In room:* TV, minibar, hair dryer, safe.

Radisson SAS Scandinavia Hotel ★★ A 5-minute walk east of Tivoli, this international deluxe hotel is rated as the finest and largest modern hotel in the Danish capital, catering primarily to businesspeople. First-class rooms are attractive and comfortable, with many luxuries including beautifully kept bathrooms with tub/shower combinations. Greater comfort is found on the top floors at the Business Club, where guests also have such complimentary amenities as free cable and Internet connections.

There are four restaurants in this mammoth hotel, each attracting a clientele of locals as well as hotel guests. The two most elegant are the **Blue Elephant,** which serves Thai food, and **The Dining Room,** a panoramic and formal eatery set on the building's 25th floor. On the lobby level are a pair of less expensive restaurants: **Mama's and Papa's,** serving Italian food, grilled steaks, and fresh seafood, much of it from the nearby North Sea; and **Kyoto,** a Japanese restaurant with a full complement of sushi. Gamblers enjoy the **Casino Copenhagen.**

Amager Blvd. 70, DK-2300 København. ℂ 800/333-3333 in the U.S., or 33-96-50-00. Fax 33-96-55-00. www.radissonsas.com. 542 units. 2,030DKK ($339) double; Fri–Sun 1,380DKK ($230) double. Business Club Mon–Thurs 2,400DKK ($401) double, 2,795DKK ($467) suite; Fri–Sun 1,690DKK ($282) double, 2,300DKK ($384) suite. Rates include buffet breakfast. 1 child stays free in parent's room. AE, DC, MC, V. Free parking. Bus: 15. **Amenities:** 4 restaurants; 2 bars; indoor heated pool; squash court; fitness center; sauna; 24-hr. room service; massage; babysitting; laundry service; dry cleaning; nonsmoking rooms; rooms for those with limited mobility; boutiques; casino; solarium. *In room:* TV, dataport, coffeemaker, iron/ironing board.

Scandic Hotel ★★ One of the tallest buildings in the neighborhood, this 18-story steel-and-glass member of a hotel chain makes a good impression in the Danish capital. Built near the Tivoli Gardens in 1972, it's a favorite among business executives, partly because of the concierge staff, who can arrange for typists, translators, and other business services quickly and conveniently. Rooms are outfitted with modern conveniences. The most expensive are located on the hotel's top two floors. The sixth floor is reserved exclusively for nonsmokers. Bathrooms tend to be small, often with showers instead of tubs.

The Blue Garden is the hotel's most prestigious dining room, while simple platters can be ordered in the **Red Lion Pub.**

Vester Søgade 6 (Box 337), DK-1601 København. ℂ 33-14-35-35. Fax 33-32-12-23. www.scandic-hotels. com. 486 units. 1,500DKK–2,100DKK ($251–$351) double; from 2,400DKK ($401) suite. Rates include continental breakfast. AE, DC, MC, V. Parking 80DKK ($13). Bus: 1 or 14. **Amenities:** Restaurant; bar; exercise room; sauna; concierge; room service (6am–10:30pm); massage; laundry service; dry cleaning; nonsmoking rooms; rooms for those with limited mobility. *In room:* A/C, TV, dataport, minibar, hair dryer, trouser press, iron/ironing board.

Sofitel Copenhagen ★ Rich with turn-of-the-20th-century atmosphere, this successful overhaul of an older hotel combines first-class comfort and antique furnishings. Opposite the Tivoli Gardens, the hotel was commissioned by King Frederik VIII in 1913, and has entertained its share of celebrities and royalty. Guest rooms of varying dimensions resemble what you might find in an English country house—but with all the modern amenities. Antiques, double-glazed windows, and views from many units make this a good choice; rooms on the top floor have dormered windows. Bathrooms are generous in size, are completely tiled, and contain tub/shower combinations and makeup mirrors. Some of the accommodations are nonsmoking.

Bernstorffsgade 4, DK-1577 København. ℂ **800/221-4542** in the U.S., or 33-14-92-62. Fax 33-93-93-62. www.accorhotel.dk. 93 units. 1,999DKK ($334) double; 2,220DKK–6,499DKK ($371–$1085) suite. 1 child stays free in parent's room. AE, DC, MC, V. Parking 165DKK ($28). Bus: 1 or 6. **Amenities:** Restaurant; bar; fitness center; car rental; 24-hr. room service; babysitting; laundry service; dry cleaning; nonsmoking rooms. *In room:* A/C, TV, dataport, minibar, hair dryer, safe.

MODERATE

Ascot Hotel ★ *Value*   This is one of the best small hotels in Copenhagen. On a side street about a 2-minute walk from Town Hall Square, it was built in 1902 (on 492 wooden pilings rescued from a medieval fortification that had previously stood on the site). In 1994, the hotel annexed an adjacent building designed in the 19th century as a boathouse; its black-marble columns and interior bas-reliefs are historically notable. The guest rooms have been renovated and modernized, and the atmosphere is inviting. The furniture is rather standard, and the finest units open onto the street. Nevertheless, the rooms in the rear get better air circulation and more light. The tiled bathrooms are generous in size and equipped with tub/shower combinations.

Studiestræde 61, DK-1554 København. ℂ **33-12-60-00**. Fax 33-14-60-40. www.ascothotel.dk. 165 units. 1,280DKK–1,480DKK ($214–$247) double; 1,695DKK–2,560DKK ($283–$428) suite. Rates include buffet breakfast. Winter discounts available. AE, DC, MC, V. Parking 50DKK ($8.35). Bus: 14 or 16. **Amenities:** Restaurant; bar; fitness center; room service (7am–9pm); laundry service; dry cleaning; nonsmoking rooms. *In room:* TV, dataport, hair dryer.

DGI-byen's Hotel ★ *Finds*   There's no hotel like this one in all Copenhagen. Right behind the Central Station and convenient to most public transportation, this government-rated three-star hotel attracts sports lovers to its precincts, which contain a bowling alley, a gigantic swim center, a spa, a "climbing wall," a shooting range, and, oh yes, a hotel. This is a dynamic, flexible so-called multicenter attracting schoolchildren, sports clubs, company executives, and regular visitors. Bedrooms, midsize to large, reflect the latest in Danish design. Interiors are simple yet tasteful and comfortable with dark wood furnishings and blond wood floors. Swimming is free to hotel guests but the spa costs extra. The onsite **restaurant,** serving good and reasonably priced food, was created from an old cattle market that stood here in 1870.

Tietgensgade 65, DK-1704 Copenhagen. ℂ **33-29-80-00**. Fax 33-29-80-80. www.dgi-byen.dk. 104 units. 825DKK–1,125DKK ($138–$188) double; 1,025DKK–1,225DKK ($171–$205) suite. AE, DC, MC, V. Parking 90DKK ($15). **Amenities:** Restaurant; bar; lounge; 5 indoor heated pools; sports center; spa; Jacuzzi; sauna; 24-hr. room service (6am–10pm); babysitting; laundry service; dry cleaning; nonsmoking rooms; rooms for those with limited mobility; solarium. *In room:* TV, VCR, hair dryer, dataport, safe.

Hotel Guldsmeden ★ *Finds*   This is a real discovery in the heart of Copenhagen, housed in a renovated 19th-century building. The structure might be old, but the bedrooms are up-to-date, ranging from small to midsize. Each is handsomely decorated in a vague French colonial style with high ceilings, stucco, and wood paneling. The best rooms contain such luxuries as four-poster beds, fireplaces, balconies with summer furniture, and bathtubs instead of showers. The friendly staff greets you, and the place is made more homelike and inviting by the original art decorating the walls and a judicious use of elegant teak furnishings.

Vesterbrogade 66, DK-1620 Copenhagen. ✆ **33-22-15-00.** Fax 33-22-15-55. 64 units. 1,295DKK ($216) double; 1,495DKK ($250) junior suite. Rates include buffet breakfast. AE, DC, MC, V. Bus: 6A. Free parking. **Amenities:** Breakfast room; bar; limited room service; laundry service; dry cleaning; nonsmoking rooms. *In room:* TV, dataport, minibar, hair dryer, safe.

Kong Arthur ★ *Value*   Built as an orphanage in 1882, this hotel sits behind a private courtyard next to tree-lined Peblinge Lake in a residential part of town. It's a terrific value. The building has been completely renovated into a contemporary hostelry; a more recent expansion offers more spacious rooms, including 20 nonsmoking units. Each of the comfortably furnished and carpeted guest rooms has in-house video. The spacious bathrooms are tiled and contain tub/shower combinations. Breakfast is served in a large greenhouse-like room that's filled with light on sunny days.

Nørre Søgade 11, DK-1370 København. ✆ **33-11-12-12.** Fax 33-32-61-30. www.kongarthur.dk. 107 units. 1,400DKK–1,600DKK ($234–$267) double; from 2,000DKK ($334) suite. Rates include buffet breakfast. AE, DC, MC, V. Free parking. Bus: 5, 7, or 16. **Amenities:** 4 restaurants; bar; sauna; car rental; 24-hr. room service; massage; babysitting; laundry service; dry cleaning; nonsmoking rooms. *In room:* TV, dataport, minibar, hair dryer, trouser press, safe.

Mermaid Hotel *Value*   In the heart of Copenhagen, close to the Town Hall, the surprisingly large Mermaid Hotel offers good value. In just 2 minutes you can walk to the Tivoli Gardens. All its refurbished rooms have a modern Danish design and contain a neatly kept bathroom with a tub/shower combination. Traditional Danish lunches or dinners are served in the hotel's restaurant, **Hattehylden.** Also on-site is the **John Bull Pub,** the oldest English pub in the city, which even has a poolroom. Just 2 minutes away is the Mermaid's sibling hotel, the Palace, where you can enjoy its roof terrace in summer.

Løngangstræde 27, DK-1468 København. ✆ **33-12-65-70.** Fax 33-15-28-99. www.mermaid-hotel.dk. 201 units. 1,399DKK–1,540DKK ($234–$257) double. Rates include buffet breakfast. Additional bed 195DKK ($33). AE, DC, MC, V. Parking 160DKK ($27). Bus: 1, 5, or 6. **Amenities:** Restaurant; bar; laundry service; dry cleaning; nonsmoking rooms. *In room:* TV, hair dryer.

Park Hotel   The Park Hotel houses our favorite breakfast room in Copenhagen. One wall is adorned with radiator covers from six vintage automobiles while other walls have an airplane propeller from 1916, a collection of antique auto headlights, and lots of machine-age posters and engravings. Rooms have tasteful furniture, thick carpeting, and well-maintained bathrooms with tub/shower combinations.

Jarmers Plads 3, DK-1551 København. ✆ **33-13-30-00.** Fax 33-14-30-33. www.copenhagenparkhotel.dk. 61 units. 1,100DKK–1,300DKK ($184–$217) double. Rates include breakfast. AE, DC, MC, V. Parking 150DKK ($25) nearby, 12DKK ($2) per hr. on street. Bus: 14 or 16. **Amenities:** Restaurant; bar; laundry service; dry cleaning. *In room:* TV, hair dryer, safe.

INEXPENSIVE

Hotel Nebo *Kids*   This hotel near the railroad station is a quiet retreat, with clean, up-to-date, although spartan, rooms. The lobby is tiny, and a lounge opens onto a side courtyard. Rooms are small, furnished in a functional, Nordic style. There are bathrooms with shower units on all floors. The hotel offers some family rooms with up to four beds per accommodation.

Istedgade 6, DK-1650 København. ✆ **33-21-12-17.** Fax 33-23-47-74. www.nebo.dk. 128 units, 88 with bathroom. 690DKK ($115) double without bathroom, 860DKK ($144) double with bathroom; 845DKK ($141) family room for 3, 1,000DKK ($167) family room for 4. Additional bed 150DKK ($25) extra. Rates include buffet breakfast. AE, DC, MC, V. Parking 40DKK ($6.70). Bus: 1, 6, 16, 28, or 41. **Amenities:** Breakfast room; lounge. *In room:* TV.

Hotel Valberg *(Value)*   The top floor of a charming building from 1903 was recently converted into a series of apartments, lying only a 10-minute walk from the Tivoli. Each of the attractively furnished accommodations comes with a kitchen, a bathroom with shower, and modern Danish furnishings that are more functional than stylish. Unlike most apartment rentals, this one features a continental breakfast and daily cleaning. The apartments are well equipped with a dinner table with chairs, a comfortable sofa, and high-quality beds.

Sønder Blvd. 53, DK-1720 København. ℭ **33-25-25-19.** Fax 33-25-25-83. www.valberg.dk. 15 apartments. From 750DKK ($125) apt. for 2. Extra bed 200DKK ($33). Rates include breakfast. DC, DISC, MC, V. Parking 50DKK ($8.35). Bus: 10. **Amenities:** Breakfast room; lounge; laundry service; dry cleaning. *In room:* TV, hair dryer, iron/ironing board.

Ibis Copenhagen Crown Hotel *(Value)*   In business for more than a century, this welcoming hotel lies only a short walk from the Tivoli Gardens and the main train station. You enter through a tranquil, beautiful courtyard, evoking Copenhagen of long ago. The traffic-clogged Vesterbrogade is a short distance away but you feel that this is a well-maintained, safe, and quiet haven once you enter. The midsize bedrooms are classically and tastefully decorated, some of them opening onto Vesterbrogade, the rest onto the courtyard. Each accommodation comes with a full bathroom with tub-and-shower combination. The most attractive feature of this hotel is its rooftop **restaurant,** where a varied Scandinavian breakfast buffet is served overlooking the rooftops of the city.

Vesterbrogade 41, DK-1620 Copenhagen. ℭ **33-21-21-66.** Fax 33-21-00-66. www.accorhotels.com. 78 units. 779DKK ($130) double. Rates include breakfast. AE, DC, MC, V. Bus: 6. **Amenities:** Restaurant; bar; laundry service; dry cleaning; nonsmoking rooms. *In room:* TV, dataport, minibar, hair dryer, safe.

Kids Family-Friendly Accommodations

Comfort Hotel Europa (p. 69)   In addition to letting children under 12 stay free in their parents' rooms, this hotel also offers a playroom for the little ones, and babysitting services.

Hotel Ansgar (p. 70)   This hotel rents out a dozen large rooms spacious enough to house up to six overnight guests, which makes the Ansgar ideal for families traveling with children.

Hotel d'Angleterre (p. 58)   This elegant hotel contains a swimming pool and in-house video; both help keep children entertained.

Hotel Nebo (p. 67)   Save money on "family rooms" for up to five people. It's also within walking distance of the Tivoli Gardens and other family attractions.

Hotel Selandia (p. 70)   This well-maintained, tidy hotel offers laundry facilities and babysitting services at affordable rates. It's a clean, safe environment.

Ibsens Hotel (p. 70)   This hotel caters to families on a budget, since many of its triple rooms are large enough to house mom, dad, and one or two kids. There are no other special features for kids, however.

Kong Arthur (p. 67)   Once a home for Danish orphans, this is a safe haven in a residential section near tree-lined Peblinge Lake.

ON HELGOLANDSGADE & COLBJØRNSENSGADE

In the 1970s this area behind the railroad station became one of the major pornography districts of Europe, but subsequent hotel renovations, much-publicized civic efforts, and the gradual decline of the porno shops have led to a continuing gentrification. Today, with the original 19th-century facades mostly still intact and often gracefully restored, the district is safer than you might think and offers some of the best hotel values in Copenhagen.

MODERATE

Comfort Hotel Europa *(Kids)*   Operated by a chain that manages several other Danish tourist hotels, this large but unpretentious hotel is composed of two connected 19th-century buildings. Rooms are simple, efficient, and modern, and include well-kept bathrooms with tub/shower combinations. There's a **bar,** plus **Restaurant City,** which serves Danish specialties. Children 12 and under stay free if sharing room with parents when no additional bedding is required.

Colbjørnsensgade 5–11, DK-1652 København. © **877/424-6423** in the U.S., or 33-21-33-33. Fax 33-31-33-99. www.choicehotels.com. 230 units. 1,415DKK ($236) double. Rates include breakfast and evening buffet Mon–Thurs. Winter discounts available. AE, DC, MC, V. Bus: 6, 10, 16, 28, or 41. **Amenities:** Restaurant; bar; lounge; children's play room; car rental; babysitting; laundry service; dry cleaning; nonsmoking rooms. *In room:* TV, iron/ironing board.

Comfort Hotel Mayfair   This older, much-respected hotel retains some of its original architectural detailing after a radical overhaul that brought it up to modern-day standards about a decade ago. Two blocks west of the main railroad station, the hotel boasts decor that might remind you of the furnishings in a well-heeled private home in England. Guest rooms are comfortable, representing better-than-expected value for a hotel that's rated three stars by the Danish government. Rooms have full marble bathrooms, which contain tub/shower combinations. Some recently upgraded accommodations have sitting areas.

Helgolandsgade 3, DK-1653 København V. © **877/424-6423** in the U.S., or 70-12-17-00. Fax 33-23-96-86. www.choicehotels.com. 105 units. 850DKK–1,525DKK ($142–$255) double; from 1,500DKK ($251) suite. Rates include breakfast. AE, DC, MC, V. Bus: 6, 16, 28, 29, or 41. **Amenities:** Breakfast room; bar; lounge; bicycle rental; babysitting; laundry service; dry cleaning; nonsmoking rooms. *In room:* TV, fax, dataport, minibar, hair dryer, trouser press, safe.

Copenhagen Star   A short walk from the railroad station, this hotel was created in 1990 when a simple older lodging was connected to a neighboring building and upgraded. Its neoclassical facade was originally built around 1880. The outside is lit with neon, and the interior is definitely postmodern, with leather chairs, teakwood tables, and granite columns. Guest rooms are traditionally furnished and well maintained, with neatly kept bathrooms with tub/shower combinations. The suites have Jacuzzis.

Colbjørnsensgade 13, DK-1652 København. © **33-22-11-00.** Fax 33-21-21-86. www.ibishotels.com. 134 units. 899DKK ($150) double; 1,395DKK–1,995DKK ($233–$333) suite. Rates include breakfast. AE, DC, MC, V. Bus: 6, 16, 28, 29, or 41. **Amenities:** Breakfast room; bar; lounge; laundry service; dry cleaning; nonsmoking rooms. *In room:* A/C, TV, safe.

INEXPENSIVE

Absalon Hotel ⭐ *(Value)*   This family-run lodging, one of the best-managed hotels in the neighborhood, consists of four townhouses that were joined into one building and became a hotel in 1938. It has a spacious blue-and-white breakfast room, and an attentive staff directed by Karen Nedergaard. The guest rooms are simple and modern, and come in various sizes ranging from cramped to spacious. Those on the fifth floor have the most character. Overflow guests are housed in one of the very simple and rather functional rooms in the Absalon Annex. Bathrooms are equipped with tub/shower combinations.

The Absalon traces its origins to a love story that unfolded at the nearby railroad station. Shortly after the yet-to-be father of the present owners began his first job as a porter at a neighboring hotel, he was asked to go to the station to pick up a new babysitter who had just arrived from Jutland. They fell in love, married, and bought the first of the buildings that became the hotel. Two of their children were born in Room 108.

Helgolandsgade 15, DK-1653 København. ℂ **33-24-22-11.** Fax 33-24-34-11. www.absalon-hotel.dk. 262 units. 1,155DKK–1,650DKK ($193–$276) double; 1,355DKK–1,936DKK ($226–$323) triple; 1,520DKK–2,429DKK ($254–$406) suite. Rates include buffet breakfast. AE, DC, MC, V. Closed Dec 19–Jan 2. Bus: 6, 10, 16, 27, or 28. **Amenities:** Breakfast room; lounge; laundry service; dry cleaning; nonsmoking rooms. *In room:* TV, dataport (in some), hair dryer (in some), trouser press.

Hotel Ansgar *(Kids)*   Although this five-story hotel was built in 1885, its comfortable, cozy rooms have modern Danish furniture. Two dozen large rooms that can accommodate up to six are perfect for families, and are available at negotiable rates. All units contain well-kept bathrooms with shower units. You'll often find free parking outside the hotel after 6pm. Guests arriving at Kastrup Airport can take the SAS bus to the Air Terminal at the Central Railroad Station, walk through the station, and be inside the hotel in less than 4 minutes.

Colbjørnsensgade 29, DK-1652 København. ℂ **33-21-21-96.** Fax 33-21-61-91. www.ansgar-hotel.dk. 81 units. 995DKK–1,200DKK ($166–$200) double. Rates include buffet breakfast. Extra bed 200DKK ($33). AE, DC, MC, V. Bus: 6, 10, 28, or 41. **Amenities:** Breakfast room; lounge; room service (7am–10pm); laundry service; dry cleaning; nonsmoking rooms. *In room:* TV.

Hotel Selandia *(Kids)*   Solidly built in 1928 behind the railroad station, the Hotel Selandia was given a new, comfortably modern format in 1992. A longtime favorite of budget-conscious families, it's well maintained and clean. The furnishings are simple, in a modern Scandinavian style. All units have well-maintained bathrooms with tub/shower combinations. A good Danish breakfast is served in a ground-floor room.

Helgolandsgade 12, DK-1653 København. ℂ **33-31-46-10.** Fax 33-31-46-09. www.hotel-selandia.dk. 87 units, 57 with bathroom. 540DKK–650DKK ($90–$109) double without bathroom, 740DKK–975DKK ($124–$163) double with bathroom. Extra bed 200DKK. Rates include breakfast. AE, DC, MC, V. Closed Dec 20–Jan 2. Bus: 1, 6, 10, 14, 16, 27, or 28. **Amenities:** Breakfast room; lounge. *In room:* TV, fridge, hair dryer, trouser press (in some).

Saga Hotel   This hotel is a reasonably priced, acceptable choice on this sometimes-troublesome street. About half of its rooms tend to be booked by groups of international visitors in the summer, and by Danish student and convention groups in the winter. The hotel was created in 1947 from two late-19th-century apartment buildings. The guest rooms are unusual—each has its own layout. All units have well-maintained bathrooms with tub/shower combinations. The five-story building has no elevator, so take that into consideration. The reception and breakfast areas are one floor above street level.

Colbjørnsensgade 18–20, DK-1652 København. ℂ **33-24-49-44.** Fax 33-24-60-33. www.sagahotel.dk. 79 units, 31 with bathroom. 480DKK–750DKK ($80–$125) double without bathroom, 600DKK–920DKK ($100–$154) double with bathroom. Rates include breakfast. Extra bed 150DKK ($25). Modest winter discounts. AE, DC, MC, V. Bus: 6, 10, 16, 28, or 41. **Amenities:** Breakfast room; lounge; nonsmoking rooms. *In room:* TV.

NEAR NØRREPORT STATION
MODERATE

Ibsens Hotel *(Kids)*   A favorite with budget-conscious travelers and families, Ibsens Hotel, built in 1906 and completely renovated in 1998, offers comfortable, well-maintained guest rooms. Most of the traditionally furnished rooms are doubles or triples. They now have private bathrooms, which are cramped but contain tub/shower combinations.

Vendersgade 23, DK-1363 København. ℂ **33-13-19-13.** Fax 33-13-19-16. www.ibsenshotel.dk. 118 units. 1,113DKK–1,330DKK ($186–$222) double; 2,100DKK ($351) suite. Rates include buffet breakfast. AE, DC, MC, V. Bus: 5, 14, or 16. **Amenities:** 2 restaurants; bar; car hire; babysitting; laundry service; dry cleaning; nonsmoking rooms. *In room:* TV.

INEXPENSIVE

Hotel Jørgensen This white stucco 1906 building, a former publishing house, became Denmark's first gay hotel in 1984. Located on a busy boulevard in central Copenhagen, the hotel also welcomes straight guests. The staff is most helpful. Prices are reasonable, and the rooms are conventional and well organized. Bathrooms, in those units that have them, are well kept and contain tub/shower combinations. The 13 dormitory rooms, which accommodate 6 to 14 people each, are segregated by gender.

Rømersgade 11, DK-1362 København. ℂ **33-13-81-86.** Fax 33-15-51-05. 24 units; 13 dorm rooms (72 beds). 700DKK ($117) double; 130DKK ($22) per person in dorm. Rates include breakfast. MC, V. Parking 90DKK ($15). Free parking. Bus: 14 or 16. **Amenities:** Breakfast room; lounge. *In room:* TV.

IN FREDERIKSBERG
INEXPENSIVE

Cab Inn Copenhagen EXPRESS This is one of three members of a small Danish chain of low-cost hotels that many readers have found cozy, comfortable, and affordable. Set within the township of Frederiksberg, a half-mile south of Copenhagen's Town Hall, this tasteful low-budget hotel, built in the early 1990s, rises three stories above the surrounding cityscape. Other than a coffee shop set near the lobby, the hotel has almost no amenities. Rooms are simple, streamlined, and illuminated by small windows overlooking the street life outside. The small bathrooms have shower units but little room to spread out your stuff.

If this hotel is overbooked on the night of your arrival, fear not, as its larger (201-room) sibling lies within about a block. **Cab Inn Scandinavia,** Vodroffsvej 57, DK-1900 Frederiksberg (ℂ **35-36-11-11;** fax 35-36-11-14), about 2 years newer than the other property, offers the same amenities (or lack thereof), the same decor, the same kind of coffee shop in the lobby, and the same streamlined, contemporary look. Each room at this other property has a bathroom with shower, TV, and coffeemaker, with doubles costing 610DKK ($102) and family units going for 870DKK ($145). Despite appearing understaffed during busy periods, this Cab Inn has managed to capture the business of budget-conscious travelers from around Europe.

Danasvej 32–34, DK 1910 Frederiksberg (Copenhagen). ℂ **33-21-04-00.** Fax 33-21-74-09. www.cab-inn.dk. 86 units. 510DKK ($85) double; 870DKK ($145) family room (up to 4 people). Rates include breakfast. AE, DC, MC, V. Parking 50DKK ($8.35). S-tog: Vesterport (plus a 5-min. walk). Bus: 29. **Amenities:** Breakfast room; bar; lounge; nonsmoking rooms; rooms for those with limited mobility. *In room:* TV, dataport (in some), coffeemaker.

4 Where to Dine

It's estimated that Copenhagen has more than 2,000 cafes, snack bars, and restaurants. Most of the restaurants are either in Tivoli Gardens or around Rådhuspladsen (Town Hall Square), around the Central Railroad Station, or in Nyhavn. Others are in the shopping district, on streets off of Strøget.

You pay for the privilege of dining in Tivoli; prices are always higher. Reservations are not usually important, but it's best to call in advance. Nearly everyone who answers the phone at restaurants speaks English.

Copenhagen Dining

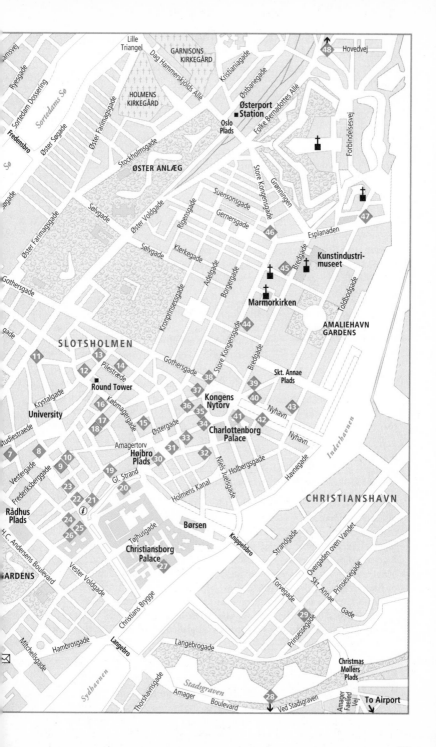

NEAR KONGENS NYTORV & NYHAVN
VERY EXPENSIVE

Era Ora ★★★ ITALIAN   This reminder of the "Golden Age" *(Era Ora)* is on virtually everyone's list as the best Italian restaurant in Denmark and is one of the best restaurants in Copenhagen. Established in 1982 by Tuscan-born partners Alessandro and Elvio, it offers an antique-looking dining room, with additional seating for parties of up to 12 in the wine cellar. You're likely to find some chic people dining here, including members of Denmark's royal family, lots of politicians, and well-known Danish writers and artists. The cuisine is based on Tuscan and Umbrian models, with sophisticated variations inspired by Denmark's superb array of fresh seafood and produce. Traditional favorites include a platter of 10 types of antipasto. Among them is a variation of *Valletta* (tender roast beef with olive oil, Parmesan, and herbs) that's one of the prides of the restaurant. All pastas are freshly made every day. Depending on the season and the inspiration of the chef, main courses include succulent veal dishes, rack of venison with balsamic vinegar and chanterelles, and ultrafresh fish.

Overgaden Neden Vandet 33B. (✆ **32-54-06-93.** Reservations required. Fixed-price menus 700DKK–815DKK ($117–$136). AE, DC, MC, V. Mon–Sat 6pm–midnight. Bus: 2 or 8.

Godt ★★★ INTERNATIONAL   A consistent small-scale favorite that's known to everyone in the neighborhood, including the Queen, this restaurant offers two floors of minimalist and very modern decor that never exceeds more than 20 diners at a time. Despite the restaurant's fame, you'll find an appealing lack of pretension and a sense of informality. Food is prepared fresh every day, based on what's best at the market. The chefs have prodigious talent and imagination, and the dishes are constantly changing. The sauces are sublime, as are the herbs and seasonings. Examples might include fried Norwegian redfish with a purée of celery and watercress sauce; roasted rack of hare with cranberries and roasted chanterelles; and fresh figs marinated with black currant liqueur, wrapped in phyllo pastry and served with a coulis of pears and chocolate mousse.

Gothersgade 38. (✆ **33-15-21-22.** Reservations required. Fixed-price menus 480DKK–600DKK ($80–$100). Tues–Sat 5:30–10pm. Closed July and Dec 23–Jan 3. Bus: 6, 10, or 14.

Kommandanten ★★★ INTERNATIONAL   This former residence of the military commander of Copenhagen, built in 1698, is the epitome of Danish chic and charm. Enjoy an aperitif in the bar before you go upstairs to dine. The menu offers an array of classical dishes as well as innovative selections. Each dish is given a pleasing personal touch. The finest ingredients are used, and the menu changes every 2 weeks. Before leaving, look at the three Andy Warhol originals of Margrethe II in the downstairs dining room. Feast on such delights as free-range pork served with pig jowl and chanterelles accompanied by baked onions, spring potatoes, and a tangy lemon sauce. The chef also succeeds with sautéed loin of veal served with tomato terrine and grilled eggplant. Perfectly cooked roasted halibut comes with gnocchi and fennel.

Ny Adelgade 7. (✆ **33-12-09-90.** Reservations required. Main courses 302DKK–340DKK ($50–$57); fixed-price 5-course menu 720DKK ($120). AE, DC, MC, V. Mon–Sat 5:30–10pm. Bus: 1 or 6.

Kong Hans Kælder ★★★ FRENCH   This vaulted Gothic cellar, once owned by King Hans (1455–1513), may be the best restaurant in Denmark. Its most serious competition is the Kommandanten (see above). Five centuries ago the site of this restaurant was a vineyard. Located on "the oldest corner of Copenhagen," the building has been restored and is now a Relais Gourmands (a member of an exclusive society of gourmet restaurants). Hans Christian Andersen once lived upstairs and even wrote some of his stories here.

The chef creates dishes that one critic claimed "to have been prepared by Matisse or Picasso." You might prefer to order the fixed-price menu; one is offered at lunch and another at 5pm. A typical three-course dinner might include smoked salmon from the restaurant's smokery, breast of duck with bigarade sauce (a classic duck sauce made with oranges and wine), followed by plum ice cream with Armagnac for dessert. The a la carte menu is divided into "country cooking," which includes such items as coq au vin, and *les spécialités*, which feature tournedos with foie gras sauce or fresh fish from the daily market, perhaps beginning with a galantine of quails with truffles.

Vingårdsstræde 6. ℂ **33-11-68-68**. Reservations required. Main courses 195DKK–345DKK ($33–$58); fixed-price menu 665DKK–875DKK ($111–$146). AE, DC, DISC, MC, V. Mon–Sat 6–10:30pm. Closed July 20–Aug 10 and Dec 24–26. Bus: 1, 6, or 9.

Pierre André ⭐⭐⭐ FRENCH Named after the two sons of the Danish/French couple who own the place, this restaurant is painted a warm shade of terra cotta and is close to Nyhavn and the Hotel d'Angleterre. Menu items are elegant and stylish, as shown by a house specialty of carpaccio of foie gras "Emilia-Romagna," served with shaved Parmesan and truffles. Other starters include a salad of curried lobster with broccoli; braised filet of turbot with mushrooms, leeks, and mango sauce; wild venison with a bitter chocolate sauce, corn, and cranberries; and a dessert specialty of chocolate cake wherein the innards are partially liquefied in a gooey but delectable concoction that runs onto your plate. Everything we've sampled has been a delight, ranking with the top restaurants of Paris or London. The chefs have considerable talent to create imaginative dishes packed with robust flavors, but nothing that's overpowering.

Ny Østergade 21. ℂ **33-16-17-19**. Reservations required. Main courses 265DKK–285DKK ($44–$48); fixed-price menus 375DKK–695DKK ($63–$116). AE, DC, MC, V. Tues–Sat noon–2:30pm and 6–10pm. Closed 3 weeks July–Aug. Bus: 6, 10, or 14.

EXPENSIVE

Leonore Christine ⭐ DANISH This restaurant, on the sunny (south) side of the canal, is the best in Nyhavn, in a building dating from 1681. The restaurant is open year-round, but seems at its best in summer when the terrace is open and you can dine overlooking the canal and the throngs of passersby. It's named Leonore Christine after the sister-in-law and bitter enemy of Sophie Amalie, the 17th-century queen of Denmark and wife of Frederik III. Although the menu changes frequently, you might try such stellar dishes as oven-baked halibut with mussels and saffron, North Sea turbot with fjord shrimp and asparagus, tournedos with spinach and a red-burgundy sauce, or warm smoked trout with lumpfish roe and Danish caviar. For dessert, you might be served white-chocolate cake with mango sorbet. There are mastery of cookery here, pure harmony, and lots of flavor.

Nyhavn 9. ℂ **33-13-50-40**. Reservations required. Main courses 195DKK–245DKK ($33–$41); 4-course fixed-price menu 425DKK ($71). AE, DC, MC, V. Daily noon–4pm and 6–10pm. Bus: 1, 6, 9, or 650.

Le Sommelier ⭐ FRENCH A 5-minute walk from Kongens Nytorv, this French restaurant and wine bar evokes a Left Bank bistro. Winner of several culinary awards, it offers one of the finest wine cellars in the city, stocked with some 850 bottles. Naturally, its sommelier is one of Copenhagen's wisest. Businesspeople predominate at lunch, with a more lively, younger crowd at dinner. The menu, the creation of chef Francis Cardenau, is short but inspired. Start with such delightful appetizers as cannelloni stuffed with salmon or a smooth and delicious terrine of foie gras. One soup, and it was a honey, recently sampled was made with red mullet. A savory stuffed rabbit appears frequently on the menu or else you may want to sample the *poisson du jour.* A specialty is a seafood paella that's even better when you can order it to be shared. The crème brûlée competes with the best of such desserts in Copenhagen.

Bredgade 63. ℂ **33-11-45-15.** Reservation recommended. Main courses 165DKK–200DKK ($28–$33). Fixed-price menus 245DKK–315DKK ($41–$53). AE, DC, MC, V. Mon–Thurs noon–2pm and 6–10pm; Fri noon–2pm and 6–11pm; Sat 6–11pm; Sun 6–10pm. Bus: 1A.

MODERATE

Café Lumskebugten ★ *Finds* DANISH   This spic-and-span, well-managed bastion of Danish charm has an unpretentious elegance that's admired throughout the capital. A now-legendary matriarch named Karen Marguerita Krog established it in 1854 as a tavern for sailors. As the tavern's reputation grew, aristocrats, artists, and members of the Danish royal family came to dine. Today a tastefully gentrified version of the original beef hash is still served.

Antique ship models decorate two glistening white dining rooms. (Two additional smaller rooms are usually reserved for private functions.) The food and service are excellent. Menu specialties include a tartare of salmon with herbs, Danish fish cakes with mustard sauce and minced beet root, fried platters of herring, sugar-marinated salmon with mustard-cream sauce, and a symphony of fish with saffron sauce and new potatoes. At lunchtime, you can order a Danish platter of assorted house specialties (275DKK/$46).

Esplanaden 21. ℂ **33-15-60-29.** Reservations recommended. Main courses 178DKK–275DKK ($30–$46); 3-course fixed-price lunch 275DKK ($46); 5-course fixed-price dinner 545DKK ($91). AE, DC, MC, V. Mon–Fri 11:30am–10pm; Sat 5–10pm. Bus: 1, 6, or 9.

L'Alsace CONTINENTAL   Established in the 1970s by an entrepreneur from Austria, within an 18th-century building on a cobble-covered courtyard, this restaurant offers dishes that provide a welcome change from too constant a diet of Danish food. Amid a striking collection of modern paintings, you can order dishes from across the culinary divides of Europe. Many derive from Alsace, including sauerkraut studded with pork knuckles and pork sausages, and a terrine of foie gras. There are also oysters from the Atlantic coast of France, Wiener schnitzels, *tafelspitz* (Habsburg-style boiled beef with horseradish), Austrian-style roulades of beef, pepper steaks, roasted duck with orange sauce, and other items that change according to the whim of the chef and the availability of ingredients. Dessert brings pastries inspired by France and Austria. What's our beef about the place? We only hope that former diners Elton John and Queen Margrethe got better service than we did on our last visit.

Ny Østerg 9. ℂ **33-14-57-43.** Reservations recommended. Main courses 105DKK–324DKK ($18–$54); set lunch 256DKK ($43); set dinner 317DKK–454DKK ($53–$76). AE, DC, MC, V. Mon–Sat 11:30am–11:45pm. Bus: 5.

Restaurant Els DANISH/FRENCH   Restaurant Els preserves its original 1854 decor. Several murals believed to be the work of 19th-century muralist Christian Hitsch, who adorned parts of the interior of the Danish Royal Theater, are displayed. Hans Christian Andersen was a regular here.

Each day there's a different fixed-price menu, but a selection of Danish open-faced sandwiches is offered at lunch for those who want a lighter meal. The cuisine at night is French, accompanied by excellent wines. A fish menu is featured nightly, including, for example, such perfectly prepared dishes as honey-smoked salmon, lobster ragout in puff pastry, and filet of Dover sole with saffron sauce, followed by black-currant sorbet with cassis. A la carte dishes are likely to include a winning combination of salted quail and sweetbreads in a bouillon with crispy vegetables. The cuisine is remarkably well crafted as exemplified by the sirloin of veal in Parma ham with a fricassee of white asparagus. Tuna fish is first marinated and then grilled to perfection before being served with a crisp salad.

Store Strandstræde 3 (off Kongens Nytorv). (ℂ) **33-14-13-41.** Reservations recommended. Main courses 198DKK–258DKK ($33–$43); sandwiches (lunch only) 45DKK–75DKK ($7.50–$13); fixed-price 2-course lunch 195DKK ($33); fixed-price 3-course lunch 215DKK ($36); fixed-price 5-course dinner 485DKK ($81). AE, DC, MC, V. Mon–Sat noon–3pm; daily 5:30–10pm. Closed July. Bus: 1, 6, or 10.

Restaurant Gilleleje INTERNATIONAL   The nautical decor is appealing but diners come for the endless procession of meats, fish, spices, garnishes, and sauces made deftly by a skilled kitchen staff. The chefs here aren't afraid of adding flavor to the food. You get tasty vittles and plenty of them. You might start with the specialty, a velvety smooth lobster soup that will make you want to order a second helping, though that would fill you up too quickly. The fish soup is always savory, as is the whisky steak flambé with grilled tomatoes. More recent items include Thai fish soup, spit-roasted Danish lamb with potatoes, and a rabbit stew with fresh vegetables. For dessert (if you have room), the Danish crepes with vanilla ice cream will make you fall in love with Copenhagen.

Nyhavn 10. (ℂ) **33-12-58-58.** Reservations required. Main courses 140DKK–150DKK ($23–$25). AE, DC, MC, V. Mon–Sat 11am–midnight. Bus: 1, 6, 9, 10, 19, or 31.

Restaurant Havfruen ⭐ _Finds_ SEAFOOD   Small and usually full because of its reputation for good fish, this restaurant is a cozy, nautically outfitted hideaway whose atmosphere is enhanced by the carved wooden mermaid hanging from the ceiling beams. Lunches are less complicated, and less expensive than dinners, and offer a more limited choice, with an emphasis on salmon, different preparations of herring, and shellfish such as clams and oysters. Dinner is fancier, with platters of whatever fish arrived fresh that day in the market. Especially flavorful is the Greenland turbot in a _beurre blanc_ (white butter) sauce, which tastes wonderful when served with a fruity white wine from the Loire valley. The staff can get rather hysterical when the place fills up.

Nyhavn 39. (ℂ) **33-11-11-38.** Reservations recommended. Main courses 125DKK–250DKK ($21–$42). DC, MC, V. Daily 11:30am–11pm. Bus: 1, 6, or 9.

Restaurant Wiinblad DANISH/INTERNATIONAL   This is the less formal of the two restaurants in the ultraupscale Hotel d'Angleterre (p. 58), and as such, many clients prefer it to the more restrictive (and more expensive) sibling, Restaurant d'Angleterre. It was named after Bjørn Wiinblad, an artist who is beloved throughout Denmark for his illustrations of children's fables. The mostly blue decor was for the most part designed and executed within Wiinblad's studios, usually featuring representations of fanciful characters that show the Danish sense of myth, legend, and fairy tale at its best.

Menu items are more formal in the evening than at lunchtime. Lunches might consist of _smørrebrød_ (open-faced sandwiches), salads, and Danish platters that combine three different food items on a plate—perhaps slices of roast beef, potatoes, and a cooked fresh vegetable. Dinners are more elaborate, and might include a simple but perfect dish—fried mullet with a warm potato salad, accompanied by a sauce of capers and truffles. Danish salmon is roasted to perfection in its skin to retain its flavor, or else you may prefer something more innovative: cockerel served with a goat-cheese tart and pickled rhubarb. The

Kids Family-Friendly Restaurants

Copenhagen Corner (p. 81)   A special children's menu features such dishes as shrimp cocktail and grilled rump steak.

Grøften (p. 91)   This is the most popular restaurant in the Tivoli, mainly because of its wholesome, traditional fare prepared and served at affordable prices on an outdoor terrace.

Ida Davidsen (p. 79)   When has your kid ever faced a choice of over 100 sandwiches for lunch? At the "*smørrebrød* queen's" cozy eatery, that's what you get—almost every conceivable sandwich, ranging from salmon to ham, from shrimp to smoked duck.

Københavner Cafeen (p. 84)   Visits from Santa are a year-round event at this reasonably-priced café.

dessert surprise is strawberries Romanoff with crispy chocolate and basil-flavored vanilla ice cream. This hotel has long been known for selecting some of Copenhagen's finest chefs, and chances are you won't be disappointed.

In the Hotel d'Angleterre, Kongens Nytorv 14. ☏ 33-12-00-95. Reservations recommended. Main courses 99DKK–295DKK ($17–$49); fixed-price 2-course lunch menu 195DKK ($33); fixed-price dinner menu 325DKK–385DKK ($54–$64). AE, DC, MC, V. Daily 11:30am–5pm; Sun–Thurs 5–10pm; Fri–Sat 5–11pm. Bus: 1, 6, or 9.

Victor's Café DANISH/FRENCH   Hip, artsy, and boasting Parisian decor and service, this is a Danish version of a bustling French bistro. There's a cafe at one end and a restaurant at the other. The arts-oriented crowd sits at the curved, illuminated bar or at tables. The popular Victor Plate, which costs 165DKK ($28), offers three food items. You can also choose from a variety of open-faced sandwiches. Look for the daily specials posted on the chalkboard. Try the breast of wild duckling with plums and celery, ragout of fish with red peppers, or baked salmon with chervil sauce and artichoke heart. The cooking may not be the finest in Copenhagen, but the atmosphere and ambience compensate.

Ny Østergade 8. ☏ 33-13-36-13. Reservations recommended. Restaurant main courses 70DKK–155DKK ($12–$26); cafe *smørrebrød* (served only at lunch) 50DKK–156DKK ($8.35–$26). AE, DC, MC, V. Mon–Wed 8am–1am; Thurs–Sat 8am–2am; Sun 11am–11pm. Bus: 1, 6, or 9.

INEXPENSIVE

Café Zeze CONTINENTAL   Set in a neighborhood with a dense collection of shops and offices, this hip bistro and cafe has a reputation for good food and brisk service. You'll find a cheerful-looking setup with a high ceiling, mirrors, and a mostly yellow interior. Noise levels can get a bit high, especially late at night when more folk seem to be drinking than eating, but overall the place can be a lot of fun. Menu items change frequently, but expect a well-prepared medley of dishes that include grilled chicken breast with mushrooms, sautéed breast of turkey with coconut and chile sauce, roasted guinea fowl with shrimp and braised arugula, and filets of lamb with shiitake mushrooms.

Ny Østergade 20. ☏ 33-14-23-90. Reservations recommended. Main courses 45DKK–80DKK ($7.50–$13) at lunch, 100DKK–139DKK ($17–$23) at dinner; fixed-price lunch 70DKK ($12); fixed-price dinner 98DKK ($16). AE, DC, MC, V. Mon–Sat 11:30am–4:30pm and 5:30–10pm (last order). Bar and cafe Mon–Thurs 9am–midnight; Fri–Sat 9am–2am. Bus: 1, 6, 9, or 10.

Ida Davidsen ★ *Kids* SANDWICHES   This restaurant has become an institution since 1888 when the forebears of its present owner, Ida Davidsen, opened a sandwich shop. Today, five generations later, the family matriarch and namesake is known as the "*smørrebrød* queen of Copenhagen," selling a greater variety of open-faced sandwiches (177 kinds) than anyone else in Denmark. If you opt for a sandwich here, you'll be in good company: Her fare has even been served at Amalienborg Castle. The vast selection includes salmon, lobster, shrimp, smoked duck with braised cabbage and horseradish, liver pâté, ham, herring, and boiled egg. Two of them, accompanied perhaps by a slice of cheese, compose a worthy lunch. If you're in doubt, a member of the service team will offer suggestions. Incidentally, the enlarged photographs that decorate the walls of this place usually come from the Davidsen family's personal scrapbook and feature *smørrebrød* authorities, in their natural element, from generations past.

Store Kongensgade 70. ⓒ **33-91-36-55.** Reservations recommended. Sandwiches 40DKK–155DKK ($6.70–$26). AE, DC, MC, V. Mon–Fri 10am–4pm. Bus: 1, 6, or 9.

Nyhavns Færgekro ★ *Finds* DANISH/FRENCH   The "Nyhavn Ferry Inn" near the harbor has a long tradition and many loyal fans. The house is old, dating from the final years of the 18th century. Diners enjoy not only their food but also a view of the surrounding 18th-century houses and the canal from the popular summer terrace. Inside, the decor is unusual, with a spiral stairway from an antique tram and a black-and-white "checkerboard" marble floor. Lights serve as call buttons to summon the staff when you want service.

The kitchen prepares a daily homemade buffet of 10 types of herring in different styles and sauces, including fried, *rollmops* (rolled or curled herring), and smoked. Some people make a full meal of the herring. You can also order *smørrebrød*—everything from smoked eel with scrambled eggs to chicken salad with bacon. A true Dane, in the tradition of Nyhavn, orders a schnapps or aquavit at lunch. Denmark has a tradition of making spicy aquavit from the herbs and plants of the land—Saint-John's-wort from Tisvilde Hegn, sloe-leaf from the wild moors, green walnuts from the south of Funen, and many other varieties. For dinner you can enjoy one of Copenhagen's most tender and succulent entrecôtes.

Nyhavn 5. ⓒ **33-15-15-88.** Reservations required. Fixed-price dinner 165DKK ($28). DC, MC, V. Daily 11:30am–4pm and 5–11:30pm. Closed Jan 1 and Dec 24–25. Bus: 1, 6, or 9.

Restaurant Ostehjørnet DANISH   This restaurant is so popular at lunchtime that dozens are turned away. The secret is to arrive early or late. There are a variety of Danish specialties, but we recommend the herring salad, the mussel salad, quiche Lorraine, veal *cordon bleu*, smoked turkey, sweetbreads, and ham-and-cheese omelets. All the dishes are served buffet-style. An excellent dessert is a delectable fruit tart with a hint of chocolate. The restaurant is located one floor above street level in an 18th-century building.

Store Kongensgade 56. ⓒ **33-15-85-77.** Reservations recommended. Main courses 110DKK ($18). DC, MC, V. June and Aug–Sept Mon–Fri 11:30am–4pm; Oct–May Mon–Fri noon–4pm, Sat 11:30am–3pm; closed in July. Bus: 1 or 10.

Restaurant Parnas DANISH   Opposite the city's largest department store, Magasin, this is a late-night refuge decorated like a warm, rustic, old-fashioned Danish *kro* (inn). Begin with three different kinds of herring or marinated salmon, followed by fried sliced pork with parsley sauce, several different preparations of sole and salmon, or the house specialty—*Parnas Gryde*, which combines grilled sirloin with bacon, marrow, and mushrooms, with béarnaise sauce on the side. This platter has been on the menu since the restaurant opened in the 1930s. After midnight a limited menu is available. Live music begins at 8:30pm.

Lille Kongensgade 16. © **33-11-49-10**. Reservations required. Main courses 98DKK–168DKK ($16–$28). AE, DC, MC, V. Mon–Thurs noon–3am; Fri–Sat noon–5am. Bus: 1, 6, 9, 10, or 29.

Skindbuksen *Moments* DANISH   This place is more Danish than the queen. Although it's in an expensive neighborhood, it not only is reasonable in price but is a down-home type of place (that is, down-home Danish style). This atmospheric landmark has long drawn beer drinkers in the neighborhood. Many locals, often old sailors, swear by its *lobscouse,* the Danish version of a meat-and-potato stew that has kept many a mariner from starvation over the years. This popular dish is often sold out at noon. A good variety of *smørrebrød* is always a luncheon favorite. You can order other dishes too, including homemade soups, pâtés, fresh shrimp, and a local favorite, tender beef served with a béarnaise sauce. There is piano live music Monday to Saturday from 8pm to 12:30am.

Lille Kongensgade 4 (off Kongens Nytorv). © **33-12-90-37**. Reservations recommended. Main courses 85DKK–149DKK ($14–$25). AE, DC, MC, V. Daily 11:30am–midnight (kitchen closes at 10pm). Bus: 1, 6, 10, 27, 28, or 29.

NORTH OF CHURCHILLPARKEN
MODERATE

Restaurant Le Saint-Jacques *Finds* FRENCH   Set in a single dignified dining room, in a building that's at least a century old, this well-respected French restaurant has a talent for defining itself as an unofficial embassy of Gallic goodwill. During mild weather, you can escape from the somewhat cramped interior in favor of a table on the street outside, adding a flavor that might remind you of something in the south of France. Menu items change frequently, based on the inspiration of the chef and the availability of ingredients. Examples include North Atlantic scallops with salmon roe and leeks in a beurre blanc sauce, filet of sole with a balsamic glaze, and filets of free-range chicken with a cream-flavored morel sauce. A steady hand in the kitchen admirably presents dishes to diners who usually have traditional tastes. Excellent ingredients also go into this skillful cuisine. The wide-ranging wine list includes vintages from around the world.

Skt. Jacobs Pladsen 1. © **35-42-77-07**. Reservations recommended. Main courses 78DKK–135DKK ($13–$23) at lunch, 135DKK–195DKK ($23–$33) at dinner; set menu 278DKK ($46). DC, MC, V. Daily noon–midnight. Bus: 6 or 14.

NEAR RÅDHUSPLADSEN & TIVOLI
MODERATE

Atlas Bar/Restaurant Flyvefisken DANISH/THAI/INTERNATIONAL   The cuisine at these two restaurants (prepared in the same kitchen) include lots of vegetarian food inspired by the fare of Thailand, Mexico, and India, with a Danish overview toward tidiness and coziness. On the street level, the cramped, cozy Atlas Bar serves a busy lunchtime crowd, but slackens off a bit at night, when the wood-sheathed Flyvefisken (Flying Fish) opens for dinner upstairs. Upstairs, expect a bit more emphasis on Thai cuisine and its fiery flavors, including lemongrass, curries, and several of the hot, spicy fish soups native to Bangkok. Although the authenticity of the Thai cuisine has lost a bit of its zest in the long jump from Thailand, it's still a change of pace from typical Danish fare. Expect crowds here, especially at lunch, when the place is likely to be full.

Lars Bjørnstræde 18. © **33-14-95-15.** Reservations recommended. Main courses 75DKK–140DKK ($13–$23) at lunch, 105DKK–175DKK ($18–$29) at dinner. AE, DC, MC, V. Atlas Bar Mon–Sat noon–10pm. Restaurant Flyvefisken Mon–Sat 5–10pm. Bus: 5, 6, or 16.

Café Ketchup ★ *Finds* INTERNATIONAL   We love the name of this cafe and restaurant, even if there aren't any bottles of ketchup in sight. The coolest bar in the city, the centrally located place (all buses to the center) draws a lively, beautiful crowd of young people, including many models. With its great drinks, including Cosmopolitans and mojitos, that minty run mixed drink, this is the place to be in Copenhagen on a Friday or Saturday night. On the ground floor is a cafe with floor-to-ceiling windows overseeing the action outside. There are restaurant tables in back and a bar along one wall, with many tables in the basement and an open kitchen. The restaurant roams the world for its culinary inspiration: There are even Danish dishes. You'd think the focus was on the drinks and atmosphere, but the food is good and well prepared. Get a load of these offerings: potato wasabi soup with crispy wasabi peas and a mango salsa bruschette or artichoke salad with grilled chicken breast and crispy Parma ham with cherry tomatoes and a chili-laced lime vinaigrette. They have less complicated dishes as well. For dessert? How many times have you had crème brûlée flavored with lemon grass and fresh basil, with apple sorbet and a crisp honey tuile (a thin cookie)?

Pilestræde 19. © **33-32-30-30.** Reservation recommended. Main courses 110DKK–285DKK ($18–$48). Fixed-price dinner menus 415DKK–725DKK ($69–$121). AE, DC, MC, V. Daily noon–10:30pm.

Cilatro Bar and Grill ★ *Finds* INTERNATIONAL   Established in 1910 as the Café Sønderborg, this restaurant was revitalized under the direction of the Michelsen family, and does a thriving business from a position near the SAS Radisson Scandinavia Hotel, east of Tivoli. It resembles a warm Danish *kro*, with dark wood trim, white stucco walls, and impeccable service. As much attention is paid to the way a dish looks as to the way it tastes. Menu items include lobster bisque with cognac; risotto with shellfish; roasted mackerel with tomatoes and garlic; carpaccio of duck; goose liver with apples and Calvados; and any of several fresh fish of the day, sometimes served with seasonal mushrooms.

Amagerbrogade 37. © **32-54-44-44.** Reservations recommended. Main courses 45DKK–85DKK ($7.50–$14) at lunch, 188DKK–265DKK ($31–$44) at dinner; fixed-price lunches 200DKK–240DKK ($33–$40); fixed-price dinners 250DKK–365DKK ($42–$61). AE, DC, MC, V. Mon–Fri noon–3pm and 5–10pm; Sat 5–10pm. Closed July. Bus: 2 or 9.

Copenhagen Corner *Kids* SCANDINAVIAN   Set amid some of the heaviest pedestrian traffic in Copenhagen, this restaurant opens onto Rådhuspladsen, around the corner from the Tivoli Gardens. Outfitted with some of the accessories of a greenhouse-style conservatory for plants, it offers well-prepared, unpretentious meals to dozens of city residents throughout the day and evening. The menu, which offers many Danish favorites, will place you deep in the heart of Denmark, beginning with three kinds of herring or freshly peeled shrimp with dill and lemon. There's even a carpaccio of filet of deer for the most adventurous palates. The soups are excellent, such as the consommé of white asparagus flavored with chicken and fresh herbs. The fish is fresh and beautifully prepared, especially the steamed Norwegian salmon with a "lasagna" of potatoes, or the baked halibut with artichokes. Meat and poultry courses, although not always equal to the fish, are tasty and tender, especially the veal liver Provençal.

H. C. Andersens Blvd. 1A. © **33-91-45-45.** Reservations recommended. Main courses 128DKK–255DKK ($21–$43); 3-course fixed-price menu 298DKK ($50). AE, DC, MC, V. Daily 11:30am–11pm. Bus: 1, 6, or 8.

Tips **Quick Bites in Copenhagen**

Copenhagen has many hot dog stands, chicken and fish grills, and *smørrebrød* counters that serve good, fast, inexpensive meals.

Hot dog stands, especially those around Rådhuspladsen, offer *polser* (steamed or grilled hot dogs) with shredded onions on top and *pommes frites* (french fries) on the side.

The *bageri* or *konditori* (bakery), found on almost every block, sells fresh bread, rolls, and Danish pastries.

Viktualiehandler (small food shops), found throughout the city, are the closest thing to a New York deli. You can buy roast beef with free *log* (fried onions). The best buy is smoked fish. Ask for a Bornholmer, a large, boneless sardine from the Danish island of Bornholm, or for *røgost,* a popular and inexpensive smoked cheese. Yogurt fans will be delighted to know that the Danish variety is cheap and tasty. It's available in small containers—just peel off the cover and drink it right out of the cup as the Danes do. *Hytte ret* (cottage cheese) is also good and cheap.

The favorite lunch of Scandinavians, particularly Danes, is the open-faced sandwich called **smørrebrød.** The purest form is made with dark rye bread, called *rugbrød.* Most taverns and cafes offer *smørrebrød,* and many places serve it as takeout food.

You can picnic in any of the city parks in the town center. Try Kongsgarten near Kongens Nytorv, the Kastellet area near *The Little Mermaid* statue, Botanisk Have (site of the Botanical Gardens), the lakeside promenades in southeastern Copenhagen, and the old moat at Christianshavn.

Søren K ✸ INTERNATIONAL   Named after Denmark's most celebrated philosopher, this is an artfully minimalist dining room that's on the ground floor of the newest addition to the Royal Library. It has the kind of monochromatic gray and flesh–toned decor you might find in Milan, and big-windowed views that stretch out over the sea. Menu items change frequently, but might include carpaccio of veal, foie gras, oyster soup, and main courses such as veal chops served with lobster sauce and a half-lobster, or venison roasted with nuts and seasonal berries and a marinade of green tomatoes. The restaurant virtually never cooks with butter, cream, or high-cholesterol cheeses, making a meal here a low-cholesterol as well as a savory experience. To reach this place, you'll have to enter the main entrance of the library and pass through its lobby.

On the ground floor of the Royal Library's Black Diamond Wing, Søren Kierkegaards Plads 1. ☎ **33-47-49-50.** Reservations recommended. Main courses 65DKK–125DKK ($11–$21) at lunch, 195DKK–225DKK ($33–$38) at dinner; fixed-price 3-course dinner 360DKK ($60); 8-course tasting menu 495DKK ($83). DC, MC, V. Mon–Sat 11am–10:30pm. Bus: 1, 2, 5, 6, 8, or 9.

Sult ✸ SOUTHERN EUROPEAN/FUSION   This fashionable, trendy eatery is inside the Danish Film Institute's center and is both a cultural and a gourmet experience. The setting is like a modern museum with wood floors, towering windows, and high lofty ceilings. Chef Alvin Bielefeldt has traveled the world for his culinary inspiration, although he specializes in a Mediterranean cuisine of southern Europe. Using market-fresh ingredients, he often elevates his cuisine to the sublime. Many of the dishes were inspired by Morocco or Asia, particularly Thailand. You might find mussels with creamy carrots or else a roast guinea fowl with yams. We recently enjoyed grilled veal medallions with fresh green beans, our dinner guest enjoying a perfectly grilled halibut. For an appetizer we suggest the terrine of foie gras. If you don't want to make decisions, opt for one of the fixed-price menus, which are innovative and engaging to the palate.

Vognmagergade 8B. ☎ **33-74-34-17**. Reservations recommended. 185DKK ($31) all main courses. Fixed-price menus 240DKK–425DKK ($40–$71). AE, DC, MC, V. Tues–Sat noon–midnight, Sun 11am–10pm. S-tog: Nørreport.

TyvenKokkenHansKoneog-HendesElsker *(Finds* ✸✸✸ INTERNATIONAL In olden days these headquarters were the seat of the most famous brothel in Copenhagen. Today, the restored 18th-century townhouse near Rådhuspladsen (Town Hall Square) is one of the city's most unusual and one of its best restaurants. Its bizarre name comes from Peter Greenaway's cannibalistic *The Cook, The Thief, His Wife and Her Lover*, a brilliant film with macabre feast scenes. The two-story restaurant offers tables with a view over old Copenhagen upstairs. The chefs here are inspired in their selection of an innovative fixed-price menu. The menu changes weekly, but we recently enjoyed the "Lobstermenu" with champagne. It began with grilled lobster's claw and turbot with green peas and pearl onions, proceeded to encompass risotto with lobster fragments and fresh chanterelles, and followed with lobster tail with seared foie gras. Everything is good here, even something simple but sublime like entrecôte with fresh vegetables. Finish off with a luscious dessert or a platter of various European farm cheeses.

Magstræde 16. ☎ **33-16-12-92**. Reservations recommended. Main courses 135DKK–235DKK ($23–$39). Fixed-price menu 595DKK ($99). DC, MC, V. Mon–Sat 6pm–2am.

INEXPENSIVE

Axelborg Bodega DANISH   Across from the Benneweis Circus and near Scala and Tivoli, this well-established 1912 Danish cafe has outdoor tables where you can enjoy a brisk Scandinavian evening. Order the *dagens ret* (daily special). Typical Danish dishes are featured, including *frikadeller* (meatballs) and pork chops. A wide selection of club sandwiches is also available, costing 48DKK to 76DKK ($8–$13) each. Although the atmosphere is somewhat impersonal, this is a local favorite; diners enjoy the recipes from grandma's attic.

Axeltorv 1. ☎ **33-11-06-38**. Reservations recommended. Main courses 78DKK–138DKK ($13–$23). AE, DC, MC, V. Restaurant daily 11am–9pm. Bar daily 11am–2am. Bus: 1 or 6.

Café Sorgenfri *(Value* SANDWICHES   Don't come here expecting grand cuisine, or even a menu with any particular variety. This place has thrived for 150 years selling beer, schnapps, and a medley of *smørrebrød* that appeal to virtually everyone's sense of workaday thrift and frugality. With only about 50 seats, the place is likely to be crowded around the lunch hour, with somewhat more space during the midafternoon. Come here for an early dinner. Everything inside reeks of old-time Denmark, from the potted shrubs that adorn the facade to the well-oiled paneling that has witnessed many generations of Copenhageners selecting and enjoying sandwiches. Between two and four of them might compose a reasonable lunch, depending on your appetite. You'll find it in the all-pedestrian shopping zone, in the commercial heart of town.

Brolæggerstræde 8. ☎ **33-11-58-80**. Reservations recommended for groups of 4 or more. *Smørrebrød* 42DKK–75DKK ($7–$13). DC, MC, V. Daily 11am–9pm. Bus: 5 or 6.

Chili AMERICAN   Boisterous, informal, and with an American theme, this is the most recent incarnation of a once-famous 19th-century establishment known to many generations of Danes as Tokanten. Chili serves at least 17 versions of burgers, available in quarter- and half-pound sizes, whose descriptions read like a map of the world. Choices include Hawaii burgers (with pineapple and curry), English burgers (with bacon and fried eggs), French burgers (with mushrooms in cream sauce), Danish burgers (with fried onions), and all the Texas burgers and chili burgers you could want. Also available are sandwiches and grilled steak platters. Service is fast, and the ambience is unpretentious.

Vandkunsten 1. (✆ **33-91-19-18.** Main courses 42DKK–165DKK ($7–$28); burgers and sandwiches 65DKK–98DKK ($11–$16). No credit cards. Mon–Sat 11am–midnight; Sun 11am–11pm. Bus: 5, 14, 16, 28, or 41.

Domhus Kælderen DANISH/INTERNATIONAL   Its good food, and a location across the square from City Hall, guarantees a large number of lawyers and their clients. That, coupled with lots of foreign visitors, makes this a bustling and old-fashioned emporium of Danish cuisine. The setting is a half-cellar room illuminated with high-laced windows that shine light down on wooden tables and 50 years of memorabilia. Menu items at lunch are more conservative and more Danish than at night. Lunch might include *frikadeller,* and heaping platters of herring, Danish cheeses, smoked meats and fish, and salads. Dinners might include pickled salmon, prime rib with horseradish, and fine cuts of beef, served with a béarnaise or pepper sauce. Also look for the catch of the day, prepared in virtually any way you like. The food is typically Danish and well prepared. You get no culinary surprises here, but then you are rarely disappointed.

Nytorv 5. (✆ **33-14-84-55.** Reservations recommended. Main courses 42DKK–128DKK ($7–$21) at lunch, 98DKK–168DKK ($16–$28) at dinner; set menus 190DKK–225DKK ($32–$38). AE, DC, MC, V. Daily 11am–4pm and 5–10pm. Bus: 5.

Husmann Vinstue (*Value* SANDWICHES   This old-fashioned, two-fisted, and bustling lunch stopover reminds city residents of the way much of Copenhagen was during the 19th century. It was founded in 1888 as a tavern and the decor hasn't changed much since. The menu focuses almost exclusively on *smørrebrød.* Combination platters, with herring, meatballs, Danish cheeses, and a small piece of steak, make especially satisfying meals. The fresh raw materials and the homemade specialties are of the highest quality.

Larsbjørnsstræde 2. (✆ **33-11-58-86.** Reservations recommended. Main courses 45DKK–94DKK ($7.50–$16). AE, DC, MC, V. Daily 11:30am–4pm (last order). Bus: 5.

Københavner Cafeen DANISH (*Kids*   One of the smallest (about 45 seats) restaurants in this pedestrians-only zone, the Københavner works hard to convey a sense of old-time Denmark. There's been an inn on this site since the 12th century, but the current structure dates from the 19th century. The setting is cozy, and you can enjoy authentically old-fashioned food items whose preparation adheres to methods practiced by many Danish grandmothers. Expect a roster of open-faced sandwiches at both lunch and dinner; *frikadeller;* grilled filets of plaice with butter sauce and fresh asparagus; roasted pork with braised red cabbage; and *biksemal,* a type of seafood hash that was served several times a week in many Danish homes throughout World War II. One of the most appealing items, and a specialty of the house, is a *Københavner platte,* which features several preparations of herring, marinated salmon, shrimp, meatballs, fresh vegetables, and fresh-baked, roughly textured bread with butter. The price of this culinary tour through Denmark is 149DKK ($25). Be warned that Santa impersonators might be entertaining the children in the crowd during your visit, even if your visit happens to fall during the month of August.

Badstuestæde 10. ⓒ **33-32-80-81**. Reservations recommended. *Smørrebrød* 44DKK–55DKK ($7.35–$9.20); main courses 79DKK–149DKK ($13–$25). AE, DC, MC, V. Daily 10am–midnight. Bus: 5 or 6.

Puk's Restaurant DANISH Solid and reliable, this restaurant is housed inside the thick stone walls of a former 18th-century brewery. You can enjoy a drink or two in the atmospheric pub next door; a pint of Danish beer costs 34DKK ($4). Most serious diners head down a flight of stairs from the street into the cellar-level restaurant. Menu selections include Danish meatballs, platters of *smørrebrød* or several kinds of smoked fish, herring offered either cold and marinated or fried and served with dill and new potatoes, and tournedos of beef with a sauce made from fresh tomatoes and herbs. This is real Danish cooking—without any particular flair, but hearty and filling.

Vandkunsten 8. ⓒ **33-11-14-17**. Reservations required in summer and Dec only. Main courses 49DKK–169DKK ($8.20–$28). AE, DC, MC, V. Daily 11am–10:30pm. Bus: 5, 28, 29, or 41.

Riz Raz (Value) MEDITERRANEAN/VEGETARIAN Bustling and unpretentious, this decidedly un-Danish hideaway offers the best all-vegetarian buffet in Copenhagen. There's additional seating outdoors during mild weather. Expect a medley of virtually every vegetable known to humankind, prepared either *au naturel* or as part of a marinated fantasy that might include the antipasti of Italy, the hummus of Lebanon, or an array of long-simmered casseroles inspired by the cuisine of the Moroccan highlands. There's also a selection of pastas, some of them redolent with garlic, oil, and Mediterranean spices, as well as a limited array of meat and fish dishes. Service staff is composed mostly of students from countries around the world. Alcohol is served.

Kompagnistræde 20 (at Knabrostræde). ⓒ **33-15-05-75**. Vegetarian buffet 59DKK ($9.85) per person; main courses 100DKK–179DKK ($17–$30). AE, DC, MC, V. Daily 11:30am–midnight. Bus: 5 or 6.

Sløtskælderne DANISH A star on the *smørrebrød* circuit, this landmark opened in 1797 but since 1910 has been owned by the same family. Habitués call the place "Gitte Kik," the name of the owner and granddaughter of the founder. Everything—the Danish wood trim, the old photographs, and the gold walls—adds up to *hygge*, a coziness that has attracted such notables as the prince of Denmark, the king and queen of Sweden, and the late Victor Borge. Try the marinated salmon, fresh tiny shrimp, or hot *frikadeller*. The smoked eel and scrambled egg sandwich is the best of its kind.

Fortunstræde 4. ⓒ **33-11-15-37**. Reservations recommended. *Smørrebrød* 36DKK–85DKK ($6–$14). AE, DC, MC, V. Tues–Sat 11am–3pm. Bus: 1, 6, or 10.

NEAR ROSENBORG SLOT
VERY EXPENSIVE

St. Gertruds Kloster (★) (Finds) INTERNATIONAL Near Nørreport Station and south of Rosenborg Castle, this is the most romantic restaurant in Copenhagen. There's no electricity in the labyrinth of 14th-century underground vaults, and the 1,500 flickering candles, open grill, iron sconces, and rough-hewn furniture create an elegant medieval ambience. Enjoy an aperitif in the darkly paneled library. The chefs display talent and integrity, their cuisine reflecting precision and sensitivity. Every flavor is fully focused, each dish balanced to perfection. Try the fresh, homemade foie gras with black truffles, lobster served in a turbot bouillon, venison (year-round) with green asparagus and truffle sauce, or a fish-and-shellfish terrine studded with chunks of lobster and salmon.

Hauser Plads 32. ℂ **33-14-66-30**. Reservations required. Main courses 250DKK–280DKK ($42–$47); fixed-price menu 468DKK–498DKK ($78–$83); children's menu 95DKK ($16). AE, DC, MC, V. Daily 5–11pm. Closed Dec 25–Jan 1. Bus: 4E, 7E, 14, or 16.

AT GRÅBRØDRETORV

Gråbrødretorv (Grey Friars Square), in the heart of Copenhagen's medieval core, is named after the monks who used to wander through its premises in medieval times. Now viewed as charming and hip, the area is a late-night destination that's not unlike what you'd find in the Latin Quarter district of Paris. The setting is low-key, unpretentious, and representative of the brown-brick architecture that fills most of the rest of historic Copenhagen.

MODERATE

Bøf & Ost DANISH/FRENCH   "Beef & Cheese" is in a 1728 building with cellars from a medieval monastery. In summer there's a pleasant outdoor terrace overlooking "Grey Friars Square." Specialties include lobster soup, fresh Danish bay strips, a cheese plate with six different selections, and some of the best grilled tenderloin in town. One local diner confided in us: "The food is not worthy of God's own table but it's so good for me I come here once a week."

Gråbrødretorv 13. ℂ **33-11-99-11**. Reservations required. Main courses 120DKK–199DKK ($20–$33); fixed-price lunch menu 118DKK ($20). DC, MC, V. Mon–Sat 11:30am–10:30pm. Closed Jan 1 and Dec 24–25. Bus: 5.

El Mesón SPANISH   This is the best Spanish restaurant in Copenhagen, with an emphasis on fresh food prepared in the Iberian style, and a staff from Murcia, Córdoba, Zaragoza, Madrid, and Valencia. The restaurant is especially appealing later at night, when lots of locals indulge themselves in the fond memories of their holidays on Spanish beaches. Menu items include tender cuts of tournedos and chateaubriand, a succulent version of lamb chops served with potatoes and fresh vegetables, and *Pinco de España,* a tenderloin of pork served with paprika and rosemary. The chef's version of paella is one of the most appealing this side of Valencia. All of the wines available at this restaurant, of course, are from Spain, and include impressive lists of Riojas and Ribera del Duero.

Hauser Plads 12. ℂ **33-11-91-31**. Reservations recommended. Main courses 135DKK–172DKK ($18–$23); fixed-price menu 206DKK ($27). DC, MC, V. Mon–Sat 5–10:30pm. Bus: 5.

Peder Oxe's Restaurant/Vinkælder Wine Bar DANISH   In the Middle Ages this was the site of a monastery, but the present building dates from the 1700s. Today this restaurant and wine bar attracts a young crowd. Selections from the salad bar cost 30DKK ($5) when accompanied by a main course, but the offerings are so tempting that many prefer to enjoy salad alone for 75DKK ($13) per person. Dishes include lobster soup, Danish bay shrimp, fresh asparagus, open-faced sandwiches, hamburgers, and fresh fish. The bill of fare, although standard, is well prepared.

Gråbrødretorv 11. ℂ **33-11-00-77**. Reservations recommended. Main courses 89DKK–189DKK ($15–$32); fixed-price lunch menu 67DKK–118DKK ($11–$20). DC, MC, V. Daily 11:30am–midnight. Bus: 5.

INEXPENSIVE

Pasta Basta *Value* ITALIAN   This restaurant's main attraction is a table loaded with cold antipasti and salads, one of the best deals in town. With more than nine selections on the enormous buffet, it's sometimes called the "Pasta Basta Table." For 79DKK ($13) you can partake of all that you can eat, plus unlimited bread. The restaurant itself is divided into half a dozen cozy dining rooms, each decorated in the style of ancient Pompeii. The restaurant is located on a historic cobblestone street off the main shopping boulevard, Strøget.

Menu choices include at least 15 kinds of fresh pasta, carpaccio served with olive oil and basil, a platter with three kinds of Danish caviar (whitefish, speckled trout, and vendace), thin-sliced salmon with a cream-based sauce of salmon roe, and Danish suckling lamb with fried spring onions and tarragon. Dessert offerings include an assortment of Danish, French, and Italian cheeses, crème brûlée, and *tartufo,* an Italian ice-cream treat.

Valkendorfsgade 22. ✆ **33-11-21-31.** Reservations recommended. Main courses 80DKK–160DKK ($13–$27). DC, MC, V. Sun–Thurs 11:30am–3am; Fri–Sat 11:30am–5:30am. Bus: 5.

NEAR KULTORVET
INEXPENSIVE

Ristorante Italiano ITALIAN   Patronized mainly by a foreign clientele under age 30 and by students from the University of Copenhagen, this restaurant is boisterous, unassuming, and often very busy. Its specialties include various pizzas and pastas, as well as platters of Italian-style veal and grilled steaks. Both the service and the turnover are rapid. You've probably had better versions of this cuisine elsewhere, but Italiano is a good value and many of the dishes are quite tasty, although never rising to a level where you'd request the recipe.

Fiolstræde 2. ✆ **33-11-12-95.** Reservations recommended. Pizzas and pastas 59DKK–118DKK ($9.85–$20); main courses 99DKK–199DKK ($17–$33); 3-course fixed-price menu 199DKK ($33). AE, DC, MC, V. Daily 11am–midnight. Bus: 5.

NEAR CHRISTIANSBORG
EXPENSIVE

Krogs Fiskerestaurant ☆ SEAFOOD   Krogs Fiskerestaurant, which is a short walk from Christiansborg Castle, is the most famous restaurant in the district, originally built in 1789 as a fish shop. (The canalside plaza where fishermen moored their boats is now the site of the restaurant's outdoor terrace.) Converted into a restaurant in 1910, it still serves fresh seafood in a single large room decorated in an antique style with old oil paintings and rustic colors. The well-chosen menu includes lobster soup, bouillabaisse, oysters, mussels steamed in white wine, and poached salmon-trout with saffron sauce. Each dish is impeccably prepared and filled with flavor. A limited selection of meat dishes is also available, but the fish is better.

Gammel Strand 38. ✆ **33-15-89-15.** Reservations required. Main courses 328DKK–585DKK ($55–$98); fixed-price 4-course menu 685DKK ($114); fixed-price 5-course menu 895DKK ($149). AE, DC, MC, V. Mon–Sat 11:30am–4pm and 5:30–10:30pm. Bus: 1, 2, 10, 16, or 29.

Nouvelle ☆☆ DANISH   In an elegant dining-room setting, Nouvelle has been one of the capital's special restaurants since 1950. It's on the first floor of a gray 1870 house beside a canal. If you've won the lottery, the restaurant has a special caviar menu, with Sevruga and Beluga. Otherwise you can explore the a la carte menu, which changes frequently but is likely to include goose liver terrine with three kinds of glazed onions or warm oysters and mussels gratinée. The fish dishes are superb, including North Sea turbot grilled or poached and served on a tomato, rosemary, and artichoke parfait. Lobster is served as a fricassee with green apples and a curry hollandaise. Meat selections are likely to include grilled goose liver with glazed spring cabbage and curry or lamb medallions with white truffles and new onions.

Gammel Strand 34. ✆ **33-13-50-18.** Reservations required. Main courses 272DKK–330DKK ($45–$55); 3-course fixed-price lunch 475DKK ($79); 4-course fixed-price dinner 610DKK ($102). AE, DC, MC, V. Mon–Fri 11:30am–3pm and 6–10pm; Sat 7:30–9pm. Closed Dec 22–Jan 6. Bus: 28, 29, or 41.

INEXPENSIVE

Cafeen Nikolaj DANISH   This cafe, which to some evokes Greenwich Village in the 1950s, is on the site that, around 1530, was the scene of the thundering sermons of Hans Tausen, a father of the Danish Reformation. Today orating has been replaced by ordering—from an array of Danish lunches including a tasty variety of open-faced sandwiches along with homemade soups. You can always count on the cook preparing various types of herring. Danish sliced ham on good homemade bread is a perennial favorite, and there is also a selection of Danish cheese. Nikolaj is a simple cafe for good-tasting food prepared with fresh ingredients and sold at a fair price.

Nikolaj Plads 12. *℃* **70-26-64-64**. Reservations not accepted. Main courses 80DKK–235DKK ($13–$39). AE, DC, DISC, MC, V. Mon–Sat 11:30am–5pm. Bus: 2, 6, 10, 27, 28, or 29.

Thorvaldsen DANISH   This restaurant, in the same building as the elegant and far more expensive Nouvelle, is hardly a citadel of grand cuisine, but it offers some of the best tasting and least expensive *smørrebrød* in town along with a changing daily array of old-fashioned Danish cookery. Against a backdrop of walls covered with old tapestries, you can partake of this hearty and very filling cuisine. Locals begin with various versions of herring or smoked salmon. You can go on to the typical dishes of the day, which almost invariably include fried plaice. An occasional special appears with flair and flavor, including, for example, free-range Danish roasted chicken with a saffron sauce and accompanied by a helping of risotto. For dessert, opt for the fresh fruit with vanilla ice cream. Tables are placed outside in a courtyard if the weather allows.

Gammel Strand 34. *℃* **33-32-04-00**. Reservations not accepted. Main courses 95DKK–185DKK ($16–$31). AE, DC, MC, V. Mon–Thurs 11am–10pm; Fri–Sat 11am–10:30pm. Bus: 28, 29, or 41.

IN NØRREBRO
INEXPENSIVE

Kasmir INDIAN   This North Indian hideaway does a thriving business with local residents. Surrounded by floors and walls lavishly decorated with handmade Indian carpets, you can order from a long list of dishes from South Asia's most populous country. Most can be ordered to the degree of spiciness you specify, from cool and mild to fiery. Examples include buttered lamb, slow-baked lamb *aloo* that's cooked in a clay pot with spices; a savory tandoori chicken with cumin; several varieties of Indian nan (bread); and a wide choice of highly flavorful vegetarian dishes served in either tomato or yogurt sauce.

Nørrebrogade 35. *℃* **35-37-54-71**. Reservations recommended. Main courses 45DKK–110DKK ($7.50–$18). Set menus (served only to 2 diners or more) 125DKK–175DKK ($21–$29). AE, DC, MC, V. Daily 2–11pm. Bus: 16.

Pussy Galore's Flying Circus INTERNATIONAL   Named after the James Bond character, this eatery is in trendy Nørrebro. From inexpensive fresh salads to some of the juiciest burgers in town, it's a great place to eat, drink, and make the scene. The location is a bit away from the center but that doesn't seem to bother one of its patrons, Prince Frederik, the playboy heir to the throne. Media types also flock here.

In summer, tables overflow onto the sidewalk. Many books that review the world's best bars, including one by "Black Bush Whiskey," list this place among the globe's best watering holes. As an attractive waiter confided to us, "Café Ketchup gets the young and beautiful; we get the younger and more beautiful." Against a 1990s minimalist decor, with Arne Jacobsen chairs, partake of great cocktails (especially those mojitos). Many regulars drop in every morning for eggs and bacon, returning in the evening for, perhaps, a wok-fried delight.

Sankt Hans Torv 30. (**C**) **35-24-53-00**. Reservations recommended. Main courses 65DKK–110DKK ($11–$18). AE, DC, MC, V. Mon–Fri 8am–2am, Sat–Sun 9am–2am. Bus: 3.

Ristorante Quattro Fontane ITALIAN   This is one of the busiest and most popular Italian restaurants in Copenhagen. Dining rooms contain marble-topped tables, artwork that celebrates Italian landscapes, and a motif of grapevines that meander across the ceilings. If you're an absolute purist about Italian authenticity, be sure to specify the degree of al dente you prefer in your pasta: The Abruzzi-born owner notes that Danish tastes prefer the spaghetti a bit softer than an Italian might want, so communication with a staff member might be a good idea. Menu items include thick-crusted pizzas; sautéed frogs' legs in the French style; succulent shrimp with garlic sauce; excellent fish, lamb, and scaloppine dishes; tenderloin steaks; and even some platters of grilled vegetables that celebrate the fruits of the Danish harvest prepared in the Italian style.

Guldbergsgade 3. (**C**) **35-39-39-31**. Reservations recommended. Main courses 98DKK–159DKK ($16–$27). DC, MC, V. Daily 4–11:30pm. Bus: 5. Also open for lunch in summer (June–Sept) daily 1–3pm.

IN FREDERIKSBERG
EXPENSIVE
Formel B. ★★ DANISH/FRENCH   In western Copenhagen and worth the short bus ride here, this restaurant is the culinary showcase for Kristian Møller and Rune Jochumsen, who seem to enjoy a love affair with the food critics of the Danish press. Their ultrastylish restaurant stands on the border separating the Vesterbro and Frederiksberg neighborhoods. No chefs in Copenhagen are as fanatical about serving fresh ingredients as this pair. They take the best of Danish raw materials and transform them into classical French dishes. They believe that dining should be "a total experience, which speaks to all the senses." Even if they don't always succeed in such a lofty ambition, the menu is divine and a treat to your palate. Our party of five, sampling many dishes, learned of the chefs' prowess by ordering such dishes as oysters, barley, and caviar, or hake with beetroot and fresh horseradish. The monkfish and mushrooms in a foamy sauce was sublime, as was the tender veal with foie gras and cherries. The dessert was a first for us: fresh raspberries with a licorice sherbet.

Vesterbrogade 182, Frederiksberg. (**C**) **33-25-10-66**. Reservations required. Fixed-price menu 600DKK ($100). AE, DC, MC, V. Mon–Sat 6–10pm. Bus: 6A.

IN TIVOLI
Food prices in the Tivoli Gardens restaurants are about 30% higher than elsewhere. To compensate for this, skip dessert and buy something less expensive (perhaps ice cream or pastry) later at one of the many stands in the park. Take bus nos. 1, 6, 8, 16, 29, 30, 32, or 33 to reach the park and any of the following restaurants. *Note:* These restaurants are open only May to mid-September.

VERY EXPENSIVE
The Paul ★★★ INTERNATIONAL   Winning a coveted Michelin star, the first for a restaurant in the Tivoli Gardens, this is the new gourmet restaurant in town. Chef Paul Cunningham's stated desire is to provide Tivoli revelers "with an intense gourmet experience." He brings fresh, new, and exciting ideas to his cuisine, spending his winters when the restaurant is closed "traveling, tasting, experiencing, and absorbing new inspirations." At elegant table settings, guests

enjoy a view of the lake. As an appetizer, try the foie gras and salted organic salmon with a side of Granny Smith apples or the warm quail salad with a poached egg and truffle butter. For a main course, opt for the Danish lamb with black olives. Desserts are always daring and innovative, especially the chocolate with Szechuan pepper, mango, and caramel sauce.

Vesterbrogade 3. ✆ 33-75-07-75. Reservations recommended. Fixed-price menus 395DKK–700DKK ($66–$117). AE, DC, MC, V. Mon–Sat noon–2:30pm and 6–8pm. Closed Oct–Mar.

EXPENSIVE

Divan II ✿✿ DANISH/FRENCH   This restaurant in a garden setting is the finest in Tivoli, and certainly the most expensive. It was established in 1843, the same year as Tivoli itself, and despite its name—Divan II—it's actually older than its nearby competitor, the less formal Divan I. The service is uniformly impeccable. The cuisine is among the most sophisticated in Copenhagen. The credo of the chefs is to create excellent meals using the best ingredients, but without audacious inventions. Try the leg of free-range cockerel from Bornholm, which is braised in white wine and served with morels and fresh shallots. The classic Danish dish, pan-fried meatballs with creamy leeks, never tastes better than it does here. But you may want something more exotic: roast breast of quail served with papaya and green beans with a flavoring of curry oil. Strawberries Romanoff finishes off the meal delightfully.

Vesterbrogade 3, Tivoli. ✆ 33-75-07-50. Reservations recommended. Main courses 95DKK–365DKK ($16–$61); fixed-price menu 365DKK ($61) at lunch; fixed-price dinner menu 465DKK–585DKK ($78–$98). AE, DC, MC, V. Daily 11am–midnight.

La Crevette ✿ SEAFOOD/DANISH   This restaurant offers more varied seafood dishes than any of its Tivoli competitors. Housed in a 1909 pavilion, it has an outdoor terrace, a modern dining room, and a well-trained staff. The seafood is fresh, flavorful, and prepared in innovative ways—pickled slices of salmon come with oyster flan and egg cream with chives, and a bisque of turbot is served with veal bacon and quail's eggs. Meat and poultry courses are extremely skimpy on the menu but you don't come here for that. Finish your repast with a selection of cheese from France, Denmark, and Italy (served with marinated prunes, a nice touch), or the fresh pastries of the day. The restaurant has its own confectionery. This restaurant is under the same management as Louise Nimb below, and has the same phone number.

Vesterbrogade 5, Tivoli. ✆ 33-14-60-03. Reservations recommended. Main courses 255DKK–315DKK ($43–$53); 4-course fixed-price dinner 455DKK ($76). AE, DC, MC, V. Daily noon–midnight.

Louise Nimb ✿ DANISH/FRENCH   Next door to its companion restaurant, La Crevette, this is the most formal restaurant in Tivoli, styled like a Moorish pavilion. Why the name Louise Nimb? She's the establishment's long-departed female chef who ladled up soup from the formerly smaller kitchen. Those modest days are long forgotten and the present menu is one of the most elaborate in the city; the chef uses only the freshest produce from Denmark and the rest of Europe. The first course is likely to include smoked Baltic salmon or freshly peeled fjord shrimp, or six oysters gratinée in a lemon zabaglione. The chef is rightfully proud of his shellfish medley, which includes Norwegian lobster, mussels, oysters, crab claws, and North Sea shrimp. Other fish choices include grilled red mullet with chive sauce or, for meat eaters, tournedos of beef with marrow and a red wine sauce.

Bernstorffsgade 5, Tivoli. ✆ 33-14-60-03. Reservations required. Main courses 210DKK–295DKK ($35–$49). AE, DC, MC, V. Daily noon–midnight.

MODERATE

Færgekroen DANISH   Nestled in a cluster of trees at the edge of the lake, this restaurant resembles a pink half-timbered Danish cottage. In warm weather, try to sit on the outside dining terrace. The menu offers drinks, snacks, and full meals. The latter might include an array of omelets, beef with horseradish, fried plaice with melted butter, pork chops with red cabbage, curried chicken, and fried meatballs. The food, prepared according to old recipes, is like what you might get down on a Danish farm. If you like honest, straightforward fare, without a lot of trimmings, and don't like to spend a lot of money, this might be the place for you. A pianist provides singalong music from Tuesday to Saturday starting at 8pm.

Vesterbrogade 3, Tivoli. ℂ **33-12-94-12.** Main courses 90DKK–195DKK ($15–$33). AE, DC, MC, V. Daily 11am–midnight (hot food until 9:45pm).

Grøften ⭐ *Kids* DANISH   Partly because of its low prices, and partly because it recalls the rustic restaurants fondly remembered by many Danes from their childhood vacations, this is the most popular spot in Tivoli. There's room for about 750 diners, equally divided between an outdoor terrace and an indoor dining room. In 1996 Grøften radically revised and improved its menus, keeping the old-fashioned favorites while adding several dishes that evoke the rich flavors and textures of the Mediterranean. We always start with the freshly peeled shrimp, though the smoked salmon with cream of morels is equally tempting. The cold potato soup with bacon and chives is the Danish version of vichyssoise. The wisest bet is to ask the waiter for the day's fish offering, based on the latest visit of the fishmonger. The chef's specialty is grilled beef tenderloin with bitter greens, tomatoes, olive oil, and black truffle essence. Old-time Danes have been coming here for years for the skipper's *lobscouse* (Danish hash). Glasses of Danish beer sell for 29DKK to 48DKK ($4.85–$8), depending on size.

Vesterbrogade 3, Tivoli. ℂ **33-12-11-25.** Main courses 105DKK–225DKK ($18–$38). AE, DC, MC, V. Sun–Thurs noon–midnight; Fri–Sat noon–1am.

4

Exploring Copenhagen

Copenhagen is a city of amusement parks, glittering shops, beer cellars, gardens, and bustling nightlife. But the city is also proud of its vast storehouse of antiquities and holds its own with the other capitals of Europe.

While there are plenty of amusing ways to while away the days, the Danish capital also offers numerous opportunities for the visitor who wants to see art, museums, and castles.

In the morning, you can wander back to classical or Renaissance days in such showcases of art as Thorvaldsen's Museum.

In the afternoon, you can head south to the town of Dragør on the island of Amager, now almost a suburb of Copenhagen. Here, in the museums and architecture, you'll see evidence of the Dutch inhabitants who lived and farmed on the island for 300 years.

On a summer evening, visitors can stroll through the Tivoli pleasure gardens, which seem to have emerged intact from the days when the world was young . . . and so were we. Apparently, the Danes love childhood too much to abandon it forever, no matter how old they get—so Tivoli keeps alive the magic of fairy lights and the wonder of yesteryear.

SUGGESTED ITINERARIES

If You Have 1 Day Take our walking tour through the old city (see p. 109 for a suggested walk), which isn't too taxing if you're still recovering from jet lag. Spend the late afternoon at Christiansborg Palace (on Slotsholmen), where the queen of Denmark receives guests. Early in the evening, head to Tivoli.

If You Have 2 Days For your first day, follow the suggestions above. On Day 2, visit Amalienborg Palace, the queen's residence. Try to time your visit to see the changing of the guard. Continue beyond the palace to the statue of *The Little Mermaid.* In the afternoon, see the art treasures of Ny Carlsberg Glyptotek. At night, visit Scala, the restaurant-and-shopping complex.

If You Have 3 Days Try some of the suggestions above for the first 2 days. On the morning of Day 3, visit the 17th-century Rosenborg Castle, summer palace of Christian IV. Afterward, wander the park and gardens. Have lunch at one of the restaurants on the canal at Nyhavn, the old seamen's quarter. In the afternoon, go to the Rundetårn (Round Tower) for a panoramic view of the city and, if time permits, stop in at the National Museum.

If You Have 4 or 5 Days For the first 3 days, see "If You Have 3 Days," above. On Day 4, head north from Copenhagen to Louisiana, the modern art museum, and continue on to Helsingør to visit Kronborg Castle, famously associated with Shakespeare's *Hamlet.* Return to Copenhagen in time for a stroll along Strøget. For dinner, eat at a restaurant in Dragør.

On Day 5, visit Frilandsmuseet, at Lyngby, a half-hour train ride from Copenhagen. Have lunch at the park. Return to Copenhagen and tour the Carlsberg brewery. Pay a final visit to Tivoli to cap your adventure in the Danish capital.

1 Seeing the Sights

IN & AROUND THE TIVOLI GARDENS

Tivoli Gardens ★★★ *Moments*   Since it opened in 1843, this 8-hectare (20-acre) garden and amusement park in the center of Copenhagen has been a resounding success. It features thousands of flowers, a merry-go-round of tiny Viking ships, games of chance and skill (pinball arcades, slot machines, shooting galleries), and a Ferris wheel of hot-air balloons and cabin seats. The latest attraction at Tivoli, "The Demon," is the biggest roller coaster in Denmark. Passengers whiz through three loops on the thrill ride, reaching a top speed of 80kmph (50 mph). There's also a playground for children.

An Arabian-style fantasy palace, with towers and arches, houses more than two dozen restaurants in all price ranges, from a lakeside inn to a beer garden. Take a walk around the edge of the tiny lake with its ducks, swans, and boats.

A parade of the red-uniformed Tivoli Boys Guard takes place on weekends at 5:20 and 7:20pm (also on Wed at 5pm), and their regimental band gives concerts on Saturday at 3pm on the open-air stage. The oldest building at Tivoli, the Chinese-style Pantomime Theater with its peacock curtain, offers pantomimes in the evening.

For more on the nighttime happenings in Tivoli—fireworks, bands, orchestras, discos, variety acts—see "Copenhagen After Dark," later in this chapter.

Vesterbrogade 3. ⓒ **33-15-10-01.** www.tivoli.dk. Admission 65DKK ($11) adults, 35DKK ($5.85) children under 14, combination ticket including admission and all rides 195DKK ($33). June 18–Aug 15 40DKK ($6.70) children. Closed mid-Sept to mid-Apr. Bus: 1, 16, or 29.

Ny Carlsberg Glyptotek ★★★   The Glyptotek, behind Tivoli, is one of the most important art museums in Scandinavia. Founded by the 19th-century art collector Carl Jacobsen, Mr. Carlsberg Beer himself, the museum includes modern art and antiquities. The modern section has both French and Danish art, mainly from the 19th century. Sculpture, including works by Rodin, is on the ground floor, and works of the Impressionists and related artists, including van Gogh's *Landscape from St. Rémy,* are on the upper floors. Egyptian, Greek, and Roman antiquities are on the main floor; Etruscan, Greek, and Cypriot on the lower floor. The Egyptian collection is outstanding; the most notable piece is a prehistoric rendering of a hippopotamus. Fine Greek originals (headless Apollo, Niobe's tragic children) and Roman copies of Greek bronzes (4th-c. Hercules) are also displayed, as are some of the noblest Roman busts—Pompey, Virgil, Augustus, and Trajan. The Etruscan collection (sarcophagi, a winged lion, bronzes, and pottery) is a favorite of ours.

In 1996 the Ny Glyptotek added a French masters' wing. Constructed of white marble and granite, it's in the inner courtyard, which can be reached only through the Conservatory. In a climate- and light-controlled environment, you'll find an extensive collection of French masterpieces including works by Manet, Monet, Degas, and Renoir, as well as an impressive collection of French sculpture, such as Rodin's *The Burghers of Calais,* and one of only three complete sets of Degas bronzes. The display features Cézanne's famous *Portrait of the Artist,* as well as about 35 paintings by former Copenhagen resident Paul Gauguin.

Copenhagen Attractions

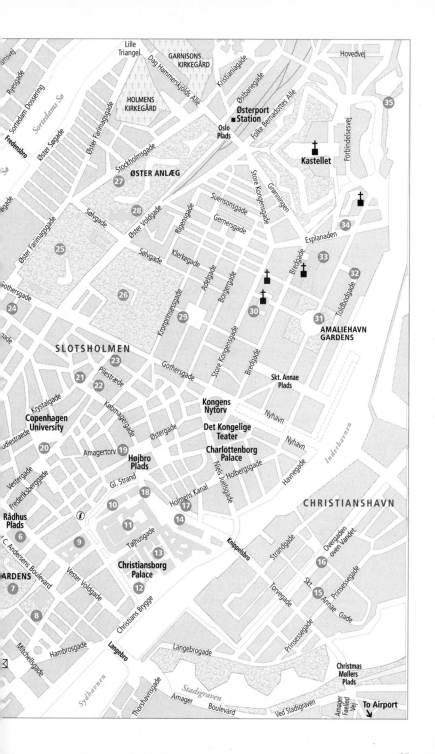

95

Dantes Plads 7. (© **33-41-81-41**. www.glyptoteket.dk. Admission 20DKK ($3.35) adults, free for children, free for everyone Wed and Sun. Tues–Sun 10am–4pm. Bus: 1, 2, 5, 6, 8, or 10.

Rådhus (Town Hall) and World Clock   Built in 1905, the Town Hall has statues of Hans Christian Andersen and Niels Bohr (the Nobel Prize–winning physicist). Jens Olsen's **World Clock** is open for viewing Monday to Friday 10am to 4pm and Saturday at 1pm. Frederik IX set the clock on December 15, 1955. The clockwork is so exact that it's accurate to within half a second every 300 years. Climb the tower for an impressive view. It's not for the faint of heart: 300 steps with no elevator.

To the east of the Rådhus is one of Copenhagen's most famous landmarks, the **Lurblæserne** (Lur Blower Column), topped by two Vikings blowing an ancient trumpet called a *lur.* There's a bit of artistic license taken here. The *lur* actually dates from the Bronze Age (ca. 1500 B.C.), while the Vikings lived some 1,000 years ago. But it's a fascinating sight anyway.

Rådhuspladsen. (© **33-66-25-82**. Admission to Rådhus 30DKK ($5). Admission to clock 10DKK ($1.65) adults, 5DKK (85¢) children. Guided tour of Rådhus Mon–Fri 3pm; Sat 10 and 11am. Guided tour of tower Oct–May Mon–Sat noon; June–Sept Mon–Fri 10am, noon, and 2pm, Sat noon. Bus: 1, 6, or 8.

AMALIENBORG PALACE & ENVIRONS

Amalienborg Palace ★★   These four 18th-century French-style rococo mansions—opening onto one of the most attractive squares in Europe—have been the home of the Danish royal family since 1794, when Christiansborg burned. Visitors flock to see the changing of the guard at noon when the royal family is in residence. A swallowtail flag on the mast signifies that the queen is in Copenhagen, and not at her North Zealand summer home, Fredensborg Palace.

The Royal Life Guard in black bearskin busbies (like the hussars) leaves Rosenborg Castle at 11:30am and marches along Gothersgade, Nørre Voldgade, Frederiksberggade, Købmagergade, Østergade, Kongens Nytorv, Bredgade, Skt. Annæ Plads, and Amaliegade, to Amalienborg. After the event, the guard, still accompanied by the band, returns to Rosenborg Castle via Frederiksgade, Store Kongensgade, and Gothersgade.

In 1994, some of the official and private rooms in Amalienborg were opened to the public. The rooms, reconstructed to reflect the period 1863 to 1947, all belonged to members of the royal family, the Glücksborgs, who ascended the throne in 1863. The highlight is the period devoted to the long reign (1863–1906) of Christian IX (1818–1906) and Queen Louise (1817–98). The items in his study and her drawing room—gifts from their far-flung children— reflect their unofficial status as "parents-in-law to Europe." Indeed, the story of their lives has been called "the Making of a Dynasty." Both came from distant sides of the then-heirless royal family to create a "love match." The verses for their 1842 wedding song (a Danish tradition) were written by Hans Christian Andersen.

Christian and Louise gave their six children a simple (by royal standards) but internationally oriented upbringing. One daughter, Alexandra, married Edward VII of England; another, Dagmar, wed Czar Alexander III of Russia. The crown prince, later Frederik VIII, married Louise of Sweden-Norway; another son became king of Greece, and yet another declined the throne of Bulgaria. In 1905 a grandson became king of Norway.

Frommer's Favorite Copenhagen Experiences

Sitting at an Outdoor Cafe   Because of Copenhagen's long gray winters, sitting at an outdoor cafe in the summer and drinking beer or eating is always a favorite pastime. The best spot is at Nyhavn (New Harbor), beginning at Kongens Nytorv. Enjoy ice cream while admiring the tall rigged ships with bowsprits moored in the canal.

Going to Tivoli   This is the quintessential summer adventure in Copenhagen, a tradition since 1843. It's an amusement park with a difference—even the merry-go-rounds are special, using a fleet of Viking ships instead of the usual horses.

Strolling Strøget   In Danish, the word *strøget* means "to stroll"—and that's exactly what all born-to-shop addicts do along this nearly 1.2km (¾-mile) stretch, from Rådhuspladsen to Kongens Nytorv.

Exploring Alternative Lifestyles   Not for everybody, but worth a look, is a trip to the Free City of Christiania, on the island of Christianshavn (bus: 8 from Rådhuspladsen). Since 1971 some 1,000 squatters have illegally taken over 130 former army barracks (spread across 8 hectares/ 20 acres) and declared the area a free city. You can shop, dine, and talk to the natives about this community with its own doctors, clubs, stores, and even its own flag. Exercise caution here, however; there are pickpockets about.

In the 1880s, members of the Danish royal family, numbering more than 50, got together regularly each summer at the Fredensborg Palace, north of Copenhagen. The children, now monarchs in their own right, brought Christian IX and Louise presents—works of art from the imperial workshops and from jewelers such as Fabergé—as well as souvenirs, embroideries, and handicrafts made by the grandchildren. All became treasures for the aging king and queen, and many are exhibited in the museum rooms today.

Also open to the public are the studies of Frederik VIII and Christian X. Thanks to his marriage to Louise of Sweden-Norway, the liberal-minded Frederik VIII (1843–1912), who reigned from 1906 to 1912, had considerable wealth, and he furnished Amalienborg Palace sumptuously. The king's large study, decorated in lavish neo-Renaissance style, testifies to this.

The final period room in the museum is the study of Christian X (1870–1947), the grandfather of current queen Margrethe II, who was king from 1912 to 1947. He became a symbol of national resistance during the German occupation of Denmark during World War II. Along with the period rooms, a costume gallery and a jewelry room are open to the public. The Amalienborg Museum rooms compose one of two divisions of the Royal Danish Collections; the other is at Rosenborg Palace in Copenhagen.

Christian VIII's Palace. © **33-40-10-10.** Admission 45DKK ($7.50) adults, 30DKK ($5) students, 10DKK ($1.65) children 5–12, free for children 4 and under. Access is by guided tours only, which leave daily at 1pm July–Sept. Bus: 1, 6, 9, or 10.

Fun Fact **Danish Design**

While there's been a massive postwar output of modern furniture in Norway and Sweden, and architectural innovations by such Finnish designers as Alvar Aalto, the streamlined, uncluttered look of modern Scandinavian design is most associated with Denmark. This is due in part to innovations made during the 1950s by such local luminaries as Hans Wegner, Poul Kjærholm, and Arne Jacobsen, who were trained as architects. Connoisseurs who appreciate their radical departures from previous styles avidly showcase their mid-century furniture and tableware designs.

The original inspiration for Danish design is believed to be the organic curves of Art Nouveau, where critics have defined sinuousness and an uncluttered elegance as "the curved line in love with itself." Danish modern managed to transform Art Nouveau from a decorative, nonessential adornment into an aesthetically pleasing, utilitarian stylistic approach that coincided with the industrial boom in Europe after World War II.

What makes a desirable and sought-after piece of Danish design? Some critics have referred to it as "structural vigor," others as "the visual expression of a socially just society" or "aesthetic functionalism," through simple and straightforward materials, including wood (usually oak, maple, ash, and, to a lesser degree, walnut and teak), steel, aluminum, silver, and copper. The best pieces of Danish modern stress flawless craftsmanship, a design that suits the ergonomics of the object's intended use, and subservience of form to function. Respect for the beauty of the components of a piece demands use of the finest materials. The artful simplicity of each piece is achieved only after laborious hours of lathering, polishing, mortise-and-tenoning, and fitting the components into a simple whole.

As the postwar years progressed, new industrial processes developed experimental materials (which later became mainstream): Bakelite,

Den Lille Havfrue (The Little Mermaid) ⭐ *Moments*   The statue *everybody* wants to see in Copenhagen is the life-size bronze of *Den Lille Havfrue,* inspired by Andersen's famous fairy tale *The Little Mermaid.* Edvard Eriksen sculpted the statue, unveiled in 1913. It rests on rocks right off the shore.

In spite of its small size, the statue is as important a symbol to Copenhageners as the Statue of Liberty is to New Yorkers. Tragedy struck on January 6, 1998. An anonymous tipster called a freelance television cameraman in the middle of the night to check out the 1.2m (4-ft.) bronze Mermaid. She'd lost her head. Most of the city responded with sadness. "She is part of our heritage, like Tivoli, the Queen, and stuff like that," said local sculptor Christian Moerk.

The Mermaid had also been decapitated in 1964. The culprits at that time were never discovered, and the head was never recovered. In the early 1900s some unknown party or parties cut off her arm. The original mold exists so it's possible to recast the bronze and weld back missing body parts. The arm was replaced.

high-grade plastics, spun aluminum, and spun steel. All these were carefully integrated into the growing canon of tenets associated with Danish modern, especially the integrity of design plus aesthetically pleasing functionalism.

Home design before World War II embodied clunky bourgeois ideals. Following the devastation of the war and its aftermath, the modern design movement emerged from the peculiar corner of the world that was Denmark, a land that during the 1950s found itself uncomfortably positioned between eastern and western Europe. Danish *joie de vivre* rose to the challenge. Within the streamlined designs, there's an implicit belief in the intelligence of the consumer as typified in the socialist idealism of the 1930s, and an implied rejection of the romantic ideals, arrogant nationalism, and imperialism that motivated some of the carnage of World War II. There's also an endearing (perhaps even quaint) sense of optimism that science and technology can alleviate many of society's problems and ills.

The style was unusual for what it was, and perhaps even more unusual for what it was not. There isn't a trace of kitschiness about it— the very fact that the best examples of the style have endured for almost half a century (with few alterations or adaptations) attests to its timelessness. In contrast, the Naugahyde sofas and Eisenhower-era "moderne" accessories that swept across other parts of the world look hopelessly outdated today.

The allure of Danish modern hasn't been lost on art historians: Most visitors to Copenhagen's Museum of Decorative and Applied Art head straight for the Danish modern exhibits, featuring works that were purchased directly from the designers and artists in the 1950s. Hot objects on the auction circuit that fetch high prices today include mid-century cocktail shakers and the ergonomically balanced "egg chairs."

Although not taking blame for the last attack in 1998, the Radical Feminist Faction sent flyers to newspapers to protest "the woman-hating, sexually fixated male dreams" allegedly conjured by the statue's bronze nudity. After the last decapitation, the head turned up at a TV station, delivered by a masked figure. In the spring, welders put her head back on, making the seam invisible. Today *The Little Mermaid*—head, fishy tail, and all—is back to being the most photographed nude woman in Copenhagen.

Near *The Little Mermaid* statue is **Gefion Springvandet** (Gefion Fountain), sculpted by Anders Bundgaard. Gefion was a Scandinavian goddess who plowed Zealand away from Sweden by turning her sons into oxen.

Also in the area is **Kastellet** at Langelinie (© **33-11-22-33**), a citadel constructed by King Frederik III in the 1660s. Some of Copenhagen's original ramparts still surround the structure. The Citadel was the capital's main fortress until the 18th century. During the Nazi occupation of Copenhagen, the Germans made it their headquarters. Today the Danish military occupies the buildings. You can, however, explore the beautiful grounds of Churchillparken surrounding Kastellet. At the entrance to the park stands St. Albans, the English church of Copenhagen. You can still see the double moats built as part of Copenhagen's defense in the wake of the Swedish siege of the capital on February 10, 1659. The ruined citadel can be explored daily from 6am to sunset. Admission is free.

Langelinie on the harbor. Bus: 1, 6, or 9.

Frihedsmuseet (Museum of Danish Resistance, 1940–45)   This museum reveals the tools of espionage and sabotage that the Danes used to throw off the Nazi yoke in World War II. Beginning softly with peace marches in the early days of the war, the resistance movement grew from a fledgling organization into a highly polished and skilled underground that eventually electrified and excited the Allied world: "Danes Fighting Germans!" blared the headlines.

The museum highlights the workings of the outlaw press, the wireless communications equipment and illegal films, relics of torture and concentration camps, British propaganda leaflets dropped in the country, satirical caricatures of Hitler, information about Danish Jews, and, conversely, about Danish Nazis, and material on the paralyzing nationwide strikes. In all, this moment in history is graphically and dramatically preserved. An armed car, used against Danish Nazi informers and collaborators, is displayed on the grounds.

Churchillparken. © 33-13-77-14. www.natmus.dk. Admission 30DKK ($5) adults, free for children under 16; free to all Wed. May–Sept 15 Tues–Sat 10am–4pm, Sun 10am–5pm; Sept 16–Apr Tues–Sat 11am–3pm, Sun 11am–4pm. Bus: 1, 6, or 9.

Kunstindustrimuseet (Museum of Decorative and Applied Art) ✪   The Kunstindustrimuseet is in a rococo building consisting of four wings surrounding a garden, a part of the former Royal Frederik Hospital built from 1752 to 1757 under King Frederik V. It was restored in the 1920s to house the collections of the museum, which consist mostly of European decorative and applied art from the Middle Ages to the present, arranged in chronological order. Pride of place is given to furniture, tapestries, other textiles, pottery, porcelain, glass, and silver. There are also collections of Chinese and Japanese art and handicrafts. Several separate exhibitions are shown within the scope of the museum. The library contains around 65,000 books and periodicals dealing with arts and crafts, architecture, costumes, advertising, photography, and industrial design.

Bredgade 68. © 33-18-56-56. www.kunstindustrimuseet.dk. Admission to museum 40DKK ($6.70) adults, free for children under 16. Free admission to library. Museum Tues–Fri 10am–4pm; Sat–Sun noon–4pm. Library Tues–Sat 10am–4pm. S-tog: Østerport. Bus: 1, 6, or 9.

Davids Samling ✪   Its status as a privately funded museum, plus the excellence of its collection, makes this a most unusual museum. Established by a Danish attorney, C. L. David (1878–1960), shortly after World War II on the premises of his house across from the park surrounding Rosenborg Castle, the collection features European art, decorative art, and the largest Islamic collection in the Nordic world.

David's other major bequest was his summer villa in the northern suburbs of Copenhagen at Marienborg, reserved for the Danish prime minister's use.

Kronprinsessegade 30. © 33-13-55-64. Free admission. Tues–Sun 1–4pm. Bus: 1, 6, 9, 10, 19, 29, 31, 42, or 43.

ROSENBORG CASTLE, THE BOTANICAL GARDENS & ENVIRONS

Rosenborg Castle ★★   Built by Christian IV in the 17th century, this red-brick, Renaissance-style castle houses everything from narwhal-tusked and ivory coronation chairs to Frederik VII's baby shoes—all artifacts from the Danish royal family. Officially, its biggest draws are the dazzling crown jewels and regalia in the basement Treasury, which houses a lavishly decorated coronation saddle from 1596 and other treasures. Try to see the Knights Hall (Room 21), with its coronation seat, three silver lions, and relics from the 1700s. Room 3, another important attraction, was used by founding father Christian IV (lucky in love, unlucky in war), who died in this bedroom decorated with Asian lacquer art and a stucco ceiling. The King's Garden (*Have*) surrounds the castle, and the Botanical Gardens are across the street.

Øster Voldgade 4A. ℂ **33-15-32-86.** www.rosenborgslot.dk. Admission 60DKK ($10) adults, 30DKK ($5) students and seniors, 10DKK ($1.65) children 5–12, free for children 4 and under. Palace and treasury (royal jewels) Jan–Apr Tues–Sun 11am–2pm; May and Sept daily 10am–4pm; June–Aug daily 10am–5pm; Oct daily 11am–5pm; Nov–Dec 17 Tues–Sun 11am–2pm. S-tog: Nørreport. Bus: 5, 10, 14, 16, 31, 42, 43, 184, or 185.

Botanisk Have (Botanical Gardens)   Planted from 1871 to 1874, the Botanical Gardens are on a lake that was once part of the city's defensive moat. Across from Rosenborg Castle, they contain greenhouses growing both tropical and subtropical plants. Special features include a cactus house and a palm house, all of which appear even more exotic in the far northern country of Denmark. An alpine garden contains mountain plants from all over the world.

Gothersgade 128. ℂ **35-32-22-40.** www.botanic-garden.ku.dk. Free admission. May–Sept daily 8:30am–6pm; Oct–Apr Tues–Sun 8:30am–4pm. S-tog: Nørreport. Bus: 5, 7, 14, 16, 24, 40, or 43.

Statens Museum for Kunst (Royal Museum of Fine Arts) ★★   This well-stocked art museum—the largest in Denmark—houses painting and sculpture from the 13th century to the present. There are Dutch golden age landscapes and marine paintings by Rubens and his school, and portraits by Frans Hals and Rembrandt. The Danish golden age is represented by Eckersberg, Købke, and Hansen. French 20th-century art includes 20 works by Matisse. In the Royal Print Room are some of the museum's 300,000 drawings, prints, lithographs, and other works by such artists as Dürer, Rembrandt, Matisse, and Picasso. In 1998, a new modern museum was erected at the rear of the century-old main building. Also new is a wing that serves as a Children's Art Museum.

Sølvgade 48–50. ℂ **33-74-84-94.** www.smk.dk. Admission 50DKK ($8.35) adults, free for children under 16. Tues and Thurs–Sun 10am–5pm; Wed 10am–8pm. Bus: 10, 14, 43, or 184.

Den Hirschsprungske Samling (Hirschsprung Collection)   This collection of Danish art from the 19th and early 20th centuries is in Ostre Anlaeg, a park in the city center. Heinrich Hirschsprung (1836–1908), a tobacco merchant, created the collection, and it has been growing ever since. The emphasis is on the Danish golden age, with such artists as Eckersberg, Købke, and Lundbye, and on the Skagen painters P. S. Krøyer and Anna and Michael Ancher. Some furnishings from the artists' homes are also exhibited.

Stockholmsgade 20. ℂ **35-42-03-36.** www.hirschsprung.dk. Admission 35DKK ($5.85) adults, free for children under 16, free to all Wed. Wed–Mon 11am–4pm. Bus: 6A, 14, 40, 42, or 43.

CHRISTIANSBORG PALACE & ENVIRONS

Christiansborg Palace ★★★   This granite-and-copper palace on Slotshol-men—a small island that has been the center of political power in Denmark for more than 800 years—houses the Danish parliament, the Supreme Court, the prime minister's offices, and the Royal Reception Rooms. A guide will lead you through richly decorated rooms, including the Throne Room, Banqueting Hall, and the Queen's Library. Before entering, you'll be asked to put on soft overshoes to protect the floors.

Under the palace, visit the well-preserved ruins of the 1167 castle of Bishop Absalon, founder of Copenhagen.

You can also visit **Kongelige Stalde & Kareter,** Christiansborg Ridebane 12 (© **33-40-10-10**), the royal stables and coaches. Elegantly clad in riding breeches and jackets, riders exercise the royal horses. Vehicles include regal coaches and "fairy tale" carriages, along with a display of harnesses in use by the royal family since 1778. Admission is 10DKK ($1.65) for adults, free for children under 12. The site can be visited May to October Friday to Sunday 2 to 4pm. During other months, visits are possible on Saturday and Sunday 2 to 4pm.

Christiansborg Slotsplads. © **33-92-64-92.** Guided tour of Royal Reception Rooms 50DKK ($8.35) adults, 20DKK ($3.35) children. Admission to castle ruins 25DKK ($4.20) adults, 10DKK ($1.65) children. Free admission to parliament. Guided tours of Reception Rooms May–Sept daily at 11am, 1pm, and 3pm; Oct–Apr Tues–Sun at 3pm. Ruins May–Sept daily 10am–4pm; Oct–Apr Tues–Sun 10am–4pm. English-language tours of parliament daily 11am, 1pm, and 3pm year-round. Bus: 1, 2, 5, 8, or 9.

Nationalmuseet (National Museum) ★   A giant repository of anthropological artifacts, this museum is divided into five departments. The first section focuses on prehistory, the Middle Ages, and the Renaissance in Denmark. These collections date from the Stone Age and include Viking stones, helmets, and fragments of battle gear. Especially interesting are the *lur* horn, a Bronze Age instrument that is among the oldest instruments in Europe, and the world-famous "Sun Chariot," an elegant Bronze Age piece of pagan art. The second area focuses on the history of the 18th-century royal palace. The third collection, the Royal Collection of Coins and Medals, displays various coins from antiquity. The fourth collection, Egyptian and Classical Antiquities, offers outstanding examples of art and artifacts from ancient civilizations. Here you'll find the Roman holy cups depicting Homeric legends. Finally, the Ethnographic section is devoted to relics of the Eskimo culture and the people of Greenland and Denmark.

Ny Vestergade 10. © **33-13-44-11.** www.natmus.dk. Admission 25DKK ($4.20) adults and students, free for children under 16. Tues–Sun 10am–5pm. Closed Dec 24–25 and Dec 31. Bus: 1, 2, 5, 6, 8, 10, or 41.

Børsen (Stock Exchange)   One of the most unusual buildings in Copenhagen, on Slotsholmen, must be seen from outside because it's not open to the public. Architects Hans and Lorenz Steenwinkel built the long, low Renaissance structure for Christian IV. The spire, 54m (177 ft.) high, resembles a quartet of intertwined dragon tails. The Stock Exchange itself is no longer here; the building is now the headquarters of the Copenhagen Chamber of Commerce.

Børsgade. Bus: 1, 2, 5, 6, 8, or 9.

Erotica Museum   This is perhaps the only museum in the world where you can go to learn about the sex lives of such famous people as Freud, Nietzsche, and Duke Ellington. Founded by Ole Ege, a well-known Danish photographer of nudes, it's within walking distance of Tivoli and the Central Railroad Station. In addition to providing a glimpse into the sex lives of the famous, the exhibits present a survey of erotica around the world as well as through the ages.

The exhibits range from the tame to the tempestuous—everything from Etruscan drawings and Chinese paintings to Greek vases depicting a lot of sexual activity. On display are remarkable lifelike tableaux created by craftspeople from Tussaud's Wax Museum, as well as a collection of those dirty little postcards Americans tried to sneak home through Customs back in the 1920s and 1930s.

As you ascend the floors of the museum, the more explicit the exhibits become. By the time you reach the fourth (top) floor, a dozen video monitors are showing erotic films, featuring everything from black-and-white films from the 1920s—all made underground—to today's triple X–rated releases.

Købmagergade 24. ℭ **33-12-03-11**. www.museumerotica.dk. Admission 89DKK ($15). Visitors 16–18 must be accompanied by an adult; no one under 16 permitted. May–Sept daily 10am–11pm; Oct–Apr Sun–Thurs 11am–8pm, Fri–Sat 10am–10pm. S-tog: Nørreport.

Tøjhusmuseet (Royal Arsenal Museum)   The museum features a fantastic display of weapons used for hunting and warfare. The ground floor's Canon Hall—the longest vaulted Renaissance hall in Europe—displays artillery equipment from 1500 up to the present day. Above this hall is the impressive Armory Hall with one of the world's finest collections of small arms, colors, and armor. The museum building was erected during the years 1598 to 1604.

Tøjhusgade 3. ℭ **33-11-60-37**. www.thm.dk. Admission 25DKK ($4.20) adults, 20DKK ($3.35) students and seniors, free for children under 15. Tues–Sun noon–4pm. Closed Jan 1, Dec 24–25, and Dec 31. Bus: 1, 2, 5, 8, and 9.

Thorvaldsens Museum ★   This museum on Slotsholmen, next door to Christiansborg, houses the greatest collection of the works of Bertel Thorvaldsen (1770–1844), the most significant name in neoclassical sculpture. Thorvaldsen's life represented the romanticism of the 18th and 19th centuries: He rose from semipoverty to the pinnacle of success in his day. He's famous for his most typical, classical, restrained works, taken from mythology: Cupid and Psyche, Adonis, Jason, Hercules, Ganymede, Mercury—all of which are displayed at the museum. In addition to the works of this latter-day exponent of Roman classicism, the museum also contains Thorvaldsen's personal, and quite extensive, collection, everything from the Egyptian relics of Ptolemy to the contemporary paintings he acquired during his lifetime (*Apollo Among the Thessalian Shepherds*). After many years of self-imposed exile in Italy, Thorvaldsen returned in triumph to his native Copenhagen, where he died a national figure and was buried here in the courtyard of his own personal museum.

Bertel Thorvaldsens Plads 2. ℭ **33-32-15-32**. www.thorvaldsensmuseum.dk. Admission 20DKK ($3.35) adults, free for children under 15, free to all Wed. Tues–Sun 10am–5pm. Closed Jan 1, Dec 24–25 and Dec 31. Bus: 1, 2, 15, 26, 29, or 650S.

IN THE OLD TOWN (INDRE BY)

Rundetårn (Round Tower)   For a panoramic view of Copenhagen, thousands of visitors climb the spiral ramp (no steps) of this 17th-century public observatory attached to a church. The tower is one of the crowning architectural achievements of the Christian IV era. Peter the Great, in Denmark for a state visit, galloped up the ramp on horseback, preceded by his carriage-drawn czarina. On the premises is a Bibliotekssalen (Library Hall), offering changing exhibits on art, culture, history, and science.

Købmagergade 52A. ℭ **33-73-03-73**. www.rundetaarn.dk. Admission 20DKK ($3.35) adults, 5DKK (85¢) children. Tower June–Aug Mon–Sat 10am–8pm, Sun noon–8pm; Sept–May Mon–Sat 10am–5pm, Sun noon–5pm. Observatory Oct 15–Mar 22 only Tues–Wed 7–10pm; June 20–Aug 10 only Sun 1–4pm. Bus: 5, 7E, 14, 16, or 42.

Vor Frue Kirke (Copenhagen Cathedral) This Greek Renaissance–style church, built in the early 19th century near Copenhagen University, features Bertel Thorvaldsen's white marble neoclassical works including *Christ and the Apostles*. The funeral of Hans Christian Andersen took place here in 1875, and that of Søren Kierkegaard in 1855.

Nørregade. ✆ **33-14-41-28**. Free admission. Mon–Fri 9am–5pm. Bus: 5.

MORE MUSEUMS

Arbejdermuseet (The Workers Museum) In the Nørrebro District, this museum traces the history of the working class of Denmark from around 1850 up to the present day. About more than just the labor movement, the exhibits re-create various times and eras. For example, there is a reconstruction of a Danish street in the 1800s, complete with a tram. There's also the re-creation of an apartment that was once inhabited by a worker in a brewery, along with his wife and eight children. The furnishings and artifacts are authentic. This homage to the working class depicts the struggle of laborers to make a living and provide for their families. See the box "Dining at Arbejdermuseet" for details on the museum's restaurant and coffee shop.

Rømersgade 22. ✆ **33-93-25-75**. www.arbejdermuseet.dk. Admission 50DKK ($8.35) adults, 30DKK ($5) children. July 1–Nov 1 daily 10am–6pm; off season Tues–Sun 10am–6pm. S-tog: Nørreport. Bus: 5, 14, 16, 31, 40, 42, 43, or 150S.

Arken Museum of Modern Art Adjacent to a popular public beach in Ishøj, a suburb south of Copenhagen, this museum houses an extensive collection of modern art. The Danish architect Søren Robert Lund designed the impressive structure while he was a student at the Royal Academy of Fine Arts. Constructed of white concrete and steel, it opened in 1996. The lines evoke the hull of a beached ship. Lund designed the structure and the interiors, including display space and furniture. In addition to gallery space, the museum has a concert hall, sculpture courtyards, and a restaurant. Recent exhibitions have included an Emil Nolde retrospective.

Ishøj Strandpark, Skovvej 100. ✆ **43-54-02-22**. www.arken.dk. Admission 60DKK ($10) adults, 30DKK ($5) children. Tues–Sun 10am–5pm; Wed 10am–9pm. Train: E or A to Ishøj Station, then bus 128. Children under 5 are not admitted.

Den Kongelige Afstøbningssamling Founded in 1895 as part of the Statens Museum for Kunst, this museum contains one of the largest and oldest cast collections in the world, comprising some 2,000 plaster casts modeled from famous sculptures from the past 4,000 years of western culture. The best known original works from antiquity and the Renaissance are scattered throughout the museums of the world, but this world of plaster unites many of them—Egyptian sphinxes, gold from Atreus's treasury, *Venus de Milo,* the Pergamon altar, and marble sculpture from the Acropolis. Most of the collection was made from 1870 to 1915 by leading European plaster workshops. In 1984 the collection was moved from its original location to the Vestindisk Pakhus, a rebuilt warehouse overlooking the harbor of Copenhagen, close to Amalienborg Palace.

Vestindisk Pakhus, Toldbodgade 40. ✆ **33-74-84-94**. www.smk.dk. Admission 50DKK ($8.35) adults, free for children under 16, free to all Wed. Tues and Thurs–Sun 10am–5pm; Wed 10am–8pm. Bus: 1, 6, or 9.

Kongelige Bibliotek (Royal Library) ⭐ The Royal Library dates from the 1600s and is the largest library in Scandinavia. The classical building with its high-ceilinged reading rooms is a grand and impressive place. The library owns original manuscripts by such Danish writers as H. C. Andersen and Karen Blixen (Isak Dinesen). In 1998, a gargantuan granite annex, the Black Diamond, expanded the library all the way to the waterfront. Likened to the Taj Mahal or Sydney's Opera House for its evocative and enigmatic appearance, the Black Diamond's progressive design suits its location on Christians Brygge—by the harbor between the bridges Langebro and Knippelsbro. A myriad of dazzling, reflective black granite tiles from Zimbabwe cover the facade, and its exterior walls slant sharply toward the water. Along with space for 200,000 books, the Black Diamond features a bookshop, a restaurant with a spectacular harborfront view, six reading rooms, a courtyard for exhibitions, and a 600-seat concert hall. After viewing the interior of the library, you can wander through its formal gardens, past the fishpond and statue of philosopher Søren Kierkegaard.

Søren Kierkegaards Plads 1. ℂ 33-47-47-47. www.kb.dk. Free admission. Mon–Fri 10am–5pm. Bus: 1, 2, 5, 6, 8, or 9.

Musikhistorisk Museum
This museum offers a journey through the history of musical instruments in Europe and worldwide from 1000 to 1900. Special recordings accompany the exhibits. Overall, the museum emphasizes the effect music has had on Danish culture. Concerts occasionally take place.

Åbenrå 30. ℂ 33-11-27-26. www.musikhistoriskmuseum.dk. Admission 40DKK ($6.70) adults, 10DKK ($1.65) children. May 2–Sept 30 Fri–Wed 1–4pm; Oct–May 1 Mon, Wed, Sat, and Sun 1–4pm. Bus: 5, 7, 14, 16, 17, 24, 31, 42, 43, 50, 84, or 384.

Orlogsmuseet (Royal Naval Museum)
This museum in Søkvasthuset, the former naval hospital, opens onto Christianshavn Kanal. Since it traces the history of the navy, and Denmark is a maritime nation, this museum practically tells the saga of the country itself. More than 300 model ships, many based on designs that date from as early as the 1500s, are on display. Some of these vessels were designed and constructed by naval engineers. They served as prototypes for the construction of actual ships later launched into the North Sea. The models are wide ranging—some are fully "dressed," with working sails, whereas others are cross-sectional with their frames outlined. You get a vast array of other naval artifacts too, including an intriguing collection of figureheads, some of which are artworks themselves. Look for the display of navigation instruments and the propeller from the German U-boat that sank the *Lusitania*. Naval uniforms worn by Danish officers and other sailors are also on display.

Overgaden Oven Vandet 58. ℂ 33-11-60-37. www.orlogsmuseet.dk. Admission 25DKK ($4.20) adults, free for children under 15. Tues–Sun noon–4pm. Bus: 2, 19, or 350S.

Teatermuseet
Theater buffs flock to this museum in the Old Court Theater. King Christian VII had it constructed in 1767 as the first court theater in Copenhagen. Hans Christian Andersen was once a ballet student here, although we can't imagine how this awkward "ugly duckling" looked onstage. In 1842 the theater was overhauled and given its present look, but the curtain went down for the last time in 1881. It made a "comeback" as a museum in 1992. The museum traces the history of the Danish theater from the 18th century to modern times. The public has access to the theater boxes, the stage, and the old dressing rooms. Some of the great theatrical performances of Europe, from Italian opera to pantomime, took place on this stage. Photographs, prints, theatrical costumes, and even old stage programs tell the story, from Ludvig Holberg to the present day.

Christiansborg Ridebane 18. ℂ 33-11-51-76. Admission 30DKK ($3.95) adults, free for children under 16. Wed 2–4pm; Sat–Sun noon–4pm. Bus: 1, 2, 12, 15, 19, 26, 29, 33, or 650.

> **Tips Dining at Arbejdermuseet**
>
> The Arbejdermuseet (p. 104) also offers a couple of memorable eateries, like a 19th-century–style restaurant where they serve old-fashioned home-style Danish specialties. There's also a 1950s-style coffee shop where you'll expect to see the Danish versions of Marilyn Monroe and James Dean walk in any minute.

W.Ø. Larsens Tobakmuseet (W.Ø. Larsens Tobacco Museum) For the pipe or cigar smoker, this place is Valhalla. It contains pipes from around the world—in all, 400 years of tobacco and the cigar industry. The museum is crammed with antiquities and rarities pertaining to tobacco. You can see old-fashioned tobacco jars, pipe racks, snuff tins, and old tobacco packaging down through the ages. One tiny pipe is no bigger than an embroidery needle.

Amagertorv 9. ✆ **33-12-20-50.** Free admission. Mon–Thurs 10am–6pm; Fri 10am–7pm; Sat 10am–5pm. Bus: 8, 28, 29, or 41.

THE CHURCHES OF COPENHAGEN

For a visit to the cathedral of Copenhagen, refer to "In the Old Town," above.

Frederikskirke (called the Marble Church) ★ This 200-year-old church, with its copper dome—one of the largest in the world—is a short walk from Amalienborg Palace. After an unsuccessful start during Denmark's neoclassical revival in the 1750s, the church was completed in Roman baroque style in 1894. In many ways, particularly in its rich decoration, it's more impressive than Copenhagen's cathedral.

Frederiksgade 4. ✆ **33-15-01-44.** Free admission to church. Admission to dome 20DKK ($3.35) adults, 10DKK ($1.65) children. Church Mon–Thurs 10am–5pm; Fri–Sun noon–5pm. Dome June 15–Aug 31 daily 1 and 3pm; Sept–June 14 Sat–Sun 1 and 3pm. Bus: 1, 6, or 9.

Grundtvigs Kirke (Grundtvig Church) Built from 1921 to 1940, this church was designed by Jensen Klint, who died before it was completed. About six million yellow bricks were used in its construction. The interior is 76m (249 ft.) wide and 35m (115 ft.) tall; the exterior resembles a huge organ. The church is a popular venue for concerts.

På Bjerget, Bispebjerg. ✆ **35-81-54-42.** Free admission. Apr–Oct daily 9am–4:45pm; Nov–Mar daily 9am–4pm. Bus: 10, 16, 43, or 69.

Holmens Kirke Built in 1619, this royal chapel and naval church lies across the canal from Slotsholmen, next to the National Bank of Denmark. Although the structure was converted into a church for the Royal Navy in 1619, its nave was built in 1562 as an anchor forge. By 1641 the ever-changing church was renovated to its current, predominantly Dutch Renaissance style. The so-called "royal doorway" was brought from Roskilde Cathedral in the 19th century. Inside, look for the baroque altar of unpainted oak and a carved pulpit by Abel Schrøder the Younger. In the burial chamber are the tombs of some of Denmark's most important naval figures, including Admiral Niels Juel, who successfully fought off a naval attack by Swedes in 1677 in the Battle of Køge Bay. Peder Tordenskjold, who defeated Charles XII of Sweden during the Great Northern War in the early 1700s, is also entombed here. On a lighter note, this is the church in which Queen Margrethe II took her wedding vows in 1967.

Holmens Kanal. ✆ **33-13-61-78.** Free admission. Mon–Fri 9am–2pm; Sat 9am–noon. Bus: 1, 2, 6, 8, 9, 10, 31, 37, or 43.

Vor Frelsers Kirken (Our Savior's Church)   This baroque church with an external tower staircase dates from 1696. Legend has it that when the encircling staircase was constructed curving the wrong way, the architect climbed to the top, realized what he'd done, and then committed suicide by jumping. The green and gold tower of this Gothic structure is a Copenhagen landmark, dominating the Christianshavn area. Inside, view the splendid baroque altar, richly adorned with a romp of cherubs and other figures. There are also a lovely font and richly carved organ case. Four hundred steps will take you to the top, where you'll see a gilded figure of Christ standing on a globe, and a panoramic view of the city.

Skt. Annægade 29. ✆ **32-57-27-98.** Free admission to church. Admission to tower 20DKK ($3.35) adults, 10DKK ($1.65) children. Apr–Aug Mon–Sat 11am–4:30pm, Sun noon–4:30pm; Sept–Oct Mon–Sat 11am–3:30pm, Sun noon–3:30pm; Nov–Mar daily 11am–3:30pm. Metro: Christianshavn. It is possible to visit the tower only Apr–Oct.

A GLIMPSE INTO THE PAST RIGHT OUTSIDE COPENHAGEN

Frilandsmuseet (Open-Air Museum) ★★   This reconstructed village in Lyngby, on the fringe of Copenhagen, recaptures Denmark's one-time rural character. The "museum" is nearly 36 hectares (89 acres), a 3km (1¾-mile) walk around the compound, and includes a dozen re-created buildings—farmsteads, windmills, and fishers' cottages. Exhibits include a half-timbered 18th-century farmstead from one of the tiny windswept Danish islands, a primitive longhouse from the remote Faroe Islands, thatched fishermen's huts from Jutland, tower windmills, and a potter's workshop from the mid–19th century.

Organized activities take place on summer afternoons. On one recent visit, folk dancers in native costume performed, and there were demonstrations of lacemaking and loom-weaving.

The park is about 14km (8⅔ miles) from the Central Railroad Station. There's an old-style restaurant at the entryway to the museum.

Kongevejen 100. ✆ **33-13-44-11.** www.natmus.dk. Admission 25DKK ($4.20) adults, free for children under 16. Tues–Sun 10am–5pm. Closed Mondays, except Mar 28–May 5 and Oct. 17 Closed Dec 24-25 and Dec. 31. S-tog: Sorgenfri (leaving every 20 min. from Copenhagen Central Station). Bus: 184 or 194.

LITERARY LANDMARKS

Admirers of **Hans Christian Andersen** may want to seek out the various addresses where he lived in Copenhagen, including Nyhavn 18, Nyhavn 20, and Nyhavn 67. He also lived for a time at Vingårdsstræde 6.

Assistens Kirkegård (Assistens Cemetery)   The largest cemetery in Copenhagen, dating from 1711, it contains the tombs of Søren Kierkegaard, H. C. Andersen, and Martin Andersen Nexø, a famous novelist of the working class. The cemetery is now a public park.

Nørrebrogade/Kapelvej 4. ✆ **35-37-19-17.** Free admission. Jan–Feb 8am–5pm; Mar–Apr 8am–6pm; May–Aug 8am–8pm; Sept–Oct 8am–6pm; Nov–Dec 8am–4pm. Bus: 5, 7E, or 16.

Københavns Bymuseum (Copenhagen City Museum)   The permanent exhibition presents the history of Copenhagen in artifacts and pictures. A smaller section is devoted to Søren Kierkegaard, the father of existentialism; you'll find exhibits of his drawings, letters, books, photographs, and personal belongings.

Vesterbrogade 59. ✆ **33-21-07-72.** www.kbhbymuseum.dk. Admission 20DKK ($3.35) adults, free for children under 14, free to all Fri. May–Sept Wed–Mon 10am–4pm; Oct–Apr Wed–Mon 1–4pm. Bus: 6, 16, 27, or 28.

Tips   **Special & Free Events**

Much of Copenhagen is a summer festival, especially at the **Tivoli Gardens** (p. 93). Although the gardens have an entrance fee, once you're inside, many of the concerts and other presentations are free. A total of 150 performances each summer are presented at the Concert Hall. Of these, more than 100 are free. Pantomime performances at the Pantomime Theater are also free. Performances on the open-air stage are free every night (closed Mon). Likewise, **Bakken Amusement Park** (below) has many free events. And you don't have to pay an admission to enter—only if you patronize the various attractions.

The **birthday of Queen Margrethe** on April 16 is a celebration with the queen and the royal family driving through the pedestrian street, Strøget, in a stagecoach escorted by hussars in regalia.

A **Ballet and Opera Festival** (mid-May to June) takes place at the Royal Theater, offering classical and modern dance, as well as operatic masterpieces.

ESPECIALLY FOR KIDS

Copenhagen is a wonderful place for children, and many so-called adult attractions also appeal to kids. **Tivoli** is an obvious choice, as is the statue of *Den Lille Havfrue (The Little Mermaid)* at Langelinie. Try to see the changing of the Queen's Royal Life Guard at **Amalienborg Palace,** including the entire parade to and from the royal residence. Kids also enjoy **Frilandsmuseet,** the open-air museum. (For details on these sights, see listings earlier in this chapter.) Other attractions great for kids include the following.

Bakken Amusement Park   On the northern edge of Copenhagen, about 12km (7½ miles) from the city center, this amusement park was created 35 years before the Pilgrims landed at Plymouth Rock. It's a local favorite, featuring roller coasters, dancing, a tunnel of love, and a merry-go-round. Open-air restaurants are plentiful, as are snack bars and ice-cream booths. Some individual attractions charge a separate admission fee—proceeds support this unspoiled natural preserve. There are no cars in the park—only bicycles and horse-drawn carriages are allowed.

Dyrehavevej 62, Klampenborg. © **39-63-73-00.** Free admission; rides cost 10DKK–50DKK ($1.65–$8.35) each. Summer daily noon–midnight. Closed late Aug to late Mar. S-tog: Klampenborg (about 20 min. from Central Railroad Station); then walk through the Deer Park or take a horse-drawn cab.

Denmark's Aquarium ★★   Opened in 1939 north of Copenhagen along the Øresund coast, this is one of the most extensive aquariums in Europe. Hundreds of salt- and freshwater species are exhibited. One of the tanks houses bloodthirsty piranhas from South America.

Strandvejen, in Charlottenlund Fort Park, Charlottenlund. © **39-62-32-83.** Admission 70DKK ($12) adults, 35DKK ($5.85) children. May–Aug daily 10am–6pm; Sept–Oct and Feb–Apr daily 10am–5pm; Nov–Jan daily 10am–4pm. S-tog: Charlottenlund. Bus: 6.

Eskperimentarium (Hands-On Science Center)   In the old mineral water–bottling hall of Tuborg breweries north of Copenhagen in Hellerup, this museum has a hands-on approach to science. Visitors use not only their hands but all five of their senses as they participate in some 300 interactive exhibitions and demonstrations divided into three themes: "Man," "Nature," and "The Interaction Between Man and Nature." Visitors hear what all the world's languages sound like, make a wind machine blow up to hurricane force, check their skin to test how much sun it can take, dance in an "inverted" disco, or visit a slimming machine. Families can work as a team to examine enzymes, make a camera from paper, or test perfume. Exhibitions change frequently.

Tuborg Havnevej 7, Hellerup. (C) **39-27-33-33**. www.experimentarium.dk. Admission 10DKK ($1.65) adults, 70DKK ($12) children 3–14, free for children under 3. Mon and Wed–Fri 9:30am–5pm; Tues 9:30am–9pm; Sat–Sun 11am–5pm. Closed Dec 23–25, Dec 31, and Jan 1. S-tog: Hellerup or Svanemøllen. Bus: 1, 14, or 21.

Louis Tussaud Wax Museum   Now a part of Tivoli, the Louis Tussaud Wax Museum (he was the great-grandson of Madame Tussaud) is a major attraction in Copenhagen. It features more than 200 wax figures—everybody from Danish kings and queens to Leonardo da Vinci. Children can visit the Snow Queen's Castle, or watch Frankenstein and Dracula guard the monsters and vampires.

H. C. Andersens Blvd. 22. (C) **33-11-89-00**. www.tussaud.dk. Admission 79DKK ($13) adults, 34DKK ($5.70) children 5–9, 58DKK ($9.70) children 10–15. Apr 16–Sept 13 daily 10am–11pm; Sept 14–Apr 15 daily 10am–6pm. Bus: 1, 2, 16, 28, 29, or 41.

Tycho Brahe Planetarium   A star projector using the planetarium dome as a screen and space theater creates the marvel of the night sky, with its planets, galaxies, star clusters, and comets. Named after the famed Danish astronomer Tycho Brahe (1546–1601), the planetarium also stages OMNIMAX film productions. There are an information center and a restaurant.

Gammel Kongevej 10. (C) **33-12-12-24**. Admission 25DKK ($4.20) adults, 15DKK ($2.50) children; OMNIMAX films 85DKK ($14) adults, 65DKK ($11) children. Daily 10am–9pm. Bus: 1 or 14.

Zoologisk Have (Copenhagen Zoo)   With more than 3,300 animals from Greenland to Africa, this zoo boasts spacious habitats for reindeer and musk oxen as well as an open roaming area for lions. Take a ride up the small wooden Eiffel Tower, or let the younger kids enjoy the petting zoo. The place is mobbed on Sundays. The Frederiksberg location is west of the inner city.

Roskildevej 32, Frederiksberg. (C) **72-20-02-00**. www.zoo.dk. Admission 90DKK ($15) adults, 50DKK ($8.35) children. Jan–Feb and Nov–Dec daily 9am–4pm; Mar Mon–Fri 9am–4pm, Sat–Sun 9am–5pm; Apr–May and Sept Mon–Fri 9am–5pm, Sat–Sun 9am–8pm; June–Aug daily 9am–6pm; Oct daily 9am–5pm. S-tog: Valby. Bus: 6, 18, 28, 39, or 550S.

WALKING TOUR 1	THE OLD CITY

Start:	Rådhuspladsen.
Finish:	Tivoli Gardens.
Time:	1½ hours.
Best Times:	Any sunny day.
Worst Times:	Rush hours (Mon–Fri 7:30–9am and 5–6:30pm).

Start in the center of Copenhagen at:

❶ Rådhuspladsen (Town Hall Square)

Pay a visit to the bronze statue of Hans Christian Andersen, the spinner of fairy tales, which stands near a boulevard bearing his name. Also on this square is a statue of two *lur* horn players that has stood here since 1914.

Bypassing the *lur* horn players, walk east along Vester Voldgade onto a narrow street on your left:

❷ Lavendelstræde

Many houses along here date from the late 18th century. At Lavendelstræde 1, Mozart's widow (Constanze) lived with her second husband, Georg Nikolaus Nissen, a Danish diplomat, from 1812 to 1820.

The little street quickly becomes:

❸ Slutterigade

Courthouses rise on both sides of this short street, joined by elevated walkways. Built between 1805 and 1815, this was Copenhagen's fourth town hall, now the city's major law courts. The main courthouse entrance is on Nytorv.

Slutterigade will lead to:

❹ Nytorv

In this famous square, you can admire fine 19th-century houses. Philosopher Søren Kierkegaard (1813–55) lived in a house adjacent to the courthouse.

Cross Nytorv, and veer slightly west (to your left) until you reach Nygade, part of the:

❺ Strøget

At this point, this traffic-free shopping street has a different name. (It actually began at Rådhuspladsen and was called Frederiksberggade.) The major shopping street of Scandinavia, Strøget is a stroller's and a shopper's delight, following a 1.2km (¾-mile) trail through the heart of Copenhagen.

Nygade is one of the five streets that compose Strøget. Head northeast along this street, which becomes winding and narrow Vimmelskaftet, then turns into Amagertorv. Along Amagertorv, on your left, you'll come across the:

❻ Helligåndskirken (Church of the Holy Ghost)

Complete with an abbey, Helligåndshuset is the oldest church in Copenhagen, founded at the beginning of the 15th century. Partially destroyed in 1728, it was reconstructed in 1880 in

a neoclassical style. Some of the buildings on this street date from 1616. The sales rooms of the Royal Porcelain Factory are at Amagertorv 6.

Next you'll come to Østergade, the last portion of Strøget. You'll see Illum's department store on your left. Østergade leads to the square:

❼ Kongens Nytorv

Surrounding Copenhagen's largest square, with an equestrian statue of Christian IV in the center, are many interesting buildings. The statue is a bronze replica of a 1688 sculpture.

At Kongens Nytorv, head right until you come to Laksegade. Then go south along this street until you reach the intersection with Nikolajgade. Turn right. This street will lead to the:

❽ Nikolaj Church

The building dates from 1530 and was the scene of the thundering sermons of Hans Tausen, a father of the Danish Reformation.

TAKE A BREAK
A mellow spot for a pick-me-up, either a refreshing cool drink or an open-faced sandwich, the **Cafeen Nikolaj**, Nikolaj Plads 12 (© **33-11-63-13**), attracts both older shoppers and young people. You can sit and linger over a cup of coffee, and no one is likely to hurry you. You can visit anytime in the afternoon, perhaps making it your luncheon stopover.

After viewing the church, head left down Fortunstræde to your next stop, a square off Gammel Strand:

❾ Højbro Plads

You'll have a good view of Christiansborg Palace and Thorvaldsens Museum on Slotsholmen. On Højbro Plads is an equestrian statue honoring Bishop Absalon, who founded Copenhagen in 1167. Several handsome buildings line the square.

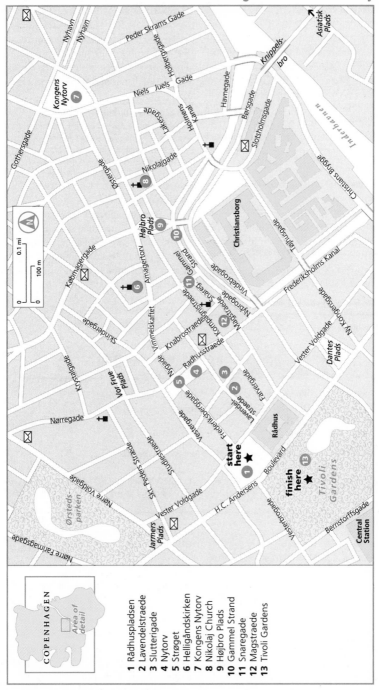

COPENHAGEN

Area of detail

1 Rådhuspladsen
2 Lavendelstraede
3 Slutterigade
4 Nytorv
5 Strøget
6 Helligåndskirken
7 Kongens Nytorv
8 Nikolaj Church
9 Højbro Plads
10 Gammel Strand
11 Snaregade
12 Magstraede
13 Tivoli Gardens

Continue west along:

⑩ Gammel Strand

From this waterfront promenade—the name means "old shore"—the former edge of Copenhagen, you'll have a good view across to Christiansborg Palace. A number of interesting old buildings line this street, and at the end you'll come upon the Ministry of Cultural Affairs, occupying a former government pawnbroking establishment, dating from 1730.

To the right of this building, walk up:

⑪ Snaregade

This old-fashioned provincial street is typical of the old city. Walk until you reach Knabrostræde. Both streets boast structures built just after the great fire of 1795. Where the streets intersect, you'll see the Church of Our Lady.

Make your way back to Snaregade, and turn right to one of Copenhagen's best-preserved streets:

⑫ Magstræde

Proceed along to Rådhusstræde. Just before you reach Rådhusstræde, notice the two buildings facing that street. These are the oldest structures in the city, dating from the 16th century.

Walk across Vandkunsten, a square at the end of Magstræde, then turn right down Gasegade, which doesn't go very far before you turn left along Farvergade. At this street's intersection with Vester Voldgade, you'll see the Vartov Church. Continue west until you reach Rådhuspladsen. Across the square, you'll see the:

⑬ Tivoli Gardens

You'll find the entrance at Vesterbrogade 3. Attracting some 4.5 million visitors every summer, this amusement park has 25 different entertainment choices and attractions and just as many restaurants and beer gardens.

WALKING TOUR 2	**KONGENS NYTORV TO LANGELINIE**

Start:	Kongens Nytorv.
Finish:	*Den Lille Havfrue (The Little Mermaid).*
Time:	1½ hours.
Best Time:	Any sunny day.
Worst Times:	Rush hours (weekdays 7:30–9am and 5–6:30pm).

Although Nyhavn, once a boisterous sailors' quarter, has quieted down, it's still a charming part of old Copenhagen, with its 1673 canal and 18th-century houses.

Begin at:

❶ Kongens Nytorv

The "King's New Market" dates from 1680. It contains Magasin, the biggest department store in the capital, plus an equestrian statue of Christian IV.

On the northeast side of the square is:

❷ Thott's Mansion

Completed in 1685 for a Danish naval hero and restored in 1760, it now houses the French Embassy. Between Bredgade and Store Strandstræde, a little street angling to the right near Nyhavn, is Kanneworff House, a

beautifully preserved private home that dates from 1782. On the west side of the square, at no. 34, is the Hotel d'Angleterre. Also here is an old anchor memorializing the Danish seamen who died in World War II.

On the southeast side of the square is:

❸ The Royal Theater

Founded in 1748, the theater presents ballet, opera, and plays. Statues of famous Danish dramatists are out front. The present theater, constructed in 1874, has a neo-Renaissance style.

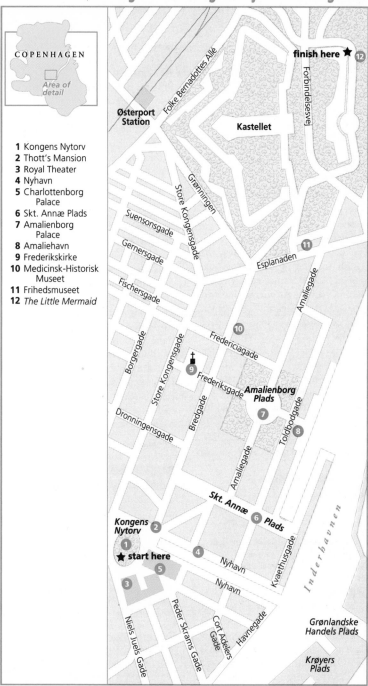

COPENHAGEN

Area of detail

1 Kongens Nytorv
2 Thott's Mansion
3 Royal Theater
4 Nyhavn
5 Charlottenborg Palace
6 Skt. Annæ Plads
7 Amalienborg Palace
8 Amaliehavn
9 Frederikskirke
10 Medicinsk-Historisk Museet
11 Frihedsmuseet
12 *The Little Mermaid*

With your back to the Hotel d'Angleterre, walk toward the water along:

④ Nyhavn

Once filled with maritime businesses and seamen's bars and lodgings, Nyhavn is now "restaurant row." First, walk along its north (left) side. In the summer, cafe tables border the canal, giving it a festive atmosphere. At the port end of the canal, you can see the Naval Dockyards, and Christianshavn across the harbor. High-speed craft come and go all day, connecting Copenhagen with Malmö, Sweden.

On the quieter (south) side of the canal, you can see:

⑤ Charlottenborg Palace

The style of the building, now the Danish Academy of Fine Arts, is pure baroque. The name comes from Queen Charlotte Amalie, who moved there in 1700. Beautiful old homes, antiques shops, and more restaurants line the southern bank. Nyhavn was the home of Hans Christian Andersen at various times. He lived at no. 20, where he wrote his first fairy tales, in 1835, and at no. 67 from 1845 to 1864. He spent the last 2 years of his life at no. 18, where he died in 1875.

Walk back to the harbor end of Nyhavn and turn left onto Kvæsthusgade, which will take you to:

⑥ Skt. Annæ Plads

Ferries depart for Oslo from this square. Many consulates, two hotels, and fine old buildings open onto it.

Walk inland along the plads and turn right onto Amaliegade, which leads under a colonnade into cobblestoned Amalienborg Plads, site of:

⑦ Amalienborg Palace

In the square's center is a statue of Frederik V. When the queen is in residence, the changing of the guard takes place here daily at noon. The palace is the official residence of the queen and her French prince, but sections of it are open to visitors. Four identical mansion-like palaces flank the square.

The queen lives in the right wing, next to the colonnade.

Between the square and the harbor are the gardens of:

⑧ Amaliehavn

Among the most beautiful in Copenhagen, these gardens were laid out by Jean Delogne, who made lavish use of Danish granite and French limestone. The bronze pillars around the fountain were the work of Arnaldo Pomodoro, an Italian sculptor.

After viewing the waterfront gardens, walk away from the water, crossing Amalienborg Plads and emerging onto Frederiksgade. Continue along this street until you reach:

⑨ Frederikskirke

This church is often called the *Marmorkirken* or "marble church." Construction began in 1740, but had to stop in 1770 because of the costs. The church wasn't completed until 1894—using Danish marble instead of more expensive Norwegian marble. The church was modeled on and intended to rival St. Peter's in Rome; indeed, it ended up with one of the largest church domes in Europe. Supported on a dozen towering piers, the dome has a diameter of 32m (105 ft.).

Facing the church, turn right and head north along Bredgade, passing at no. 22 the:

⑩ Medicinsk-Historisk Museet (Medical History Museum)

The collection is gruesome, with fetuses, dissected heads, and the like.

TAKE A BREAK
Before you approach *The Little Mermaid,* consider tea and a snack at **Café Lumskebugten,** Esplanaden 21 (**✆ 33-15-60-29;** see "Where to Dine," in chapter 3). Dating from 1854, this cafe offers a cold plate served throughout the afternoon. There are five specialties: beef tartare, fish cakes with mustard sauce, marinated salmon, baked cod, and shrimp.

Bredgade ends at Esplanaden, which opens onto Churchillparken, a green belt bordering the water. Turn right and walk along Esplanaden until you come to Churchill-parken and the:

⓫ Frihedsmuseet

The Danish Resistance museum commemorates the struggle against the Nazis from 1940 to 1945.

After leaving the museum, walk toward the water along Langelinie, where signs point the way to:

⓬ *The Little Mermaid*

Perched on rocks just off the harbor bank, *Den Lille Havfrue,* the most photographed statue in Scandinavia, dates from 1913. The bronze figure, by Edvard Eriksen, was modeled after the figure of prima ballerina Ellen Price. In time, this much-attacked and abused statue became the symbol of Copenhagen.

ORGANIZED TOURS

BUS & BOAT TOURS   The boat and bus sightseeing tours in Copenhagen range from get-acquainted jaunts to in-depth excursions. Either of the following tours can be arranged through **Copenhagen Excursions** (✆ **32-54-06-06**) or **Vikingbus** (✆ **32-66-00-00**). Inexpensive bus tours depart from the *lur* blowers' statue at Town Hall Square, and boat trips leave from Gammel Strand (the fish market) or Nyhavn.

For orientation, hop on a bus for the 1½-hour **City Tour,** which covers scenic highlights like *The Little Mermaid,* Rosenborg Castle, and Amalienborg Palace. Monday through Friday, tours also visit the Carlsberg Brewery, which adds 1 hour to the time if you choose to continue. Tours depart from the City Hall Square daily at 9:30am, 11:30am, and 1:30pm May 15 to September 30. They cost 130DKK ($22) for adults, 65DKK ($11) for children under 12.

We heartily recommend the **City and Harbor Tour,** a 2½-hour trip by launch and bus that departs from Town Hall Square. The boat tours the city's main canals, passing *The Little Mermaid* and the Old Fish Market. It operates May 15 to September 30, daily at 9:30am, 11:30am, and 1:30pm. It costs 175DKK ($29) for adults, 80DKK ($13) for children under 12.

Shakespeare buffs may be interested in an afternoon excursion to the castles of North Zealand. The 7-hour tour explores the area north of Copenhagen, including Kronborg (Hamlet's castle), a brief visit to Fredensborg, the queen's residence, and a stopover at Frederiksborg Castle and the National Historical Museum. Tours depart from Town Hall Square. They run February to April and October to December Wednesday and Sunday at 9:30am; May to September Wednesday, Saturday, and Sunday at 9:30am. The cost is 420DKK ($70) for adults, 225DKK ($38) for children under 12.

For more information about these tours and the most convenient place to buy tickets in advance, call **Vikingbus** or **Copenhagen Excursions.** For more information about the sightseeing tours in Copenhagen visit www.sightseeing.dk.

GUIDED WALKS THROUGH COPENHAGEN   Staff members of the Copenhagen Tourist Information Office conduct 2-hour guided walking tours of the city every Monday and Friday to Sunday at 10am, between May and September. The price is 80DKK ($13) for adults, 25DKK ($4.20) for children. For information, contact the **Copenhagen Tourist Information Center,** Vesterbrogade 4A (✆ **70-22-24-42;** www.woco.dk).

A VISIT TO COPENHAGEN'S MOST FAMOUS BREWERY   Carlsberg is the most famous beer in Denmark. You can take a self-guided tour of the brewery that turns out three million bottles of beer a day, walking around an observation gallery whose English-language signs explain the brewing process. The factory is open for visits Tuesday to Sunday 10am to 4pm. Entrance is free, and each visitor is given a free beer at the end of the tour, with the option of buying more at the on-site pub. The entrance to the factory is graced with a pair of sculpted elephants, each with armored regalia that includes a swastika. That doesn't mean the company was a Nazi sympathizer—Carlsberg used the symbol as part of its image long before Hitler. Take bus no. 26 from Copenhagen Central Station or from the Town Hall Square in Copenhagen to **Carlsberg Brewery,** Gamle Carlsberg Vej 11 (© **33-27-13-14**).

ACTIVE SPORTS

BICYCLING   The absence of hills and the abundance of parks and wide avenues with bicycle lanes make cycling the best way to explore Copenhagen. Bike-rental shops and stands are scattered throughout the city. Two suggestions are **Københavns Cyker,** Reventlowsgade 11 (© **33-33-86-13;** bus: 6 or 10), and **Dan Wheel,** Colbjørnsensgade 3 (© **33-21-22-27;** bus: 28 or 41). A deposit of 200DKK ($33) is required.

FITNESS   Form & Fitness, Øster Allé 42E (© **35-55-00-78;** bus: 9 or 10), offers a day pass for 150DKK ($25). Aerobics, weights, and fitness machines are available Monday to Thursday 6:30am to midnight, Friday 6:30am to 9pm, Saturday and Sunday 8am to 6pm.

GOLF   Denmark's best-known golf course, and one of its most challenging, is at the **Rungsted Golf Klub,** Vestre Stationsvej 16, Rungsted (© **45-76-85-82;** bus: 3, 16, or 45). It's in the heart of Denmark's "Whisky Trail," a string of homes and mansions known for their allure to retirees, about 21km (13 miles) north of Copenhagen. Golfers visit from around the world. Some degree of competence is required, so beginners and intermediate golfers might want to hold off. If you're an advanced golfer, call for information and to arrange a tee time. Greens fees run 375DKK and 550DKK ($63 and $92) for a full day's use of the club's 18 holes. To play, you must present evidence of a 20 handicap on Saturday and Sunday, or 25 on weekdays. With advance notice, you can rent clubs for 250DKK ($42). No carts are allowed on the ecologically fragile course. It's open year-round, except when it is snowing.

JOGGING   The many parks (known to locals as "green lungs") of Copenhagen provide endless routes for joggers. Our favorite, just west of the city center, circles Lakes Sortedams, St. Jorgens, and Peblinge. The paths that wind through the Frederiksborg gardens are also well suited for joggers.

SWIMMING   Swimming is a favorite Danish pastime. The **Frederiksborg Svømmehal,** Helgesvej 29 (© **38-14-04-04;** bus: 6 or 18), is open to the public Monday to Friday 8am to 8pm, Saturday 8am to 2pm, Sunday 9:30am to 2:15pm. Tickets cost 32DKK ($5.35). You can also try **Sundby Swimming-pool,** Sundbyvestervej 50 (© **32-58-55-68;** bus: 30 or 31); or **Kildeskovshallen,** Adolphsvej 25 (© **39-77-44-00;** bus: 165).

TENNIS   Visitors usually pay a large supplement to play tennis at hotels and clubs in Copenhagen. There's a high hourly rate, and courts must be reserved in advance. At the **Hotel Mercur,** Vester Farimagsgade 17 (© **33-12-57-11;** bus:

40 or 46), visitors pay 130DKK ($22) for the first hour, 100DKK ($17) for each additional hour. Another club is **Københavns Boldklub,** Peter Bangs Vej 147 (© **38-71-41-50;** bus: 1); this club is in Frederiksberg, a neighborhood west of central Copenhagen.

2 Shopping

Copenhagen is in the vanguard of shopping in Europe, and much of the action takes place on **Strøget,** the pedestrian street in the heart of the capital. Strøget begins as Frederiksberggade, north of Rådhuspladsen, and winds to Østergade, which opens onto Kongens Nytorv. The jam-packed street is lined with stores selling everything from porcelain statues of *Youthful Boldness* to Greenland shrimp to Kay Bojesen's teak monkeys.

Between stops, relax with a drink at an outdoor cafe, or just sit on a bench and watch the crowds.

In two nearby walking areas—**Gråbrødretorv** and **Fiolstræde**—you can browse through antiques shops and bookstores.

Bredgade, beginning at Kongens Nytorv, is the antiques district. Prices tend to be very high. **Læderstræde** is another shopping street that competes with Bredgade in antiques.

BEST BUYS   In a country famed for its designers and craftspeople, the best buys are in stainless steel, porcelain, china, glassware, toys—especially Kay Bojesen's wooden animals—functionally designed furniture, textiles, and jewelry (decorative, silver, and semiprecious stones).

SHIPPING IT HOME & RECOVERING VAT   Denmark imposes a 25% tax on goods and services, a "value-added tax" known in Denmark as **MOMS** (pronounced "mumps"). Tax-free exports are possible. Many stores will mail goods to your home so you can avoid paying the tax. If you want to take your purchases, look for shops displaying Danish tax-free shopping notices. Such shops offer tourists tax refunds for personal export. This refund applies to purchases of over 300DKK ($50) for visitors from the United States and Canada—spent at the same store, but not necessarily all at once. For more information, see "Taxes" in "Fast Facts: Denmark," in chapter 2. For answers to tax refund questions, call **Global Refund** (© **32-52-55-66**).

STORE HOURS   In general, shopping hours are 9:30 or 10am to 5:30pm Monday to Thursday, to 7 or 8pm on Friday, and to 2pm on Saturday. Most shops are closed Sunday, except the kiosks and supermarket at the Central Railroad Station. Here you can purchase food until 10pm or midnight. The Central Railroad Station's bakery is open until 9pm, and one kiosk at Rådhuspladsen, which sells papers, film, and souvenirs, is open 24 hours.

SHOPPING A TO Z
AMBER
The Amber Specialist   The owners, known to customers as the "Amber Twins," will sell you "the gold of the north." This petrified resin originated in the large coniferous forests that covered Denmark some 35 million years ago. The forest disappeared, but the amber lasted, and is now used to create handsome jewelry. This shop carries a large collection of amber set in 14-karat gold. Frederiksberggade 28. © **33-11-88-03.** Bus: 28, 29, or 41.

ART GALLERIES & AUCTION HOUSES

Bruun Rasmussen Established shortly after World War II, this is Denmark's leading auction house. July is usually quiet, although the premises remain open for appraisals and purchases. The season begins in August, with an auction of paintings and fine art. Viewing time is allowed before auctions, which are held about once a month. There are also auctions of art, wine, coins, books, and antique weapons. Bredgade 33. ✆ **33-13-69-11**. Bus: 1, 6, 9, or 10.

Galerie Asbaek This modern-art gallery has a permanent exhibit of the best local artists, along with changing shows by Scandinavian and foreign artists. A bookshop and cafe serving French-inspired Danish food is on the premises. Graphics and posters are for sale. Bredgade 20. ✆ **33-15-40-04**. Bus: 1, 6, 9, 10, 28, 29, or 41.

Kunsthallens Auktioner Established in 1926, this is Europe's leading dealer in the pan-European school of painting known as COBRA (an acronym for Copenhagen, Brussels, and Amsterdam, where the artists originated). These works, produced from 1948 to 1951, were a precursor of abstract expressionism. The gallery holds 12 auctions yearly, 8 with modern art; others concentrate on the 19th century. Gothersgade 9. ✆ **33-32-46-70**. Bus: 1, 6, 9, or 10.

BOOKS

Boghallen This big store at Town Hall Square carries many books in English, as well as a wide selection of travel-related literature, including maps. It stocks books in English on Danish themes, such as the collected works of Hans Christian Andersen. Rådhuspladsen 37. ✆ **33-47-25-60**. Bus: 2, 8, or 30.

DEPARTMENT STORES

Illum One of Denmark's top department stores, Illum is on Strøget. Take time to browse through its vast store of Danish and Scandinavian design. There are a restaurant and a special export cash desk at street level. Østergade 52. ✆ **33-93-37-67**. Bus: 1, 6, 9, or 10.

Magasin An elegant department store, Magasin is the biggest in Scandinavia. It offers a complete assortment of Danish designer fashion, a large selection of glass and porcelain, and souvenirs. Goods are shipped abroad tax-free. Kongens Nytorv 13. ✆ **33-11-44-33**. Bus: 1, 6, 9, or 10.

FASHIONS

Sweater Market Take your pick from top-grade Scandinavian and Icelandic cardigans, pullovers, hats, scarves, and mittens, hand-knit in Denmark of 100% wool. There's also a large selection of Icelandic wool jackets and coats. Frederiksberggade 15. ✆ **33-15-27-73**. Bus: 2, 8, or 30.

FLEA MARKETS

Det Blå Pakhus Copenhagen's largest indoor marketplace has 325 booths, selling a little bit of everything. The motto of "The Blue Warehouse" is that you can find "everything between heaven and earth here," and they're probably right. It's a flea market paradise, complete with secondhand furniture, antiques, carpets, assorted bric-a-brac, and all sorts of knickknacks. It is open only Saturday and Sunday 10am to 5pm, and charges an entrance of 15DKK ($2.50). Holmbladsgade 113. ✆ **32-95-17-07**. Bus: 5 or 37.

FURS

Birger Christensen   This is one of Scandinavia's leading fur shops. It has its own designer line and also features furs and fashions by some of the world's leading designers, including Sonia Rykiel, Yves Saint Laurent, Diane von Furstenberg, Chanel, Hermes, and Donna Karan. You can also purchase—cheaper than the furs—a selection of cashmere or wool blended coats with fur lining and fur trim. This is swank shopping and very, very, expensive. Østergade 38. ℂ **33-11-55-55.** Bus: 1, 6, 9, 10, 19, 29, 31, 42, or 43.

GLASSWARE, PORCELAIN & CRYSTAL

Holmegaards Glasværker   This is Denmark's only major producer of glasswork. Its Wellington pattern, created in 1859, is available again, after not being produced for 50 years. The Holmegaard glasses and the Regiment Bar set reflect solid craftsmanship. In the Royal Copenhagen retail center, Amagertorv 6 (Strøget). ℂ **33-12-44-77.** Bus: 1, 6, 8, 9, or 10.

Rosenthal Studio-Haus   You'll find an array of ceramic works here, especially by well-known Danish artist Bjørn Wiinblad, whose figures we find whimsical and delightful. You can also get some good buys on Orrefors crystal, including some stunning bowls. The sculptural reliefs, handmade in lead crystal, range from miniatures to giant animals in limited world editions of 199 pieces. They often depict the animals of the far north. Frederiksberggade 21. ℂ **33-14-21-01.** Bus: 28, 29, or 41.

Royal Copenhagen Porcelain   Royal Copenhagen's trademark, three wavy blue lines, has come to symbolize quality. Founded in 1775, the factory was a royal possession for a century before passing into private hands in 1868. Royal Copenhagen's Christmas plates are collectors' items. The factory has turned out a new plate each year since 1908, most of the designs depicting the Danish countryside in winter. There's a huge selection of seconds on the top floor, and unless you're an expert, you probably can't tell the difference. Visitors are welcome at the **factory** at Søndre Fasanvej 5 (ℂ **38-14-48-48**), where tours are given Monday to Friday from 9am to 3pm. (These tours can be arranged by contacting the Royal Copenhagen store at the phone number listed above.) Purchases cannot be made at the factory.

There are also various porcelain and silver retailers in this same location, as well as the Royal Copenhagen Antiques shop, which specializes in buying and selling antique Georg Jensen, Royal Copenhagen, Bing & Grøndahl Porcelain, and Michelson Christmas Spoons. In the Royal Scandinavia retail center, Amagertorv 6 (Strøget). ℂ **33-13-71-81.** www.royalcopenhagen.com. Bus: 1, 2, 6, 8, 28, 29, or 41 for the retail outlet; 1 or 14 for the factory.

Skandinavisk Glas/A. B. Schou   This store carries porcelain pieces from Royal Copenhagen, Baccarat crystal, porcelain from Ginovi in Italy, Hummels from Germany, Orrefors from Sweden, Lladró from Spain, and Wedgwood from England. If you like to comparison-shop among famous names, this is the place. The exhibition of collectors' plates is the largest in Scandinavia. Ny Østergade 4. ℂ **33-13-80-95.** Bus: 1, 6, 9, or 10.

GOOSE-DOWN COMFORTERS

Ofelia   If you'd like to snuggle under a goose-down comforter on a winter's night, head for this shop noted for its traditional craftsmanship and quality. You'll find it along the Strøget. Amagertorv 3. ℂ **40-29-91-50.** Bus: 28, 29, or 41.

HOME FURNISHINGS

Illums Bolighus   A center for modern Scandinavian and Danish design, this is one of Europe's finest showcases for household furnishings and accessories. It stocks furniture, lamps, rugs, textiles, bedding, glassware, kitchenware, flatware, china, jewelry, and ceramics. The store also sells women's and men's clothes and accessories. There's even a gift shop. Amagertorv 10 (Strøget). ℂ **33-14-19-41.** Bus: 28, 29, or 41.

Lysberg, Hansen & Therp   This major interior-decorating center offers fabrics, carpets, and furniture. The model apartments are furnished in impeccable taste. The company manufactures its own furniture in traditional design and imports fabrics, usually from Germany or France. The gift shop has many hard-to-find creations. Bredgade 77. ℂ **33-14-47-87.** Bus: 1, 6, 9, or 10.

Paustian   Copenhagen's leading furniture showroom, in the somewhat distant industrial Nordhavn section, will ship anywhere in the world. The finest of Scandinavian design is on display, along with reproductions of the classics. There's a well-recommended adjoining restaurant. Kalkbrænderiløbskaj 2. ℂ **40-38-20-90.** S-tog: Nordhavn.

INTERIOR DESIGN

Hanne Gundelach   At this house of art and design, you can purchase works by David Marshall, the well-known sculptor and designer. Handmade interior design objects are hand-cast in a method dating back to the Romans, producing a rustic appearance. The outlet also represents the well-known artist Guillermo Silva, known for beautiful sculptures, tableware, candlesticks, and bowls. Bredgade 56. ℂ **33-11-33-96.** Bus: 28, 29, or 41.

JEWELRY

Hartmann's Selected Estate Silver & Jewelry   This shop buys silver and jewelry from old estates and sells it at reduced prices. Sometimes it's possible to purchase heirloom Georg Jensen estate silver. Ulrik Hartmann, the store's owner, launched his career as a 10-year-old trading at a local flea market, but went on to greater things. The shop is near Kongens Nytorv. While in the neighborhood, you can walk for hours, exploring the auction rooms, jewelry shops, and art galleries in the vicinity. Bredgade 4. ℂ **33-33-09-63.** Bus: 1, 6, 9, or 10.

Kaere Ven   One of the city's oldest diamond dealers, in business for more than 100 years, this outlet advertises itself as offering "prices from another century." That's a bit of an exaggeration, but you can often find bargains in antique jewelry, even old Georg Jensen silver. An array of rings, earrings, necklaces, and bracelets are sold, along with other items. A few items in the store are sold at 50% off competitive prices, but you have to shop carefully and know what you're buying. Star Kongens Gade 30. ℂ **33-11-43-15.** Bus: 1, 6, 9, or 10.

MUSIC

Axel Musik   One of the best-stocked music stores in the Danish capital, Axel also has a newer branch in the city's main railway station. In Scala Center (ground floor), Axeltorv 2. ℂ **33-14-05-50.** Bus: 1, 6, or 8.

NEEDLEWORK

Eva Rosenstand A/S–Clara Wæver   You'll find Danish-designed cross-stitch embroideries here. The materials are usually linen, in medium or coarser grades, but cotton is also available. The free needlework museum is the only one of its kind in Europe. Østergade 42. ℂ **33-13-29-40.** Bus: 1, 6, 9, or 10.

Travel Tip: He who finds the best hotel deal has more to spend on facials involving knobbly vegetables.

Hello, the Roaming Gnome here. I've been nabbed from the garden and taken round the world. The people who took me are so terribly clever. They find the best offerings on Travelocity. For very little cha-ching. And that means I get to be pampered and exfoliated till I'm pink as a bunny's doodah.

travelocity®

1-888-TRAVELOCITY / travelocity.com / America Online Keyword: Travel

PEWTER & SILVER

Georg Jensen   Legendary Georg Jensen is known for its silver. For the connoisseur, there's no better address. On display is the largest and best collection of Jensen holloware in Europe. The store also features gold and silver jewelry in traditional and modern Danish designs. In the Royal Scandinavia retail center, Amagertorv 6 (Strøget). ℂ 33-11-40-80. www.georgjensen.com. Bus: 1, 6, 8, 9, or 10.

SHOPPING CENTER

In addition to the centers described above, for excellent buys in Scandinavian merchandise, as well as tax-free goods, we recommend the **shopping center at the airport.** A VAT-refund office is located nearby.

3 Copenhagen After Dark

Danes know how to party. A good night means a late night, and on warm weekends, hundreds of rowdy revelers crowd Strøget until sunrise. Merrymaking in Copenhagen is not just for the younger crowd; jazz clubs, traditional beer houses, and wine cellars are routinely packed with people of all ages. Of course, the city has a more highbrow cultural side as well, exemplified by excellent theaters, operas, ballets, and one of the best circuses in Europe.

To find out what's happening at the time of your visit, pick up a free copy of *Copenhagen This Week* at the tourist information center. The section marked "Events Calendar" has a week-by-week roundup of the most interesting entertainment and sightseeing events in the Danish capital.

TIVOLI GARDENS ✪✪

In the center of the gardens, the large **open-air stage** books vaudeville acts (tumbling clowns, acrobats, aerialists) who give performances Monday to Thursday at 7 and 9:30pm; Saturday at 4:30, 7, and 10pm; and Sunday at 7 and 10pm. Spectators must enter through the turnstiles for seats, but there's an unobstructed view from outside if you prefer to stand. Jazz and folklore groups also perform here during the season. Admission is free.

The 150-year-old outdoor **Pantomime Theater,** with its Chinese stage and peacock curtain, is near the Tivoli's Vesterbrogade 3 entrance and presents shows Tuesday to Thursday at 6:15 and 8:15pm; Friday at 7:30 and 9pm; Saturday at 8:15 and 8:30pm; and Sunday at 4:30 and 6:30pm. The repertoire consists of 16 different commedia dell'arte productions featuring the entertaining trio Pierrot, Columbine, and Harlequin—these are authentic pantomimes that have been performed continuously in Copenhagen since 1844. Admission is free.

The modern **Tivolis Koncertsal** (concert hall) is a great place to hear top artists and orchestras, led by equally famous conductors. Opened in 1956, the concert hall can seat 2,000, and its season—which begins in late April and lasts for more than 5 months—has been called "the most extensive music festival in the world." Performances of everything from symphony to opera are presented Monday to Saturday at 7:30pm, and sometimes at 8pm, depending on the event. Good seats are available at prices ranging from 200DKK to 400DKK ($33–$67) when major artists are performing—but most performances are free. Tickets are sold at the main booking office on Vesterbrogade 3 (ℂ **33-15-10-12**).

Tivoli Glassalen (ℂ **33-15-10-12**) is housed in a century-old octagonal gazebo-like building with a glass, gilt-capped canopy. Shows are often comedic/satirical performances by Danish comedians in Danish, and these usually don't interest non-Danish audiences. But there are also musical revues. Tickets range from 205DKK to 240DKK ($34–$40).

THE PERFORMING ARTS

For **discount seats** (sometimes as much as 50% off), go in person to a ticket kiosk at the corner of Fiolstraede and Nørre Voldgade, across from the Nørreport train station. Discount tickets are sold the day of the performance and may be purchased Monday to Friday noon to 5pm and Saturday noon to 3pm.

Copenhagen Opera House ★★★ Opened by Queen Margrethe, this new $441-million, 1,700-seat opera house is the new and luxurious home of the Royal Danish Opera. The opera house is the gift of the AP Møller and Chastine McKinney Møller Foundation, which is headed by Maersk McKinney-Møller, one of the wealthiest men in the country. Designed by Danish architect Henning Larsen, the opera house uses precious stones and metals, including 105,000 sheets of gold leaf. In addition to the international artists, the opera house also showcases the works of such Danish composers as Carl Nielsen and Poul Ruders. You can dine at the on-site **Restauranten** before curtain time, with a three-course menu costing 399DKK ($67). In addition there is an **Opera Café,** serving sandwiches, salads, and light Danish specialties. The season runs from August until the beginning of June. Ekuipagemesteruej 10. ✆ 33-69-69-33. Tickets 70DKK–440DKK ($12–$73). Box office (✆ 33-69-69-69; Mon–Sat noon–6pm).

Det Kongelige Teater (Royal Theater) Performances by the world-renowned **Royal Danish Ballet** and **Royal Danish Opera,** dating from 1748, are major winter cultural events in Copenhagen. Because the arts are state-subsidized in Denmark, ticket prices are comparatively low, and some seats may be available at the box office the day before a performance. The season runs August to June. Kongens Nytorv. ✆ 33-69-69-69. www.kgl-teater.dk. Tickets 70DKK–615DKK ($12–$103), half-price for seniors over 66 and people under 26. Bus: 1, 6, 9, or 10.

THE CLUB & MUSIC SCENE
DANCE CLUBS

Baron & Baroness A short walk from Tivoli, this is a relatively upscale nightclub whose decor incorporates faux-medieval crenellations, wrought-iron replicas of the bars on boudoir windows, suits of armor, and lots of hunting trophies. It attracts a crowd that's a bit older and more prosperous than nearby competitors catering to teens. Full meals cost from 168DKK to 238DKK ($28–$40). On nights when there's no disco, you'll find a solo musician playing a fiddle, piano, or harmonica. The bars are open nightly 6pm to at least 3am; the restaurant, 6 to 11pm. There's a disco above the restaurant Thursday to Saturday, 10pm to dawn. Vesterbrogade 2E. ✆ **33-16-01-01.** No cover. Bus: 250E or 350E.

Cavi ★ Some of Copenhagen's best DJs, often from abroad, entertain at this fashionable dance lounge with R & B, funk, soul, hip-hop, or whatever. There's a dance floor at one section of the principal room, although most of the crowd in their 20s and 30s are found enjoying one of the more secluded sofas or else the large panoramic roof terrace, ideal on a summer night. The location is on a side street in the vicinity of the Magasin department store. Weekends are packed here. The big drawback is that you have to look like Paris Hilton (or Colin Farrell) to get by the doorman. Open Thursday and Friday 11pm to 5am, Saturday 11pm to 6am. Lille Kongensgade 16. ✆ **33-11-20-20.** Cover 50DKK ($8.35) men Thurs–Fri, 100DKK ($17) Sat; 50DKK ($8.35) women Thurs, free Fri–Sat. Bus: 1, 6, 9, or 10.

Den Røde Pimpernel The lively, clublike atmosphere of "The Scarlet Pimpernel" makes it a good place for dancing or dining. You'll be admitted only after being inspected through a peephole. A live band plays a variety of dance music. It's open daily noon to 4am. Bernstorffsgade 3, Tivoli ℂ **33-75-07-60**. Cover 50DKK ($8.35) Fri–Sat. Bus: 2, 8, or 30.

Enzo Few other nightclubs in Copenhagen offer as many bars. In this case, each has a different theme, ranging from plush hideaways whose upholstery encourages intimacy to more spartan stand-up affairs where patrons compete elbow-to-elbow to see how fast they can consume a shot of liquor. Come here for an all-around introduction to Copenhagen's night owls, then gravitate to the Couch Lounge (where you'll probably sit, and where secluded booths are reserved); the Cigar Lounge (where you can puff up a storm); a disco bar (where you'll dance between drinks); a Water Bar (where you can, despite the bar's name, still get a drink of whiskey); and the Shot Bar, which boasts a comprehensive collection of tequilas, rums, and vodkas. It's open to the public Thursday to Saturday 11pm to 5am—the rest of the week, it's reserved for private parties. Nørregade 41. ℂ **33-13-67-88**. Cover 60DKK ($10) Thurs, 75DKK ($13) Fri–Sat after 11pm. S-tog: Nørreport Station.

NASA Its name has changed several times in the past decade, but even so, this is the most posh and prestigious of three nightclubs that occupy three respective floors of the same building. The late-night crowd of 25- to 40-year-olds includes many avid fans of whatever musical innovation has just emerged in London or Los Angeles. The decorative theme includes lots of white, lots of mirrors, and lots of artfully directed spotlights. Don't be surprised to see a room full of expensively, albeit casually, dressed Danes chattering away in a cacophony of different languages. Technically, the site is a private club, but polite and presentable newcomers can usually gain access. It's open only Friday and Saturday midnight to 6am. Gothersgade 8F, Bolthensgaard. ℂ **33-93-74-15**. Cover 100DKK ($17) for nonmembers. Bus: 1, 6, or 9.

Rosie McGee's Across the boulevard from Tivoli, this is a funky, American-style nightclub that caters to youthful (ages 18–25), high-energy scenesters. There is a jukebox near the entrance, and lots of gum-chewing teeny-boppers with braces, decked out in jeans and sneakers, come here to mingle, compare notes, and dance, dance, dance. There's a simple restaurant on-site, serving mostly Mexican food and frothy, foamy drinks that might help ease the shyness of striking up a conversation with a stranger. The bars and restaurant open nightly from noon (*note:* Mon–Sat the restaurant closes at 11pm, Sun at 10pm), with the disco featured Sunday to Tuesday 11pm to 3am, Wednesday and Thursday 11pm to 4am, Friday 11pm to 5am, and Saturday 11pm to 6am. Vesterbrogade 2A. ℂ **33-32-19-23**. Cover 60DKK ($10) on disco nights only. Bus: 250E or 350E.

Rust Rust sprawls over a single floor in the Nørrebro district where the clientele is international and high-energy. There are a restaurant, several bars, a dance floor, and a stage where live musicians perform every Thursday night beginning around 9pm. Meals are served Wednesday to Saturday 5:30pm to around midnight, and at least someone will begin to boogie on the dance floor after 9:30pm, as drinks flow. The setting is dark and shadowy. There are places to sit, but none so comfortable that you'll stay in one place for too long. No one under age 21 is admitted but you'll spot very few over age 45. Open 5:30pm to at least 2am Wednesday to Saturday. Guldbergsgade 8. ℂ **35-24-52-00**. Cover 50DKK–110DKK ($8.35–$18) Wed–Sat. Bus: 5 or 6.

Value   **Nighttime Experiences for Free (Well, Almost)**

You don't have to go to clubs or attend cultural presentations to experience Copenhagen nightlife. If you want to save money and have a good time, too, consider doing as the Danes do: Walk about and enjoy the city and its glittering lights for free, perhaps stopping at a lovely square to have a drink and watch the world pass by.

Copenhagen's elegant spires and tangle of cobbled one-way streets are best viewed at night, when they take on the aura of the Hans Christian Andersen era. The old buildings have been well preserved, and at night they're floodlit. The city's network of drawbridges and small bridges is also particularly charming at night.

One of the best places for a walk is **Nyhavn** (New Harbor), which until about 25 years ago was the haunt of sailors and some of the roughest dives in Copenhagen. Today it's gone upmarket and is the site of numerous restaurants and bars. In summer you can sit out at one of the cafe tables watching life along the canal and throngs of people from around the world passing by—all for the price of your Carlsberg. Along the quay you can also see a fleet of old-time sailing ships. Hans Christian Andersen lived at three different addresses along Nyhavn: nos. 18, 20, and 67.

Another neighborhood that takes on special magic at night is **Christianshavn,** whose principal landmark is **Christiansborg Slot** or **Castle,** a massive granite pile surrounded by canals on three sides. The ramparts of Christianshavn are edged with walking paths, which are lit at light. This neighborhood, which glows under the soft, forgiving light of antique street lamps, is the closest Copenhagen comes to the charm of the Left Bank in Paris. You can wander for hours through its cobbled streets and 18th-century buildings. The area also abounds with cafes,

---

Subsonic   Thanks to an armada of designers who developed it, and thanks to its self-appointed role as a "Design Disco," its interior is more artfully outfitted than any other in Copenhagen. Expect lots of postmodern gloss, references to the California rave movement, an occasional emphasis on dance music of the 1980s, a small corner outfitted like a cozy beer hall, and a clientele that seems familiar with the music and ambience of some very hip clubs in Europe and the United States. Part of its interior was based on a waiting room of a 1970s Scandinavian airport, complete with then-innovative streamlined design that's been associated with Denmark ever since. It's open Friday and Saturday 11pm till at least 5:30am. Skindergade 45. ☎ **33-13-26-25.** Cover 60DKK ($10). Bus: 1 or 6. No changes.

JAZZ, ROCK & BLUES

Copenhagen JazzHouse   The decor is modern and uncomplicated and serves as a consciously simple foil for the music and noise. This club hosts more performances by non-Danish jazz artists than any other jazz bar in town. Shows begin relatively early, at around 8:30pm, and usually finish early, too. Around

bars, and restaurants. Originally the section was built by King Christian IV to provide housing for workers in the shipbuilding industry, but in the past decades real-estate prices here have soared.

For a more offbeat adventure—although it's not the safest place at night—you can head for the commune of **Christiania,** a few blocks to the east of Vor Frelsers Kirke. This area once housed Danish soldiers in barracks. When the soldiers moved out, the free spirits of Copenhagen moved in, occupying the little village, even though—technically speaking—they are squatters and in violation of the law. They declared the area a "free city" on September 24, 1971. Copenhagen authorities have not moved in to oust them in all this time, fearing a full-scale riot. The area is a refuge for petty criminals and drug dealers. But there has been success in the community as well, evoking the communes of the 1960s. For example, the villagers have helped hundreds of addicts kick heroin habits.

At night, adventurous tourists enter Christiania to eat at one of the neighborhood's little restaurants, many of which are surprisingly good. Prices here are the cheapest in Copenhagen, because the restaurant managers refuse to pay taxes. You can also wander through some of the shops selling handmade crafts. Because most establishments are small and personal, you can also invite yourself in, perhaps to listen to innovative music or see some cultural presentation. Currently your best bet for dining is **Spiseloppen.** Later you can visit the jazz club, **Loppen,** where you'll hear some of the best jazz in the city. If you're a vegetarian, as are many members of the commune, head for the vegetarian restaurant, **Morgensted.** (These two restaurants and the club don't have addresses, but they're easy to spot.)

midnight on Friday and Saturday, the club is transformed from a live concert hall into a disco (it's open until 5am). It's closed Mondays; otherwise, it keeps a confusing schedule that changes according to the demands of the current band. Niels Hemmingsensgade 10. (C) **33-15-26-00.** Cover charge 70DKK to 260DKK ($12–$43) when live music is performed, depending on the artist. Bus: 10.

La Fontaine This is a dive that hasn't changed much since the 1950s, but it's the kind of dive that—if you meet the right partner, or if you really groove with the music—can be a lot of fun. Small, and cozy to the point of being cramped, it functions mostly as a bar, every Tuesday to Saturday 8pm to 6am or even 8am. Sunday hours are 9pm to 1am. Live music is performed on Friday and Saturday, when free-form jazz artists play starting around 11:30pm. Kompagnistræde 11. (C) **33-11-60-98.** Cover 50DKK ($8.35) Fri–Sat. Bus: 5 or 10.

Mojo Blues Bar Mojo is a candlelit drinking spot that offers blues music, 90% of which is performed by Scandinavian groups. It's open daily 8pm to 5am. Løngangstræde 21C. (C) **33-11-64-53.** Cover 50DKK ($8.35) Fri–Sat. Bus: 2, 8, or 30. No changes.

THE BAR SCENE
PUBS

Det Lille Apotek This is a good spot for English-speaking foreign students to meet their Danish counterparts. Although the menu varies from week to week, keep an eye out for the prawn cocktail and tenderloin, both highly recommended. The main courses run about 88DKK to 188DKK ($15–$31). It's open Monday to Saturday 11am to midnight, Sunday noon to midnight; closed December 24 to 26. Stor Kannikestræde 15. © **33-12-56-06.** Bus: 2, 5, 8, or 30.

Library Bar Frequently visited by celebrities and royalty, the Library Bar was once rated by the late Malcolm Forbes as one of the top five bars in the world. In a setting of antique books and works of art, you can order everything from a cappuccino to a cocktail. The setting is the lobby level of the landmark Hotel Plaza, commissioned in 1913 by Frederik VIII. The bar was originally designed and built as the hotel's ballroom, and Oregon pine was used for the paneling. The oversized mural of George Washington and his men dates from 1910. It's open Monday to Friday 4pm to midnight; Saturday and Sunday 4pm to 2am. Beer costs 26DKK ($4.35); drinks begin at 30DKK ($5). In the Hotel Plaza, Bernstorffsgade 4. © **33-14-92-62.** Bus: 6.

Nyhavn 17 This is the last of the honky-tonks that used to make up the former sailors' quarter. This cafe is a short walk from the patrician Kongens Nytorv. In summer you can sit outside. It's open Sunday to Thursday 10am to 2am and Friday and Saturday to 3am. Beer costs 35DKK ($5.85), and drinks start at 45DKK ($7.50). Nyhavn 17. © **33-12-54-19.** Bus: 1, 6, 27, or 29.

The Queen's Pub Cozy, traditional, and imbued with a sense of Baltic history, this is the kind of bar where a businessperson could feel at home after a transatlantic flight. The older members of the staff have served nearly every politician and journalist in Denmark. It's on the ground floor of one of Copenhagen's most legendary (and discreet) hotels, and its decor includes English walnut, red brocade, and etched Victorian glass. Open Monday to Saturday from noon to 11pm. Beer costs 27DKK to 47DKK ($4.50–$7.85); drinks begin at 55DKK ($9.20). In the Kong Frederik Hotel, Vester Voldgade 25. © **33-12-59-02.** Bus: 1, 2, 6, 8, or 28.

A WINE BAR

Hvids Vinstue Built in 1670, this old wine cellar is a dimly lit safe haven for an eclectic crowd, many patrons—including theatergoers, actors, and dancers—drawn from the Royal Theater across the way. In December only, a combination of red wine and cognac is served. It's open Monday to Saturday 10am to 1am; closed Sunday in July and August. Beer is 35DKK ($5.85); wine costs 30DKK ($5). Kongens Nytorv 19. © **33-15-10-64.** Bus: 1, 6, 9, or 10.

GAY & LESBIAN CLUBS

Catwalk This is one of the newest and hippest of the gay clubs in Copenhagen. The bartender assured us, "It's filled every night with the cutest boys in town if you're partial to blonds." The house DJ is in action throughout the evening playing your favorite tunes and some newly released music. As the night wears on, the club gets hotter and the cruising more uninhibited. Open Monday to Saturday midnight to 10am; in summer Wednesday to Saturday from 7pm (no set closing time). Kattesundet 4. © **33-12-20-32.** Cover 50DKK ($8.35). S-tog: Central Station.

Cosy Bar   It runs a fine line between a crowd that favors leather, and what you'd expect from a working crew of men performing manual labor down by the harborfront. Popular and cruisy, it's open daily 11pm till 8am, dispensing ample amounts of schnapps and suds during the course of a working night. Studiestræde 24. © **33-12-74-27.** Bus: 6 or 29.

The Men's Bar   This is the only leather bar in town, filled with an unusual collection of uniforms, leather, and Levi's. It's open daily 3pm to 2am. A beer will set you back 20DKK ($3.35). Teglgaardstræde 3. © **33-12-73-03.** Bus: 2, 8, or 30.

Pan Club   This nationwide organization was established in 1948 for the protection and advancement of gay and lesbian rights. Its headquarters is a 19th-century yellow building off of the Strøget. A dance club occupies three of its floors, and a modern cafe is on the ground level. Every night is gay night, although a lot of straights come here for the music. The cafe is open Thursday 9pm to 4pm; Friday and Saturday 10pm to 5am. The dance club is open Friday 10pm to 5am and Saturday 10pm to 6am. Knabrostræde 3. © **33-11-37-84.** Cover 55DKK ($9.20) for dance club. Bus: 28, 29, or 41.

SLM (Scandinavia Leather Men) Club   Set amid the densest concentration of gay bars in Denmark, just around the corner from the also-recommended Men's Bar, this is technically a private club that caters to men interested in the way other men look and act in leather. Nonmembers visiting from other countries, if they're dressed properly, can usually pay 100DKK ($17) for a temporary membership that will get them past the doorman. It's open Friday and Saturday nights only, 10pm to at least 4am, and usually later. Entrance is allowed until 2am. Studiestræde 14. © **33-32-06-01.** Bus: 6 or 29.

XXX COPENHAGEN

The heady "boogie nights" of the '70s, when pornography aficionados flocked to Copenhagen to purchase X-rated materials, are long gone. Copenhagen is no longer the capital of sex, having long ago lost out to Hamburg and Amsterdam. But it's still possible to take a walk here on the wild side any night of the week. Two of the city's streets are **Istedgade** and **Helgolandsgade,** both of them near the rail terminus in the center of the city. Ironically, the sex shops peddling magazines and X-rated films stand virtually adjacent to decent family hotels. Mothers can often be seen hustling their sons past the window displays.

GAMBLING

Casino Copenhagen   Danish authorities allowed the country's first fully licensed casino to open in the first-class SAS Scandinavia Hotel in 1990. Today gamblers play such popular games as roulette, baccarat, punto banco, blackjack, and slot machines. The whole operation is overseen by Casinos of Austria, the largest casino operator in Europe. It's open daily 2pm to 4am. In the SAS Scandinavia Hotel, Amager Blvd. 70. © **33-96-59-65.** Cover 80DKK ($13); guests at any of Copenhagen's SAS hotels enter free. Bus: 5, 11, 30, or 34.

4 Side Trips from Copenhagen

BEACHES

The beach closest to Copenhagen is **Bellevue** (S-tog: Klampenborg), but the water is not recommended for swimming. If you want to take a dip at a sandy beach, take a trip (by train or car) to the beaches of North Zealand—**Gilleleje, Hornbæk, Liseleje,** and **Tisvildeleje.** Although these are family beaches, minimal bathing attire is worn.

To reach any of these beaches, take the train to Helsingør and then continue by bus. Or you can make connections by train to Hillerød and switch to a local train; check at the railroad station for details. If you drive, you may want to stay for the evening discos at the little beach resort towns dotting the north coast of Zealand.

DRAGØR
5km (3 miles) S of Copenhagen's Kastrup Airport

This old seafaring town on the island of Amager is filled with well-preserved half-timbered ocher and pink 18th-century cottages with steep red-tile or thatched roofs, many of which are under the protection of the National Trust.

Dragør (pronounced *Drah*-wer) was a busy port on the herring-rich Baltic Sea in the early Middle Ages, and when fishing fell off, it became a sleepy little waterfront village. After 1520, Amager Island and its villages—Dragør and Store Magleby—were inhabited by the Dutch, who brought their own customs, Low-German language, and agricultural expertise to Amager, especially their love of bulb flowers. In Copenhagen you still see wooden-shoed Amager locals selling their hyacinths, tulips, daffodils, and lilies in the streets.

ESSENTIALS
GETTING THERE   By Bus   Take bus nos. 30, 33, or 73E from Rådhus-pladsen (Town Hall Square) in Copenhagen (trip time: 35 min.).

SEEING THE SIGHTS
Amager Museum   A rich trove of historic treasures is found in this museum outside Dragør. The exhibits reveal the affluence achieved by the Amager Dutch, with rich textiles, fine embroidery, and such amenities as carved silver buckles and buttons. The interiors of a Dutch house are especially interesting, showing how these people decorated their homes and lived in comfort.

Hovedgaden 4–12, Store Magleby. ℂ **32-53-93-07.** www.amagermuseet.dk. Admission 20DKK ($3.35) adults, 10DKK ($1.65) children. May–Sept daily noon–4pm; Oct–Mar Wed and Sun noon–4pm; Closed in April. Bus: 30, 33, or 350S.

Dragør Museum   The exhibits at this harborfront museum show how the Amager Dutch lived from prehistoric times to the 20th century. Farming, goose breeding, seafaring, fishing, ship piloting, and ship salvaging are displayed through pictures and artifacts.

Havnepladsen 2–4. ℂ **32-53-41-06.** www.dragoer-information.dk. Admission 20DKK ($3.35) adults, 10DKK ($1.65) children. May–Sept Tues–Sun and holidays noon–4pm. Closed Oct–Apr. Bus: 30, 32, or 350S.

WHERE TO STAY
Dragør Badehotel   Built around 1901, this establishment near the sea is more popular as a restaurant than a hotel, yet it offers comfortably old-fashioned rooms with good beds, but a shortage of private bathrooms. Naturally, the rooms with private (shower-only) bathrooms are booked first, since they cost no more than units without. You'll get a real feel for a country Danish inn here, only 20 minutes from the Copenhagen Town Hall. Nonguests are welcome to enjoy the hotel's excellent cuisine. There are six different preparations of herring to get you going, followed by a Dragør Plate of mixed meats and pâtés, tender schnitzels, homemade soups, and a selection of *smørrebrød* (open-face sandwiches) at lunch.

Drogdensvej 43, DK-2791 Dragør. ℂ and fax **32-53-05-00.** www.badehotellet.dk. 33 units, 3 with bathroom. 795DKK–2,070DKK ($133–$346) double with or without bathroom. Rates include breakfast. AE, DC, MC, V. Bus: 30, 33, or 73E. **Amenities:** Restaurant; lounge; laundry service; nonsmoking rooms. *In room:* TV, minibar.

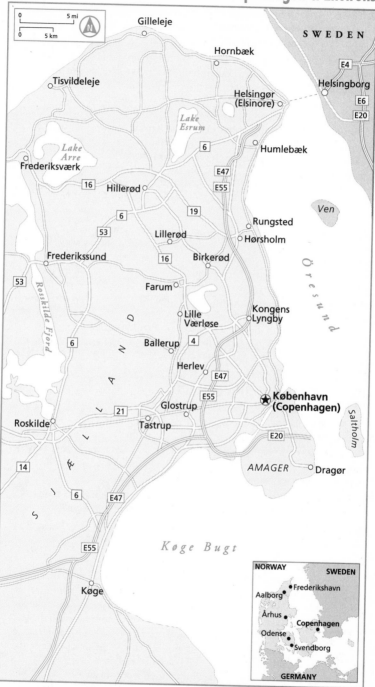

WHERE TO DINE

The **Dragør Badehotel** (see above) also offers an excellent cuisine.

Restaurant Beghuset DANISH   This cafe and restaurant on a cobblestone street in the center of town looks like an idyllic cottage. To reach the restaurant section, you walk through the cafe. Although the menu changes every 2 to 3 months to accommodate seasonal items, a weary traveler in search of sustenance will be tempted by selections like fish soup, Swedish caviar, thinly sliced smoked lamb with a balsamic dressing on a bed of seasonal greens, and fresh oysters. Main courses include a perfectly cooked guinea fowl braised in red wine served with bacon of veal (their own invention) and herbs, and Dragør plaice roasted in butter and served with either parsley sauce or a bacon-thyme sauce.

Strandgade 14. ✆ **32-53-01-36.** Reservations recommended. 1-platter lunch 138DKK–189DKK ($23–$32); 2-course lunch 198DKK ($33); 3-course lunch 225DKK ($38); dinner main courses 178DKK–198DKK ($30–$33); 3-course fixed-price dinner 348DKK ($58); 4-course fixed-price dinner 398DKK ($66). AE, DC, MC, V. Tues–Sun noon–3pm and 6–9:45pm. Bus: 30, 33, or 73E.

Strandhotel DANISH   One of Dragør's most visible restaurants is the Strandhotel (which, ironically, has no bedrooms). A longtime favorite, it has welcomed such guests as Frederik III (who usually ordered eel soup) and Kierkegaard. At lunchtime an ample spread of *smørrebrød* is served, although other offerings include filet of pork in paprika sauce, a savory smoked filet of eel, fried or poached plaice, and a delectable trout with almonds. At dinner the chefs tempt you with such dishes as grilled tuna with raspberries or oven-baked whitefish served in a banana leaf, the flavor enhanced by a saffron cream sauce.

Strandlinbyn 9, Havnen. ✆ **32-53-00-75.** Reservations recommended. Main courses 158DKK–196DKK ($26–$33); lunch *smørrebrød* 78DKK–188DKK ($13–$31); "quick lunch" 188DKK ($31). AE, DC, MC, V. Daily 9am–9:30pm. Closed Oct–Mar. Bus: 350S.

HUMLEBÆK (LOUISIANA MUSEUM)

32km (20 miles) N of Copenhagen

ESSENTIALS

GETTING THERE **By Train**   Humlebæk is on the Copenhagen–Helsingør train line; there are two trains per hour that leave Copenhagen's main railway station heading toward Humlebæk (trip time: 40 min.). Once you reach Humlebæk, the Louisiana Museum is a 10-minute walk.

By Bus   Take the S-tog train, line A or B, to Lyngby station. From there, take bus no. 388 along the coast road. There's a bus stop at the museum.

By Car   Follow the Strandvej (coastal road no. 152) from Copenhagen. The scenic drive takes about 45 minutes.

SEEING THE SIGHTS

Louisiana Museum of Modern Art ★★★ *Kids*   This museum is situated in a 19th-century mansion on the Danish Riviera surrounded by elegant gardens, opening directly onto the Øresund. Exhibits include paintings and sculptures by modern masters (Giacometti and Henry Moore, to name two) as well as the best and most controversial works of modern art. Look for paintings by Carl-Henning Pedersen. The museum name derives from the fact that the first owner of the estate, Alexander Brun, had three wives—each named Louise.

The museum has one of the largest exhibition spaces in Europe, and major exhibitions of contemporary art are staged here. There is also an extensive program of concerts, lectures, films, discussions with authors, and public debates. Children find their own haven here, especially at the **Børnehuset,** or children's house, and the **Søhaven,** or Sea Garden. The museum's cafe is on a terrace with Alexander Calder's sculptures. Current exhibits include paintings and sculptures by Jørn Utzon, the man behind Sydney's famous Opera House.

Gl. Strandvej 13. © **49-19-07-19.** Admission 74DKK ($12) adults, 67DKK ($11) students, 20DKK ($3.35) children 4–16, free for children 4 and under. Wed 10am–10pm; Thurs–Tues 10am–5pm. Closed Dec 24–25 and Dec 31.

WHERE TO DINE

Louisiana Café DANISH   This is the most obvious luncheon choice for anyone visiting the Louisiana Museum, which is just a short walk away. Built in 1722, the inn is composed of one large dining room and three hideaway rooms richly adorned with rustically elegant accessories. Food selections include a range of open-faced sandwiches, deep-fried filet of plaice with shrimp and mayonnaise sauce, Wiener schnitzel, medallions of veal with morel sauce, and herring with sherry sauce. The cookery is very satisfying in an old-fashioned sort of way.

Gl. Strandvej 13. © **49-19-07-19.** Reservations recommended. Main courses 178DKK–225DKK ($30–$38). AE, DC, MC, V. Daily 11:30am–9:30pm.

RUNGSTEDLUND: HOME OF KAREN BLIXEN
21km (13 miles) N of Copenhagen

GETTING THERE   By Train   From Copenhagen's Central Railroad Station, trains run to Rungsted Kyst every 30 minutes. However, since this rail stop is still half a mile from the museum, it is better to take the train to Klampenborg, where you can board **bus** no. 388, which offers frequent service to a bus stop about a block from the entrance to the museum.

By Car   Head north from Copenhagen along the E4 to Helsingør until you reach the turnoff east marked RUNGSTED.

THE MUSEUM

Since the 1985 release of *Out of Africa,* starring Robert Redford and Meryl Streep, thousands of fans have visited the former home of Baroness Karen Blixen, who wrote under the pen name Isak Dinesen. Her home, Rungstedlund, at Rungsted Strandvej III (© **45-57-10-57**), is midway between Copenhagen and Helsingør on the coastal road.

Karen's father, Wilhelm Dinesen, purchased the estate in 1879. She left in 1914 for Kenya when she married Bror van Blixen Finecke, but returned in 1931 and stayed until her death in 1962. It was at Rungstedlund that Blixen wrote her first major success, *Seven Gothic Tales,* which many consider more memorable than *Out of Africa.* She also wrote collections of stories, *Winter's Tales* and *Last Tales,* here. Before Blixen's father acquired the property, it was called Rungsted Kro (an inn), attracting travelers going north from Copenhagen to Helsingør.

Blixen wrote in Ewald's Room, named in honor of poet Johannes Ewald, who stayed at the place when it was an inn. Before her death, Blixen established the Rungstedlund Foundation, which owns the property and its 16-hectare (40-acre) garden and bird sanctuary. The gardens have long been open to the public, but in 1991 the foundation invited Queen Margrethe to open the museum.

In one part of the museum is a small gallery with exhibits in oil, pastel, and charcoal—all by Blixen. The museum is filled with photographs, manuscripts, and memorabilia that document Blixen's life in both Africa and Denmark.

Visitors pay 40DKK ($6.70) to enter, although children under 12 go free. It's open May to September, Tuesday to Sunday 10am to 5pm; October to April, Wednesday to Friday 1 to 4pm and Saturday and Sunday 11am to 4pm.

Blixen is buried in the grave at the foot of Edwaldshøj.

WHERE TO DINE

Restaurant Nokken ★★ DANISH/SEAFOOD   Amid light-grained paneling and nautical accessories, a short walk downhill from Karen Blixen's house, with views that extend across the water as far as Sweden, you can enjoy one of the best meals to be found along the Danish Riviera. You'll find it near the sea-battered piers next to the harbors, a fact that gives it a raffish feeling despite its reputation for well-prepared, savory fish and seafood. There's a bar near the entrance that's a hangout for boat owners and local residents, and when you eventually get hungry, head for the dining room. The specialty is a seafood platter piled high with mussels, shrimp, oysters, and lobster. There are also fish dishes, including filets of lemon sole with hollandaise sauce, or you can try the roasted Danish lamb, the scampi with sweet-and-sour sauce. The cuisine is generous, uncomplicated, and always fresh.

Rungsted Havn 44. ℂ **45-57-13-14.** Reservations recommended. Lunch platters 79DKK–190DKK ($13–$32); dinner main courses 190DKK–215DKK ($32–$36); fixed-price menu 285DKK ($48). AE, DC, MC, V. Daily noon–4:30pm and 5:30–10:30pm.

5

North Zealand

Close to seashores, lakes, fishing villages, and woodlands, North Zealand is often called "Royal North Zealand," because of its associations with the royal family of Denmark. In July, the Queen throws open the doors of her summer place at Fredensborg and invites the public in. Of course, many rushed visitors, after seeing Copenhagen, schedule a brief visit to "Hamlet's Castle" at Helsingør—and that's it for North Zealand.

But those with more time and interest will find a wealth of attractions here. Two of the more famous, the Louisiana Museum of Modern Art at Humlebæk and the home of Isak Dinesen (Karen Blixen) at Rungstedlund, are so close to Copenhagen that they're practically viewed as part of the capital itself. For information on them, refer to "Side Trips from Copenhagen," in chapter 4.

It will take days just to see some of the highlights, which range from Frederiksborg Castle at Hillerød (not to be confused with Helsingør); the home of explorer Knid Rasmussen, near Hundested; and the cathedral and the Viking Ship Museum at Roskilde, the old capital of Denmark.

Don't overlook the possibility of a beach outing, although you may at first think the water is better suited for polar bears. Wherever you stay in North Zealand, you are not far from a beach. A blue flag flying over the beach indicates that its waters are clean. Danes don't use their beaches just on summer days. Even on a blustery autumn afternoon, or when the Nordic winds of spring are still cold, you'll find them walking along the strands, smelling the fresh air, and listening to the crashing of waves. They even visit their beaches on crisp, fresh winter days for long walks.

If you can't make it to Norway, you can sample "Fjord Country" in Denmark. Around the fjords of Roskilde and Isefjord are charming towns such as Hundested, with its beautiful light (praised by artists) and its bustling harbor, and Frederiksværk, with its canal system. On the gentle banks of Isefjord you'll find such lively centers as Holbæk and Roskilde itself ("the town of kings").

For North Zealand rail information, you can call the main station in Copenhagen (see chapter 4). For train and bus information within Denmark call © **70-13-14-15.**

1 Hillerød

35km (22 miles) NW of Copenhagen

Hillerød offers some interesting sights, including one of Scandinavia's most beautiful castles. The ideal time to visit is during its summer Viking festival (see below). But there's always something of interest here, as Hillerød lies in the heart of North Zealand, surrounded by some of the most beautiful and extensive woodlands in Denmark.

The city's history goes back 4 centuries; its status rose significantly in 1602 when Christian IV began the construction of Frederiksborg Castle (see below).

The wide forests around Hillerød remain as vestiges of the prehistoric North Zealand wilderness. To the south sprawl the woodlands of Store Dyrehave, and to the north stretch the forests of **Gribskov,** the second largest in the country. The forests are still rich in game, notably the pale, tail-less roe deer. Gribskov forest contains some 800 fallow deer distinguished by their white-speckled hide. The philosopher Søren Kierkegaard reveled in the tranquillity of these forests.

Leaflets outlining the best walks and trails to follow in Gribskov and Store Dyrehave are available at the tourist office (see below).

Close at hand is **Esrum Sø,** a lake popular with bathers, sail-sports enthusiasts, and anglers alike. The western shores of the lake are fringed by Gribskov. The parklands of Fredensborg Palace and Skipperhuset (Skipper's Cabin) lie on the eastern shores, the point of embarkation for a sailing trip on Esrum Sø.

ESSENTIALS

GETTING THERE   The S-tog from Copenhagen arrives every 10 minutes throughout the day (trip time: 40 min.).

By Train   Trains link Hillerød with Helsingør in the east, and there are also rail links with Gilleleje and Tisvildeleje.

By Bus   Hillerød has good bus connections with the major towns of North Zealand: bus no. 305 from Gilleleje; bus nos. 306, 336, and 339 from Hornbæk; and bus nos. 336 and 339 from Fredensborg.

By Car   From Copenhagen, take Route 16 north.

VISITOR INFORMATION   The **tourist office,** Møllestræde 9 (© **48-24-26-26**), is open daily Monday to Friday 10am to 5pm and Saturday 10am to 1pm.

SPECIAL EVENTS   One of the most important Viking festivals in Scandinavia takes place every year near Hillerød. **Frederikssund** is a town 13km (8 miles) southwest of Hillerød and 48km (30 miles) northwest of Copenhagen. It stages a 2-week **Viking festival** ✵ each summer where Nordic sagas are revived—and the record is set straight about who "discovered" America 5 centuries before Christopher Columbus. The festival features a series of plays, medieval and modern, about the Vikings.

The festival begins in mid-June. The traditional play is performed nightly at 8pm, and a Viking banquet follows. Tickets for the festival are 110DKK ($18) adults, 25DKK ($4.20) children 5 to 12 (it's not suitable for children 4 and under). The dinner costs 150DKK ($25) adults, 75DKK ($13) children 5 to 12. Trains depart for Frederikssund at 20-minute intervals from Copenhagen's Central Railroad Station (trip time: 50 min.), and there are enough trains back to Copenhagen after the spectacle ends to allow commutes from the capital. From the station at Frederikssund, it's a 20-minute walk to the site of the pageant. For details, contact the tourist information office in Copenhagen or phone the Frederikssund Tourist Office (© **47-31-06-85**).

SEEING THE SIGHTS

Det Nationalhistoriske Museum på Frederiksborg (Frederiksborg Castle) ✵✵✵   This *slot* (castle) with a moat, known as the Danish Versailles, is the major castle in Scandinavia, constructed on three islands in a lake. Like Kronborg, it was built in Dutch Renaissance style (red brick, copper roof, sandstone facade). The oldest parts date from 1560 and the reign of Frederik II. His son, Christian IV, erected the main part of the castle from 1600 to 1620. Danish

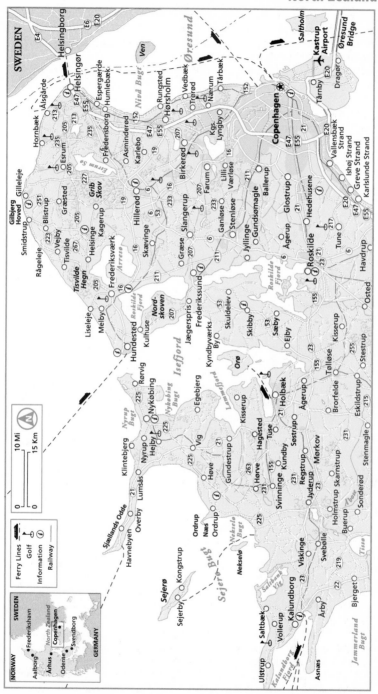

monarchs used it for some 2 centuries. From 1671 to 1840, Danish kings were crowned in Christian IV's chapel, which is still used as a parish church. Since 1693 it has been a chapel for the knights of the Order of the Elephant and of the Grand Cross of Danneborg. Standing in the gallery is an old organ built by Esaias Compenius in 1610. Every Thursday from 1:30 to 2pm, the chapel organist plays for museum visitors.

Since 1878 the castle has housed the Museum of National History. Founded by the brewer J. C. Jacobsen as part of the Carlsberg Foundation, it encompasses the Great Hall and the former Audience Chamber of Danish monarchs. The museum contains the most important collection of portraits and historical paintings in the country. The collection illustrates Danish history from the 16th century to today. The 20th-century collection was added on the third floor in 1993.

The castle is a 15-minute walk or a short taxi ride from the train station.

In Frederiksborg Slot. ✆ **48-26-04-39**. Admission 60DKK ($10) adults, 15DKK ($2.50) children 6–15, free for children under 6. Nov–Mar daily 11am–3pm; Apr–Oct daily 10am–5pm. Bus: 701 from Hillerød Station.

Frederiksborg Castle Garden ✿   This baroque garden north of the castle, laid out by Frederik IV in the early 18th century, became one of the finest in the country. The royal architect and landscape designer, Johan Cornelius Krieger, was responsible for its final appearance.

The gardens were built around a central axis, creating a sense of continuity between building, garden, and the open land. A cascade with water canals and fountains was built along the main axis. Symmetrically surrounding the cascades were avenues, groves, and a parterre sporting royal monograms. The parterre was planted with box hedges in the exact manner in which King Frederik had seen similar gardens in France and Italy. The garden existed for 40 years and enjoyed the patronage of three kings—Frederik IV, Christian VI, and Frederik V.

The last remains of the cascade were removed during the reign of Christian VII (1766–1808), presumably because the garden had grown out of style and become too expensive to maintain. By 1993, only the terraced ground, avenues in decay, and deformed box hedges remained from the original baroque garden. But in 1996, the baroque garden was re-created. As many as 65,000 box plants and 166 pyramid-shaped yews have been planted in the parterre, while 375 limes and 7,000 hornbeam plants create the avenues and groves. The cascade floor consists of nearly half a kilometer (¼ mile) of dressed granite stones. During the summer, the Frederiksborg Castle Garden forms the venue for several recurring concerts, maypole celebrations, and other cultural events.

Rendelæggerbakken 3. ✆ **48-26-04-39**. Free admission. May–Aug daily 10am–9pm; Sept and Apr daily 10am–7pm; Oct and Mar daily 10am–5pm; Nov–Feb daily 10am–4pm. Bus: 701 from Hillerød Station.

Nordsjællandsk Folkemuseet (North Zealand Folk Museum)   This museum's collections depict the rural history of North Zealand, with special emphasis on the pre-industrialization era in Hillerød.

There are supplementary displays at **Sophienborg,** Sophienborg Allé (✆ **48-24-34-48;** bus: 734 from Hillerød station), an estate on the western outskirts of Hillerød. By car, take either Frederiksværksgade or Herredsvejen, turn right at Tulstrupvej, and follow the signs to the Folkemuseet Sophienborg. It keeps the same hours as the folk museum, and admission is on the same ticket.

Abelholt Klostermuseum, Abelholt 4 (✆ **48-21-03-51**), the ruins of an Augustinian monastery founded in 1175, is 6km (3¾ miles) west of Hillerød. A museum on this site—housed in the ruins—exhibits skeletons dating from the medieval period. Healing methods used by these early monks are also revealed. You can wander through a medicinal garden adjoining the museum. This satellite keeps different hours from the other two locations: In March, April and October, its hours are Saturday and Sunday 1 to 4pm; from May to August, hours are Tuesday through Sunday 10am to 4pm; and in September, hours are Tuesday through Sunday 1 to 4pm.

Helsingørsgade 65. (℃ **48-24-34-48.** Admission 15DKK ($2.50) adults, free for children. Tues–Sun 11am–4pm. Closed Nov–Feb.

SHOPPING

The town is loaded with shopping possibilities. In the town center is the sprawl-ing **SlotsArkaderne** shopping center, close to Frederiksborg Castle, with an entrance on Nordstensvej. Opened in 1992, its distinctive interior design has been hailed throughout Denmark. It is definitely shopper-friendly. Within the center are some 50 specialty shops. The center is one of the most beautiful shop-ping malls in Europe. Shops here are open Monday to Friday 10am to 7pm and Saturday 10am to 4pm.

There are a number of specialty stores throughout the town. Right in front of the castle, **Sweater House,** Slangerupgade 1 (℃ **48-25-51-25**), offers the town's best selection of Scandinavian sweaters, often in blue and white patterns. The best selection of leather goods is at **Laederhuset Husted,** Helsingørsgade 11 (℃ **48-26-02-54**). Since Danish toys enjoy world renown, you might want to check out the selection at **Fætter BR,** SlotsArkaderne 27 (℃ **48-26-07-55**).

WHERE TO STAY

Although the hotel recommended below is fine, many guests prefer the more glamorous Fredensborg Store Kro (see below).

Hotel Hillerød   This hotel offers clean, well-maintained accommodations within a modern design, and it's just a short walk south of the town's commer-cial and monumental core. Low-slung, and evocative of a motel you might find on the outskirts of a large American city, it offers rooms with Danish modern furniture and neatly kept bathrooms with shower units. Each has a terrace or balcony, and most have a small kitchenette. Breakfast is the only meal served.

Milnersvej 41, DK-3400 Hillerød. (℃ **48-24-08-00.** Fax 48-24-08-74. www.hotelhillerod.dk. 74 units, 63 with kitchenette. 1,081DKK ($181) double. Rates include breakfast. AE, DC, MC, V. **Amenities:** Breakfast room; lounge; laundry service; dry cleaning; nonsmoking rooms; rooms for those with limited mobility. *In room:* TV, minibar, coffeemaker, hair dryer, trouser press, safe.

WHERE TO DINE

John F. Kennedy Pub-Café DANISH/INTERNATIONAL   Set on the main square of Hillerød, its name was selected in 1996 by the owner, an avid fan of virtually everything associated with the memory of JFK. During the day this place mainly functions as a cafe and restaurant, where menu items include New Orleans–style barbecue, grilled shrimp, club sandwiches, and pastas. However, when the food service winds down, beginning around 7pm, it transforms itself into a bar designed for drinking, talking, and flirting. Action spills over onto an outdoor terrace, and every Friday and Saturday an annex room is transformed into a dance club, **Club Annabell.** Entry is 50DKK ($8.35); a bottle of Carls-berg goes for 25DKK ($4.20). No one under age 25 is allowed inside.

Torvet 4. (℃ **48-26-04-05.** Fixed-price meals 68DKK–175DKK ($11–$29). AE, DC, MC, V. May–Sept Mon–Sat 2–11pm; Oct–Apr Tues–Sat 11am–7pm. Bar until 2am year-round.

Spisestedet Leonora 🍴 DANISH   Since the 1970s this well-managed tavern has flourished in the former Frederiksborg Castle stables. It's the most sought-after dining spot in town for anyone visiting the castle, partly because of its array of carefully crafted open-faced sandwiches. The place also serves grilled meats, salads, and platters of food, which usually compose meals in themselves.

Frederiksborg Slot. (℗ **48-26-75-16.** Main courses 55DKK–125DKK ($9.20–$21); lunch plate 98DKK ($16); smørrebrød 42DKK–98DKK ($7–$16). DC, MC, V. Daily 10am–5pm. Closed 1 week at Christmas. Bus: 701.

Slotskroen 🍴 DANISH   Either before or after a visit to the castle, this is the nearest, most convenient, and most appealing luncheon stopover. It has been serving hungry passersby since 1794, when it was inaugurated as an inn. Nowadays, food is served only at lunchtime (although on rare occasions, dinner is served). Within a trio of cozy and historic-looking dining rooms, some of whose windows open onto direct views of the nearby castle, you can enjoy access to a smörgåsbord that's laden with hot and cold dishes, several kinds of open-faced Danish sandwiches, *frikadeller* (meatballs), and salads. Otherwise, fixed-price menus might include any of several kinds of herring, Wiener schnitzel, and a well-flavored version of beefsteak with mushrooms, bacon, bread, and butter. There's also an outdoor terrace for use during warm weather.

Slotsgade 67. (℗ **48-26-01-82.** Smörgåsbord buffet 395DKK ($66). AE, DC, MC, V. Daily noon–5pm.

HILLERØD AFTER DARK

The best place to go is the **John F. Kennedy Pub-Café** (see "Where to Dine," above), which transforms itself into **Club Annabell** at night.

A CASTLE, AN ART MUSEUM & RUINS

Hillerød makes a good center for exploring neighboring attractions.

From the center of Hillerød, take Route 6 south, following the signs to København. At Route 53, turn west. Fifty-five kilometers (34 miles) from Hillerød you'll come to **Selsø Slot,** Selsøvej 30 ((℗ **47-52-01-71**), Denmark's first Renaissance castle, built in 1576 and renovated in the baroque style in 1733. Located at Hornsherred, east of Skibby, south of Skuldelev, and 56km (35 miles) west of Copenhagen, Selsø is one of the few private manor houses on Zealand that can be thoroughly explored.

The Great Hall and adjoining rooms are maintained as they were in 1733, with 4-meter (13-ft.) marble panels, ornate plaster ceilings, and fine paintings. A children's room with hundreds of tin soldiers, the cellar, vaults dating from around 1560, an old manor kitchen with open fireplace and a scullery, old tools, and a dungeon below the gatehouse—all these features are worth seeing. Cultural events, such as orchestral concerts, are staged annually.

Admission is 40DKK ($6.70) adults, 10DKK ($1.65) children. The castle is open mid-June to mid-August, daily 1 to 4pm; and mid-August to late October, Saturday and Sunday 1 to 4pm (closed otherwise).

Frederikssund (see above) is usually visited at the time of its Viking pageant. But the opening of an art museum here in 1957 made the hamlet a year-round attraction. **J. F. Willumsen's Museum,** Jenriksvej 4 ((℗ **47-31-07-73**), is devoted to the paintings, drawings, engravings, sculpture, ceramics, and photographs of the well-known Danish artist, J. F. Willumsen (1863–1958), one of Denmark's leading symbolists. The artist spent most of his creative years in France. The museum also displays the works of other artists which were once part of Willumsen's private collection. Hours are daily year-round 10am to 4pm.

Admission is 35DKK ($5.85) adults, 15DKK ($2.50) students, free for children under age 15. From Hillerød, take Route 6 south, following the signs to Copenhagen. At Route 53 head west. The total distance is 40km (25 miles).

2 Fredensborg (⋆)

9.5km (6 miles) W of Helsingør; 40km (25 miles) N of Copenhagen

On the southeast shore of Esrum Sø, the country's second largest lake, Fredensborg is visited mainly for its royal palace. Many visitors rush through, visiting the palace and then departing immediately. However, you can stay and dine in the area and enjoy a number of other attractions as well (see below).

The first inhabitants of the town were people who helped serve the royal court. But over the years others moved in, and today the town is a lively little place even when the Queen isn't in residence. To Denmark, it occupies a position somewhat similar to Windsor in England. The town is home to some 40 specialty shops.

The palace is a major backdrop for events in the life of the royal family—weddings, birthday parties, and the like. Heads of states from many of the countries of the world are received here when they pay state visits. And foreign ambassadors present their credentials to the monarch here as well.

ESSENTIALS

GETTING THERE   By Train   From Copenhagen's Central Railroad Station, frequent trains run to Fredensborg. There are no buses.

By Car   From Copenhagen, head north on the E55 toward Helsingør, turning west on Route 6.

VISITOR INFORMATION   The **Fredensborg Turistinformation,** Slotsgade 2 (© **48-48-21-00**), is open Monday to Friday 10am to 4pm.

EXPLORING THE AREA

Esrum Sø ⋆ not only is the second largest lake in Denmark, but it's also exceptionally deep: 22m (72 ft.) in some places. Since 1949, the land around the lake has been protected by the government. Increasingly it is a winter feeding ground for large numbers of waterfowl. You can enjoy a trip on the lake if for no other reason than to admire the flocks of noble swans—there's not an "Ugly Duckling" among them.

If the weather is good enough and there's enough business to warrant its departure, a local outfitter, **Færgefart Bådudlejning på Esrum Sø,** Skipperhuset, in the village of Sørup (© **48-48-01-07**), leads tours in an open boat through the lake's shallow waters. The emphasis is on ecology, and the tour is conducted in Danish with halting English and German explanations added afterward. The duration of the tour is around 45 minutes, and the cost of participating is 50DKK ($8.35).

Esrum Kloster, Klostergade 11, Esrum (© **48-36-04-00**), was founded in 1151 and has a long and ancient history. Eleven monks arrived to lay the foundation stone of what later became the abbey, surrounded by forest, meadows, lake, and fields. The Middle Ages come alive here as you view the second-floor exhibit of the monastic period. Until the Reformation, the cloisters functioned as one of the most important Cistercian monasteries in Scandinavia.

The mounted exhibition gives you an idea of the layout of the monastery and the everyday life of the monks. The exhibition on the main floor deals with Esrum Abbey after the Reformation. The cloisters underwent many changes, becoming a royal hunting lodge, a base for a regiment of dragoons, a stud farm for horses, even a post office and district tax office. As a result of King Frederik II's horse-breeding interests, the fabled Frederiksborg horse was produced, highly prized for its skill and stamina.

In addition to the exhibitions, regular concerts and theatrical performances are staged here, both inside and outside the monastery.

The abbey is open January 6 to May 14 Thursday to Sunday 10am to 4pm; May 15 to June 16 and August 1 to October 17 Tuesday to Sunday 10am to 4pm; June 17 to 30 Friday to Wednesday 10am to 4pm, Thursday 10am to 9pm; July Friday to Wednesday 10am to 5pm and Thursday 10am to 9pm; October 18 to December 18 Thursday to Sunday 10am to 4pm. It's closed December 19 to January 5. Admission is 40DKK ($6.70), 20DKK ($3.35) for children.

From Fredensborg, you can get to Esrum by bus (marked ESRUM), getting off at Hovedgaden. From here, walk for less than half a kilometer (¼ mile) along the Klostergade, which leads you to the entrance of the abbey. Motorists can take Route 205 north from Fredensborg.

From Hillerød to Esrum, you can take bus nos. 305, 306, or 331, a 25-minute ride, for around 20DKK ($3.35).

Fredensborg Slot ★   This is the summer residence of the Danish royal family. Although the palace has been added on to many times, it still retains its baroque, rococo, and classic features. The palace was celebrated during the reign of Christian IX, who assembled the greats of European royalty here in the days of Queen Victoria. When the queen is in residence, visitors assemble at noon to watch the changing of the guard. On Thursdays, except in July, the queen often appears to acknowledge a regimental band concert in her honor.

The Danish architect J. D. Krieger built the palace for King Frederik IV. Originally there was only the main building with a Cupola Hall. Over the years the palace was extended with such additions as the Chancellery House and the Cavaliers Wing. Though hardly one of the impressive royal palaces of Europe, it has its own charm, especially in the Domed Hall and the Garden Room.

The palace opens onto a 275-year-old baroque garden. A public part of the palace garden is open year-round, but the private, reserved royal garden is open only in July, daily 9am to 5pm. The orangery in the royal garden is also open in July, daily 1 to 4:30pm. These are some of the largest and best-preserved gardens in Denmark. Note how strictly symmetrical and geometrical the shapes are. Drawing on Italian designs for their inspiration, Frederik IV and J. C. Krieger laid out the palace gardens in the 1720s. In the 1760s Frederik V redesigned the garden, adding elements from French baroque horticulture.

Slottet. ② **33-40-31-87.** Admission 40DKK ($6.70) adults, 15DKK ($2.50) children. Palace July daily 1–5pm. Joint ticket for the Palace and the Orangery and Herb Garden: 60DKK ($10) for adults and 25DKK ($4.20) for children.

WHERE TO STAY

Endruplund Country House ★ *(Finds*   Set less than a kilometer (about ½ mile) northeast of Fredensborg's center, this is a former farmhouse (ca. 1900) that was purchased by the present owner's parents in 1926. Today, you'll find comfortable, charmingly eccentric rooms, each personalized by the hardworking efforts of the inn's owner, Karen Windinge, whose critically acclaimed dried-flower arrangements are artfully scattered throughout her comfortable and eclectically decorated guesthouse. About half of the rooms share a bathroom with a shower unit. No meals are served other than breakfast.

Holmeskovvej 5, DK-3480 Fredensborg. ℂ **48-48-02-38**. Fax 48-48-35-17. www.countryhouse.dk. 17 units, 11 with bathroom. 380DKK ($63) double without bathroom; 420DKK ($70) double with bathroom. MC, V. From Fredensborg's center, follow the signs to Helsingør. **Amenities:** Breakfast room; lounge. *In room:* No phone.

Fredensborg Store Kro ★★

A 10-minute walk from the train station and 5 minutes from Esrum Lake, this is one of the most venerable old inns in Zealand. It was commissioned in 1723 by Frederik IV. Since it was right next door to Fredensborg Castle, many guests of the royal family have stayed here. No two rooms are alike, but all are equally charming. Taste and elegance rule throughout. Over the years such modern extras as private bathrooms with tub/shower combinations have been added. Ask for a room with a view of the palace—although only five are available, and they are of course the most requested. In 1997 President Clinton dropped into the inn for a look when he was visiting the queen at Fredensborg. The hotel restaurant is the finest in the area (see "Where to Dine," below). Concierge, billiards, and a dart room are available.

Slotsgade 6, DK-3480 Fredensborg. ℂ **48-40-01-11**. www.fredensborg.storekro.dk. 49 units. 1,500DKK–1,700DKK ($251–$284) double; 2,100DKK ($351) suite. Rates include breakfast. AE, DC, MC, V. Bus: 336 or 733E. **Amenities:** Restaurant; bar; room service (7am–11pm); laundry service; dry cleaning; rooms for those with limited mobility. *In room:* TV, dataport, minibar, hair dryer.

Pension Bondehuset

This compound of Dutch-roofed buildings at the edge of Esrum Lake was originally constructed in the 1700s by the local shipbuilder less than a kilometer (about ½ mile) south of the center of Fredensborg. For years, it functioned as a boatyard and repair site for watercraft on the lake, but since the Larsen family took over, it has been a cozy and sought-after hotel. Part of its allure derives from its brightly colored public areas with plush furnishings. Rooms are outfitted in sedate, eminently tasteful motifs similar to what you'd expect in a private manor house. All units have well-maintained bathrooms with tub/shower combinations.

Sørupvej 14, DK-3480 Fredensborg. ℂ **48-48-01-12**. Fax 48-48-03-01. www.bondehuset.dk. 15 units. 1,350DKK ($225) double. Rates include half-board. DC, MC, V. **Amenities:** Dining room; bar; lounge. *In room:* Hair dryer.

WHERE TO DINE

Fredensborg Store Kro Restaurant ★ DANISH/INTERNATIONAL

When the weather is warm, the garden here is ideal for lunch and dinner; otherwise, you can retreat into the elegant dining room where the service and staff are top-rate. The cooking is not only delicious—it's sometimes inspired. You might start with pigeon stuffed with apricots and served with arugula and balsamic vinegar. Go on to such delights as grilled veal with kidney and spinach, accompanied by a Madeira sauce, or else grilled angler served with a tomato compote and a mussel cream sauce. The specialty here is *canard a la presse,* using the same recipe as the celebrated dish served at the Tour d'Argent in Paris. Here it comes with a red wine sauce, cayenne, lemon and orange flavors, and, of course, foie gras. The fresh salmon and monkfish served with beet root, spinach leaves, and salmon roe—delicately flavored with dill—is worthy enough to invite the Queen over from the palace to join you. For dessert, there's nothing better than the meringue pie stuffed with fresh fruit sorbet.

Slotsgade 6. ℂ **48-40-01-11**. Reservations recommended. Main courses 215DKK–275DKK ($36–$46). AE, DC, MC, V. Daily noon–3pm and 6–10pm.

Prinsessen DANISH/FRENCH   This small, family-run restaurant a short walk from Fredensborg Castle has a lot of panache, verve, and sensitivity. Originally built in the 1930s, the premises might remind you of a small-scale villa. Inside, you'll find a trio of cozy dining rooms, a cuisine that focuses on Danish and French dishes, and food items that include chateaubriand, Wiener schnitzels, French-style beef with horseradish sauce, several different preparations of herring and salmon, and freshly made dessert pastries. At any time, if the more substantial offerings don't appeal to you, you can order any of at least a dozen artfully contrived *smørrebrød* (open-faced sandwiches).

Slotsgade 3A. ℭ **48-48-01-25.** Reservations recommended. Main courses 80DKK–286DKK ($13–$48). Fixed-price menu 268DKK–289DKK ($45–$48). MC, V. Daily noon–11pm.

Restaurant Skipperhuset ✭ *Finds*   DANISH/FRENCH   Part of the experience of dining at this restaurant is the pleasant path you'll use to reach it—a long promenade lined with trees originally laid out as one of the decorative avenues associated with Fredensborg Palace. Today, this much-altered former boathouse functions as a well-respected restaurant where cuisine manages to combine elements of both the Danish and the French traditions. The cooks here have experience and an expert sense of precise, clear flavors. Menu items include breast of chicken stewed with young vegetables and summer cabbage; fried mackerel with spinach, apples, olives, and lemon-thyme sauce; and a dessert specialty of stewed rhubarb with sugared biscuits.

Skipperallee 6. ℭ **48-48-17-17.** Reservations recommended. Main courses 168DKK–188DKK ($28–$31); fixed-price menus 288DKK–368DKK ($48–$61). AE, MC, V. Tues–Sun noon–5pm and 6–9:30pm (last order).

3 Helsingør (Elsinore): In Search of Hamlet ✭

40km (25 miles) N of Copenhagen; 24km (15 miles) NE of Hillerød; 72km (45 miles) NE of Roskilde

Once you reach Helsingør, usually by train from Copenhagen, you'll be in the center of town and can cover all the major attractions on foot. Helsingør ("Elsinore" in English) is visited chiefly for "Hamlet's Castle." Aside from its literary associations, the town has a certain charm: a quiet market square, medieval lanes, and old half-timbered and brick buildings—remains of its once-prosperous shipping industry.

In 1429 King Erik of Pomerania ruled that ships passing Helsingør had to pay a toll for sailing within local waters. The town quickly developed into the focal point for international shipping, bringing in a lot of revenue. King Erik also constructed the Castle of Krogen, later rebuilt by Christian IV as the Castle of Kronborg. For a while Helsingør prospered and grew so much that it was the second-largest town in the country.

ESSENTIALS

GETTING THERE   By Train   There are frequent trains from Copenhagen (trip time: 50 min.).

By Car   Take E-4 north from Copenhagen.

By Ferry   Ferries ply the waters of the narrow channel separating Helsingør (Denmark) from Helsingborg (Sweden) in less than 25 minutes. They're operated around the clock by **Scandlines** (ℭ **33-15-15-15;** www.scandlines.dk), which charges 18DKK ($3) each way for a pedestrian without a car, and

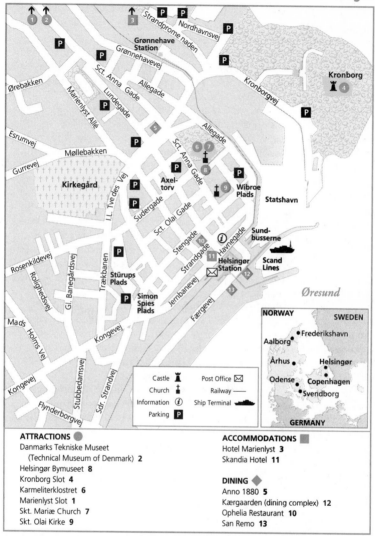

ATTRACTIONS ●
Danmarks Tekniske Museet
  (Technical Museum of Denmark) **2**
Helsingør Bymuseet **8**
Kronborg Slot **4**
Karmeliterklostret **6**
Marienlyst Slot **1**
Skt. Mariæ Church **7**
Skt. Olai Kirke **9**

ACCOMMODATIONS ■
Hotel Marienlyst **3**
Skandia Hotel **11**

DINING ◆
Anno 1880 **5**
Kærgaarden (dining complex) **12**
Ophelia Restaurant **10**
San Remo **13**

230DKK ($38) each way for a car with up to five persons inside. Between 6am and 11pm, departures are every 20 minutes; 11pm to 6am, departures are timed at intervals of 40 to 80 minutes. The process is simple and straightforward: You simply drive your car onboard and wait in your car. Border formalities during the crossing between Denmark and Sweden are perfunctory, and although you should carry a passport, you might not even be asked for it.

VISITOR INFORMATION   The **tourist office,** at Havnepladsen 3 (© **49-21-13-33**), is open Monday to Thursday 9am to 5pm; Friday 9am to 6pm; and Saturday 10am to 3pm.

SEEING THE SIGHTS

Kronborg Slot ★★★   There is no evidence that Shakespeare ever saw this sandstone-and-copper Dutch Renaissance–style castle, full of intriguing secret passages, but he made it famous in *Hamlet*. If Hamlet had really lived, it would have been centuries before Kronborg was built (1574–85). Over the years a number of productions of the Shakespearean play have been staged here, with Richard Burton and Claire Bloom in 1954 and Sir Derek Jacobi in 1979.

The castle, on a peninsula jutting out into Øresund, was restored in 1629 by Christian IV after it had been gutted by fire. Other events in its history include looting, bombardment, occupation by Swedes, and use as a barracks (1785–1922). The facade is covered with sandstone, and the entire castle is surrounded by a deep moat. You approach the castle via a wooden bridge and by going through Mørkeport, a gate from the 16th century. This will lead you to the main courtyard of Kronborg. Instead of entering the castle at once, you can walk around the moat to the waterfront, where you can view a spectacular vista of the Swedish coast. At the platform—backed by massive bronze guns—Hamlet is said to have seen the ghost of his father, shrouded in pea-soup fog.

The starkly furnished Great Hall is the largest in northern Europe. Originally 40 tapestries portraying 111 Danish kings were hung around this room on special occasions. They were commissioned by Frederik II and produced around 1585. Only seven remain at Kronborg; the rest have disappeared except for seven in the Nationalmuseet in Copenhagen. The church, with its original oak furnishings and the royal chambers, is worth exploring. The bleak and austere atmosphere adds to the drama. Holger Danske, a mythological hero who is believed to assist Denmark whenever the country is threatened, is said to live in the basement. Also on the premises is the **Danish Maritime Museum** (✆ **49-21-06-85**), which explores the history of Danish shipping.

Guided tours are given every half-hour October to April. In summer you can walk around on your own. The castle is less than a kilometer (about ½ mile) from the rail station. On November 30, 2000, Kronborg was added to UNESCO's World Heritage List.

Kronborg. ✆ **49-21-30-78.** www.kronborgcastle.com. Admission 50DKK ($8.35) adults, 15DKK ($2.50) children 6–14, free for children under 6. Joint ticket for the castle and the Danish Maritime Museum 75DKK ($13) adults, 25DKK ($4.20) children. May–Sept daily 10:30am–5pm; Apr and Oct Tues–Sun 11am–4pm; Nov–Mar Tues–Sun 11am–3pm. Closed Dec 25.

Karmeliterklostret   This 15th-century former Carmelite monastery is the best of its kind in Scandinavia. After the Reformation it became a hospital, but by 1630 it was a poorhouse. It's at the intersection of Havnegade and Kronborgvej.

Skt. Annagade 38. ✆ **49-21-17-74.** Admission 20DKK ($3.35) adults, 5DKK (85¢) children. Guided tours mid-May to mid-Sept daily at 2pm.

Skt. Mariæ Church   A monastery complex with late-15th-century frescoes, St. Mary's also contains the organ—which is still in use—played by baroque composer Dietrich Buxtehude from 1660 to 1668. The church is located near the intersection of Havnegade and Kronborgvej.

Skt. Annagade 38. ✆ **49-21-17-74.** Free admission. Thurs 4–6pm; Fri–Wed 9am–noon. Guided tours May 16–Sept 15 Mon–Fri at 2pm, 20DKK ($3.35) adults, 5DKK (85¢) children.

Skt. Olai's Kirke   Built between 1480 and 1559, this christening chapel is worth a visit. The interior of the church, and the baptistery in particular, are one-of-a-kind. The spired church is connected to the Carmelite cloisters. The church lies near the intersection of Havnegade and Kronborgvej.

Skt. Annagade 12. Ⓒ **49-21-04-43**. Free admission. May–Aug Mon–Sat 10am–4pm; Sept–Apr daily 10am–2pm.

Helsingør Bymuseet   Installed in part of the Karmeliterklostret (see above), this museum houses the town's historic archives and various exhibits. Of special interest are 15th-century items related to Helsingør's collection of duties in the sound. The exhibits present materials on the various trades practiced in days gone by, including a printing house. There's a collection of about 200 antique dolls, and the museum also has a fine-scale model of the town around 1801. It's a short walk from bus, train, and ferryboat stations.

Helsingørsgade 65. Ⓒ **49-28-18-30**. Admission 15DKK ($2.50) adults, free for children. May–Oct Tues–Sun 11am–4pm.

Marienlyst Slot   The French architect N. H. Jardin built Marienlyst from 1759 to 1763 in a neoclassical style. The building was intended to be a royal summer home, but was never used as such. Up until 1953 it served as a private residence. Today it's a museum, with well-preserved interiors in the original Louis XVI style and a permanent collection of paintings from Helsingør, along with an exhibit of silver works. Special exhibits are arranged upstairs in summer. A fine park surrounds the castle, and there's a panoramic view of the sound from the top of a steep slope behind the castle.

Marienlyst Allé 32. Ⓒ **49-28-18-30**. Admission 30DKK ($5) adults, free for children. Daily noon–4pm.

Danmarks Tekniske Museet (Technical Museum of Denmark) ★ (Finds)   This museum offers technical, industrial, scientific, and transportation exhibits, including the oldest Danish airplanes and trains, the world's first typewriter, and the world's first electromagnetic sound recorder (tape recorder). There's also an 1888 Danish automobile, the Hammelvognen. In the southern part of town, the museum has taken over a former iron foundry. There is an impressive collection of steam engines, electric appliances, bicycles, cars, and airplanes. A pewter workshop has been installed as well. In the exhibit devoted to communications, you can see Valdemar Poulsen's invention, the Telegraphone, which is the forerunner of the modern tape recording. In the aviation area, there are some 30 airplanes displayed, ranging from gyrocopters to helicopters, even a complete Caravella airliner. As a curiosity, seek out an airplane, the "Danish Edison," invented by J. C. Ellhammer. Danes will tell you he was the first in flight in Europe in 1906, but his feats were never recorded. Among the automobiles on display, the best known is the Hammel car from 1888. This is thought to be the oldest original automobile in running condition.

Fabriksvej 25. Ⓒ **49-22-26-11**. Admission Jan 2–Apr 30 and Oct 1–Dec 30 50DKK ($8.35) adults, 25DKK ($4.20) children; May–Sept 65DKK ($11) adults, 25DKK ($4.20) children. Tues–Sun 10am–5pm.

WHERE TO STAY

Hotel Marienlyst ★   On the western outskirts of town beyond the castle, this hotel is about as close to Las Vegas as you'll get in Denmark. Composed of three buildings, its headquarters and oldest core were built around 1850, while the largest of its annexes went up in the mid-1970s. With a panoramic view over the gray sea toward Sweden, this hotel contains a glossy outbuilding with one of only six gambling casinos in Denmark. Rooms are a study in sleek Nordic styling—comfortable and beautifully maintained. The bathrooms are neatly kept, with tub/shower combinations. Many rooms have balconies or terraces, and 86 have a view of the sound. The suites and apartments have a kitchen and dishwasher.

Nordre Strandvej 2, DK-3000 Helsingør. (C) **49-21-40-00.** Fax 49-21-49-00. www.marienlyst.dk. 233 units. 995DKK–1,550DKK ($166–$259) double; 2,000DKK–2,750DKK ($334–$459) suite. Rates include breakfast. AE, DC, MC, V. Bus: 340. **Amenities:** 2 restaurants; bar; water park; indoor heated pool; 9-hole putting green; sauna; room service (7am–11pm); babysitting; laundry service; dry cleaning; nonsmoking rooms; rooms for those with limited mobility; casino. *In room:* TV, dataport, hair dryer.

Skandia Hotel *Value*   Attracting the economy-minded, this hotel provides simple but clean and cost-conscious accommodations in an amply proportioned building erected in 1922. Only half of its rooms have been renovated, so your opinion of this hotel may depend on your room assignment. Naturally, the renovated ones go first. Rooms are neat and functionally furnished. Each unit has a well-kept bathroom with a tub/shower combination. Ask for one on the fifth floor if you'd like a good view of the sound. If you need to make a phone call, you can do so at the reception desk. The hotel lies behind a red-brick facade along a street running parallel to the port near the bus and train station and the departure point for the ferryboat to Sweden.

Bramstræde 1, DK-3000 Helsingør. (C) **49-21-09-02.** Fax 49-26-54-90. 44 units, 9 with bathroom. 550DKK ($92) double without bathroom; 660DKK ($110) double with bathroom; 725DKK ($121) 3-bed family room without shower; 825DKK ($138) 3-bed family rooms with shower. No credit cards. **Amenities:** Lounge; nonsmoking rooms. *In room:* TV.

WHERE TO DINE

Typical Danish hot meals, such as *hakkebof* (hamburger steak), *frikadeller* (Danish rissoles or meatballs), rib roast with red cabbage, cooked or fried flounder or herring, and *æggekage* (egg cake) with bacon, are served in the local restaurants. In Helsingør you'll also find many fast-food places, and you won't want to miss the celebrated ice-cream wafers.

Anno 1880 DANISH   Set within a long, narrow, half-timbered building that originally functioned as a greengrocery, this is a comfortable and traditional restaurant that's owner-managed and always alert to the freshness of its ingredients. Within old-fashioned dining rooms, you'll enjoy seasonal meals that might include cream of clam soup with saffron; filets of salmon, haddock, or plaice in butter sauce with herbs; fried steak with fried onions and boiled potatoes; and such desserts as a kirsch-flavored parfait.

Kongensgade 6. (C) **49-21-54-80.** Reservations recommended. Main courses 120DKK–200DKK ($20–$33); fixed-price menu 250DKK ($42). DC, MC, V. Mon–Sat noon–4pm and 6–9:30pm.

Ophelia Restaurant DANISH/FRENCH   The Ophelia is one of the most appealing restaurants in town. In the elegantly rustic dining room, photos of *Hamlet* productions from around the world line the brick walls. Specialties of the house include "Hamlet veal steak" and calorie-rich desserts. Lunches cost half as much as dinner. Although not overly imaginative, the cookery is very competent, with dish after tasteful dish emerging from the kitchen.

In the Hotel Hamlet, Bramstræde 5. (C) **49-21-05-91.** Reservations recommended. Main courses 90DKK–190DKK ($15–$32). AE, DC, MC, V. Daily noon–9:30pm. Bus: 801 or 802.

San Remo DANISH   A down-to-earth self-service establishment that nevertheless sports crystal chandeliers, the San Remo offers 35 different meals, including *frikadeller* (ping-pong ball sized meatballs) and potatoes. The fare is robust, filling, and cheap—nothing more. The cafeteria is set in a traffic-free shopping mall half a block from the harbor, in a Dutch-inspired building dating from 1904.

Stengade 53 (at Bjergegade). (C) **49-21-00-55.** Main courses 32DKK–95DKK ($5.35–$16). MC, V. June–July daily 9am–9pm; Aug–May daily 11am–6pm. Bus: 801 or 802.

A DINING COMPLEX

Færgaarden is the setting for a trio of international restaurants in what was Helsingør's Customs House back in 1770. This complex enjoys the dining monopoly in Helsingør and is frequented by passengers going to and from Sweden. In addition to Samos, Færgaarden also offers **Gringo's Cantina** (© **49-26-14-47**), a Mexican restaurant where main courses cost 98DKK to 159DKK ($16–$27), with a fixed-price menu going for 149DKK to 349DKK ($25–$58). There is also the very competent **Bamboo** (© **49-21-22-82**), a Chinese restaurant offering main courses for 100DKK to 150DKK ($17–$25). Both are open daily from noon to 10pm. All accept American Express, Diners Club, MasterCard, and Visa.

HELSINGØR AFTER DARK

The major center of nightlife is the previously recommended **Hotel Marienlyst,** which has a casino usually filled with Swedes. Charging an admission of 50DKK ($8.35), it is open daily from 7pm to 4am. Games of chance include blackjack, roulette, Seven Card Stud poker, and 60 slot machines. Bring a photo ID, and know that the minimum age is 18. A casino package, costing 449DKK ($75), includes a welcoming drink, a three-course dinner in the Seaside restaurant, admission to the casino, and cash chips at a value of 200€ ($240).

4 Hornbæk

50km (31 miles) N of Copenhagen; 12km (7½ miles) west of Helsingør

A 500-year-old fishing hamlet turned modern holiday resort, Hornbæk is one of the best places for a vacation on the north coast of Zealand—sometimes called the Kattegat coast. Coastal woodlands, heath, and sand dunes make for a uniquely Danish holiday.

Hornbæk has the best beach along the north coast, a wide expanse of soft white sands that runs the full length of the resort, set against a backdrop of beach grass and sand dunes. *Rosa rugosa,* a wild pink rose that flourishes in this salty air, blooms here all summer. The beach is pristine and is beautifully maintained; all the kiosks and facilities lie inland from the dunes.

The light found in Hornbæk attracted and continues to attract artists to this fishing hamlet. In 1870, the town was discovered by such artists as Kristian Zartmann, P. S. Krøyer, Viggo Johansen, and Carl Locher. Krøyer often depicted the work of fishermen at sea and down the shore. Locher was so fascinated with his marine subjects that he lived at Hornbæk from 1881 to 1889; his home still stands at Østre Stejlebakke but is not open to the public.

ESSENTIALS

GETTING THERE By Train From Helsingør (see above), which has frequent connections to Copenhagen, trains arrive about twice an hour during the day, pulling into the station at Hornbæk (trip time: 22 min.).

By Bus Bus no. 340 journeys here about once an hour, taking 30 minutes.

By Car Drive NE along the coastal road (Rte. 237) from Helsingør, following the signs to Hornbæk and/or Gilleleje.

VISITOR INFORMATION Providing information for the area, **Hornbæk Turistbureau,** Vester Stejlebakke 2A (© 49-70-47-47), is found inside the local library. Hours are Monday 10am to 7pm, Tuesday to Friday 10am to 5pm, Saturday 10am to 2pm.

FUN ON THE BEACH & ELSEWHERE

The beach is the big attraction, and swimming conditions are good. The dunes protect the beach from heavy winds. Danes, often from Copenhagen, flock here in summer, but there's always space for sunbathing. The beach offers views over the sea toward Kullen, the rocky promontory jutting out from the Swedish coast.

The municipality cleans the beach daily, and for several years it has been voted one of the cleanest beaches in Scandinavia. A host of activities are available, including water biking. Windsurfing can be arranged at **Surfudlejning** (© **49-70-33-75**), at Drejervej 19. Kiosks sell food and drinks; there are toilets, and, for persons with disabilities, catwalks that are wheelchair-friendly lead to the sea.

The **Havnen** or **Hornbæk Harbour** is a modern, well-equipped harbor with mooring for 200 boats. It lies next to "shanty town," a collection of huts where fishers check their tackle or hang flatfish out to dry. Facilities with showers are beside the harbormaster's office. Charters for fishing trips can be arranged here. The harbor here is the starting point of an annual Zealand regatta in June.

If you've arrived by train from Helsingør, the harbor is only a 5-minute walk from the depot. Head down Havnevej. After crossing the dunes, you're on the beach, and we hope the day is a sunny one.

At the harbor, you'll see a monument honoring the poet Holger Drachmann, who died here in 1908.

If you'd like to walk through the village you'll come upon some old fishers' cottages still standing, and a church from the 17th century with many votive ships hanging from the ceiling. Votive ships are scaled-down replicas that have been blessed by a priest or minister and are designed to honor the sacrifices of men who labor at sea. The church was built in 1737 to take the place of two buildings that were blown down in fierce winds. A bit inland, many Danes have erected summer villas. City officials have planted tree plantations to give shelter from the frequent gales.

SHOPPING

The best outlet for handicrafts is found at **Sylvest Stentøj,** Klosterrisvej 2, Havreholm (© **49-70-11-20**), which specializes in stoneware.

WHERE TO STAY

Ewaldsgaardeny   Small-scale and deliberately rustic, this hotel prides itself on its role as a simple pension with few if any of the extras of a full-fledged hotel. It was originally built in 1814 as a post office, with enough stables to house the horses needed for keeping mail deliveries timely. You'll be thrown into a closer series of contacts with the other guests here than in a more anonymous setting, thanks to the small dimensions and rather cramped rooms. Each of these is outfitted with a combination of wallpaper and painted surfaces, sometimes in bright colors, and contains many of the trappings of a thoughtfully decorated private home. Overall, thanks to genuine cheerfulness and thoughtful management, you can have a happy and successful overnight stay here.

Johs. Ewaldswej 5, DK-3100 Hornbæk. © and fax **49-70-00-82**. 12 units, none with bathroom. 675DKK–695DKK ($113–$116) double. Rates include breakfast. V. *In room:* No phone.

Havreholm Slot ⭐ *finds*   The most elaborate and best-accessorized hotel in Hornbæk occupies what was originally built in the 1870s as the private home of a lumber baron and paper manufacturer, Valdemar Culmsee. Designed with a mock-fortified tower and vaguely ecclesiastical Victorian-style ornaments, it sits 4km (2½ miles) south of Hornbæk, within a large expanse of privately owned field and forest. Overnight accommodations are in a series of independent bungalows set on the hillsides sloping down to a widening of the river on which the property sits. Each is cozy and attractively decorated in a way befitting an upscale private home. All units have well-kept bathrooms with shower units.

Klosterrisvej 4, Havreholm DK-3100 Hornbæk. ℂ 49-75-86-00. Fax 49-75-80-23. www.havreholm.dk. 30 units. 1,790DKK ($299) double; 2,200DKK ($367) suite. DC, MC, V. Take bus from central Hornbæk marked "Havreholm." **Amenities:** Restaurant; bar; 2 pools (1 indoor heated); 9-hole golf course; squash course; fitness room; Jacuzzi; sauna; laundry service; dry cleaning; nonsmoking rooms; rooms for those with limited mobility; solarium. *In room:* TV, dataport, minibar, hair dryer, safe.

WHERE TO DINE

Havreholm Slot ✿ FRENCH/INTERNATIONAL   One of the most appealing restaurants in the region is in the previously recommended Havreholm Slot hotel, in a grand 19th-century dining room whose original accessories remain for the most part intact. Part of its allure for art historians and Danish nationalists derives from the wall murals commissioned in 1872 by the owner of the house and painted by Danish artist Joakim Skovgaard. The result was an interpretation of the Creation and the Garden of Eden in 12 panels. In addition to the mural-decked dining room, there are three other dining areas, each with a fireplace. A well-trained chef produces the best food in town, with menu items that change with the seasons. Examples include a salad of fresh mussels, fresh salmon served with a vegetable terrine, breast of chicken cooked with mushrooms and red wine sauce, and an especially delectable choice, roasted oxtail in red wine sauce.

Klosterrisvej 4, Havreholm. ℂ 49-75-86-00. Reservations recommended. Main courses 110DKK–135DKK ($18–$23); fixed-price menu 405DKK ($68). DC, MC, V. Daily noon–2pm and 6–9pm.

Hornbæk Bodega DANISH/INTERNATIONAL   Set near the water, in a century-old building in the center of town, this bodega resembles an English pub more closely than anything else in Hornbæk. Surrounded by forest green walls, you'll be seated on the black leather upholstery of what used to serve as seats for an old-fashioned English train. No one will mind if you drop in for a drink. But if you're hungry, menu items include lots of American-derived items such as club sandwiches and burgers, and such Danish standards as *frikadeller,* fish filets with shrimp and asparagus, liver pâté with bacon and mushrooms, and fried plaice.

A.R. Friisvej 10. ℂ 49-70-28-88. Main courses 65DKK–129DKK ($11–$22). DC, MC, V. Daily 11am–5pm.

⌒ *Tips* **Insider's Tip**

After you've explored the town of Hornbæk and hit the beach, consider taking a trail through a vast track of public forest, **Hornbæk Plantage** ✿, 3km (1¾ miles) east of the center of Hornbæk. The tourist office will give you a free map outlining the best hiking trails. You'll come across Scotch broom, wild roses, and hundreds of pine trees as you follow one of the trails along the coast. We recommend the coastal trail because of its more dramatic scenery, although some of the hiking routes cut inland.

Søstrene Olsen ⭐ DANISH/CONTINENTAL   Set near the sea, close to the center of town, the building that houses this restaurant was originally constructed in the 1880s as the summer home of a wealthy woman who spent most of her winters in Copenhagen. Today, it's one of the most appealing restaurants in town, partly because of its low-key elegance, partly because of the flavorful cuisine that emerges on steaming platters from the hardworking kitchens. The menu changes at least every 2 weeks, but might include such dishes as a gratin of lobster with green sauce, filets of monkfish served with shrimp and liquefied spinach, filet of beef with a tomato-cream sauce, fried eel with mashed potatoes, *moules marinière* (mussels marinara), and crème brûlée.

Øresundsvej 10. ℰ **49-70-05-50.** Reservations recommended. Main courses 198DKK–245DKK ($33–$41); fixed-price dinner 388DKK ($65). AE, DC, MC, V. Daily noon–4pm and 5:30–9pm. Closed Nov–Mar.

HORNBÆK AFTER DARK

Two of the busiest and oft-mentioned watering holes in Hornbæk are particularly active during the summer months. The more historic of the two is **Hornbæk Bodega,** A.R. Friisvej 10 (ℰ **49-70-28-88**), a previously recommended restaurant (see "Where to Dine," above). Set within what was originally conceived as the town's movie theater, it attracts socializing Danes like a magnet every evening as the dinner service begins to wind down. Come here for a drink of beer or schnapps, or for some dance music if your visit happens to fall on a Friday or Saturday night (10pm to around 5am year-round). When there is dance music, a cover charge of 50DKK ($8.35) pays for the first drink. The Bodega's most visible competitor is **Café Paradiso,** Havnevej 3 (ℰ **49-70-04-25**). This is a lively and gregarious English-inspired pub that offers live music every Friday and Saturday night 9pm to 5am, with no cover.

5 Gilleleje

59km (37 miles) N of Copenhagen; 30km (19 miles) NW of Helsingør

The northernmost town in Zealand, Gilleleje offers Blue Flag beaches (meaning their waters are not polluted), the leafy glades of the nearby Gribskov forest in the south, and a typical Danish landscape with straw-roofed houses and a large fishing harbor. In all, there are 14km (8⅔ miles) of coastline with plenty of sandy beaches for water lovers of all ages.

Gilleleje Harbour is the center of local life. As soon as dawn breaks, fishing boats of all sizes make their way into North Zealand's largest industrial port, and they can be seen unloading their catch. Look for the fish auction hall to see the night's catch being sold in a unique language understood only by the initiated. There are many smokehouses along the harbor used for smoking the fish.

Later you can go for a walk in the town itself, with its many small and large shops. On Thursdays and Saturdays you can experience a Zealand *mylder* (market), when the town square becomes a marketplace with stalls and booths vying to take your *kroner.* Horse-drawn carriage rides and street music provide an added bonus.

ESSENTIALS

GETTING THERE   By Train   During the day, two trains an hour arrive from Hillerød (trip time: 30 min.). There is also frequent service from Helsingør (40 min.).

By Bus   Buses link all the towns of North Zealand. For example, bus no. 340 links Gilleleje with Hornbæk (20 min.), and with Helsingør (50 min.). Bus no. 363 links Gilleleje with Tisvildeleje, but the awkward route takes about an hour. The bus and train depot in Gilleleje adjoin each other. It's only a 5-minute walk from the bus and train stations down to the harbor.

By Car   Follow Route 237 west from Helsingør (see above).

VISITOR INFORMATION   The **Gilleleje Turistbureau** is at Gilleleje Hovedgade 6F (© **48-30-01-74**). May to August, it's open Monday to Friday 10am to 5pm and Saturday 10am to 6pm; September to April, it's open Monday to Friday 9am to 4pm and Saturday 9am to noon.

EXPLORING THE AREA

When you tire of the beaches, take a stroll through the old town, with its narrow streets and well-preserved old houses, no two alike. In the center of town stands the Sladrebænken or "gossip bench" where you can rest and spread some gossip.

From the harbor you can take the signposted Gilbjergstien path, offering panoramic views over the sea. This will take you to the Søren Kierkegaard Stone, a monument to Denmark's most renowned philosopher. As long ago as 1835, he was one of the first tourists to appreciate the beauty and tranquillity of this place.

But most summer visitors come here for the beaches. Gilleleje has an unbroken coastline on either side, stretching from Gilbjerg to Kullen, running from Kattegat in the north to Øresund in the southeast. The city has lifeguards posted in several places along the coast. Many of the bathing beaches have modern toilets, little kiosks, and, often, proper restaurants. Several beaches also have ramps leading down to the water for the benefit of wheelchair users.

Within a green space adjacent to the sea, an area that forms part of the landscaping around the recommended Gilleleje Museum and the town's public library, stands a bronze statue called *Teka Bashofar Gadol,* a Hebrew name meaning "Let the mighty *Shofar* proclaim." The statue was donated by a wealthy Israeli patron of the arts, Yul Ofer, and was unveiled in the spring of 1997 to commemorate the flight of Danish Jews from the Nazis in 1943. Gilleleje was the point of departure for some 2,000 Jews who fled to Sweden from the town and other places along the North Coast. Risking their own lives, people in the town and country harbored Jews until they could secure passage on a ship to Sweden.

Gilleleje Museum, Vesterbrogade 56 (© **48-30-16-31**), traces the development of the area from the early Middle Ages, although some exhibits go back before recorded history. Panoramas present both shorebirds and migratory birds. The museum, along with Gilleleje's library, is housed in the Pyramiden, the Pyramid cultural center where traditional and modern buildings have been integrated into a harmonious whole.

There is a fascinating exhibit related to the rescue of the Danish Jews in 1943. The museum is open year-round, Tuesday through Sunday, 1 to 4pm. Admission costs 25DKK ($4.20) for adults; children ages 12 and under are free.

Less than a kilometer (about ½ mile) east of town stands the world's first coalfired lighthouse, **Nakkehoved Østre Fyr,** Fyrvej 20 (© **48-30-16-31**). Dating from 1772, it has been restored and turned into a nautical museum. You can drive there—its location 2.5km (1½ miles) east of town is marked from the town center (follow the signs to NAKKEHOVED ØSTRE FYR). But the more invigorating method of reaching the lighthouse involves walking along a coastal footpath beginning in Gilleleje at Hovedgade on the east side of the fishing museum. It's only open June to September, Wednesday to Monday 1 to 4pm, charging an admission of 10DKK ($1.65) for adults; children ages 12 and under are free.

Fiskerhuset (Old Fisherman's House) and **The Skibshallen** (Ship Hall) are at Hovedgade 49 (© 48-30-16-31). This is a restored fisherman's dwelling from the 1820s. The Hall presents the history of fishermen in the area from the Middle Ages to the present day, using the fishing hamlets between Hundested and Helsingør as the points of departure. The museum—on the main street—uses a variety of panoramic scenes, models of the boats, and exhibits on trades associated with fishing, to reveal how the industry has dominated local life. The hours and prices are the same as those previously mentioned for the lighthouse.

One of the most interesting museums in the region is the **Rudolph Tegnersmuseum** ★, Museumsvej 19, in Villingerød (© 49-71-91-77; bus: 340). Set 7km (4⅓ miles) southwest of Gilleleje, you can reach it by driving southwest along the coastal route (no. 237) and then following the signs pointing south to the museum from Dronningmølle. Surrounded by heather-covered hills that might remind you of Scotland (although this region of Zealand is often referred to as "Russia"), this museum is devoted to the artist Rudolph Tegner (1873–1950). Fourteen of his bronzes are displayed in an adjacent sculpture park, 17,000 hectares (42,000 acres) of protected countryside. The museum houses Tegner's collection of 250 sculptures in plaster, clay, bronze, and marble, some of monumental proportions. Selected pieces of furniture from the artist's home and a sarcophagus containing his body make the museum a monument to this individual and controversial avant-garde artist. It's open April 15 through May, Tuesday to Sunday noon to 5pm; June to August, Tuesday to Sunday 9:30am to 5pm; September to the third Sunday in October, Tuesday to Sunday noon to 5pm. It's closed the rest of the year. Admission costs 40DKK ($6.70) for adults and is free for children under age 12.

OUTDOOR ACTIVITIES

A wealth of possibilities in North Zealand await you, none finer than the **Gilleleje Golf Klub,** Ferlevej 52 (© 49-71-80-56), one of Denmark's best golf courses, with 18 holes situated in gently undulating terrain. The course is of very high quality and often used for both national and international tournaments. A bar, restaurant, and golf shop are on-site. Greens fees are 350DKK ($58) from Monday through Friday, rising to 450DKK ($75) on weekends.

Gilleleje Tennis Klub, Øster Allé, is a few minutes' walk from the beach. This tennis complex has eight hard courts, plus bathing and club facilities.

Many other sporting possibilities are available—the tourist office (see "Visitor Information," above) has full details. The use of jet skis is prohibited, but the coast of Rågeleje is ideal for windsurfing. The beaches of Gilleleje and Dronningmølle also attract windsurfers, although you must exercise caution to avoid swimmers. If you'd like to go horseback riding across heath and sand dunes, contact the **Enggården Ridecenter,** Hellebjergvej 27, Dronningmølle (© 49-70-46-60).

SHOPPING

There are more shops in Gilleleje, per capita, than in virtually any other small town in Zealand. At least part of that is attributable to the discretionary income of many of the vacationers who flock here, or perhaps it's the tradition of buying and selling antiques that has been a part of the civic consciousness here since the 1960s. In any event, a walk up and down the length of the Vesterbrogade will reveal lots of small boutiques whose collective inventories might enrich the aesthetics of your home or office.

J.S. Antiques, Ferlevej 55–57, Ferle (*© **49-71-79-79**), is one of the biggest and most visible antiques stores in town. Another store that has garnered a devoted clientele from all around the world because of its knowledge of antique Danish porcelain, especially Royal Copenhagen, is **Antik Ulla,** Vesterbrogade 94 (*© **48-30-07-58**). Looking for something more contemporary, but hand-made? Check out the modern stoneware and ceramics, especially the depictions of fish and boats, at **Radoor Keramik,** Havnevej 13 (*© **48-30-20-87**).

Know in advance, before you begin your barnstorming of Gilleleje's antiques stores, that opening hours are relaxed to the point of being almost chaotic. In *most* cases, shops open daily except Monday and Tuesday, roughly 11am to 4 or 5pm, depending on business and the mood of the shopkeeper. Most, however, maintain extensions of the phone numbers listed that ring in their homes, so a call in advance will sometimes do the trick in getting a shop to open.

WHERE TO STAY

Hotel Strand   Because of frequent rebuilding and a radical renovation that was completed in 1984, it's sometimes hard to get a sense of the 1896 origins of this well-established hotel. But despite the fact that most of the old-time architectural embellishments were long ago ripped out, it's still a popular, well-managed hotel whose simple, efficiently decorated rooms are usually booked fairly heavily throughout the summer. Both the beach and the harbor lie within a 2-minute walk. Breakfast is the only meal served. All rooms in the hotel have private bathrooms with shower units except for three singles.

Vesterbrogade 4D, DK-3250 Gilleleje. *© **48-30-05-12.** Fax 48-30-18-59. 25 units, 22 with bathroom. 880DKK ($147) double with bathroom; 760DKK ($127) double without bathroom; 1,000DKK ($167) suite. Rates include breakfast. AE, DC, MC, V. **Amenities:** Breakfast room; bar; lounge; laundry service; dry cleaning; nonsmoking rooms. *In room:* TV.

WHERE TO DINE

Fyrkroen *⋆* DANISH   Much of the allure of this place derives from its his-toric charm and the fact that it affords diners panoramic views stretching as far away as the coast of Sweden. It was built in 1772 as a lighthouse. Today, the low-slung white-painted stone building adjacent to the lighthouse tower contains a well-recommended restaurant where patronage is especially brisk on days with the best visibility. There are an indoor dining room, an outdoor terrace, and a sense of the old-time days of the long-ago sailing ships. Menu items include a medley of soups (especially shrimp, asparagus, tomato, and goulash); smoked salmon; several kinds of salads; steaks; and a roster of such fish as halibut, salmon, and perch. The cookery is competent, made with market-fresh ingredients.

Fyrvejen 29. *© **48-30-02-25.** Reservations recommended, especially when weather is clear. Main courses 128DKK–178DKK ($21–$30). DC, MC, V. May–Oct daily noon–9pm; Nov–Dec and Mar–Apr Thurs–Sun noon–9pm. Closed Jan–Feb. From Gilleleje, drive 4km (2½ miles) west, following signs to Hornbæk.

Hos Karen & Marie *⋆* DANISH/FRENCH   This is our favorite restaurant in Gilleleje, thanks to its hardworking staff and a sophisticated international flair. The setting is a 110-year-old yellow-brick building that was originally a general store for the maritime industry. Menu items change with the seasons and the moods of the chef but focus to a large extent on fish and, in virtually every case, at least two meat dishes. The restaurant's signature dish is a local whole plaice, served with parsley sauce and new potatoes. Alternatively, you might appreciate the sea devil prepared with rum, thyme, and basil; or the beef ten-derloin served with forest mushrooms and red wine sauce. A worthy beginning to a meal here is virgin lobster bisque garnished with cognac.

Nordre Havnevej 3. ✆ **48-30-21-30.** Reservations recommended. Main courses 187DKK–248DKK ($31–$41); fixed-price menus 228DKK–258DKK ($38–$43). AE, DC, MC, V. May–Oct daily 1–4pm and 6–10pm; Nov–Apr Tues–Sat 1–4pm and 6–10pm, Sun 1–4pm.

6 Tisvildeleje

59km (37 miles) NW of Copenhagen; 25km (16 miles) W of Helsingør; 18km (11 miles) NW of Hillerød; 71km (44 miles) N of Roskilde

This is one of the most idyllic seaside villages along the north coast of Zealand. Against a backdrop of low-lying sand dunes, Tisvildeleje—the largest settlement in the region known as Tisvilde—opens onto one of the broadest stretches of white sandy beaches in Zealand, although the waters, even in July, will be too cold for you if you're accustomed to Florida-like temperatures. The best beach is less than 1.5km (1 mile) west of the center of the resort. It has a changing room and toilets and also a spacious parking lot. People also come here for walks through **Tisvilde Hegn,** a wind-swept forest of heather-covered hills and trees twisted by the cold Nordic winds.

ESSENTIALS

GETTING THERE   By Train   From Hillerød trains run to Tisvildeleje at the rate of once an hour during the day (trip time: 30 min.).

VISITOR INFORMATION   Tisvilde Turistinformation, Banevej 8 (✆ **48-70-74-51**), is open Monday to Friday noon to 5pm and Saturday 10am to 3pm, but only from June to August.

GETTING AROUND   Bike rentals are available at **Servicehjørnet,** Hovedgade 54 (✆ **48-70-80-13**). You can rent one for 75DKK ($13) per day.

EXPLORING THE AREA

To the west of the center, running alongside Tisvilde Hegn, one of Denmark's largest forests, is a 1.2km (¾-mile) stretch of white sandy beaches lapped by clean salty waters and fringed by dunes and woodland. The surroundings here are exceptionally clean and unspoiled. Volunteers work to see that this whole area of coastline is the most thoroughly inspected and litter-free in Denmark. A blue flag flies over the beach, meaning that the waters are not polluted.

In town you can visit **Tibirke Kirke,** Tibirke Kirkevej (✆ **48-70-62-94**), which is open Monday through Saturday 8am to 4pm, with Sunday devoted to a church service. Admission is free. This church was probably built around 1120 on a pagan site. In the latter part of the 14th century, it was enlarged and the nave provided with arches. At that time, the small Roman windows were replaced with larger Gothic ones. In the middle of the 15th century a larger choir also replaced the original one. The tower was built during the first half of the 16th century, but has been reconstructed many times since. During a period of terrible sand drifts, the church was laid waste. But it was eventually restored, and in 1740 a baroque altarpiece was added, with a picture by J. F. Krügell depicting the Last Supper.

At the foot of the church is a spring that may have been the place where pilgrims came in olden days.

Tisvilde Hegn is enchanting and usually windblown. The forest is crossed with many trails, our favorite being a dirt path south to Troldeskoven, a distance of about 2.4km (1.5 miles). Nordic winds have turned the trees into "sculptures" of rather haunting shapes—one is called "Witch Wood." The tourist office (see "Visitor Information," above) will provide trail maps.

SHOPPING

Every Saturday between June and September, 10am to 2pm, a large, lively flea market, **Tisvilde Loppemarked** (Tisvilde Flea Market), is held at Birkepladsen, in front of Tisvildeleje's railway station. This is the time locals empty their attics, divesting themselves of things they might have inherited or acquired and don't really want. There's also a collection of crafts and, in some cases, used clothing.

WHERE TO STAY

Kildegaard ★ *Finds*   This is an engaging and likable small hotel whose owners, the Tetzschner family, work hard to create an intimate, cozy environment for guests who tend to return several years in a row. The centerpiece of the complex is a century-old farmhouse whose space is supplemented with outbuildings. Guests spend their days swimming at the nearby beach, playing volleyball or sleeping in hammocks strung across the garden, and enjoying a menagerie of family pets. Rooms are unpretentious and summery, and each is outfitted with a mishmash of simple contemporary furniture. Dinner platters are served only to residents who request them in advance. The establishment is located in the heart of town, a short walk from the tourist information office.

Hovedgaden 52, DK-3220 Tisvildeleje. ✆ 48-70-71-53. 23 units, none with bathroom. 650DKK ($109) double. Rates include breakfast. No credit cards. **Amenities:** Dining room; lounge. *In room:* No phone.

Tisvildeleje Strand Hotel   This is one of the few structures in Tisvildeleje that precedes the building boom of the 1920s, when wealthy Copenhagen families bought up much of the seafront and constructed summerhouses. Conceived in 1897 as a grocery store and livery stable, it has been rebuilt and expanded many times since until it reached its present form: four interconnected buildings encircling a verdant courtyard and a massive chestnut tree. Don't expect a lot of amenities to amuse and entertain you, as the focus is on beach life (the sea is only 90m/295 ft. away) and back-to-the-earth walks in the nearby forest. Rooms are simple, summery, and unpretentious. All units have neatly kept bathrooms with shower units. The in-house restaurant is surprisingly good and aggressively international in its tastes (see "Where to Dine," below).

Hovedgaden 75, DK-3220 Tisvildeleje. ✆ 48-70-71-19. Fax 48-70-71-77. 29 units, 8 with bathroom. 640DKK ($107) double without bathroom; 750DKK–975DKK ($125–$163) double with bathroom. Rates include breakfast. MC, V. **Amenities:** Restaurant; bar; lounge. *In room:* No phone.

WHERE TO DINE

Bio-Bistro DANISH/INTERNATIONAL   This well-respected dinner-only bistro next to a movie theater offers food that is often praised by the owners of various B&B hotels in town without restaurants of their own. In a setting that's vaguely reminiscent of the kind of brasserie you might expect in Paris or Lyons, you can order simple lunches (sandwiches, burgers, croque-monsieur), but only during the peak of midsummer. Menus feature a mixture of French and Danish dishes, and usually include chicken with wine sauce, salmon with a mousseline sauce, and several different kinds of steak.

Hovegården 38. ✆ 40-46-99-47. Main courses 95DKK–225DKK ($16–$38). DC, MC, V. June–Aug daily 11:30am–10pm; Sept Wed–Sun 6–10pm; Oct Fri–Sun 6–10pm; Nov–May Fri–Sat 6–10pm.

Tisvildeleje Strand Hotel INTERNATIONAL   Set in a big-windowed area of the previously recommended hotel, this brasserie-like eatery is the most cosmopolitan and internationally conscious restaurant in town. About the only thing that's Danish here is the clientele; menu options include selections from Thailand, the Philippines, Australia, and France, and all of the well-crafted dishes use very fresh ingredients. Expect an array of stir-fried fish and vegetable dishes, lemongrass soup and both green and red curry dishes from Thailand, satay skewers of beef and chicken served with peanut sauce, and, whenever the chef feels particularly French, an old-fashioned coq au vin or pepper steak.

Hovedgåden 75. (*C*) **48-70-71-19.** Reservations recommended. Main courses 65DKK–150DKK ($11–$25); 2-course menu 175DKK ($29); 3-course menu 205DKK ($34). MC, V. June to late Sept daily 11:30am–10pm. Closed Oct–May.

7 Roskilde ⭐/⭐

32km (20 miles) W of Copenhagen

Roskilde, once a great ecclesiastical seat, was Denmark's leading city until the mid–15th century. Today the twin spires of **Roskilde Cathedral** stand out from the Danish landscape like elegantly tapered beacons. These towers are the first landmark you see when approaching the city that celebrated its 1,000th anniversary in 1998.

Roskilde may be centuries past its peak, but it is no sleepy museum town. It's filled with a dynamic student community, boutique-filled walking streets, several landmarks and major sights, and a population of more than 52,000 people who call themselves *Roskildenser*.

Toward the end of the first millennium (A.D.), the Vikings settled the area, drawn, no doubt, by its sinuous coastline, where they could launch their ships. In 1957 divers in the Roskilde Fjord came upon shards of wood and reported their findings. Their discovery turned out to be bigger than anyone imagined. Here, sunken and mud-preserved, were five Viking ships that presumably had been put there to block the passage of enemy ships.

Archeologists began the painstaking job of building a water-tight dam and draining that section of the fjord, while keeping the chunks of splinters of wood wet enough so as not to cause them to disintegrate. Splinter by splinter they began the reconstruction and reassembly of the boats—a process that continues today. You can see their efforts on display at the **Viking Ship Museum** (see below), a modern museum that contains the five found ships.

Between A.D. 990 and A.D. 1000, Roskilde's prominence grew, becoming the home of the royal residence. By the 11th century, a Catholic church and a Bishop's Seat resided at Roskilde, which was to remain Denmark's capital until the Reformation in 1536.

At that time all the parish churches were abolished and the Catholic hierarchy disappeared. The government and the monarchy moved to Copenhagen. Nonetheless, at its peak, Roskilde's importance was expressed in its architecture. By 1150, it was surrounded by an embankment and a moat, inside of which stood 12 churches and a cathedral. In 1170, Bishop Absalon built a new church on the site where Harald Bluetooth had erected his church 2 centuries before. Though it took 300 years to construct, and was subsequently burned, destroyed, ravaged, and rebuilt, Absalon's cathedral laid the foundation for the existing Roskilde Cathedral or Domkirche, which today is a UNESCO World Heritage Site.

ESSENTIALS

GETTING THERE **By Train** Trains leave three times an hour from Copenhagen's Central Railroad Station on the 35-minute trip to Roskilde.

By Bus Buses depart from Roskilde several times daily from Copenhagen's Central Railroad Station.

By Car Take the E-21 express highway west from Copenhagen.

Roskilde

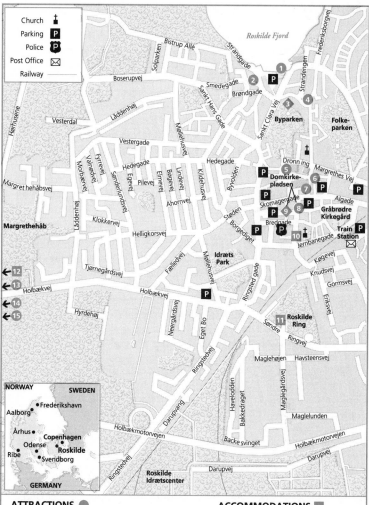

ATTRACTIONS ●

Ledreborg Park og Slot **14**
Lejre Research Center **13**
Museet for Samtidskunst
(Museum of Contemporary Art) **8**
Palæsamlingerne (The Palace Collections) **7**
Roskilde Domkirke **5**
Roskilde Museum **6**
Skt. Lbs Kirke **4**
Skt. Jørgensbjerg Kirke **2**
The Tramway Museum **15**
Vikingeskibshallen
(Viking Ship Museum) **1**

ACCOMMODATIONS ■

Hotel Prinsden **10**
Scandic Hotel Roskilde **11**
Svogerslev Kro **12**

DINING ◆

Le Brasserie **10**
Raadhuskælderen **9**
Restaurant Toppen **3**

VISITOR INFORMATION   The **Roskilde-Egnens Turistbureau,** Gullandsstræde 15 (© **46-35-27-00**), provides pamphlets about the town and the surrounding area. The office is open January 1 through March 31 and August 23 to December 31 Monday to Thursday 9am to 5pm, Friday 9am to 4pm, and Saturday 10am to 1pm; April 1 to June 27 Monday to Friday 9am to 5pm and Saturday 10am to 1pm; June 28 to August 22 Monday to Friday 9am to 6pm and Saturday 10am to 2pm. While at the tourist office inquire about a Roskilde card, which costs 150DKK ($25) adults or 75DKK ($13) children. The card admits you to the 11 attractions in the area and is valid for 7 days from the date of issue. Without the card, it would cost 439DKK ($73) to visit these same attractions.

SPECIAL EVENTS   The **Roskilde Festival** (© **46-35-27-00;** www.roskilde-festival.dk), held outdoors June 30 to July 3 on a large grassy field, attracts fans of rock and techno music. To get information on the festival—dates and performances—call the above number or contact the Roskilde-Egnens Turistbureau (see "Visitor Information," above).

SEEING THE SIGHTS

Roskilde Domkirke ★★★   This cathedral made Roskilde the spiritual capital of Denmark and northern Europe. Today it rises out of a modest townscape like a mirage—a cathedral several times too big for the town surrounding it. Construction started in 1170 when Absalon was bishop of Roskilde. Work continued into the 13th century, and the building's original Romanesque features gave way to an early Gothic facade. The twin towers weren't built until the 14th century.

Today the cathedral's beauty goes beyond a single architectural style, providing almost a crash course in Danish architecture. Although damaged by a fire in 1968, the cathedral has been restored, including its magnificent altarpiece.

The Domkirke is the final abode of 38 Danish monarchs whose tombs are here, ranging from the modest to the eccentric. Not surprisingly, the tomb of Christian IV, the builder king, who was instrumental in the construction of nearly all of Copenhagen's famous towers and castles, is interred in a grandiose chapel here with a massive painting of himself in combat, a bronze likeness by the Danish sculptor, Bertel Thorvaldsen. In humble contrast is the newest addition, from 1972, of the simple brick chapel of King Frederik IX, which stands outside the church. This chapel is octagonal in shape and decorated with hand-painted tiles designed by the architects Johannes and Inger Exner and Vilhelm Wohlert. Other notable tombs include the white marble sarcophagus of Queen Margrethe I.

In King Christian I's Chapel, which dates from the 15th century, there is a column marked with the heights of several kings. The tallest monarch was Christian I, at 2.1m (6 ft., 9 in.). This, no doubt, was an exaggeration, as his skeleton measures only 1.9m (6 ft., 2 in.). A large, bright cupola graces the late-18th- and early-19th-century chapel of King Frederik V. Note also the Gothic choir stalls, each richly and intricately carved with details from both the Old and New Testaments.

The gilded winged altar in the choir was made in Antwerp in the 1500s and was originally intended for Frederiksborg Castle. Pictures on the wings of the altar depict scenes from the life of Jesus, ranging from the Nativity to the Crucifixion. Following the fire, the renowned artist Anna Thommesen created a new altar cloth.

The most charming aspect of the cathedral is its early-16th-century clock poised on the interior south wall above the entrance. A tiny St. George on horseback marks the hour by charging a dragon. The beast howls, echoing through the cavernous church, causing Peter Doever, "the Deafener," to sound the hour. A terrified Kirsten Kiemer, "the Chimer," shakes in fright but pulls herself together to strike the quarters.

Insider's tip: Free concerts on the cathedral's pipe organ, which dates from the 1500s, are often presented at 8pm on Thursdays in summer. They are presented less frequently throughout the rest of the year. Check with the tourist office.

Domkirkestræde 10. ℂ **46-31-65-65.** Admission 25DKK ($4.20) adults, 15DKK ($2.50) children. Apr–Sept Mon–Fri 9am–4:45pm, Sat 9am–noon, Sun 12:30–4:45pm; Oct–Mar Tues–Sat 10am–3:45pm, Sun 12:30–3:45pm. Bus: 602, 603, or 604.

Viking Ship Museum (Vikingeskibshallen) ★★   Displayed here are five vessels found in Roskilde Fjord and painstakingly pieced together from countless fragments of wreckage. It's presumed that the craft were deliberately sunk about 20km (12 miles) north of Roskilde at the narrowest section of the fjord to protect the settlement from a sea attack. The discovery was relatively unprotected and unpublicized until 1957, when the Danish National Museum carried out a series of underwater excavations.

A merchant cargo ship used by the Vikings, a small ferry or fishing boat, and a Danish Viking warship similar to the ones portrayed in the Bayeux Tapestry are also displayed, and a "longship," a Viking man-of-war that terrorized European coasts, was also discovered. Copies of Viking jewelry may be purchased in the museum gift shop, and there's also a cafeteria.

To understand the attraction better, you can see a short film, *The Ships of the Vikings,* about the excavation and preservation of the ships and the building and navigation of *Roar Ege,* a Viking ship replica.

In 1997 the Viking Ship Museum opened a museum harbor for its collection of Nordic vessels, including *Roar Ege,* plus another Viking ship replica, *Helge Ask.* The museum's restored sloop, *Ruth,* is also moored here. And workshops where you can try your hand at old maritime crafts, such as rope- and sail-making, woodwork, and other activities, are located opposite the Boat Yard.

Vindebader 12. ℂ **46-30-02-00.** www.vikingeskibsmuseet.dk. Admission May–Sept 75DKK ($13) adults, 190DKK ($32) family ticket; Oct–Apr 45DKK ($7.50) adults, 125DKK ($21) family ticket; 25 DKK ($4.20) children 4–15; free for children under 4. Daily 10am–5pm. Bus: 216 or 607.

Roskilde Museum   Located 90m (295 ft.) from the Town Square, this museum, in a former merchant's house, features exhibits of the celebrated Hedebo embroidery, regional costumes, and antique toys. Displays also include an *aurochs* (an ancient European ox) skeleton, a unique Viking tomb, and a large number of medieval finds from the town. The museum also has a grocer's courtyard, with the shop in operation.

Skt. Ols Gade 15–18. ℂ **46-31-65-00.** www.roskildemuseum.dk. Admission 25DKK ($4.20) adults, free for children under 12. Daily 11am–4pm. Closed Dec 24–25 and Dec 31–Jan 1. Bus: 601, 602, 603, or 605.

Museet for Samtidskunst (Museum of Contemporary Art)   In a beautiful palace from the 18th century, this museum of modern art has frequently changing exhibitions, together with performances, film shows, and dance and classical-music concerts. It also houses a screening room presenting programs with Danish and foreign artists. "The Palace Collections" (see below) are also housed here.

Stændertorvet 3D. ℂ **46-36-88-74.** Admission 30DKK ($5) adults, 15DKK ($2.50) seniors, free for children. Tues–Fri 11am–5pm; Sat–Sun noon–4pm. Bus: 601, 602, 603, or 605.

Palæsamlingerne (The Palace Collections)   After a visit to the Museet for Samtidskunst (see above), you can view the collections in Roskilde Palace at the same site. Most of these objets d'art and paintings date from the era of great prosperity Roskilde merchants enjoyed in the 1700s and 1800s, when such local families as the Bruuns and the Borchs amassed a great deal of art and antiques, which you can see today.

Stændertorvet 3E. ℂ 46-35-78-80. Admission 25DKK ($4.20) adults, free for children. May 15–Sept 14 daily 11am–4pm; off season Sat–Sun 2–4pm. Bus: 601, 602, 603, or 605.

MORE ATTRACTIONS

The **St. Jørgensbjerg quarter** was originally a small fishing village, and a number of old, half-timbered houses, some with thatched roofs, remain. These houses cluster around **Skt. Jørgensbjerg Kirke,** Kirkegade, which stands on the top of a hill with a panoramic view of Roskilde Fjord. This is one of the oldest and best-preserved stone buildings in Denmark. The nave and choir of the church date from the beginning of the 12th century, but the walled-up north door is even older, possibly dating from 1040. Slender billets, found only in wooden churches, are in the corners of the church and in the center of the nave. A model of a *kogge,* a medieval merchant vessel, has been engraved in a wall. The church is open only June 22 to August 31, Monday through Friday 10am to noon. To get there from Roskilde, take bus no. 607 toward Boserup.

The same bus will deliver you to **Skt. Ibs Kirke** ("The Church of St. James"), Skt. Ibs Vej (ℂ 46-35-29-66), also in the north of Roskilde. Although no longer in use as a church, this ruin dates from around 1100. Abolished as a church in 1808, it was later a field hospital and a merchant's warehouse. Regrettably, the merchant destroyed the tower, the chancel, the porch, and the church vaults of this medieval relic, but spared the nave. It is open for visits only April 4 to October 17, from sunup to sundown.

NEARBY ATTRACTIONS

Ledreborg Park Og Slot ✮   A baroque manor house and French/English-style park 7km (4⅓ miles) southwest of Roskilde and 43km (27 miles) west of Copenhagen, Ledreborg is one of the best-preserved monuments in Denmark. Built by Johan Ludwig Holstein, a minister to Christian IV, the Holstein-Ledreborg family has owned this 33-room house with a landscaped garden and 88-hectare (217-acre) park for eight generations. Between 1741 and 1757 it was turned from a farmhouse into a baroque manor. Inside are a collection of 17th- and 18th-century antiques and a gallery of Danish paintings. It's approached by a 6km (3¾-mile) alley of lime trees, some 2 centuries old. Near the manor is a grave dating from the late Stone Age, approximately 3000 B.C.

Allé 2, Lejre. ℂ 46-48-00-38. Admission 60DKK ($10) adults, 35DKK ($5.85) children 3–14, 170DKK ($28) family ticket. Mid-June to Aug daily 11am–5pm; May to mid-June and Sept Sun 11am–5pm. Closed Oct–Apr. From Copenhagen's Central Railroad Station, take the direct train to Lejre, which leaves hourly and takes 35 min.; from Lejre station, take the 3-min. bus 233 to the castle and park. From Roskilde, there are frequent buses to Lejre, followed by the short bus ride to the castle and park. Combined ticket for Ledreborg Park Og Slot and Lejre Research Center (see below) 115DKK ($19) adults, 60DKK ($10) children.

Lejre Research Center   Eight kilometers (5 miles) west of Roskilde, this archaeological research center, Lejre Research Center, is the site of a reconstructed Iron Age community on 10 hectares (25 acres) of woodland. The main feature is clay-walled and thatch houses built with tools just as they were some 2,000 years ago. Staffers re-create the physical working conditions as they thatch Iron Age huts, work fields with *ards* (oxen-pulled plows), weave, and make pottery by an open fire. They also sail in dugout canoes, grind corn with a stone, and bake in direct fire. Visitors can take part in these activities. Jutland black pottery is produced here, and handicrafts and books are for sale at the gift shop. There are tables where you can enjoy a picnic lunch.

Slagealléen 2, Lejre. ✆ **46-48-08-78.** Admission 75DKK ($13) adults, 45DKK ($7.50) children. Tues–Fri 10am–4pm; Sat–Sun 11am–5pm. Closed mid-Sept to Apr. Take the train from Copenhagen to Lejre, then bus 233 to the center. From Roskilde, there are frequent buses to Lejre; then take bus 233.

The Tramway Museum   In the town of Justrup, some 16km (10 miles) southwest of Roskilde, in a pleasant woodland area close to Glydenveshj, the Tramway Museum with its collection of antique trams is situated on the highest point on Zealand, 127m (417 ft.) above sea level. To reach the museum, board an old tram at the entrance and travel the 305m (1,001 ft.) to the main building.

Skjoldenæsvej 107, Skjoldenæsholm. ✆ **57-52-88-33.** www.sporvejsmuseet.dk. Admission 70DKK ($12) adults, 35DKK ($5.85) children. May 1–June 21 and Aug 6–Oct 8 Sat 1–5pm, Sun 10am–5pm; June 22–Aug 5 Tues–Thurs 10am–5pm; Oct 9–17 daily 10am–5pm. Closed Oct 18–Apr 30. Take a train from Copenhagen to Borup, and then bus 249 from the station.

A BOAT TOUR OF THE ROSKILDE FJORD

You'll get a leisurely waterside view of the southern parts of Roskilde Fjord by participating in one of the frequent warm-weather tours offered aboard the *Sagafjord,* a steamer from the 1950s whose profile evokes a paddle-wheel steamer on the Mississippi. You can opt for either a lunch or a dinner cruise (2–2½ hr. long, and 3½ hr. long, respectively), or a shorter mid-afternoon cruise (90 min.), depending on your schedule. Regardless of what you select, you'll pay a base rate of 85DKK ($14), after which your (optional) food costs are extra. Platters of food aboard the lunch cruise cost 76DKK to 235DKK ($13–$39) each. Evening three-course fixed-price menus cost 299DKK to 395DKK ($50–$66) each. Tours are conducted only April to October. They operate daily in June, July, August, and September, and depending on the schedule, 3 to 5 days a week in April, May, and October. Cruises depart from a prominently signposted (SAGAFJORD TOURS) pier in Roskilde Harbor. For schedules, information, and reservations, contact **Rederiet Sagafjord,** St. Valbyvej 154 (✆ **46-75-64-60**).

SHOPPING

The best streets for shopping are the pedestrian thoroughfares Algade and Skomagergade. Of these, we find Skomagergade the more interesting. It dates from the 12th century. Its name, which literally means "shoemaker street," was where the cobblers of Roskilde plied their trade in the Middle Ages.

At either end of the street, a **triskelion** within a circle has been placed in the pavement. The symbol is three curved lines radiating from the center. It comes from the coins struck in Roskilde from 1018 to 1047. Today this silver coin has been re-created by one of the goldsmiths of Roskilde and is sold as a piece of jewelry at the tourist office (see "Visitor Information," above).

The best time for shoppers to be in Roskilde is for the market days every Wednesday and Saturday morning (go after 8am). Fresh fruit and vegetables of the season are sold from stalls on Stændertorvet, the main square by the cathedral, along with many stalls hawking fresh fish and Danish cheese. You can purchase the makings of a picnic, along with beautiful pieces of jewelry, and even mugs and pottery. Vendors also peddle a number of well-made children's clothes.

Roskilde also abounds in specialty shops, notably **Bydr. Lützhøfts,** Køb-mandsgård, Ringstedgade 6–8 (© **46-35-00-61**), a cozy old grocer's shop selling herring and other delicacies across the counter. The interior of the shop looks as it did during the 1920s, and goods for sale are typical of that era. The building at Ringstedgade 8 is a butcher's shop, **Slagterbutikken O. Lunds,** selling goods made according to recipes from about 1920. You can also explore the merchant's yard with 18th- and 19th-century buildings. Sometimes exhibitions are staged here—for example, depictions of merchants and trade in Roskilde over the past 1,000 years. This shop is open Monday through Friday 11am to 5pm and Saturday 10am to 2pm. Even if you don't purchase anything, this is one of the town's tourist attractions.

The town also has very excellent buys in handicrafts. Head first for **Glasgallerjet,** Skt. Ibs Vej 12 (© 46-35-65-36), a former gasworks near the harbor that now houses the open workshop of a glass blower. Here, the glass blower, who displays marvelous skill, shapes the most beautiful glasses, dishes, vases, and other items. Spectators are able to watch the transformation of a lump of melted glass into a beautiful Danish handicraft on sale at the gallery.

An unusual selection of crafts is found at **Jeppe,** Skomagergade 33 (© **46-36-94-35**), which is run collectively by 20 craftspeople from Roskilde and its environs. They make and sell their own crafts. These are definitely nonfactory goods, and exhibitions are always changing.

SWIMMING

You can swim both in- and outdoors in the Roskilde area, although outdoors might be a bit cool if you're not a Dane. There are several small bathing beaches along Roskilde Fjord, notably **Vigen Strandpark,** directly north of the town. Here you'll find a sandy beach with a jetty, set against the backdrop of green salt meadows. The blue flag flying at this beach means the waters are not polluted.

If you'd like to swim indoors, head for the **Roskilde Badet,** Bymarken 37 (© **46-35-63-92;** bus: 601 toward Vindinge from the center). Admission is 26DKK ($4.35) adults and 13DKK ($2.15) children. Hours are Monday and Wednesday 1 to 6pm, Tuesday and Thursday 1 to 8:30pm, Friday 1 to 6:30pm, Saturday 7am to 4pm, and Sunday 8am to 1:30pm. Closed July 1 to 25.

WHERE TO STAY

Hotel Prinsden ✦ Although its stucco-covered facade looks only about a century old, the foundations of this hotel date from 1695, when it functioned as a smaller version of what you'll see today. Most of its interior was renovated in 2000, and today it offers medium-size, smartly furnished rooms with bathrooms containing tub/shower combinations. Though a bit small, all in all the rooms are cozy nests. Five rooms on the top floor have a view of the fjord. All the guest rooms in the newer wing are decorated in a Nordic style with wooden floors. Those in the older section are furnished in a more classic style. Rooms in both sections are equally comfortable. Our favorite pocket of posh here is the extremely spacious and elegant Hans Christian Andersen suite.

Algade 13, DK-4000, Roskilde. © **46-30-91-00.** Fax 46-30-91-50. www.hotelprindsen.dk. 77 units. 1,275DKK–1,425DKK ($213–$238) double; from 1,950DKK ($326) suite. Rates include breakfast. AE, DC, MC, V. Bus: 602 or 603. **Amenities:** Restaurant; bar; sauna; 24-hr. room service; laundry service; dry cleaning; nonsmoking rooms. *In room:* TV, dataport, minibar, hair dryer, trouser press.

Scandic Hotel Roskilde ★   The best in Roskilde, this chain hotel, built in 1989, offers a sleek modern decor and good facilities. Rooms are average size, traditionally furnished, and very comfortable, with medium-size bathrooms containing shower units. The hotel also has a good restaurant serving Danish and international dishes, plus a bar. It's on the ring road less than a kilometer (about ½ mile) south of the green belt, Roskilde Ring, on the southern outskirts of the city.

Søndre Ringvej 33, DK-4000 Roskilde. ☎ **46-32-46-32.** Fax 46-32-02-32. www.scandic-hotels.com. 98 units. 690DKK–1,465DKK ($115–$245) double; 990DKK–2,090DKK ($165–$349) suite. Rates include breakfast. AE, DC, MC, V. Free parking. **Amenities:** Restaurant; bar; fitness center; sauna; children's playroom; babysitting; laundry service; dry cleaning; nonsmoking rooms; rooms for those with limited mobility; solarium. *In room:* TV, minibar, hair dryer, trouser press, iron/ironing board.

Svogerslev Kro ★ *Finds*   Since 1727 this old-time inn has been welcoming visitors who make the 4km (2½ miles) journey west of Roskilde's center. Rooms are medium size (some are a bit small), decorated in modern Danish styling, and well maintained. Many open onto the inn's garden. Bathrooms come equipped with tub/shower combinations. The well-respected kitchen serves Danish open-faced sandwiches at lunch and an array of international dishes at night, including regional specialties, with main courses 98DKK to 210DKK ($16–$35). If you're adventurous, request the fried eel; if not, you might happily settle for the breast of guinea fowl with fresh herbs and a red pepper cream sauce. The chef's stew is made with bacon, onions, and mushrooms, in a paprika sauce. You can always count on baked salmon and some good steak dishes.

Hovedgaden 45, Svogerslev, DK-4000 Roskilde. ☎ **46-38-30-05.** Fax 46-38-30-14. www.svogerslevkro.dk. 18 units. 800DKK ($134) double. Rates include breakfast. AE, DC, MC, V. Bus: 602 with hourly connections to the town center. **Amenities:** Restaurant; bar; laundry service; dry cleaning. *In room:* TV, dataport, hair dryer.

NEARBY ACCOMMODATIONS

Gershøj Kro ★ *Finds*   The only problem with this atmospheric hotel is that it's open to individual travelers only 3 months a year, farming its simple and old-fashioned rooms out to members of corporate conventions the rest of the time. If you're lucky enough to arrive during midsummer, you'll be welcomed at an inn (dating from 1830) that's only a few paces from the docks of the fishing hamlet of Gershøj. Expect old-fashioned charm and a restaurant that's known for the variety of ways in which it prepares a time-tested local favorite, eels hauled in from the harbor. June to August, the restaurant is open daily for lunch and dinner.

Havnevej 14, Gershøj, DK-4050 Skibby. ☎ and fax **47-52-80-41.** 11 units, none with bathroom. 550DKK–625DKK ($92–$104) double. Rates include breakfast. AE, DC, MC, V. Closed Sept–May. Free parking. From Roskilde, drive 14km (8⅔ miles) NW, following the signs to Frederikssund. **Amenities:** Restaurant; bar. *In room:* No phone.

Osted Kro & Hotel   There has been a hotel on this site since 1521, functioning as a refreshment stopover for travelers migrating between Roskilde and Ringsted. The roadside inn you'll see today is much newer than that, with a much-rebuilt original core and a modern annex (constructed in 1985) that holds the establishment's 16 deliberately old-fashioned rooms. All units have well-maintained bathrooms with tub/shower combinations. Don't expect too many distractions here; other than a restaurant and bar, there isn't a lot to do. Nonetheless, meals are savory and prepared according to old-time Danish recipes.

Hovedvejen 151B, Osted, DK-4000 Roskilde. ℂ **46-49-70-41.** Fax 46-49-70-46. 16 units. 725DKK ($121) double. Rates include breakfast. AE, DC, MC, V. From Roskilde, drive 12km (7½ miles) south along Rte. 151, following the signs to Ringsted. **Amenities:** Restaurant; lounge. *In room:* TV.

Skuldelev Kro   Solid and reliable, and set behind a pale yellow facade in the hamlet of Skuldelev, less than 1.5km (1 mile) from the sea, this Danish inn was built in 1778 and was reconfigured and upgraded from a virtual ruin in the early 1990s. Since its reopening, several branches of Denmark's governmental bureaucracy have designated it as the site for some of their conferences. When one of these isn't going on, you can rent any of the simple but comfortable rooms. All units have well-kept bathrooms with tub/shower combinations.

Østergade 2A, Skuldelev, DK-4050 Skibby. ℂ **47-52-03-08.** Fax 47-52-08-93. www.hotel-skuldelevkro.dk. 31 units. 750DKK ($125) double. Rate includes breakfast. AE, DC, MC, V. From Roskilde, take Rte. 53 for 26km (16 miles), heading north, following the signposts to Skibby. **Amenities:** Restaurant; bar; outdoor pool; sauna; nonsmoking rooms. *In room:* TV, hair dryer.

WHERE TO DINE

La Brasserie ✿ STEAK/DANISH/INTERNATIONAL   In this previously recommended hotel, this is one of the best dining places in town. The food is well-prepared with market-fresh ingredients. The staff is perhaps the friendliest and most helpful in town, and the decor is in the stylish bistro decor like something in modern Paris. Everything is prepared from scratch, and hand-picked Danish raw materials are used whenever possible. The chefs even get their butter from a special dairy; their herring is cured for 8 months in Iceland, and their virgin olive oil comes from a small privately owned farm near Madrid.

It's simple and standard but ever so good: the grilled entrecôte with baked herb butter, baked potato, and grilled tomatoes. For a hefty, succulent meal, opt for the sirloin steak cut from Angus beef. Tiger prawns are a delightful concoction served with a raw tomato salsa with lime and cilantro flavorings. Chicken breast with homemade pesto is another reliable dish, as is a lamb kebab marinated in garlic and rosemary. In fair weather, you can dine outside.

Algade 13. ℂ **46-30-91-00.** Reservations recommended. Main courses 120DKK–210DKK ($20–$35). AE, DC, MC, V. Daily noon–10pm.

Raadhuskælderen ✿ DANISH   One of the oldest restaurant venues in Roskilde occupies the street level of a building erected in 1430 across the street from the town's cathedral. Although it's tempting to remain within the vaulted interior, there's also an outdoor terrace that is pleasant during midsummer, especially because of its view of the cathedral. Menu items are carefully prepared using very fresh ingredients. Some of the chef's best dishes include salmon steak with tartar sauce and grilled and marinated filet of young chicken with sautéed vegetables and a cream sauce flavored with ginger and citrus. Rack of lamb is delectably roasted and served with a sauce made from fresh summer berries.

Stændertorvet, Fondens Bro 1. ℂ **46-36-01-00.** Reservations recommended. Main courses 148DKK–218DKK ($25–$36); lunch menu 128DKK–158DKK ($21–$26). AE, DC, MC, V. Mon–Sat 11am–11pm.

Restaurant Toppen DANISH   At the top of a 1961 water tower, 84m (276 ft.) above sea level, Restaurant Toppen offers a panoramic view of the whole town, the surrounding country, and Roskilde Fjord—all from the dining room. Begin with a shrimp cocktail served with dill and lemon. Main dishes include sirloin of pork a la Toppen with mushrooms and a béarnaise sauce. For dessert, try the chef's nut cake with fruit sauce and sour cream. The cookery has much improved in recent months, and there is a finesse and consistency that wasn't here before. The restaurant is less than 1.5km (1 mile) east of the town center between Vindingevej and Københavnsvej. The water tower doesn't revolve electronically, but some clients, in the words of the management, "get the feeling that it's turning if they drink enough." There's a free elevator to the top.

Bymarken 37. © **46-36-04-12.** Reservations recommended. Main courses 62DKK–117DKK ($10–$20). DC, MC, V. Mon–Fri 3:30–10pm; Sat–Sun noon–10pm. Bus: 601.

A NEARBY PLACE TO DINE

Langtved Færgekro DANISH   This isolated Danish inn, a short walk from the hamlet of Munkholm Bro, 5km (3 miles) southwest of the town of Kirke Såby, was inaugurated 250 years ago when a need arose to feed passengers on a nearby ferryboat route. Clients who appreciate a walk in the surrounding forest or along the nearby shoreline before or after enjoying a meal in this historic dining room favor this black-and-white half-timbered restaurant. The seasonal menu items have received several awards for their flavors. Examples include shrimp cocktails; crepes stuffed with baby shrimp, feta cheese, and herbs; marinated salmon with homemade bread; steak with fried onions; and either halibut or plaice with hollandaise sauce.

Munkholmvej 138, 5km (3 miles) SW of Kirke Såby. © **46-40-50-53.** Reservations recommended. Main courses 130DKK–200DKK ($22–$33). No credit cards. Fri–Sun noon–8pm. From Roskilde, drive 26km (16 miles) NW, following the signs to Holbæk and then to Munkholm Bro.

ROSKILDE AFTER DARK

One of the most consistently fun and popular nightlife venues in Roskilde is the **Gimle Musikcafe,** Ringstedgade 30 (© **46-35-12-13**), where the trappings and ambience of a much-used, much-battered English pub combine with recorded— and in rare instances live—music. A 5-minute walk west from the center of town, it serves simple lunches and dinners, endless steins of Danish and international beer, and a dose of good cheer that's often welcomed by the many regulars who define this place as their "local."

6

South Zealand & Møn

The largest of the Danish islands—about the size of the state of Delaware—Zealand was said to have been carved from Sweden by the goddess Gefion. From Copenhagen, almost any point of Zealand can be reached in an hour and a half. For convenience of touring, we have divided the island into North Zealand (see chapter 5) and South Zealand.

The north of the island, admittedly, has more drama, including sites like Hamlet's Castle and the cathedral at Roskilde. But the less-developed south offers more tranquillity, with its rural towns and small farms that edge up to communities with white sandy beaches. And when you're this far south, you can also visit the offshore islands of Falster and Lolland.

One of the most history-rich parts of Denmark, South Zealand was especially important in the Viking age. It was also vital in the Middle Ages, especially as a center for the Valdemar dynasty. In the 1600s, some of the most epic battles between Sweden and Denmark took place here, especially in the seas off Køge. One of Denmark's greatest moments of shame came in 1658 when King Gustave of Sweden marched across the fields of South Zealand heading for Copenhagen. Once there, he forced a treaty that nearly cost Denmark its sovereignty.

If your time is limited, you may want to confine your visit to the highlights, which would include the former witch-burning town of Køge and the sleepy town of Sørø, one of the area's most charming. South Zealand is also filled with medieval churches (we've selected the best of them) and has a 1,000-year-old ring fortress at Trelleborg.

Motorists from Køge in the east heading to Korsør in the west (perhaps to cross the bridge over the Great Belt into Funen) would be wise to steer clear of the dull E20 motorway and follow the scenic and greener Route 150, which will take you through South Zealand's best villages and farmlands.

There's much to see and do here, and much that awaits discovery, as the area is almost ignored by the rushed North American visitor. But for those with the time to explore, there are rewards ranging from climbing the "Goose Tower" in the old town of Vordingborg to exploring Præstø with its charming harbor and well-preserved market-town atmosphere. There are often festivals of fine food and music throughout the summer, and there are seemingly endless sailing clubs, which give the ports a real maritime atmosphere, filled with the heady scents of seaweed and tar.

For Zealand rail or bus information, you can call ℂ **70-13-14-15.**

1 Køge ★

40km (25 miles) S of Copenhagen; 24km (15 miles) SE of Roskilde

This old port city, now peppered with many industries, is south of Copenhagen on Køge Bay on the east coast of Zealand.

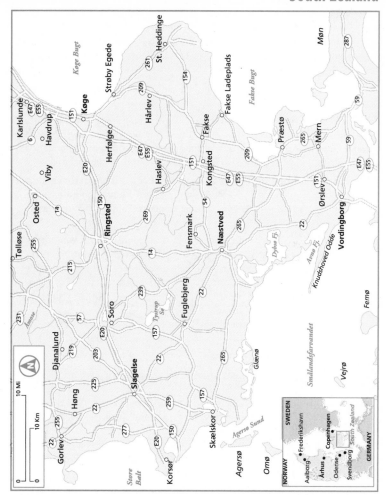

Better known in the Middle Ages than it is today, Køge was granted a charter by King Erik VI in 1288. The area grew up around a bustling natural harbor, a hub of trade with Germany and a thriving fishing center. In the Middle Ages it was known as a witch-burning town, similar to Salem, Massachusetts.

The Battle of Køge Bay was fought here in 1677, one of the major conflicts in the eternal wars with Sweden. The Danish admiral, Niels Juel, defeated the attacking Swedish navy, thwarting their attempt to conquer Denmark. He subsequently became a national hero, like Admiral Nelson to the British.

Køge, a bustling city of 40,000 with a modern commercial harbor, is visited mainly because it has preserved the narrow, historic streets of its inner core. A fire in 1633 leveled many of the buildings, but others were spared and greet visitors today, and still others were restored to their original appearance. The heart of the city is its Torvet, or town square. The streets worth exploring, such as Kirkestræde, radiate from this main square.

ESSENTIALS

GETTING THERE   By Train   Take the S-tog extension from Copenhagen. Service is every 20 minutes throughout the day (trip time: 35 min.). You can also reach Køge by train from Roskilde (25 min.). There are also rail links with Næstved (35 min.).

By Bus   Bus no. 21 departs for Køge frequently from Copenhagen's Central Railroad Station.

By Car   From Copenhagen, head south along the express highway E47/E55. Motorists from Roskilde can take Route 6, connecting with Route 151 south into the heart of Køge. Parking is available at Torvet (but only for an hour at a time). You'll find less restrictive parking at Havnen, north of the yacht harbor.

VISITOR INFORMATION   Guided tours of Køge are arranged through the **Tourist Office,** Vestergade 1 (© **56-67-60-01**), open Monday to Friday year-round 9am to 5pm. June to August Saturday hours are 9am to 2pm; off season, Saturday hours are 10am to 1pm. English is spoken.

GETTING AROUND   By Bicycle   While at the tourist bureau you can ask for a free brochure published by the Dansk Cyklist Forbund (Danish Cyclists' Union). It's in English and outlines five biking tours of the nearby area, ranging from a 40km (25-mile) tour that features Vallø Slot, or Castle (see "Easy Excursions from Køge," later in this chapter), to a 6km (3¾-mile) route that visits the grave of Danish philosopher Nikolai Frederik Grundtvig.

For bike rentals in Køge, contact **HH-Cykler,** Nørre Blvd. 59 (© **56-65-06-10**). The cost is 65DKK ($11) per day, plus a deposit of 400DKK ($67).

EXPLORING THE TOWN

Køge Bay is mainly a recreational area with a pleasure-boat harbor and kilometers of lovely but chilly beaches.

The harbor is only a short walk from the medieval center, and it has the same significance for the people of Køge as Nyhavn does for Copenhageners. We enjoy the atmosphere here and like watching the action in the busy harbor, which is filled with Baltic freighters, fishing boats, and pleasure craft. If you walk to the North Pier, you'll find a number of eating places and cafes in old-fashioned houses. You can relax here over a meal or order a cold Danish beer.

Opening onto the bay is a monument commemorating the battle in Køge Bay. You'll see it standing some 9m (30 ft.) high near the harbor. This granite obelisk bears the names of maritime heroes Niels Juel and Ivar Huitfeldt. Huitfeldt commanded the *Danebrog,* which burst into flames when bombarded by Swedish forces in 1710.

Before taking a look at the bay, explore the historic medieval core of the old town. You'll pass fish markets selling freshly caught flatfish, herring, and eel, as you experience the bustling atmosphere of this busy yacht harbor. Stroll through the city parks and surrounding woodland and peek into the courtyards of the old buildings left from the Middle Ages. In summer, live street entertainment will amuse you (giving a few kroner to the young musicians is always appreciated).

The best street for wandering is **Kirkestræde,** lined with graceful old houses. A small building on the street, no. 20, is reputed to be the oldest half-timbered house in Denmark, dating back to 1527. A couple of porch stones from the Middle Ages, said to be the only pair in Denmark in their original position, are in front of a house at Smedegarden 13, near an ancient tree.

Of the town's churches, **Sankt Nicolai Church,** Kirkestræde 29 (© **56-65-13-59**), 2 blocks north of Torvet, is of the most interest. This Gothic structure dates from 1450 to the early 16th century and was named after St. Nicholas, patron saint of mariners. History records that King Christian IV watched the Battle of Køge, in which Niels Juel sank many Swedish vessels, from the church tower. The church has a number of art treasures, including an altarpiece by Lorents Jørgensen and 100 tombs of Køge merchants. Note the carved angels on the pews. They are without noses, thanks to drunken Swedish troops who in the 1600s came this way, cutting off the noses with their swords. Look for a little brick projection at the east end of the church tower. Called *Lygten,* it was for centuries a place where a burning lantern was hung to guide sailors safely back into the harbor. Hours mid-June to late August are Monday to Friday 10am to 4pm, Sunday noon to 4pm; off season, Monday to Friday 10am to noon. Admission is free.

All streets lead to the **Torvet,** or town square. This is the marketplace where stocks once stood. Trials of witches—they were almost always found guilty—were conducted here, followed by their executions. Those dank memories are all but forgotten today, especially on Wednesday and Saturday morning when a lively market takes place here. The Saturday market is the far livelier of the two.

On the north side of the market square (Torvet) is the **Køge Rådhus,** believed to be the oldest town hall in Denmark still in use. The building in the rear was erected very early in the 17th century to serve as accommodations for King Christian IV on his trips between the royal palaces in Copenhagen and Nykøbing F (the "F" refers to the island of Falster). You can wander into the courtyard at the town hall to see a modern sculpture created by Jens Flemming Sørensen.

A path for walkers and cyclists leads along the Køge River with access from the center in several places. Go here to enjoy some peace and quiet—and take along a picnic lunch if the weather's fair. There are several delis in town where you can pick up some open-faced sandwiches and drinks to take along. The park, Lovparken, is only a 5-minute walk from the Torvet. A wooden bridge takes you across the river, where you have a charming view of the riverside and its gardens.

The coastline near Køge offers several fine spots for bathing. For example, directly north of Køge you'll come upon a land of dunes and lyme grass, with an excellent sandy beach on Ølsemagle Revle. Near the city center, Køge Syd-strand, or south beach, offers camping sites. A bit farther south, the beach at Strøby Ladeplads is ideal for windsurfers.

Among specific attractions, consider a visit to the following:

Køge Museum   This fine museum in an old merchant's home from 1610 is surrounded by a beautiful garden near the town square and is devoted to the cultural history of South Zealand. It consists of six well-furnished rooms and a kitchen with implements used between 1640 and 1899. Displays of costumes, textiles, carriages, farm equipment, crafts from artisan's guilds, and other historical artifacts of the area are featured. Curiously, there's a windowpane where H. C. Andersen scratched the words OH, GOD, OH, GOD IN KØGE. The museum also has a desk once owned by Nikolai Frederik Grundtvig, the Danish philosopher and theologian who used to live on the outskirts of Køge. Also on display are hundreds of recently discovered silver coins, forming a treasure-trove that may have been hidden for safekeeping during the wars with Sweden in the 1600s.

There's also a collection of 322 coins from all over Scandinavia and Europe—the oldest coin is a Palatinate taler from 1548. Your museum ticket, incidentally, is valid—if you use it on the same day—for admission to Vallø Slot, a charming castle that's recommended separately at the end of this section in "Easy Excursions from Køge."

Nørregade 4. (℃ 56-63-42-42. Admission 30DKK ($5) adults, free for children under 16. June–Aug Tues–Sun 11am–5pm; Sept–May Tues–Sun 1–5pm.

Kunstmuseet Køge Skitsesambling *Finds* This major modern art museum exhibits drawings, sculptures, and models by important Danish artists of the 20th century. A changing roster of special exhibitions is also presented. In English the museum's name translates as "art and sketch collection." What makes this museum unique is that it traces the artist's creative process from conception to execution, from the advent of the idea to the unfolding of the "vision." Original drawings, clay models, and even mock-ups of a particular work are included so that the public can see how a piece of art looks while it's still in the conceptual stage. This approach is particularly fascinating to see when a piece of art undergoes a tremendous conceptual change along the way.

Nørregade 29. (℃ 56-63-34-14. Admission 30DKK ($5) adults, free for children. Thurs–Tues 10am–5pm; Wed 10am–8pm.

SHOPPING

The best time to go shopping here, even if you don't buy anything, is on Saturday morning, the market day—a tradition going back to the Middle Ages. The town is crowded with people, many from the surrounding area. Most activity is found at Torvet, the main market square, but it spills over into neighboring streets as well. Fruits and vegetables, cheese, and smoked fish are sold side by side with Danish crafts and secondhand goods. You can wander from stall to stall as street musicians—most often jazz artists—entertain you from courtyards nearby.

The best and largest selection of Danish gifts is found at **Jørgen Müller's,** Torvet 3–5 (℃ 56-65-25-80), on the market square. Here you can pick up Georg Jensen silver, Royal Copenhagen porcelain, Holmegaard glass—you name it. The best selection for women's fashion is **Rokkjoer,** Torvet 2 (℃ 56-65-02-58), which has an impressive array of continental coats, blouses, and dresses—many in what they call "oversize."

If you'd like to survey some South Zealand antiques, the best outlet is **Antik Bahuset,** Brogade 16E (℃ 56-66-17-19), which sells old furnishings, pewter, brass, and a lot of pre-1900 items. It's open only Saturday 10am to 1pm unless you call for an appointment.

Another antiques store worth a visit is **Tamalat Antik,** Brogade 22 (℃ 56-65-63-10), with a wide selection of antiques, and good buys in paintings, jewelry, glass, and porcelain. Finally, **Krybben,** Torvet 19 (℃ 56-63-02-01), offers a wide selection of clothing, crafts, shoes, and antiques—an odd mixture, but intriguing nonetheless. A special feature of Krybben is an upstairs gallery exhibiting the works of a talented local painter, Anne Kureer.

For the novelty alone, you might want to visit **Købmandshandel,** Vestergade 6 (℃ 56-66-30-67), a grocer's shop of yesterday. Two hundred different sorts of tea, spices from around the world, and everything from olive oils to licorice root to rock candy are on sale. You'll even find syrups, jams, and handmade candles.

Køge used to be known for its goldsmiths. Thriving since 1979, **Guldsmedien Ejvind Sørensen,** Nørregade 31 (℃ 56-66-19-91), is in a charming old building dating from 1612. A selection of gold and silver jewelry is sold here.

For the very best of Scandinavian design, not only furnishings but home accessories, head for **Hjelm's Bolighus,** Nørregade 32 (© **56-65-06-30**). This has been the leading Scandinavian design outlet in Køge for 40 years.

WHERE TO STAY

Because of the demand from business travelers, some of these hotels charge higher rates in winter, the off season for tourists.

Best Western Hotel Niels Juel   Built in 1989, in a harborfront location, this attractive, stylish, modern hotel was named after a 17th-century naval hero. Catering to business travelers and, to a lesser degree, vacationers, it contains a bar and a cozy restaurant, the **Quintus,** specializing in Danish and French food, including fresh salmon, oysters, and mussels. On the hotel's ground floor is a well-stocked wine cellar that is often the setting for wine tastings for hotel guests. Rooms are not overly large, but are very clean and well maintained, with bathrooms with tub/shower combinations. The bedrooms and the public rooms are designed after Feng Shui style, the famous Chinese interior art. Guests relax over newspapers in the library or amuse themselves in the billiard and dart room. The staff can also make arrangements for guests to play at a golf course less than a kilometer (about ½ mile) from the hotel.

Toldbodvej 20, DK-4600 Køge. © 800/528-1234 in the U.S., or 56-63-18-00. Fax 56-63-04-92. www.hotel nielsjuel.dk. 51 units. Sept–June Sun–Thurs 1,195DKK ($200) double; July–Aug and Fri–Sat year-round 875DKK ($146) double. Rates include breakfast. AE, DC, MC, V. **Amenities:** Restaurant; bar; sauna; laundry service; dry cleaning; nonsmoking rooms; rooms for those with limited mobility; solarium; wine cellar. *In room:* TV, dataport, minibar, hair dryer.

Centralhotellet Køge   Set behind a pale blue facade in the heart of town, only a few feet from the tarmac of the street, this hotel was converted into a hotel only relatively recently and still has the feel of a cozy 19th-century house. Its main allure involves its low rates, ample justification for ultrasimple, stripped-down but clean rooms. The hotel doesn't have any real electronic extras—neither phones nor TVs—but it is reasonably comfortable, if a bit small.

Vestergade 3, DK-4600 Køge. © 56-65-06-96. Fax 56-65-59-84. 12 units, 3 with bathroom. 530DKK ($89) double without bathroom; 630DKK ($105) double with bathroom. Rates include breakfast. MC, V. **Amenities:** Breakfast room; bar; lounge. *In room:* No phone.

Hotel Hvide Hus   Built in 1963, less than a kilometer (about ½ mile) east of Køge's center, this is a two-story, white-brick hotel constructed in an angular, glass-and-chrome style that evokes a tasteful version of the kind of architecture dating from the peak of the Cold War. Set about 180m (591 ft.) from the beach, the hotel has blandly furnished but comfortable rooms outfitted in a Nordic modern style, with well-kept bathrooms equipped with tub/shower combinations. Many clients are business travelers from other parts of Scandinavia on overnight sales trips. Views encompass either the forest and garden, or the sea as seen through clusters of trees.

Strandvejen 111, DK-4600 Køge. © 800/528-1234 in the U.S., or 56-65-36-90. Fax 56-66-33-14. www.hotel hvidehus.dk. 126 units. 875DKK–1,275DKK ($146–$213) double; 2,150DKK ($359) suite. Rates include buffet breakfast. AE, DC, MC, V. **Amenities:** Restaurant; bar; sauna; room service (6am–9:30pm); laundry service; dry cleaning; nonsmoking rooms; rooms for those with limited mobility. *In room:* TV, dataport, minibar, hair dryer.

Vallø Slotskro ⭐ *Finds*   Enveloped by some of the most magnificent landscapes in South Zealand, this little B&B is a discovery. It's 8km (5 miles) south of Køge near the Vallø Slot, a Renaissance castle from the 16th century, long the stomping ground of Danish nobility. Built by King Christian VII in 1781, Vallø Slotskro often housed overflow guests from the main castle. Over the years it has been modified and changed, its last wholesale rejuvenation occurring in 2004. Each room is furnished differently, but all are comfortably appointed. Only seven come with private bathrooms, each with a tub/shower combination. Guests in the accommodations without private bathrooms will find the shared facilities in the hallway adequate. The best rooms here (and these are assigned first) are spacious, with minibars, Jacuzzis, and four-poster antique beds.

Slotsgade 1, DK-4600 Køge. © **56-26-70-20.** Fax 56-26-70-71. www.valloeslotskro.dk. 13 units, 7 with bathroom. 750DKK ($125) double without bathroom; 925DKK ($154) double with bathroom. Rates include breakfast. AE, DC, MC, V. Free parking. **Amenities:** Restaurant; bar. *In room:* TV, minibar (in some).

WHERE TO DINE

Horizonten Café & Restaurant ★★★ DANISH/FRENCH   This restaurant is ranked as the finest dining room in Køge. It's best to dine here on a summer day. That way, you can request a table on the terrace that opens onto the harbor, where much of Denmark's history took place. The chefs are extremely skilled, especially with seafood, and Danish specialties are the best, although they borrow recipes from continental—especially French—kitchens as well. This restaurant offers the best series of fixed-price menus in South Zealand. Most clients wisely request that their fish be grilled, and it's done to perfection here. Of course, you can also order seafood dishes in all sorts of other concoctions as well. On our recent visit, we found the halibut meunière a special delight.

Havnen 29A. © **56-63-86-28.** Reservations required. Main courses 175DKK–235DKK ($29–$39); fixed-price menus 345DKK–355DKK ($58–$59). MC, V. Tues–Fri 6–10pm; Sat–Sun 6–9pm.

Restaurant Arken DANISH/FRENCH   Set at the edge of the smaller of Køge's two harbors, this is a modern, big-windowed restaurant built in 1979, whose name, "The Ark," derives from its likeness to a large wooden boat that Noah might have envied. Within an interior that's flooded with sunlight, surrounded by lots of varnished wood that's reminiscent of what you might find aboard a yacht, you can order dishes that are tried-and-true to local Danish traditions. Menu items include *frikadeller* (Danish meatballs), grilled salmon with butter sauce, sautéed beefsteak with mashed potatoes and golden-fried onions, and English-style roast beef with horseradish sauce. During warm-weather months, a local version of fried eel with stewed potatoes is available as well, and a terrace that overlooks the harbor is available for additional seating.

Køge Lystbådehavn 21. © **56-66-05-05.** Reservations recommended. Main courses 100DKK–188DKK ($17–$31); fixed-price menu 178DKK ($30). DC, MC, V. Daily 11:30am–10pm.

Skipperkroen DANISH/INTERNATIONAL   Set across the road from the edge of Køge's harbor, within a much-renovated 17th-century building, this is a well-maintained, well-managed testimonial to the pleasures of Danish wine, beer, and cuisine. There's a garden for dining and drinking outdoors (weather permitting), although throughout most of the year, clients dine in one of two areas inside. Menu items depend on the availability of local ingredients. One of the most appealing is plaice stuffed with shrimp, asparagus, and lobster meat; and the chef elevates the Danish staple of *bixemad* (beef hash with potatoes and onions, traditionally made with whatever happened to be lurking in a family's larder) to a high art form. Here, a platter of *bixemad,* with the promise of as many refills as you want, makes this one of the best dining values in town.

Havnen 25. © **56-65-02-64.** Main courses 155DKK–185DKK ($26–$31). AE, DC, MC, V. Daily 11:30am–9:30pm.

KØGE AFTER DARK

Begin your nightly pub-crawl, as the locals do, at **Toldboden,** Havnen 27 (© **56-65-50-75**), a pub and bar built between 1833 and 1847. Carlsberg is served on draft, and you can also order Guinness. In summer you can use the courtyard. Live music is presented every Friday evening and on Saturday afternoons, but mostly it's a place to gather and meet the locals, most of whom speak English.

Our favorite spot to meet friends for a friendly chat at night is **La Fontaine,** Torvet 28 (© **56-65-51-00**), which somehow always manages to have the coldest beer in town. It's right on the market square by the old fountain and stays open Sunday to Thursday 10am to midnight, and Friday and Saturday 10am to 2am—late hours for sleepy Køge.

For young people, the hottest place to be at night is the **Ritz Rock Café,** Torvet 22 (© **56-65-33-77**). It's Køge's version of the fabled Hard Rock cafes. People come here for the dance music and to eat and drink, partaking of the American and Tex-Mex cuisine. On a busy night, it holds up to 1,000 patrons. On the ground floor you'll find the most impressive sound and light equipment. The second floor is smaller and more elegant, attracting a more mature clientele.

Fun Fact   **Zealand's Link to the Continent**

On June 14, 1998, one of the world's largest bridge links opened on the west coast of Zealand near the town of Korsør. Queen Margrethe II was there to cut the ribbon shortly before driving across the 18km-long (11-mile) **Great Belt Bridge.** After 10 years of construction, Zealand is linked to the mainland of Europe via Funen, which already has a bridge link to Jutland on the mainland. From Jutland, one can drive south into Germany.

The bridge has cut traveling time across the Belt by more than 1 hour compared to the ferries, which ceased operations with the opening of the bridge. At a speed of 105kmph (65 mph), crossing the Great Belt into Funen now takes only 10 minutes. By contrast, crossing by ferry took 1 hour, not including the waiting time at the port and embarkation and disembarkation from the ferries.

For crossing the bridge, a one-way fare for a private car costs 250DKK ($42). About 10,000 cars now cross the bridge each day.

The rail link across the Great Belt was opened in 1997. Since then, Danish State railways has seen a 60% rise in passenger volume on trains across the Great Belt. An average of 20,000 rail passengers cross the Great Belt each day.

Besides joining east and west Denmark, the bridge link across the Great Belt represented the first stage of an improved infrastructure between Scandinavia and the rest of Europe. The **Øresund Fixed Link** between Denmark and Sweden opened in 2000, creating a coherent traffic network and establishing even more vital links between Copenhagen on the island of Zealand and Malmö, southern Sweden's largest city. With three million people living within a 50km (30-mile) radius of the link, the region has the largest population concentration in Scandinavia.

For more information about the bridge, call © **33-93-52-00.**

One of the most charming places for a quiet drink at night is **Hugos Vinkaelder,** Brogade 19 (© **56-65-58-50**), which opens its courtyard in fair weather. This cozy little wine bar retreat is found in the cellar of an antique building dating from 1392. Filled with atmosphere, it always has an interesting selection of wine, which it will sell by the half bottle if desired. Many locals come here to drink beer, however. It's open Monday through Thursday 10am to 11pm, Friday and Saturday 10am to 1am.

Ask at the tourist office if there are any presentations of interest going on at **Køge Bugt Kulturhus,** Portalen 1 (© **43-97-83-00**). This is the Køge Bay Cultural Center and the venue for a wide range of concerts and theatrical performances. An exhibit of Danish and international art is displayed in its exhibition hall. Tickets for all types of cultural events are sold at the tourist office. Of course, you might want to skip the theatrical performances if you don't speak Danish, but concerts and other entertainment might interest English-speakers.

EASY EXCURSIONS FROM KØGE
VALLØ & ITS CASTLE ✿

Just 7km (4⅓ miles) south of Køge, Vallø is the most charming hamlet in this part of Denmark, a little village of mustard-yellow houses and cobblestone streets from the Middle Ages.

Many visitors come here to see **Vallø Slot,** a castle that dominates the town. This castle was built between the 16th and 18th centuries, with sweeping French-style gardens containing lakes, moats, rare trees, and rose and dahlia flower beds. Following a disastrous fire in 1893, the castle had to be completely rebuilt. Its towers—one square, another round—are a Vallø landmark. Once a royal palace, the castle was converted in 1738 into housing for "spinsters of noble birth." These days it houses old-age pensioners. You can't go inside since it's a private residence, but you can enjoy the elegant gardens, which are free and open April to October 10am to dusk.

On the grounds at the stables, **Hestestalden** (© **56-26-74-62**), there's an exhibition on the history of the castle from the days when it was the property of Queen Sophie Magdalene in 1737. It's open April to October 11am to 4pm. Admission is 20DKK ($3.35) adults and 10DKK ($1.65) children. The ticket, incidentally, is valid for a visit to the Køge Museum as well—but only if you use it on the same day.

GETTING THERE **By Train** Vallø station is two stops from Køge.

By Car Head south on Route 209, turning right onto Billesborgvej and left onto Valløvej.

By Bicycle Bicycling is the ideal way to reach Valløvej, as there's a cycle route signposted from Køge.

THE CHALK CLIFFS OF STEVNS KLINT ✿

Only 24km (15 miles) south of Køge, near Rødvig, lie the chalk cliffs of Stevns Klint. These are not as impressive as the ones farther south on the island of Møn but are a worthy substitute if you can't visit the latter. This chalk escarpment extends along the coastline, opening onto a panoramic vista of the sea.

A white chalk crag, rising nearly 43m (141 ft.) in the vicinity of Højerup, is the most stunning. A little church, **Højerup Kirke,** was built here in 1357. Legend claims this church was erected by fishermen in gratitude for having been rescued at sea. There's another legend about this church as well. The sea continues to erode the chalk cliffs, and locals claim that each New Year's Eve the church moves a fraction inland to keep from falling into the sea. In 1928 it didn't move far enough and the choir collapsed, but the church has since been reinforced and made relatively safe. Hours are daily 11am to 5pm, but only April to September.

For more information about the area, consult the **Turistbureau** in Stevns at Havnevej 21 (© **56-50-64-64**).

GETTING THERE   By Train and Bicycle   To get to Stevns Klint from Køge: Take the train to Rødvig, where you'll rent a bicycle from the tourist office. From there, it's only about 5 panoramic kilometers (3 miles), heading east, following the signs to Højerup, to the cliffs. This is an easy bike ride and offers the best way to experience the bracing sea air and wind-swept panoramas.

By Car   From Køge to Stevns Klint: Take Highway 261 to the village of Store Heddinge, then detour to the cliffs, following the signs to Højerup.

2 Ringsted

69km (43 miles) SW of Copenhagen; 24km (15 miles) W of Køge; 16km (10 miles) E of Søro; 28km (17½ miles) N of Næstved

An important settlement in Viking times and a medieval ecclesiastical center, today Ringsted is a sleepy provincial town. But it has its aristocratic memories. This modern town of 30,000 people makes an ideal center for touring the heart of Zealand, offering excellent rail and road conditions. Route 14 from Næstved (see below) to Roskilde intersects the east–west highway (E20) from Køge to Korsør, where you can take the bridge over the Great Belt into Funen.

As late as the 4th century, Ringsted was the site of "the thing," or *Landsting,* as the regional governing body was called. Justice was dispensed here. In Torvet, the market square, you can still see a trio of three stones, the *Tingstener,* or "thing stones," recalling the days when Ringsted was a center of power in Denmark. Also on the square is a 1930s statue of Valdemar I sculpted by Johannes Bjerg.

In times gone by, Ringsted was where Valdemar kings and many of their successors were laid to rest, in Skt. Bendts Kirke (St. Benedict's Church), which dates from the 12th century.

After a long period of slumber following the loss of its royal patronage, Ringsted revived again in the 19th century with the coming of the railway.

ESSENTIALS
GETTING THERE   By Train   Trains run frequently from Roskilde (trip time: 18 min.). Dozens of daily trains from Copenhagen pass through to Roskilde (see chapter 5, "North Zealand"). There are also rail connections from Næstved (20 min.). The center of Ringsted can be reached in a 10-minute walk north from the train depot.

By Car   Ringsted lies on Route 150 just off of the E20 motorway coming in from Copenhagen in the east or Funen in the west. From Roskilde follow Route 14 to Ringsted.

VISITOR INFORMATION   The **Ringsted Turistbureau,** Sankt Bendtsgade 6 (© **57-62-66-00**), stands opposite Skt. Bendts Kirke. May to August, its hours are Monday to Friday 10am to 5pm and Saturday 10am to 1pm. Off-season hours are Monday to Friday 9am to 2pm. The tourist office will advise you of the best cycling routes in the Ringsted area.

EXPLORING THE TOWN

Ringsted grew up around **Skt. Bendts Kirke** ⚜, Sankt Bendtsgade (© **57-61-40-19**), which was constructed by King Valdemar I (1157–82) on the site of a previous abbey church. His original intent was that the church serve as a burial site for his father, Duke Knud Lavard, who was slain by Magnus the Strong, son of King Niels (1104–34). The beloved Knud Lavard was entombed here, beginning a tradition of using the church as a burial site for the Valdemar dynasty. In 1169 Knud Lavard was canonized by the pope. The tradition of burying kings and queens of Denmark here continued until 1341. Valdemar I's larger motive in building the church was to use it to bring together the influences of the Catholic hierarchy and the Valdemar dynasty.

In the early 20th century, ill-advised restorers altered the style of the original church, but much remains from the Middle Ages, even the 11th-century travertine blocks from the older abbey church built on this site.

In 1885, King Frederik VII ordered that the royal tombs be opened. In a church chapel you can see the treasures found in these tombs, including a lead tablet from the tomb of Valdemar the Great, plus silks from the grave of Valdemar the Victorious.

The tombs themselves—marked by a series of flat stones—were buried beneath the nave on the aisle floor. Such notables as Valdemar III and his queen, Eleonora; the twice-married Valdemar II with his queens, Dagmar and Benegærd; Knud VI; Valdemar I and his queen, Sofia; and the already mentioned Duke Knud Lavard are all entombed here. Many long-forgotten royals suffered the indignity of having their tombs removed to make way for later royal personages. Chief among these was the beloved Queen Dagmar, born a princess in Bohemia and still revered in Danish folk ballads. Much loved by the people of Denmark, she died prematurely in 1212. When her grave was removed to make way for the tomb of Erik VI (Menved) and his Queen Ingeborg, a gold cross with detailed enamel work was found. Called the Dagmar Cross, it's believed to date from A.D. 1000. Today, brides marrying in Skt. Bendts often wear replicas of the Dagmar Cross.

In the choir and on the cross vaulting you can see some notable chalk paintings. Some of Zealand's most interesting church frescoes are in the nave, especially a series depicting events in the life of King Erik IV. He was called "King Ploughpenny," because of a tax he imposed on ploughs throughout his kingdom. These frescoes were painted at the beginning of the 14th century in a failed attempt to have the king canonized (the pope said no). One fresco shows Queen Agnes, wife of Erik IV, seated on a throne; another immediately to her left depicts the murder of Erik IV, his attackers stabbing him with a spear. In another fresco the king's corpse is being rescued at sea by fishermen.

Other notable features in the church include pews from 1591 with dragon motifs. The richly adorned altarpiece is from 1699, and the even older pulpit dates from 1609. The baptismal font is the oldest relic of all, believed to date from some time in the 1100s. May to mid-September the admission-free church is open daily 10am to noon and 1 to 5pm. Off-season hours are daily 1 to 3pm.

The other major attraction in town is the **Ringsted Museum,** Køgevej 37 (© **57-61-94-04**), within walking distance of both the train station and the central market square. A modern museum of local culture and history, it presents artifacts gathered throughout the area, displaying the workaday life of locals long since departed. Beside the museum is a restored 1814 Dutch windmill, still in working order and still grinding flour that is sold at a kiosk on-site. There's also a cafe. Hours are Tuesday to Thursday 10am to 4pm, Sunday 10am to 4pm; admission is 25DKK ($4.20; closed in Jan).

The town hall, of minor interest, was built in 1937 on land that once belonged to a Benedictine Monastery whose origins stretch back to the early Middle Ages. Designed by Steen Eiler Rasmussen, the Danish architect, the two-story brick building with a copper roof stands near a statue of Valdemar the Great.

A most unusual mechanized display lies a mile northwest of Ringsted, the **Eventyrlandet Fantasy World,** Eventyrvej 13 (© 57-61-19-30; bus: 14 or 401). It's especially appealing to families, who appreciate its mixture of fantasy and fairy tales. Within a large, echoing room, you'll walk along simulations of paths through a magic forest. In the forest's clearings, mechanical dolls, each about 5m (16 ft.) high, simulate characters from the stories of Hans Christian Andersen as they dance, pirouette, and interact in their stiff but charming way. The assumption is that onlookers will have memorized the tales behind each tableau, but if you've forgotten one of them, virtually any Dane in the crowd will be able to recap it for you. There are also tableaux depicting folkloric dances in Mexico and China, plus hunting scenes in Greenland. Opening times are only from February 7 to 15, daily 10am to 5pm; May 29 to August 29, daily 10am to 5pm; and October 2 to December 30, daily 10am to 5pm. Admission is 75DKK ($13) adults; 50DKK ($8.35) children ages 2 to 11; and 25DKK ($4.20) children under 2. There are also an outdoor playground, a cafe, and a gift shop.

SHOPPING

Ringsted has a number of specialty shops. A covered shopping center, **Ringsted Centret,** Nørregade 15 (© 57-67-38-05), stands right in the middle of town, enabling you to shop and browse without having to worry about the weather. This is where you'll find the widest array of Danish products in various stores. The best place to go for copies of the Dagmar Cross (see Skt. Bendts Kirke, above) is **Klints Guld & Sølv,** Torvet 2 (© 57-61-01-83). The cross comes in gold, silver, and gold with enamel. In 1683 the cross—believed to date from A.D. 1000—was discovered when Queen Dagmar's tomb site was moved. Today nearly all brides married in Ringsted wear a reproduction of this cross, which makes an intriguing piece of jewelry even if you aren't a bride.

WHERE TO STAY

Scandic Hotel Ringsted *Kids* This four-story red-brick hotel, a 5-minute walk south of the town center, opened in 1986 and has been the preferred choice in central Ringsted ever since. Despite the fact that it's newer and a lot less historic than the also-recommended **Sørup Herregård,** we prefer it for its location near the town center and because the staff is a lot better organized. Its public areas host many of the region's conventions and business meetings. Rooms are uncluttered and streamlined, with writing tables, efficient modern furniture, bathrooms with showers, and comfortable beds. Its restaurant, Klosterhavn, is open for lunch and dinner daily. Each child is given a "surprise" when checking in, and activities are planned for children of all ages.

Nørretorv 57, DK-4100 Ringsted. © **57-61-93-00.** Fax 57-67-02-07. www.scandic-hotels.com. 75 units. 1,225DKK ($205) double. Rates include breakfast. AE, DC, MC, V. **Amenities:** Restaurant; bar; fitness center; sauna; children's playroom; laundry service; dry cleaning; nonsmoking rooms; solarium. *In room:* TV, minibar, coffeemaker (in some), hair dryer, trouser press (in some).

Sørup Herregård ★ *Finds* The most atmospheric hotel in the area lies 6km (3¾ miles) east of town, in a red-brick building that was originally a manor house. Surrounded by 385 hectares (951 acres) of rolling fields and forests, it was enlarged in the 1980s with lots of glassed-in additions that send light streaming into the interior. Rooms are conservatively decorated with comfortable beds, well-kept bathrooms with shower units, and the kind of furniture you might find in an upscale private home.

Sørupvej, DK-4100 Ringsted. © 800/528-1234 in the U.S., or 57-64-30-02. Fax 57-64-31-73. 102 units. June to mid-Aug 590DKK ($99) double; mid-Aug to May 1,198DKK ($200) double; year-round suite 2,050DKK ($342). AE, DC, MC, V. **Amenities:** Restaurant; bar; indoor heated pool; tennis court; sauna; 24-hr. room service; laundry service; dry cleaning; nonsmoking rooms; rooms for those with limited mobility; solarium. *In room:* TV, dataport, minibar, hair dryer.

WHERE TO DINE

Italy & Italy ★ ITALIAN Thanks to good food and an emphasis on the olive oil–based cuisine of Italy, this is the most consistently popular restaurant in Ringsted. It sits very close to Ringsted's most famous church, in a dining room that's flooded with sunlight from big windows and lined with paintings that commemorate the architectural grandeur of Italy. Menu items cover all aspects of a well-orchestrated Italian meal, and include marinated seafood and vegetarian antipasti, and such pastas as lasagna and fettuccine with Bolognese sauce. Medallions of veal "Sct. Elisabeth" are flambéed in cognac, and veal with Gorgonzola sauce is a perennial favorite.

Torvet 1C. © **57-61-53-53.** Reservations recommended. Main courses 129DKK–189DKK ($22–$32); fixed-price menu 239DKK ($40). MC, V. Mon–Thurs 11am–10pm; Fri–Sat 11am–11pm; Sun 7–9pm.

Rådhus Kro DANISH Set across the street from the Rådhus (City Hall), after which it's named, this restaurant occupies one large room of a modern-looking building erected in the mid–1980s. The menu is very, very Danish, and traditional, and the restaurant is the haunt of Ringsted's business and government community. Menu items include mushroom bouillon with garlic croutons, Norwegian haddock with red wine sauce, veal steak with mushroom sauce, and filets of pork with white sauce and boiled potatoes.

Sct. Bendtsgade 8. © **57-61-68-97.** Reservations recommended. Main courses 105DKK–122DKK ($18–$20). AE, DC, MC, V. Mon–Sat 11am–9:30pm; Sun 4–8pm.

RINGSTED AFTER DARK

You'll find pubs in virtually every neighborhood, but one of our favorites is the **Kong Valdemar Pub,** Nørregade 5 (© **57-61-81-32**), an antique-looking watering hole that has welcomed generations of drinkers to its paneled interior.

Established in 1999, **Crazy Daisy,** Sct. Hansgade 31 (© **57-61-25-47**), is a two-floor drink and dance emporium that contains an active bar area, sometimes with live music, on its street level, and a busy dance club upstairs. Every night owl in town between the ages of 20 and 40 is likely to show up here to enjoy relaxed conversation and hot music. It's open only Friday to Sunday, 11pm to around 4am. Cover is 50DKK ($8.35) per person.

3 Slagelse

99km (62 miles) SW of Copenhagen; 37km (23 miles) SE of Kalundborg; 19km (12 miles) NE of Korsør

In the Middle Ages, this was a major trading center, with trade routes to Næstved in the south, Copenhagen in the east, and Kalundborg in the north. In the 11th century the town had its own mint, and its municipal charters were granted in

1288. Slagelse lies in the heart of Viking country and is the best center for visiting the nearby fortress at Trelleborg (see below).

Today the town of some 36,000 people is prospering, thanks largely to a lively economy. The area around here might be called Hans Christian Andersen Country, like Odense in Funen: The writer attended the local grammar school for several years but found the town a "nuisance." The school was founded after the Reformation and remained important until it closed in 1852.

After its heyday in the Middle Ages, Slagelse declined considerably, the victim of various wars and some raging fires that burned its major buildings. But with the coming of the rail lines, the economy recovered. Canning factories, distilleries, and breweries beefed up its economy.

Today it's a major city of West Zealand, a route along the important traffic artery, the E20, linking Copenhagen with the bridge across the Great Belt into Funen and the continent. Though often bypassed by rushed motorists, Slagelse has a number of treasures for those interested in the Viking period.

ESSENTIALS

GETTING THERE   By Train   Slagelse lies on the main east–west rail line between Copenhagen and the neighboring island of Funen (its subsequent link to the continent), and trains run here frequently (trip time: 1 hr.). There are also easy connections from Roskilde (35 min.) and from Korsør, near the bridge over the Great Belt (12 min.).

VISITOR INFORMATION   A 10-minute walk south of the train depot, the **Slagelse Turistbureau,** Løvegade 7 (© **58-52-22-06;** www.vikingelandet.dk), provides information about its own attractions and Trelleborg (see below) to the west. It's also helpful in hooking you up with any activities you may want to pursue and in providing directions for hiking and walking. Hours are Monday to Friday 9am to 5pm and Saturday 9am to 1pm, mid-June to August. Off season, it's open Monday to Friday 10am to 5pm and Saturday 10am to 1pm. The tourist office can arrange rooms in private homes with prices beginning at around 150DKK ($25) per person for B&B, plus a 35DKK ($5.85) booking charge. You can rent bikes here or at **HJ Cykler,** Løvegade 46 (© **58-52-28-57**).

EXPLORING THE TOWN

Sct. Mikkels Kirke (St. Michael's Church), Rosengade 4 (© **58-52-05-11**), dominates this town. Admission is free, and you can visit daily 8:30am to 5pm. The church was constructed in 1333 in the red-brick Gothic style on the tallest hill in Slagelse. By the 1870s it had fallen into serious disrepair, however, and was restored. Although hardly the most interesting church in Zealand, it makes a worthy stop. A memorial here honors the Danish Resistance Movement in World War II. The sculptor, Gunnar Slot, designed it in 1959. Next to it is another sculpture titled *Woman,* the work of Keld Moseholm Jørgensen.

Slagelse has an even older church, **Sct. Peders Kirke** (St. Peter's Church), Bredegade 7A (© **58-52-08-81**), open daily 9am to 5pm. Admission is free. It was originally built in the Romanesque style around 1150, and later given a Gothic overlay. The vestry and porch date from around 1500. After its collapse, the church's original tower was reconstructed in 1664. The building contains many medieval graves, some of which can be viewed within an area used during the Middle Ages for storage of armaments that could be employed in the event of an attack upon the town or church. The most important tomb is that of St. Anders, who died in 1205, the first in a long line of vicars, and a major figure in the development of Slagelse. His tomb is in the northern part of the church.

Another attraction, lying south of Nytorv, the main commercial square of town, is the **Slagelse Museum,** Bredegade 11 (© **58-52-83-27**), inaugurated in 1984. It's an intriguing museum of local history with exhibitions devoted to arts and crafts, trade, and industry. Everything is here from a grocer's shop to a carpenter's and joiner's workshop. The butcher, the barber, and even the blacksmith also get in on the act. Note the exquisitely set dining room. In all, there are 22 stands with exhibits. Admission is 25DKK ($4.20) for adults, 5DKK (85¢) for children. June 15 to August, hours are Tuesday to Sunday noon to 4pm. Otherwise, only Saturday and Sunday noon to 4pm.

If you follow the street, Fisketorv, it will lead to Gammel Torv, which, for many decades, was the thriving main part of town and a meeting place of locals. It's said that Queen Margrethe I crowned her 6-year-old son, Oluf, on this spot.

SHOPPING

Slagelse is home of the **Vestsjællands Center,** Jernbanegade 10 (© **58-50-63-90**), a shopping mall with about 40 stores that occupies a prominent position in the town center, and whose only real competitor is an equivalent shopping center 40km (25 miles) away.

If you're in the market for gold and silver jewelry, as well as the elegant products of Georg Jensen and Royal Copenhagen, the preferred outlet is **Guildsmed Carl Jensens,** Rosengade 17 (© **58-52-02-97**).

Finally, **Bahne,** City Arkaden (© **58-52-00-75**), is located in the shopping complex in the heart of Slagelse. It houses the largest collection of applied art in Slagelse, along with a wide range of pieces from Holmegaard glassworks and the Royal Danish Porcelain Factory.

WHERE TO STAY

Hotel Frederik den II   Set a 10-minute drive south of the center of town, at the junction of Route 22 and the E20 highway leading to Korsør, this is a sprawling, brick, motel-style establishment that's clean, convenient, well managed, and without historic charm. Rooms are comfortable, clean, respectable, and standardized, but with excellent beds and bathrooms with shower units. Those on the ground floor have private patios; those upstairs contain balconies.

Idagårdsvej 3, DK-4200 Slagelse. © **800/528-1234** in the U.S., or 58-53-03-22. Fax 58-53-46-22. www.frederik2.dk. 74 units. Mon–Fri 1,200DKK ($200) double; Sat–Sun 963DKK ($161) double; suite 1,700DKK ($284) (2 people). AE, DC, MC, V. **Amenities:** Restaurant; bar; sauna; laundry service; dry cleaning; nonsmoking rooms; rooms for those with limited mobility. *In room:* TV, dataport (in some), hair dryer.

WHERE TO DINE

Nytorv 2 ✦ DANISH   Set in the heart of town, within the all-pedestrian shopping district, this is the only full-fledged restaurant in town that specializes in Danish food. You can dine on a brick-floored patio in back, surrounded by verdant potted plants, or in a conservatively decorated but comfortable dining room with a high ceiling and a polite, attentive staff. The house specialty is a "plank steak" that's prepared with ratatouille and a combination of béarnaise and pepper sauce and served on an oaken board. Several different preparations of plaice, as well as grilled salmon with spinach and rice, are also appealing, as are such desserts as fresh pastries with ice cream.

Nytorvet 2. © **58-52-04-45**. Main courses 95DKK–195DKK ($16–$33). AE, MC, V. Daily noon–10pm.

Pulcinilla ITALIAN   This is a simple and likable dinner-only trattoria in the heart of Slagelse, with a white-walled interior whose roster of Italian art includes a blown-up version of the Mona Lisa. Menu items are flavorful and fun, and include a number of pizzas and pastas such as lasagna and fettuccine Bolognese, soups and salads, and such main courses as veal parmigiana and entrecôte with pepper sauce. We won't pretend that this will be the finest Italian meal you've ever been served, but the food is well prepared with fresh ingredients, and it's good as a change of pace if you've tired of too much Danish fare.

Rosengade 7C. © **58-53-08-07.** Reservations recommended. Main courses 119DKK–179DKK ($20–$30). AE, DC, MC, V. Daily 5–11pm.

SLAGELSE AFTER DARK

The municipality of Slagelse has converted an old power station into a splendid concert center. **Slagelse Musikhus,** Træskogården, Sdr. Stationsvej 1–3 (© **58-50-10-70**), is the venue for frequent musical events and also for changing art exhibitions. The old turbine hall can seat more than 400 patrons, and a cafe on-site serves refreshments. Ask at the tourist bureau (see "Visitor Information," above) if any events are being staged at the time of your visit.

SIDE TRIPS: MEDIEVAL RUINS & VIKING RECONSTRUCTION

Slagelse makes a good base for exploring one of Scandinavia's major Viking reconstructions, Trelleborg, as well as a center for exploring Antvorskov, the ruins of a former royal palace and monastery. While still based at Slagelse, you can view both of these attractions in one very busy day.

TRELLEBORG

Although it's merely a mock representation, you can experience Viking life as lived 1,000 years ago at **Trelleborg Allé** ★ (© **58-54-95-06**), the reconstructed fortress of **Trelleborg.** Trelleborg is the best preserved of the quartet of Viking ring fortresses in Denmark. Expect an agenda-loaded schedule once you arrive: You can feel replicas of Viking tools, see household items used by Mrs. Viking, view the inevitable weapons of the day, soak up the atmosphere in a re-created Viking house, and, best of all, enjoy the beautiful Danish countryside surrounding Trelleborg. You can also take part in various events staged throughout the summer, including longbow archery, Viking cooking, sailing, martial arts, games, a Viking pageant, and a Viking market.

A reconstructed Viking house stands at the entrance. It was built in the Viking stave style, with rough oak timbers rising above mud floors. Warriors and their families used the earthen benches inside for both sitting and sleeping. The central hearth, as in this house, usually had an opening in the roof for venting smoke. This house and other reconstructions were based on finds excavated from an actual settlement on this site, which dated from 1000 to 1050.

The ring fortress consisted of a circular rampart with wooden stakes inserted in the earth. It could be entered through four different gates. From these entrances four lanes led to the heart of the fortress. This divided the ring into four quadrants, with about 16 houses laid out in each quadrant. A moat protected the eastern side of the fortress, whereas two small rivers and a marshland secured the other three sides.

The relatively new Trelleborg Museum contains a shop selling Viking jewelry, books on the era, a film room, Viking exhibitions, ship models, ancient artifacts, and a cafe. The 20-minute video shown here will help you understand Trelleborg better before you actually explore it.

Visits are possible Saturday to Thursday 10am to 5pm. Allow at least an hour for a visit, and perhaps more if you find it intriguing. Admission is 45DKK ($7.50) adults, 30DKK ($5) children. A family ticket costs 120DKK ($20).

GETTING THERE   By Car   Trelleborg is 6km (3¾ miles) west of Slagelse. If you're driving from Slagelse, follow Strandvejen until its termination at the village of Hejininge, where you'll see signs for Trelleborg, which is less than a kilometer (about ½ mile) away.

By Bus   You can take bus no. 312 from Slagelse right to the gate. There are several buses daily.

By Bicycle   You can cycle your way to Trelleborg on a rented bike from Slagelse. The tourist office will give you a brochure outlining points of interest along the cycle trail.

ANTVORSKOV

Today only the ruins of this former monastery and royal palace can be viewed, but much of Danish history happened on this spot, 2km (1¼ miles) south of the center of Slagelse near the road to Næstved. In 1164 King Valdemar I founded a monastery here, dedicated to the Order of St. John of Jerusalem. In time it became the major seat of the Order of St. John throughout the Nordic countries.

The monastery's chief legend centers on Hans Tausen (1494–1561), who preached a sermon in Antvorskov that paved the way for the Reformation in Denmark. This renegade monk, who trained at Antvorskov, then one of the richest monasteries in the country, became a disciple of Martin Luther, whom he had heard preach in Wittenberg. He became so inflamed at the abuses of the Catholic church that he delivered a fiery speech upon his return to Antvorskov.

When the Reformation did come, the king confiscated Antvorskov. It eventually was turned into a hunting manor. King Frederik II died here in 1588. In time it fell into disrepair and its buildings were sold and carted off. When it was deemed unsafe, the monastery church was torn down. The E20 motorway from Copenhagen buried about half of the former grounds of the monastery. However, you can still see some of the brick foundations.

Don't expect a formalized museum if you opt to visit this site, as it's little more than a ruin, with no guardian, no fence or barricades, no telephone contact point, no formal hours, and no admission fee.

GETTING THERE   By Bicycle   To reach the site from Slagelse, follow Slotsalleén from the heart of town, turning right when you reach the end of this road, and then follow the signposts into Antvorskov.

BIRKEGÅRDENS HAVER ⊛

This is a large, privately owned park set in one of the most beautiful parts of West Zealand, 23km (14 miles) north of Slagelse. The grounds contain a stunning Japanese garden designed by the Danish landscape architect H. C. Skovgård. The grounds also include a young oak forest with a woodland lake. There are plenty of benches throughout the park, and packed lunches may be eaten in the courtyard garden. Here you can also see cows being milked, horses grazing, and goats, rabbits, and calves that come right up to you. There are also a playground for children, a cafe offering refreshments, plus a kiosk selling ceramics, porcelain, and jewelry. Birkegårdens Haver lies at Tågerupvej 4 at Tågerup, near Kongsted (© **58-26-00-42**). It's open from April 10 to September 12 daily 10am to 6pm. Admission is 60DKK ($10) for adults, 20DKK ($3.35) for children.

GETTING THERE   By Car   To reach the gardens from Slagelse, drive north for 27km (17 miles) from the town center, following the signs that point to Kalundborg.

4 Næstved

80km (50 miles) SW of Copenhagen; 25km (15½ miles) S of Ringsted; 27km (17 miles) N of Vordingborg

The largest town in South Zealand, Næstved lies in an unspoiled countryside setting. With a population of some 45,000 and a historic core worth exploring, this port and industrial town stands on the southwest coast of Zealand at a point where the River Suså flows into the Karrebaek Fjord. This waterway forms a link between Næstved and Karrebæksminde Bay.

Næstved sprouted up around a Benedictine monastery, whose buildings today house Herlufen, Denmark's most famous boarding school, similar in prestige to Eton in Britain. In time, it became a major Hanseatic trading port. After a decline of fortunes, it came back with the coming of the rail lines in the 19th century.

Today it's a garrison town and home to the Gardehussar Regiment or Hussars of the Household Calvary. The best time to catch these guards is on Wednesday morning when they ride through the center of town amid much fanfare.

Today much of the outlying area of the town is industrial, devoted to such businesses as wood, paper, engineering, and even ceramics. But in the immediate surroundings, beyond the fringe of town, lie a number of charming places to visit, ranging from manors to mansions, and from abbeys to beautiful parks (see "Easy Excursions," below).

ESSENTIALS

GETTING THERE By Train Næstved lies on two major train routes, one going via Ringsted (trip time: 20 min.), the other going via Køge (38 min.). Of course, Køge (see earlier in this chapter), as well as Ringsted (see earlier in this chapter), enjoy frequent rail connections from Copenhagen.

By Car From Copenhagen, head south along E55 (also known as E47), cutting west along Route 54 into Næstved.

VISITOR INFORMATION South of Axeltorv, **Næstved Turistbureau,** Havnen 1 (✆ **55-72-11-22**), is open January to June 14 and September to December, Monday to Friday 9am to 4pm, Saturday 9am to noon. June 15 to 30 and August, it's open Monday to Friday 9am to 5pm, Saturday 9am to 2pm. July it's open Monday to Friday 9am to 6pm, Saturday 9am to 2pm.

GETTING AROUND By Bicycle Bicycling is especially popular in Næstved, thanks to a relatively flat landscape and the fact that everyone in town seems to view it as a part of everyday life. You can rent a bike from **Brotorvets Bicycles,** Brotorvet 3 (✆ **55-77-24-80**). Bikes rent for 50DKK ($8.35) a day, plus a 100DKK ($17) deposit.

EXPLORING THE TOWN

Our favorite pastime here is a canoe ride on the River Suså, with its calm waters. The river runs through the west side of Næstved. It doesn't have rapids and its current is negligible, so maneuvering by canoe is fairly easy. On summer weekends, the river is crowded with others who like to go canoeing too. Canoes can be rented at **Suså Kanoudlejning,** Næsbyholm Allé 6, near Glumsø (✆ **57-64-61-44**). Charges are 100DKK ($17) per hour or 350DKK ($58) per day. The outlet for rentals lies at Slusehuset, at the southern end of Rådmanshavn.

As you stroll through the town, you'll come upon some interesting old structures, the most notable of which is **Apostelhuset,** a half-timbered house on Riddergade (just south of Sct. Mortens Kirke) that dates from the Middle Ages. "Apostle House" has carved figures of the apostles on the beams of its 16th-century facade;

each carries an object that symbolizes his martyrdom. These are some of the oldest, and certainly the best-preserved, timber-frame carvings in the country. Nearby you'll see **Løveapoteket,** an old pharmacy in a restored half-timbered structure from 1853. The building is in the Dutch Renaissance style, and medicinal herbs and spices are still grown in a garden out back.

The central square of town is Axeltorv. All of the major sights of town are within a short walk of this historic area. The town center is graced with two Gothic churches, notably **Sct. Peders Kirke,** Sct. Peders Kirkeplads (© 55-72-31-90), lying just to the south of Axeltorv. This is the largest Gothic church in Denmark, dating from the 1200s. When it was restored in the 1880s, wall paintings from 1375 were uncovered in the choir area. One of these paintings depicted Valdemar IV and his consort, Hedwig, kneeling at a penitent's stool. A Latin inscription reads, "In 1375, the day before the feast of St. Crispin, King Valdemar died—do not forget that!" You can also see a choir screen by Abel Schrøder the Elder (ca. 1600), plus a crucifix by an unknown artisan dating from the 1200s, and a pulpit dated 1671. The church is open year-round, Tuesday to Friday 10am to noon. May to September, it's also open Tuesday to Friday 10am to noon and 2 to 4pm. Admission is free.

The other church worth a visit is **Sct. Mortens Kirke,** Kattibjerg 2 (© 55-73-57-39), lying halfway between the train depot and the landmark Axeltorv. Its facade is similar to that of Sankt Peders Kirke. The artistic highlight inside is a tall altar carved in 1667 by Abel Schrøder the Younger; the pulpit, even more ancient, was the work of his father, Abel Schrøder the Older. Admission is free, and the church is open year-round Monday to Friday 9 to 11am. July and August, it's also open Monday to Friday 2 to 5pm.

The town museum, **Næstved Museum,** Ringstedgade 4 (© 55-77-08-11), is also worth a visit. North of Axeltorv, it's divided into two sections. One of these, in the 14th-century Helligåndshuset or "House of the Holy Ghost" (the town's oldest building), is devoted to the cultural history of the area. Once this building was the town hospital. Its collection is known for its medieval woodcarvings, although some contemporary works are also featured. Other artifacts illustrate the agricultural history of the region and the tools the peasants used. The second section, Boderne, at Sct. Peders Kirkeplads, displays local silver and crafts. The Holmegaard glass on display was made locally. The buildings housing this section of the museum are period pieces, made of medieval brick with arched windows imbedded in mortar. Called *Stenboderne,* these 15th-century "stone booths" are the only remaining medieval terrace houses in Denmark. Craftspeople used to occupy them before they were turned into a museum. Charging 20DKK ($3.35) entrance for both sections of the museum (free for children under age 18), the museum is open Tuesday to Sunday 10am to 4pm.

SHOPPING
The things to purchase here are products made by Holmegaards Glasvaerker (see "Easy Excursions," below).

Of course, there's plenty of shopping in Næstved itself, with no fewer than three major shopping centers. Every day in summer the streets in the heart of town echo with the sounds of a jazz band, and there's a market at Axeltorv Wednesday and Saturday mornings. All the shopping malls in Næstved stage free exhibitions and shows.

The most important mall is the **Næstved Stor-Center,** Holsted Allée (© 55-77-15-00; bus: 2), which is widely recognized as the major shopping center for all of South Zealand, and attracts shoppers from Møn, Falster, and various hamlets for many kilometers around. Located about less than a kilometer (½ mile) north of the center, it's dominated by the giant Bilka supermarket (it's so large that they refer to it as a "hypermarket"). The mall's more than 50 specialist shops sell handicrafts, glass, jewelry, clothing, gifts, and dozens of other items.

WHERE TO STAY

Hotel Kirstine ★ *Finds*   The most appealing hotel in Næstved originated in 1745, when a local alderman created it as a venue for town meetings in a carpenter-derived design that's part neoclassical, part country baroque. Throughout most of the 1800s, it functioned as the home of the town's mayors, until around 1909, when it was transformed into a hotel that strictly prohibited any kind of alcohol on its premises. Today, the site is a half-timbered and romantic-looking monument to the elegant country life, thanks to a meticulous allegiance in all the public areas to a kind of well-scrubbed, prosperous-looking integrity that many visitors associate with rural Denmark. Rooms are conservatively and comfortably furnished, with private bathrooms with shower, but without the richly accessorized glamour of some of the public areas.

Købmagergade 20, DK-470 Næstved. ✆ 55-77-47-00. Fax 55-72-11-53. www.hotelkirstine.dk. 31 units. 850DKK ($142) double; 1,150DKK ($192) suite. Rates include buffet breakfast. AE, MC, V. **Amenities:** Restaurant; bar; laundry service; dry cleaning. *In room:* TV, dataport, minibar, hair dryer, safe.

Hotel Vinhuset ★ *Finds*   One of the most distinctive hotels in the region was built in 1768 atop vaulted cellars that monks used to store wine as long ago as the 1400s. And although the site has always had a tradition of housing overnight guests and the worldly goods of an order of monks, it entered the world of modern tourism in earnest sometime after World War II, when it was transformed into a working hotel. You'll find it across the square from Sankt Peders Kirke. Inside, Persian carpets, antique furniture, and a romantic atmosphere add to the allure. Rooms are comfortable, high ceilinged, and outfitted with a combination of modern furniture—especially good beds—and reproductions of antiques. All units also have neatly kept bathrooms with tub/shower combinations.

Sct. Peders Kirkeplads 4, DK-4700 Næstved. ✆ 55-72-08-07. Fax 55-72-03-35. www.hotelvinhuset.dk. 57 units. 700DKK–995DKK ($117–$166) double. Rates include breakfast. AE, DC, MC, V. **Amenities:** Restaurant; bar; room service (7am–10pm); babysitting; laundry service; dry cleaning; nonsmoking rooms. *In room:* TV, hair dryer.

Mogenstrup Kro   With origins that go back to its role as an old-time inn more than 200 years ago, this is a solid, well-respected resort that does a decent trade with weekenders escaping the urban congestion of Copenhagen. Rooms are medium in size with big windows, good beds, fine plumbing, and tub/shower combinations in the bathrooms.

Præstø Landevej 25, DK-4700 Næstved. ✆ 55-76-11-30. Fax 55-76-11-29. www.firsthotels.com. 99 units. 878DKK–1,276DKK ($147–$213) double. AE, DC, MC, V. **Amenities:** Restaurant; bar; sauna; room service (7am–9pm); laundry service; dry cleaning; nonsmoking rooms; rooms for those with limited mobility. *In room:* TV, dataport, minibar (in some), hair dryer.

WHERE TO DINE

Restaurant Bytinget/Restaurant Les Baraques ★ DANISH (Bytinget); FRENCH/CONTINENTAL (Les Baraques)   In this small town, it's unusual to have one organization (the previously recommended Hotel Vinhuset) with two separate restaurants. Both lie within the 18th-century precincts of a country-baroque building that originally functioned as a warehouse for the wine and worldly goods of an order of Danish monks. The more Danish, and folkloric, of the two venues is Bytinget, where Danish staples such as *frikadeller*, Danish hash, browned steak with onions, and filet of plaice with parsley-butter sauce are among the culinary choices. The more formal and prestigious of the lot is Les Baraques, where the fare is upscale Danish and French. On the frequently changed menu you get morel cream sauce and foie gras accompanying many dishes, and such delights as tender veal filets and lobster. Both the roast lamb and the duckling are superb here. The chefs are known for selecting only the finest ingredients on the market that day, but you'll pay for such culinary luxuries.

In the Hotel Vinhuset, Sct. Peders Kirkeplads 4. ⓒ **55-72-08-07**. Bytinget main courses 108DKK–198DKK ($18–$33). Les Baraques main courses 198DKK–278DKK ($33–$46). AE, DC, MC, V. Mon–Sat noon–3pm and 6–9:30pm.

NÆSTVED AFTER DARK

Each of the hotels recommended above maintains a bar, but in addition to those, you'll find easy access to at least three pubs, any of which might act as a backdrop for some drinks, dialogue, and people-watching. Each of them follows an unpredictable, frequently changing schedule that incorporates an hour or two of live music, usually on Friday and/or Saturday nights beginning around 9pm. Everything in town, however, is very spontaneous, so be alert to whatever musical venue your hotel staff says is happening during the time of your arrival. A worthwhile bet for nautical atmosphere and camaraderie is **Rådhus Kroenm,** Skomagerrækken 8 (ⓒ **55-72-01-56**), rivaled only by **Underhuset Bar,** Axeltorv 9 (ⓒ **55-72-79-19**). Equally appealing is the **Step Inn,** Ramsherred 14 (ⓒ **55-77-01-08**).

EASY EXCURSIONS

An excursion is to **Herlufsholm,** known to educators throughout Europe as the site of a famous prep school. Set about less than a kilometer (about ½ mile) northwest of the center of Næstved, it was founded at the dawn of the 13th century as a Benedictine monastery known as Skovkloster. The monastery, which was abandoned at the time of the Reformation, was eventually transformed into the **Herlufsholm Academy,** Herlufsholm Allée (ⓒ **55-72-60-97**; bus: 6A). To reach it from Næstved, follow the Slagelsevej from the town center. You can wander around the grounds, assuming you don't interrupt the flow of the academics, but if your time is limited, the crown jewel of the academy grounds is the monastery church, **Stiftskirke Herlufsholm.** Constructed in the late Middle Ages, it is one of the oldest brick churches in Denmark. It's noteworthy for its tombs, especially those of Admiral Herluf Trolle, who left an endowment to the monastery, and his wife, Birgitte Goye. The ivory Gothic crucifix inside dates from around 1230; the baroque pulpit was the creation of Ejler Abelsen in 1620. The church, which has an unusually wide nave, can be visited daily—except during religious services—during daylight hours. Admission is free.

Of the many stately homes surrounding Næstved, none is more interesting than **Gavnø Slot & Park** ⚜, Gavnørej (ⓒ **55-70-02-00**; bus: 1A). Located 4km (2½ miles) south of town, it lies on a peninsula, on the opposite bank of the Karrebæk fjord from the rest of Næstved. The old rococo castle is surrounded by a delightful botanical garden and is also the site of Butterfly World, where exotic tropical butterflies are allowed to fly free. A former nunnery, Gavnø reverted to private ownership in 1584. When Otto Thott (1703–85) took over the property, he had it converted into the rococo-style mansion you see today. Thott also accumulated one of the largest picture collections and private libraries (about 140,000 volumes) in Denmark. The premises also contain a valuable altar and pulpit carved by Abel Schrøder the Elder. Although part of the interior remains a private residence, much of the castle can be visited, and much of the old collection is on display. The best time to visit is when the tulips bloom in spring. Later, these flowers give way to ornamental shrubs and roses. A ticket that combines admission to the castle, the castle gardens with its butterfly collection, and a nearby church (Gavnø Kirke) that has been associated with the castle for many generations costs 55DKK ($9.20) adults, free for children under 12. All three places are open May to August, daily 10am to 4pm.

The manor house that we'd like to own is **Gisselfeld Slot** ⭐, Gisselfeldvej 3, Haslev (© **56-32-60-32**). It's a beautiful, step-gabled, brick Renaissance home dating from 1557. Although it has been much altered and changed over the centuries, it forms an impressive sight today, set in a well laid-out park that evokes the countryside of England. The park contains a fountain, a small lake, a grotto, and even a waterfall. You will have to be content to view the house from the outside, but you can wander through one of Denmark's finest private gardens, with some 400 different species of trees and bushes, including a rose island and a bamboo grove. The gardens are at their best in the late spring. It's said that it was here that Hans Christian Andersen found inspiration for his fairy tale "The Ugly Duckling." The gardens can be visited daily 10am to 5pm (mid-June to mid-Aug to 6pm). It costs 20DKK ($3.35) adults, free for children under 12. The only time the interior can be visited is during July, when guided tours can be arranged, on a rotating and oft-changing schedule that must be reconfirmed prior to your arrival.

5 Vordingborg ⭐

104km (65 miles) S of Copenhagen; 27km (17 miles) S of Næstved; 13km (8 miles) W of Møn

The little town of Vordingborg was much more important in the Middle Ages than it is today. It was from Vordingborg that the Danish kingdom was reunited in 1157—after several years of division—when Valdemar I (the Great) ascended the throne. Denmark's first constitution was written here in 1282. Before that, in 1241, the Jutland Code was first proclaimed here. This was one of the most significant doctrines of medieval times, codifying traditional law. The code's preamble—*"Mæth logh skal land byggiæs,"* or "with law shall a land be built"—is as familiar to Danish schoolchildren as the opening line of the Pledge of Allegiance is to American youth.

Because of its natural harbor, Vordingborg was an important launching point for the military campaigns of Bishop Absalon in the late 1100s against the warring Wends of eastern Germany. During the reign of the Valdemar kings, Vordingborg continued to remain in favor as a royal residence. The royal castle here was part of the system of Danish fortifications constructed along the Baltic as a protection against the Wends.

Valdemar IV (Valdemar Atterdag) was the king who in the 1360s extended the ring fortifications of the castle to their present-day dimensions. But in the 1400s the town lost its strategic importance when the Kalmar Union came into being. From that point on, Danish kings had such an expanded territory to be concerned about that they seemed to forget little Vordingborg, which declined in fortune.

The railroad came to the town in 1870, and by 1937 the Storstrøm Bridge replaced the ancient ferry link to the island of Falster. Today, about 20,000 people live in and around Vordingborg. Although no longer the capital of Denmark, Vordingborg is thriving and is the site of many well-known local companies. Since it's only an hour's ride by rail from Copenhagen, many locals commute to the capital for work using Vordingborg as a bedroom community.

ESSENTIALS

GETTING THERE   By Train and Bus   Frequent trains throughout the day serve Vordingborg from the Danish capital (trip time: 80 min.) and Næstved (20 min.). If you're planning to go on to Møn, you'll need to switch here from the train to the bus.

By Car   From Copenhagen, take E55 south, cutting west when you reach the junction of Route 22.

VISITOR INFORMATION   Just east of the Gåsetårnet, or Goose Tower, **Vordingborg Turistbureau,** Algade 96 (© **55-34-11-11**), is open Monday to Friday 9am to 4pm and Saturday 9am to noon. June to August it's also open to 5pm Monday to Friday and to 2pm on Saturday.

EXPLORING THE TOWN

Most of the town has been rebuilt in recent years in a modern but not unappealing style. The town's **Nordhavnen** or yacht harbor is the southernmost harbor of Zealand. Founded during the Valdemar kingdom, it still retains some of its old character, in spite of the many new facilities added.

Most tourists visit Vordingborg with one reason in mind, and that is to see the fabled "Goose Tower," but there are other attractions as well. Once part of the sprawling royal castle and fortress that stood here during the Middle Ages, the 14th-century **Gåsetårnet** (Goose Tower), Slotsruinen 1 (© **55-37-25-54**), is the best-preserved medieval tower in Scandinavia. It's the only structure that remains intact from the Valdemar era. The tower gets its name from 1368, when the king, Valdemar IV, ordered that a golden goose be placed on top of the tower to show his disdain for a declaration of war against Denmark by the Hanseatic League of Germany. He was hoping to suggest that the threats coming from the Hanseatic League were no more ominous to him than a flock of cackling geese. The pointed copper roof of the 37m (121-ft.) tower is still crowned by a golden goose, and the tower, of course, remains the town's landmark and source of historic pride.

From the top of the tower a panoramic view of the countryside unfolds. In its heyday, the fortress had seven more towers, but they were demolished over the centuries. In recent years excavations have uncovered the ruins of the castle. Queen Margrethe visited in 1997 to view the excavation of a Viking quay.

Visiting hours are June to August daily 10am to 5pm; off season, Tuesday through Sunday 10am to 4pm. If you arrive by train, stroll north from the station to the post office and then turn southeast onto Algade leading to Slotstorvet, in front of the fortress. An admission of 30DKK ($5) for adults and 10DKK ($1.65) for children under 11 covers entrance to the tower and the Sydsjællands museum.

Opposite the Goose Tower and standing on the fortress grounds, the **Sydsjællands Museum** (South Zealand Museum) displays regional artifacts gathered from South Zealand since the Stone Age. It's a history not only of Vordingborg but also of nearby Langebæk and Præstø. Local antique tools are displayed in a number of rooms. The trade and crafts exhibits from medieval to Renaissance times are particularly interesting, including ecclesiastical decorations and also textiles. Look for a showcase exhibiting an *aquamanile*, a vessel from medieval times used to pour water over a priest's hands at mass.

When the castle fell into disrepair after the war with Sweden in 1660, a new fort and cavalry barracks were constructed. One of these buildings contains the museum. The museum keeps the same hours as the tower (see above).

After, you can stroll through the adjoining Botanical Garden, the first in Denmark, laid out in 1921. Plants grown here were once used for medicinal reasons.

The town's most important church is **Vor Frue Kirke (Church of Our Lady),** standing on the Kirketorvet 14A (© 55-37-06-02), on ground that was formerly the town moat. Its exact date of construction isn't known but was probably at the dawn of the 15th century. Letters of indulgence (that the pope allowed parishioners) financed this brick church; financial contributions were essentially rewarded with forgiveness for sins. Apparently, there were enough sinners in Vordingborg to finance the construction of the church. The nave and the aisle date from 1432 to 1460, the church tower was added around 1600, and the sacristy around 1700. In the choir, note the frescoes from the mid–15th century, depicting the Adoration of the Magi and the Nativity among other events. The altarpiece depicting the Crucifixion was the creation of Abel Schrøder the Younger and dates from 1642. The choir lattice gate was also created by Schrøder to isolate the clergymen from the laymen. Visiting hours are daily 10am to 2pm.

The town is also noted for its **Prince Jørgen's Guard,** which comprises 50 boys from 8 to 23 years of age. In 1676 the chief of the regiment was Prince Jørgen, the youngest son of Frederik III and Queen Sophie Amalie. At his father's death in 1670 he inherited Vordingborg Castle. In recent times the guard has been revived, winning some 70 trophies for its marching, drumming, and prancing. Normally your chance of seeing the guard is best on Saturday mornings, when they often parade down the main pedestrian street of the town, Algade.

Many interesting old sites await those who explore the environs of Vordingborg. **Knudshoved Odde (Knudshoved Point),** a 14km-long (9-mile) peninsula west of Vordingborg, which is owned by the Rosenfeldt Estate and has been protected to preserve its unique Bronze Age landscape. Almost any type of Danish tree grows here—brackens as tall as people; thickets of brambles, honeysuckle, and ivy; and a wealth of wildflowers. The curiously named "zo tree frog" also survives here. A small herd of American buffalo was also imported to live here. You can park your car for 12DKK ($2) and explore the park. The car park is halfway down the peninsula where the trail begins.

SHOPPING

Shopping here is limited but worthwhile. **Sandbirk,** Algade 48 (© 55-37-02-62), is the exclusive outlet for the best porcelain, silver, and gold items in town, with all the big names represented: Jacob Jensen, Georg Jensen, and Flora Danica. If you don't find what you like here, a leading competitor is **Boe Andersen,** Algade 72 (© 55-37-05-73). Finally, the best place for glass and porcelain is **IMERCO** (© 55-37-01-14), which is particularly strong in Royal Copenhagen products and Holmegaard Glas (glassware).

WHERE TO STAY

Hotel Kong Valdemar From the front, this hotel—the only one in town—looks like a moderate-size row house nestled comfortably among its neighbors. It's much bigger, however, than you might have thought, thanks to an enlargement in the 1980s, and thanks to the fact that it sprawls out across a garden in back. Rooms are streamlined and efficiently decorated, not plush in any way, and vaguely reminiscent of a modern, no-frills college dormitory. All units have clean bathrooms with shower units. On the premises are a bar and a restaurant (see "Where to Dine," below).

Slotstorvet, DK-4760 Vordingborg. © **55-34-30-95.** Fax 55-34-04-95. www.hotelkongvaldemar.dk. 60 units. 629DKK ($105) double. Rate includes breakfast. DC, MC, V. **Amenities:** Restaurant; bar. *In room:* TV, minibar, hair dryer.

WHERE TO DINE

Den Gylden Gås (The Golden Goose) DANISH This competent, if not exciting, dining room is associated with the Hotel Kong Valdemar. Comfortably decorated, with views that sweep out over some of the medieval buildings nearby, it offers such tried-and-true Danish specialties as shellfish and lobster soup with Noilly Prat; seafood salad (with salmon, sole, shellfish, herbs, and vinaigrette); Greenland halibut with white wine, chives, and new potatoes; pork cutlets with curry sauce and rice; and cognac-flamed pepper steak. Guests, many of whom are locals, enjoy the food here. It's a good place to take your Danish mother (if you have one)—the chefs probably cook like she does.

In the Hotel Kong Valdemar, Slotstorvet. ② 55-34-30-95. Main courses 136DKK–210DKK ($23–$35). DC, MC, V. Tues–Sun 5–8pm.

Restaurant Babette (⭐ (Finds) DANISH/INTERNATIONAL It was inevitable that at least one restaurant within this guide bears a name inspired by the brilliant European film *Babette's Feast*, in which Danish and French characters interact with one another's appetites. And in Vordingborg, the most appealing and most interesting restaurant pays homage to the Babette of that film. It lies about a kilometer (⅔ mile) north of the town center, near the headquarters of a local TV station (Channel 2), and within sight of Vordingborg's famous "Goose Tower." Cuisine is noteworthy for its zeal and intelligence and its sheer sense of style. Our most recent meal consisted of lobster cocktail with herbed Nantua sauce; filets of halibut in a mousseline sauce; free-range chicken from a nearby organic farm, served with white truffles, spicy spinach, and new Danish potatoes; a selection of French and Danish cheeses; and a finale of fresh summer berries from nearby bogs, served with homemade ice cream.

Kildemarksvej 5. ② 55-34-30-30. Reservations recommended. Fixed-price menus 375DKK–550DKK ($63–$92). DC, MC, V. Tues–Fri noon–midnight; Sat 6pm–midnight.

Restaurant Påfuglen INTERNATIONAL/DANISH This restaurant occupies a long, low, modern-looking veranda attached to a striking red-brick building that was a movie theater in the 1890s. Within a room that might remind you of a greenhouse because of its many windows along one side, you can enjoy a menu based mostly on seafood, but with lots of emphasis on steaks as well. Examples include grilled shrimp on a stick with sage sauce, fried Norwegian salmon with lobster sauce, and garlic steak with spicy butter and fried entrecôte with grilled tomatoes and béarnaise sauce. The place lives up to its moderate price tag and adheres to a fundamentally classical style of cookery. The dishes may be typical but the kitchen staff shows care and finesse in their preparations.

Algade 88. ② 55-37-01-90. Reservations recommended. Main courses 75DKK–195DKK ($13–$33). DC, MC, V. Daily 11am–9pm (last order).

VORDINGBORG AFTER DARK

A good place to begin your evening is **Amigo Bar,** Algade 35 (② **55-37-60-65**), right in the center of town. It seems to attract the most simpatico crowd. The best alehouse is nearby: **Slots Kroen,** Algade 119 (② **55-37-02-61**). A lot of the locals will also direct you to **Willy Nilly,** Algade 1 (② **55-34-20-40**), a friendly English pub that seems to have the coldest beer in town, attracting a 20 to 40 age group. It's also the site of **Prinsen Diskotek,** Algade 1 (② **55-34-20-40**), which opens at 10 or 11pm, often staying open until 3 or 4am. It rarely charges a cover.

6 Møn

128km (80 miles) S of Copenhagen

The island of **Møn** lies just off of Zealand, in the southeast corner of Denmark. Its big attraction is the 122m (400-ft.) **Møns Klint,** 6km (3¾ miles) of white chalky cliffs that rise dramatically from the Baltic Sea. Møns Klint was formed by the Baltic, and made up of ice-transported chalk masses and glacial deposits. The chalk was formed from calcareous ooze 75 million years ago. The ooze enclosed shells of marine animals that are now fossils. The glacial deposits date from a million years ago. They originated partly as boulder clay deposited by inland ice and partly as bedded clay and sand containing marine mussels. The boulders on the beach have dropped from the cliff and have been rounded by wave erosion.

Although Møn's white chalk cliffs seem to be its main appeal, once you get here you'll find an island of rustic charm and grace well worth exploring. Fewer than 12,000 people live here, and the residents of Møn zealously guard their natural environment; the beauty of their landscapes remains largely unspoiled. Sheltered by dunes, the white sandy beaches are a summer attraction, so it's not just the wild cliffs that draw visitors here. The island also boasts beautiful forests with a wide variety of wildlife and a trio of churches with the best frescoes in the country (more about that later), plus a lively market town in Stege.

Møn is also known for the prehistoric remains that are scattered about the island. For detailed information, the tourist office (see "Visitor Information," below) publishes a booklet called *Prehistoric Monuments of Møn.* Several Neolithic chambered tombs known as "giants' graves" were discovered. As the legend goes, the western part of the island was ruled by a "jolly green giant" called the Green Huntsman, and the eastern part of the island was the domain of another giant, Upsal.

Møn lies at the eastern edge of the Størstrommen, a channel dividing the island of Zealand and the island of Falster.

ESSENTIALS

GETTING THERE   By Train and Bus   From Copenhagen's Central Rail Station, take a train departing once an hour for Vordingborg in South Zealand. From Vordingborg take bus nos. 62 or 64 to Stege, the capital of Møn. Once on the island, bus service is meager; you'll need a car to explore.

By Car   Cross over from the island of Zealand on the Dronning Alexandrines Bridge, then proceed through the old country town of Stege.

VISITOR INFORMATION   The local tourist office, **Møns Turistbureau,** Storegade (© **55-81-44-11**), is open Monday to Friday 10am to 5pm and Saturday 9am to noon.

Finds   Pottery Sales

As you drive about Møn, note the many signs advertising *keramik.* On this slow-paced island, people everywhere seem to have taken up ceramics and pottery and are only too willing to sell their products to you. This interest in ceramics originated because of the rich clay deposits found here.

GETTING AROUND   By Bus   The major bus station is at Stege. This is the departure point for all the island's bus routes. Fares are based on the number of zones traveled. Bus service is unreliable and varies according to weather conditions and the time of the year. Bus no. 52 traverses the most popular route, going from Stege to Klintholm Havn via Elmelunde and Magleby. Monday through Friday service on this route is hourly, dropping to about every other hour on weekends. Magleby is the most easterly town on Møn. Bus no. 54 operates only in the peak of summer, usually late June to mid-August, taking passengers from Stege to the island's major attraction, Møns Klint. Service is about six times daily Monday through Friday, or four times daily on weekends. Finally, bus no. 53 goes from Stege to Ulvshale, with bus no. 64 serving the route from Stege to Bogø.

By Bicycle   Many Danes prefer to explore Møn by bike. The best trail to follow is the signposted bike route going from the capital, Stege, to Møns Klint. Ask at the tourist office for a pamphlet outlining the best cycling tours of the island, which take in all of Møn's principal attractions. In Stege, bikes can be rented at **Dækaingen Cykler,** Storegade 91 (© **55-81-42-49**). Rates average 35DKK ($5.85) a day.

STEGE: THE ISLAND'S CAPITAL

After crossing the bridge from "mainland" Zealand on Route 59, take an immediate left and follow the road to the ancient market town of Stege, which is the ideal gateway to the island and the source of the best information about Møn (see "Visitor Information," above).

Time seems to have forgotten this sleepy little capital, and that is part of its charm. To the surprise of first-time visitors, Stege has preserved its moat and ramparts from the Middle Ages, whereas other Danish towns have torn them down. One of its original trio of town gates, Mølleporten, is still here to greet guests as in olden days. Mølleporten, which once allowed (or prohibited) entry to the town, stands on Storegade. Meaning "mill gate" in English, the gate bears a resemblance to the Stege church tower. It's made of red brick and lined with horizontal strips of white chalk from (where else?) Møns Klint.

EXPLORING THE TOWN

Known for its primitive frescoes, **Stege Kirke** ⊛, Kirkepladsen (© **55-81-40-65**), is one of the largest churches in the country, with a massive tower striped in brick and chalk. Its oldest section, built in the Romanesque style, dates from the early 1200s. It was constructed by the ruler of the island, Jakob Sunesen, who was a member of the powerful Hvide family, which also laid claim to Bishop Absalon. In the latter 1400s the church was expanded to its present size.

The principal nave is flanked by two smaller naves on each side and is filled with pointed arched windows and high vaulted ceilings. Rich frescoes by the Master of Elmelunde are found in the choir and main nave. Long covered with whitewash, they were discovered and restored in 1892. Many are quite whimsical in nature. In the post-Reformation era, Lutheran ministers found the frescoes "too evocative of Catholic themes," and ordered that they be whitewashed. Although this sounds bad, it was the whitewashing that actually preserved the frescoes so that they can still be enjoyed today. They were restored under the supervision of Denmark's national museum. Charging no admission, the church is open April to September Tuesday to Sunday 9am to 5pm; October to March Tuesday to Sunday 9am to 1pm.

Next to the old Mølleporten or town gate stands **Empiregården,** Storegade 75 (© **55-81-40-67**), housing the rather elegant **Møn Museum,** a repository of

local cultural history. The collection is rich in artifacts from the Middle Ages, including coins and old pottery, but it also goes back to the Stone Age, displaying items like ancient fossilized sea urchins. The museum also displays Møn house interiors from the 1800s. It's open daily 10am to 4pm, charging 30DKK ($5) adults, free for children.

SHOPPING

The island is known for its ceramics and pottery, whose production keeps dozens of artisans working long hours. Two of the best places to see, and buy, some of the goods produced here include a warehouse-sized emporium 4km (2½ miles) east of Stege on the road leading to Møns Klint. **Ympelese,** Klintevej 110 (© **55-81-30-05**), stocks some of the most appealing handmade candles in Zealand, as well as a variety of ceramic pots, plates, and vessels. There's even men's, women's, and children's clothing for sale, some of it fabricated by local seamstresses, and some of it designed to protect its wearer from the midwinter gales that sweep in from the Baltic and North Seas.

WHERE TO STAY & DINE

Hotel Ellens Cabaret ★   An inviting town inn, long accustomed to putting up wayfarers, this is the leading choice in the capital. The three-story motel-style building stands at the edge of town near the sea. The English-speaking staff is helpful and welcoming. Rooms are fairly streamlined with modern pieces and all the comfort you'll need. The most desirable have large windows with balconies. All units have neatly kept bathrooms with tub/shower combinations. There are also a bar with a large TV and a clientele of sports fans and traveling salespeople.

Langelinie 48, DK-4780 Stege. © 55-81-54-54. Fax 55-81-58-90. 27 units. 700DKK ($117) double. Rates include breakfast. MC, V. **Amenities:** Bar; lounge; laundry service; dry cleaning. *In room:* No phone.

Præstekilde Kro & Hotel ★   Its fans define this as the most opulent and glamorous hotel on Møns—partly because of its upscale comforts and partly because of its association with the island's nearby golf course. Built in the early 1970s in a rambling compound of big-windowed, low-slung buildings, it lies 5km (3 miles) east of Stege, about 2.5km (1½ miles) from the nearest beach, Strand Wengensgaardsvej. Many, but by no means all, of the clients spend their day on the golf links; others decompress from urban life in Copenhagen, walking through nearby fields and forests or relaxing beside the seacoast. Rooms are more plush than those at most of the island's hotels. The bathrooms are beautifully kept and equipped with tub/shower combinations.

Klintevej 116, DK-4780 Stege. © 55-86-87-88. Fax 55-81-36-34. www.praestekilde.dk. 46 units. 925DKK–1,025DKK ($154–$171) double; 1,225DKK ($205) junior suite. Rates include breakfast. AE, DC, MC, V. **Amenities:** Restaurant; bar; indoor heated pool; sauna; 24-hr. room service; laundry service; dry cleaning; nonsmoking rooms; solarium. *In room:* TV, minibar, hair dryer.

STEGE AFTER DARK

Persons under age 25 on the island are quick to point out that there are no full-time dance clubs on Møn, unless a local church or civic group opts to hold a youth-group gathering in a communal basement somewhere. In lieu of that, you'll probably find that the most convivial gathering place is the bar at the previously recommended **Præstekilde Kro & Hotel,** Klintevej (© **55-86-87-88**). Here you'll find an inkling of big-city style a la Copenhagen, but not so much that you won't realize that you're far from urban life. Still, the drinks taste good, and you're likely to meet a handful of other urbanites to swap stories with.

ULVSHALE & NYORD

After leaving Stege, you can follow a minor little road directly north 6km (3¾ miles) with signposts that will lead you to Ulvshale, or "Wolf's Trail" in English, a peninsula jutting west toward Zealand. It's one of the most beautiful spots on Møn, now preserved as a nature reserve, with gnarled old trees and rare birds such as snipe, razorbills, water-rails, and others, which prefer to live on the mud-flats. Ulvshale boasts one of the best beaches on the island and it also is home to one of the few virgin forests left in the country. The beach is Ulvshale Strand, and the main road, Ulvshalevej, runs right along it. The forest is crisscrossed with a network of hiking routes.

Once at Ulvshale you'll see a bridge connecting Møn with the little offshore island of **Nyord.** You can walk across the bridge to get to this tiny speck of an island, which means "New Word" in English. It's been set aside as a bird sanctuary for rare birds, including rough-legged buzzards, snow buntings, hen harriers, and others.

The birds are seen mainly in the east marshes. On the north side of the road, about a kilometer (⅔ mile) after crossing the bridge, you'll come to a tower that is the best vantage point for watching the birds. The bridge itself is also a good bird-watching site.

The little village on the island is called Nyord, too, and it's a time capsule from the 1800s, with old thatched houses. Other than a tiny yacht harbor and a little church from 1846, there aren't a lot of attractions, but it's such an idyllic place it's worth the effort to get here.

After a look at the birds, head back in the direction of Stege, but when you see a turnoff to Keldby, follow the signs into this hamlet, 5km (3 miles) east of Stege.

KELDBY

This agrarian community is mainly visited by those who want a look at **Keldby Kirke** ⚘, Præstegårdstræde 1, Keldby (℗ **55-81-33-05**). Built of brick between 1200 and 1250, this is one of the island's special churches, celebrated for its frescoes that span 200 years, the oldest dating from 1275. Both Old and New Testament scenes are included. No church in Denmark quite equals Keldby in medieval frescoes—note especially the dramatic representation of Cain and Abel and the horror show depicting Doomsday. Shepherds pictured with their flocks create a more bucolic scene. In addition to the frescoes, the church also contains a number of other treasures, notably a carved pulpit dated 1586, and, in the vaulting, paintings by the Master of Elmelunde, including a tender depiction of Joseph preparing gruel for his newly born infant son. A tombstone at the north side of the church dates from the mid–14th century. The church can be visited from April to September daily from 7am to 5pm; off season daily 8am to 4pm. Admission is free.

If you have time after viewing the church, consider a visit to the manor **Hans Hansens Gård,** Skullebjergvej 15 (℗ **55-81-40-67**), which lies about a mile south of Keldby Church. (Follow the signs to Keldbylille to reach it.) Dating from 1800, this is a thatch-covered building whose wings enclose an inner courtyard. Originally conceived as a farmhouse, it's the home of Møns Museumsgården, a monument that depicts what family life was like for homesteaders during the 1800s. The farm was kept in the same family for generations. When its last owner, a bachelor, Hans Hansens (for whom the property is named), died, he willed it to the people of Møns (who converted it into a museum. Furniture and utensils used by the Hansens family are on display. It's open from April to September, Tuesday to Sunday from 10am to 4pm. Admission is 30DKK ($5).

The highway (Rte. 287) continues directly east to Elmelunde.

ELMELUNDE

This tiny rural hamlet, roughly equivalent to Keldby in size and layout, is about 7km (4⅓ miles) east of Stege and is the site of the island's second-most-visited church, **Elmelunde Kirke** ⚘, Klintevej, Elmelunde (℗ **55-81-33-05**). Dating from around 1080, it's one of the oldest stone churches in Denmark. During the Romanesque era, the nave was expanded. In the early 1300s, the distinctive tower was added, transforming it into a prominent landmark for sailors coming in from the sea. The interior of the church is known for its frescoes painted by the Master of Elmelunde. Here this rather mysterious artist left some of his masterpieces, including *Last Judgment, St. Peter with the Key to Heaven, Christ in Majesty, St. Paul with a Sword,* and his charming *Entry into Jerusalem,* along with the more sobering *Flagellation of Christ.*

He also painted lighter subjects, including autumn harvest and some plowing-the-fields scenes. Other frescoes depict Adam and Eve being thrown out of the Garden of Eden. The feudal lord, Corfitz Ulfeldt, and his consort, Queen Leonora Christina, donated the altar and pulpit. The intricately carved and painted altar dates from 1646; the pulpit was created about 3 years later. The carved pulpit is supported entirely on a figure of St. Peter. In 1460 the three-pointed vaults (seen over the altar) were added, and the Master of Elmelunde painted them as well. Year-round, the church is open daily 8am to 4pm. Admission is free.

WHERE TO STAY

Hotel Elmehøj   Set about 4km (2½ miles) inland, midway between Stege and Møns Klint, adjacent to the stop for buses that interconnect the two, this is one of the most stately looking guesthouses in Møn. It occupies a former retirement home built between 1928 and 1930. In 1991, it was acquired by Brit Olifent, a woman born and reared on Møn, who runs it today with her husband, Jonathan, who was born in Perth, Australia. Rooms are simple and very clean, with few frills and a sense of regimented orderliness. There's little to do on the property, other than taking promenades in the well-tended garden, exploring the nearby beach and forest, and visiting the 12th-century interior of the Elmelunde church, a short walk away. A communal TV room and a public kitchen that some guests use to prepare light lunches and snacks are on the premises.

Kirkebakken 39, Elmelunde, DK-4780 Stege, Møn. © **55-81-35-35.** Fax 55-81-32-67. www.elmehoj.dk. 23 units, none with bathroom. 450DKK ($75) double; half-board 440DKK ($73) (double occupancy). Rates include breakfast. MC, V. Closed Jan. **Amenities:** Breakfast room; lounge; laundry service; dry cleaning. *In room:* No phone.

WHERE TO DINE

Kaj Kok DANISH   Set within a big-windowed building from the 1970s, about a kilometer (⅔ mile) from the hamlet of Elmelunde, this highly recommended restaurant has earned a reputation for serving well-prepared versions of time-honored Danish specialties. You'll recognize it by its red facade and a large garden in which tame goats munch on vegetables. Within an interior whose modernity is disguised by a roster of old-fashioned decorative accessories, you can order crab and garlic bisque, marinated and/or smoked salmon, filets of halibut in white wine parsley sauce, and a flavorful version of pepper steak. Lighter appetites appreciate the *smørrebrød* (open-face sandwich), which usually sell for 30DKK ($5), except for a deluxe version, with lobster, that costs 61DKK ($10).

Klintevej 151, Elmelunde. © **55-81-35-85.** Reservations recommended. Main courses 89DKK–161DKK ($15–$27). AE, DC, MC, V. Daily noon–9pm. Closed Oct–Apr Mon–Wed.

LISELUND

After a meal at Kaj Kok, continue east along Route 287 through the hamlet of Borre, where you'll pass a brick church built in the early 1200s. Continue through the village but turn left at the signpost to Sømarke. The next road to the right leads to Sømarkedyssen. At this point you'll come upon a round dolmen crowned by a huge capstone over an open chamber. From here there's a panoramic view over the entire island. After a look at the dolmen continue on the same road, going left up a very narrow lane. At the peak, turn right along the road for about 90m (295 ft.), which will lead to the entrance of Liselund.

This thatched palatial summer home from 1795 is surrounded by lovely park grounds with artificial lakes and canals in the northeastern part of the island. H. C. Andersen wrote *The Tinder Box* while staying at Swiss Cottage here. The park is called a "folly" of the 18th century, when it was constructed by Bosc de la Calmette, a royal chamberlain who was inspired by Marie Antoinette's Hamlet at Versailles. You can buy refreshments at a small chalet filled with antlers and antiques. The admission-free park is open daily until sunset year-round.

Other structures in the park were destroyed by a rockfall in 1905, but guided tours of the **Gamle Slot** (Old Castle) are available. Call © **55-81-21-78** for more details. Inside you'll find an architectural mélange of styles, with tiny canopied beds, a *trompe l'oeil* painting, and a Monkey Room painted with a jungle scene. Visits are possible May to October at 10:30am, 11am, 1:30pm, and

2pm. On Sunday there are two extra visits at 4 and 4:30pm. No visits are possible on Monday or Saturday. Admission is 30DKK ($5) adults, free for children.

WHERE TO STAY & DINE

Liselund Ny Slot   Set amid the trees and rolling hills of a national park, this manor house was built in 1887 as an annex to a much older castle. Since the transformation of the original castle into a museum, most of the region's overnight guests seek accommodations in the yellow-colored stucco walls and soaring tower of the Ny Slot (New Castle). Rooms are very simple, outfitted with minimalist furniture and neatly kept bathrooms with shower units, and afford views over fields, forests, a pond with swans, and the sea. Many of the public areas have high, frescoed ceilings that give a sense of the place's original grandeur.

You don't have to stay at the hotel to eat lunch in the establishment's basement-level cafe (served noon–6pm), or for dinner in the more formal dining room (6:30–8pm). Menu items include preparations of Danish lamb in rosemary sauce, Baltic or North Sea fish, and steaks. There's also an occasional Chinese or Asian dish. The restaurant is open daily in summer, with an occasional (unscheduled) closing 1 or 2 days a week in winter.

Langebjergvej 6, DK-4791 Borre. ℭ **55-81-20-81.** Fax 55-81-21-91. 15 units. 1,125DKK ($188) double. MC, V. **Amenities:** Dining room; cafe; lounge. *In room:* No phone.

MØNS KLINT ★★

After a visit or even an overnight stay at Ny Slot, drive back to Route 287 and follow the road east to the highlight of the tour, **Møns Klint.** These impressive white chalk cliffs (see the introduction to Møn) stretch for several kilometers, with a sheer drop of 120m (394 ft.) at their highest point. Formed by glacial deposits combined with the action of a turbulent sea, they are one of the most dramatic natural sights in Denmark. Møns Klint was pocked throughout with nearly 100 Neolithic burial mounds. Paths lead through woodland to the towering edge of the cliffs, where one of the most spectacular views in all of Denmark awaits you. For decades photographers have delighted in capturing the image of these brilliantly white cliffs against the azure blue of the sea. When the sun is out, the scene is especially breathtaking.

Footpaths are cut into the cliffs, and visitors are fond of hiking these towering trails. It takes about an hour's walk to appreciate the magnificence of the site. There's a wide expanse of beech trees along the top of the cliffs, providing shelter for rare plants, including 20 species of orchids hidden in the undergrowth. For the best view, follow the signs to the peak called Sommerspiret and hope that the sky is clear at the time of your visit. Fossils of marine animals—some long extinct—have also been discovered on the beach below these cliffs. Two steep flights of steps lead from both Storeklint and Jydeleje down to the sea, but be prepared for an exhausting climb back to the top. Once you're at the bottom, you can join Danish families who hunt for blanched fossils on the beach, usually sea urchins. Captains at sea use the cliffs as a navigational point since they stand out from Zealand's relatively flat topography.

The most dramatic hike, of course, is along the towering cliffs. But if time remains, you can also hike through Klinteskoven (Klinte Forest), a woodland area that grows right up to the edge of the cliffs. Horse trails and a network of paths have been cut through this forest. Trails start from the edge of the cliffs, and the most interesting track to follow is a about a kilometer (⅔ mile) west of Storeklint, which will take you to Timmesø Bjerg. Here you'll see the ruins of a castle built around 1100. If you visit, facilities for tourists are found at Storeklint, including a cafeteria and a parking lot, along with some souvenir kiosks.

At **Rent-A-Horse,** Langebjergvej 1 (© **55-81-25-25**), an outfitter near a local youth hostel at Møns Klint, you can book 2-hour guided horseback tours of Møns Klint or the bay at its base, the Klinteskoven. Equestrian treks are priced at 250DKK ($42) per person per 1½ hours (including a guide).

KLINTHOLM HAVN

Returning to the parking lot at Møns Klint, you can continue south along a minor little road to the hamlet of Sandvej. Once here, turn right at the T-junction in the direction of Mandemarke. Before reaching this village, take a left turn down a lane marked KLINTHOLM HAVN. This will take you to an old village on the coast with a bustling fishing harbor and a modern marina. The seaside village, a bit of a holiday center, opens onto Hjelm Bay. It's best to visit here on a sunny day, as Klintholm Havn is mainly known for its beach.

Many wealthy Germans use the marina here to station their yachts. One harbor is filled with fishing boats, the other with these yachts, and the beach runs in both directions from these two harbors. We prefer the beach extending to the east. It's well maintained and set against a backdrop of low-lying dunes; the sands aren't pure white, however, but more of an oyster gray. But if you want to venture into these usually cold waters, the safest swimming is on the beach extending to the west of the harbors. The marina has public toilets and showers.

WHERE TO DINE

Chances are you'll be in the area for lunch. There are a few slightly formal places to eat, but our suggestion for a meal is to walk east along the coastal road from the fishing harbor until you come to a little outlet called **Klintholm Røgeri.** Here you can purchase fried or smoked fish and wash it down with a cold Carlsberg. This is an ideal place to enjoy a picnic, and there are picnic tables on-site.

If you prefer, however, you can return to the village and have more formal service in a regular dining room.

Klintholm Søbad ★ (Finds   Set in the center of Klintholm Havn, about 3km (1¾ miles) southeast of Borre, this yellow-walled *kro* (inn) is one of the most appealing and charming restaurants on Møn. Built a few steps from the sea, with views that extend southward as far as the coast of eastern Germany, it dates from 1927 and has been feeding visitors with traditional Danish-style food ever since. If you opt for the buffet, you won't be disappointed: It's laid out smörgåsbord-style and includes many of the traditional culinary specialties of Denmark. But if you opt for a la carte, the inn's signature dish is fried flatfish (a form of plaice) that's served with parsley-enriched butter sauce and new potatoes. Even more appealing, if it's to your taste, is the "herring buffet." Priced at 40DKK ($6.70) per person, it includes four different preparations of herring (fried, marinated, in cream sauce, and in curry sauce), and satisfying chunks of fresh whole-wheat bread and butter. It's the kind of culinary experience that can be delectable, if you love this most Scandinavian of fish.

On the premises are two simple, not very frequently occupied rooms, priced at 695DKK ($116) for a double, and six cottages, built in the 1980s, for 795DKK ($133) for between one and four occupants. Each comes with few amenities, although there are a TV and kitchenette in all cottages. You might consider these if you're looking for old-fashioned, bare-bones accommodations by the sea.

Thyravej 19, Klintholm Havn, DK-4791 Borre. © 55-81-91-23. Reservations recommended. Main courses 99DKK–149DKK ($17–$25); 3-course fixed-price menu 159DKK ($27). AE, MC, V. Daily 8:30am–11pm. Closed Oct–Apr. Free parking.

SIGHTS IN WEST MØN

After a visit to Møns Klint, you'll have to take the same route back into Stege. But there are other attractions in Møn if time remains. From Stege, head south along Route 287 to Grønjægers Høj, an impressive long barrow surrounded by a stone circle, 6km (3¾ miles) south of Stege near the hamlet of Æbelnæs. It's signposted. Called "The Hill of the Green Huntsman," it's a Stone Age "passage grave." Nearly 150 large stones surround the megalithic tomb with three chambers, one of the largest such grave sites in all of Scandinavia.

The third church of Møn to have been decorated by the Master of Elmelunde lies in the area. To reach it, continue on Route 287 to Damsholte, then go left on a minor road following the sign to **Fanefjord Kirke** ✿, Fanefjordkirkevej, Fanefjord (© **55-81-70-05**). The frescoes in the chancel date from the mid–14th century, but the rest are by the master himself. The cycle of paintings was called "Biblia Pauperum," or "Bible of the poor," since many of the peasants who formed the congregation did not read. Most of the themes were taken from the Old and New Testaments. Some are loosely based on Christian legends.

Depicted are the Adoration of the Magi, the Baptism of Jesus, the Birth of Jesus, and the Annunciation, among other subjects. The Slaughter of the Innocents is particularly moving. The most fun and amusing fresco is St. George and the Dragon. In the choir arch are some frescoes from the High Gothic period, around the mid–14th century, depicting St. Martin and St. Christopher, among other subjects. St. Christopher is seen carrying Christ across a fjord. The imagination that went into these frescoes shows amazing creativity and massive talent, and the refinement of color is also an outstanding achievement. They are well worth the detour here to reach them. The church itself overlooks Fanefjord and was constructed in the mid–13th century in the Gothic style. The church can be visited daily 8am to 4pm. Admission is free.

After viewing the church, head 8km (5 miles) north in the direction of Tostenæs, where you'll see a sign to **Kong Asgers Høj,** a large passage grave, with a passageway leading to a vast burial chamber. The site lies in a farmer's field on Kong Asgers Vej. The burial chamber is 10m (33 ft.) long and some 2m (6½ ft.) wide. Duck as you go in or you'll crown yourself.

One final attraction remains for Møn, and it's actually an island unto itself. The island of **Bogø** at the southwestern edge of Møn is reached by continuing along Route 287. A causeway leads to what is called "The Island of Mills." Once many mills peppered the little island, but now there's only one remaining, Bogø Molle, which was constructed in 1852 and looks like a windmill from Holland.

Other than its bucolic charm, there isn't a lot to see and do on Bogø, but it has some of the most unspoiled scenery around and makes for a satisfying drive.

In the little hamlet you can pass by a medieval village church with some late-15th-century murals, but you will have seen better and more intriguing churches if you've already toured Møn. It isn't necessary to return to Møn to get back to Zealand. You can drive straight through Bogø until you come to the Farø bridges, which will connect you with Copenhagen in the north or to Falster in the south.

As you approach the ramp to the bridges, you'll see the **Farobroen Welcome Center,** with a cafeteria, money-exchange office, and toilets. At the tourist kiosk here you can pick up brochures about Denmark.

7

Bornholm

Surrounded by the Baltic Sea, astride the important shipping lanes that connect St. Petersburg with Copenhagen and the Atlantic, Bornholm sits only 37km (23 miles) off the coast of Sweden, but about 153km (95 miles) east of Copenhagen and the rest of Denmark. Prized as a strategic Baltic military and trading outpost since the early Middle Ages, but sadly the site of many bloody territorial disputes among the Danes, Germans, and Swedes, it's home to 45,000 year-round residents. An additional 450,000 visitors arrive during the balmy months of summer. Besides tourism, which is growing rapidly, the economy relies on trade, fishing, herring processing, agriculture, and the manufacture of ceramics. Thanks to the island's deep veins of clay, ceramics has been an important industry since the 1700s.

Covering a terrain of granite and sandstone is a thin but rich layer of topsoil; the island's rock-studded surface is made up of forests and moors. The unusual topography and surprisingly temperate autumn climate—a function of the waters of the Baltic—promotes the verdant growth of plants: figs, mulberries, and enough lavish conifers to create the third-largest forest in Denmark (right in the center of the island). This forest, Almindingen, has the only rocking stone which still rocks. Rocking stones are giant erratic boulders weighing up to 40 tons that were brought to Bornholm by the advancing glaciers during the last Ice Age. In addition, one of Denmark's largest waterfalls, Døndalen, lies in the north

of Bornholm in a rift valley. It can best be viewed from spring through fall.

The island covers 945 sq. km (365 sq. miles), and most of the inhabitants live along 140km (87 miles) of coastline. Not only do the flora and fauna differ in many respects from the rest of Denmark, but its geology is unique as well. The island is divided into two geologic zones: 1,500-million-year-old bedrock to the north and a 550-million-year-old layer of sandstone to the south.

Bornholmers traditionally have been fishers and farmers. Today their villages are still idyllic, evocative of the old way of life in their well-kept homesteads, as are fishing hamlets with their characteristic smokehouse chimneys, often used for smoking herring.

The island is still sparsely populated. Grand Canary, a Spanish island off the coast of Africa, for example, is the same size as Bornholm, but while that resort hosts some two million residents in high season, the greatest number of people ever seen on Bornholm at one time is 100,000.

The best beaches of Bornholm lie in the southwestern section of the island, between the towns of Balka and the main beach town of Dueodde.

Because of its location at the crossroads of warring nations, Bornholm has had a turbulent history, even as recently as 1945. Strongholds and fortified churches protected local inhabitants when the island was a virtual plaything in the power struggle between royal and religious forces. It was plundered by pirate fleets, noblemen, and the

Hanseatic towns of Pomerania. It didn't experience peace until after it revolted against Swedish conquerors at the end of Denmark's war with Sweden in 1658. A group of liberators shot the island's Swedish Lord, and the Bornholmers handed their land over to the king of Denmark.

On a more modern and rather fanatical note, the liberation of Bornholm—unlike the rest of Denmark—was slow to come in 1945. Even when the Nazis had surrendered, the local German commandant on Bornholm refused to give up the island to the Allies. In response, the Soviets rained bombs down on Rønne and Nexø (the two main towns) and then invaded the island and occupied it for several months before returning it to the crown of Denmark. During the long

Cold War, the Danes indulged in a little payback time with the Russians. Bornholm became one of NATO's key surveillance bases, spying on what Ronald Reagan called "The Evil Empire."

The island's cuisine is obviously influenced by the surrounding sea. Baltic herring, cod, and salmon are the traditional dishes. One of the most popular local dishes is called *Sun over Gudhjem,* a specialty of smoked herring topped with a raw egg yolk in an onion ring. It's served with coarse salt and chives, or, most often, radishes. In autumn, the small Bornholm herring are caught and used for a variety of spiced and pickled herring dishes. Another local dish is salt-fried herring served on dark rye bread with beetroot and hot mustard.

ESSENTIALS
GETTING THERE

By Ferry   The most popular means of reaching the island from Copenhagen is the 7-hour ferryboat ride. Maintained by the **Bornholmstraffiken** (✆ **33-13-18-66**), these ferries depart year-round from the pier at Kvæsthusbroen once per evening at 11:30pm, with scheduled arrival the following morning at 6:30am. Late-June to mid-August there's an additional departure at 8:30am every day except Wednesday. Passage costs 32DKK ($5.35) per person each way, plus an optional supplement of 221DKK ($37) to rent a private cabin. These ferries are most often used to transport a car from Copenhagen, which costs 174DKK ($29) each way.

Bornholm Ferries, Havnen, at Rønne (✆ **56-95-18-66**), operates 2½-hour ferries from Ystad on the southern coast of Sweden, with up to four departures daily. These ferries have tax-free shops onboard. A car with a maximum of five passengers costs 122DKK ($20) each way. You can also travel from Sassnitz-Mukran (Rügen) in north Germany for a 3½-hour crossing to Bornholm, arriving at Rønne. Tax-free shopping is also found onboard on this crossing. From Germany, one-way passage for a car with a maximum of five passengers is 1,135DKK ($190). Each of these ferries has a restaurant or bistro featuring a buffet with Danish and Bornholm specialties.

By Plane   **Cimber Air** (✆ **70-10-12-18** for reservations and information) has about nine flights a day from Copenhagen to Bornholm's airport, 5.5km (3½ miles) south of Rønne. Depending on restrictions, round-trip fares range from 465DKK to 1,680DKK ($78–$281).

VISITOR INFORMATION

The tourist office, known as **The Bornholm Welcome Center,** Kystvej 3, Rønne (✆ **56-95-95-00**), is open June to August daily 10am to 5:30pm; April, May, September, and October Monday to Friday 9am to 4pm, Saturday 10am to 1pm; November to March Monday to Friday 9am to 4pm.

> **Tips** Hassle on Bornholm
>
> Don't expect to enjoy a holiday on Bornholm without some inconvenience: Boats from Copenhagen take either 5½ or 7 hours each way. And if you plan to visit in midsummer, firm reservations are essential because of the large numbers of Danes who come for the sandy beaches and the Baltic sunshine.

GETTING AROUND

By Car   The best place on the island for car rentals is **Europcar,** Nodre Kystvej 1 in Rønne (✆ **877/940-6900** in the U.S., or 53-95-43-00). Its least expensive rentals begin at 2,750DKK ($459) per week, including unlimited mileage and insurance coverage as well as the government tax. In addition, **Avis** is located at Snellemark 19, in Rønne (✆ **800/230-4898** in the U.S., or 56-95-22-08).

By Bicycle   During nice weather, biking around the island is almost as popular as driving. If you want to do as the Danes do, rent a bike; the prices are pretty much the same throughout the island—about 60DKK ($10) a day. A suggested bike-rental company in Rønne is **Bornholms Cykleudleijning,** Nordre Kystvej 5 (✆ **56-95-13-59**). Open daily 8am to 4pm and 8:30 to 9pm.

EXPLORING THE ISLAND

Even if you have a car available, you might want to bike the tour we've outlined later in this chapter. Ask at any tourist office for a map of the island's more than 190km (118 miles) of bicycle trails and divide this tour into several days, hitting the highlights mentioned below at your own pace.

The tour begins at Rønne, but you could join in at almost any point; basically, the route goes counterclockwise around the island's periphery. Be aware that Bornholm's highways do not have route numbers; even though some maps show the main east–west artery as Route 38, local residents call it "the road to Nexø." Consistent with local custom, this tour suggests that you follow the directional signs pointing to towns you'll eventually reach en route.

1 Rønne

The capital and administrative city of Bornholm, Rønne lies on the western coast facing the island of Zealand. The island's major harbor and airfield are found here.

Rønne is an elongated town with many single-family dwellings, both large and small. If you arrive by boat, you'll notice St. Nicolai Church, dedicated to the patron saint of seafarers, on Harbour Hill, towering over the small South Boat Harbor just below.

It wasn't until the 18th century that locals moved ahead with plans for a large trading harbor here. Even today the harbor is still expanding to service ferries and the many cruise ships that call at Rønne in increasing numbers.

Soviet aerial attacks in 1945, mentioned previously, left most of Rønne in shambles. What you see today is essentially a modern town with a population of 15,000. Many of the houses look older than they are because the town was carefully rebuilt in the post-war years in the old style. The town is full of narrow streets with cross-timbered houses, and many are painted in bright colors such as yellow and orange.

On the vast stretches of sand both south and north of Rønne are popular bathing beaches.

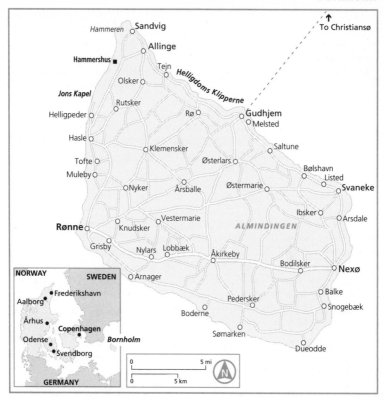

SEEING THE SIGHTS

Ericksson's Gård (Farm) *Finds*   Set on the outskirts of Rønne, just a short walk from the town center, this is the island's best-preserved example of an old-fashioned farm—the kind that once flourished on Bornholm. Originally constructed in 1806, it's a half-timbered, tile-covered building filled with antique furniture and oil paintings, and flanked with a garden that horticulturists admire for its 160 species of old-fashioned (that is, nonhybrid) roses and flowers. Some of the objects inside commemorate the marriage of a descendent of the farm's original owners—the Ericksson family. An Ericksson daughter married the Danish poet Holger Drachmann (1846–1908), whose works are studied by virtually every schoolchild in Denmark.

Laksegade 7. ② **56-95-97-35**. Admission 35DKK ($5.85) adults, 10DKK ($1.65) children. June to mid-Oct Mon–Fri 10am–4pm, Sat 10am–2pm. Closed mid-Oct to May.

Forsvarsmuseet   Housed within a citadel built around 1650 by the Danish king, this Defense Museum is in the southern part of town. With its massive round tower, this old castle is filled with weapons, maps, and models of fortifications. There is also a collection of antique armaments and military uniforms. In our view, the most interesting displays depict the Soviet aerial bombardment of Bornholm in 1945 and the subsequent Russian occupation of the island.

If you have a car or are a great biker you can also view some attractions in the environs. **Borgårdsten** lies 9km (5⅔ miles) north of Rønne along the road to the hamlet of Hasle. This is the most significant runic stone on the island. First found in 1868, it dates from the beginning of the 12th century. Some long-ago Viking inscribed "Svenger had this stone placed here for his father Toste and for his brother Alvlak and for his mother and sisters." Apparently, women weren't considered important enough to list their actual names.

If you visit Borgårdsten you might as well go another 2.5km (1½ miles) up the coast to the little port of **Hasle,** with its stone church from the 1300s and a half-timbered tower. Inside the church is an intricately carved and painted altar, the work of an unknown Lübeck artist, dating from the mid–15th century. In July a "herring festival" is celebrated here.

If you'd like to check out a west coast Bornholm beach, you'll find one south of Hasle. It's quite sandy and set against a backdrop of pine trees.

While at Hasle you can see five smokehouses in a row, lying on the coastline. One of the smokehouses (which can be visited for free) is preserved as it was originally built in 1897. It is **Silderøgerierne I Hasle,** Sdr. Bæk 16–20 (© **56-96-44-11**). In one of the other smokehouses, you can watch herring and other kinds of fish being smoked the traditional way, in open chimneys. Afterward you can purchase smoked fish, pick up a beer, and find a nearby spot for an idyllic and quintessential Bornholm experience.

Kastellet Galløkken. © **56-95-65-83**. Admission 35DKK ($5.85) adults, 10DKK ($1.65) children 6–12, free for children under 6. May–Oct Tues–Sat 11am–5pm.

Hjorth's Fabrik (Bornholm Ceramic Museum)   The unusual geology of Bornholm includes deep veins of clay that potters have appreciated for many generations. Since the 1700s hundreds of island residents have produced large numbers of unusual pots, plates, and cups—many of which are whimsical and highly idiosyncratic reminders of another way of life. In 1858 a small-scale factory, Hjorth's Ceramics, was established to make pottery from the island's rich deposits of clay, and it survived until 1993. In 1995 the island's newest museum was established in the company's original factory, a simple but solid building dating back to 1860. Inside, you'll find an intriguing hybrid between an art gallery and an industrial museum. You'll see the island's best examples of the dark-brown, yellow, and gray pottery that was produced in abundance beginning in the 1700s; samples of the dishes and bowls made by the Hjorth company over the years; and some of the work of Bornholm's modern-day potters. Throughout the year several ceramic artists maintain studios inside, casting, spinning, or glazing pots in full view of visitors. Two women descendants of the Hjorth family run the charming small-scale museum. The museum shop sells modern-day replicas of Hjorth ceramics, and many exhibits trace the production process from start to finish.

Krystalgade 5. © **56-95-01-60**. Admission mid-Apr to mid-Oct 35DKK ($5.85) adults, 10DKK ($1.65) children; mid-Oct to mid-Apr 10DKK ($1.65) adults, free for children. May–Oct Mon–Fri 10am–5pm, Sat 10am–2pm; Nov–Apr Mon–Fri 10am–5pm, Sat 10am–1pm.

Museum of Bornholm (Bornholms Museum) ✿   This is the largest and most distinguished museum on Bornholm. It focuses on the island's unique position in the Baltic. Set in what was formerly the island's hospital, it has displays on archaeology, local traditions and costumes, ethnology, and the seafaring and agrarian traditions that made the island what it is today. Several rooms are outfitted with 19th-century antique furniture, toys, island-made silverware, and accessories. Of special interest is the collection of Bornholm-made clocks, copied from a shipment of English clocks that was salvaged from a Dutch shipwreck in the late 1700s.

Skt. Mortensgade 29. (✆ **56-95-07-35**. www.bornholmsmuseum.dk. Admission 35DKK ($5.85) adults, 10DKK ($1.65) children. Mid-Apr to mid-Oct Mon–Fri 10am–5pm, Sat 10am–2pm; mid-Oct to mid-Apr Mon–Sat 1–4pm.

SHOPPING

Despite its isolation in the middle of the Baltic, Bornholm offers many opportunities for acquiring some serious merchandise. Most of the island's shops line either side of streets funneling into the Lille Torv and the Store Torv. Part of the fun involves wandering aimlessly from shop to shop, but if you want specific addresses and ideas, consider any of the following.

Want to offer some flowers to the object of your most recent affections? Head for **Lilliendal Plantecenter,** Sagavej 1 (✆ **56-95-47-24**). Some of the most unusual and eccentric kitchen- and housewares in Bornholm are available at **Inspiration,** Lille Torv 1 (✆ **56-95-01-11**). Expect Danish functionalism combined with wrought iron, glass, ceramics, textiles, and wood; much of it is made within Scandinavia.

If you're looking for a garment of any degree of formality for the child or children you left behind, the best children's clothing store on the island is **Kids' Shop,** Sct. Mortensgade 4 (✆ **56-91-00-17**). Is your camera running out of film? Film supply or development is available at **Ilsted Bech,** Snellmark 25 (✆ **56-95-00-23**).

A major outlet for some of the art glass produced in abundance on Bornholm is **Pernille Bülow Glas,** Lille Torv (✆ **56-95-43-05**). For a catch-all emporium selling everything from cheap souvenirs to rather exotic handmade goods that you're not likely to find on the Danish "mainland," head for **Joker,** Torvegade 4 (✆ **56-95-09-13**).

The island is known for its unique Bornholmer grandfather clocks. The tradition began in 1744 when a Dutch ship was stranded on the way from Helsingør in Denmark to Tallinn in Estonia. In its hold were five clocks and a cask with weights for them. Dexterous young men made models of the clocks and, in so doing, founded a Bornholm clockmaking tradition, a craft that virtually disappeared at the end of World War II. The craft has now been revived, and the island's largest clockmaker workshop is located in Rønne. **Nye Bornholmerure,** Torneværksvej 26 (✆ **56-95-31-08**), sells the finest handmade grandfather clocks in Denmark, although they can be very expensive depending on the model. These clocks sound the hour with music—everything from Mozart to Andrew Lloyd Weber.

Many Swedes come over to Bornholm just to shop for the island's famous ceramics. **Michael Andersen,** Lille Torv 7 (✆ **56-95-00-01**), still preserves the old ceramics-making traditions but also manufactures many modern products as well.

The island's best goldsmith—and he's a stunning talent—is Jørn-Ole Thomsen, who works at **Guldhuset,** Bornholmercentret (✆ **56-95-02-70**), on Store Torv. Thomsen makes fine jewelry not only for the local shop but also for Georg Jensen, the world-famous silver and goldsmith company.

WHERE TO STAY

The island is essentially a fair weather destination, and most hotels are likely to be closed in winter except for a few diehards.

Hotel Griffen ⭐ Near the heart of Rønne, a 5-minute walk from the beach, the town center, and an upscale marina, this hotel is the largest on Bornholm. Built in the 1970s, its buildings vaguely resemble 18th-century hip-roofed manor houses. Two of the four buildings contain only lodgings, and because of their separation from the from dining, drinking, and convention facilities, they tend to be quiet and peaceful. Guest-room furnishings are contemporary and minimalist but with occasional touches of elegance enhanced by floor-to-ceiling windows and glass doors that afford views of the sea. All units have well-managed bathrooms with tub/shower combinations.

Ndr. Kystvej 34, DK-3700 Rønne. ✆ **56-95-51-11.** Fax 56-95-52-97. www.hotelgriffen.dk. 140 units. 1,045DKK ($175) double; 1,650DKK ($276) suite. AE, DC, MC, V. **Amenities:** Restaurant; bar; indoor heated pool; sauna; room service (7am–9pm). *In room:* TV, hair dryer.

Hotel Hoffman Built in the 1970s about a block from the city's inner harbor and the ferry terminal, this hotel is mainly appealing for its well-designed, monochromatic rooms. The apartments here have kitchenettes and are more bare-boned than the conventional rooms; they require the payment of a one-time cleaning fee that's imposed at the end of every rental even if it's only 1 day. Bathrooms are well maintained and contain tub/shower combinations.

Ndr. Hystvej 32, DK-3700 Rønne. ✆ **56-95-03-86.** Fax 56-95-25-15. 69 units, 16 apts with kitchen but without maid service. 715DKK ($119) double with breakfast; 795DKK ($133) apt with kitchen (double occupancy). In apts, breakfast 70DKK ($12) extra per person. One-time expense of 350DKK ($58) for end-of-rental cleaning costs. AE, DC, MC, V. **Amenities:** Bar; lounge. *In room:* TV.

Hotel Ryttergaarden Set about 2km (1¼ miles) south of Rønne, less than 180m (591 ft.) from a sandy beach, this hotel was built between 1986 and 1998 as a compound of angular, big-windowed modern structures. Parts of its architecture might remind you of the buildings surrounding an international airport, because of their boxy, hyper-modern shapes and their ample use of glass. Overall, it's a good, albeit somewhat anonymous, choice for a holiday beside the sea. Rooms are cozy and modern, with varnished blond wood and sliding glass doors that open onto balconies facing the sea. All units have well-kept bathrooms with tub/shower combinations.

Strandvejen 79, DK-3700 Rønne. ✆ **56-95-19-13.** Fax 56-95-19-22. www.hotel-ryttergaarden.dk. 102 units, 28 apts with kitchenette. 770DKK–970DKK ($129–$162) double; rates include breakfast. Apts for up to 6 occupants 2,595DKK–5,495DKK ($433–$918) per week, without breakfast, plus an obligatory one-time fee per apt of 350DKK ($46) for cleaning, plus 195DKK–310DKK ($33–$52) per apt per week for electricity. AE, DC, MC, V. Closed Oct–Apr. Bus from Rønne: 23 or 24. **Amenities:** 2 restaurants; bar; indoor heated pool; tennis court; fitness center; sauna; laundry service; dry cleaning; nonsmoking rooms; rooms for those with limited mobility; solarium. *In room:* A/C, TV, minibar, hair dryer, trouser press.

Radisson Hotel Fredensborg This is one of the few hotels on the island that remains open year-round. In a quiet forest, adjacent to a beach less than a kilometer (about ½ mile) south of the Rønne harbor, it was built during the 1960s. There's Danish modern furniture in the comfortable guest rooms; each contains a bathroom with a tub/shower combination. Prices vary according to season and views of the water.

Strandvejen 116, DK-3700 Rønne. ✆ **800/333-3333** in the U.S., or 56-95-44-44. Fax 56-95-03-14. www.radissonsas.com. 72 units. 1,195DKK ($157) double; 1,495DKK–1,795DKK ($196–$235) suite. Rates include buffet breakfast. AE, DC, MC, V. **Amenities:** Restaurant; bar; tennis court; sauna; room service (7am–10pm); babysitting; laundry service; dry cleaning; nonsmoking rooms. *In room:* TV, dataport, minibar, hair dryer.

Sverres Small Hotel Set about a block from Rønne's harbor, this ocher-colored antique building was originally established as a coaching inn around 1850. This is a clean, well-maintained, and completely unpretentious hotel that's an extremely good choice if you don't mind a 1km (⅗-mile) trek to a worthwhile beach. Rooms are simple but cozy. Units with bathrooms have well-kept shower units. Breakfast is the only meal served, although the neighborhood around the hotel offers many different dining choices.

Snellmark 2, DK-3700 Rønne. © 56-95-03-03. Fax 56-95-03-92. www.sverres-hotel.dk. 22 units, 12 with bathroom. 390DKK–460DKK ($65–$77) double without bathroom; 510DKK–580DKK ($85–$97) double with bathroom. MC, V. Rates include breakfast. **Amenities:** Breakfast room; lounge; room service (7am–10pm). *In room:* TV, no phone.

WHERE TO DINE

De 5 Stâuerna ★★ DANISH/INTERNATIONAL This is the best and most upscale restaurant in Rønne, with a clientele that tends to select it for celebratory meals and family gatherings. Its name translates as "the five rooms," each of which is outfitted in a rustic country-Danish style. There's always a platter of the proposed fish of the day, which is usually fried in butter and served with new potatoes—a style that Bornholmers have witnessed since their childhood. Other more elaborate options include Hereford beefsteak prepared cordon bleu style, with salted cured ham and Emmenthaler cheese; tournedos of beef flambéed in Calvados and served with apples and onions; an exotic sautéed filet of ostrich with Mexican pimentos and peppers; marinated and minced beefsteak with chiles; and a dish that we personally prefer more than almost anything else on the menu: Bornholm lamb served with a sauce concocted from rosemary, olive oil, and tarragon.

In the Hotel Fredensborg, Strandvejen 116. © 56-95-44-44. Reservations recommended. Main courses 75DKK–210DKK ($13–$35); fixed-price menu degustation 265DKK ($44). AE, DC, MC, V. Daily 11am–10pm. No changes.

Rådhuskroen ★ *(Finds* DANISH This is the most visible and, in its own way, most charming restaurant in Rønne. It's situated in the darkened and intimately illuminated cellar of the Town Hall, a 140-year-old building with a long history of feeding island residents in a cozy setting protected from blustering midwinter winds. Wall sconces cast romantic shadows over a collection of antique furniture and accessories, as a well-trained service staff serves such dishes as super filet of salmon in a "summer sauce" of fresh tomatoes, chives, and herbs, and two different sizes of tender and well-prepared beefsteak ("Mr. Beef" and "Mrs. Beef").

Nørregade 2. © 56-95-00-69. Reservations recommended on weekends. Main courses 10DKK–171DKK ($1.65–$29). AE, DC, MC, V. Mon–Sat noon–3pm and 5–9pm.

RØNNE AFTER DARK

Its role as Bornholm's largest settlement forces Rønne into the sometimes unwanted role as nightlife capital of the island. But don't expect too much glitter, as things on Bornholm tend to stay quiet.

For high-energy members of the under-30 generation, the most visible and popular dance club on the island is **Red Barone,** Sct. Mortensgade 48, in Rønne (© **56-95-06-88**). Victim to oft-changing ownership within the past decade, it offers high-volume mania that's associated with nightlife in bigger cities. The venue is a dark-painted, much-used environment with prominent bars, battered sofas and chairs, and a dance floor lit by colored lights that just might tempt you to get up and dance. A 40DKK ($6.70) cover charge is imposed on Friday and Saturday; other times, entrance is free. If you're less interested in hanging out with the young crowd, consider a pint of Guinness at **O'Malley's Irish Pub,** Store Torvegade, in Rønne (℃ **56-95-00-16**), where clients older than 30 appreciate the Celtic conviviality and the recorded music.

Calm, cool, and mellow, **Dr. Jazz,** Snelle Mark 26 (℃ **56-95-50-26**), is Bornholm's leading emporium of jazz, which is produced by local combos as well as groups imported from other parts of Europe. Expect a crowd of drinkers and smokers over 25, and a spontaneity that can be rather charming. It's open daily 11pm to 5am. There's usually no cover charge.

FROM RØNNE TO NEXØ

From Rønne, drive east along the island's modern highway, A38, following the signs toward Nexø. Stop in **Nylars** (about 5km/3 miles from Rønne), a town that's known as the site of the best-preserved of Bornholm's four round churches. The **Nylarskirke** (℃ **56-97-20-13**), built around 1250 and rising prominently from the center of a community with no more than about 50 buildings, contains frescoes that depict the Creation and the expulsion of Adam and Eve from the Garden of Eden. The cylindrical nave has three floors, the uppermost of which was a watchman's tower in the Middle Ages. You can also view two fragments of a runic stone. From Rønne, you can take bus no. 6 if you don't have a car; the bike path from Rønne to Åkirkeby also passes by the church. It's open mid-April to October 20, Monday to Friday 9am to 5pm. Admission is free.

Continue driving another 5km (3 miles) east until you reach **Åkirkeby,** the only inland settlement of any size. Its economy is based on farming. Small-scale and sleepy, this is Bornholm's oldest settlement (its town charter dates from 1346). The little town was important in medieval times when islanders had to move inland to avoid attacks from enemies at sea. The island's regional council met here until 1776, and Åkirkeby was also the ecclesiastical center of Bornholm.

It's also home to the island's oldest and largest church, **Åkirke,** Torvet (℃ **56-97-41-03**), originally built around 1250. This church isn't as eccentric as some of the others. It's a sandstone-fronted monument built with defense in mind, as you'll note from the small windows. Note the Romanesque baptismal font incised with runic inscriptions believed to be carved by the master craftsman Sigraf on the island of Gotland. Other runic inscriptions appear on the cloverleaf-shaped arches. The church is open daily 10am to 4pm; there is a charge of 6DKK ($1) for visitors.

Åkirkeby is a good point to cut inland if you wish to see some of Bornholm's woodlands, among the densest in Denmark. Forests are filled with oak, hemlock, fir, spruce, and beech trees. The tourist office in Rønne (see "Visitor Information," earlier in this chapter) will give you a map outlining the best of the trails that cut through Bornholm's largest forest, **Almindingen,** in the center of the island. It can be reached by following a signposted road north from Åkirkeby. The forest is also the location of the island's highest point, **Rytterknægten,** a 160m (525 ft.) hill with a lookout tower, Kongemindet, with a staircase you can climb for a panoramic view of the dense woodlands.

You can also pick up information at a minor, rarely used tourist office that's much less visible than the island's main office in Rønne. It's the **Sydbornholms Turistbureau,** Torvet 2 (℃ **56-97-45-20**), at Åkirkeby. Mid-May to mid-September, it's open Monday through Friday 9am to 6pm and Saturday 8am to 1pm. The rest of the year, it's open Monday through Friday 10am to 6:30pm and closed Saturday and Sunday.

A minor museum that's interesting to specialists and devoted automobile fans is the **Bornholms Automobilmuseum,** Grammegardsvej 1 (© **56-97-45-95**). Its displays include vintage cars and motorcycles, plus some farm equipment and tractors that highlight the 20th century's advances in agrarian science. Antique cars and tractors derive from such manufacturers as Delahaye, Opel, Ford, Adler, Singer, Jaguar, and Fiat. It's open May to October, Monday through Saturday 10am to 5pm. The rest of the year it's closed. Admission costs 30DKK ($5) per person.

From Åkirkeby, cut southeast for 4.5km (2¾ miles), following the signs to **Pedersker,** a hamlet with only three shops (which close down during the cold-weather months). Six kilometers (4 miles) later you'll reach **Dueodde,** the name of both a raffish beachfront community and the entire region around the south-ernmost tip of the island. The village of Dueodde marks the southern edge of a stretch of coastline that some people believe is the finest beach on the island. The oceanfront bounty—and the best beaches on the island—stretch northward and eastward to the town of **Balka,** 5km (3 miles) beyond, encompassing stretches of white sand whose grains are so fine that they were used for genera-tions to fill hourglasses. The towns themselves are little more than backdrops for seasonal kiosks and a scattering of holiday homes for mainland Danes and Swedes. Most of the landscape is a virtual wilderness of pine and spruce trees, salt-tolerant shrubs, and sand dunes, some of which rise more than 12m (39 ft.) above the nearby sea.

The focal point of this southeastern coastline is the **Dueodde Fyr** (Dueodde Lighthouse), the tallest lighthouse on the island, built in 1962 to warn ships away from the extreme southern tip of the island. Weather permitting, you can climb to its top during daylight hours May to October for a fee of 5DKK (85¢), which you pay directly to the lighthouse keeper. For information, call the tourist office in Dueodde © **56-49-70-79.**

From Dueodde, continue along the coast in a northeasterly direction, passing through the unpretentious fishing hamlets of **Snogebæk** and **Balka.** Immedi-ately north of Balka the road will deliver you north to Nexø, the second major town of the island after Rønne, opening onto the eastern coast facing Sweden.

2 Nexø ⟨★⟩

Nexø, 26km (16 miles) east of Rønne, has a year-round population of 3,900, which makes it the largest fishing port on the island. Part of the charm of this community can be found in the excellent replicas of the privately owned 17th- and 18th-century buildings that were architectural highlights of the island before World War II.

In May 1945, Nexø was heavily bombed by the Russians during 2 days of horror; this happened several days after the rest of Denmark had been liberated from the Nazis. Nexø was a final holdout of Nazi soldiers in the closing days of the war. Ironically, Bornholm was the last area of Denmark to get rid of its Rus-sian "liberators," who didn't completely evacuate the island until 1946.

The destruction of most of the town's 900 buildings and their subsequent restoration along original lines is the stuff of legends.

Before exploring the area, you can pick up good information at the **Nexø-Dueodde Turistbureau,** Sdr. Hammer 2A (© **56-49-70-79**). May to August, it's open Monday through Friday 10am to 5pm and Saturday 9am to 2pm. The rest of the year, it's open Monday to Friday 10am to 5pm and closed Saturday and Sunday.

One of the town's more eccentric and idiosyncratic monuments is the **Nexø Museum,** Havnen (② **56-49-25-56**), open only May to October, daily 10am to 4pm. For an entrance fee of 35DKK ($5.85), you'll see displays of fishing-related equipment that has sustained the local economy, and memorabilia of the Danish author Martin Andersen (1869–1954)—better known as Martin Andersen Nexø, a pen name he adopted in honor of his native village. His novel *Pelle the Conqueror,* set in Bornholm and later made into an acclaimed film, revealed how Danish landowners in the early 20th century exploited Swedish newcomers to the island.

WHERE TO STAY

In this southeastern corridor of Bornholm you aren't limited just to Nexø. In summer you can also stay at the seaside hamlets of Dueodde or Snogebæk immediately south of Nexø. These are more scenic places to stay, and they also open onto the island's best beaches. Dueodde is Bornholm's number one beach area, and the entire stretch of coast is filled with rolling dunes and endless strips of white sand. Snogebæk is a little seaside settlement with holiday homes, but there's no village attached to Dueodde. For the most part, residents who live in Dueodde or Snogebæk use Nexø for their services and supplies. All these destinations are essentially summer ones, and most of the places to stay (except for the Hotel Balka Strand) close for the winter.

AT NEXØ

Hotel Balka Søbad *Kids*   Set in an isolated position on a flat and sandy seafronting plain, this hotel consists of five white modern buildings constructed between 1972 and 1976, encircling a common guest area. This beach resort caters to families with children. Rooms have bathrooms with tub/shower combinations, wall-to-wall carpeting, kitchenettes, a balcony or terrace, and simple, durable furniture. Most of the guests here spend the bulk of their time on the sands of the beach, the waters of which lie no more than 90m (295 ft.) from the hotel.

Vestre Strandvej 25, DK-3730 Nexø. ② **56-49-22-25.** Fax 56-49-22-33. www.hotel-balkasoebad.dk. 106 units. 810DKK–1,550DKK ($135–$259) double. Rates include breakfast. MC, V. Closed Nov–Apr. From Nexø, drive 3km (1¾ miles) south, following the signs to Snogebæk. **Amenities:** Restaurant; bar; outdoor heated pool; tennis court; sauna; laundry service; dry cleaning. *In room:* TV.

Hotel Balka Strand   This is the only hotel along Bornholm's beach-fringed eastern coast that remains open year-round, so it stays busy even in midwinter. Originally built in the 1970s and doubled in size in 1992, accommodations here are well maintained with comfortable beds and neatly kept bathrooms containing tub/shower combinations. Meals are served, with an emphasis on Danish recipes, in a big-windowed, modern dining room that concludes most of its evenings with live music, dancing, or some kind of entertainment.

Boulevarden 9, DK-3730 Nexø. ② **56-49-49-49.** Fax 56-49-49-48. 96 units, half with kitchenettes. 910DKK–1,030DKK ($152–$172) double without kitchenette; 970DKK–1,260DKK ($162–$210) double with kitchenette. Rates include breakfast and dinner. MC, V. From Nexø, drive 2.5km (1½ miles) south along the coastal road, following the signs to Balka and Dueodde. **Amenities:** Restaurant; bar; outdoor heated pool; tennis court; sauna; 24-hr. room service; laundry service; dry cleaning; nonsmoking rooms; rooms for those with limited mobility. *In room:* TV, dataport, hair dryer.

AT SNOGEBÆK

Snogebæk Hotelpension   Set about a kilometer (⅔ mile) west from the center of Snogebæk, in an inland position a kilometer (⅔-mile) walk, drive, or bike ride from the beach, this hotel originated around 1900 as a rustic-looking farmhouse. After a massive renovation in the late 1980s, the farmhouse's beamed interior was converted into a restaurant and social center, and newer, motel-style wings were added, extending into the garden. Rooms, which contain shower-only bathrooms, are small and not at all plush, and would be more claustrophobic if they didn't open directly into the well-maintained greenery that surrounds the hotel. Most clients spend most of their days at the nearby beach.

Ellegade 9, DK-3730 Snogebæk. ✆ **56-48-80-80.** Fax 56-48-81-31. www.bornholm.net/snogebaek-hotel pension. 25 units. 570DKK–700DKK ($95–$117) double. Rates include breakfast. MC, V. Closed Oct–Apr. **Amenities:** Restaurant; bar; indoor heated pool. *In room:* TV.

AT DUEODDE

Dueodde Badehotel ★ *Finds* Well-designed and tasteful, this two-story motel-like structure was built in 1978 and remains the most southerly hotel in Bornholm. It's surrounded by scrub-covered sand dunes and is a short walk from the beach. Each accommodation is laid out something like an efficiently designed suite aboard a cruise ship, with compact dimensions, a color scheme of blue and white, modern furniture, and in every case, a separate seating area and a balcony or terrace. Each has a neatly kept bathroom equipped with a shower unit. There's a comfortable restaurant that charges 100DKK to 200DKK ($17–$33) for well-prepared Danish meals.

Poulsker, DK-3730 Nexø. ✆ **56-48-86-49.** Fax 56-48-89-59. www.dueodde-badehotel.dk. 48 apts, each with kitchenette. 700DKK–1,100DKK ($117–$184) double; 3,360DKK–5,350DKK ($561–$893) for 3 people; 3,500DKK–6,410DKK ($585–$1,070) apt for 5 people. AE, DC, MC, V. Closed Nov–Apr. From Nexø, drive 9km (5½ miles) south along the coastal road, following the signs for Dueodde. **Amenities:** Restaurant; bar; tennis court; sauna; coin-operated laundry; nonsmoking rooms; rooms for those with limited mobility. *In room:* TV, safe.

Hotel Bornholm *Kids* Set beside the white sands of the island's most popular beach (Dueodde), this hotel was built between 1972 and 1982, in a design that evokes a stateside motel, albeit one surrounded by a verdant garden. Each room opens directly onto a garden replete with roses, flowering shrubs, and small patches of lawn, an effect that gives the impression of camping out in a natural setting. Furnishings are durable, efficient, and practical—designed for hard use by couples and families on holiday at the beach. All rooms have well-kept bathrooms with tub/shower combinations.

Pilegårdsvej 1, Dueodde, DK-3730 Nexø. ✆ **56-48-83-83.** Fax 56-48-85-37. E-mail fax56488537@turist bornholm.dk. 44 apts, 7 cottages. 795DKK–1,195DKK ($133–$200) double; 2,975DKK–5,975DKK ($497–$998) cottage for 4 people. Rates include breakfast; half-board 175DKK ($29) extra per person per day. MC, V. Closed Oct–Apr. From Nexø, drive 5.5km (3½ miles) south along the coastal road, following the signs to Dueodde. **Amenities:** Breakfast room; bar; 2 heated pools (1 indoor); tennis court; exercise room; sauna; coin-operated laundry. *In room:* TV, safe.

WHERE TO DINE
AT NEXØ

Hotel Balka Strand DANISH Although residents of the (previously recommended) hotel occupy much of its dining room, this restaurant opens its doors to nonresidents who phone ahead for reservations. Within an airy, sparsely decorated dining room, you can enjoy such traditional menu items as marinated or fried herring, various kinds of omelets, soups such as a creamy version of borscht, fried steak with onions, and a roster of fresh fish that includes halibut with herbed wine sauce. Dessert might be a slice of chocolate layer cake, or perhaps a flan inspired by the chef's most recent visit to Spain. The cuisine, although not richly varied, is always reliable. Portions tend to be quite large and filling. If you're lucky enough to arrive when there's live music, you might enjoy dancing at least part of the night away.

Boulevarden 9. ✆ **56-49-49-49.** Reservations required for nonhotel guests. Main courses 100DKK–150DKK ($17–$25). AE, DC, MC, V. Daily noon–3pm and 6:30–9:30pm.

Tre Søstre ⭐ DANISH/SEAFOOD   Right at the bustling little harborfront, The Three Sisters brightens the dining scene in Bornholm considerably. The large dining room was created from a former storage warehouse, and it's named Tre Søstre, or The Three Sisters, for the model of an old Danish ship on display. The decor honors artists of Bornholm, and even the ceramic plates and candlesticks are locally made by craftspeople on the island working through a long dark winter. Island artist Kirsten Clemann, quite well known locally, created the ceramic fish suspended from the ceiling.

The rustic, somewhat nautical decor sets the stage for the tasty seafood you are likely to be served here. We recently took delight in the fresh turbot, which was roasted to perfection and served with "fruits of the sea," in this case shellfish. The grilled salmon was equally delectable and served with a homemade hollandaise. Nothing is finer, however, than the sautéed scampi splashed with cognac and flavored with curry powder and fresh garlic. The meat eater can always order a grilled sirloin of beef with mushroom sauce.

Havnen 5. ℂ **56-49-33-93.** Reservations recommended. Main courses 100DKK–200DKK ($17–$33). AE, DC, MC, V. Daily 11:30am–10pm.

AT SNOGEBÆK

Den Lille Havfrue ⭐ *Finds* DANISH   Housed in a cozy, modern building erected in the 1980s, this is one of the least-pretentious but best-recommended restaurants on the island. Local artist Kirsten Kleman accents its woodsy setting with dozens of pottery pieces. The hardworking staff will suggest any of various fish and meat dishes, including salmon with lobster sauce (a perennial favorite), codfish with potatoes and onions, beefsteak and calves' liver, and broiled plaice with lemon and parsley-butter sauce. The menu includes an ample selection of soups, salads, and simple desserts. The cookery is always reliable here, and never makes any pretense of being anything but that.

Hovedgaden 5, Snogebæk. ℂ **56-48-80-55.** Reservations recommended. Main courses 100DKK–170DKK ($17–$28). AE, DC, MC, V. Daily 11:30am–10pm. Closed Oct–Apr.

3 Svaneke ⭐

After Nexø, the topography of the island gradually changes from tawny sandstone to a more heavily forested area with thin topsoil, deep veins of clay, and outcroppings of gray granite.

From Nexø drive 5.5km (3½ miles) north along the coastal road, following the signs to **Svaneke,** Denmark's easternmost settlement, with fewer than 1,200 year-round residents. It lies 20km (12 miles) east of Rønne. It bears some resemblance to certain eastern regions of the Baltic with which it has traded, and it still has many 17th- and 18th-century cottages along cobblestone streets leading to the harbor, where fishing boats bob idyllically at anchor.

Many writers, sculptors, and painters are acquiring homes in Svaneke, an idyllic retreat from the urban life of Copenhagen. Svaneke is the most photogenic town on Bornholm; in 1975 it won the European Gold Medal for town preservation. Its most famous citizen was J. N. Madvig, Denmark's influential philologist, who was born here in 1804.

For information about the area, contact **Svaneke Turistbureau,** Storegade 24 (ℂ **56-49-32-00**). It's open Monday to Friday 12:30 to 4:30pm.

Sights are few here and easily covered on foot. It's the appealing town itself, filled with red-tile buildings, that's the attraction. The town's main square is the Torv. Directly south of here is Svaneke Kirke, which has a runic stone dating from the mid–14th century. The church itself was largely reconstructed in the 1800s and is only of minor interest.

In and around the area are a number of windmills, including an old post mill on the north side of town. At a point 3km (1¾ miles) south of Svaneke, in the hamlet of Årsdale, there is an old working windmill where corn is still ground and sold to locals.

SHOPPING

Bornholm's east coast, particularly around Svaneke, contains the highest percentage of artists, many of whom display their creations within such art galleries as **Gallerie Hvide Hus,** Rand Kløvej 15, Saltuna (© **56-47-03-33**). Set midway between Svaneke and Gudhjem, it specializes in crafts, ceramics, and paintings, usually by Danish or Swedish artists, many of whom reside on the island. On the antiques front, **Svaneke Antikvitetshandel,** Kirkebakken 4 (© **56-49-60-91**), is the most appealing store on Bornholm, with an inventory of nautical memorabilia, plus some of the curios and furnishings that long-ago merchant ships hauled here from all parts of the world.

WHERE TO STAY

Hotel Østersøen ★ *Finds*   Rich with many of the architectural quirks of its original construction 300 years ago, this complex of apartments with kitchenettes is more charming and more authentically old-fashioned than its nearby competitors. It sprawls along a goodly portion of Svaneke's harbor, wrapping itself around three sides of an open-air courtyard. Apartments contain an appealing blend of old-fashioned buttresses, modern kitchenettes, and summery, airy furnishings. All units contain well-kept shower-only bathrooms. Overall, the venue is comfortable, cozy, and attractively positioned.

Havnebryggen 5, DK-3740 Svaneke. © **56-49-60-20.** Fax 56-49-72-79. www.ostersoen.dk. 21 apts. 2,395DKK–4,895DKK ($400–$817) double per week; 2,795DKK–5,995DKK ($467–$1,001) quad per week. Obligatory end-of-rental cleaning fee of 400DKK ($67) for 2 persons, 450DKK ($75) for 4. AE, DC, MC, V. **Amenities:** Lounge; outdoor heated pool; laundry service; dry cleaning. *In room:* TV, kitchenette.

Pension Solgården   The only problem with this solidly built guesthouse is that it's open only 3 months a year, during the peak of midsummer. It was originally conceived in the 1930s as the quintessential red-brick schoolhouse, with a panoramic position adjacent to the sea, 3km (1¾ miles) south of Svaneke, beside the road leading south to Nexø. The simple but cozy rooms are outfitted with the kind of furnishings you might see in a college dormitory of long ago. There's a dining room, but it's open only to residents of the hotel. Outside you'll find lawns strewn with tables for sea gazing and sun worshipping.

Skolebakken 5, Årsdale, DK-3740 Svaneke. © **56-49-64-37.** Fax 56-49-65-37. E-mail: fax56496537@turist bornholm.dk. 18 units, 9 with bathroom. 540DKK ($90) double without bathroom; 620DKK ($104) double with bathroom. Rates include breakfast. No credit cards. Closed Sept–May. **Amenities:** Dining room; lounge. *In room:* No phone.

Siemsens Gaard   Until about 6 years ago, this hotel sported one of the oldest physical structures on Bornholm. In the early 1990s, however, lightning struck one of the two buildings, burning it to the ground, and necessitating a rebuilding of about half of the hotel rooms. Today, you'll face a hotel with old and new rooms; both types are cozy and rustically appealing as weather-tight getaways. All units have well-maintained bathrooms with shower units. Its location a few steps from the Svaneke harbor adds a lot of charm to this property, as does the publike cocktail lounge and restaurant (see "Where to Dine," below).

Havnebryggen 9, DK-3740 Svaneke. © **56-49-61-49.** Fax 56-49-61-03. www.siemsens.dk. 50 units. 760DKK–1,095DKK ($127–$183) double. Rates include breakfast. AE, DC, MC, V. **Amenities:** Restaurant; bar; sauna; room service (7:30am–9:30pm); coin-operated laundry; all nonsmoking rooms. *In room:* TV, hair dryer, safe.

WHERE TO DINE

Siemsens Gaard ★ *Value* DANISH   Set directly on the Svaneke harbor, the building that contains this restaurant is one of the oldest in town. Half-timbered, and with a pale yellow facade that evokes a historic *kro* (inn), it was constructed 400 years ago as the home of a wealthy merchant. The artfully rustic and simple dining rooms have thick walls and harbor views that evoke early-20th-century Denmark. If you're not sure what to order at lunch, consider a medley of *smørrebrød* (open-faced sandwiches) that some culinary experts think are almost too attractive to eat. An average lunch might consist of two or three of these. More substantial fare might include a selection of herring arranged onto the same platter, steaming bowls of cream of shellfish soup, smoked and marinated salmon with crème fraîche, grilled monkfish or haddock with herbs and red wine sauce, grilled sirloin with herbs and mustard sauce, and a dessert specialty of crepes with almond cream and fresh berries.

Havnebryggen 9. © **56-49-61-49.** Reservations recommended. Main courses 90DKK–110DKK ($15–$18) at lunch, 150DKK–200DKK ($25–$33) at dinner; lunch *smørrebrød* 45DKK ($7.50). AE, DC, MC, V. Daily 7am–10:30pm.

FROM SVANEKE TO GUDHJEM

From Svaneke, you can leave the Baltic coastline and head inland through the northern outskirts of the third largest forest in Denmark, **Almindingen.** (The western part of this forest is best explored by heading north from Åkirkeby; see "From Rønne to Nexø," earlier in this chapter.) Dotted with creeks and ponds, and covered mostly with hardy conifers, it's known for the profusion of its wildflowers—especially lily of the valley—and well-designated hiking trails. Head first for **Østerlars,** home to the largest of the island's distinctive round churches, the **Østerlarskirke,** at Gudhjemsveg 28 (© **56-49-82-64;** bus: 9 from Gudhjem). It's open early April to mid-October, Monday to Saturday 9am to 5pm. Admission is 10DKK ($1.65) adults, free for children. The Vikings originally built it around 1150, using rocks, boulders, and stone slabs. The church was dedicated to St. Laurence and later enlarged with chunky-looking buttresses; it was intended to serve in part as a fortress against raids by Baltic pirates. Inside are several wall paintings that date from around 1350, depicting scenes from the life of Jesus.

After exploring the area and dipping south along forest roads, you can follow the signposts to Østerlars, southwest of Gudhjem, or else drive back along the coast to Svaneke and take the coastal road northwest into Gudhjem.

4 Gudhjem

From Østerlars, drive 3km (1¾ miles) north, following the signs to **Gudhjem** ("God's Home"), a steeply inclined town that traded with the Hanseatic League during the Middle Ages. Most of its population died as a result of plagues in 1653 and 1654, but Danish guerrilla fighters and sympathizers, following territorial wars with Sweden, repopulated the town some years later. You'll find a town that—because of its many fig and mulberry trees, plus steep slopes—has a vaguely Mediterranean flavor.

Before setting out to explore actual sights, you might want to call first at the **Gudhjem Turistbureau,** Åbogade 9 (© **56-48-52-10**), a block inland from the harbor. It's open only in summertime, May to September. May to mid-June, and mid-August to September, hours are Monday through Saturday 1 to 4pm. During the peak of midsummer, from mid-June to mid-August, hours are Friday through Wednesday 10am to 4pm.

SEEING THE SIGHTS

Especially charming are Gudhjem's 18th-century half-timbered houses and the 19th-century smokehouses, known for their distinctive techniques of preserving herring with alderwood smoke. Its harbor, blasted out of the rocky shoreline in the 1850s, is the focal point for the town's 1,200 permanent residents.

Gudhjem Museum   This museum is housed in Gudhjem's old railway station, an early-20th-century building that closed in 1952. Its exhibits honor the now-defunct railways that once crisscrossed the island. There are locomotives and other train-related memorabilia.

Stationsvej 1. ℂ **56-48-54-62.** Admission 25DKK ($4.20), 10DKK ($1.65) children. Mid-May to mid-Sept Mon–Sat 10am–5pm, Sun 2–5pm. Closed mid-Sept to mid-May.

Landsbrugs Museum (Bornholm Agricultural Museum)   This museum is located inside a half-timbered, thatched-roof farmhouse originally built in 1796. It displays the kind of farm implements that were commonplace as recently as 1920; also on view are a group of pigs, goats, cows, and barnyard fowl that are genetically similar to those that were bred on Bornholm a century ago.

Melstedvej 25 (1km/½ mile south of Gudhjem). ℂ **56-48-55-98.** Admission 30DKK ($5) adults, 10DKK ($1.65) children. Mid-May to mid-Oct Tues–Sun 10am–5pm. Closed mid-Oct to mid-May.

SHOPPING

For some of the best glass objects in the area, head for **Gallerie Baltic See Glass,** Melstedvej 47 (ℂ **56-48-56-41**), lying 3km (1¾ miles) south of Gudhjem along the coastal road. Although much of this glass has a practical value, some works are so stunningly beautiful that they should be treated like objects of art.

One of the best art galleries in the area is **Gallerie Kaffslottet,** Duebakken 2 (ℂ **56-48-56-18**).

WHERE TO STAY

Casa Blanca   Efficient, matter-of-fact, and carefully scrutinized throughout its summer-only rental season by owners Elly and Preben Mortensen, this is a three-story, red-roofed, motel-style structure in the center of Gudhjem. The white rooms are somewhat cramped and outfitted with simple furniture that, in some instances, is covered with leather upholstery. Glass doors in every room open onto private balconies or terraces. All units have clean shower-only bathrooms. The hotel restaurant, the Flagermusen (see "Where to Dine," below), functions as a social center for residents.

Kirchevej 10, DK-3760 Gudhjem. ℂ **56-48-50-20.** Fax 56-48-50-81. E-mail: casablanca@adr.dk. **33 units.** 700DKK–760DKK ($117–$127) double. Rates include breakfast; supplement for half-board 100DKK ($17) per person. AE, DC, MC, V. Closed Oct–Apr. **Amenities:** Restaurant; bar; outdoor heated pool. *In room:* TV, no phone.

Gudhjem Hotel & Feriepark   This holiday complex consists of a tastefully designed compound of masonry-sided cottages, each with a steep, often sky-lit, terra-cotta roof, and a cement patio that extends the living area out onto the carefully clipped lawns. It sits a short walk south of Gudhjem, about midway between it and the satellite hamlet of Melsted, a 5-minute walk from the center of either. Many guests seem to frequent the wide, sandy expanse of beachfront that lies just a few steps from the hotel. Inside, accommodations are cozy and simple, contain bathrooms with tub/shower combinations, and are just a bit anonymous, although because of the wide expanses of beachfront a short walk from the hotel, most clients tend to spend most of their time outdoors anyway.

Jernkåsvej 1, DK-3760 Gudhjem. © **56-48-54-44.** Fax 56-48-54-55. www.bornholmbest.net. 102 apts. 490DKK–950DKK ($82–$159) double. Supplemental charges include 175DKK ($29) for electricity, a nominal fee for the rental of linens and towels, and a one-time cleaning charge of 325DKK ($54). Discounts available for stays of 3 days or more. AE, DC, MC, V. Closed Nov–Apr. **Amenities:** Lounge; outdoor heated pool; 2 tennis courts; sauna; coin-operated laundry. *In room:* TV, kitchen.

Jantzens Hotel ★ Opened in 1872, this buttercup-yellow structure with wrought-iron balconies is the town's oldest hotel and also one of the longest running on the island. The main building faces the Baltic Sea. In the rear yard is a rock garden enveloped by a trio of small cottages with private terraces. The hotel has recently been restored and is welcoming, although service is very laid-back. A lot of the feel of the early 20th century has been recaptured here, with its hardwood floors and rattan furnishings. Some of the rooms open onto balconies looking out over the town. Bathrooms were added as an afterthought to this old building and are rather cramped. You don't have to journey outside at night but can dine at the on-site Andi's Kokken, serving a Danish and French menu.

Brøddeg 33, DK-3760 Gudhjem. © **56-48-50-17.** 16 units. 700DKK–975DKK ($117–$163) single; 1,100DKK ($184) double. Rates include breakfast. MC, V. Closed Nov–Apr. **Amenities:** Restaurant. *In room:* TV (in some).

Melsted Badehotel Originally built in 1942, during the darkest days of World War II, in a boxy, modern format with white-painted bricks and soft blue trim, this is the most prominent and visible building in the seaside hamlet of Melsted, a kilometer (⅝ mile) south of Gudhjem. Part of its allure derives from its location just 12m (39 ft.) from the edge of the sea—occupants of its well-maintained and cozy rooms can hear the sounds of the surf throughout the night. Most rooms have private terraces or balconies; all units contain well-kept bathrooms with shower units. There's a coffee shop/bistro that serves simple lunches every day when the hotel is open, but never dinner. Much of this establishment's conviviality is exhibited on the wooden terrace that extends out over the sands, where outdoor tables, sun parasols, and chairs provide a space for sunbathing, people-watching, and dining on meals from the hotel's bistro.

Melstedvej 27, DK-3760 Gudhjem. © **56-48-51-00.** Fax 56-48-55-84. www.melsted-badehotel.dk. 21 units. 980DKK–1,380DKK ($164–$230) double; 1,580DKK ($264) apt. Rates include breakfast. MC, V. Closed Nov–Apr. Bus: 7. **Amenities:** Restaurant; cafe; lounge; all nonsmoking rooms. *In room:* TV.

WHERE TO DINE

Bokulhus DANISH Its name derives from the Bokul, which in Gudhjem refers to the highest elevation in town—an undulating, gentle knoll that's within a 5-minute walk of the harbor. It was built in 1932 as a private home. Menu items are authentically Danish and, in many cases, designed so that a platter of food is all most warm-weather diners really want. An example includes a *Dansk-platte,* which is loaded with herring, salmon, an assortment of cheeses, chickpeas, and hand-peeled shrimp. Other well-prepared choices include beef tournedos with baked sweet peppers, yellowfin tuna with saffron sauce, and veal cutlets with potatoes and a shallot and parsley sauce. Overall, this is our favorite restaurant in Gudhjem.

Bokulvej 4. © **56-48-52-97.** Reservations recommended. *Smørrebrød* platters 75DKK ($13); main courses 160DKK ($27). AE, DC, MC, V. Daily 11:30am–10pm. Closed mid-Apr to May and Sept to mid-Oct Tues; closed mid-Oct to mid-Apr.

Restaurant Flagermusen DANISH   Some locals consider this wood-paneled restaurant the highlight of the simple (and also-recommended) hotel that contains it. Some aspects might remind you of a brasserie with a Danish accent. Meals might begin with mushroom or cream of clam soup, followed by smoked salmon, grilled Norwegian haddock with béarnaise sauce, turkey croquettes, fried herring or steak, or filets of plaice with butter and parsley sauce. Service is personalized and polite, although a bit slow.

In the Casa Blanca, Kirchevej 10. ℰ 56-48-50-20. Main courses 100DKK–160DKK ($17–$27); fixed-price menu 80DKK ($13). AE, DC, MC, V. May–Sept daily 11:30am–9pm. Closed Oct–Apr.

GUDHJEM AFTER DARK

Consider a drink at the **Café Klint,** Egn Mikkelsensvej (ℰ 56-48-56-26), where a cozy ambience that might remind you of a Danish version of an English pub welcomes you with pints of ale in an old-fashioned setting. And for something a bit more electronic, with more emphasis on rock-'n'-roll music, have a drink or two at the **Café Gustav,** St. Torv 8 (ℰ 56-91-00-47), where at least one or two of the many artists living on the island's east coast are likely to congregate.

FROM GUDHJEM TO ALLINGE

Drive west along the coastal road. Between Gudhjem and Allinge, a distance of 14km (8⅔ miles), you'll enjoy dramatic vistas over granite cliffs and sometimes savage seascapes. The entire coastline here is known as **Helligdoms Klipperne** (Cliffs of Sanctuary), for the survivors of the many ships that floundered along this granite coastline over the centuries.

Midway along the route you'll see the island's newest museum, the **Bornholms Kunstmuseet** (Art Museum of Bornholm), Helligdommen (ℰ 56-48-43-86). Opened in 1993, it contains the largest collection of works by Bornholm artists, including Olaf Rude and Oluf Høst. It's open June to August, daily 10am to 5pm; April, May, September and October, Tuesday to Sunday 10am to 5pm; November to March, Tuesday and Thursday 1 to 5pm, Sunday 10am to 5pm. Admission is 50DKK ($8.35) adults, free for children ages 15 and under. From the rocky bluff where the museum sits, you can see the isolated and rocky island of **Christiansø** (see below), about 11km (6¾ miles) offshore, the wind-tossed home to about 120 year-round residents, most of whom make their living from the sea.

5 Christiansø

Tiny Christiansø lies in the open sea east of Bornholm and is part of the archipelago known as Ertholmene. One of the most remote sites in Denmark, Christiansø is one of only two inhabited islands within the Ertholmene chain, the others being set aside as bird sanctuaries.

Ferryboats depart between one and seven times a day, depending on the season. For ferries from Allinge and Gudhjem, call ℰ 56-48-51-76. For ferryboats from Svaneke, call ℰ 56-49-64-32. Round-trip transit of 60 to 90 minutes costs 160DKK ($27). No cars are allowed on any of the Ertholmene islands. Christiansø, the largest, can be circumnavigated on foot in about half an hour. Once you're here, the most charming accommodation is recommended below.

WHERE TO STAY & DINE

Christiansø Gæstgiveriet ⭐ *Finds*   The most desirable place to stay in the archipelago is this solidly built, antique-looking inn, which was originally constructed in the 1700s as the home of the local naval commander. Rooms are cozy, contain well-maintained bathrooms with shower units, and are outfitted in a style that is reminiscent of a room within a 1910 private home. There's a nautically decorated bar on the premises, as well as a restaurant that serves lunch platters for 50DKK to 60DKK ($8.35–$10), dinner platters for 89DKK to 160DKK ($15–$27). Basically, the only entertainment you'll find here is what you'll create for yourself, talking with fellow guests, or exploring the local bird and wildlife habitats. Don't even consider, especially during July and August, heading out here from Bornholm without an advance reservation, as it's very popular in midsummer.

DK-3740 Christiansø. ℂ 56-46-20-15. Fax 56-46-20-86. 7 units. 800DKK ($134) double. Rates include breakfast. MC, V. Closed mid-Dec to mid-Feb. **Amenities:** Restaurant; bar; coin-operated laundry; all non-smoking rooms. *In room:* No phone.

6 Allinge & Sandvig

Continue driving northwest until you reach the twin communities of **Allinge** and **Sandvig.** Allinge, whose architecture is noticeably older than that of Sandvig, contains 200- and 300-year-old half-timbered houses built for the purveyors of the long-ago herring trade, and antique smokehouses for preserving herring for later consumption or for export abroad.

The newer town of Sandvig, a short drive to the northwest, flourished around 1900 when many ferryboats arrived from Sweden. Sandvig became a stylish beach resort, accommodating guests at the Strandhotellet.

The forest that surrounds these twin communities is known as the **Trolleskoe** (Forest of Trolls), home to wart-covered and phenomenally ugly magical creatures that delight in brewing trouble, mischief, and the endless fog that sweeps over this end of the island.

From Allinge, detour inland (southward) for about 4km (2½ miles) to reach **Olsker,** site of the **Olskirke** (Round Church of Ols), Lindesgordsvej (ℂ **56-48-05-29**). Built in the 1100s with a conical roof and thick walls, it's the smallest of the island's round churches. It was painstakingly restored in the early 1950s. Dedicated to St. Olav (Olav the Holy, king of Norway, who died in 1031), it looks something like a fortress, an image that the original architects wanted very much to convey. June to September, and October 12 to 16, it's open Monday to Saturday 9am to noon and 2 to 5pm. April and May, and October 1 to 11, it's open Tuesday to Thursday 9am to noon. It's closed the rest of the year. Entrance costs 10DKK ($1.65).

Now retrace your route back to Allinge and head northward toward Sandvig, a distance of less than a kilometer (½ mile). You'll soon see **Madsebakke,** a well-signposted open-air site containing the largest collection of Bronze Age rock carvings in Denmark. Don't expect a building, any type of enclosed area, or even a curator. Simply follow the signs posted beside the main highway. The carvings include 11 depictions of high-prowed sailing ships of unknown origin, and were made in a smooth, glacier-scoured piece of bedrock close to the side of the road.

From here, proceed just less than a kilometer (½ mile) to the island's northernmost tip, **Hammeren,** for views that—depending on the weather—could extend all the way to Sweden. Here you'll see the island's oldest lighthouse, **Hammerfyr** (built in 1871).

WHERE TO STAY IN SANDVIG

Strandhotellet ★★ *(Finds)*   The foundations and part of the core of this historic hotel were built as stables in 1896; a decade later it became the largest, most stylish hotel on Bornholm. It's a reminder of a former way of life, when Sandvig was the main point of access from abroad. Nowadays Rønne has that role, and Sandvig is less commercial and more isolated than it was a century ago. A worthy detour for diners who drive from other parts of the island, the hotel offers three floors of spartan accommodations with lots of exposed birch wood and (in most cases) sea views. Each unit has a well-maintained bathroom with a tub/shower combination. The interior was modernized in 1991, making it suitable for a secluded getaway.

Strandpromenaden 7, DK-3770 Sandvig. © **56-48-03-14**. Fax 56-48-02-09. 49 units. 650DKK–950DKK ($109–$159) double; 1,000DKK–1,275DKK ($167–$213) suite. AE, DC, MC, V. **Amenities:** Restaurant; bar; sauna. *In room:* TV.

WHERE TO DINE IN SANDVIG

Strandhotellet Restaurant DANISH/SEAFOOD   This hotel dining room was designed in the 1930s as a dance hall and supper club. Big windows overlook the sea, and you'll sense the care and attention to detail that's consistent with the Strandhotellet's role as a special dining destination on Bornholm. Choices include smoked filet of wild salmon with tomato tapenade, a platter of mixed fish that varies according to the daily catch, and medallions of beef with a ragout of fresh vegetables. The abundance of food and flavor make this a good value.

Strandpromenaden 7, Sandvig. © **56-48-03-14**. Main courses 59DKK–69DKK ($9.85–$12) at lunch, 93DKK–130DKK ($16–$22) at dinner. AE, DC, MC, V. Daily noon–10pm.

FROM ALLINGE & SANDVIG BACK TO RØNNE

Now turn south, following the signs pointing to Rønne. After less than a kilometer (½ mile) you'll see the rocky crags of a semiruined fortress that Bornholmers believe is the most historically significant building on the island—the **Hammershus Fortress** ⚘, begun in 1255 by the archbishop of Lund (Sweden). He planned this massive fortress to reinforce his control of the island. Since then, however, the island has passed from Swedish to German to Danish hands several times; it was a strategic powerhouse controlling what was then a vitally important sea lane. The decisive moment came in 1658, when the Danish national hero Jens Kofoed murdered the Swedish governor and sailed to Denmark to present the castle (and the rest of the island) to the Danish king.

Regrettably, the fortress's dilapidated condition was caused by later architects, who used it as a rock quarry to supply the stone used to construct some of the buildings and streets (including Hovedvagten) of Rønne, as well as several of the structures on Christiansø, the tiny island 11km (6¾ miles) northeast of Bornholm. The systematic destruction of the fortress ended in 1822, when it was "redefined" as a Danish national treasure. Much of the work that restored the fortress to the eerily jagged condition you'll see today was completed in 1967. Interestingly, Hammershus escaped the fate of the second-most-powerful fortress on the island, Lilleborg. Set deep in Bornholm's forests, Lilleborg was gradually stripped of its stones for other buildings after its medieval defenses became obsolete.

Some 4km (2½ miles) south of Hammershus—still on the coastal road heading back to Rønne—is a geological oddity called **Jons Kapel** (Jon's Chapel); it can be seen by anyone who'd like to take a short hike (less than a km/½ mile) from the highway. Basically it's a rocky bluff with a panoramic view over the island's western coast, where, according to ancient legend, an agile but reclusive hermit, Brother Jon, preached to the seagulls and crashing surf below. For those who would like to enjoy a marvelous view, signs point the way from the highway.

From here, continue driving southward another 13km (8 miles) to Rønne, passing through the hamlet of **Hasle** en route.

8

Funen

Funen, the second-largest Danish island, separates Zealand from the mainland peninsula, Jutland. Known as *Fyn* in Danish, it offers unique attractions, from a Viking ship to runic stones.

Hans Christian Andersen was born in Funen in the town of Odense. A visit to the storyteller's native island is a journey into a land of roadside hop gardens and orchards, busy harbors, market towns, castles, and stately manor houses.

Funen has some 1,125km (700 miles) of coastline, with wide sandy beaches in some parts, and woods and grass that grow all the way to the water's edge in others. Steep cliffs provide sweeping views of the Baltic or the Kattegat.

Although ferryboats have plied the waters between the islands and peninsulas of Denmark since ancient times, recent decades have seen the development of a network of bridges. In 1934 the first plans were developed for a bridge over the span of water known as the **Storebaelt** (Great Belt), the 19km (12-mile) silt-bottomed channel that separates Zealand (and

Copenhagen) from Funen and the rest of continental Europe. After many delays caused by war, technical difficulties, and lack of funding, and after the submission of 144 designs by engineers from around the world, construction began in 1988 on an intricately calibrated network of bridges and tunnels.

On June 14, 1998, her majesty, Queen Margrethe II, cut the ribbon shortly before driving across the Great Belt Bridge. The project incorporated both railway and road traffic divided between a long underwater tunnel and both low and high bridges. (The rail link has operated since 1997.) Only some aspects of the Chunnel between England and France are on par with the staggering scale of this project.

Visitors can view exhibitions about the bridge at the **Great Belt Exhibition Center** (*C* **58-35-01-00**), located at the entrance to the bridge and hard to miss. It's open May to September, daily 10am to 7pm; and October to April, daily 10am to 5pm. Admission is 25DKK ($4.20) adults, 10DKK ($1.65) children.

1 Nyborg: Gateway to Funen

130km (81 miles) W of Copenhagen; 34km (21 miles) E of Odense

After crossing the bridge from Zealand to Funen, you'll arrive at this old seaport and market town, a perfect place to explore before you head to Odense. Founded some 700 years ago, Nyborg is one of the oldest towns in Denmark. Its location in the middle of the trade route between Zealand in the east and Jutland in the west has helped boost its importance. In medieval times, about 1200 to 1413, Nyborg was the capital of Denmark. Medieval buildings and well-preserved ramparts are testaments to that era. Nyborg's town square, the **Torvet,**

was created in 1540, when a block of houses was demolished to make room for the royal tournaments of Christian III.

In summer, Denmark's oldest open-air theater, **Nyborg Voldspil,** is the setting for an annual musical or operetta under the leafy beeches on the old castle ramparts. Throughout the summer, classical music concerts (featuring international soloists) are performed in the castle's Great Hall. Inquire at the tourist office (see "Essentials," below) for further details.

Dating from the mid-1600s, the "Tattoo" is an ancient military ceremony with musical accompaniment. This old custom has been revived to honor the corps who played an important role in the Schleswig wars in 1848 and again in 1864. In tribute to the old corps, the present-day Tattoo participants wear a green uniform with its characteristic cap, or *chakot.* The corps marches through the center of town at 9pm each year on June 30, thereafter every Tuesday in July and August.

ESSENTIALS

GETTING THERE   By Train or Bus   You can reach Nyborg by train or bus (via ferry). Trains leave Copenhagen every hour, and there's frequent bus service from Copenhagen as well. Trains arrive twice an hour from Odense.

VISITOR INFORMATION   The **Nyborg Turistbureau,** Torvet 9 (© **65-31-02-80;** www.nyborgturist.dk), is open June 15 to August, Monday to Friday

---

> **Tips   Around the Island by Rail & Bus**
>
> Funen has a good system of buses and trains that fan out from the central depot in Odense in all directions. Although public transport obviously takes longer than driving a car, it's possible to see the highlights of Funen without your own vehicle. It's also possible to base yourself in Odense, and visit the island's intriguing towns such as Svendborg as day trips. See the individual town listings for more details. For rail information or schedules throughout Funen, call ℂ **70-13-14-15.** For bus routes on the island, call the tourist office (ℂ **65-31-02-80**).

9:30am to 5:30pm and Saturday 9am to 2:30pm; September to June 14, Monday to Friday 9:30am to 4pm and Saturday 9am to 12:30pm.

GETTING AROUND   Bus nos. 1, 3, and 4 serve all in-town destinations listed below.

SEEING THE SIGHTS

Mads Lerches Gård (Nyborg Og Omegns Museet) ★   The finest and best-preserved half-timbered house in Nyborg, this building rises two floors and was built in 1601 by Mads Lerche, the town mayor. The 30 rooms of the house, painted a reddish pink, contain exhibitions on local history.

Slotsgade 11. ℂ **65-31-02-07.** Admission 30DKK ($5) adults, 15DKK ($2.50) children 6–14, free for children under 6. June–Aug daily 10am–4pm; Apr–May and Sept–Oct daily 10am–3pm. Closed Nov–Mar. Bus: 1, 3, or 4.

Nyborg Slot   Founded in 1170, Nyborg Castle, with its rampart still intact, is the oldest royal seat in Scandinavia. King Erik Glipping signed Denmark's first constitution in this castle with moat in 1282, and it was the seat of the Danish parliament, the *Danehof,* until 1413. The present furnishings date primarily from the 17th century, when Nyborg was a resplendent Renaissance palace. It's located directly north of Torvet in the town center.

Slotspladen. ℂ **65-31-02-07.** Admission 30DKK ($5) adults, 15DKK ($2.50) children. June–Aug daily 10am–4pm; Apr–May and Sept–Oct daily 10am–3pm. Closed Nov–Mar. Bus: 1, 2, or 3.

Vor Frue Kirke   Dating from the late 14th and early 15th centuries, the church of Our Lady has a fine Gothic spire, three aisles, woodcarvings, old epitaphs, candelabra, and model ships. Nightly at 9:45, the Watchman's Bell from 1523 is rung—a tradition that dates far back in the town's history. Opposite the church is the 12th-century **Korsbrødregård** (chapter house) of the Order of St. John, with a vaulted cellar now converted into a gift shop. The church, located at the end of Kongegade in the town center, can be entered through the south door.

Adelgade. ℂ **65-31-16-08.** Free admission. June–Aug Mon–Sat 9am–6pm, Sun 9am–1pm; Sept–May Mon–Sat 9am–4pm, Sun 9am–1pm.

SHOPPING

A wide range of antiques and gift items are found at **Nyborg Antik,** Nørregade 11 (ℂ **65-30-31-40**). Look especially for the Royal Copenhagen figurines, china, and old Funen furniture. The open workshop of a talented potter and ceramicist can be visited at **Ida Rostgård,** Holken Havn 1 (ℂ **65-30-23-02**).

WHERE TO STAY

Hotel Hesselet ★★   Set among beech trees, with a view across the Great Belt, this red-brick building with a pagoda roof is one of the most stylish hotels in

Denmark. It offers spacious rooms, good-sized bathrooms with tub/shower combinations, and firm beds. The Oriental carpets, leather couches, fireplace, tasteful library, and sunken living rooms create a glamorous aura. The hotel's gourmet **restaurant,** with a view of the Great Belt, is one of the finest on Funen.

Christianslundsvej 119, DK-5800 Nyborg. (℅ **65-31-30-29.** Fax 65-31-29-58. www.hesselet.dk. 43 units. Mon–Thurs 1,280DKK–1,780DKK ($214–$297) double; Fri–Sun 1,180DKK–1,680DKK ($197–$281) double; 2,400DKK–2,800DKK ($401–$468) suite. Rates include breakfast. AE, DC, MC, V. Free parking. **Amenities:** Restaurant; bar; indoor heated pool; 2 tennis courts; sauna; room service (7am–10pm); babysitting; laundry service; dry cleaning; nonsmoking rooms; solarium. *In room:* TV, dataport, minibar, hair dryer, safe.

Hotel Nyborg Strand ⭐   Dating from 1899, the Nyborg Strand is one of the largest and most popular conference hotels in Funen, but it provides a suitable overnight stopover for casual visitors as well. Less than a kilometer (about ½ mile) east of the train station, near the beach, it's a solid and reliable choice. Surrounded by forests, it offers modern comforts in its medium-size rooms, which have standard furnishings and good-size bathrooms equipped with tub/shower combinations. There are also two junior suites, one of which has its own sauna.

Østersvej 2, DK-5800 Nyborg. (℅ **800/528-1234** in the U.S., or 65-31-31-31. Fax 65-31-37-01. www.nyborg strand.dk. 282 units. Mon–Thurs 970DKK–1,350DKK ($162–$225) double; Fri–Sun 680DKK–850DKK ($114–$142) double; 1,640DKK–1,930DKK ($274–$322) junior suite. Rates include breakfast. AE, DC, MC, V. Closed Dec 16–Jan 3. **Amenities:** 2 restaurants; bar; indoor heated pool; fitness center; sauna; room service (4am–4pm in summer; 4am–11pm in winter); babysitting; laundry service; dry cleaning; nonsmoking rooms; rooms for those with limited mobility. *In room:* TV, dataport (in some), hair dryer.

WHERE TO DINE

Central Cafeen ⭐ DANISH   This place is many notches better than a translation of its unpretentious name (Central Café) would imply, It's actually a cozy, well-recommended restaurant, with a sense of local history, and a deep-seated pride in its Danish origins. Set directly across the street from City Hall, within a circa 1787 house that has contained some kind of restaurant since the 1850s, it offers four separate dining rooms, each outfitted with sepia-toned photographs of four generations of Danish monarchs, plus a somewhat quirky collection of ladies' hats, tucked away, museum-style, behind glass cases. Come here for old-fashioned Danish cuisine that's been just a bit influenced by France. The composition of the set-price menus changes every month, but ongoing staples include, among others, New Orleans–style shrimp in a garlic sauce, creamy lobster bisque, fried pork cutlets with boiled potatoes and parsley sauce, and fried plaice with lobster-and-shrimp sauce.

Nørregade 6. (℅ **65-31-01083.** Reservations recommended. Main courses 128DKK–198DKK ($21–$33). Set-price menus 208DKK ($35) and 238DKK ($40) 3-courses. AE, DC, MC, V. Mon–Sat 11:30am–8:45pm. Bus: 1, 3, or 4.

Danehofkroen DANISH/FRENCH   A well-managed dining choice since the Jensen family took over in 1993, this restaurant was originally built as a barracks in 1815 for the soldiers who guarded the nearby castle. Painted a vivid yellow, with a red-tile roof, it's a low-slung building with two dining rooms outfitted like an elegantly old-fashioned country tavern. The tasty menu items include fish soup with saffron, fried duck liver flavored with bacon and leeks, turbot with mushroom sauce, a delectable veal fried with chanterelle mushrooms, and a dessert specialty of raspberry parfait with fresh melon.

Slotsplads. (℅ **65-31-02-02.** Reservations recommended. Main courses 150DKK–200DKK ($25–$33). MC, V. Tues–Sun 12:30–9pm (last order).

Restaurant Østervemb DANISH/FRENCH   This restaurant in the heart of town has flourished since it was established in 1924. Inside, on two floors devoted to dining and drinking facilities, you can order platters piled high with three different preparations of herring, cold potato soup with bacon and chives, breast of Danish hen served with spinach and mushrooms, curried chicken salad with bacon, and slices of grilled beef tenderloin with a fricassee of oyster mushrooms and tarragon-flavored glaze. The cookery is as heart-warming as that provided by a nourishing Danish aunt.

Mellemgade. ☎ 65-30-10-70. Reservations recommended. Lunch platters 184DKK ($24); dinner main courses 182DKK–226DKK ($30–$38); fixed-price 2 course menu 272DKK ($45), 3 course 319DKK ($53). DC, MC, V. Tues–Sat noon–3pm and 6–10:30pm.

NYBORG AFTER DARK

The town's most consistently popular bar and pub is **Café Anthon,** Mellemgade 25 (☎ **65-31-16-64**), where sports enthusiasts, students, and anyone who happens to want to be convivial gather in a publike ambience that's cozy and warm. For the release of spontaneous energy, head for **Crazy Daisy,** Strandvejen 10 (☎ **63-31-08-28**), open Friday and Saturday from 11pm till dawn.

2 Odense: Birthplace of Hans Christian Andersen ★ ★

96km (60 miles) W of Copenhagen; 34km (21 miles) W of Nyborg; 43km (27 miles) NW of Svendborg

Leaving Nyborg, our next stop is Odense. This ancient town, the third largest in Denmark, has changed greatly since its famous son, H. C. Andersen, walked its streets. However, it's still possible to discover a few unspoiled spots.

In the heart of Funen and home to more than 185,000 inhabitants, Odense is one of the oldest cities in the country, with a history stretching back some 1,000 years. The Danish king Canute, or Knud, was murdered in St. Alban's Church here in 1086, and some 15 years later the Pope canonized him. Long before Odense became a pilgrimage center for fans of Hans Christian Andersen, it was an ecclesiastical center and site of religious pilgrimage in the Middle Ages.

Although Odense's tourism virtually lives off of the memory of the fairy-tale writer, Andersen never felt appreciated in his native town, a resentment which some claim to discern in his story *The Ugly Ducking*.

Odense today is no fairy-tale town, but rather an industrial center in Denmark. Its harbor is linked by a canal to the Odense Fjord and thus the Great Belt. It's a center of electro-technical, textile, steel, iron, and timber production.

In summer Odense takes on a festive air, with lots of outdoor activities, including all types of music, drama, and street theater taking place on its squares and in its piazzas. Cafes and pubs are lively day and night.

The city's name stems from two words—*Odins Vi* (Odin's shrine), suggesting that the god Odin must have been worshipped here in pre-Christian times.

ESSENTIALS

GETTING THERE   By Train or Bus   You can easily reach Odense by train or bus from Copenhagen. About 12 trains or buses a day leave Copenhagen's Central Railroad Station for Odense (trip time: 3 hr.).

By Car   From Nyborg, head west on E20 to Allerup and then follow Route 9 north to Odense.

VISITOR INFORMATION   Odense Tourist Bureau is at Rådhuset, Vestergade 2A (☎ **66-12-75-20;** www.visitodense.com). It's open mid-June to August, Monday through Friday 9am to 6pm, Saturday and Sunday 10am to 3pm;

Odense

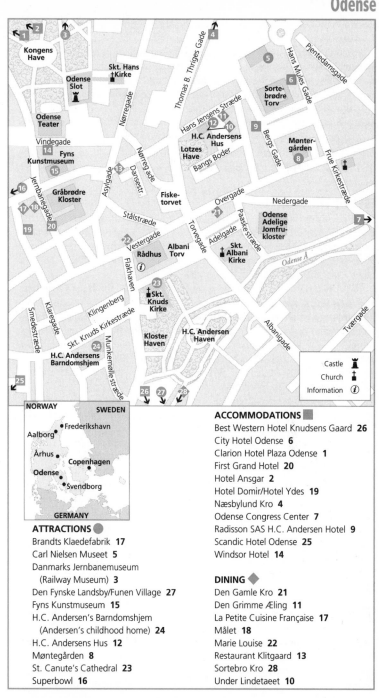

ACCOMMODATIONS ■
Best Western Hotel Knudsens Gaard **26**
City Hotel Odense **6**
Clarion Hotel Plaza Odense **1**
First Grand Hotel **20**
Hotel Ansgar **2**
Hotel Domir/Hotel Ydes **19**
Næsbylund Kro **4**
Odense Congress Center **7**
Radisson SAS H.C. Andersen Hotel **9**
Scandic Hotel Odense **25**
Windsor Hotel **14**

DINING ◆
Den Gamle Kro **21**
Den Grimme Æling **11**
La Petite Cuisine Française **17**
Målet **18**
Marie Louise **22**
Restaurant Klitgaard **13**
Sortebro Kro **28**
Under Lindetaeet **10**

ATTRACTIONS ●
Brandts Klaedefabrik **17**
Carl Nielsen Museet **5**
Danmarks Jernbanemuseum
   (Railway Museum) **3**
Den Fynske Landsby/Funen Village **27**
Fyns Kunstmuseum **15**
H.C. Andersen's Barndomshjem
   (Andersen's childhood home) **24**
H.C. Andersens Hus **12**
Møntegården **8**
St. Canute's Cathedral **23**
Superbowl **16**

September to mid-June, Monday through Friday 9:30am to 4:30pm and Saturday 10am to 1pm.

Besides helping you arrange excursions, the tourist bureau sells the **Odense Adventure Pass,** giving you access to 16 of the city's museums, the Odense Zoo, six indoor swimming pools, and unlimited free travel on the city buses and DSB trains within the municipality. It also entitles you to discounts on river cruises and admission to the summer-only presentation of the city's Hans Christian Andersen plays (see "Seeing the Sights," below). Passes are valid for 1 or 2 days. A 1-day pass is 110DKK ($18) for adults, 60DKK ($10) for children under 14; 2-day passes cost 150DKK ($25) and 80DKK ($13).

GETTING AROUND   By Bus   Bus no. 2 serves all in-town destinations listed below.

SEEING THE SIGHTS

The Odense Tourist Bureau (see above) offers a 2-hour **walking tour** conducted in July and August, every Tuesday, Wednesday, and Thursday at 11am and Friday at 3pm, from a meeting place behind the tourist office. Advance reservations are recommended. Covering the town's major sites, it costs 50DKK ($8.35) adults and 25DKK ($4.20) children.

Also at the tourist office, you can get information about the **Hans Christian Andersen plays,** which are presented every year mid-July to mid-August. The plays are given on an outdoor stage in the Funen Village, where members of the audience sit on blankets on the grass (if it's dry) or stand (if it's raining or if the ground is wet). Even if you don't understand Danish, there's lots of entertainment value in the visuals. Plays begin every day at 4pm, last around 90 minutes, cost 60DKK ($10) adults and 35DKK ($5.85) children, and are usually mobbed with H. C. Andersen fans.

Less than a kilometer (½ mile) west of the city center is **Superbowl,** Grøneløkkenvej (© **66-19-16-40;** bus: 91 or 92), a complex of amusements and diversions that are entirely devoted to popular American culture. It incorporates facilities for indoor go-cart racing, an indoor version of American-style miniature golf, several bowling alleys, and a small-scale collection of rides and games inspired by the theme parks of Florida. Each individual attraction within the park maintains its own hours and entrance policies, but the best way to appreciate this site's activities is to head here anytime between 10am and 6pm, when for an all-inclusive fee of 70DKK ($12), you'll have unlimited access to all of them.

Brandts Klaedefabrik ✦   An antique textile factory has been successfully converted into an art-filled compound with four museums spread across its precincts. You can spend 3 or more hours here and only scratch the surface of its exhibits. The **Danish Museum of Printing** and the **Danish Press Museum** (© **66-12-10-20**) show the development of the printing press in the country for at least 3 centuries. The museum also houses papermaking, bookbinding, and lithography workshops. Also on-site is the **Kunsthallen Brandts** (© **66-13-78-97**), the art gallery filling four spacious rooms that once housed weaving machines. The exhibitions vary here depending on the season. The **Museum of Photographic Art** (© **66-13-78-97**), the only one of its kind in the country, offers not only a permanent collection but at least 10 special exhibits a year. Finally, "The Time Collection" (© **65-91-19-42**) allows you to travel through time from the turn of the 20th century up to the '70s by following its exhibitions of housing interiors and changing fashions. Tableaux present various eras in fashion.

Brandts Passage 37–43. ✆ **66-13-78-97**. Combined ticket 50DKK ($8.35), or else 25DKK–30DKK ($4.20–$5) for each admission. July–Aug daily 10am–5pm; Sept–June Tues–Sun 10am–5pm.

Bymuseet Møntegården (Odense City Museum)   Not the typical dull city museum with dusty artifacts, this museum traces Odense's history back to the Viking era and has a number of half-timbered houses from the 1500s and 1600s you can actually walk through. It's particularly rich in artifacts from the Middle Ages, and there are interiors from the 17th and 18th centuries, as well as exhibits that go right up to the 1950s. In the Nyborgladen—the open storehouse of the museum—there are thousands of items exemplifying everyday life from the Middle Ages to the present day. The coin collection virtually spans a millennium.

Overgade 48–50. ✆ **66-14-88-46**. Admission 30DKK ($5) adults, 15DKK ($2.50) children 5–11, free for children under 5. Tues–Sun 10am–6pm.

Carl Nielsen Museet   Adjoining the Odense Concert Hall, this museum documents the life and work of composer Carl Nielsen (1865–1931) and his wife, the sculptor Ann Marie Nielsen. Visitors hear excerpts of Nielsen's music while they look at the exhibits and a biographical slide show. Parking is available outside the concert hall.

Claus Bergsgade 11. ✆ **65-51-46-01**. Admission 25DKK ($4.20) adults, 10DKK ($1.65) children 5–14, free for children under 5. Tues and Fri 4–8pm; Sun noon–4pm. Bus: 2.

Danmarks Jernbanemuseum (Railway Museum) *Kids*   Original locomotives and carriages depict Denmark's railway history from the first railroad in 1847. One of the oldest locomotives in the collection, a "B-Machine," dates from 1869. Also on display are three royal coaches, a double-decker carriage, and a model railway. The museum is adjacent to the train station.

Dannebrogsgade 24. ✆ **66-13-66-30**. Admission 40DKK ($6.70) adults, 16DKK ($2.65) children. Daily 10am–4pm. Bus: 2.

Funen Village/Den Fynske Landsby ★★ *Kids*   A big open-air regional culture museum, this is an archive of 18th- and 19th-century Funen life. Located in the Hunderup Woods, old buildings—a tollhouse, weaver's shop, windmill, farming homestead, jail, vicarage, village school, and even brickworks—were reassembled and authentically furnished. Plays and folk dances are staged at the Greek theater. In addition, you can visit workshops and see a basket maker, spoon cutter, blacksmith, weaver, and others at work.

Sejerskovvej 20. ✆ **66-14-88-14**. Admission 55DKK ($9.20) adults, 15DKK ($2.50) children. Mid-June to mid-Aug daily 9:30am–7pm; Apr to mid-June and mid-Aug to mid-Oct Tues–Sun 10am–5pm; mid-Oct to Mar Sun 11am–3pm. Bus: 21 or 22 from Flakhaven.

Fyns Kunstmuseum   Showcased in a dignified Greco-Roman-style building, this museum displays Danish art from 1750 to the present. Everything is here, from paintings by old masters to the most abstract modern works of today. An array of artists whose names are widely familiar in Denmark but only in art circles elsewhere includes Jens Juel, C. W. Eckersberg, Dankvart Dreyer, Franciska Clausen, and Henrik B. Andersen. A collection of works by young Danish sculptors has been set up, and there are also special exhibits devoted to Danish and international art.

Jernbanegade 13. ✆ **66-14-88-14**. Admission 30DKK ($5) adults, 15DKK ($2.50) children. Tues–Sun 10am–4pm.

H. C. Andersens Barndomshjem (H. C. Andersen's Childhood Home) *Kids*
Visit Andersen's humble childhood home, where the fairy-tale writer lived from

age 2 to 14. From what is known of Andersen's childhood, his mother was a drunken, superstitious washerwoman, and Andersen was a gawky boy, lumbering and graceless, the victim of his fellow urchins' cruel jabs. However, all is serene at the cottage today; in fact, the little house has a certain unpretentious charm, and the "garden still blooms," as in *The Snow Queen.*

Munkemøllestraede 3. ⓒ **66-14-88-14.** Admission 10DKK ($1.65) adults, 5DKK (85¢) children. June–Aug daily 10am–4pm; Sept–May daily 11am–3pm. Bus: 2.

H. C. Andersens Hus ★★ *(Kids* The object of most Funen pilgrimages is the *hus* and museum of H. C. Andersen, popular with both adults and children. A lot of Hans Christian Andersen memorabilia is here: his famous walking stick, top hat, and battered portmanteau, plus letters to his dear friend Jenny Lind and fellow writer Charles Dickens. In addition, hundreds of documents, manuscripts, and reprints of his books in dozens of languages are displayed.

Hans Jensensstraede 37–45. ⓒ **66-14-88-14.** Admission 50DKK ($8.35) adults, 20DKK ($3.35) children 5–14, free for children under 5. June 16–Aug daily 9am–7pm; Sept–June 15 daily 10am–4pm. Bus: 2.

Hollufgård   Lying 10km (6¼ miles) to the south of Odense (reached by bus no. 61), this is the archaeological museum of Odense, housed on an estate going back to the 16th century. It's not possible to tour the inside of the manor but you can wander the grounds, taking in exhibits in various barns and outbuildings. Many of the artifacts are from the prehistoric days of Funen. One building houses one of Denmark's finest collections of coins and medallions. You can wander through a sculpture garden, and can also visit sculptor workshops with working artists.

Hestelhaven 201. ⓒ **66-14-88-14.** Admission 25DKK ($4.20) adults, 15DKK ($2.50) children. May–Oct Tues–Sat 10am–5pm; Nov–Apr Sun 11am–4pm.

Møntegården   This is Odense's museum of urban history. A group of row houses—four in all—from the 1600s were joined around a cobblestone-paved courtyard to form the nucleus of the museum. Some of the more interesting artifacts are from the Viking Age, although the later medieval period is also represented. Several interiors were re-created showing how people lived in the 16th and 17th centuries. The exhibitions go up until the 1950s. We are especially intrigued with the relics of the Nazi occupation of Denmark in the early '40s.

Overgade 48. ⓒ **66-14-88-14.** Admission 30DKK ($5) adults, 15DKK ($2.50) children. Tues–Sun 10am–4pm.

St. Canute's Cathedral   Despite its unimpressive facade, this is the most important Gothic-style building in Denmark. A popular feature of this 13th-century brick building is the elegant triptych gold altar screen, carved by Calus Berg in 1526 at the request of Queen Christina. King Canute, the patron of the church, was killed by angry Jutland taxpayers in 1086 and then canonized 15 years later. The church stands opposite the Town Hall.

Klosterbakken 2. ⓒ **66-12-61-23.** Free admission. June–Aug Mon–Sat 10am–5pm, Sun and holidays noon–3pm; May 15–30 and Sept 1–14 Mon–Sat 10am–5pm; Apr–May 14 and Sept 15–30 Mon–Sat 10am–4pm; Oct–Mar Mon–Fri 10am–4pm, Sat 10am–2pm. Bus: 21 or 22.

NEARBY ATTRACTIONS

Carl Nielsen's Barndomshjem   Thirteen kilometers (8 miles) from Odense, the childhood house of the famous composer is now a museum and archive of his life. Nielsen lived here during the last 5 years of his childhood until his confirmation in 1879. Two studies have been made into commemorative rooms, where the collections illustrate the composer's life.

Odensevej 2A, near Lyndelse. ✆ **65-51-46-01**. Admission 25DKK ($4.20) adults, 10DKK ($1.65) children. Tues–Sun 11am–3pm. Closed Oct–Apr. Bus: 960 or 962.

Egeskov Castle ★★ This 1554 Renaissance castle with magnificent gardens, northeast of Faaborg at Kvaerndrup, is the most romantic and splendid of Denmark's fortified manors. The castle was built on oak pillars in the middle of a moat or small lake. International experts consider it the best-preserved Renaissance castle of its type in Europe.

Every year some 200,000 visitors roam the 12-hectare (30 acre) park and castle located on the main road between Svendborg and Odense. There's a vintage automobile, horse carriage, and airplane museum on the grounds as well. Chamber-music concerts are held in the Great Hall of the castle on 10 summer Sundays beginning in late June, starting at 5pm.

The most dramatic story in the castle's history is about an unfortunate maiden, Rigborg, who was seduced by a young nobleman and bore him a child out of wedlock. Banished to the castle, she was imprisoned by her father in a tower from 1599 to 1604.

Egeskovgade 18, Kvaerndrup. ✆ **62-27-10-16**. Admission including castle, park, and maze 225DKK ($38) adults, 115DKK ($19) children 4–12; park, maze, and museum 140DKK ($23) adults, 70DKK ($12) children 4–12. Free for children under 4. July park daily 10am–8pm, castle daily 10am–7pm; June and Aug park daily 10am–6pm, castle daily 10am–5pm; May and Sept park and castle daily 10am–5pm. Closed Oct–Apr. Train: From Odense or Svendborg every hour. Bus: 920 from Nyborg.

Frydenlund *Kids* This bird sanctuary and park is 20km (12 miles) southwest of Odense near the village of Tommerup. Some 200 different species of pheasants, ducks, geese, storks, ostriches, parrots, owls, and other birds from all parts of the world live here. There are more than 120 aviaries and some 20 parkland areas in an old farm setting, with many flowers, bushes, and trees. You can enjoy coffee and homemade pastries in the cafe or bring your own lunch.

Skovvej 50, Naarup, near Tommerup. ✆ **64-76-13-22**. Admission 50DKK ($8.35) adults, 25DKK ($4.20) children. Daily 10am–6pm.

Ladbyskibet Ladby, 19km (12 miles) northeast of Odense, is the site of a 22-meter (72-ft.) 10th-century Viking ship, discovered in 1935. Remains of the ship are displayed in a burial mound along with replicas from the excavation (the originals are in the National Museum in Copenhagen). A skeleton of the pagan chieftain buried in this looted ship was never found, just the bones of his nearly dozen horses and dogs.

Vikingevej 123, Ladby. ✆ **65-32-16-67**. Admission 25DKK ($4.20) adults, free for children under 15. May 15–Sept 14 daily 10am–5pm; Mar–May 14 and Sept 15–Oct daily 10am–4pm; Nov–Feb Wed–Sun 11am–3pm. Bus: 482 from Kerteminde.

SHOPPING

Inspiration Zinch, Vestergade 82–84 (✆ **66-12-96-93**), offers the widest selection of Danish design and handicrafts on the island of Funen. All the big names are here, everything from Royal Copenhagen to Georg Jensen, but you will also come across younger and more modern designers, with whose names you might be unfamiliar. In the heart of the old town, opposite Hans Christian Andersen's house, you'll find a display of Danish crafts and Christmas decorations in a typical atmosphere of Old Funen at **Klods Hans,** Hans Jensens Staede 34 (✆ **66-11-09-40**). Another interesting outlet is **Smykker,** 3 Klaregade (✆ **66-12-06-96**), which offers museum copies of Bronze Age, Iron Age, and Viking jewelry—all made in gold, sterling silver, and bronze in the outlet's own workshop.

College Art, Grandts Passage 38 (✆ **66-11-35-45**), has assembled a unique collection of posters, lithographs, silk-screens, original art, and cards. The best gallery for contemporary art is **Galleri Torso,** Hasselvej 25 (✆ **66-13-44-66**). Finally, if none of the above shops has what you want, head for **Rosengårdcentret** at Munkerisvej and Ørbaekvej. It's Denmark's biggest shopping center, with nearly 110 stores all under one roof.

WHERE TO STAY

Some hotels in Odense charge higher rates in winter because of the demand from business travelers at that time.

EXPENSIVE

Clarion Hotel Plaza Odense ★★   Less than half a kilometer (about ¼ mile) from the town center, Odense's classic hotel, built in 1915, is one of its most alluring hostelries. The rooms evoke an English country home, and open onto scenic views. Some are quite spacious and all contain well-kept bathrooms with tub/shower combinations. Units for nonsmokers can be requested. The terrace overlooks a park and garden.

Østre Stationsvej 24, DK-5000 Odense. ✆ **877/424-6423** in the U.S., or 66-11-77-45. Fax 66-14-41-45. www.hotel-plaza.dk. 68 units. July–Aug 840DKK ($140) double, 1,775DKK ($296) suite; Sept–June 1,275DKK ($213) double, 1,775DKK ($296) suite. Rates include breakfast. AE, DC, MC, V. Free parking. Bus: 31, 33, 35, or 36. **Amenities:** Restaurant; bar; 24-hr. room service; laundry service; dry cleaning; nonsmoking rooms. *In room:* TV, dataport, minibar, hair dryer, safe.

Radisson SAS H.C. Andersen Hotel ★   With a 1960s Nordic modern design throughout, this brick structure in the heart of the old city lies next to a former Hans Christian Andersen residence. It's one of the premier hotels of Funen. The reception area, with its glass-roofed section and southern exposure, is inviting and welcoming. Rooms come in a variety of sizes, some large, others a bit cramped. The quietest rooms open onto the interior. Bathrooms tend to be small but have thoughtful extras such as makeup mirrors and tub/shower combinations.

Overlooking the market square, the hotel's formal **restaurant** is known for catering to special requests, such as vegetarian or other special diets. It serves a refined international and Danish cuisine and does so exceedingly well, using market-fresh ingredients.

Claus Bergs Gade 7, DK-5000 Odense. ✆ **800/333-3333** in the U.S., or 66-14-78-00. Fax 66-14-78-90. www. radissonsas.com. 145 units. 1,395DKK–1,595DKK ($233–$266) double. Rates include breakfast. AE, DC, MC, V. Bus: 4 or 5. **Amenities:** Restaurant; bar; fitness center; sauna; room service (7am–10pm); laundry service; dry cleaning; nonsmoking rooms; rooms for those with limited mobility; solarium; casino. *In room:* TV, dataport, minibar, hair dryer, safe.

Scandic Hotel Odense ★ *Kids*   Comfortable and international, and designed in a low-slung, three-story format that dates from 1986, this hotel lies 5km (3 miles) southwest of the center, in a drab industrial neighborhood that's conveniently close to the E20 highway. Inside, you'll find a polite and accommodating staff, a comfortable and uncontroversial contemporary decor, and tasteful rooms with good-size bathrooms equipped with shower units, seating areas, and writing tables. For children, there is a big playroom with a large selection of books and toys.

Hvidkærvej 25, DK-5250 Odense SV. ✆ **66-17-66-66**. Fax 66-17-25-53. www.scandic-hotels.com. 100 units. 1,325DKK–1,525DKK ($221–$255) double; 2,150DKK ($359) suite. Rates include breakfast. AE, DC, MC, V. Bus: 835 or 840. **Amenities:** Restaurant; bar; fitness center; sauna; children's playroom; room service (7am–10pm); babysitting; laundry service; dry cleaning; nonsmoking rooms; rooms for those with limited mobility; solarium. *In room:* TV, dataport, minibar, hair dryer, trouser press.

MODERATE

Best Western Hotel Knudsens Gaard   This motel, built in 1955 and renovated in the early 1990s, lies on Route 1A at the A9 junction, less than a kilometer (½ mile) south of the town center. This family favorite grew out of a half-timbered farmhouse. Rooms are compact and well furnished, and all contain neatly kept bathrooms with tub/shower combinations. There's a well-appointed first-class restaurant serving French and Danish cuisine.

Hunderupgade 2, DK-5230 Odense. © 800/528-1234 in the U.S., or 63-11-43-11. Fax 63-11-43-01. www. bestwestern.com. 62 units. 1,045DKK–1,550DKK ($175–$259) double. Rates include breakfast. AE, DC, MC, V. **Amenities:** Restaurant; bar; room service (7am–10pm); laundry service; dry cleaning; nonsmoking rooms; rooms for those with limited mobility. *In room:* TV, dataport, minibar, hair dryer.

City Hotel Odense   In the heart of the city, less than 2 blocks from the train station, this postmodern cluster of old-fashioned style Danish cottages was built in 1988. Favored by many of Odense's corporations for lodging conventioneers, it offers a sun deck, and bland, not particularly large but comfortably modern rooms. Each unit has a neatly kept bathroom with a shower unit. Other than breakfast, no meals are offered, although a 300-year-old Danish inn, Den Gamle Kro, run by the same owner, serves flavorful meals a 5-minute walk away.

Hans Mules Gade 5, DK-5000 Odense. © 66-12-12-58. Fax 66-12-93-64. www.city-hotel-odense.dk. 43 units. Mon–Fri 895DKK ($149) double; Sat–Sun 795DKK ($133) double. From 995DKK ($166) apt. Rates include breakfast. AE, DC, MC, V. Bus: 41 or 42. **Amenities:** Breakfast room; bar; game room; laundry service; dry cleaning; nonsmoking rooms. *In room:* TV, dataport, hair dryer.

First Grand Hotel ✮ *Value*   Near the rail depot, this 100-year-old hotel has been considerably rejuvenated and is now one of the better and more affordable choices in town. Rising four floors, the brick structure is shaped like a triangle and studded with old-fashioned dormers. Some of the Belle Epoque elements, such as crystal chandeliers, stone floors, and a broad stairwell, are still in place, but much has been modernized with today's comforts. The ground-floor reception will provide you with an ornately shaped brass key for your bedroom door. Bedrooms, in the 19th-century tradition, are large, and each is comfortably furnished, with an adjoining good-sized bathroom with tiles and a tub/shower combination. On-site are a relatively good restaurant serving Danish regional food and a cozy bar that makes an ideal place for a rendezvous.

Jernbanegade 18, DK-5000 Odense. © 66-11-71-71. Fax 66-14-11-71. www.firsthotels.com. 147 units. 1,179DKK–1,203DKK ($197–$201) double; 1,653DKK–2,503DKK ($276–$418) suite. Rates include breakfast. AE, DC, MC, V. Parking 50DKK ($8.35). **Amenities:** Restaurant; bar; sauna; room service (7am–10pm); nonsmoking rooms. *In room:* TV, dataport (in some), minibar.

Hotel Ansgar   Built in 1902 as an affiliate of a local church, this hotel dropped its religious connections years ago. In the heart of town, behind a brick-and-stone facade, it boasts a modern interior. Double-glazed windows cut traffic noise considerably. The rooms are well furnished and vary in size from small to spacious. Likewise, bathrooms are variously cramped and medium-size. All rooms have well-kept bathrooms with tub/shower combinations. The hotel's reasonably priced restaurant serves Danish food. A good value is the two-course fixed-price dinner for 150DKK ($25). The hotel is a 5-minute walk from the train depot.

Østre Stationsvej 32, DK-5000 Odense. © 66-11-96-93. Fax 66-11-96-75. www.hotel-ansgar.dk. 64 units. June–Aug 650DKK ($109) double; Sept–May 895DKK ($149) double. Rates include breakfast. Extra bed 200DKK ($33). AE, DC, MC, V. Free parking. Bus: 31, 33, 35, or 36. **Amenities:** Restaurant; bar; laundry service; dry cleaning; nonsmoking rooms. *In room:* TV, dataport, minibar, hair dryer.

Odense Congress Center   This hotel is connected to the largest convention and conference facility in Funen. Set 5km (3 miles) east of Odense's center, it has an angular red-brick facade, bland-looking but well-designed public areas that might remind you of an airport, and comfortably contemporary rooms filled with enough electronic extras to keep you entertained and diverted during your stay. All units have well-managed bathrooms equipped with tub/shower combinations.

Ørbækvej 350, DK-5220 Odense. (**65-56-01-00.** Fax 65-56-01-99. www.occ.dk. 109 units. 1,175DKK–1,750DKK ($196–$292) double. Rates include breakfast. Bus: 61. **Amenities:** Restaurant; bar; exercise room; sauna; game room; room service (7am–10pm); laundry service; dry cleaning; nonsmoking rooms; rooms for those with limited mobility. *In room:* TV, dataport (in some), minibar, hair dryer, iron/ironing board.

INEXPENSIVE

Hotel Domir/Hotel Ydes   There are so many similarities between these nearly adjacent hotels that many travel journalists simply describe them as different manifestations of the same organization. Each was built in the early 20th century, and they share the same owner. Each has cozy, comfortable rooms, with the Ydes (28 rooms) focusing a bit more on old-fashioned decor, and the Domir (35 rooms) going for brighter colors and a more indulgent approach to pop culture. Every room has a well-kept bathroom with a shower unit. You'll have a greater sense of camaraderie at the Domir, where a live receptionist will check you in; at the Ydes, a TV monitor will beam you the instructions from the manager (who works in the Domir). The two are literally steps from each other.

Hans Tausensgade 11 and 19, DK-5000 Odense C. (**66-12-14-27.** Fax 66-12-14-13. www.domir.dk. 63 units. 545DKK ($91) double at Domir, 495DKK ($83) double at Ydes. Rates include breakfast. AE, DC, MC, V. **Amenities:** Breakfast room; bar. *In room:* TV, dataport, trouser press.

Næsbylund Kro   Despite its self-image as a *kro* (usually suggesting an antique Danish inn), this roadside hotel 4km (2½ miles) north of Odense was built in 1983 in a style that's unabashedly modern. Rooms, which have balconies, are conservatively modern and comfortable, if relatively impersonal looking. Each unit is also equipped with a neatly kept shower-only bathroom. In a separate building, the Carolinenkilde restaurant serves dinner nightly 5 to 9:30pm, with a fixed-price menu going for 158DKK ($26).

Bogensevej 105–117, DK-5270 Odense. (**66-18-00-39.** Fax 66-18-29-29. 53 units. 760DKK ($127) double. Rates include breakfast. AE, DC, MC, V. Bus: 91 or 92. **Amenities:** Restaurant; lounge. *In room:* TV.

Comfort Windsor Hotel   Built in 1898, this cozy, well-furnished red-brick hotel occupies a street corner close to the center of town near the rail station. It's not plush in any sense, but is cozily comfortable. The high-ceilinged rooms are well maintained and inviting, although small for many tastes, with equally small shower-only bathrooms. Furnishings are in a sleek Nordic style. Double-glazing cuts down the noise level. There's a good restaurant serving dinner Monday through Thursday 6 to 9:30pm; a two-course Danish meal costs only 155DKK ($26). The food is simple but prepared with fresh ingredients.

Vindegade 45, DK-5000 Odense. (**66-12-06-52.** Fax 66-91-00-23. 62 units. www.hotel-windsor.dk. 795DKK–895DKK ($133–$149) double. Rates include breakfast. AE, DC, MC, V. **Amenities:** Restaurant; bar; laundry service; dry cleaning; nonsmoking rooms. *In room:* TV, dataport (in some), minibar.

WHERE TO DINE
EXPENSIVE

Den Gamle Kro ⊕ DANISH/FRENCH   With a history of serving food and drink that goes back to 1683, this inn has little in common with the postmodern 10-year-old hotel with which it shares its management. Set within the city limits, a 5-minute walk from the center, it offers separate drinking and dining facilities, and a complex that includes a cellar-level bar that's lined with antique masonry and a street-level restaurant with a beamed ceiling and references to old-fashioned Danish values. Two of the best menu items here are trout fried in butter and herbs, served with creamed potatoes, asparagus, and parsley; and beef tenderloin with herbs and green vegetables.

Overgade 23. ✆ **66-12-14-33.** Reservations recommended. Main courses 169DKK–258DKK ($28–$43); fixed-price meals 158DKK–348DKK ($26–$58). AE, DC, MC, V. Mon–Sat 11am–10:30pm; Sun 11am–9:30pm.

La Petite Cuisine ★ FRENCH   Small and intimate, with only 55 seats, this well-groomed and highly conscientious restaurant evokes the kind of bistro you might expect in a medium-sized city in France. Set on a narrow, partially covered passageway in the heart of Odense, it offers a contemporary-looking decor and a soothing color scheme. Menu items are elegant and carefully planned. Your meal might begin with marinated wild Scottish salmon served with pickled watercress and a mild mustard sauce with passion fruit oil, or thin-sliced scallops with foie gras, wild watercress, and slices of pickled pumpkin. Main courses include a duet of Danish veal and French duck aromatically served with anise-poached fennel, and crisp-fried filet of redfish with roasted artichoke hearts and lobster bisque.

Brandts Passage 13. ✆ **66-14-11-00.** Reservations recommended. Main courses 198DKK–250DKK ($33–$42); 4-course fixed-price menu 435DKK ($73). DC, MC, V. Mon–Sat 5pm–midnight. Bus: 2.

Marie Louise ★★ FRENCH   A centrally located antique house is the home of Odense's smallest and most exclusive restaurant. Its dining room is a white-walled re-creation of an old-fashioned country tavern, although closer inspec-tion reveals a decidedly upscale slant to the furnishings, accessories, silver, and crystal. A polished staff serves well-planned dishes based on French recipes. Delectable specialties include a salmon-and-dill mousse with shrimp sauce, plat-ters of fresh fish, turbot in Riesling or champagne sauce, lobster in butter or Provençal sauce, and an array of delectable desserts, many laid out like tempo-rary (and well-flavored) works of art.

Lottrups Gaard, Vestergade 70–72. ✆ **66-17-92-95.** Reservations recommended. Main courses 318DKK–387DKK ($53–$65); fixed-price menu 395DKK–610DKK ($66–$102). MC, V. Mon–Sat noon–mid-night. Closed July. Bus: 2.

Restaurant Klitgaard ★ *Finds* CONTINENTAL   Since its establishment in 1998, this restaurant has become one of the most stylish and innovative restau-rants in Odense. The setting is a woodsy, appealingly simple dining room out-fitted in monochromatic tones of brown and beige, with room for only 30 guests at a time. The feeling you might get, except for its view over the other buildings of Odense's historic core, is that of a Tuscan farmhouse. Jacob Klitgaard, born about 30km (20 miles) from the town of Svendborg, is the chef and very hip namesake of this place, personally selecting impeccably fresh ingredients, many of them produced or cultivated in and around Odense. Menu items make ample use of both foie gras and shellfish. The best examples include roasted local trout, served with roasted zucchini and with a rosemary-scented olive oil. Also look for saltwater catfish served with a ragout of basil-flavored minestrone and a mar-velous braised pheasant with wild mushrooms in beer sauce, and a fricassee of guinea fowl with herb sauce.

Gravene 4. ✆ **66-13-14-55.** Reservations recommended. Fixed-price menus 355DKK–585DKK ($59–$98). DC, MC, V. Tues–Sat 6–9pm (last order). Closed July. Bus: 2.

Under Lindetraeet ★ DANISH/INTERNATIONAL   This inn, con-structed in 1704, is located across the street from Hans Christian Andersen's house. Since the 1960s this has been a landmark restaurant, whose menu is based on fresh and high-quality ingredients. Skillfully prepared dishes include tender Danish lamb, filet of plaice with butter sauce, shrimp, *escalope* of veal in sherry sauce, fried herring with new potatoes, and an upscale version of *laubscaus,* the famed sailors' hash. The atmosphere is Old World, and in summer, meals and light refreshments are served outside under linden trees. Artists often sit here to sketch Andersen's house.

Ramsherred 2. © **66-12-92-86.** Reservations required. Main courses 225DKK–495DKK ($38–$83); fixed-price menus 395DKK–595DKK ($66–$99). DC, MC, V. Tues–Sat 11am–11pm. Closed July 4–24. Bus: 2.

MODERATE

Sortebro Kro *Value* DANISH/FRENCH   Outside the entrance to Funen Village, the open-air culture museum, about 2.5km (1½ miles) south of the center, Sortebro Kro is a coaching inn that dates from 1807. The interior is an attraction in its own right: long refectory tables, sagging ceilings with overhead beams, three-legged chairs, florid handmade chests, and crockery cupboards. Country meals are served featuring a popular all-you-can-eat Danish cold board.

Sejerskovvej 20. © **66-13-28-26.** Reservations required. Main courses 265DKK–385DKK ($44–$64). AE, DC, MC, V. Apr–Dec Mon–Sat noon–10pm, Sun noon–4pm; Jan–Mar daily noon–4pm. Closed Dec 23–26. Bus: 21 or 22 from Flakhaven.

INEXPENSIVE

Den Gremme Æling ★ *Kids* DANISH   Part of its charm derives from its name (which translates as "The Ugly Duckling"), and its location is very close to the former home of Hans Christian Andersen. It's set on a cobble-covered street in Odense's historic core, in an ocher-colored building from around 1850 that emulates an old-fashioned Danish *kro.* Attracting a large family trade, it specializes in well-stocked buffets manned by uniformed staff members who will cook your steak, fish, omelet, or whatever into virtually any Danish-inspired configuration you want. There are no *smørrebrød* (open-face sandwiches), but because the lunch buffet contains a roster of sliced cheeses, breads, meats, and condiments, you can always make your own. The staff speaks excellent English, and if buffet dining appeals to you, you might have a wonderful time here.

Hans Jensens Stræde 1. © **65-91-70-30.** Mon–Fri buffets 109DKK ($18), Sat–Sun 120DKK ($20). MC, V. Daily noon–2:30pm and 5:30–10:30pm.

Målet DANISH   One of the most vivid theme restaurants in Odense is guaranteed to please sports aficionados because of its tongue-in-cheek admiration for the nuances of soccer in general and Odense municipal soccer teams in particular. Don't expect the high-tech, big-screen prowess of sports bars you might visit in the U.S. Instead, you'll see a cramped bar for around 15 drinkers in one corner, two small-screen TVs projecting sports events from around the world, and years of collected memorabilia pertaining to soccer. No one will mind if you simply drink your way through the evening with the locals. But if you want a meal, try the house specialty, a large portion of pork schnitzel, priced at 89DKK ($15), served with potatoes, and prepared in any of 10 different ways. Otherwise, you can order fish or beefsteak, and even an occasional vegetarian dish, but the schnitzels are simply the most appealing dish in the house. *Målet,* incidentally, translates as "soccer goalpost," and management has erected one as an admittedly ugly decorative centerpiece in a prominent position against one wall.

Jernbanegade 17. © **66-17-82-41.** Reservations recommended. Main courses 55DKK–135DKK ($9.20–$23). No credit cards. Mon–Sat 11am–11pm. Bar daily until midnight.

ODENSE AFTER DARK

There are lots of cultural events in Odense, foremost among which are performances by the **Odense Symphony Orchestra.** Throughout much of the year, concerts are presented in the **Carl Nielsen Hall,** Claus Bergs Gade 9 (✆ **66-12-00-57** for ticket information). Tickets cost 60DKK–160DKK ($10–$27), depending on the event. During the warm-weather months, the orchestra's role is less formal. In August, for example, the group is more likely to play outdoors at the marketplace in front of the vegetable stands. Because of their location, these performances have been referred to as "the Vegetable Concerts." On Saturdays at 11am in August the orchestra presents free live music at Skovsoen park.

The **Casino** at the Radisson SAS H.C. Anderson Hotel, Claus Berg Gade 7 (✆ **66-14-78-00**), is one of only six casinos in the entire country. Dress is casual, and it is open daily from 7pm to 4am, charging a cover of 50DKK ($8.35). A driver's license or passport is required to enter.

Odense offers several places for dancing. By far the most popular and entertaining is **Congress Disco,** Asylgade 9 (✆ **66-11-63-02**), which opens at 11pm only on Friday and Saturday and offers a sometimes crowded dance floor in its cellar; upstairs, very high ceilings help reduce the noise a bit. Only a bit less visible is **Boogies,** Nørregade 21-23 (✆ **66-14-00-39**), which attracts the most mixed crowd in town, including some of Odense's gay and lesbian population, who blend in with an otherwise straight clientele. More rowdy, sometimes so much so that you might want to avoid it altogether, is the **James Dean Dansebar,** Mageløs 12 (✆ **66-11-90-54**), which features punk rock and high-volume electronic rock music inspired by London clubs. Other than hanging out at Boogies (see above), gay people either drive to Copenhagen for evening events, or stay alert to the special activities sponsored by **Lambda** (✆ **66-17-76-92**), which offers a Friday and/or Saturday (depending on the schedule) dance club in the cellar of Vindegade 100.

At Odense's railway station, **Frank A.'s Café,** Jernbanegade 4 (✆ **66-12-27-57**), operates as a cafe throughout the day, and as such, draws a respectable crowd of drinkers and diners who appreciate the simple Danish platters which cost from 69DKK to 190DKK ($12–$32). But the real heart and soul of the place doesn't become visible until after 10pm, when all pretenses of culinary skill are abandoned, and the place is transformed into one of the loudest, wildest, and most raucous nightlife venues in town. Then, live music—either Brazilian, Latin, or simple rock 'n' roll—transforms the place into everybody's favorite rendezvous. Come here to be convivial, amid a setting that's loaded with kitschy bric-a-brac and dozens of single or wannabe-single local residents. Food service is daily 10am to 10pm; nightlife action runs 10pm to at least 2am, and sometimes later.

3 Svendborg

43km (27 miles) S of Odense; 146km (91 miles) W of Copenhagen

This old port on Svendborg Sound has long been a popular boating center where you can see yachts, ketches, and kayaks in the harbor. The town still retains some of its medieval heritage, but much of it has been torn down in the name of progress. Visitors find that Svendborg makes a good base for touring the Danish châteaux country and the South Funen archipelago as well.

With 42,000 inhabitants, Svendborg is the second biggest town in Funen and the major commercial hub for south Funen. Until 1915, Svendborg was the home port for a big fleet of sailing ships because of its position on the lovely Svendborg Sound, which provides convenient access to Baltic ports.

Today Svendborg is a lively modern town, with much of interest, including museums, constantly changing art exhibitions, and sports. It has swimming pools, a brand-new beach resort, and a yachting school. Its beach, Christiansminde, is one of several in Funen flying the blue flag that indicates nonpolluted waters.

Svendborg is a market town. On Sunday morning, visit the cobblestone central plaza where flowers and fish are sold. Wander through the many winding streets where brick and half-timbered buildings still stand. On **Ragergade** you'll see the old homes of early seafarers. **Møllergade,** a pedestrian street, is one of the oldest streets in town, with about 100 different shops.

Literary buffs will be interested to know that the German writer Bertolt Brecht lived at Skovsbo Strand west of Svendborg from 1933 to 1939, but he left at the outbreak of World War II. During this period he wrote *Mother Courage and Her Children.*

ESSENTIALS

GETTING THERE **By Train** You can take a train from Copenhagen to Odense, where you can get a connecting train to Svendborg, with frequent service throughout the day.

By Car From our last stopover in Odense, head south on Route 9, following the signs into Svendborg.

VISITOR INFORMATION Contact the **Svendborg Tourist Office,** Centrumpladsen (℃ **62-21-09-80;** www.visitsydfyn.dk), open June 14 to August, Monday to Friday 9:30am to 6pm and Saturday 9:30am to 3pm; January 2 to June 13 and September to December 22, Monday to Friday 9:30am to 5pm, and Saturday 9:30am to noon (closed Dec 23–Jan 1). Biking routes and maps are available at this office. Bike rentals for hotel guests, at 60DKK ($10) per day, can be obtained at the Hotel Svendborg, Centrumpladsen 1 (℃ **62-21-17-00;** bus: 200 or 204).

GETTING AROUND **By Bus** Bus no. 200 serves all in-town destinations listed below, except for Vester Skerninge Kro, for which you need a car.

SEEING THE SIGHTS

Anne Hvides Gård The oldest secular house in Svendborg, a branch of the County Museum, was built around 1558. It's a beautiful half-timbered structure with 18th- and 19th-century interiors and collections of Svendborg silver, glass, copper, brass, and faience. It's located in the center of Torvet, the old market square.

Fruestraede 3. ℃ **62-21-76-15.** Admission 25DKK ($4.20) adults, 15DKK ($2.50) seniors, free for children when accompanied by an adult. Apr–Sept Tues–Sun 10am–5pm; off season by arrangement with the main office.

St. Jørgen's Church Only the Church of St. Nicolaj (see below) exceeds the beauty of St. George's church. The core of the church is a Gothic longhouse with a three-sided chancel from the late 13th century. During restoration of the church in 1961, an archaeological dig of the floor disclosed traces of a wooden building believed to be a predecessor of the present house of worship. Note the glass mosaics in the interior.

Strandvej 97. ℃ **62-21-14-73.** Free admission. Mon–Fri 8am–4pm.

St. Nicolaj Church Svendborg's oldest church is situated among a cluster of antique houses off Kyseborgstraede, in the vicinity of Gerrits Plads. Built before

Svendborg

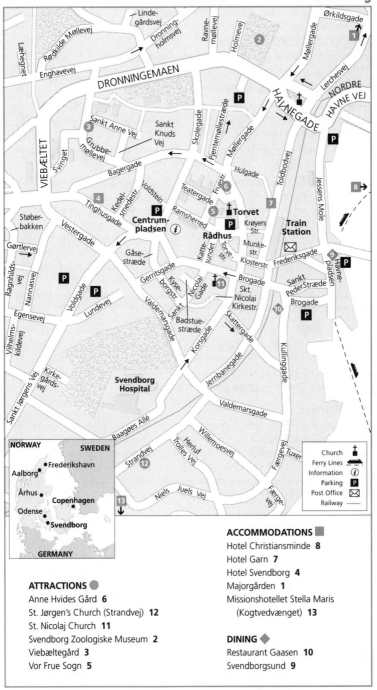

ATTRACTIONS ●
Anne Hvides Gård **6**
St. Jørgen's Church (Strandvej) **12**
St. Nicolaj Church **11**
Svendborg Zoologiske Museum **2**
Viebæltegård **3**
Vor Frue Sogn **5**

ACCOMMODATIONS ■
Hotel Christiansminde **8**
Hotel Garn **7**
Hotel Svendborg **4**
Majorgården **1**
Missionshotellet Stella Maris
   (Kogtvedvænget) **13**

DINING ◆
Restaurant Gaasen **10**
Svendborgsund **9**

1200 in the Romanesque style and last restored in 1892, its red-brick walls and white vaulting complement the fine altarpiece and stained-glass windows. Enter through the main door.

Skt. Nicolajgade 2B. (C) **62-21-12-96**. Free admission. May–Aug daily 10am–4pm; Sept–Apr daily 10am–noon.

Svendborg Zoologiske Museum   Danish zoological specimens and large dioramas showing animal migration and habitats are displayed. Many exhibits have sound effects. Make sure to stop in at the whale house where you can view the skeleton of a 17m (56-ft.) whale that beached itself on Tåsinge island in 1955.

Dronningemaen 30. (C) **62-21-06-50**. Admission 50DKK ($8.35) adults, 25DKK ($4.20) children. Apr–Sept daily 9am–5pm; Oct–Mar Mon–Fri 9am–4pm, Sat–Sun 10am–4pm. Bus: 205, 206, or 208.

Viebaeltegård   The headquarters for the Svendborg County Museum's four branches, Viebaeltegård, is in the town center, housed in a former poor-house/workhouse constructed in 1872, the only one of its kind still existing in a Danish town. These social-welfare buildings, including the garden, are now historical monuments. Inside, see displays from ancient times and the Middle Ages, including excavation finds from old Svendborg and south Funen. You can also visit crafts workshops, and watch goldsmiths, potters, and printers at work. There's a big museum shop, and you can picnic in the garden.

Grubbemøllevej 13 (near Dronningemaen). (C) **62-21-02-61**. Admission 40DKK ($6.70) adults, free for children when accompanied by an adult. Open year-round Tues–Sun 10am–5pm.

Vor Frue Sogn   On the hill where the old Castle Swineburg stood, this Romanesque-Gothic church, dating from 1253, has a carillon of 27 bells, which ring four times a day. From the tourist office at Torvet, walk up the steps leading to the rise on which the church stands, overlooking the Old Town and the harbor.

Frue Kirkestraede 4. (C) **62-21-11-67**. Free admission. Daily 8am–4pm.

SHOPPING

The widest selection of Danish design, from household utensils to prestigious china from Royal Copenhagen, and even silver from Georg Jensen, is found at **Inspiration Zinck,** in the Svendborg Bycenter, Tinghusgade ((C) **62-22-35-93**). The best source of glass is **Glasblaeseriet,** Brogade 37 ((C) **62-22-83-73**), where glass can be blown to your own design specifications. Of course, regular glass products, created by others, are also for sale.

WHERE TO STAY

Hotel Christiansminde   Clean-cut, modern, accommodating, and comfortable, this hotel was built in the 1970s about 3km (1¾ miles) east of Svendborg's center, on a grassy slope that's close to the sea. Many visitors come here for a summer holiday beside the beach; others arrive as part of corporate conventions whose sponsors rent virtually every room for inspiration-building discussions over long weekends. Rooms have balconies or private terraces, neatly kept bathrooms with shower units, and simple, functional, unpretentious furniture. Some contain small kitchens, although there's no additional cost for such added luxuries. There are a restaurant and a series of convention rooms with up-to-date electronic and broadcast facilities. Walks into Svendborg are made easier thanks to a network of hiking trails, most of which avoid active roadways. Other than that, there aren't a lot of sport facilities and diversions at this property—only easy access to the great Danish outdoors and the nearby sea.

Christiansmindvej 16, DK-5700 Svendborg. ℂ **62-21-90-00.** Fax 62-21-60-82. www.christiansminde.dk. 98 units. 795DKK ($133) double. Rates include breakfast. AE, MC, V. Bus: 201 from Svendborg. **Amenities:** Restaurant; lounge; indoor heated pool; laundry service; dry cleaning; solarium. *In room:* TV, dataport. Closed Jan–Mar.

Hotel Garni   A 1930s hotel of modest comforts, this is for those who prefer a central location opposite the bus and rail stations. Rooms are simply furnished, with those in front having a harbor view. All units contain well-equipped bathrooms with shower units. Only breakfast is served.

Toldbodvej 5, DK-5700 Svendborg. ℂ and fax **63-20-30-50.** 18 units. 650DKK ($109) double. Rates include breakfast. MC, V. Bus: 200, 208, or 980. **Amenities:** Breakfast room; lounge. *In room:* TV, hair dryer.

Hotel Svendborg ⭐   This stylish hotel offers the best accommodations in Svendborg. Built in the 1950s, it rises four floors above the commercial core of town. Except for five or six rooms that missed out on an overhaul in 1994 (and are priced accordingly), the comfortable accommodations have Scandinavian modern furniture and good bathrooms with tub/shower combinations. The hotel also rents suites and apartments, the latter housing up to four guests. On the premises are a restaurant that serves international food, and a cafe-bar with a glassed-in front terrace. There's also an on-site tanning facility.

Centrumpladsen 1, DK-5700 Svendborg. ℂ **62-21-17-00.** Fax 62-21-90-12. www.hotel-svendborg.dk. 132 units. 995DKK–1,195DKK ($166–$200) double; 1,600DKK–1,995DKK ($267–$333) suite; 1,200DKK ($200) apt for 2; 1,400DKK ($234) apt for 4. Rates include breakfast. AE, DC, MC, V. Free parking. Bus: 200 or 204. **Amenities:** Restaurant; bar; room service (7am–10pm); laundry service; dry cleaning; nonsmoking rooms. *In room:* TV, dataport, minibar, hair dryer, safe.

Majorgården ⭐ *Finds*   On the coast road, 4.3km (7 miles) from Svendborg and 32km (20 miles) from Nyborg, such illustrious Danes as tenor Lauritz Melchior have cherished this 1761 white-brick inn. Outside, a bower of roses grows against the walls, low white tables sit on the lawn for coffee, and a little pond at the rear is filled with ducks. An old horse stable has been turned into a bar. The rooms sit cozily above the restaurant under the roofline. If you're just driving by, stop in for a "plate of the inn"—two kinds of herring, plaice, meatballs, meat sausages, liver paste, and cheese. A large selection of fish and meat dishes is also available. Fixed-price menus cost 100DKK to 145DKK ($17–$24) and meals are served every day noon to 9:30pm.

Landevejen 155, DK-5883 Oure. ℂ **62-28-18-19.** Fax 62-28-18-13. 4 units, none with bathroom. 450DKK ($75) double. Rates include breakfast. MC, V. Bus: 910 from Svendborg and Nyborg. **Amenities:** Restaurant; bar; lounge. *In room:* No phone.

Missionshotellet Stella Maris *Value*   This is an old-fashioned place, the former servants' house of a large estate, built in 1904. Rooms are comfortable, if dated, each coming with a small bathroom with shower stall. Seaview rooms opening onto Svendborg Sound are more expensive options. A private park leads directly to the sound. In the southwest of the city, this lovely old seaside villa, part of a Christian hotel chain, maintains a smoke-free and alcohol-free atmosphere.

Kogtvedvaenget 3, DK-5700 Svendborg. ℂ **62-21-38-91.** Fax 62-22-41-74. www.stellamaris.dk. 25 units, 15 with bathroom. 650DKK ($109) double without bathroom; 713DKK–855DKK ($119–$143) double with bathroom. Rates include breakfast. DC, MC, V. Bus: 202. From Svendborg head west along Kogtvedvej. **Amenities:** Breakfast room. *In room:* No phone.

WHERE TO DINE

Restaurant Marco Polo ⭐ ITALIAN   Set at the edge of Svendborg's harbor, and housed in a former ironmonger's smithy, this is one of the most appealing and congenial restaurants in town. Chef and owner, Mr. Nikolaj invents many of the dishes that attract a steady stream of local business. We were recently delighted with the grilled lamb entrecôte with whiskey sauce and the fettuccini with salmon. The chef also tempted our large table with his ravioli with a pesto and tomato sauce and his baked chicken with a Gorgonzola sauce.

Kullinggade 1B. ℰ 62-22-92-11. Reservations recommended. Main courses 99DKK–139DKK ($17–$23). MC, V. Mon–Sat 5–10pm.

Svendborgsund DANISH/FRENCH   A 5-minute walk south of the commercial center, this waterfront restaurant is the oldest in town, built in the 1830s in a stone house painted white. From its windows or summer terrace you can see the harbor with its ferryboats, trawlers, and pleasure yachts. The chef specializes in fresh fish and meat, and does so exceedingly well, especially with the very filling *biksemad* (meat, potatoes, and onions). The separate bar is popular with the locals.

Havnepladsen 5A. ℰ 62-21-07-19. Reservations recommended. Main courses 100DKK–188DKK ($17–$31); lunch *smørrebrød* 60DKK–100DKK ($10–$17). MC, V. Daily 11am–10pm.

Vester Skerninge Kro *Value* DANISH   In the hamlet of Vester Skerninge, 11km (6¾ miles) west of Svendborg along Route 44, this *kro* was established in 1772, and has been dispensing generous portions of simple Danish food ever since. Behind a half-timbered facade, the chef tempts you with his perfectly roasted filet of pork. You can also enjoy fried pork in a parsley sauce. That same parsley sauce tastes even better over the fried plaice. The halibut is from Greenland, and it's served with a savory caper sauce. You might also be tempted by the tenderloin of steak with vegetables or the baked veal in a mushroom sauce.

Kravej 9, Vester Skerninge. ℰ 62-24-10-04. Main courses 89DKK–178DKK ($15–$30). AE, MC, V. Wed–Mon noon–2:30pm and 5–9pm.

SVENDBORG AFTER DARK

The most popular dance club in town, with the most appealing clients, is **Crazy Daisy,** Frederiksgade 6 (ℰ 62-21-67-60). Outfitted with bright lights and loud music deriving from Los Angeles, New York, and London, it spreads its clients—mostly people ages 20 to 35—over two floors that have easy access to three separate bars. Upstairs is disco music from the 1980s; downstairs, the dance music is newer, more cutting-edge, and more experimental. It's open only on Wednesdays, Fridays, and Saturdays 10pm till dawn. Cover is 50DKK ($8.35). Also popular, but never as much as Crazy Daisy, is **Chess,** Vestergade 7 (ℰ 62-22-17-16), which offers music that alternates between disco from the '70s and '80s and more cutting-edge fare. It's open Wednesday, Friday and Saturday from 11pm till dawn. Attracting a diverse age group, the town's best pub, Børsen, Gerritsgata 31 (ℰ 62-22-41-41), is also the largest. The tavern itself dates from 1620. We like its old-style atmosphere, but as the night ages, the patrons grow younger and rowdier. And during the warm-weather months, the outdoor decks of the ship **Orangi,** Jessens Mole (ℰ 62-22-82-92), is a late-night venue for drinks and live jazz, but only May to September, 9pm to around 1am.

NEARBY ATTRACTIONS
ON THURØ ⊛

This horseshoe-shaped island, connected to Funen by a causeway, is filled with orchards and well-cared-for gardens, sometimes called the "Garden of Denmark." The island was once the property of the manor house, Bjornemose, but the Thurineans wanted liberty, so they joined together to buy back Thurø in 1810, an event commemorated by a stone proclaiming freedom from manorial domination.

It's the island itself that's the attraction, because of its scenic beauty. However, if you want a specific target to visit, make it **Thurø Kirke** (✆ **62-20-50-92**), open daily 7:30am to 4pm, charging no admission. The best beaches can be found at Smørmosen, Thurø Rev, and Grasten.

ON TÅSINGE ✰

The largest island in the south Funen archipelago, Tåsinge has been connected to Funen by the Svendborg Sound Bridge since 1966. **Troense,** the "skipper town" of Tåsinge, is one of the best-preserved villages in Denmark, where many half-timbered houses still stand on Badstuen and Grønnegade, the latter declared Denmark's prettiest street.

The island was the setting for a famous tragic love story depicted in the film *Elvira Madigan.* After checking out of a hotel in Svendborg, Danish artist Elvira Madigan and her lover, Sixten Sparre, a Swedish lieutenant, crossed by ferry to Tåsinge, where together they committed suicide. The Romeo and Juliet of Denmark were buried in the Landet Kirkegård, Elvira Madigansvej, at Landet, in the middle of Tåsinge, where many brides, even today, throw their wedding bouquets on their graves. The 100th anniversary of the death of these two lovers was widely observed in 1989 throughout Scandinavia; many ballads were written to commemorate the date.

The island is best explored by car—follow Route 9 and drive over the causeway, or you could take local bus no. 980. However, the most important attraction, Valdemars Slot, can be seen by taking the vintage steamer MS *Helge* (✆ **62-21-09-80** for information), which departs several times daily from the harbor at Svendborg. The steamer operates from May 7 to September 5. A one-way ticket costs 35DKK ($5.85); a round-trip, 70DKK ($12). Tickets are sold onboard or at the Svendborg Tourist Office (see above).

Seeing the Sights

Bregninge Kirkebakke If the weather is clear, be sure to climb the **Bregninge church tower** for panoramic views of the island and the Funen archipelago. To the south are the Bregninge Hills, whose wooded slopes are popular for outings. Originally Romanesque, the church has a porch that dates from the 16th century, and its north wing dates from the 18th century. Inside you'll see a Romanesque granite font, a head of Christ on the north wall dating from about 1250, and a 1621 pulpit with rich ornamentation. In the porch is a tombstone with arcade decoration, the image of a vicar, and runic letters.

Kirkebakken 1, Bregninge. Admission to tower 7DKK ($1.15) adults, 3DKK (50¢) children; free admission to church. Tower daily 6am–10pm. Church Apr–Sept Mon–Sat 8am–6pm, Sun 8am–noon; Oct–Mar Mon–Sat 8am–4pm, Sun 8am–noon. Bus: 980 from Svendborg.

Sofartssamlingerne I Troense The Maritime Museum (a branch of the County Museum), housed in a 1790s school, traces maritime history from the early 19th century to the present. Pictures of ships, panoramas, yachting models, and memorabilia of the trade routes to China and East India—including Staffordshire figures, Liverpool ware, Sunderland china, rope-work art, and ships in a bottle—are displayed.

Strandgade 1, Troense. ✆ 62-22-52-32. Admission 25DKK ($4.20) adults, free for children. Mid-Apr to mid-Oct daily 10am–5pm. Cross the causeway to Tåsinge, turn left and then left again, heading down Bregingevej toward the water; turn right at Troensevej and follow the signs to the old port of Troense and to the village school (now the museum) on Strandgade.

Tåsinge Skipperhjem og Folkemindesamling Set in an 1826 school building, this private historical collection contains model and bottled ships, a coin collection, and archives of Tåsinge history. A small collection of memorabilia is associated with the tragic love drama of Elvira and Sixten. In another building you can see what a typical sea captain's house looked like some 100 years ago.

Kirkebakken 1, Bregninge. ℂ 62-22-71-44. Admission 30DKK ($5) adults, 5DKK (85¢) children. June–Aug daily 10am–5pm. Bus: 980 from Svendborg. From Valdemars Slot (see below), turn right by 2 thatched cottages and left again at the next junction; follow the signs to Bregninge.

Valdemars Slot   Valdemars Slot was built between 1639 and 1644 by order of Christian IV for his son, Valdemar Christian. In 1678 it was given to the naval hero Niels Juel for his third victory over the Swedes in a Køge Bay battle. The Juel family still owns the slot, which is in considerably better condition than when the admiral arrived. He found that the enemy Swedes had occupied the estate, sending the copper roof home to make bullets and stabling horses in the church. The castle is now a museum.

Valdemars Castle Church, in the south wing, was cleaned up by Admiral Juel, was consecrated in 1687, and has been used for worship ever since. Two stories high, it's overarched by three star vaults and illuminated by Gothic windows.

Slotsalléen 100, Troense. ℂ 62-22-61-06. Admission 95DKK ($16) adults, 45DKK ($7.50) children. Apr–June and Aug daily 10am–5pm; July daily 10am–6pm; Sept Tues–Sun 10am–5pm; Oct 1–19 Sat–Sun 10am–5pm. Take the MS Helge from Svendborg Harbor. By car, from Troense, follow Slotsalléen to the castle.

Where to Stay

Det Lille Hotel ⋆ *Finds*   Beside the harbor in the center of Troense, this is one of the most appealing small hotels in the district. The half-timbered building with a straw roof was built 150 years ago to house a family that worked at a nearby castle (Valdemar Slot). The hotel's quirky old age, and the kindness of its owner, Birgit Erikssen, more than compensate for the lack of private bathrooms. Rooms are cozy, cramped, but comfortable, and very likable. Other than breakfast, the only meals served are those prepared by Ms. Erikssen herself, which are priced at 160DKK ($27) each, but only if you announce your intention of dining in-house several hours in advance.

Badstuen 15, Troense, Tåsinge, DK-5700 Svendborg. ℂ 62-22-53-41. Fax 62-22-52-41. www.detlillehotel. dk. 8 units, none with bathroom. 550DKK ($92) double. Rates include breakfast. AE, DC, MC, V. **Amenities:** Breakfast room; lounge. *In room:* No phone.

Where to Dine

Restaurant Slotskaelderen DANISH/FRENCH   Inside the thick stone walls of one of the region's most foreboding castles, this restaurant is divided into an unpretentious Danish bistro and an upscale French restaurant. The bistro serves such dishes as schnitzels, *lobscouse* (hash), and roulades of beef with Danish beer and aquavit. The views over the tidal flats and sea are better from the restaurant, but most visitors prefer the informality and lower prices of the bistro.

If you'd like to stay overnight, there are five luxurious rooms (four with private bathrooms) and one suite located in a modern outbuilding of the historic castle. Expect luxury, charm, and grace if you decide on an overnight stay here. Doubles without bathrooms cost 840DKK ($140), doubles with bathrooms are 950DKK ($159), and the suite goes for 1450DKK ($242).

In Valdemars Slot, Slotsalléen Troense. ℂ 62-22-59-00. Restaurant main courses 75DKK–350DKK ($13–$58); bistro main courses 75DKK–175DKK ($13–$29). MC, V. June to mid-Sept daily 11am–9pm; Apr–May and mid-Sept to mid-Dec Tues–Sat 11am–9pm. Closed mid-Dec to Mar.

4 Faaborg

27km (17 miles) W of Svendborg; 179km (112 miles) W of Copenhagen; 37km (23 miles) S of Odense

Like Svendborg, Faaborg (also written Fåborg), a small seaside town of red-roofed buildings, is a good base for exploring southwestern Funen. Crowned by an old belfry, Faaborg has a number of well-preserved buildings, among them the medieval **Vesterport,** all that's left of Faaborg's walled fortifications.

You'll find one of the best collections of Funen paintings and sculpture here, particularly the work of Kai Nielsen, an important modern Danish sculptor. One controversial sculpture by Nielsen that has been denounced as obscene by some and praised by others is *Ymerbrond* (Ymer Wall), displayed in the market square (a copy is displayed in the Museum of Faaborg). The sculpture depicts a man drinking from the udder of a bony cow while the cow licks a baby.

ESSENTIALS

GETTING THERE   By Bus   From Odense, bus nos. 960, 961, or 962 run hourly from sunrise to about 11pm (trip time: 1¼ hr.). Bus no. 930 from Svendborg also arrives frequently throughout the day (40 min.). The bus station lies on Banegårdspladsen, site of the old rail train depot at the southern rim of town. (There is no longer train service to Faaborg.)

By Car   From Svendborg, head west on Route 44; from Odense, go south on Route 43.

VISITOR INFORMATION   The **Faaborg and District Tourist Association,** Banegårdspladsen 2A (© **62-61-07-07;** www.faaborg.dk), is open May to mid-September Monday to Saturday 9am to 5pm, Sunday 10am to 3pm.

GETTING AROUND   You can cover the sites below **on foot** from the Faaborg bus station with the exception of Korinth Kro, which can be reached by **bus** no. 930.

SEEING THE SIGHTS

Den Gamle Gaard (The Old Merchant's House)   This 1725 house was established as a museum in 1932 and displays exhibits on Faaborg life in the 18th and 19th centuries. Various furnishings (some of which were the property of Riborg Voight, an early love of H. C. Andersen's), glass, china, and faience indicating Faaborg's past importance as a trade and shipping center are also on view. Exhibits from Lyk, including beautiful textiles and embroidery, are in the back. The museum lies in the town center near the marketplace and harbor.

Holkegade 1. © **62-61-33-38.** Admission 30DKK ($5) adults, free for children. May 15–Sept 15 daily 10:30am–4:30pm; Sept 16–Oct 31 Sat–Sun 11am–3pm. Closed Nov 1–May 14.

Faaborg Museum   Near the bus station, the museum has a rich collection of work by Kai Nielsen. Aside from his work, the museum displays paintings by such outstanding local artists as Peter Hansen, Johannes Larsen, and Fritz Syberg. In the octagonal rotunda of the museum is a huge statue, commissioned by Mads Rasmussen, a wealthy art patron who bore the nickname "Mads Tomato." The museum has a cafe serving lunch and coffee.

Grønnegade 75. © **62-61-06-45.** Admission 35DKK ($5.85) adults, free for children under 15. Apr–Oct daily 10am–4pm; Nov–Mar Tues–Sun 11am–3pm.

Klokketårnet   This old belfry is the Faaborg's main landmark—it's all that's left of the 13th-century Church of St. Nicolai, the first church in town, which was demolished around 1600. The town's old fire sledge is also here. The caril-lon bells play hymns four times a day. The belfry is in the town center near the marketplace.

Tarnstraede. © **62-61-04-78**. Admission 10DKK ($1.65) adults, 2DKK (35¢) children. Mon–Fri 11am–4pm; Sat 10am–1pm. Closed mid-Sept to mid-June.

WHERE TO STAY

Falsled Kro ★★★ The epitome of a Danish roadside inn, this former 15th-century smuggler's inn has been converted into a premier hotel, the finest in Funen. It's west of Faaborg on Route 329. A Relais & Châteaux property, it offers tradition and quality in its colony of thatched buildings clustered around a cobblestone courtyard with a fountain. Rooms are elegantly furnished and comfortable—some in converted outbuildings, others in cottages across the road. All units have neatly kept bathrooms with mostly tub/shower combina-tions. A garden leads to the water and a yacht harbor.

Assensvej 513, Falsled, DK-5642 Millinge. © **62-68-11-11**. Fax 62-68-11-62. www.falsledkro.dk. 19 units. 1,200DKK–2,300DKK ($200–$384) double; 2,550DKK–2,850DKK ($426–$476) suite. AE, DC, MC, V. Bus: 930. **Amenities:** Restaurant; bar; 24-hr. room service; babysitting; laundry service; dry cleaning. *In room:* TV, dat-aport (in suites), minibar, hair dryer.

Hotel Mosegaard *Value* Built in the 1960s, this hotel is in an isolated spot surrounded by fields and forests, beside the sea, about 5km (3 miles) east of Faaborg. Most clients are Danes on holiday, and many opt for stays of at least a week or more. Rooms are clean, conservative, comfortable, and snug. Those with private shower-only bathrooms also contain TVs. Most on the top floor have a sea view, and some have their own private balconies. Fixed-price meals in the hotel's dining room cost 195DKK ($33) for two courses or 225DKK ($38) for three courses. The cuisine is Danish regional fare, including roast veal in a brown sauce with mixed vegetables and boiled potatoes or breaded plaice meu-nière with lime and boiled potatoes.

Nabgyden 31, DK-5600 Faaborg. © **62-61-56-91**. Fax 62-61-56-96. www.hotelmosegaard.dk. 20 units, 10 with bathroom. 500DKK ($84) double without bathroom; 650DKK–950DKK ($109–$159) double with bath-room. Rates include breakfast. AE, DC, MC, V. **Amenities:** Breakfast room; lounge. *In room:* TV, hair dryer (in some).

Hvedholm Slot ★★ One of the region's most evocative castles enjoys a recorded history going back to 1231, and a sweeping view over the fjord and the Faaborg harbor. The grand and ornate brick-and-sandstone facade you'll see today was rebuilt during the late 19th century, when it gained the soaring tower and elaborate gables and ornamentation that make it so charming. When its owners ran out of money after World War I, the contents were sold at auction by the Danish government, and the site functioned as a mental hospital begin-ning in 1928. In 1996, it was bought by a team of bold and imaginative entre-preneurs, Gorm Lokdam and Ann Vibeke, who added it to their already-functioning chain of three other stately hotels in Denmark. Today, you'll find a tasteful medley of conservative reproductions vaguely inspired by the stately homes of England. Bedrooms are spacious and comfortably and tastefully furnished, containing well-kept bathrooms with tub/shower combinations.

Breakfast and dinner are the only scheduled meals, although someone on the staff might prepare you a platter of food around noontime if you ask. Dinner is daily 6 to 10pm, and priced as part of table d'hôte meals at 325DKK ($54), plus drinks. Nonguests who phone in advance are welcome. During our visit, the din-ner consisted of a platter of smoked fish with an avocado cream sauce, followed by breast of duck with a spinach soufflé, mushrooms, and fried potatoes, followed by a medley of Danish cheeses and pastries. There's a great deal of charm about this place, and a vivid history, despite a certain spartan look.

Hvedholm Slot 1, DK-5600 Faaborg. ℂ **63-60-10-20.** Fax 63-60-10-29. 42 units. 1,000DKK–1,300DKK ($167–$217) double. Rates include breakfast. AE, DC, MC, V. Drive 7km (4⅓ miles) west of Faaborg, following Rte. 8 and the signs pointing to Bøjden. Bus: 920 from Faaborg center will drop you off less than .5km (¼ mile) from the hotel. **Amenities:** Restaurant; room service (7am–10pm); laundry service; dry cleaning; rooms for those with limited mobility. *In room:* TV, dataport (in some), hair dryer.

Korinth Kro *Kids*   Eight kilometers (5 miles) northeast of Faaborg along Route 8, this hotel features comfortably old-fashioned rooms equipped with well-kept shower-only bathrooms, a children's playground, and a garden. The 1758 building was originally intended as a school where local farm girls could learn weaving, but it became an inn in 1801. Today it's shielded from the main road by a screen of architectural gingerbread, a red-tile roof, and scores of climbing vines. If you wish, you can just drop in for lunch or dinner.

Reventlowsvej 10, DK-5600 Faaborg. ℂ **62-65-10-23.** 30 units, 12 with bathroom. 500DKK ($84) double without bathroom; 675DKK ($113) double with bathroom; 775DKK ($129) suite. Rates include breakfast. DC, MC, V. Bus: 930. **Amenities:** Restaurant; bar. *In room:* TV.

Quality Hotel Faaborg Fjord   Set in its own park at the eastern edge of town across the road from a sweeping view over one of Denmark's most famous fjords, this modern year-round hotel has comfortable rooms, each with a well-maintained bathroom containing a shower unit and a balcony/terrace. An indoor pool and sauna are among the amenities. The restaurant offers a panoramic sea view, good food, and an excellent wine cellar. Dishes are typically Danish but often with a French influence, including poached trout in beurre blanc sauce or poached fish delicately flavored with lemon.

Svendborgvej 175, DK-5600 Faaborg. ℂ **62-61-10-10.** Fax 62-61-10-17. www.hotelfaaborgfjord.dk. 131 units. 1,125DKK ($188) double. Rates include breakfast. AE, DC, MC, V. **Amenities:** Restaurant; bar; indoor heated pool; fitness center; sauna; laundry service; dry cleaning; nonsmoking rooms; rooms for those with limited mobility. *In room:* TV.

Steensgaard Herregaardspension ⭐ *Finds*   Few places in Denmark are evocative of a bygone manorial life as much as this brick-and-timber house, one of the most ideal places in Funen for a relaxing weekend. It's set in an area of scenic beauty in a very large park with a private lake. About 6.5km (4 miles) northwest of Faaborg, the oldest section dates from 1310, possibly earlier. Rooms are comfortably and tastefully furnished, often with antiques. All units contain well-managed bathrooms with tub/shower combinations.

Dinner is served nightly 6:30 to 9:30pm. If you aren't a guest you should reserve a table. You can also visit for lunch daily 12:30 to 2pm. Typical dishes include champagne soup, roe deer with juniper berries, or salmon *en papillote* with local herbs. Fresh from the sea, Danish lobster or baby shrimp are also featured.

Steensgaard, DK-5642 Millinge. ℂ **62-61-94-90.** Fax 63-61-68-61. www.herregaardspension.dk. 18 units. 1,050DKK–1,600DKK ($175–$267) double. Rates include breakfast. AE, DC, MC, V. Bus: 920 or 930. **Amenities:** Restaurant; bar; 24-hr. room service; laundry service; dry cleaning; nonsmoking rooms. *In room:* Dataport, minibar, hair dryer.

WHERE TO DINE

Falsled Kro ⭐⭐⭐ DANISH/FRENCH   Hailed as Denmark's finest dining choice, this *kro* may well be the culinary highlight of your stay. Growing many of its own vegetables, the *kro* uses only fresh, seasonal produce. Food preparation is inspired by French cuisine. Some of this restaurant's most noted dishes are among the simplest—for example, a succulent salmon smoked on the premises in one of the outbuildings. Other choices include a warm salad of smoked haddock with roast eggplant, scallop salad with basil sauce, a fish-and-shellfish soup with sorrel, spicy lobster "Tiger Lee," French duck liver with wild rice and sweet corn relish, and a saddle of rabbit or braised beef in red wine sauce. The owners breed quail locally and cook and serve them with a port wine sauce. The chef's seafood platter is a gift to put before Neptune. Try salmon grilled or flamed over fennel. Game dishes predominate in autumn. The kitchen also bakes its own bread and cakes, and the wine list is well chosen.

Assensvej 513, Falsled, Millinge. ℂ **62-68-11-11.** Reservations required. Main courses 260DKK–390DKK ($43–$65); fixed-price menus 525DKK–695DKK ($88–$116) for 3 courses, 850DKK ($142) for 6 courses. AE, DC, MC, V. Mon noon–2:30pm; Tues–Sun 6–9:30pm. Closed Oct–Mar Mon.

Restaurant Klinten ✿ DANISH   This attractive restaurant, overlooking the water less than half a kilometer (¼ mile) east of the commercial center, enjoys a forest setting near the sea. The restaurant is known for its big windows and panoramic view of a verdant offshore island. The cooking has a lot of flavor and shows a respect for fresh ingredients. Try the fresh salmon in puff pastry with spinach and lobster as a starter, following with such main courses as spicy steak in a tomato sauce, served with a medley of fresh vegetables, or else the salmon cutlet in a white wine sauce. In summer the terrace is popular when the weather's right. On the terrace is a barbecue grill with a salad bar. Occasionally they have all-you-can-eat barbecues here for 150DKK ($25).

Klintallée 1. ℂ **62-61-32-00.** Reservations recommended. Main courses 120DKK–175DKK ($20–$29); fixed-price lunch 150DKK ($25), fixed-price dinner 198DKK ($33). MC, V. Daily 11am–9pm. Bar closes at 11pm.

Tre Kroner DANISH   This is the oldest pub and restaurant in Faaborg, with a pedigree going back to 1821, when it was established as an inn, and a stone-sided architectural layout that dates back to sometime in the 1600s. The venerable, informal, and somewhat cramped setting is the first to be cited by townsfolk as a cozy site for drinks. Meals focus on traditional Danish recipes, and include a lunchtime roster of *smørrebrød,* platters of herring, soups, and salads. Dinners are more elaborate, featuring chicken breasts in mushrooms and brandy sauce, grilled steaks, calves' liver with onions, and roasted pork with braised red cabbage.

Strandgade 1. ℂ **62-61-01-50.** Reservations recommended. Main courses 50DKK–80DKK ($8.35–$13) at lunch, 130DKK–150DKK ($22–$25) at dinner. No credit cards. Daily 11am–3pm and 6–9pm. Bar daily 10am–11pm or midnight, depending on business.

FAABORG AFTER DARK

Our leading choice for a drink in comfy and historic surroundings is the previously recommended restaurant, **Tre Kroner.** Even at the peak dinner hours, someone is likely to be here just for drinks, and after the rush of the evening meal service ends (around 9:15pm), the entire place is reinvented as a pub until closing at around midnight.

A viable competitor for the after-dark favors of Faaborgians is **The Train,** Banegårdspladsen 21 (no phone), occupying a former movie theater. Its pub section opens daily at noon and continues until at least midnight. Live music is heard on Fridays and Saturdays 9pm till closing. A weekend nightclub transforms the place into a rock-'n'-roll emporium every Friday and Saturday 10pm to around 6am. Admission to the club is 30DKK to 60DKK ($5–$10).

5 Ærø ⓐⓐⓐ

29km (18 miles) across the water S of Svendborg; 176km (110 miles) W of Copenhagen; 74km (46 miles) S of Odense

An interesting Denmark excursion is to the Baltic Sea island of Ærø, 35km (22 miles) long and 10km (6¼ miles) wide. The island has little seaside and country hamlets linked by winding, sometimes single-lane roads, with thatch-roofed farmhouses in pastures and fields. Ærø possesses both sand and pebble beaches. The best towns to base yourself in are Søby, Ærøskøbing, or Marstal.

There are many good places on Ærø to eat and sleep—cozy inns in the country and comfortable little hotels in town. Try some of the local rye bread; it's said to be the best in Denmark. With your aquavit, ask for a dash of Riga balsam bitters, a tradition that started when Ærø men sailed to Riga, found these bitters, and used them ever since in their aquavit.

As you drive across Ærø, you'll note the landscape dotted with a number of windmills evoking the fields of Holland. Some of the mills are new; others, much older but well preserved. Regrettably, they are not open for interior visits but they can be viewed from the outside. The mills are particularly visible at Risemark, where you can see 11 of them. There are other mills outside the towns of Bregninge, Søby, Haven, and Marstal. All these mills still provide power for the people of Ærø, creating as little pollution as possible.

ESSENTIALS

GETTING THERE   By Ferry   The only way to reach Ærø is by ferry. Car ferries depart from Svendborg six times daily. The trip takes about an hour. For a schedule, contact the tourist office or the ferry office at the harbor in Svendborg. Bookings are made through **Det Æroske Faergegraf-Ikselskab** in Ærøskøbing (ⓒ **62-52-40-00**).

GETTING AROUND   By Bus   It's best to take a car on the ferry since there's limited bus service on Ærø (ⓒ **62-53-10-10** in Ærøskøbing for bus information). Bus no. 990 runs every hour on the hour in the afternoon between Ærøskøbing, Marstal, and Søby. There's only limited morning service. Tourist offices (see below) provide bus schedules, which change seasonally. Tickets are 62DKK ($10) for the day and can be bought on the bus.

If you'd like to take a bus tour of the island, call **Jesper "Bus" Jensen** (ⓒ **62-58-13-13**). His bus holds 12 to 14 passengers, and the tour costs 50DKK ($8.35) per person.

EXPLORING THE ISLAND

Most visitors go to Ærøskøbing, or perhaps Marstal, then return to the pleasures of south Funen. But if you like to cycle or have rented a car in Funen you can explore the southern tier of the island, going from Marstal, the port in the east, all the way to Søby at the northern and far western tip of Ærø. There are several attractions along the way, although you can just enjoy the landscape for its own idyllic beauty.

Take the coastal road going west from Marstal (signposted VEJSNAES). From here continue west, following the signs to Store Rise, where you can stop and visit **Rise Kirke,** originally a Romanesque church dating from the latter part of the 12th century. Later, vaults were added and the church was enlarged twice, the last time in 1697. The altarpiece inside dates from 1300 and depicts the suffering and resurrection of Christ. Its carved work is from the town of Schleswig in northwestern Germany. The tower is similar to that of the church at Breg-ninge. It was originally roofed in oak tiles but these were replaced in 1957. In the churchyard wall facing the vicarage garden an old porch known as "the Monks Door" (ca. 1450) can be seen.

In a field in the rear of the church you can view **Tingstedet,** a 54m (177-ft.) Neolithic passage grave. It's believed that this site is at least 5,000 years old. Archaeologists have claimed that the cuplike markings in the biggest stone (close to the church) indicate the site may have been used by a "fertility cult." A foot-path leading from the church to the Neolithic site is clearly marked, and it's only a short walk.

If you'd like to break up the driving tour, you can drive less than a kilometer (½ mile) south of the village to **Risemark Strand,** one of the island's few sandy beaches. Many of the other beaches on Ærø consist of shingles.

CYCLING AROUND THE ISLAND

Ærø is one of the best islands in Denmark for cycling because of its low-lying terrain and scenic paths. Local tourist offices provide maps outlining routes for 15DKK ($2.50). You can use these maps for bike rides but also for walks. Num-bers 90, 91, and 92 mark cycle trails around the coast. Bike rentals cost 45DKK ($7.50) a day, and rentals in Ærøskøbing are available at the **Ærøskøbing Van-drerhjem,** Smedevejen 15 (© **62-52-10-44**); at Marstal at **Nørremark Cykelforretning,** Møllevejen 77 (© **62-53-14-77**); and at **Søby Cykelforret-ning,** Langebro 4A (© **20-29-17-53**).

The road continues west to Tranderup, where you can visit **Tranderup Kirke,** a Romanesque building with Gothic vaulting. Inside, the large carved figure depicting Mary and the infant Jesus dates from around the 14th century and is one of the oldest ecclesiastical pieces on the island. The triptych is from around 1510, and the large mural over the chancel arch reveals the date of its execution in 1518. Originally, the spires of Tranderup resembled those of Bregninge (see below). But they were rebuilt in a neoclassical style in 1832; the largest bell was cast in 1566 and is still in use.

After a visit follow the signs west to the village of **Vodrup,** which originally was founded in the 13th century and is mentioned for the first time in 1537 as "Wuderup." The village disappeared in the 17th century when the land became part of Vodrup Estate. When the estate was dissolved, the village came back.

The cliffs at Vodrup, **Vodrup Klint** ★★, have an unusual geology: Large blocks of land have slipped down and resemble huge steps. The soil lies on top of a layer of gray clay, which can be seen at the base of the cliffs by the beach. The layer of clay is full of snail and cockleshells, left there by the sea. Water seep-ing down through the earth is stopped by the clay. When the clay absorbs enough water, it becomes so "movable" that it acts as a sliding plane for the lay-ers above. The last great landslide here occurred in 1834.

Vodrup Klint is one of the most southerly points in Denmark, attracting crea-tures such as lizards and many species of plants that thrive here—the carline thistle grows on these cliffs, blooming from July to September. An unusual char-acteristic of the cliffs is a proliferation of springs, where water bubbles out by the foot of the slopes. When the cattle need water, farmers need only push a pipe into the cliff face and let the water collect in a pool.

Fyn County has bought the cliffs, roughly 35 hectares (86 acres), and set them aside for the use of the public, which has access to the area. Animals are allowed to graze the fields in the summer months. You can walk on all areas of the land. Cycle trail 91 runs right past Vodrup Klint, so it's often a stopover for bikers.

The route continues west to Bregninge and **Bregninge Kirke,** a 13th-century building with grandiose vaults that were added during the late 15th century. Its impressive spire shows the influence of east Schleswig (Germany) building traditions, and is roofed with oak tiles. The murals inside date from around 1510—one, for example, depicts the Passion of Christ, another the life of John the Baptist. The magnificent triptych dates from shortly before the Reformation, and was made by Claus Berg. The crucifix in the nave is from the latter Middle Ages, and the 1612 pulpit was executed in the Renaissance style.

After your visit along the southern part of Ærø, you can continue northwest into Søby.

ÆRØSKØBING

The neat little village of **Ærøskøbing** ★★★ is a 13th-century market town, which came to be known as a skippers' town in the 17th century. Called "a Lilliputian souvenir of the past," with its small gingerbread houses, intricately carved wooden doors, and cast-iron lamps, few Scandinavian towns have retained their heritage as much as Ærøskøbing. In the heyday of the windjammer, nearly 100 commercial sailing ships made Ærøskøbing their home port.

Lying in the middle of the island, the town looks as if it were laid out by Walt Disney—in fact, it's often known as "the fairy-tale town" because it looks more like a movie set than a real town. Filled with cobblestone streets, hollyhocks, and beautifully painted doors and windows, the town itself is far more interesting to wander and explore at random than are any of its minor attractions.

During the summer its shops, cafes, and restaurants are bustling with life. At the old market square you can still see the pumps that supplied the town with its water until 1952; they are still in working order.

The marina and nearby beach are ideal spots for enjoying outdoor activities. At the end of a busy day, we suggest you stroll over to the Vesterstrand, where the sunset (in our view) is the most romantic and evocative in all of Denmark.

The town of Ærøskøbing was founded in the 12th century, and it was granted town privileges in 1522 on orders of King Christian II. As visitors wander through the town, many wonder why the houses are still original and weren't torn down to make way for modern structures. The main reasons were the hard times and poverty that prevented many citizens from tearing down their old structures and rebuilding. However, when prosperity did come, the locals realized their old buildings were a treasure, so instead of tearing them down they restored them—and they're waiting for you to see them today. Preservation societies are particularly strong on the island.

ESSENTIALS

VISITOR INFORMATION   The **Ærøskøbing Turistbureau,** Vestergade 1 (© **62-52-13-00**), is open June 15 to August, Monday to Friday 9am to 3:30pm, Saturday 10am to 1pm; September to June 14, Monday to Friday 9am to 1pm, Saturday 9:30am to 12:30pm.

SEEING THE SIGHTS

Ærøskøbing Kirke, Søndergade 43 (© **62-52-11-72**), was built between 1756 and 1758 to replace a rather dilapidated church from the Middle Ages. In the present reconstructed church, the 13th-century font and the pulpit stem from the original structure. They were donated by Duke Philip of Lyksborg in 1634, the year he bought Gråsten County on the island of Ærø. The year before, he had inherited the market town of Ærøskøbing and an estate in Vodrup. The altarpiece is a copy of Eckersberg's picture hanging in Vor Frue Kirke in Svendborg. The colors selected for the interior of the church, along with the floral motifs, were the creation of Elinar V. Jensen in connection with an extensive restoration project carried out in 1950. The church can be visited every day 8:30am to 5pm; admission is free.

Flaskeskibssamlingen, Smedegade 22 (© **62-52-29-51**), is a nautical museum. The seafaring life is documented in this museum of Peter Jacobsen's ships in bottles, which represent his life's work. Upon his death in 1960 at the age of 84, this former cook, nicknamed "Bottle Peter," had crafted more than 1,600 bottled ships and some 150 model sailing vessels built to scale, earning him the reputation in Ærøskøbing of "the ancient mariner." The museum also has Ærø clocks, furniture, china, and carved works by sculptor H. C. Petersen. Admission is 30DKK ($5) adults, 15DKK ($2.50) children; open daily 10am to 5pm.

Ærø Museum, Brogade 35 (© **62-52-29-50**), is the best local museum, found at the corner of Nørregade and Brogade. In the old days it was inhabited by the bailiff, but today you'll find a rich collection of the island's past. The collection includes antiques and paintings from the mid-1800s. It's open Tuesday through Sunday June 13 to August 23, 10am to 4pm. Off-season hours are Tuesday through Sunday 10am to 1pm. Admission is 20DKK ($3.35).

Of minor interest, **Hammerichs Hus,** Gyden 22 (© **62-52-27-54**), stands on the corner of Brogade and Gyden. It was the home of sculptor Genner Hammerich and is now a museum with a collection of his art and tiles. The half-timbered house also has a collection of period furnishings, antiques, and china, all gathered by the artist in Funen and Jutland. In one of the rooms you'll find a pair of porcelain dogs, which were brought home from England by sailors. It's said that prostitutes placed these dogs on their windowsills. If the dogs faced each other, callers were welcome. Since prostitutes were not allowed to charge for their favors, they sold the dogs to their customers instead. It's said that the North Sea is paved with porcelain dogs that the sailors did not dare bring home. It's open June to August, Wednesday through Monday noon to 4pm. Admission is 20DKK ($3.35).

SHOPPING

Shopping options in Ærøskøbing blossom like flowers in summer, but are greatly reduced after the crush of seasonal tourists retreats. Two particularly worthwhile options that remain open most of the year include **Ærøskøbing Antiks,** Vestergade 60 (© **62-52-10-32**), which sells a remarkable collection of antiques, many of them nautical in their inspiration, and some of them imported from faraway St. Petersburg, Estonia, or northeastern Germany during Ærø's maritime heyday. Gift items, souvenirs of Ærø, newspapers, and books in Danish, German, and English are available from **Creutz Boghanel,** Vestergade 47 (© **62-52-10-22**). And in addition to those year-round staples, some of the best shopping is available simply by wandering among the seasonal kiosks and boutiques that line either side of the Søndergade and the Vestergade, the town's main shopping emporiums.

WHERE TO STAY

Det Lille Hotel ★ (Value) Lying 90m (295 ft.) from the ferry and harbor, Det Lille Hotel was built in 1844 as a private home. Today it offers simple but cozy guest rooms. All units contain well-kept bathrooms with tub/shower combinations. The hotel is also a good dining choice. It serves meals daily from 11:30am to 2pm and 6 to 9pm. Try asparagus soup, pork chops with vegetables, ham cutlets with mushrooms, beefsteaks, fried chicken, or hash.

Smedegate 33, DK-5970 Ærøskøbing. ⓒ **62-52-23-00.** 6 units, none with bathroom. 565DKK ($94) double. Rates include breakfast. MC, V. Free parking on street. **Amenities:** Restaurant; lounge. *In room:* TV.

Hotel Ærøhus ⭐   This typical Danish inn is charming, with many traditional features, such as copper kettles hanging from the ceiling and warm lamps glowing. The guest rooms are traditional—in vaguely French boudoir style—although they've been modernized. Most units have a well-kept bathroom with a tub/shower combination. You can also enjoy good Danish meals here. In the summer there's dining in the large garden. The hotel, a 3-minute walk from the harbor, offers live music on summer weekends.

Vestergade 38, DK-5970 Ærøskøbing. ⓒ **62-52-10-03.** Fax 62-52-21-23. 65 units, 50 with bathroom. 650DKK ($109) double without bathroom; 1,190DKK ($199) double with bathroom. Rates include breakfast. MC, V. Free parking. **Amenities:** Restaurant; bar *In room:* TV, dataport, hair dryer, safe.

Pension Vestergade 44 ⭐ *Value*   One of the most historically appealing buildings of downtown Aeroskøbing is in the center of the village, 183m (600 ft.) from the ferryboat piers, within an antique (built in 1784) half-timbered structure that the Danish historical authority considers almost sacrosanct. This allegiance to maintaining the building in its pristine original condition has restricted its owner, English-born Susanna Greve, from adding private bathrooms to its venerable interior. But because of its history and atmosphere, the guests don't seem to mind. This enormous apricot-colored building was built by a local sea captain for each of his two daughters, and it's divided into two almost exactly equal halves. Only half of the house is occupied by this B&B. (The other half is the home of a local doctor, and is not open for view.) Within Susanna's half, you'll find scads of Danish and English antiques, substantial and bracing breakfasts, midafternoon coffee that's served every day, and a distinctive (and rather philosophical) sense of humor. Local fire codes demand an absolute no-smoking policy on the building's upper floors. As for plumbing issues, know in advance that the inn maintains five bathrooms, each opening onto corridors and public areas, for six accommodations, more than most other B&Bs in Denmark, so most visitors find the bathroom situation acceptable. Susanna knows the ins and outs of virtually every tourist facility in town, and is generous about transmitting information about local restaurants and bike-rental facilities to her guests. None of the rooms has TV or phone, but there's a communal TV in one of the public areas.

Vestergade 44. DK-5970, Aeroskøbing. ⓒ **62-52-22-98.** www.pension-vestergade44.dk. 6 rooms, none with private bathroom. 680DKK–780DKK ($114–$130) double. No credit cards. *In room:* Dataport.

Vindeballe Kro   This charming country inn, built in 1888, is located on the road between Søby and Marstal, 4km (2½ miles) south of Ærøskøbing and close to the sea. Rooms with shower-only bathrooms are without frills, but comfortable, and guests share the lounge, which has a TV. The inn also has a simple restaurant (see "Where to Dine," below).

Vindeballe Vej 1. DK-5970 Ærøskøbing. ⓒ **62-52-16-13.** Fax 62-52-23-49. vindeballe.kro@get2net.dk. 6 units, none with bathroom. 420DKK ($70) double. Rates include breakfast. MC, V. **Amenities:** Restaurant; bar. *In room:* Hair dryer, no phone.

WHERE TO DINE

Ærøskøbing Røgeri *Value* SMOKED FISH   The setting is anything but glamorous, and the food you order will be served on paper plates with plastic knives and forks. And if you're looking for wine to accompany your meal, forget it, as the beverage of choice is beer. Nevertheless, this is one of the most popular places in town, a culinary landmark that nearly everyone describes with nostalgia and affection. Set beside the harbor in a raffish-looking house built in the old Ærø style, it serves only fresh fish that has been smoked (usually that morning) in electric and wood-fired ovens on the premises. You specify what kind of fish you want (salmon, herring, filet or whole mackerel, trout, or shrimp) and which of a half-dozen seasonings you want (dill, parsley, pepper, paprika, garlic, or "Provençal"), then you carry your plate to outdoor seating overlooking the harbor, or haul it back to wherever you're staying. The most expensive thing on the menu is a slab of fresh-smoked salmon accompanied with bread, butter, and a portion of potato salad; the least expensive is a make-it-yourself *smørrebrød* that includes a smoked herring, a slice of rough-textured bread, and Danish butter.

Havnen 15. ℂ 62-52-40-07. Platters 19DKK–26DKK ($3.15–$4.35). No credit cards. Daily 10am–6pm (until 8pm mid-June to mid-August). Closed Sept–Apr.

Restaurant Mumm AMERICAN/INTERNATIONAL   In a simple house whose foundation dates from 1780, this restaurant enjoys a reputation for well-prepared dishes that sometimes carry a North American (or at least an international) flavor. Inside, you'll find a pair of dining rooms; the less formal one offers a view into a very busy kitchen. There's also a terrace set up in the garden in back, where parasols and candles usually adorn the outdoor tables. The restaurant offers an unusual combination of American- and Danish-style dishes (a former owner was a chef at a Florida resort). There are a copious salad buffet, well-flavored steaks, and an abundance of seafood (most of which comes from local waters), including filet of plaice, grilled salmon with hollandaise sauce, sole in parsley-butter sauce, and various preparations of shrimp and snails.

Søndergade 12. ℂ 62-52-12-12. Ærøskøbing. Main courses 120DKK–188DKK ($20–$31). AE, DC, MC, V. June–Sept daily 11:30am–2:30pm and 6–9:30pm; May and Sept Tues–Sun 11:30am–2:30pm and 6–9:30pm. Closed Oct–Apr.

Vindeballe Kro DANISH   The restaurant is better known, and better recommended by local residents, than the previously recommended hotel, especially since it's one of the few die-hard eateries that's open year-round, even after the hordes of tourists go home for the winter. There's room for only about 30 diners. Menu items include "flat fish" (a form of plaice) with parsley and butter sauce, Danish beef that's fried with onions, beef tenderloin with baked potatoes, veal schnitzels fried in butter, pan-fried eel (a specialty of Ærø) served with potatoes, turkey steak with Gorgonzola sauce, and grilled steaks with your choice of béarnaise, tomato, or Mexican-style sauce. Some of the tables are arranged around a bar (separate from the restaurant) that attracts a local clientele.

Vindeballe Vej 1, Vindeballe. ℂ 62-52-16-13. Reservations recommended. Main courses 100DKK–165DKK ($17–$28). AE, DC, MC, V. Daily 8am–midnight. From Ærøskøbing, drive 4km (2½ miles) south, following the road signs to Søby.

ÆRØSKØBING AFTER DARK

In summertime, you'll find sidewalk cafes and bars that come and go with the seasons (and which sometimes don't return the following year) along either side of the Vestergade and the Søndergade. One of the most reliable and enduring of these seasonal joints is the **Café Andelen,** Søndergade 28A (ℂ 62-52-17-11), which presents live jazz that begins around 9pm most nights June to August. Two year-round pubs that tend to be favored by local residents and fishers are **Aarebo Pub,** Vestergade 4 (ℂ 62-52-28-50), which offers some kind of live music every Friday and Saturday throughout the year, and its nearby competitor, **Landborgården Pub,** Vestergade 54 (© **62-52-10-41**), which is a site just for drinking and socializing.

MARSTAL

Marstal, a thriving little port on the east coast of Ærø, has been a center for sailing since the days of the tall ships. The harbor, protected by a granite jetty, is still busy, with a shipyard producing steel and wooden vessels, an engine factory, a ferry terminal, and one of Denmark's biggest yacht basins. The street names of Marstal attest to its seafaring background: Skonnertvej, Barkvej, and Galeasevej (Schooner, Bark, and Ketch roads).

ESSENTIALS

VISITOR INFORMATION   The **Marstal Turistbureau,** Havnegade 5 (© **62-53-19-60**), a 5-minute walk south of the harbor, is open mid-June to August Monday to Friday 10am to 4pm and Saturday 10:30am to 2:30pm. In July, the peak month to visit Ærø, it's also open Sunday 10am to noon. Off-season hours are Monday to Friday 10am to 3pm.

SEEING THE SIGHTS

In summer, consider a side trip to **Birkholm Island.** It's ideal for exploring, relaxing, and swimming. Twice a day a mail boat takes a limited number of passengers on this 45-minute trip from Marstal. Except for service and utility vehicles, there are no cars allowed on the island. For information and reservations, call Birkholm Færgen at © **62-54-17-77.** The price of round-trip passage from Marstal to Birkholm Island is 130DKK ($22).

Maren Minors Minde   This is the once-prosperous, once-private home of a successful sea captain, Rasmus Minor, whose other bequests to Ærø included an orphanage and a retirement home. In the 1950s his widow, Maren Minor, willed the house and its collection of nautical artifacts to the municipality as a museum.

Teglgade 9. © **62-53-23-31**. Admission 10DKK ($1.65) adults, 5DKK (85¢) children. Daily 11am–3pm. Closed Sept to mid-June.

Marstal Kirke   Built in 1738, the church was enlarged twice—once in 1772 by adding an extension and later in 1920 with a tower to commemorate the reunification of southern Jutland with Denmark. Seven votive ships inside indicate the growth of shipping in the town from the 18th to the 20th centuries, and the town's close links to the sea. The front dates from the Middle Ages. The blue color of the benches symbolizes the sea and eternity, whereas the red colors of the altar and pulpit are supposed to evoke the blood shed by Christ. Red is also the color of love. Carl Rasmussen, a maritime artist who usually specialized in the motifs of Greenland, painted the 1881 altarpiece. It depicts Christ stilling a storm. In the old churchyard are memorials and tombstones honoring the sailors of Marstal who died at sea during two world wars.

Kirkestrade 14. © **62-53-10-38**. Free admission. Daily 9am–5pm.

Marstal Søfartsmuseum   This museum, of only passing interest, contains collections of ship models, old maritime equipment, objets d'art, and junk brought home by sailors from foreign shores.

Prinsensgade 1. © **62-53-23-31**. Admission 40DKK ($6.70) adults, 10DKK ($1.65) children. Oct–Apr Tues–Fri 10am–4pm, Sat 11am–3pm; May and Sept daily 10am–4pm; June and Aug daily 9am–5pm; July daily 9am–8pm.

SHOPPING

Marstal's most densely packed shopping streets are the Kirkestræde (which is transformed into a pedestrians-only walkway July–Aug) and Kongensgade. Many of the boutiques and kiosks that flourish there during midsummer disappear altogether the rest of the year, so the best way to appreciate the shopping scene involves spontaneously dropping in and out of boutiques as they catch your fancy. The best, and more enduring, venue for souvenirs from Ærø and the rest of Denmark is **Emerto,** Kirkestræde 10 (© **62-53-13-91**). Its owner, Bille Knusen, accumulates porcelain, crystal, woodcarvings, nautical memorabilia, and pots and pans into an all-inclusive emporium. Nearby is **Fruhøst,** Kongensgade 22 (© **62-53-24-09**), a store specializing in odd bits of handmade paraphernalia that for the most part are made on Ærø. Owner Elizabeth Jørgensen sells weavings, homemade wine, homemade chocolates, candles, and bric-a-brac.

WHERE TO STAY

Ærø Kongreshotel   A 5-minute walk south of the center of town and less than half a kilometer (¼ mile) from the beach, this hotel, opened in 1989, is the largest and most up-to-date on the island. Surrounded by sea grass and sweeping vistas, the rooms are first-class, decorated in pastel colors, with well-maintained bathrooms containing tub/shower combinations. The suites are twice the size of regular rooms.

Egehovedvej 4, DK-5960 Marstal. © **62-53-33-20.** Fax 62-53-31-50. 100 units. 845DKK ($141) double; 1,195DKK ($200) suite. Rates include breakfast. DC, MC, V. Free parking. Closed Dec 20–Jan 2. Bus: 990 to Marstal. **Amenities:** Restaurant; bar; indoor heated pool; sauna. *In room:* TV.

Hotel Marstal   This old-fashioned hotel is in the town center, 2 minutes from the harbor. It contains medium-size clean and functionally furnished rooms with large windows. The two that open onto a view of the sea are the most frequently requested. Bathrooms are a bit small, but are well kept and equipped with tub/shower combinations. The good news is that the hotel operates one of the most reliable restaurants in town. You may want to patronize it even if you aren't a guest. (See "Where to Dine," below.)

Droningstraede 1A, DK-5960 Marstal. © **62-53-13-52.** 7 units, none with bathroom. 500DKK ($84) double. Rates include breakfast. MC, V. **Amenities:** Restaurant; bar. *In room:* TV, no phone.

WHERE TO DINE

Den Gamle Vingård ☆ DANISH   On the Torvet (main square) of Marstal, this restaurant is set in a relatively new building, despite the fact that its name means "the old vineyard." It is, nonetheless, one of the best restaurants in Marstal, with engravings and oil paintings of antique ships and lots of woodsy-looking memorabilia of old Ærø. Your meal might consist of something as simple as pasta or a pizza, or more substantial fare, which includes steaks, veal, chicken, fried filets of pork, or any of a half-dozen kinds of fresh fish. Each is prepared with the sauce or preparation best suited to its individual flavors: Salmon, for example, is grilled and accompanied with an herb-and-butter sauce; herring is best either marinated, or fried and served with a lime-vinegar sauce. Plaice, depending on the mood of the chef, might be stuffed with shrimp and asparagus.

Skolegade 15. © **62-53-13-25.** Reservations recommended. Pizzas and pastas 50DKK–68DKK ($8.35–$11); main courses 64DKK–142DKK ($11–$24). No credit cards. May and Sept daily 5–10pm; June–Aug daily noon–10pm. Closed Oct–Apr.

The Restaurant in the Hotel Marstal ✦ STEAKS/SEAFOOD   One of the best restaurants in town is this dark-toned replica of an English pub, where lots of varnished paneling, flickering candles, and nautical accessories contribute to a general coziness at all times of the year. There's lots of beer on tap, as well as a menu that focuses on grilled steaks, some of them with pepper sauce; veal cordon bleu; and fresh seafood that might have arrived that morning from local fishers. Especially flavorful are any of the beef dishes, or the grilled salmon steak with potatoes, asparagus, and either a lemon-butter or hollandaise sauce.

Dronningestræde 1A. ☎ 62-53-13-52. Reservations recommended. Main courses 104DKK–178DKK ($17–$30); fixed-price menus 110DKK–175DKK ($18–$29). AE, DC, MC, V. Daily noon–2pm and 5:45–11pm.

MARSTAL AFTER DARK
One of our favorite pubs on Marstal is **Toldbohus,** Prinsensgade 7 (☎ **62-53-15-41**), which opens every day at 8am and which transforms itself from a cafe into a bar and pub as the day progresses.

6 Langeland & Rudkøbing

125km (77½ miles) SW of Copenhagen; 18km (11 miles) SE of Svendborg; 50km (31 miles) SE of Odense

Southeast of Funen, surrounded by the waters of the Great Belt, this long and narrow island attracts visitors to its beaches, its bird-watching, and its biking possibilities. It has a year-round population of about 15,000 people, which swells in summer to 40,000. At the northern tip of Hov to its southern rim at Dons Klint is a distance of 50km (31 miles). From Tåsinge a bridge connects Langeland with the rest of Funen, funneling traffic into Langeland's capital, Rudkøbing.

GETTING THERE   By Bus or Car   Route 9, via the Langeland Bridge, links Rudkøbing to Tåsinge and ultimately Svendborg (see earlier in this chapter). From Svendborg buses make the 30-minute run every hour during the day.

By Ferry   It's also possible to take one of the frequent daily ferries that make the run from Marstal to Rudkøbing on the west coast of Langeland. Ferryboats are operated year-round five to six times a day (trip time: 1 hr.). One-way transit costs 179DKK ($30) for a car with a driver, or 487DKK ($81) for a car with a driver and up to four passengers. Pedestrians without cars pay 81DKK ($14) each way. For information and departure times, contact **Det Ærøske Færgetrafikselskab,** Vestergade 1, Ærøskøbing (☎ **62-52-40-00**).

GETTING AROUND   By Bus   Bus no. 910 runs between Lohals in the north and Bagenkop in the south, passing through Rudkøbing and linking all the major villages of Langeland. From Rudkøbing, make sure you're heading in the right direction before hopping aboard.

By Car   If you're a motorist, once on Langeland you'll find that Route 305 runs from Lohals in the north to Bagenkop in the south, nearly the full north–south length of Langeland.

By Bicycle   If you're biking you'll find asphalt cycling paths from Rudkøbing running north to Lohals, south to Bagenkop, and even east to Spodsbjerg, which is a little port facing east toward the Danish island of Lolland. Bike rentals are available at the cycle shop operated by **Ole Dægehn,** Spodsbjergvej 186 (☎ **62-50-21-10**), in the hamlet of Spodsbjerg, 8km (5 miles) east of Rudkøbing. Depending on what you rent, bikes cost 60DKK ($10) per day.

RUDKØBING

Although this is the island's capital, with a population of 6,000, it's really just a country town, albeit an old one, having been granted its charter back in 1287. Because of a bad economy, the town was allowed to stagnate for a long time, as its buildings fell into disrepair. This turned out to be a blessing, as the buildings weren't torn down and many have now been restored, giving Rudkøbing a look of one of the most unspoiled towns in Denmark.

You can wander through its narrow winding streets, with some incredibly small houses, which today are often filled with craftspeople. You can steal a glance into a garden here or a yard there. There are a number of stately mansions as well. The best streets for seeking out the old homes are Gåsetorv, Østergade, and Brogade.

To the north of the ferry harbor is a fishing harbor, and close at hand is a 260-berth yacht harbor. Many Zealanders come here in summer to sail the waters, as do German yachters to the south.

ESSENTIALS

VISITOR INFORMATION   The center for information is the **Langelands Turistforening,** Torvet 5 (© **62-51-35-05**), open mid-June to August Monday to Friday 9am to 5pm, Saturday 9am to 3pm; off season Monday to Friday 9:30am to 4:30pm and Saturday 9:30am to 12:30pm. You can purchase fishing licenses here for 30DKK ($5) per day and cycling maps for 30DKK ($5).

SEEING THE SIGHTS

Attractions are rather thin within Rudkøbing itself. If your time is severely limited it would be better to use it to explore the island than to seek out individual attractions here. Nevertheless, there are some amusements, but none better than walking the antique streets at the historic core.

On Brogade, just east of Ramsherred, is a statue of Dr. Hans Christian Ørsted (1777–1851), who discovered electromagnetism. Across the street at Brogade 15 is the old **Rudkøbing Apotek** (© **63-51-10-10**), which was Ørsted's birthplace. Today it houses a small museum with replicas of the interiors of pharmacy shops—one from the 1700s, another from the 1800s—and a collection of pharmacy equipment, some of it dating back 3 centuries. The museum itself is open June 15 to August Monday to Friday 11am to 4pm, charging 20DKK ($3.35) adults; free for children under 12.

The island's history museum is the **Langelands Museum,** Jens Wintheersvej 12 and Østergade 25 (© **63-51-10-10**). It's the virtual "attic" of Langeland, displaying everything from prehistoric artifacts to exhibits from the early part of the 20th century. From the Stone Age you can view flint axes of various sizes, finely worked daggers, amber ornaments, various skulls, and wooden tools, plus huge earthenware vessels made during the Iron Age. A unique double tomb is exhibited together with ornaments and highly decorated riding equipment found in the tombs of Viking chiefs. There's also an array of medieval objects and beautiful Renaissance and 18th-century marquetry furniture. The museum is open Monday to Thursday 10am to 4pm, Friday 10am to 1pm. Admission is 25DKK ($4.20) adults, free for children under 12.

During the Cold War Fort Langeland was responsible for the surveillance of the Baltic and was a military command center for the area. In the '90s it was closed, but the Langelands Museum has reopened the site. Boys of all ages love to stand by the huge guns or descend into the emplacements with their cramped crew's quarters and ammunition storage depots. Set near the island's most southerly tip, 32km (20 miles) from Rudkøbing, **Museum Langelandsfort,**

Vognsbjergvej 4B, Bagenkop (© **63-51-10-10**), is open only May to October, Monday through Friday 10am to 5pm. (It's usually closed on Sat, except in July, when it's open Sat 11am–5pm.) The setting for the fort is idyllic, surrounded by an untouched marsh and woodland that's a prime migration stopover for birds. There is also a panoramic view of the Baltic Coast from the old fort site. Admission costs 35DKK ($5.85) adults, free for children under 12.

WHERE TO STAY

Hotel Rudkøbing Skudehavn   At the very edge of a historic harbor, this hostelry is composed of 30 wooden cottages, each containing two apartments. Rooms feature indestructible furnishings (the kind even children have a hard time damaging) and, in some cases, additional sleeping space—usually for a child—beneath the peak of the roofline. Don't expect glamour. What you'll get, however, is a comfortable, well-managed family-style hotel. The reception staff is well versed in the sports and holiday diversions within the region. There is a recommended in-house restaurant (see "Where to Dine," below).

Havnegade 21, DK-5900 Rudkøbing. © **62-51-46-00**. Fax 62-51-49-40. 76 apts, each with kitchenette. 735DKK–815DKK ($123–$136) double. Extra bed 165DKK ($28). Rates include breakfast. AE, DC, MC, V. **Amenities:** Restaurant; bar; indoor heated pool; fitness center; sauna; solarium. *In room:* TV.

Skrøbelevgaard ⭐ *(Finds* This appealing former 17th-century manor house is a centerpiece for hundreds of acres of surrounding forests and field. You'll be invited to wander around the estate, admiring the half-timbered outbuildings that were once stables, barns, and shelters belonging to herdsmen and bailiffs. The original dining room has been carefully preserved and is the site of well-prepared dinners that will be served, if reservations are given several hours in advance. The mood here is like a private, tastefully arranged dinner party. The relatively inexpensive rooms are cozy, old-fashioned, and charming, personalized with knickknacks collected by the family that maintains the place. Each unit has a well-kept bathroom with a tub/shower combination.

Skrøbelev Hedevej 4, Ny Skrøbelev, DK-5900 Rudkøbing. © **62-51-45-31**. 10 units. 500DKK–700DKK ($84–$117) double. Rates include breakfast. No credit cards. From Rudkøbing, drive 3km (1¾ miles) east of town, following the signs to Spodsbjerg, turning off when you see the signs for Skrøbelevgaard. **Amenities:** Breakfast room; lounge. *In room:* TV (in some).

WHERE TO DINE

Hotel Rudkøbing Skudehavn DANISH   This is a well-managed, unpretentious restaurant whose soaring glass windows illuminate a high-ceilinged, peak-roofed interior and look out over one of the most historic harbors in the region. Menu items are based on the culinary traditions of old-time Denmark, and include such dishes as fried Danish-style filets of plaice, fresh-fried fish cakes, heaping platters of fresh-peeled shrimp, brisket of beef with horseradish, and roast pork with red cabbage or fried onions, and potatoes. Any of these might be followed with an assortment of Danish cheeses produced by local farmers.

Havnegade 21. © **62-51-46-00**. Reservations recommended. Main courses 79DKK–189DKK ($13–$32); fixed-price menus 145DKK–270DKK ($24–$45). AE, DC, MC, V. June–Sept daily noon–10pm; Oct–May daily 5:30–8:30pm.

NORTHERN LANGELAND

This is great farming country, and the area is dotted with windmills as in Holland. The two main goals for the motorist here are the hamlet of Tranekær and the northern town of Lohals.

After leaving Rudkøbing, Route 305 continues 12km (7½ miles) north to the hamlet of Tranekær, with its many old framed houses. The area is dominated by

Tranekær Slot (Tranekær Castle), Slotsgade 95, Tranekær (© **63-51-10-10**). Sited on a big hill and surrounded by water, parts of the castle were constructed as a fortress in the 13th century. In the 15th century thick walls were built to withstand the enemy's cannonballs. Tranekær Castle has belonged to the Ahlefeldt-Laurvig family for almost 350 years, and today is the seat of Count Preben Ahlefeldt-Laurvig.

The history of the castle is filled with legend and lore. Originally Frederik Ahlefeldt, who was later to become chancellor of Denmark, fell in love with Margrethe Rantzau, the 15-year-old daughter of the owner of the estate. However, her father would not let them get married, so Frederik abducted the teenager and they were wed in Germany. A previous owner is said to have fathered 92 illegitimate children.

Since the interior is a private residence, the castle cannot be toured. However, the grounds and a museum are open to the public. One of Denmark's largest parks (80 hectares/198 acres) surrounds the castle. The estate contains many rare trees, ranging from California sequoia to Norway spruce. Laid out in a 19th-century English style, the landscape today has been converted into a sculpture park called **Tickon.**

In one of the castle's outbuildings, just across the road, the **Tranekær Slotsmuseum,** Slotsgade 95 (© **63-51-10-10**), contains various artifacts from the estate and provides details about the fascinating former occupants of the castle. It's open during the same hours as the above-mentioned Museum Langelandsfort. Admission to the museum and the park is 45DKK ($7.50) adults, free for children under 12.

Half a mile north of the castle, under the same administration as the above-mentioned Slotsmuseum, is the **Tranekær Slotsmølle,** Lejbøllevej 3 (© **63-51-10-10**), the mill that once belonged to the estate but which now functions as a small museum. You can see the massive and phenomenally heavy millstones that once pulverized wheat and barley into flour. From an outside balcony there's a panoramic view of the coastline. The Dutch-style windmill dates from 1846. It's open June to September, Monday through Friday 10am to 5pm and Sunday 1 to 5pm. Admission is 35DKK ($5.85) adults, free for children under 12.

At Hou, directly to the north of Lohals, you can see a lighthouse from 1893 that rises 12m (39 ft.) above the coast. Back in Lohals, the harbor in summertime is often filled with yachts. You'll also see some fishermen still at work.

Also in Lohals, an interesting but controversial place to visit is **Tom Knudsen's Safarimuseum,** Houvej 49 (© **62-59-16-99**), open June to September daily 2 to 4pm. Born in Langeland in 1890, Tom Knudsen emigrated to the United States when he was 20, made a fortune, and eventually returned to Langeland to display the dozens of hunting trophies he collected during safaris in India, the Arctic, the Americas, and Africa. Inside, you'll find the largest collection of mounted game in Denmark outside Copenhagen. Admission is 30DKK ($5) adults, free for children under 12.

SOUTH LANGELAND

Most Danes visit the southern part of the island mainly for its beaches. But there are some attractions as well. The first stop after heading south along Route 305 from Rudkøbing is the hamlet of **Lindese.**

Three kilometers (2 miles) southeast of here stands **Skovgård,** Skovgårdsvej, Humble (© **62-57-24-60**), a publicly owned manor estate that specializes in organic farming, and which welcomes visitors during the same hours and seasons as the Museum Langelandsfort (see above). Ellen Fuglede, former owner of

(Moments) Visiting Working Artists

Although all Danish islands have devotees who spend much of their lives in lonely isolation creating arts and crafts, Langeland seems to have more than most. Many are drawn to Langeland because they view it as an inexhaustible source of inspiration. Many of their workshops welcome visitors. Check with the tourist office in Rudkøbing for detailed directions and guidance, whether you're seeking glass, ceramics, or whatever.

Although there are some addresses to visit in the capital, many of the finest galleries are farther out on the island. In Rudkøbing itself, you'll find one of the best collections of ceramics—certainly the most imaginatively conceived—at the studio of **Lizzi and Leif Larsen,** Sidsel Bagersgade 10 (© **62-51-41-53**).

If you take our tour of North Langeland (p. 257), you can combine sightseeing with your search for crafts. Many artists are centered at Tranekær. The finest art studio at Tranekær is **Galleri Benedict,** Snødevej 9 (© **62-55-10-03**). Some of the most elegant and graceful ceramics made on Langeland are found at the **Tranekær studio of Poul Erik Eliasen,** Strandbyvej 3 (© **62-59-15-59**). The cozy place has over the years built up a circle of regular customers. This half-timbered house lies in Strandby, right outside Tranekær, deep in a forest. The house is painted red and is hard to miss. Just follow Strandbyvej south of Tranekær. The calm of this potter's home is reflected in the ceramics, which in shape and decoration have a rigidly defined but very harmonious expression.

Lothals in the far north is the equal of Tranekær for the quality of its artisans. For the best art, you can visit **Galleri Sharp,** Stoense Udflyttervej 25 (© **62-55-25-25**). If you go to the very northern tip of Langeland, you'll come upon the studio of **Karin and Erling Heerwagen,** Hovvej 52 (© **62-55-12-63**), at Hov. These artisans turn to nature for their inspiration and produce ceramics that you may want to pass on to the next generation. Here you enter an imaginative universe. Whether big or small, you'll find the same friendly expression on their frogs, birds, fish, and even in their ceramic flowering apple trees.

If you're heading into south Langeland, you'll find an equal number of workshops that welcome visitors. At Humble, **Brangstrup Stentøj,** Vagebjergvej 4 (© **62-57-28-20**), has the widest collection of ceramics and Danish glass.

At the southern tip of the island, in the port of Bagenkop, artists proliferate. One of the finest of them is **Ulla Keramik,** Daemningen 1 (© **62-56-12-98**), a ceramics workshop with elegant offerings. There is a boutique attached. A regular circle of friends is always dropping in to see what Ulla and Knud have created.

Skovgård, died in 1979 after spending most of her secluded life here. Wanting to preserve the lands around her manor, she willed it to the Danish Nature Fund, and the Danish Society of Conservation of Nature administers it today.

In 1989, the society switched to organic farming. Today, the estate is open to all. Several footpaths take you through the landscape, and you can also learn about environmentally friendly forestry. You can also visit a cafe where only ecological products are served, and later enjoy a picnic in the well-manicured park grounds. In a Carriage Museum some old horse-drawn carriages are exhibited, and a small Forestry Museum reveals developments in that industry in the past century. The grounds surrounding the mill farm include demonstration fields and botanical gardens. The garden of the mill farm, also open to visitors, has a marvelous collection of ancient types of roses. Admission is 30DKK ($5).

Route 305 continues south to the hamlet of **Kaedeby,** where you'll see a sign pointing south to Langeland's most important prehistoric find, **Kong Humbles Grav,** the biggest dolmen on the island, dating from 3000 B.C. "King Humble's Grave" (its English name) is an impressive Megalithic "corridor grave"—the barrow edged with 77 stones, extending 55m (180 ft.). It has a single burial chamber. In spite of its name and in spite of popular legend, archaeologists cannot support the legend that a king was buried here. Although the dolmen technically lies on private lands, the owner allows visitors to walk across his fields to the site. The path to the ancient site begins right near the little Humble Kirke. From here, it's about a 25-minute walk, but makes for a pleasant stroll.

Back on Route 305 heading south, you'll pass through the little commercial center of **Humble,** which has a number of service facilities such as a gas station. After leaving Humble, you can detour from 305 and take a minor road west signposted RISTINGE, a small seaside village with thatched houses. It's the best place for visiting those sandy beaches referred to earlier. The islanders themselves view Ristinge as their favorite place for sea bathing.

While here, you can take in **Ristinge Klint.** You can see the 20m (66-ft.) cliffs by walking along the beach. Layers of ice formed during the Ice Age built up the cliffs so that they are almost vertical. Some of the layers are rich in fossils, including gigantic mussels. Steps lead from the beach up to the cliff. From here is a panoramic view over the sea. Denmark protects the cliff as a natural wonder, but there is access to it from the beach car park southeast of Ristinge village.

If you have time remaining, you can explore the southern tip of Langeland, virtually one big nature reserve with cliffs, forest, marshlands, and coves. There's also a large sanctuary where serious "birders" from throughout Denmark and Europe come to spot birds year-round.

Within walking distance of the town, just beyond Bagenkop at the southernmost point of the island, lies **Dovns Klint,** a 16m (52-ft.) cliff towering toward the southeast. Surprisingly, it changes its shape every time a storm ravages Langeland. The beach here is filled with pebbles, but it's a scenic spot to visit nevertheless. It's especially popular at the time of the massive migrations of birds in the autumn, when they leave the chilly north to fly south for the winter.

To the southeast of Dovns Klint you'll see **Kels Nor Fyr,** one of the last Danish lighthouses still in use.

9

South Jutland

South Jutland (Jylland in Danish) is the part of Denmark that's on Continental Europe, with Germany its immediate neighbor to the south. It's the southernmost part of the Jutland peninsula, dotted with heather-covered moors, fjords, farmlands, lakes, and sand dunes. It's 402km (250 miles) from the northern tip of Jutland to the German frontier. The North Sea washes up on kilometers of sandy beaches, making this a favorite holiday place.

The meadows of Jutland are filled with rich bird life and winding rivers. Nature walks are possible in almost all directions. Gabled houses in the marshlands of South Jutland add to the peninsula's charm. Two of the most popular vacation islands are Rømø and Fanø, off of the southwestern coast. Here many traditional homes of fishermen and sea captains have been preserved. Of all the towns of South Jutland, none has more particular appeal and charm for the tourist than Ribe, fabled for its storks' nests.

You can do as the Danes do and cycle through the countryside of South Jutland, which is crisscrossed by a fine network of bicycle paths. Stop in at one of the tourist offices and pick up a detailed map of the region, which often outlines the best bike paths.

A dike evocative of the Netherlands stretches along the coast of southwest Jutland. It was built to protect the land here from the tempestuous North Sea. Nature lovers flock here to enjoy walks along the Wadden Sea, and at low tide they can even explore the seabed itself. You can also bicycle along the dike, but the westerly winds make this a difficult run.

Some of the finest beaches in northern Europe are found in South Jutland, especially on the island of Rømø. When the winds blow, these long beaches are ideal for kite flying.

In the little villages and towns, the past meets the present, as you walk along narrow, cobbled streets, admiring the half-timbered houses that look as if they've emerged from a Hans Christian Andersen fairy tale. To experience an authentically Danish meal, order the traditional lunch of pickled herring, rye bread, and schnapps.

There are many museums of local history, showing you how life was lived long before you arrived. Many include workshops where artisans still practice the old crafts—for example, the lacemaking that made Tønder famous in the 18th century.

Mainly, South Jutland is a place to go to recharge your batteries.

1 Kolding

208km (130 miles) SW of Copenhagen; 91km (57 miles) E of Esbjerg; 82km (51 miles) N of the German border; 70km (43½ miles) SW of Århus

The lively port of Kolding in the east is the gateway to South Jutland. Nestled on a fjord of the same name, Kolding dates from 1321. Several roads converged here in the Middle Ages, and in 1248 the crown ordered that Koldinghus Slot be erected here. It was torn down and rebuilt several times over the centuries. In wars over the disputed territory of Schleswig-Holstein, Kolding was occupied by Prussian troops, but the Treaty of Vienna in 1864 left the town in Danish hands.

Today, Kolding, a city of some 60,000 people, is the fifth largest city of Jutland. The town continues its role as Denmark's largest cattle exporter, and has a number of prosperous industries, including engineering, iron, and textiles.

On November 4, 2004, Kolding made headlines when a blaze at a fireworks factory caused a mammoth explosion, leaving one person dead and destroying nearly two dozen homes. As many as 350 buildings were damaged. The explosion in Kolding took place in the residential suburb of Seest, 3km (1¾ miles) west of Kolding's harborfront and historic core.

ESSENTIALS

GETTING THERE By Train Trains run frequently between Kolding and Padborg on the northern German border (trip time: 70 min.). Frequent trains also arrive from Frederikshavn in the north of Jutland (4 hr.). Trains also cut across Jutland, reaching Esbjerg (see later) in the west in just under an hour.

By Car After taking the bridge from Funen in the east, follow Route 161 into Kolding. If you're already in West Jutland, perhaps in Esbjerg, you can cut across Jutland along motorway E20 until you reach Kolding as you near the east coast.

VISITOR INFORMATION Kolding Tourist Information, Akseltorv 8 (℗ **76-33-21-00;** www.visitkolding.dk), is open Monday through Friday 9:30am to 7pm and Saturday 9:30am to 2pm.

SEEING THE SIGHTS

Kolding Fjord attracts anglers, swimmers, and boaters, and **Kolding Marina** is one of the largest in Denmark. The fjord is also lined with beaches with plenty of recreational areas.

The town's major sight remains its castle, **Koldinghus Slot,** in the center of town (℗ **76-33-81-00**), immediately to the north of Akseltorv. In 1268 King Erik V ordered that a fortress be built on this site to protect Danish interests against the Duchy of Schleswig to the south. Christian IV spent much of his boyhood here, adding a landmark tower around 1600. Over the years the castle was attacked and destroyed many times. The oldest parts of the present building are from around the mid–15th century. In 1808, Denmark was allied with France under Napoleon Bonaparte. Napoleon commanded Spanish troops because his brother occupied the Spanish throne, and at the time Spanish soldiers were billeted in Koldinghus Slot. The Spanish soldiers, not used to Danish winters, built a roaring fire that not only kept them warm, but set the castle on fire.

Until 1890 the castle was left in ruins. A north wing was restored to house a museum. Reconstruction continued slowly over much of the 20th century, with the Christian IV tower restored by 1935. Today the castle shelters a Historical and Cultural Museum, with exhibitions tracing the town's history. The exterior has a baroque facade evocative of the 18th century. The castle is rich in Romanesque and Gothic sculptures, plus such handcrafted articles as silver, stoneware, and porcelain. A special exhibit documents the wars against Prussia from 1848 to 1850 and in 1864. Special exhibitions, theatrical and operatic performances, and classical concerts are held in the great hall and courtyard. From the top of the tower there are panoramic views over the town and surrounding area. Hours are daily 10am to 5pm. Admission is 60DKK ($10) adults, 30DKK ($5) for students, free for children under 13.

Equally intriguing as the castle is the **Kunstmuseet Trapholt,** Æblehaven 23 (© **76-30-05-30**), reached by bus no. 4 from the center of the city. On the eastern periphery of Kolding, it opens onto the north side of Kolding Fjord. Situated in a park, and launched in 1988, it's home to a vast collection of contemporary Danish paintings and applied art, such as textiles, design, and ceramics. Its angular glass walls and stark white interiors flood the art with natural light. You'll see works by such artists as Egill Jacobsen, Anna Archer, and Richard Mortensen. Trapholt also houses a Museum of Furniture that opened in 1996, and is dedicated to modern Danish furniture design. Furniture from as far back as 1900 is exhibited, but the collection is centered mainly on some of the biggest names in Danish design, including Arne Jacobsen, Finn Juhl, Poul Kjærholm, Mogens Koch, Børge Morgensen, and Hans J. Wegner. May to September the museum is open daily 10am to 5pm. During other months, hours are Monday through Friday noon to 4pm and Saturday and Sunday 10am to 4pm. Admission is 60DKK ($10) adults, free for children under 16.

Also worth a visit is **Geografisk Have og Rosehave (Geographical Garden)** ★, Chr. d. 4 Vej (© **76-30-05-30;** bus: 2). Axel Olsen, the owner of a local tree nursery, laid out this garden on the southern periphery of town. Today it has some 2,000 species of trees and shrubs from all over the globe, including North and South America and Burma. It gets its name because it was laid out like world map. It is home to the largest bamboo grove in Northern Europe. You can also enjoy a picnic lunch outdoors or in one of the on-site garden pavilions. The gardens are open May to September daily 10am to 6pm. Admission is 35DKK ($5.85) adults, 15DKK ($2.50) children ages 10 to 16, free for children 9 and under.

SHOPPING

There is a network of pedestrian streets flanked with shops in the town center. On Tuesday and Friday 7am to 1pm there's an open-air market at Akseltorv where traders sell flowers, fruit, vegetables, cheese, fish, and much more.

One of the largest shopping malls in Denmark, **Kolding Storcenter,** Skovvangen 42 (℃ **75-50-96-06**), lies 4km (2½ miles) north of Kolding's center (follow the signs to Vejle from the town center). Home to some 60 shops, it attracts an astonishing 80,000 visitors a week. In a style that might remind you of a megamall in California, it's especially crowded whenever it's raining, when hundreds of local residents come here just to hang out.

Another intriguing shopping possibility is the **Kolding Antiques & Stall Market** held at Haderslevvej and Sdr. Ringvej on Saturday and Sunday from 10am to 5pm.

The best art galleries in town are **Galleri Elise Toft,** Låsbygade 58 (℃ **20-96-54-14**), and **Galleri Pagter,** Adelgade 3 (℃ **75-54-09-30**).

WHERE TO STAY

Comwell Kolding   This hotel is just northwest of the town center, adjacent to a small lake. The place is saturated with contemporary Danish design, sophisticated (usually halogen) lighting, exposed and varnished pine-wood trim with touches of brass, big windows, and, at least in the public areas, a stylish kind of minimalism. Rooms aren't particularly spacious, but are comfortable, bright, cheerful, and well maintained. Each unit has a well-kept bathroom that contains a tub/shower combination. There's a wood-burning fireplace in one of the public lounges, and a restaurant, **Repos.**

Skovbrynet 1, DK-6000 Kolding. ℃ 76-34-11-00. Fax 76-34-12-00. www.comwell.com. 180 units. 1,425DKK ($238) double. Rates include breakfast. AE, DC, MC, V. Bus: 1, 5, or 6. **Amenities:** Restaurant; bar; indoor heated pool; exercise room; sauna; room service (7am–10pm); laundry service; dry cleaning; nonsmoking rooms; solarium. *In room:* TV, dataport, minibar, hair dryer.

Hotel Byparken   This early 1970s hotel might remind you of an American-style motel. Bordered by one of Kolding's public parks on one side and a group of quiet private homes on the other, it affords a chance to relax in calm, quiet surroundings that seem very far from the urban world. Rooms are comfortable but anonymous-looking, outfitted with contemporary Danish furnishings and neatly kept bathrooms with shower units.

Byparken, DK-6000 Kolding. ℃ 75-53-21-22. Fax 75-50-40-64. www.hotelbyparken.dk. 76 units. 750DKK–1,095DKK ($125–$183) double. AE, DC, MC, V. **Amenities:** Restaurant; bar; fitness center; sauna; room service (7am–10pm); laundry service; dry cleaning; nonsmoking rooms; rooms for those with limited mobility. *In room:* TV, dataport, safe.

Kolding Byferie 🏆 *Finds*   One of the most unusual hotels in the district sits at the edge of the water, in a roughly defined "amphitheater" created by the other, older buildings of the town center. The hotel consists of about 15 modern cement-and-glass buildings, erected in 1994 and shaped into different forms, including squares, rectangles, octagons, circles, and stars. The result is an award-winning compound that has drawn great interest in architectural circles, and which provides unusual floor plans for occupants, who are required to stay at least 3 nights. The oversize windows of each room slide open, virtually transforming it into an outdoor terrace. Furnishings inside are simple, angular, and virtually indestructible, and as such, are often occupied by families with children. Each unit also has a well-kept bathroom with a shower unit. There are few luxuries (no restaurant, bar, pool, or sauna) on the premises, but the dining, drinking, and public sports facilities of Kolding are close by, and the staff is well versed in providing ideas on how and where clients might want to spend their free time.

Kedelsmedgangen 2, DK-6000 Kolding. ℃ 75-54-18-00. Fax 75-54-18-02. www.kolding-byferie.dk. 114 units. 1,025DKK–2,325DKK ($171–$388) double. AE, DC, MC, V. *In room:* TV, safe.

Radisson SAS Koldingfjord Hotel ⭐⭐   Set on the opposite bank of the Kolding Fjord, a 5km (3-mile) drive from the center, this is one of the most ostentatiously grandiose buildings in the region. In 1911, a neoclassical palace was erected on 20 hectares (49 acres) of forested land adjacent to the Kolding Fjord in an area noted for its pure air. After a long stint as a hospital and school, the site was transformed in 1988 into a comfortable hotel that's one of the most appealing in the region. Rooms, scattered between the main building and three of its original outbuildings, have comfortably unfussy furnishings and well-kept bathrooms with shower units. Also on the premises are a brand-new, very large, convention center, and a recommended restaurant (see "Where to Dine," below).

Fjordvej 154, Strandhuse, DK-6000 Kolding. ℂ **75-51-00-00.** Fax 75-51-00-51. www.radissonsas.com. 134 units. 950DKK–1,459DKK ($159–$244) double. AE, DC, MC, V. From Kolding, follow the signs to the E45 hwy., then (before you reach it), detour northward along the Lushojalle and drive 3km (1¾ miles). **Amenities:** Restaurant; bar; indoor heated pool; tennis court; sauna; room service (7am–10:30pm); laundry service; dry cleaning; nonsmoking rooms; rooms for those with limited mobility; solarium. *In room:* TV, dataport, minibar, hair dryer, safe.

Saxildhus Hotel ⭐   Right at the train station, this landmark and architecturally graceful hotel has long been the preferred stopover in Kolding. Under a rooftop studded with dormers, it earns four stars from the government. Major renovations in 2001 and 2002 have returned the hotel to some of the glory it knew before World War II. Not all bedrooms are the same; some have a nostalgic decor with antique mahogany four-poster beds and others are furnished with Danish modern. Regardless of the style, all the rooms are comfortable and tasteful, each with a private bathroom with tub or shower. Even if you're not a guest, consider stopping off at the hotel **restaurant,** as it features superb Danish regional specialties, most of which come from the sea.

Banegaardsplatz, DK-6000 Kolding. ℂ **75-52-12-00.** Fax 75-53-53-10. www.saxildhus.dk. 87 units. 895DKK–1,195DKK ($149–$200) double; 1,295DKK ($216) suite. Rates include buffet breakfast. AE, DC, MC, V. **Amenities:** 2 restaurants; bar; 24-hr. room service; laundry service; dry cleaning; nonsmoking rooms. *In room:* TV, minibar.

Scandic Hotel   Its brochures refer to it as "the gem of the motorway," and while that might not exactly thrill you, it is a reliable provider of clean, safe, predictable lodgings that are convenient for motorists. Rooms are clean, well maintained, comfortable, and streamlined, with good beds and small but adequate bathrooms with shower units.

Kokholm, DK-6000 Kolding. ℂ **75-51-77-00.** Fax 75-51-77-01. www.scandic-hotels.com. 120 units. 1,295DKK–1,395DKK ($216–$233) double. Rates include breakfast. AE, DC, MC, V. From the E45 hwy., 6.5km (4 miles) north of Kolding, the hotel lies adjacent to Exit 63. **Amenities:** Restaurant; bar; fitness center; sauna; room service (7am–10pm); laundry service; dry cleaning; nonsmoking rooms; rooms for those with limited mobility; solarium. *In room:* TV, minibar, trouser press; suites have dataport, coffeemaker, hair dryer, iron/ironing board.

WHERE TO DINE

Hotel Koldingfjord ⭐ DANISH/CONTINENTAL   Set in one of the high-ceilinged formal reception rooms of the previously recommended hotel, this is one of the most appealing restaurants in Kolding. Food is well prepared, but a dining experience here has the added benefit of a view over the fjord. Seasonal menu items might include a garden salad garnished with lobster and fresh asparagus, warm salmon pudding with spinach, crabmeat bouillon with fresh tomatoes, filet of monkfish with either citrus sauce or beurre blanc, gratin of fresh tuna with a ragout of fish roe and tomatoes, and a dessert specialty consisting of a medley of summer berries with freshly made vanilla cream.

Fjordvej 154, Strandhuse. ℂ **75-51-00-00**. Reservations recommended. Main courses 80DKK–260DKK ($13–$43). AE, DC, MC, V. Daily noon–2pm and 6–10:30pm. From Kolding, follow the signs to the E45 hwy., then (before you reach it), detour northward along the Lushojalle and drive 3km (1¾ miles).

Repos DANISH/FRENCH   The only drawback to this well-orchestrated restaurant is its lack of a view over the nearby lake. Other than that, the place is cozy, inviting, and appealing, thanks to well-prepared food. The copious lunchtime buffet (the best in town) includes an all-Danish medley of hot and cold dishes that feature *frikadeller* (meatballs), many different preparations of herring, salads, casseroles, an impressive collection of fresh-baked breads, and an artful medley of Danish and European cheeses. Seasonal a la carte dishes are likely to include such choices as Dover sole meunière; tournedos of beef with onions and a confit of sweet peppers; a ragout of angler-fish with scallops and fresh vegetables; and North Sea turbot with white asparagus stalks, baby cabbage, and a reduction of fresh tomatoes.

In the Hotel Comwell, Skovbrynet 1. ℂ **76-34-11-00**. Reservations recommended. Lunch buffet 165DKK ($28) per person; fixed-price dinners 300DKK–410DKK ($50–$68); main courses 160DKK–210DKK ($27–$35). AE, DC, MC, V. Mon–Sat noon–10pm; buffet Mon–Sat noon–2pm. Bus: 1, 5, or 6.

KOLDING AFTER DARK

Three sites compete with one another for the title of most popular nightlife option in Kolding. They include the **English Pub,** A. L. Passagen (ℂ **75-50-80-44**), which is open 2pm to 2am Monday through Friday, 2pm to 4am Saturday and 2 to 8pm Sunday, and serves hundreds of pints of English and Danish beer every night until closing around midnight. Equally popular, but with shorter hours, is the **Crazy Daisy,** Jernbanegade 13 (ℂ **75-54-16-88**), a pub and nightclub that's open for drinking every night 9pm to midnight, and which functions as a dance club every Tuesday, Friday, and Saturday night 9pm to around 4am. A fashionable venue that combines hi-tech decor with food service and occasional bouts of live jazz is the **Blue Café,** Lilletorv (ℂ **75-50-65-12**). Light platters of simple food are served daily 10am to around 9:30pm; cappuccino, wine, beer, and schnapps are available every day till at least midnight, and sometimes later, depending on the size of the crowd.

AN EASY EXCURSION FROM KOLDING

Directly to the south of Kolding, a distance of 9km (5⅗ miles)—follow the signs pointing to Christiansfeldt—is one of the most powerful but understated monuments of Denmark, **Skamlingsbanken.** A rolling hill that rises to a height of 113m (371 ft.), it commemorates the survival of the Danish language and the Danish nation against German incursions throughout the centuries. Its location marks the frontier between Denmark and North Schleswig, a hotly contested territory that was bounced around between Germany and Denmark repeatedly throughout modern times. In 1920, as part of the settlement at the end of World War I, the Danish-German border was moved 82km (51 miles) to the south, where it has remained ever since. Today, few Danes can articulate the reason for the emotion associated with this site. (In the words of one tourist official, "Today, we're all part of the European Community, and we really don't like to talk about that.") For reasons of tact, since the 1960s, the site has been downplayed within the Danish national psyche. Beginning in 1998, it has been the site of a concert presented the first Sunday in August, where the Royal Danish Opera travels down from Copenhagen to present operatic works by archetypal German and Danish composers Richard Wagner and Karl Nielsen. The event is free, with further details available at the tourist office in Kolding (see above).

2 Haderslev /★

248km (155 miles) SW of Copenhagen; 31km (19 miles) S of Kolding; 51km (32 miles) E of Ribe

At the head of the Haderslev Fjord, this appealing town of 32,000 inhabitants is known for having one of the oldest and best-preserved historic cores in Denmark. In 1995 it was awarded the Europa Nostra Prize for its old, beautifully restored buildings. In spite of some minor attractions, there's nothing more interesting here than walking through its narrow cobbled streets with buildings dating back all the way to 1570. As a result of a massive preservation effort launched in 1971 the town of Haderslev looks better than ever.

Although built on the banks of a fjord, Haderslev actually lies 15km (9½ miles) inland. It has always depended on trade for its livelihood, and by 1292 it already had a city charter. Christian I came here in 1448, signing a charter that allowed him to become king of Denmark. Another Christian (this time King Christian IV) came here in 1597 to celebrate his wedding to Anne-Catherine of Brandenburg. From 1864 to as late as 1920 Haderslev was part of the duchy of Schleswig-Holstein and controlled by Prussia. When the Duchy of Schleswig was divided in 1920, Haderslev became part of Denmark.

ESSENTIALS

GETTING THERE   By Train   The nearest train depot is at the town of Vojens. It is possible to arrive by train at Vojens, then take a 30-minute bus ride over to Haderslev.

By Bus   Bus no. 34 runs hourly between Kolding and Haderslev (trip time: 45 min.).

By Car   From Kolding, head south on Route 170 or go east from Ribe along Routes 24 and 47.

VISITOR INFORMATION   The **Haderslev Turistbureau,** Honnørkajen (© **74-52-55-50;** www.haderslev-turist.dk), is open January 2 to March, Monday through Friday 9:30am to 4:30pm; April to mid-June and September to December 22, Monday through Friday 9:30am to 4:30pm, Saturday 9:30am to 12:30pm; mid-June to August, Monday through Friday 9:30am to 6pm and Saturday from 9:30am to 2pm.

EXPLORING THE AREA

Haderslev is situated in a **subglacial stream trench** ★ that is 24km (15 miles) long and stretches from the Little Belt to the neighboring town of Vojens. A beautiful landscape has been created by nature. In 1994, Denmark's second-largest nature reserve opened south of Haderslev Dam, stocked with fallow deer. Near the reserve, the large marsh area of Hindemade was flooded. Today, the whole area has a rich bird and animal life, and Hindemade has been designated a bird sanctuary by the European Union. You can walk about in the area along the Tunneldal paths, which run through most of the subglacial trench between Haderslev and Vojens.

Back in the center of Haderslev, you can, as mentioned, wander through the town's historic core, an area so well preserved it was voted European town of the year in 1984. The old town grew up around its Domkirke (see below), which stands on high ground. One of the oldest and most interesting houses, dating from the 16th century, is now the **Ehlers-samlingen (Ehlers Collections),** Slotsgade 20 (© **74-53-08-58**), a museum of Danish pottery dating from the medieval era to the beginning of the 20th century. At this point, regional distinctions in Danish pottery began to erode. This is an attractive timber-framed building from 1577 that has preserved many of its original decorative wall panels. You can also see many antique domestic items and some 16th-century wall paintings. The collection can be viewed Tuesday through Sunday 10am to 5pm and Saturday and Sunday 1 to 5pm. It's closed Monday in winter. Admission is 25DKK ($4.20) adults, free for children under 16.

Haderslev Domkirke ★★, Torvet (© **74-52-36-33**), is a red-brick cathedral that's one of the most interesting buildings of its kind in the country. The structure has been entirely whitewashed, enhancing the light coming through the tall windows in the 15th-century chancel. The transept and nave are the most ancient parts of the cathedral, dating from the mid–13th century. Many additions, however, were made over the years. The bronze font is from the late 1400s, and the baroque pulpit was added in 1636. A restored Sieseby organ has a beautifully clear sound, and is played regularly. At the altar you'll see a Romanesque crucifix, probably from the beginning of the 14th century, and statues of Mary and John along with alabaster figures of the Apostles. The church played an important part in the Reformation, becoming the first Lutheran church in the country. A disastrous fire swept over the Domkirke in 1627, destroying much of the building, but a restoration was completed by 1650. When Haderslev reunited with Denmark in 1920, a new diocese was established, making the Domkirke a true cathedral. Admission is free, and the cathedral is open May to September Monday through Saturday 10am to 5pm, and Sunday 11:30am to 5pm. It's open daily off season 10am to 3pm. In August concerts are given on the previously mentioned church organ at 8pm on Tuesday and at 4:30pm Friday. These days might vary, depending on the availability of performers, so a call in advance to the tourist office might clear up any confusion. The Friday concert is usually free, while admission to the Tuesday concert is 80DKK ($13).

Less than a kilometer (½ mile) northeast of the Torvet stands the **Haderslev Museum,** Dalgade 7 (© **74-52-75-66**). This has one of the peninsula's best collections of archaeological artifacts gathered in the region. There are also local historical exhibitions and reconstructed street scenes, with entire rooms decorated as they would have been in the 19th century. In addition, there are an open-air museum with an old farm, and even a windmill, among other period structures. June to August hours are Tuesday through Sunday 10am to 4pm; off season, Tuesday through Sunday 1 to 4pm. Admission is 25DKK ($3.30) adults, free for children 16 and under.

SHOPPING

Two of the most appealing shops in Haderslev include **Stentebjerg,** Storegade 8 (© **74-52-02-09**), which specializes in pottery from the region and from throughout Denmark. For more options on how to make your home or apartment look a little more Danish, head for **Stolen,** Møllepladsen 2 (© **20-16-02-16**).

WHERE TO STAY

Hotel Harmonien ★ (Finds)   Haderslev's most charming hotel lies in the town center. Established in 1793, it was the site of a visit from King Christian VII in the late 19th century and a full-blown dinner attended by Queen Margrethe II and her family in May 1998. Although much of the allure of this place derives from the cozy restaurant (see "Where to Dine," below), its rooms are attractively decorated with comfortable furnishings and a sense of the off-the-beaten-track Europe of long ago. Each unit also contains a well-kept bathroom with a shower unit. There are virtually no additional facilities associated with this hotel, but in view of the hotel's sense of history, none of the clients really seems to mind.

Gåskærgade 19, DK-6100 Haderslev. © **74-52-37-20.** Fax 74-52-44-51. www.harmonien.dk. 28 units. 795DKK–1,100DKK ($133–$184) double. AE, DC, MC, V. **Amenities:** Restaurant; bar; room service (7am–10pm); laundry service; dry cleaning; nonsmoking rooms. *In room:* TV, dataport (in some), hair dryer.

Hotel Norden This is the biggest and best-accessorized hotel in Haderslev, large enough to accommodate many corporate conventions, and even the occasional tour bus making stops at historic sites throughout Jutland. A 5-minute walk north of the town center, it has a well-trained staff and clean, comfortable accommodations. All units contain well-maintained bathrooms with shower units.

Storegade 55, DK-6100 Haderslev. © **74-52-40-30.** Fax 74-52-40-25. www.hotel-norden.dk. 67 units. 1,145DKK ($191) double year-round. Rates include breakfast. AE, DC, MC, V. **Amenities:** Restaurant; bar; indoor heated pool; exercise room; sauna; room service (7am–10pm); laundry service; dry cleaning; nonsmoking rooms; 1 room for those with limited mobility; solarium. *In room:* TV, dataport, minibar, hair dryer.

WHERE TO DINE

Restaurant Harmonien ⭐ DANISH The most charming historic restaurant in Haderslev occupies a *kro* (inn) built around 1844. Set in the town center, it's the restaurant most often cited as a place for a cozy, country-style Danish meal without too much emphasis on big-city glamour. In a long and narrow dining room that contains only about 10 tables and an oversized fireplace that's usually blazing on cold evenings, you can order such Danish specialties as venison with red wine sauce, tournedos of beef with several kinds of peppercorns, filet of Dover sole prepared meunière-style, and roasted breast of duck with a piquant sauce. These dishes are expertly prepared and exquisitely seasoned. There isn't culinary greatness here, but you get the sense that the kitchen staff really cares about what it serves its guests.

In the Hotel Harmonien, Gåskærgade 19. © **75-52-37-20.** Reservations recommended. Main courses 80DKK–250DKK ($13–$42). Daily 6–9:30pm. AE, DC, MC, V. Closed Dec 20–Jan 2.

The Restaurant of the Hotel Norden DANISH/FRENCH Modern, airy, high-ceilinged, and spacious, this restaurant's setting is radically different from that of its leading competitor, the also-recommended antique dining room of the Hotel Harmonien. Surrounded with unusual art and a welcome sense of space, you'll be offered a roster of well-prepared menu items that might include North Sea turbot roasted with lemon juice and wine, served with white asparagus and braised cabbage; beef tournedos with baked sweet peppers; Danish veal cutlet with ham, shallots, parsley, and morel sauce; and noisettes of lamb sautéed in virgin olive oil, served with Dijon mustard and Swiss-style *spätzle* (noodles). On our last visit, everything was flawlessly prepared and beautifully presented by a helpful staff, which is both unobtrusive and prompt.

Storegade 55. © **74-52-40-30.** Reservations recommended. Main courses 76DKK–218DKK ($13–$36). AE, DC, MC, V. Daily 6–10pm.

HADERSLEV AFTER DARK

Most of the after-dark activities in town take place at one of only two hangouts. One of them, **Buch's Vinstue,** Nørregade 9 (© **74-53-09-53**), is an old-fashioned Danish beer and wine house that gets very crowded with friends and acquaintances from throughout the district. They select it as a rendezvous point for ongoing discussions about politics, art, business, or just casual conversation. It opens daily at 2pm. A competitor that's a bit more modern in its approach to entertainment is **Huset,** Nørregade 10 (© **74-53-43-73**). Opening around 6pm, it functions as a well-used bar most nights, except on Thursdays and Fridays, when live music is presented beginning around 10pm. There's never any cover charge, and the under-40 residents of Haderslev tend to flock to the changing musical fare at this local landmark.

3 Tønder (★

277km (173 miles) SW of Copenhagen; 77km (48 miles) S of Esbjerg; 85km (53 miles) SW of Kolding

Tønder, on the banks of the River Vidå, is called the capital of the marshland, the oldest town in Denmark holding official town rights, with a municipal charter granted in 1243. In medieval times, it was an important port and a place of disembarkation for horses and cattle. Its surrounding marshland, even Tønder itself, was often flooded by the North Sea. By the middle of the 15th century, townspeople started to erect dikes. But the end result was that Tønder lost its position as a port. The sea eventually receded, leaving Tønder landlocked.

In the 17th century, the townsfolk turned to lacemaking, and eventually 12,000 lacemakers were employed in and around the town. The many rich lace dealers built the beautiful patrician houses adorning the streets today.

From 1864 Tønder and the region of North Slesvig were part of Germany. But a plebiscite in 1920 led to the reunion of North Slesvig with Denmark. Even so, Tønder is still influenced by German traditions, as it is only 4km (2½ miles) north of the German frontier. The town still has a German school, kindergarten, and library, and a German vicar is attached to Tønder Christ Church.

ESSENTIALS

GETTING THERE   By Train   The train depot lies on the west side of Tønder, less than a kilometer (½ mile) from Torvet (the market square) and reached by going along Vestergade. Monday through Friday, trains arrive every hour during the day from Ribe (trip time: 50 min.) and Esbjerg (trip time: 1½ hr.). There's less frequent service on Saturday and Sunday.

By Car   From Kolding (see earlier in the chapter), take Route 25 southwest to the junction with Route 11, which will carry you for the final lap to the turnoff for Tønder, reached along Route 419 heading west.

VISITOR INFORMATION   The **Tønder Turistbureau,** Torvet 1 (© 74-72-12-20; www.tdr-turist.dk), is open June 15 to August Monday through Friday 9:30am to 5:30pm and Saturday 9:30am to 3pm. Otherwise, hours are Monday through Friday 9am to 4pm and Saturday 9am to noon.

GETTING AROUND   By Bicycle   Tønder Campingplads, Holmevej 2A (© 74-72-18-49), rents bikes and, mid-May to mid-August, water bikes from 50DKK ($8.35) a day. Bicycling maps are available at the tourist office.

SPECIAL EVENTS   Beginning rather modestly in 1975, the **Tønder Festivalen,** Vestergade 80 (© 74-72-46-10), held every year August 25 to 29, has turned into an international musical event. The Tønder Festival covers a wide range of music styles. Musicians from all over the world present blues, bluegrass, Cajun, zydeco, jazz, gospel, and traditional Irish, Scottish, English, and American folk music. Names as well as unknowns play their instruments in the streets, squares, pubs, and on seven official stages. More than 25,000 visitors flock to Tønder annually for this event. Tickets cost 100DKK to 275DKK ($17–$46).

SEEING THE SIGHTS

To see the antique homes built by the lacemakers during the heyday of Tønder's prosperity, wander up and down the main street, which changes its name several times: Østergade becomes Storegade, and finally Vestergade. Most of these stately mansions, which are characterized by richly carved portals, were built in the 17th and 18th centuries. The actual lacemakers lived on the smaller side streets, Uldgade and Spikergade, and their houses were more modest, but still interesting to explore. Most of these houses on the latter two streets were built in the 1600s with bay windows. Actually, in our view, Uldgade is the most colorful lane in Tønder. A narrow cobblestone lane, it is in many ways the street in Tønder most evocative of old Denmark.

The best collection of regional artifacts is showcased at the **Tønder Museum,** Kongevej 55 (© **74-72-89-89**), in the gatehouse of the old Tønder Castle, all that remains of the former *slot.* Exhibitions reflect the local history of the area, and naturally there is an emphasis on the city's lacemaking heyday. You can also view regional costumes, wall tiles, antiques, and even elegant table silver once owned by prosperous merchants in the area. The wooden figure with the cane, Kagmand, once stood at Torvet, the marketplace. At one time any citizen who had committed a crime was tied to this figure and publicly whipped.

In the same building as the Tønder Museum is the **Sønderjyllands Kunstmuseum,** Kongevej 55 (© **74-72-89-89**), which holds a fine collection of Danish surrealistic art and a collection of contemporary works. Besides the permanent exhibitions, changing art shows are staged here as well.

A short walk away is the **Museumstårnet & H. J. Wedgner udstilling,** Kongevej 55 (© **74-72-89-89**). In 1995, the town's old water tower was converted into an exhibition center for the works of the celebrated furniture designer, native son H. J. Wedgner, whose designs during the 1950s and 1960s were precursors of the style that became known as Danish modern. The top floor of the tower offers panoramic views over the surrounding marshlands.

The price of an all-inclusive admission to all three of Tønder's museums is 40DKK ($6.70) adults, free for children. May to October, all three museums are open daily 10am to 5pm; the rest of the year they're open Tuesday through Sunday 1 to 5pm.

Dröhse's Hus, Storgade 14 (© **74-72-49-90**), is a small museum in Tønder's pedestrian zone. The exhibitions inside focus on artifacts relating to lacemaking, antiques, and old glass. The painstaking art of old-fashioned lacemaking that once made the town famous is demonstrated by women in period costumes. It is open April to December Monday through Friday 10am to 5pm, and Saturday 10am to 1pm. Admission costs 20DKK ($3.35) adults, free for children under 16.

Kristkirken ⚓, Kirkepladsen (© **74-72-20-80**), is on the northeast side of Torvet. This church from the 1500s is one of the richest in Denmark in terms of furnishings from the Renaissance and baroque era. The 50m (164-ft.) tower is actually from an earlier church that stood on this site. In the old days, when Tønder was a port (before the North Sea receded), the tower served as a navigational marker for mariners. Inside are a mid-14th-century font, a pulpit from 1586, and a series of memorial tablets or epitaphs hung by wealthy cattle and lace dealers in the 15th and 16th centuries. The church is open Monday to Saturday 10am to 5pm; admission is free.

SHOPPING

According to long tradition, the shopkeepers of Tønder—dressed in old-fashioned costumes—arrange a pedestrian zone market in the center of town July 17 and 18. On Saturday, the final market day, there are live music and drinks in the main square, Torvet. Another shopping adventure occurs on August 1 when there's a feast in the pedestrian zone. Shops remain open until 10pm, offering amusements to visitors. There is plenty of food and drink, climaxed by a concert in the main square.

On Tuesday and Friday local vendors sell fish, fruit, cheese, and fresh vegetables in the main square. We always like to gather the makings for a picnic here, to be enjoyed later in the marshland surrounding Tønder.

For such a small town, Tønder has a large number of specialty shops. Many Germans drive across the border to shop here. Various gifts and souvenirs can be purchased at **Andersen & Nissen,** Storegade 26 (© 74-72-13-42).

Back in 1671 **Det Gamle** Apotek (The Old Pharmacy), Østerg 1 (© 7472-51-11), opened as a pharmacy. But today it's been converted into one of the best Danish handcrafts shops in the area, although the landmark antique structure was left as it used to be, just restored. Even the medicine jars and pharmaceutical equipment are intact, except instead of headache remedies and cures for the gout, you get Danish glassware, handmade ceramics, and various other quality crafts. Din **Grønne Skobutik,** Østergade 3 (© 74-72-48-93), features one of the best collections of women's shoes in town, everything from high heels to the kinds of boots a woman might want for treks through the marshes and forests of Denmark.

Gaveboden, Østergade 10–12 (© 74-72-58-29), sells sweaters—the kind of garments that ward off the fog and damp of a Danish winter yet still manage to make a wearer look appealing. Specialties of the store include alpaca, Angora, and woolen tops with unusual patterns, including plaids. There's even a scattering of garments by Finnish designer Marimekko.

WHERE TO STAY

Bowler Inn   Few hotels pursue as aggressive a devotion to one particular sport. In this case, the passion is for bowling, and the hotel has 10 state-of-the-art bowling alleys. Don't fret that you won't fit in if you opt not to go bowling, as rooms are more modern, more comfortable, and better-accessorized than those of many nearby competitors in the same price range. Each room also has a clean bathroom with a shower unit. The complex, just north of the city center, contains an English-inspired pub, a restaurant serving mostly Danish food, and the above-mentioned bowling alleys. Rental of a bowling alley for up to six players costs 100DKK to 145DKK ($17–$24), depending on the time of day.

Ribe Landevej 56, DK-6270 Tønder. © **74-72-00-11.** Fax 74-72-65-11. www.hotelbowlerinn.dk. 10 units. 795DKK ($133) double. MC, V. **Amenities:** Restaurant; bar. *In room:* TV, dataport (in some), minibar.

Hostrups Hotel   Set on the southern perimeter of town, where the river widens to one of its broadest points, this hotel was built in 1904, and today projects an aura of calm, manicured charm. Rooms are modern and contribute to a restful sense of tranquillity. All have good beds and well-maintained bathrooms with tub/shower combinations. There are a restaurant and bar, and, unusual for Denmark, a staff that speaks virtually no English.

Søndergade 30, DK-6270 Tønder. © **74-72-21-29.** Fax 74-72-07-26. www.hostrupshotel.dk. 18 units. 725DKK ($121) double. Rates include breakfast. MC, V. **Amenities:** Restaurant; bar. *In room:* TV, hair dryer.

Hotel Tønderhus   Built in 1818, this is the best hotel within the Tønder city limits, and the hotel that most people in town tend to recommend. It has well-maintained and unpretentious rooms equipped with neatly kept bathrooms with tub/shower combinations. There's also a basement-level party room with a glass ceiling that was originally conceived as a cistern. A glass-sided cafe serves simple snacks and coffee, and there's a cozy **restaurant** (see "Where to Dine," below).

Jomfrustien 1, DK-6270 Tønder. © **74-72-22-22.** Fax 74-72-05-92. www.hoteltoenderhus.dk. 42 units. 900DKK–1,050DKK ($150–$175) double. AE, DC, MC, V. **Amenities:** Restaurant; lounge; room service; laundry service; dry cleaning. *In room:* TV, minibar, hair dryer, trouser press.

WHERE TO DINE

Hotel Tønderhus DANISH   One of Tønder's many appealing restaurants lies on the street level of this previously recommended hotel. In an artfully old-fashioned setting, accessorized with rustic farm implements, you can order copious portions of such tried-and-true Danish specialties as cold potato soup with bacon and chives, fresh-fried fish cakes of the house, a platter of assorted marinades of herring, brisket of beef with horseradish, and a savory afterthought that might include fried Camembert with black currant jam. Between the lunch and dinner hour, the place remains open for coffee, tea, drinks, and a selection of such cold platters as marinated herring with various types of Danish cheeses.

Jomfrustien 1. ✆ **74-72-22-22.** Main courses 169DKK–229DKK ($28–$38); fixed-price menus 238DKK–279DKK ($40–$47). AE, DC, MC, V. Daily noon–2pm and 6–9:30pm.

Torvets Restaurant ★ *(Finds* DANISH   The stately main floor of this former 1930s bank is divided into a formal, antiques-laden restaurant and a less elegant bistro where food is cheaper and culinary pretensions are a lot lower. In the bistro, you can order platters of *smørrebrød* (open-face sandwich), pastas, pizzas, and cold assortments of Danish cheese, herring, and fresh vegetables. In the restaurant, expect more elaborate concoctions that change with the season and are likely to include fried plaice with hollandaise sauce and boiled potatoes; roasted, spiced salmon with boiled potatoes; grilled trout with roasted tomatoes, shrimps, asparagus and mushrooms; and steak stuffed with roasted onions, bacon, and mushrooms.

Storegade 1. ✆ **74-72-43-73.** Reservations recommended in restaurant, not necessary in bistro. Restaurant main courses 89DKK–218DKK ($15–$36); bistro platters 45DKK–69DKK ($7.50–$12). AE, DC, MC, V. Daily noon–11pm.

Victoria Restaurant DANISH   Set in a century-old building in the heart of town, this restaurant serves well-prepared, unpretentious platters of Danish food that arrive cheerfully and in generous portions. In summer, tables and chairs are set in front, creating the aura of a Tivoli-style bistro-cafe in faraway Copenhagen. Menu items reflect time-tested Danish traditions, and usually include such dishes as smoked salmon with a morel-flavored dill sauce, platters heaped with three different kinds of herring, egg salad with shrimp from the waters off Greenland, breast of Danish hen with spinach and mushrooms, and a dessert specialty that might include a citrus-flavored *bavarois* (custard) with wild berry sauce.

Storegade 9. ✆ **74-72-00-89.** Reservations recommended. Main courses 89DKK–139DKK ($15–$23). AE, DC, MC, V. Mon–Fri 10:30am–11pm; Sat 10:30am–1am; Sun 2–11pm.

TØNDER AFTER DARK

There isn't much activity here at night. Your best bet is **Hagge's Musik Pub,** Vestergade 80 (✆ **74-72-44-49**), which lies opposite the post office. You can order pub grub and both Irish and Danish beer on draft here. Although it's not a nightly event, it's a frequent venue for live music including blues, jazz, and Danish or Scottish folk. Open Tuesday to Thursday 4 to 11pm; Friday 3 to 11pm; Saturday noon to 11pm.

A VISIT TO OLD-WORLD MØGELTØNDER

Even if you have to skip Tønder itself, head for the little village of **Møgeltønder** ★★, only 4km (2½ miles) west of Tønder via Route 419. Bus no. 66 from Tønder runs here about every hour during the day (trip time: 10 min.).

Once at Møgeltønder, you'll find a charming old-world village. Filmmakers have called it a fairy-tale setting, with its long and narrow street, called Slotsgade, lined with low gabled houses, some with thatched roofs and most dating from the 1700s. The street is also planted with a double row of lime trees, making it even more colorful and photogenic.

At the end of the street stands a small castle, **Schackenborg Slot,** which can only be viewed from the outside, as it's owned by the Queen of Denmark and currently functions as the principal residence of her younger son, Prince Joachim, and his wife, Alexandra. The king presented Field Marshall Hans Schack with the castle in 1661, in the wake of his victory over the Swedes during the battle of Nyborg. His descendants occupied the castle for centuries. Although security is tight and you can't visit the interior of the castle, you can tour the moat-enclosed grounds that begin on the opposite side of the street. June, July, and August, two 30-minute tours are conducted daily at 11:30pm and noon. The price is 25DKK ($4.20) for adults, 20DKK ($3.35) for children, for the carefully supervised trek. The rest of the year, visits to the gardens are not possible.

At the other end of the Slotsgade stands the 12th-century **Møgeltønder Kirke,** Slotsgade (© **74-73-81-39**), which contains some interesting frescoes (the oldest of which dates from 1275) under the chancel's arch. In the chancel itself are some mid-16th-century frescoes. The altarpiece is probably early 16th century, and you can also see such treasures as a Romanesque font and a late-17th-century baroque pulpit. The church organ was made in Hamburg in 1679. The church is open daily from 8am to 5pm, closing at 4pm October to March. Admission is free.

WHERE TO STAY

Schackenborg Slotskro ★★★ *Finds*   This venerable, thick-walled 17th-century structure is set on the historic, picture-perfect main street of the hamlet Møgeltønder. Owned but not operated by the queen's son, Prince Joachim, and his Hong Kong–born wife, Alexandra, the Royal licensed coaching inn takes great pains to project an aura of aristocratic well-being and glamour, despite occasional streamlined, modern touches in an otherwise old-world setting. Each room is named after one of the palaces or fortresses of Denmark and contains a condensed history of its namesake. Both the furnishings and the bathrooms with tub/shower combinations are tidily kept. Expect a relatively luxurious Danish manor house at its most intimate. Even if you opt not to spend the night, consider a meal in the formal **dining room,** which, frankly, is a lot more appealing than the hotel (see "Where to Dine," below).

Slotsgaden 42, Møgeltønder, DK-6270 Tønder. © **74-73-83-83.** Fax 74-73-83-11. www.slotskro.com. 25 units. 1,090DKK–1,290DKK ($182–$215) double. Rates include buffet breakfast. AE, DC, MC, V. **Amenities:** Restaurant; bar; car rental; room service (7am–10pm); laundry service; dry cleaning; nonsmoking rooms. *In room:* TV, hair dryer, safe.

WHERE TO DINE

Schackenborg Slotskro ★★★ DANISH/INTERNATIONAL   The most stylish and prestigious restaurant in the neighborhood lies on the street level of the inn owned by Prince Joachim. In an ocher-colored dining room that reeks of 18th-century respectability, you'll be seated at formally accessorized tables. The restaurant is famous for a distinctive specialty—salmon soufflé encased in a fish mousse. Yours will come with a number indicating where it falls on the historical tally (at this writing, the restaurant had served more than 70,000). Other items include quail cooked in Madeira sauce, and various versions of seafood. Expect a leisurely, rather elegant reflection of the image that's preferred by Denmark's royal family, and a bit of social posturing on the part of the other guests.

Slotsgaden 42, Møgeltønder. © **74-73-83-83**. Reservations recommended. Main courses 175DKK–260DKK ($29–$43); fixed-price menus 295DKK–495DKK ($49–$83). AE, DC, MC, V. Daily noon–2pm and 6–8:30pm. Closed occasional Mon for private parties.

A TRIP TO LØGUM KLOSTER & MEMORIES OF A MONASTERY

A final and worthwhile excursion is to the hamlet of Løgum, 18km (11 miles) north of Tønder. (From Tønder, follow the road signs to Ribe, then to Kolding and, a bit later, to Løgum Kloster.) **Løgum Kloster (Løgum Abbey),** Klostervej (© **74-74-41-65**), once competed with Tønder as a lacemaking center. Built in what was then an uninhabited and marshy plain, the abbey—today an ecclesiastical administrative center—was founded in 1173. Once impressive in size, the abbey today has been reduced to its east wing, with the sacristy, library, chapter house, and church remaining. Constructed from red brick, the abbey church grew and changed over a period of years from 1230 to 1330. It was built when Europe was changing from the Romanesque to the Gothic style, so the abbey reflects both periods of architecture. In the nave are traces of frescoes, and other treasures include a winged altar and elegantly carved choir stalls from the early 16th century, and a reliquary with wings and a Gothic triumphal cross (ca. 1300). Opposite the main building stands a 24m (79-ft.) tower with a carillon named in honor of King Frederik IX. It strikes a concert every Wednesday at 8pm (only June–Aug).

Between May and October, the abbey church can be visited Monday through Saturday from 10am to 6:30pm; Sunday from noon to 5pm. The rest of the year, it can be visited Monday to Saturday from 10am to 4pm and Sunday noon to 4pm. Admission is free.

4 Rømø ★

288km (180 miles) SW of Copenhagen; 15km (9 miles) W of Skærbæk; 5km (3 miles) N of Sylt

Off the west coast of Jutland, **Rømø,** a North Frisian island, is the largest Danish island in the North Sea. It is about 9km (5⅝ miles) long and 6.5km (4 miles) wide. The western shore opens onto the North Sea, whereas the east coast facing the mainland is bounded by tidal shallows. The northwest corner of the island is a restricted military zone.

The island, which is separated from the German island of Sylt by the **Lister Dyb (Lister Deep),** has a wild, windswept appearance and is particularly known for its nude sunbathing, as is the German island of Sylt. In summer, Rømø is filled with tourists, especially Germans, but off season it's one of the sleepiest places in Europe.

Midway between Ribe and Tønder, Rømø is connected to the mainland by a 10km (6¼-mile) causeway that passes over a panoramic marshland filled with wading seabirds and grazing sheep in summer. Exposed to the North Sea, the western edge of the island is the site of the best sandy beaches and is a magnet for windsurfers. The most popular beach area is at Lakolk on the central western coastal strip. Here the beach is under a kilometer (½ mile) wide. The main hamlets are on the eastern coast along a 6km (3¾-mile) stretch from the causeway south to the little port of Havneby.

ESSENTIALS

GETTING THERE   By Train   Skærbæk is linked by rail to the towns of Tønder, Ribe, and Esbjerg.

Moments Wildlife on Rømø

Many visitors come to Rømø to seek out its plentiful bird life on the west coast, which is also home to some 1,500 seals. You can see them sunbathing during the day.

By Bus You can take a bus south from Ribe to Skærbæk and then bus no. 29 across the tidal flats to Rømø.

By Car Take the 10km (6¼-mile) stone causeway from mainland Jutland, a half-hour's drive on Route 175 from either Tønder or Ribe (there are no tolls en route).

By Ferry If you'd like to continue your trip to Sylt from Rømø, a car ferry departs six times daily from the Danish fishing village of Havneby to the far northern German town of List (trip time: 1 hr.). For schedules and more information, call **Rømø/Sylt Linie** (© **74-75-53-03**). The price for a car (up to 5 passengers) is 279DKK to 312DKK ($47–$52), depending on the size of the car.

VISITOR INFORMATION **Rømø Turistbureau,** Havnebyvej 30 (© **74-75-51-30;** www.romo.dk), is open June to August daily 9am to 6pm. It's closed every Sunday off season November to April.

GETTING AROUND **By Bicycle** The best way to get around Rømø is by bike. Rentals, costing from 40DKK ($5.25) a day, are available at **Garni,** Nørre Frankel at Havneby (© **74-75-54-80**).

SEEING THE SIGHTS

The island of Rømø has one of the widest beaches in Denmark flying the blue flag (indicating nonpolluted waters). The nude beach, often frequented by Germans, is at Sønderstrand on the southwestern tip of the island. Windsurfing is popular here, mainly on the west coast. The best area for windsurfing is at the southern side of Lakolf. *Note:* windsurfers must bring their own equipment to Rømø, as there is no outlet locally to rent equipment.

Other than the beaches and windsurfing, the most popular outdoor pursuit is horseback riding, available at **Rømø Ranch,** Lakolk Strand (© **74-75-54-11**), a stable right on Lakolk Beach. It offers rides to experienced as well as novice riders, and most rides take place right on the beach, for 50DKK to 80DKK ($8.35–$13) per hour.

At the rear of the tourist office (see "Visitor Information," above) you'll find the **Naturcentret Tønnisgård,** Havnebyvej 30 (© **74-75-52-57**), in an old thatched farmhouse from the island of Rømø. It contains modest displays of the island flora and fauna, and there is also a cafeteria serving drinks and Danish pastries. Tønnisgård is open Monday to Friday 10am to 4pm except November to January. Admission is 15DKK ($2.50) adults and 5DKK (85¢) children. The center also conducts 90-minute nature tours of the local wetlands June to September. Four or five of these depart every day during that period, depending on demand, for 45DKK ($7.50) adults, 20DKK ($3.35) children 13 and under. Phone ahead for schedules and departure times.

Other attractions include **Kommandørgården** (The National Museum's Commander House), Guvrevej 60, in the hamlet of Toftum (© **74-75-52-76**). The house dates from 1748 and is evocative of the great prosperity enjoyed by ship commanders in the sailing heyday of Rømø in the 18th century. The house

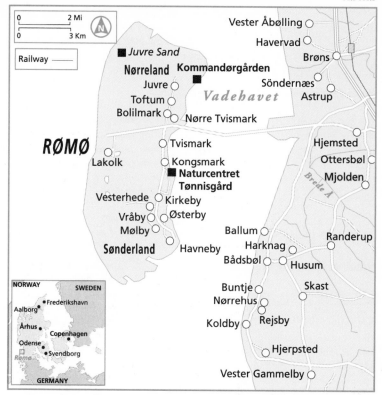

is fully restored, including its panels, ceilings, and doors. The walls are covered with Dutch tiles and the furnishings are lavish. About 50 sailors from Rømø served simultaneously as captains on Dutch and German ships that sailed on whaling expeditions to Greenland. May to September the house is open Tuesday through Sunday 10am to 6pm. In October it's open Tuesday through Sunday 10am to 3pm and closed off season. Admission costs 15DKK ($2.50) adults, 10DKK ($1.65) seniors and students, free for ages 15 and under.

In the village of **Jurve,** there is a fence of whale jawbone made in 1772. It has been preserved and is now under the protection of the National Museum in Copenhagen. As no wood or stone was available on the island at the time, the locals made use of this unusual building material, a remnant of the whaling ships' catches in Greenland.

Rømø Kirke at Kirkeby also merits a visit. The church was originally built in the late Gothic style, but was greatly extended in the 17th and 18th centuries. It is consecrated to St. Clemens, the patron saint of seafarers, and contains a number of ship models, as well as three large chandeliers, all donated by sailors. Admission is free, and it is open year-round Tuesday through Friday 8am to 4pm.

SHOPPING

At the center of the island in Kongsmark, you'll find Rømø's major gallery, known by the English name **Art House,** Gamle Skolevej, 8A (© **74-75-61-36**). Here you can experience and purchase Danish and European handicraft products. April to

October, a new exhibition of glass and pottery by leading Danish and international artisans is presented every month. If weather allows, you can enjoy freshly brewed coffee and other refreshments in a beautiful garden surrounding the Art House. The only way to stop in is by appointment.

WHERE TO STAY

Hotel Færgegaarden ★ *Finds*   Set on the southern stretches of the island, a short drive from the island's best beaches, one of the most charming hotels on Rømø is an authentic, thatch-roofed inn that has welcomed overnight guests since it was originally built in 1813. Although the cozy, much-restored rooms with tub/shower combination bathrooms are comfortable and solid, the real appeal of the place derives from its restaurant, where beamed ceilings and many other reminders of the Denmark of long ago contribute to a feeling of well-being. You'll also find a clientele that's more cosmopolitan than you might expect, with visitors from as far away as Florida, Washington, and California.

Vestergade, DK-6792 Havneby. ⓒ 74-75-54-32. Fax 74-75-58-59. 35 units. 900DKK ($150) double. Rates include breakfast. AE, DC, MC, V. **Amenities:** Restaurant; bar; indoor heated pool; tennis court; sauna; room service (7am–10pm); laundry service; dry cleaning; solarium. *In room:* TV, minibar, hair dryer.

Hotel/Motel Rømø *Value*   This is one of the least expensive and simplest hotels on Rømø. Built in the early 1970s on the island's eastern shore, it has virtually no architectural fantasy, no sense of old-time Denmark, and no decorative frills or graceful notes. Despite that, the place is usually booked solid, thanks to low prices, clean rooms that have big windows, well-kept bathrooms with shower units, and a feeling of isolation from the cares and concerns of mainland Europe. There's a simple restaurant that serves generous portions of traditional Danish food daily noon to 9:30pm. A fixed-price menu is a relative bargain at 120DKK ($20). Although the sea is only a few steps from the hotel, the nearest beach lies 4km (2½ miles) to the south, on Rømø's southern tip.

Kongsmark, DK-6792 Rømø. ⓒ 74-75-51-14. 35 units. 401DKK–587DKK ($67–$98) double. No credit cards. Closed Nov–Apr. **Amenities:** Restaurant; lounge. *In room:* TV, safe.

Hotel RIM & Feriecenter   This is the largest and most visible hotel on Rømø, with a northern European clientele (Danish, Dutch, and German) that tends to stay for several days or more. The setting is a compound of gabled brown-brick houses, each of which contains between two and four apartments. Inside, you'll find simple, angular furnishings, lots of exposed wood, neatly kept bathrooms with shower units, and an overall unfrilly, anonymous setting. Don't expect verdant gardens or forests, as the venue is based on the fragile ecology of tenacious sea grasses that grow under streaming sunlight and almost constant ocean winds. There's easy access to the largest beach in northern Europe, a windswept stretch of sand almost 3km (1¾ miles) wide by 7km (4⅓ miles) long. Unlike many other apartment-style beachfront hotels in Denmark, this one remains open year-round.

Vestergade 159, DK-6792 Rømø. ⓒ 74-75-57-75. Fax 74-75-57-36. 207 units, each with kitchenette. 618DKK–1,090DKK ($103–$182) apt for 1–4 occupants; 713DKK–1,227DKK ($119–$205) apt for 1–6 occupants. AE, DC, MC, V. **Amenities:** Restaurant; bar; 4 pools (2 heated indoor); fitness center; sauna; laundry service; dry cleaning; nonsmoking rooms; solarium. *In room:* TV.

WHERE TO DINE

Hotel Færgegaarden ★ CONTINENTAL   This hotel offers not only the best accommodations on the island, but also the finest cuisine. Service rituals are more elaborate here than elsewhere on Rømø. The place has been feeding wayfarers since 1813, and doing so admirably. Fresh fish, in our view, is the best item on the menu, especially the salmon cutlets with fresh spinach and lime sauce. The meat dishes also get tender, loving care, especially the breast of chicken with a mushroom cream sauce, or the tournedos Rossini with a pâté of goose liver and wild mushrooms. There are three dining rooms; we prefer the oldest and most atmospheric, called the Pejsestuen.

Vestergade. ⓒ **74-75-54-32.** Reservations recommended. Main courses 65DKK–100DKK ($11–$17) at lunch, 115DKK–305DKK ($19–$51) at dinner; fixed-price menus 188DKK–298DKK ($31–$50). AE, DC, MC, V. Daily noon–9pm.

Otto & Ani's Fisk SEAFOOD You'll find this place either authentic and appealingly raffish, or hopelessly informal, depending on your temperament. Expect a self-service format in a brown-brick building that's among the least stately looking in Rømø. English-speaking proprietor Susan Jensen will help you select from a Danish-language menu that lists various platters of fish, most of which compose a filling meal in their own right. Examples include everything from a simple filet of cod served sandwich-style, with fresh bread, butter, and a handful of freshly peeled shrimp, to a dinner-sized filet of sole with baked potato, mixed salad, and—again—a handful of shrimp. Beer or wine might accompany your meal, which you'll consume either at picnic tables set up outside, or in a severe all-white room. Despite its shortcomings, the place has thrived for more than a dozen years because of its low prices and flavorful fish.

Havnepladsen, Havneby. ⓒ **74-75-53-06.** Main courses 55DKK–135DKK ($9.20–$23). No credit cards. Apr–Oct daily 11am–9pm.

RØMØ AFTER DARK

There are very few options for nightlife on this island that is notoriously sleepy, even by the Danish island standards. Our best suggestion is to have a drink and do some dancing at **Make Up Diskotek,** Lakolk Butikstorv (ⓒ **74-75-59-23**), open summer only Thursday through Saturday 10pm to 4am and Sunday through Wednesday 10:30pm to 2am. Cover is 60DKK ($10).

5 Ribe ⭐⭐

32km (20 miles) S of Esbjerg; 298km (186 miles) W of Copenhagen; 47km (29 miles) N of Tønder

Ribe, a town of narrow cobblestone lanes and half-timbered and crooked houses, became legendary because of the graceful (and endangered) storks that build their nests on top of its red-roofed medieval houses. Every year the residents of Denmark's oldest town ponder the question: Will the storks return in April?

This port was an important trading center during the Viking era (around A.D. 900) and became an Episcopal see in 948, when one of the first Christian churches in Denmark was established here. It was also the royal residence of the ruling Valdemars around 1200.

In medieval days, sea-trade routes to England, Germany, Friesland, the Mediterranean, and other ports linked Ribe, but then its waters receded. Today it's surrounded by marshes, much like a landlocked Moby Dick. The town watchman still makes his rounds—armed with his lantern and trusty staff— since the ancient custom was revived in 1936.

ESSENTIALS

GETTING THERE By Train and Bus There's hourly train service from Copenhagen (via Bramming). The schedules of both trains and buses are available at the tourist office.

By Car   From Kolding (see earlier in this chapter), head west across Jutland on the motorway (E20), but cut southwest when you reach Route 32, which will carry you into Ribe.

VISITOR INFORMATION   The **Ribe Turistbureau,** Torvet 3 (© **75-42-15-00;** www.ribetourist.dk), is open June 15 through August, Monday to Saturday 9:30am to 5:30pm, and Sunday 10am to 2pm; April to June 14 and September to October, Monday to Friday 9am to 5pm and Saturday 10am to 1pm; and November to March, Monday through Friday 9:30am to 4:30pm and Saturday 10am to 1pm.

GETTING AROUND   **By Bicycle**   If you'd like to bike your way around the area, you can rent bikes for 60DKK ($10) at **Ribe Vandrerhjem** (Youth Hostel), Sct. Pedersgade 16 (© **75-42-06-20**).

SEEING THE SIGHTS

Det Gamle Rådhus (Town Hall Museum)   In the oldest existing town hall in Denmark, originally built in 1496, the medieval Town Hall Museum houses Ribe's artifacts and archives. Included are a 16th-century executioner's sword, ceremonial swords, the town's money chest, antique tradesmen's signs, and a depiction of the "iron hand," still a symbol of police authority.

Von Støckends Plads. © **79-89-89-55.** Admission 15DKK ($2.50) adults, 5DKK (85¢) children 7–14, free for children under 7. June–Aug daily 1–3pm; May and Sept Mon–Fri 1–3pm. Closed Oct–Apr.

Ribe Domkirke ✦   This stone-and-brick cathedral, this little town's crowning achievement, was under construction from 1150 to 1175. Inspired by Rhenish architecture, it's a good example of the Romanesque influence on Danish architecture, despite its Gothic arches. A century later a tower was added; climb it if you want to see how the storks view Ribe—and if you have the stamina. Try to see the legendary "Cat's Head Door," once the principal entranceway to the church, and the granite tympanum—*Removal from the Cross*—the most significant piece of medieval sculpture left in Denmark. The mosaics, stained glass, and frescoes in the eastern apse are by the artist Carl-Henning Pedersen.

Torvet (in the town center off Sønderportsgade). © **75-42-06-19.** Admission 12DKK ($2) adults, 5DKK (85¢) children. June–Aug daily 10am–5:30pm; May and Sept daily 10am–5pm; Oct–Apr Mon–Sat 11am–3pm, Sun 1–3pm.

Ribe Kunstmuseet   An extensive collection of Danish art is displayed at the Ribe Kunstmuseet, including works by acclaimed Danish artists like Eckersberg, Kobke, C. A. Jensen, Hammershøj, and Juel. Housed in a stately mid-19th-century villa in a garden on the Ribe River, many paintings are from the golden age of Danish art. Occasionally the museum changes exhibitions.

Skt. Nicolai Gade 10. © **75-42-03-62.** Admission 35DKK ($5.85) adults, free for children under 16. Sept–June Tues–Sun 11am–4pm, July–Aug Tues–Sun 11am–5pm. Closed Jan 1–Feb 11.

Ribe Legetøjsmuseum (Toy Museum)   This exhibition on two floors contains a unique collection of several thousand toys from 1850 to 1980. There are more than 500 dolls alone, along with toy cars ranging from the first horseless carriages to today's model cars. Motorcycles are also represented. There are also wooden toys, old games, robots, antique teddy bears, and much more.

Von Støckens Plads 2. © **75-41-14-40.** Admission 35DKK ($5.85) adults, 15DKK ($2.50) children 3–12, free for children under 3, family ticket 100DKK ($17). Jan–Mar and Nov–Dec Mon–Sat 1–4pm; Apr–May and Sept–Oct daily 1–5pm; June–Aug daily 10am–noon and 1–5pm.

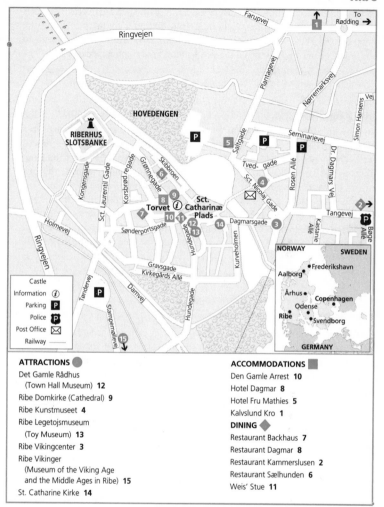

ATTRACTIONS ●

Det Gamle Rådhus
(Town Hall Museum) **12**

Ribe Domkirke (Cathedral) **9**

Ribe Kunstmuseet **4**

Ribe Legetøjsmuseum
(Toy Museum) **13**

Ribe Vikingcenter **3**

Ribe Vikinger
(Museum of the Viking Age
and the Middle Ages in Ribe) **15**

St. Catharine Kirke **14**

ACCOMMODATIONS ■

Den Gamle Arrest **10**

Hotel Dagmar **8**

Hotel Fru Mathies **5**

Kalvslund Kro **1**

DINING ◆

Restaurant Backhaus **7**

Restaurant Dagmar **8**

Restaurant Kammerslusen **2**

Restaurant Sælhunden **6**

Weis' Stue **11**

Ribe Vikingecenter Lying less than a kilometer (½ mile) south of the town's historic core, this Viking center is affiliated with Ribe Vikinger (see below). The highlight of the center is a re-created Viking town from 1050, showing the type of houses you would find in the early Middle Ages. The centerpiece of the town is a so-called "great house," showing a type of Danish manor that would have been occupied by the town's most powerful baron.

Lustrupvej 4. ℂ **75-41-16-11**. Admission 60DKK ($10) adults, 30DKK ($5) children 3–14, free for children under 3. May–June and Sept Mon–Fri 10am–3:30pm; July–Aug daily 11am–5pm. Guided tours in English are offered in May–June and Sept daily at 10:10am; July–Aug daily at 11:10am. Tours cost 200DKK ($33) for 30 min. or 375DKK ($63) for 1 hr.

Ribe Vikinger (Museum of the Viking Age and the Middle Ages in Ribe) Opened in 1995, this museum traces the story of Ribe through exhibitions. Beginning in A.D. 700, it depicts the Viking age and the medieval period.

Actual archaeological finds are displayed, along with such reconstructed scenes as a Viking marketplace, dating from around 800, and a church building site from around 1500. A multimedia room, "Odin's Eye," introduces the visitor to the world of the Vikings through a vivid sound and vision experience.

Odins Plads. ✆ 75-42-22-22. Admission 50DKK ($8.35) adults, 20DKK ($3.35) children, family ticket 120DKK ($20). Apr–June and Sept–Oct daily 10am–4pm; July–Aug Thurs–Tues 10am–6pm, Wed 10am–9pm; Nov–Mar Tues–Sun 10am–4pm.

Skt. Catharine Kirke   The Black Friars (Dominicans) came to Ribe in 1228 and began constructing a church and chapter house (the east wing of a monastery). Parts of the original edifice can still be seen, especially the southern wall. The present church, near Dagmarsgade, with nave and aisles, dates from 1400 to 1450, the tower from 1617. Extensive restorations have made this one of the best-preserved abbeys in Scandinavia. Only the monks' stalls and the Romanesque font remain from the Middle Ages. The pulpit dates from 1591 and the altarpiece from 1650. You can walk through the cloisters and see ship models and religious paintings hanging in the southern aisle. Tombstones of Ribe citizens from the Reformation and later can be seen along the outer walls of the church.

Skt. Catharine's Plads. ✆ 75-42-05-34. Free admission to church; cloisters 3DKK (50¢) adults, 1DKK (15¢) children under 14. May–Sept daily 10am–noon and 2–5pm; Oct–Apr daily 10am–noon and 2–4pm. Closed during church services.

OUTDOOR ACTIVITIES

You can evoke yesteryear by riding a horse-drawn carriage through the cobble-covered streets of Ribe. In summer, you can hire a carriage in Torvet, the central market square. The cost is 50DKK ($8.35) per person for a ride of about 15 minutes. Carriages hold up to five passengers each. For more information, call ✆ 75-42-19-94.

Anglers and fishers head for **Storkesøen,** an interconnected trio of artificial lakes that are kept well-stocked with fish, especially trout. Known for their appeal to escapists and for their verdant beauty, they lie less than 1.5km (¾ mile) south of Ribe. A permit allowing 4 consecutive hours of fishing costs 100DKK ($17); 7 hours costs 160DKK ($27); 9 hours costs 200DKK ($33); and a permit good for 24 hours of fishing costs 420DKK ($70). For more information, contact Storkesøen, Haulundvej 164 (✆ 75-41-04-11).

Horseback riding in the area can be arranged through **Gelsådalens Ridelejr,** Ribelandevej 17 at Gram (✆ 74-82-21-22). The cost is 100DKK ($17) per hour.

SHOPPING

Ribe has some of the best shopping in Jutland. The best selection of antiques is at **Antik Gaarden,** Overdammen 5 (✆ 75-41-18-08). The best clothing store is **Mr. Lundgaard,** Saltgade 3 (✆ 75-42-42-40), which has the town's largest selection, everything from high-quality clothes to Marlboro classics. The shop caters to both women and men. A wide range of footwear for adults and children is available at **Sara Sko,** Skoringen Ribe, Tømmergangen 3 (✆ 75-42-11-24). At **Ribe's Broderi & Garn,** Dagmarsgade 4 (✆ 75-42-16-75), you'll find the finest selection of needlework—some of the pieces are exquisite—and woolen items. **Bentzons Boghandel,** Mellemdammen 16 (✆ 75-43-57-51), is the best bookstore, with many English-language titles. **Alisson-Dansk Naturkosmetik,** Nederdammen 32 (✆ 75-41-09-01), is an intriguing store with a varied selection of products from a well-known Danish company, Alisson of Denmark. They are makers of skin-care and cosmetic products.

If your tastes run to handicrafts, gifts, and souvenirs, you'll find that Ribe is loaded with boutiques. The most amusing outlet is **Ryk Ind,** Sønderportsgade 7 (© **75-42-29-69**), which is stuffed with gifts—everything from classic model cars to china dolls. A large assortment of artwork, porcelain, glass, paper collages, and mobiles, plus other decorative items for the home, is sold at **Overdammens Idebutik,** Overdammen 5 (© **75-42-14-14**). For generations, Ribe citizens have patronized **Børge Bottelet Guldsmedie,** Mellemdammen 14 (© **75-42-02-26**), for jewelry.

WHERE TO STAY

Weis Stue and Restaurant Backhaus (see "Where to Dine," below) also rent rooms. Parking at the following hotels is available on the street.

Den Gamle Arrest ⭐⭐   One of the town's most charming hotels occupies a structure built in 1546 as the town jail. Set on the main square of Ribe, and constructed of the same russet-colored bricks that formed most of the town's important buildings, it functioned as a jail until 1989. The present owners transformed it into a cozy hotel. The guest rooms are snug, often with exposed brick and enough old-fashioned amenities to remind you of a gentrified version of the building's original function.

Torvet 11, DK-6760 Ribe. © **75-42-37-00.** Fax 75-42-37-22. www.dengamlearrest.dk. 11 units, 2 with bathroom. 590DKK–740DKK ($99–$124) double without bathroom; 840DKK–940DKK ($140–$157) double with bathroom. Rates include breakfast. No credit cards. **Amenities:** Bar. *In room:* TV (in some), no phone.

Hotel Dagmar ⭐⭐⭐   Once the most famous hotel outside Copenhagen, this 1581 building is the most glamorous address in the region. Converted from a private home in 1850, it's named after a medieval Danish queen. The guest rooms are comfortable and roomy, with traditional furniture and state-of-the-art bathrooms with tub/shower combinations. On Friday and Saturday nights (except in summer), there's music and dancing. The hotel has a restaurant (see "Where to Dine," below).

Torvet 1, DK-6760 Ribe. © **75-42-00-33.** Fax 75-42-36-52. www.hoteldagmar.dk. 50 units. 1,045DKK–1,395DKK ($175–$233) double. Rates include breakfast. AE, DC, MC, V. **Amenities:** 3 restaurants; bar; room service (7am–10pm); laundry service; dry cleaning; nonsmoking rooms. *In room:* TV, minibar, hair dryer, safe.

Hotel Fru Mathies   Set behind a bright yellow stucco facade, a very short walk from the city's pedestrian zone, this hotel was named after its present guardian and supervisor, Fru (Mrs.) Inga Mathies. There's a shared TV/living room on the premises, and bedrooms are simple but cozy affairs, each with a bathroom equipped with a tub/shower combination and modest numbers of old-fashioned accessories. Breakfast is the only meal served.

Saltgade 15, DK-67660 Ribe. © **75-42-34-20.** 6 units, 4 with bathroom. 490DKK ($82) double without bathroom; 640DKK ($107) double with bathroom. Rates include breakfast. AE, DC, MC, V. **Amenities:** Breakfast room; bar; lounge. *In room:* TV, minibar, no phone.

Kalvslund Kro   This 1865 inn offers comfortable rooms but few frills. The furniture, according to the management, "is old but not antique." Each unit contains a neatly kept bathroom with a tub/shower combination. The restaurant serves home-style cooking that is well prepared and presented. Full meals include such dishes as asparagus soup, Danish beef with sautéed onions, and pork cutlets.

Koldingvej 105 (at Kalvslund), DK-6760 Ribe. © **75-43-70-12.** 5 units, none with bathroom. 300DKK ($50) double. Rates include breakfast. No credit cards. Free parking. May–Sept daily 11am–10pm; other times of year by advance reservation only. Bus: 57 or 921 from Ribe. 9km (5⅗ miles) north of Ribe on Rte. 52. **Amenities:** Breakfast room; bar; lounge. *In room:* No phone.

WHERE TO DINE

Restaurant Backhaus DANISH   This place has served as a restaurant or an inn for as long as anyone in Ribe can remember. Today, steaming platters of all-Danish food arrive in generous portions at reasonable prices. Menu specialties include a Danish platter containing artfully arranged presentations of herring, cheeses, and vegetables that taste wonderful with the establishment's earthy, rough-textured bread; tomato soup with sour cream and a surprising but refreshing dab of horseradish; tender pork schnitzels served with potatoes and braised red cabbage; and sautéed strips of beef tenderloin with fried onions that hit the spot on a cold, windy day. Dessert might be a hazelnut pie with vanilla ice cream.

On the premises are seven simple rooms, stripped-down but comfortable hideaways that are very clean. With breakfast included, doubles cost 750DKK ($125). With the exception of about a week every year at Christmas, the hotel is open year-round.

Grydergade 12, DK-6760 Ribe. ℂ **75-42-11-01.** Reservations recommended. Main courses 100DKK–170DKK ($17–$28). MC, V. Daily 11am–9:30pm.

Restaurant Dagmar DANISH/INTERNATIONAL   Opposite the cathedral and near the train station, the Hotel Dagmar's four dining rooms are a 19th-century dream of ornate furnishings and accessories. The international cuisine is the best in town, and it's impeccably served and complemented by a good wine list. Two fresh North Sea fish dishes of the day are usually offered. Among meat and poultry selections, try the fried quail stuffed with mushrooms on beurre blanc, or veal tenderloin with shallot mousse in port sauce. There's also a cozy cellar restaurant.

In the Hotel Dagmar, Torvet 1. ℂ **75-42-00-33.** Reservations required. Main courses 165DKK–265DKK ($28–$44); fixed-price lunch 165DKK ($28); fixed-price dinner 325DKK–565DKK ($54–$94). AE, DC, MC, V. Daily noon–10pm.

Restaurant Kammerslusen DANISH   Built in 1997, this restaurant is between the seacoast and the canal that connects Ribe to the sea. To reach it, drive 15km (9½ miles) east of Ribe, across flat and sandy terrain, until you eventually reach a red-brick, old-fashioned-looking hideaway. There's no public transport to this hotel. Menu items derive from long-standing regional traditions, and include fried filets of eel with white sauce and new potatoes, poached red salmon with au gratin potatoes, and a popular house specialty of grilled steak with barbecue sauce and fried onions. The cookery is always reliable and tasty, and it's easy to understand why this place has blossomed into a local favorite.

Bjerrumvej 30. ℂ **75-42-07-96.** Fax 75-42-29-32. Reservations recommended. Main courses 98DKK–215DKK ($16–$36); fixed-price menu 190DKK ($32). DC, MC, V. Daily 11am–9pm.

Restaurant Saelhunden DANISH/INTERNATIONAL   One of the most evocative and cheerful restaurants in Ribe occupies a venerable but cozy brick building whose history goes back to 1634. Set beside the river that flows through Ribe, within full view of the craft that kept its commerce alive during its mercantile heyday, it has flourished as a restaurant since 1969. Today, you're likely to find an engaging staff hailing from every corner of Europe, and an old-fashioned format whose size is doubled during mild weather thanks to an outdoor terrace. Menu items include at least three kinds of steaks that include T-bone, French-style entrecôte, and something known as "English steak." There are also fried filets of plaice with boiled potatoes and hollandaise sauce; platters of meatballs or smoked salmon; and a local delicacy, smoked and fried dab, a flat fish not unlike flounder that flourishes in the local estuaries. The cookery is imaginative and versatile, using fresh, quality ingredients. No one will mind if you come here just for a beer or a simple snack. In summertime, it's one of the closest approximations in town to the kind of beer garden you might expect to find in Hamburg.

Skibbroen 13. ✆ **75-42-09-46.** Reservations recommended. Main courses 56DKK–186DKK ($9.35–$31). DC, MC, V. Apr–Oct daily 11am–9:45pm (last food order); Nov–Mar 11am–8:45pm (last food order). Beer served till 11pm.

Weis Stue ★ *Finds* DANISH   Small, charming, and rich with history, this brick-and-timber inn is on the market square next to the cathedral. Originally built in the 1500s, it was gradually enlarged over the centuries. The food in the ground-floor restaurant is plentiful and well prepared. You might try shrimp with mayonnaise, marinated herring with raw onions, smoked Greenland halibut with scrambled eggs, liver paste with mushrooms, sliced ham and Italian salad, filet of beef with onions, and two cheeses with bread and butter.

The inn also has four upstairs guest rooms. They're cozy but don't have private bathrooms. A double costs 595DKK ($99), including breakfast.

Torvet 2, DK-6760 Ribe. ✆ **75-42-07-00.** Reservations recommended. Main courses 109DKK–215DKK ($18–$36); 2-course fixed-price menu 200DKK ($33). DC, MC, V. Daily 11am–10pm.

RIBE AFTER DARK

The Hotel Dagmar is the most happening place in Ribe. If it's winter, visit **Vægterkælderen,** Torvet (✆ **75-42-14-00**), the place to enjoy a good meal in informal and traditional surroundings, or else to savor a glass of frothy, newly drawn ale in the company of locals. The kitchen serves homemade pickled herring, fresh fish dishes, and juicy steaks, but many locals just come in for a drink. In the summer months you might want to sit outside in the Dagmar's courtyard, enjoying the **Pavillionen,** Torvet (✆ **75-42-00-33**). Hot drinks are served on cooler days, but if it's hot you can order draft beer or lemonade. Light summer meals, including fresh fish, are served. You can listen to the bells in the cathedral tower, admire the storks in their nests, and, if you're still around at 10 o'clock at night, see the night watchman as he prepares for his rounds.

The market square is also the home of the **Stenbohus Pub & Bar,** entered at Stenbogade 1 (✆ **75-42-01-22**), where live music can be heard at least once a week—folk, rock, soul, or blues. Otherwise, it's one of the most congenial taverns in town to meet locals over a glass of beer with a good head on it. Vægterkælderen (see above) is a classier joint for a drink; this one is more informal, attracting a more youthful crowd.

A SIDE TRIP TO MANDØ ★

The island of Mandø, 10km (6¼ miles) off the coast of Jutland southwest of Ribe, is one of the most tranquil island hideaways in Denmark. Surrounded by the Wadden Sea, it has remained almost untouched by tourism, partly because of the awkwardness involved in getting here. Other than privately owned watercraft, the only way to reach the island is via a bumpy stone-and-gravel drive (the Låningsvejen) that's completely submerged during high tide, usually twice a day.

Under normal conditions, and whenever seas aren't particularly rough, access is possible some 15 to 18 hours during every 24-hour period in summertime. The island itself is a low-lying marshland that's protected from erosion by a man-made dike that surrounds it. Massive sandbanks and dunes that are infertile, uninhabited, completely surrounded by water during high tides, and change their size and locations after storms also protect the island.

To reach Mandø from Ribe, drive 10km (6¼ miles) southwest of town to the coastal hamlet of Vester Vedsted, which marks the beginning of the Låningsvejen. The distance from Vester Vedsted to Mandø is 11km (6¾ miles), of which 5.5km (3½ miles) are submerged by the high tides of the Wadden Sea. If you respect the clearly posted safety notices and the schedule of tides, a conventional car can make the trip out to Mandø without incident. You can also get there as a passenger in the **Mandø Bussen (Mandø Bus),** a heavy-duty tractor-bus that's equipped with large-tread tires. It departs from the parking lot just to the west of Vester Vedsted at least twice a day May to September, charging 50DKK ($8.35) per passenger. Except under optimum circumstances, it doesn't run at all from October to April. For information about departure times, call either the tourist office in Ribe or the Mandø Bussen at © **75-44-51-07.**

The first recorded mention of Mandø appeared in 1231, when it was claimed in its entirety by the Danish monarchs. In 1741, the inhabitants purchased the island from the king at auction. Then, and throughout the rest of the 18th and 19th centuries, the island's men were involved with shipping while the women took care of the farms. In 1890, the island's population was 262; today, the island has a year-round population of only 70.

A few meters from where the bus stops in Mandø village stands **Mandøhuset** (© **75-42-60-52**), an old skipper's home, now a museum of local artifacts. Entrance is 15DKK ($2.50) adults and 5DKK (85¢) children. Visits are possible Monday through Friday from 10am to 4pm.

To the south stands **Mandø Kirke** (© **75-44-51-80**), dating from 1639. The entrance costs 4DKK (65¢), but you have to call ahead to have the church opened. An old mill, built in 1860, can be seen in the northern part of the village.

Bird life here is outstanding, with thousands of breeding pairs, including eider ducks, sandpipers, and oystercatchers.

The tidal flats on the island are neither land nor sea. One moment they are dry, but for 6 hours a day they are covered by vast quantities of water. These flats are spawning grounds for several species of edible fish, including plaice and cod. It is estimated that every year 10 to 12 million birds fly over these tidal flats.

These flats are Denmark's largest nature reserve. For those who like birdwatching, the spring and autumn migration periods are the best times to visit.

If you look anywhere to the southwest of Mandø, you'll get a view of what's sometimes referred to as Denmark's largest desert, an uninhabited expanse of sand dunes surrounded like an island by tidal flats that are submerged during high tides and storms. With borders and *prieler* (channels) whose positions are constantly changing because of storm and wave actions, the dunes and sand deposits are known as **Koresand.** Although a visit in winter is not advisable, during calm seas in summer, the site attracts ecologists and bird-watchers as part of twice-per-week half-day tours that are arranged by the same entrepreneurs who manage the above-mentioned **Mandø Bussen** (© **75-44-51-07** for reservations and departure times).

Visitors depart from and return to Mandø in open trailers drawn by tractors that resemble the Mandø Bussen. En route, you'll pass some of the largest seal colonies in the Baltic. (These are most active and interesting during August) You'll also be able to see the island of Rømø to the south and the island of Fanø to the northwest. There's usually the chance to search for amber on the beaches of Koresand, depending on the waves and the weather. The whole experience covers about 25km (15½ miles) and takes about 2 hours. The cost of the excursion is 60DKK ($10) adults and 40DKK ($6.70) children under 12.

6 Esbjerg

93km (58 miles) W of Vejle; 168km (105 miles) SW of Århus; 277km (173 miles) W of Copenhagen

Esbjerg's harbor, on the west coast of Denmark, with its easy accessibility to the North Sea, is a perfect shipping point for large agricultural exports to Great Britain, making it Denmark's largest fishing port. In recent years, the oil and natural gas deposits in the North Sea have made Esbjerg the country's oil city. Many ships here are used as supply vessels for Danish oil rigs.

Esbjerg is laid out with straight, wide streets, square town sections, and a large town square. There's a long pedestrian street, plus many specialty shops and large shopping centers. Within the town are parks and lakes with wooded areas.

Denmark's youngest major city can also be used as a base for exploring one of the country's prime holiday areas, a landscape of beaches, nature experiences, medieval towns, and amusement parks.

After Denmark lost Schleswig-Holstein to Germany in 1864, it needed an export harbor for shipping grain to Britain. In what had previously been farmland, the town at Esbjerg was founded in 1868, with the port opening in 1874. It was granted its city charter in 1898. The population has steadily grown to 82,000, making Esbjerg the fifth largest city of Denmark. The downside here is that since the city is relatively new, it doesn't have the old-time historic core that attracts visitors to cities such as Ribe (see earlier in this chapter). There is still much here to amuse.

ESSENTIALS

GETTING THERE   By Train   About three trains depart every day for Esbjerg from Frederikshavn, Aalborg, Viborg, and Herning.

By Car   From all corners of Denmark, highways lead to Esbjerg. From the German border in the south, take Route 11 north, heading left at the junction with Route 24. From Funen, take the E20 express highway west across Jutland.

By Ferry   Throughout the year, Harwich, England, has three weekly ferry departures heading for Esbjerg (trip time: 19 hr.). For information and reservations, contact **DFDS Ferries** at ℂ 79-17-79-17 (www.dfdsseaways.com). You can also connect by ferry with Fanø. Ferries from Fanø leave every 20 minutes during the day year-round (trip time: 12 min.).

VISITOR INFORMATION   The **Esbjerg Tourist Office,** Skolegade 33 (ℂ **75-12-55-99;** www.visitesbjerg.dk), is open Monday through Friday 9am to 5pm and Saturday 9am to 1pm (to 5pm in summer).

SEEING THE SIGHTS

The town landmark is the **Esbjerg Vandtårn,** or Esbjerg Watertower, 2 blocks south of Torvet (market square) at Havnegade 22 (ℂ **75-12-78-11**). C. H. Clausen, the town architect at the time, erected it in 1897, so don't be deceived by its appearance, which is evocative of the Middle Ages. Since Esbjerg was so new, town fathers at the time wanted the tower to give the town a more medieval look. You can climb the tower June 1 to September 15 daily 10am to 4pm. Off-season hours are only Saturday and Sunday 10am to 4pm. Admission is 30DKK ($5) adults, 15DKK ($2.50) children.

Esbjerg Havn (Esbjerg Harbor) is one of the most important in Denmark—Christian IX in 1868 called it "Denmark's gateway to the west." The oldest section is Den gamle Dokhavn and England Quay, the latter being the terminal that sees the arrival of some 200,000 ferry passengers between Denmark and England annually.

Just west of the Den gamle Dokhavn are the ferry terminals taking passengers to the holiday-island of Fanø (see later).

Close to the ferryboat terminal for boats headed to Fanø, at Esbjerg Havn, the museum lightship, **_Horns Rev_** (ℂ **75-45-91-88**), lies permanently anchored. The vessel offers visitors an excellent impression of what life was like onboard the ship, which helped protect shipping off the dangerous west coast of Jutland until 1984. It can be visited April, May, and September Monday to Friday 10am to 3pm; June to August Monday through Friday 10am to 4pm. Entrance costs 20DKK ($3.35) adults, 10DKK ($1.65) for children.

If you have a passion for things maritime, and if the idea of a waterside view of the port of Esbjerg appeals to you, consider a round-trip passage aboard M/S _Sønderho,_ which leaves from the docks at Færgehavnen. Tours of the harbor last 75 minutes each, are conducted late June to early September, and depart Monday, Tuesday, and Thursday at 11am and 1pm, Wednesday at 1, 3, and 5pm. Adults pay 45DKK ($7.50), children under 25DKK ($4.20). For further information call the tourist office (ℂ **75-12-55-99**).

At the southern end of the harbor lies Vestkraft power plant, which boasts Denmark's highest smokestack—248m (814 ft.) tall. Vestkraft supplies the entire south and west Jutland area with electricity as well as providing inexpensive heat for some 80,000 of the region's inhabitants. At the far end of the harbor lies Østerhavn, which is used as a base for shipping supplies and equipment to the many offshore oil and gas production facilities in the North Sea.

Although the fish auctions aren't what they used to be when the industry was more important for Esbjerg, they are still held at 9:30am on Wednesdays in July and August in a large, clearly visible auction hall at the harbor. Fishing for edible fish has declined, although Esbjerg is still a leading producer of fish meal and fish oil—some 600 tons of fish are processed here annually for that purpose.

The newest landmark in Esbjerg—also at the harbor—has attracted a lot of attention, from both visitors and locals. Called "Esbjerg's new giants," they are four chalky-white figures, the late Svend Wiig Hansen's enormous sculpture, _Man Meets the Sea_ ⍟, at Sædding Strand, on a 150 sq. m (1,615 sq. ft.) area of the shore opposite the fishing museum (see below). These concrete figures, gazing out across the mysterious sea, are 79m (259 ft.) high. They sit upright like Greek columns. The four figures are completely alike, radiating a kind of classical beauty. The images evoke the massive monuments of ancient Egypt, perhaps something found in the Valley of the Kings.

Bogtrykmuseet (The Museum of Printing)   The largest working presswork museum in Denmark, it's built and furnished like a medium-size Danish printing office. Exhibits of printed work and presses trace the craft of printing through 500 years. You can see the process as it developed from handset type and printing on cumbersome manpowered presses to today's fast, accurate production with state-of-the-art equipment.

Borgergade 6. ℂ **75-12-78-11**. Admission 30DKK ($5) adults, free for children. Tues–Fri 1–4pm; Sat–Mon noon–4pm. Bus: 1, 5, 6, 8, or 9.

Esbjerg Kunstmuseum (Esbjerg Art Museum)   The city's museum of art focuses both on its permanent collection and on constantly changing exhibitions of contemporary art, mainly from Europe. The museum is one of the finest in Denmark for displaying the works of the country's artists. Outstanding artists on exhibit include Richard Mortensen, Robert Jacobsen, and Per Kirkeby. The museum lies in the central park area of the city.

Havnegade 20. ✆ **75-13-02-11.** Admission 40DKK ($6.70) adults, 35DKK ($5.85) seniors, free for children under 19. Daily 10am–4pm.

Esbjerg Museum   From the train and bus station, follow the signs for less than a kilometer (about ½ mile) to this museum, off Torvegade. It tells the story of amber, called "the Danish gold." The museum exhibits hundreds of amber objects, some nearly 10,000 years old. The west coast of Jutland is famed for its amber, and the museum tells how amber was gathered over the centuries, and how people have used it from the Mesolithic Age until today. A Viking Age exhibition is also presented.

Torvegade 45. ✆ **75-12-78-11.** Admission 30DKK ($5) adults, free for children under 16; free for all Wed. Tues–Sun 10am–4pm. Closed Jan 1, June 5, and Dec 24–25. Bus: 1, 5, 6, 8, or 9.

Fiskeri-og-Søfartsmuseet, Salt-Vandsakvariet & Sælarium (Museum of Fishing & Shipping)   Lying 4km (2½ miles) northwest of the city center, this unusual attraction is an aquarium containing some 50 species of fish. There's an outdoor sea pool where you can attend seal feedings at 11am and 2:30pm daily. Down below you can watch the antics of the seals underwater and through glass.

Tarphagvej 2. ✆ **76-12-20-00.** Admission 75DKK ($13) adults, 35DKK ($5.85) children. July–Aug daily 10am–6pm; Sept–June daily 10am–5pm. Bus: 1, 3, or 8.

SHOPPING

Esbjerg is the major city for shopping in South Jutland. Everything from fresh food and delicacies to fashion and decorative art is found along **Torvegade,** a main shopping thoroughfare. If you don't find it here, chances are Esbjerg doesn't sell it. The other major shopping venue is **Kongensgade,** one of the biggest centers for shopping in West Jutland, with some 156 specialty shops. If you're planning to do a lot of picture taking in South Jutland, replenish your camera supplies at **PhotoCare,** Kongensgade 21 (✆ **75-13-50-44**).

WHERE TO STAY
EXPENSIVE

Hotel Hjerting ★ *(Finds)*   One of the most appealing hotels in Esbjerg lies 6.5km (4 miles) northwest of the center, a short walk from the beach, at the top of a rocky seawall that breaks up the power of destructive waves during storms. Capped with a red roof and painted the traditional yellow of a Danish *kro,* it was built in 1898, and expanded in 1987 and again in 1992 with two additional extensions and wings containing traditionally furnished, spacious, and comfortable rooms with medium-size bathrooms equipped with shower units. Today, most clients come here to unwind from urban stress and experience the sea, either through swimming during mild weather or by gazing over its surface from the hotel's terraces or from either of its highly recommended restaurants.

The more formal restaurant is the **Strandpavilion,** where chefs focus on fresh ingredients, seasonal variety, and Danish and French traditions. Less formal, and cheaper, is the cozy, brick-and-wood–sheathed **Ship Inn,** an English-style pub. Both are open daily, year-round, for lunch and dinner.

Strandpromenaden 1, DK-6710 Esbjerg V. ✆ **75-11-70-00.** Fax 75-11-76-77. www.hotelhjerting.dk. 48 units. 995DKK–1,095DKK ($166–$183) double; 1,395DKK ($233) suite. Rates include breakfast. AE, DC, MC,

V. Bus: 3 from Esbjerg. **Amenities:** Restaurant; bar; room service (7am–10pm); laundry service; dry cleaning; nonsmoking rooms. *In room:* TV, dataport, minibar, hair dryer.

Hotel Scandic Olympic Esbjerg ⚡ Built in a bulky, boxy-looking, four-story format in the 1970s, this is the largest hotel in Esbjerg center. Drawing on the experience of other Scandic hotels in other parts of Scandinavia, it's the best bet in the town center for clean, well-maintained accommodations with a blandly standardized, uncontroversial international flavor. Rooms are color-coordinated, conservatively modern, very comfortable, and often occupied by business travelers from other parts of Scandinavia. Each unit also has a well-kept bathroom with a tub/shower combination.

Both Danish and international food is served in the dining room, **Restaurant Scandic Olympic,** which offers a fixed-price two-course menu for 174DKK ($29). The restaurant is spacious, stylish, and formal, relying on good, well-trained chefs and market-fresh ingredients. There's also a cozy bar for relaxation.

Strandbygade 3, DK-6700 Esbjerg. ⓒ or fax **75-18-11-08.** www.scandic-hotels.com. 90 units. Late Aug to early June Sun–Thurs 1,225DKK ($205) double; mid-June to mid-Aug Sun–Thurs 775DKK ($129) double; Fri–Sat year-round 875DKK ($146) double. Rates include breakfast. AE, DC, MC, V. **Amenities:** Restaurant; bar; exercise room; sauna; 24-hr. room service; laundry service; dry cleaning; nonsmoking rooms; rooms for those with limited mobility; solarium. *In room:* TV, dataport (in some), minibar, coffeemakers (in some), hair dryer, trouser press, iron/ironing board.

MODERATE

Hotel Ansgar ⚡ Set behind an elaborate and dignified white-painted facade near the town's most centrally located square, this is Esbjerg's grande dame hotel, with a pedigree that goes back to the 1920s and architecture that evokes early-20th-century building styles. In 1997, it was radically renovated, and in some cases, walls were knocked out as a means of making some rooms bigger than they had been originally. Rooms are impeccably maintained, clean, cozy, and modern. Each contains a well-kept bathroom with a tub/shower combination. There's an appealing restaurant (see "Where to Dine," below). The hotel lies a 5-minute walk from the sea.

Skolegade 36, DK-6700 Esbjerg. ⓒ **75-12-82-44.** Fax 75-13-95-40. www.hotelansgar.dk. 53 units. Mon–Fri 875DKK–960DKK ($146–$160) double; Sat–Sun 690DKK ($115) double. Rates include breakfast. AE, DC, MC, V. **Amenities:** Restaurant; bar; 24-hr. room service; laundry service; dry cleaning; nonsmoking rooms. *In room:* TV, dataport, minibar.

Hotel Britannia One of the best hostelries in town for those seeking mid-priced lodgings, this four-story hotel was constructed in a bland format typical of the 1960s, but was enlarged, upgraded, and improved in 1985. The medium-size rooms with small, shower-only bathrooms are comfortable and outfitted in a traditional international modern style. On the premises is a decent restaurant serving standard international fare, with some Danish regional specialties.

Torvet, DK-6701 Esbjerg. ⓒ **75-13-01-11.** Fax 75-45-20-85. 79 units. June–Aug 898DKK ($150) double; Sept–May 1,248DKK ($208) double. Rates include breakfast. AE, DC, MC, V. **Amenities:** Restaurant; bar; room service (7am–10pm); babysitting; laundry service; dry cleaning; nonsmoking rooms; rooms for those with limited mobility. *In room:* TV, minibar, hair dryer.

INEXPENSIVE

Palads Hotel Cab Inn Although its accommodations are far from being the most plush or luxurious in town, the exterior of this hotel retains all the dignity and quirky stateliness it had when constructed in 1912, when it functioned as the most upscale and glamorous hotel in town. Today, numerous renovations and many, many stripping-downs of its original opulence have turned this "palace" into efficient, cost-effective lodgings. The larger and more gracious rooms are identified as "Palace Rooms" and lie near the front. The smaller, more bare-boned rooms are in back, and are known as Cab Inn rooms after the nationwide chain (the Cab Inns). Regardless of which category you select, there's something akin to the feel of a college dormitory about both, partly because of the Formica-sheathed extras that are durable but not glamorous, and a sense of budget-conscious living that pervades the place. All rooms have neatly kept shower-only bathrooms. Breakfast is the only meal served.

Skolegade 14, DK-6700 Esbjerg. ✆ **75-18-16-00.** Fax 75-18-16-24. www.cabinn.dk. 121 units. 630DKK–730DKK ($83–$96) double. Rates include breakfast. AE, DC, MC, V. Bus: 1 or 2. **Amenities:** Cafe; lounge; laundry service; dry cleaning; nonsmoking rooms; rooms for those with limited mobility. In room: TV, dataport, hair dryer, coffeemaker.

WHERE TO DINE

Papa's Cantina MEXICAN   It's clear that the locals appreciate the Mexican theme that dominates this place, using it as an excuse to really let down their hair and play at being faux Latinos. Outfitted with Mexican wall-hangings and rustic Mexican artifacts, it's one of the most consistently popular restaurants in town, thanks to a well-prepared roster of nachos, empanadas, tostadas, chimichangas, and tortillas. Recorded salsa and merengue music plays as you enjoy any of four kinds of margaritas (banana, lime, strawberry, and a mélange of fruits that the local Danes refer to as a "tutti-frutti") at a large bar that's positioned in the center of the dining room. Many clients head for the all-you-can-eat Mexican buffet, which includes both a salad bar and an ice-cream bar, the best value in town. On Friday and Saturday nights, midnight to 6am, the site is transformed into a dance club. Entrance is 40DKK ($6.70) on Friday and Saturday night.

Torvet. ✆ **75-13-08-00.** Main courses 78DKK–179DKK ($13–$30). All-you-can-eat Mexican buffet (available Mon–Thurs only) 129DKK ($22). MC, V. Daily noon–10pm.

Restaurant Ansgar DANISH/INTERNATIONAL   Set at the street level of the previously recommended hotel, this is a solidly reliable, eminently respectable restaurant that has at one time or another received visits from virtually every politician or businessperson in the region. High-ceilinged and formal-looking, it offers dishes that include clear soup with meatballs, shrimp cocktail with home-baked bread, French-style steaks sizzled in butter sauce, Indian-style curried chicken, chateaubriand with morels, and, for dessert, a medley of ice creams and pastries made on the premises. The cooking is dependable and the ingredients are fresh, but the kitchen rarely creates any culinary excitement.

In the Hotel Ansgar, Skolegade 36. ✆ **75-12-82-44.** Reservations recommended. Main courses 80DKK–165DKK ($13–$28). AE, DC, MC, V. Daily 11:30am–2pm and 5:30–9:30pm.

Restaurant Pakhuset (Finds DANISH   The red-brick building was constructed in 1902 as an auction hall for the tons of fish hauled from nearby waterways. Set a few paces from the ferries that depart for Fanø, the building (whose name means "warehouse") now functions as a restaurant and art gallery. In a heavily trussed and beamed interior similar to that of a high-ceilinged chapel, paintings by Danish artists are displayed. Launch yourself with a summer salad with a confit of baby onions, going on to a perfectly prepared Danish filet of veal with an essence of basil, or perhaps steamed filets of fjord salmon with red bibb lettuce. Many Danes prefer to end their repast with a selection of Danish or eastern French cheeses; others request something from the dessert trolley, perhaps an assortment of chocolates perfumed with essence of orange and orange zest, often garnished with the sorbets of the day.

Dokvej 3. ℭ **75-12-74-55.** Reservations required. Main courses 60DKK–190DKK ($10–$32); 3-course fixed-price menu 298DKK ($50). AE, DC, MC, V. Tues–Sat noon–3pm and 6–10pm.

Sands Restaurant ✿ DANISH   One of the oldest—and also one of the best—restaurants in Esbjerg was founded in 1907. You get not only an excellent cuisine here but also the same pleasure enjoyed by visiting an art gallery. The owners cover the walls with dozens of works of art by leading and aspiring painters from West Jutland. These paintings add to the cozy atmosphere of this intimate and softly lit place. Local specialties, most often seafood, are featured on the menu, with those delectable Danish open-faced sandwiches being the most preferred orders at lunchtime. During our most recent visit, our sautéed halibut came in a sweet-and-sour sauce and was a tasty choice indeed. Unusual dishes often appear, including, for example, ostrich steak that has been marinated in a savory brew before being cooked and served in a red wine sauce. Fried filet of plaice is the fish of choice for most diners. It can be served either with smoked salmon and spinach in a cream sauce or else with prawns and fresh asparagus. *Frikadeller,* those ping-pong ball sized meatballs, are always featured, as are some tasty pork rissoles. A slice of lightly salted, tender beef appears in summer with fresh cabbage in a white sauce.

Skolegade 60. ℭ **75-12-02-07.** Reservations required. Main courses 90DKK–165DKK ($15–$28). MC, V. Mon–Sat 11am–10pm.

ESBJERG AFTER DARK

If there's a major cultural event being presented in Esbjerg—ballet, opera, or whatever—its venue will be the stunningly designed **Musikhuset Esbjerg,** Havnegade 18 (ℭ **76-10-90-00**). The tourist office (see "Visitor Information," earlier in this chapter) will have complete details of what (if anything) will be presented at the time of your visit. The chalk-white tiled building—the work of Jørn and Jan Utzon—rises up like some huge, tempting lump of sugar in the old city park area between the main square and the waterfront. Jørn was the architect of the world-famous Sydney Opera House. Jan, his son, is also an architect.

The city boasts several symphony orchestras, and the Esbjerg Ensemble presents numerous concerts throughout the year. On a number of Wednesdays in summer, city officials offer free entertainment under an open sky (the tourist office will have details).

Rock and jazz concerts, along with theatrical performances, are also presented at **Multihus Tobaksfabrikken,** Gasværksgade 2 (ℭ **75-18-02-22**), a spectacular mecca seating an audience of 750. Musical events are presented here year-round, with ticket prices depending on the different shows booked here.

A pub that can provide conversation and diversion for a while is **You'll Never Walk Alone,** Kongensgade 10 (ℭ **75-45-40-60**), which celebrates Esbjerg's close ties with Britain and Ireland, thanks to English and Celtic folk musicians who sometimes appear here. Also, don't forget to indulge in a little dance fever, beginning at midnight on Fridays and Saturdays, within the premises of what was previously recommended as a restaurant, **Papa's Cantina,** Torvet (ℭ **75-13-08-00**). Cover charges rarely exceed 30DKK ($5), and the Cantina attracts as hard-core a crowd of nightlife addicts as Esbjerg can provide.

WALKING TOURS IN MARBÆK ✿

Eleven kilometers (7 miles) north of Esbjerg between Ho Bay and the Varde River is the scenic Marbæk area, spread over 1,315 hectares (3,249 acres). This area is now a designated a nature reserve. The name first appears in the 17th century, but it wasn't until the beginning of the 20th century that interest was shown in this wide, desolate stretch of heath where all traces of the original forests have long disappeared. In 1904, a local barrister, E. M. Hansen, began to plant trees, and today these woodlands cover 455 hectares (1,124 acres) of the total. Trees range from sitka spruce to different types of pine.

During the last Ice Age, waters of the melting snows of the Arctic spring largely leveled the area. Up until around the time of Christ, the North Sea came right into the mainland. But gradually the sea deposited new sand flats along the coast. In time Ho Bay was formed, and the cliffs of Marbæk became relatively sheltered.

In a relatively small space one can view many different species of plants, such as lyme grass, sea purslane, sea milkwort, and the stalkless obione. The area ranges from dry crowberry heath to swampy heath. Gorse is also found. Wildlife abounds here, notably foxes, deer, hares, kestrels, and the common buzzard, along with pheasants, snipe, and sparrow hawks. In the spring by the lakes and ponds you can see web-footed birds such as the pochard, tufted duck, mute swan, coot, and moorhen.

The best trails to follow are named after colors. The red trail, called the *Strandtur* (beach trail), is 5km (3.1 miles) long and takes about 90 minutes to walk. The trail starts on the beachfront at Hjerting. The green trail, called the *Nordturen* (north trail), is 5km (3.1 miles) long and also takes about 90 minutes to walk. It starts at the parking area, called Pax. The blue trail, or *Søtur* (sea trail), is 4km (2.5 miles) long and takes about 70 minutes to walk. This trail runs from the parking area near Marbækgård. The yellow trail, called *Skovtur* (woodland trail), is also 4km (2.5 miles) long and also takes about 70 minutes to walk. This trail starts at the parking lot in the middle of Marbæk plantation.

GETTING THERE   By Car   From Esbjerg you can drive in the direction of Oksbol along a road called Vestkystvejen as far as the Varde River, or along the coast road through Hjerting and Sjelborg, then take minor roads (signposted) into the area itself. Bus no. 8 also runs here from Esbjerg.

7 Fanø ★★

47km (29 miles) NW of Ribe; 282km (176 miles) W of Copenhagen

Off the coast of South Jutland, this is one of the most beautiful North Sea islands. Consisting of a landmass of some 54 sq. km (21 sq. miles), with a population of 3,500, it is known for its white sandy beaches, which have made it a popular holiday resort in summer. In addition to its beaches, heath and dunes dominate the landscape. The best beaches are in the northwest, mostly in and around the hamlets of Rindby Strand and Fanø Bad.

Nordby, where the ferry arrives, is a logical starting point for exploring the island of Fanø. Here you'll find heather-covered moors, windswept sand dunes, fir trees, wild deer, and bird sanctuaries. From Ribe, Fanø makes for a great day's excursion (or longer if there's time).

Fanø is a popular summer resort among the Danes, Germans, and English. **Sønderho,** on the southern tip, and only 14km (8½ miles) from Nordby, with its memorial to sailors drowned at sea, is our favorite spot—somewhat desolate, but that's its charm.

It was a Dutchman who launched Denmark's first bathing resort at Nordby in 1851. It consisted of a raft on which some bathing huts had been set up. The bathers entered the huts, undressed, put on different clothes, pulled down an awning to the water's surface, and bathed under the awning.

Until 1741 Fanø belonged to the king, who, when he ran short of money, sold the island at auction. The islanders themselves purchased it, and the king then granted permission for residents to build ships, which led to its prosperity.

From 1741 to 1900, some 1,000 sailing vessels were constructed here, with the islanders often manning them as well. Inhabitants built many beautiful houses on Fanø with monies earned. Some of these charming, thatched Fanø homes stand today to greet visitors. There are some in the northern settlement of Nordby, but more in the south at Sønderho.

Although Nordby and Sønderho are the principal settlements, beach lovers head for the seaside resort of Fanø Bad. This is also a popular camping area. From Fanø Bad the beach stretches almost 4km (2½ miles) to the north. Bathing here is absolutely safe as a sandy bottom slopes gently into the North Sea. There are no ocean holes and no dangerous currents.

Fanø adheres to old island traditions almost more than any other island in Denmark. As late as the 1960s some of the elderly women on Fanø still wore the "Fanø costume," the traditional dress, although today you'll see it only at special events and festivals. This dress originally consisted of five skirts, but today's costumes are likely to have only three. When the skirt was to be pleated, it was wet, laced up, and sent to the baker, who steamed it in a warm oven.

ESSENTIALS

GETTING THERE   **By Car and Ferry**   From Ribe, head north on Route 11 to Route 24. Follow Route 24 northwest to the city of Esbjerg, where you can board a ferry operated by **Scandlines** (© **70-10-17-44;** www.scandlines.dk for information and schedules). May to October, ferries depart Esbjerg every 20 minutes during the day (trip time: 12 min.). In winter, service is curtailed, with departures during the day every 45 minutes. A round-trip ticket costs 30DKK ($5) adults or 15DKK ($2.50) children. One average-size car, along with five passengers, is carried for 325DKK ($54) round-trip.

VISITOR INFORMATION   The **Fanø Turistbureau,** Færgevej 1, Nordby (© **75-16-26-00**), is open Monday through Friday 8:30am to 5:30pm, Saturday 9am to 1pm, and Sunday 11am to 1pm, except from June 6 to August 23, when hours are Monday through Friday 8:30am to 6pm, Saturday 9am to 7pm, and Sunday 9am to 5pm.

GETTING AROUND   **By Bus**   Local buses meet passengers at the ferry dock. They crisscross the island about every 40 minutes, with vastly curtailed service in winter. The bus will take you to the communities of Nordby in the north and Sønderho in the south, with stops at Rindby Strand and Fanø Bad. For information, call **Fanø Rutebiler** at Sønderho (© **75-16-40-10**). The tourist office also keeps a bus timetable.

By Bicycle   Many visitors like to explore Fanø by bike. Bikes, costing from 60DKK ($10) per day, can be rented at **Unika Cykler,** Mellemgaden 12 (© **75-16-24-60**).

SPECIAL EVENTS   A summer highlight on Fanø is the **Fannikerdagene festival,** the second weekend in July, which offers traditional dancing, costumes, and events connected with the days when sailing ships played a major part in community life.

If you miss the festival, try to be on Fanø the third Sunday in July for **Sønderho Day.** The high point of the festival day is a wedding procession that passes through the town to the square by the old mill. Traditional costumes and bridal dances are some of the attractions.

SEEING THE SIGHTS

Most explorations of the island begin where the ferry docks at the settlement of Nordby. While here, and before setting out to explore the rest of Fanø, you can stop in at the **Fanø Skibsfarts-og Dragtsamling** (Fanø Shipping & Costume Collection), Hovedgaden 28 (℃ **75-16-22-72**). The museum traces the maritime heyday of the island in the 19th century, its boom period. You'll learn that Fanø at the time had the largest fleet outside of Copenhagen. Exhibits reveal that husbands often left their families for years at a time for a life at sea. The maritime collection incorporates many ship models, details of Fanø's fleet, and displays depicting a sailor's life aboard ship and in port. The costume collection shows both the working dress of the island women and those special costumes they wore for festivals. May to September, the museum is open daily 11am to 4pm. Off season, it's open Monday through Saturday 11am to 1pm. Admission is 15DKK ($2.50) adults and 5DKK (85¢) children under age 12.

Housed in a 300-year-old building, another interesting museum at Nordby is the **Fanø Museum,** Skolevej 2 (no phone). This museum houses a comprehensive collection of period furniture, utensils, tools, and other island artifacts. There's also an exotic collection of mementos sailors have gathered on their voyages. The museum is open in June, Monday through Saturday 10am to 1pm, and July and August, Monday through Friday 11am to 4pm and Saturday 10am to 1pm. In September it's open Monday through Friday 10am to 1pm. Admission is 15DKK ($2.50) adults, 5DKK (85¢) children under age 12.

Near the most southerly tip of the island, in the settlement of Sønderho, you can visit what's often called the island's most beautiful building, **Sønderho Kirke,** Strandvejen (℃ **75-16-40-32**), open daily during daylight hours. The church has a strong maritime influence—in fact, it displays 14 votive ships, more than any other church in Denmark. The baroque altarpiece dates from 1717, the pulpit from 1661, and the organ loft with a painting from 1782. This is an assembly-hall church, seating some 800 members of a congregation. There's no charge for admission.

While at Sønderho you can also visit **Fanø Kunstmuseum,** Norland 5 (℃ **75-16-40-44**). In 1992 this museum opened in Kromanns Hus, a former store and factory. The old shop dating from 1868 has been restored and now serves as the entrance to the museum. Fanø attracted a number of artists who moved here, and this museum showcases the most outstanding of their work. The collection is based on pictures first assembled by Ruth Heinemann, who founded an art association on Fanø. The aim of the museum is to show art inspired by the Frisian coast, past and present, with both permanent and temporary exhibitions. April 3 to October, the museum is open Tuesday through Sunday 2 to 5pm. Admission is 25DKK ($4.20) adults, 15DKK ($2.50) children under age 12.

Less than half a kilometer (¼ mile) north of Sønderho, on the road to Nordby, stands the **Sønderho Mølle,** Vester Land 44 (no phone), a restored windmill. Once islanders were obliged to use the crown's mill at Ribe, but in 1701 they received permission to construct one here. Several mills have stood on this site since then. One burned down in 1894 but was replaced by another the following year, which was in use until 1923. A preservation-minded group purchased the mill in 1928 and restored it. It's open to the public June 26 to August 29 and during October, daily 3 to 5pm; and from August 30 to September 30, Wednesday, Saturday, and Sunday 3 to 5pm. Admission is 15DKK ($2.50) adults, 5DKK (85¢) children under age 12.

Hannes Hus, Østerland 7 (© **75-16-44-29**), is one of the most typical of old Fanø structures, and it's in Sønderho, which contains Denmark's highest proportion of protected buildings. Hannes Hus faithfully maintains the atmosphere of a 17th-century captain's home. Hanne, a captain's widow, and her daughter, Karen, lived here until 1965, when it was acquired by the Village Trust. Inside are original furnishings, a stove, pictures, a sheep stable, and souvenirs from the captain's travels. Here's your chance to see what a Fanø sailor's private home looked like. It's open July and August, daily 3 to 5pm and in September, Saturday and Sunday 3 to 5pm. Admission is 15DKK ($2.50) adults, 5DKK (85¢) children under age 12.

SHOPPING

For an antiques store, combined with a flea market, head for **Vestergårdens Antik,** Vestervejen 47 (© **75-16-68-00**), also at Nordby.

For the best collection of the tiles for which the island is known, head for **Den lille butik,** Landevejen 3 (© **75-16-43-58**), at Sønderho. You'll also find an array of exquisite silk items, many of them handmade, at **Jane Heinemann,** Landevejen 15 (© **75-16-42-90**), also at Sønderho. An art gallery at Sønderho, **Galleri Anne,** Østerland 15 (© **75-16-43-05**), is open in July and August, Monday to Friday noon to 3pm.

WHERE TO STAY

Fanø Krogaard ★ This old-fashioned inn has welcomed wayfarers ever since 1624. Located 90m (295 ft.) from the ferry dock, its rooms are simple but comfortable. They come equipped with a well-kept bathroom with a tub/shower combination. The inn has the best food on the island; main dishes cost 60DKK to 150DKK ($10–$25). The restaurant is open May to September, Monday to Thursday and Sunday noon to midnight, Friday and Saturday noon to 1am; October to April, Monday to Thursday 3 to 11pm, Friday 3pm to midnight, Saturday noon to midnight, Sunday noon to 11pm. There are also a popular bar, open daily from 8am to midnight, and a terrace that's used in the summer.

Langelinie 11, Nordby, DK-6720 Fanø. © **75-16-20-52.** Fax 75-16-23-00. www.fanokrogaard.dk. 11 units, 9 with bathroom. Apr–Oct 595DKK–795DKK ($99–$133) double, 995DKK ($166) suite; Nov–Mar 495DKK–695DKK ($83–$116) double, 895DKK ($149) suite. Rates include breakfast. MC, V. Free parking. **Amenities:** Breakfast room; lounge. *In room:* Hair dryer.

Hotel Fanø Badeland This hotel takes no chances with the quite likely possibility that fog or rain might ruin the swimming. Although it sits on Fanø's western edge, close to one of the best beaches on the island, it has the added benefit of a glass-enclosed complex of indoor pools creating an impressive array of year-round swimming options. Located 3.2km (2 miles) south of the hamlet of Nordby, it was built amidst windswept scrubland. Rooms are urban-looking, minimalist, and angular, with clean shower-only bathrooms and small kitchenettes nestled into the corners of the living rooms. Each has either one or two bedrooms outfitted with simple, durable furniture and no-nonsense accessories. You'll pay an additional 55DKK ($7.20) per person for a package containing sheets and towels, unless you opt to bring your own.

Strandvejen 52–56, DK-6720 Fanø. © **75-16-60-00.** Fax 75-16-60-11. www.fanoebadeland.dk. 126 units, each with kitchenette. 795DKK–845DKK ($133–$141) 1-bedroom unit for up to 4 occupants; 845DKK–1,095DKK ($141–$183) 2-bedroom unit for up to 6 occupants. Discounts offered for stays of 5 nights or more. MC, V. Bus: 631. **Amenities:** Restaurant; bar; swimming complex; tennis court; fitness center; sauna; room service (8am–10pm); laundry service; dry cleaning. *In room:* TV.

Sønderho Kro ★★★   This is an unbeatable choice. The 1722 thatched-roof, ivy-covered inn, a National Trust House, nestles behind the sand dunes. Each room has a distinctive character, yet all suit the inn's traditional atmosphere. Antiques add a nice touch. The first-floor lounge offers views of the tidal flats. The dining room's cuisine is superb and plentiful; meals begin at 235DKK ($39) for three courses. Sønderho Kro is 13km (8 miles) south of the Nordby ferry dock; a bus connects with ferry arrivals.

Kropladsen 11, Sønderho, DK-6720 Fanø. ℂ 75-16-40-09. Fax 75-16-43-85. www.sonderhokro.dk. 14 units. 1,090DKK–1,410DKK ($182–$235) double. Rates include full breakfast. AE, DC, MC, V. Free parking. **Amenities:** Restaurant; lounge; room service (7am–10pm); laundry service; dry cleaning. *In room:* TV, hair dryer.

WHERE TO DINE

Café Nanas Stue ★ *Finds* DANISH   If it's a summer night and you're on Fanø, head to this 1855 half-timbered farmhouse for a rollicking good time. It's likely that a group of local musicians will be playing typical island music using such instruments as the harmonica and the bagpipe. You get not only entertainment, but a display of tiles as well. The cafe is also the site of the Fanø Tile Museum, and its walls and handmade wood cupboards are filled with Dutch blue-and-white tiles brought by Fanø sailors from the 1600s to the 1800s. Each tile depicts a representational scene, often taken from the Bible.

Wooden tables fill up with both islanders and visitors who come here to enjoy a typical Fanø kitchen that offers regional specialties. At lunch you can partake of those Danish open-faced sandwiches—count on three making a really satisfying meal. At night you can enjoy more elaborate fare such as a tender and perfectly cooked pepper steak topped with a cognac sauce. Other tasty dishes include shrimp and salmon with asparagus or else a "Paris steak" with such accompaniments as horseradish and capers. Most habitués finish off their repast by asking the bartender to make his specialty, which is a powerful *aquavit* ("water of life") flavored with coffee beans, vanilla, and orange zest.

Sønderland 1. ℂ 75-16-40-25. Reservations recommended. Main courses 95DKK–148DKK ($16–$25). MC, V. July–Sept Tues–Sat 11am–midnight, Sun 11am–5pm; off season Fri–Sun 5pm–midnight.

Fanø Krogaard ★★ DANISH   Set within 90m (295 ft.) of the point where ferryboats arrive from the Danish "mainland," this is one of the most historic inns on the island. Originally built of russet-colored bricks in 1624, with a well-deserved patina that has accumulated thanks to many generations of diners and drinkers, it offers three cramped but cozy dining rooms that specialize exclusively in Danish food. You'll find the usual array of herring, fried beef with onions, and roasted chicken you'd expect in such a conservative setting. But you'll also find a house specialty of roasted rack of veal with a cream sauce, fresh green beans, two kinds of potatoes, and a garnish that's a hollowed-out apple filled with red currant jelly. The food is good, filling, reasonably priced, well-prepared, and nutritious.

Langelinie 11, Nordby. ℂ 75-16-20-52. Reservations recommended. Main courses 50DKK–180DKK ($8.35–$30). MC, V. May–Sept Mon–Thurs and Sun noon–midnight, Fri–Sat noon–1am; Oct–Apr, Mon–Thurs 3–11pm, Fri 3pm–midnight, Sat noon–midnight, Sun noon–11pm.

Kromann's Fisherestaurant DANISH/GERMAN   In the heart of the village, near its famous church, this restaurant occupies a red-brick building originally constructed as a private house during the early years of World War I. Menu items include a wide roster of meats and fish, especially plaice and salmon, which the chef prepares in any of at least three different ways. There are also shrimp, crayfish, and fried eel served in the traditional way—with potatoes and parsley. The cookery is solid and reliable—nothing more, nothing less.

Kropladsen, Sønderho. ℂ **75-16-44-45**. Reservations recommended. Main courses 110DKK–170DKK ($18–$28). No credit cards. Easter–Oct daily 11am–midnight. Closed Nov–Easter.

Sønderho Kro ★★★ INTERNATIONAL   A Relais & Châteaux property, this is the most prestigious and elegant restaurant on the island. The setting is adjacent to the harbor within what was established as an inn in 1722; it has gained steadily in influence and glamour ever since. Your meal is likely to include some form of smoked fish, prepared in-house with smoke from juniper wood, in a custom-built oven whose construction was inspired by designs perfected by the Inuit of Greenland.

Only the best local produce is used by the hotel chefs, who make their own jams and preserves. You can purchase some of the hotel's products to take home—like strawberry jam with almonds and French black currant liqueur. All of their dishes are good, especially some of the best beef sausage you are likely to taste—it's smoked with juniper wood. A juniper schnapps sausage and a superb smoked leg of lamb are also likely to be offered. These meats are without artificial coloring and have a low-fat content. Move on to an array of perfectly prepared dishes, a splendid gourmet feast that comes as a surprise in a country inn. Save room also for one of the harmoniously composed desserts. The international wine list is no less delightful than the friendly, efficient service.

Kropladsen 11, Sønderho. ℂ **75-16-40-09**. Reservations necessary. Main courses 235DKK–255DKK ($39–$43); fixed-price menus 298DKK–378DKK ($50–$63). AE, DC, MC, V. Apr–Sept daily noon–2:30pm and 6–9pm; Oct–Mar Thurs–Tues noon–2:30pm and 6–9pm.

FANØ AFTER DARK

Your best bet is any event sponsored by the **Fanø Jazzklub,** Bavnebjergtoft 7 (ℂ **75-16-28-52**), at Fanø. The club has various events in summer. The tourist office will have a schedule. Tickets cost 75DKK ($13) and can be purchased at the door.

Don't expect glitter or glamour on Fanø, as virtually everyone who lives here seems to believe in honest industry and an early-to-bed kind of entertainment agenda. But in Nørdby, two possible contenders for your nightlife include the previously recommended **Fanø Krogaard,** Langelinie 11 (ℂ **75-16-20-52**), where a cozy bar with a cold-weather fireplace keeps you warm. In Sønderho, a worthwhile bar is **Nanas Stue** (ℂ **75-16-40-25**), a comfy and old-fashioned environment where the winds blowing in from the North Sea seem a lot less blustery, thanks to stiff drinks and friendly conversations.

10

Central Jutland

The central part of Jutland cuts across a broad swath of the country, extending from the gateway city of Fredericia in the south to Viborg and Limfjord (a large inland fjord) in the north. The east side of Central Jutland is more populous than the west, which is a wide plain of windswept moors bordered by a rugged coastline of beach flats and sand dunes.

Small farms and rich fertile land characterize the rolling hills of the central belt's eastern shores. But since the 19th century, much of the land in the west has also been reclaimed; great parts of it have been transformed into pastureland and fields against the competition of North Sea winds.

Central Jutland contains some of the most sparsely populated regions of Denmark, although it has cities too—notably Århus (the largest city in the region), as well as Silkeborg, Viborg, Randers, and others.

It is also one of the most hospitable regions of Denmark. Locals are proud of a landscape that ranges from wide expanses of heath to lovely fields of heather to charming, clean towns. Central Jutland also has some of the best beaches in Denmark, with vast stretches of white sand. Art museums, galleries, concerts, and beautiful old churches add to the allure.

The best and most interesting towns in east Central Jutland are Jelling, Vejle, and Århus. If you'd like to base your travels in the Lake District, favorite spots include Ebeltoft, Silkeborg, and Ry. In the interior, Randers and Viborg make the best stopovers, and if you want a base on the central west coast, make it Ringkøbing.

Jelling is one of the most historic spots in Denmark, and **Legoland** is Jutland's most visited attraction. The liveliest and most diverse cultural scene is found in Århus, Denmark's second largest city with some quarter of a million residents.

For rail and bus information to any town, call ✆ **70-13-14-15.**

1 Vejle ✸

199km (124 miles) W of Copenhagen; 72km (45 miles) SW of Århus; 30km (18½ miles) N of Kolding; 25km (15½ miles) NW of Fredericia

The thriving town of Vejle is near the top of the blue waters of Vejle Fjord and stands in an area of scenic beauty, with tall wooded slopes, dales, and deep gorges. Since ancient times, it's been something of a holiday resort.

Lying in a sheltered hollow, the city has a thriving economy based on exports of bacon, textiles, and chewing gum, among other products, as well as an ever-increasing tourist industry. Highway 3 goes through the town, and the railway also brings passengers and goods here.

Vejle is close to the coast of East Jutland, and lies north of Kolding and northwest of Fredericia. The entire Vejle region stretches from the Vejle Fjord through Grejsdalen to Jelling, going through the river valley of Vejle Ådal to Egtved. This area in Denmark is known for its beautiful, hilly countryside.

The town was granted its charter in 1327. But wars with Prussia hurt its economy, and Vejle suffered great hardship in the 1600s. In the 1820s the construction of a new harbor brought it increased prosperity. By that time, the making of *aquavit* (schnapps) played an important role in its economy. In the wars of the 19th century with Schleswig-Holstein in the south, Vejle was occupied several times by German troops. Until 1956, it was a garrison town.

ESSENTIALS

GETTING THERE   By Train   Trains arrive frequently throughout the day from Copenhagen, as Vejle is on the main Jutland line. The town also has good rail links to the other major towns in Jutland—it's only 45 minutes by rail to Århus or 35 minutes to Kolding.

By Car   If you've used Fredericia as your gateway to Central Jutland, follow Route 28 northwest into Vejle.

VISITOR INFORMATION   The **Vejle-engens Turistbureau,** Banegårdspladsen 6 (© 75-82-19-55; www.visitvejle.dk), is open June to August, Monday to Friday 9:30am to 5:30pm, Saturday 9:30am to 1:30pm; off season, Monday to Thursday 9:30am to 5pm, Friday 9:30am to 4:30pm, Saturday 9:30am to 12:30pm.

SEEING THE SIGHTS

Charming small squares, old houses, courtyards, and one of the most attractive pedestrian streets in the country provide the town center with a distinctive atmosphere. Even from the center of town, there are views of the blue waters of Vejle Fjord and its forest-clad hills.

Vejle Kunstmuseum, Flegborg 16 (© 75-82-43-22), founded in 1899, is an art museum housing some 12,000 prints and drawings, including foreign prints from 1450 to 1800. In addition, there's a good collection of Danish paintings and sculpture—mostly from the 20th century. A variety of exhibitions is also mounted every year. Hours are Tuesday through Friday 10am to 3pm; admission is free.

Another notable attraction, **Vejle Museum,** Flegborg 18 (© 75-82-43-22), also founded in 1899, offers an exhibit called "Man and Nature—Archaeology in the Vejle Area." Other special exhibitions are also held here. The rest of its attractions, at Søndergade 14, trace the history of the town over the past 8 centuries, including medieval life, Vejle as a 17th-century theater of war, and Vejle as a 19th-century industrial town. The Flegborg address is open Tuesday through Sunday 10am to 4pm. The Søndergade 14 address is open April to October, Tuesday through Sunday 11am to 3pm. Admission is free at both.

Another intriguing attraction is **Sankt Nicolai Kirke,** Kirketorvet (© 75-82-41-39), a 10-minute walk from the tourist office. The Gothic church is one of the town's oldest buildings, its north wall dating back to the mid–13th century. The church contains one of Denmark's finest bog findings, an Iron Age woman from 450 B.C., discovered in the Haraldskaier bog in 1835. She can be seen through a glass-topped case. Many guidebooks report that this is the preserved body of the Viking queen, Gunhilde. However, recent scientific studies have shown that the corpse is much older, dating from the early Iron Age. The skulls of 23 beheaded robbers caught in the Nørreskoven woods some 3 centuries ago have been bricked into the outer north wall of the church. Special features of the church include a classical reredos (the screen behind the altar), the work of sculptor Jens Hiernoe in 1791, plus a 16th-century Renaissance pulpit

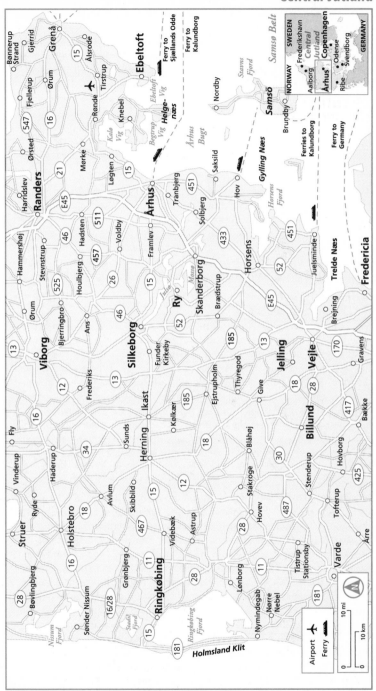

and a processional crucifix. It's open Monday through Friday 9am to 5pm, Saturday and Sunday 9am to noon. Admission is free.

For your farewell to Vejle, you can take a moving stairway in town up to the "mountain" known as **Munkebjerg,** to the southeast of Vejle. At an elevation of 90m (295 ft.), you'll enjoy a panoramic view of Vejle and the fjord. The yew— that most Scandinavian of trees—and other rare trees and plants can be seen here.

If you have a car, arm yourself with a good map (available at the tourist office) and explore **Grejsdalen,** 7km (4⅓ miles) from Vejle. This valley is one of Denmark's most beautiful areas, with densely wooded hillsides and many lookout points. The preserved part of the valley is also the home of a richly varied bird life. Near Grejs itself are some limestone deposits resembling cliff caverns.

SHOPPING

The main pedestrian street alone features more than 220 specialty shops, restaurants, and department stores, so there's a wealth of shopping opportunities here, more so than nearly any other place in Jutland.

The best and most sophisticated ceramics are sold at **Ulla Møller,** Havnegade 21 (© **75-83-71-21**). For a gift shop featuring local crafts, head to **Allehånde,** Søndergade 14 (© **75-83-83-66**). An intriguing collection of antiques is always on display at **Borring Antiques,** Grejsdalsvej 326A (© **75-85-34-00**).

WHERE TO STAY

Best Western Torvehallerne   Its construction in 1993 was viewed as a vital part of the success of the Torvehallerne—Vejle's largest conglomeration of cultural, dining, drinking, and nightlife facilities. Consequently, in any season or weather you'll be able to migrate from your room at this three-story hotel through the big-windowed, greenhouse-inspired spaces of the market hall for drinking, dining, or diversions of the kind you might expect in a mall in California (it really looks like a mall; see the picture on the website). Rooms are well maintained and comfortable, and contain simple, angular furnishings. All the accommodations have a private bathroom with a neatly tiled shower unit.

In the Torvehallerne, Kirketorvet 12, DK-7100 Vejle. © **800/528-1234** in the U.S., or 79-42-79-10. Fax 79-42-79-01. www.bestwestern.com. 43 units. 1,195DKK ($200) double. Rates include breakfast. AE, MC, V. **Amenities:** Restaurant; bar; 24-hr. room service; laundry service; dry cleaning; nonsmoking rooms; rooms for those with limited mobility. *In room:* TV, dataport, minibar, hair dryer.

Munkebjerg Hotel ★★   This is the most stylish and prestigious hotel in the region, with the most panoramic setting, and a professional and sensitive staff that's capable of dealing with delicate temperaments. South of the center, it sits in isolated but contemporary grandeur on a panoramic hilltop within the Munkebjerg Forest. Originally built in 1967, and renovated and enlarged many times since, it's the preferred stopover for clients as diverse as Little Richard and Chuck Berry, as well as the prime minister of Denmark. Expect dramatic, impeccably maintained public areas in a big-windowed and angular modern style, and very comfortable, soothing accommodations. Rooms are flooded with sunlight thanks to sliding glass windows, and offer private balconies overlooking the forest. The furniture is soft and comfortable, with deep cushions, and each bathroom has a tub and shower.

Munkebjergvej 125, DK-7100 Vejle. © **76-42-85-00.** Fax 75-72-08-86. www.munkebjerg.dk. 149 units. 1,395DKK–1,795DKK ($233–$300) double; 2,705DKK–3,450DKK ($452–$576) suite. Rates include buffet breakfast. AE, DC, MC, V. From Vejle's center, drive 7km (4⅓ miles) south, following the signs to Vejle Sid. **Amenities:** 3 restaurants; 2 bars; indoor heated pool; gym; sauna; room service (7am–10pm); babysitting; laundry service; dry cleaning; nonsmoking rooms; casino. *In room:* TV, dataport, minibar, hair dryer.

Quality Hotel Australia ★★★   This is one of the most modern and state-of-the-art hotels in Central Jutland, and the only government-rated four-star hotel in the Interscan chain. It rises 11 stories and is in a central location in the heart of town. Originally built in 1958, and radically upgraded in 1996, the hotel has a name that derives from its creator's fascination for Australia, thanks to the many trips he took there. As such, the hotel has (unofficially) spurred a flood of Danish visitors to Australia. Inside, you'll find all the amenities that several corporations would need to host simultaneous conventions. Public areas are spacious and modern. Rooms are larger than usual, clean, and well maintained with small bathrooms containing a shower. Surprisingly for a hotel of this size and stature, there is no swimming pool or health club.

Dæmningen 6, DK-7100 Vejle. ✆ **76-40-60-00.** Fax 76-40-60-01. www.choicehotels.com. 102 units. 990DKK–1,150DKK ($165–$192) double. Extra bed 200DKK ($33) all week long. Rates include breakfast. AE, DC, MC, V. **Amenities:** Restaurant; bar; exercise room; sauna; room service (7am–10pm); laundry service; dry cleaning; babysitting; nonsmoking rooms; 1 room for those with limited mobility. *In room:* TV, dataport, minibar, hair dryer, trouser press, iron/ironing board.

WHERE TO DINE

Restaurant Baghuset *Value* DANISH/INTERNATIONAL   Before it was transformed into this well-managed steakhouse, this address functioned as Vejle's community center, providing a grangelike meeting space whose walls and ceilings are massively trussed with heavy beams. Food items include several kinds of steak, each seasoned with your choice of sauces; roasted turkey and lamb; and such seafood as steamed or fried salmon, lobster, and trout. Every Friday and Saturday, 5:30pm to closing, the establishment's otherwise unused second floor is opened as a buffet with a meat carver on hand. It's one of the best weekend food values in town.

Dæmningen 42. ✆ **75-72-41-41.** Reservations recommended. Main courses 100DKK–179DKK ($17–$30); Fri–Sat buffet 169DKK–199DKK ($28–$33) per person. MC, V. Wed–Sun 5–11pm.

Treetops Restaurant ★★ DANISH/INTERNATIONAL   This restaurant in the previously recommended Munkebjerg hotel is celebrated throughout the region for its contemporary glamour and its devotion to fine cuisine. A meal is always prefaced with a guided tour of the establishment's wine cellar, where a glass of something tasty is part of the experience. After that, a table is prepared within a high-ceilinged room that's spanned with artfully arranged tree limbs that provide a cozy, forest-like tone. Menu items change frequently. Examples include lime-marinated salmon with sun-dried tomatoes and olives; crisp red snapper on summer lettuce, served with a frothy and whipped crayfish bouillon; or poached filets of sole with lobster and a tomato-flavored beurre blanc sauce. More substantial fare includes a succulent version of filet of lamb roasted with garlic and served with a lemon grass gravy, and tournedos of veal with ratatouille and balsamic vinegar. Dessert might be lemon tart with preserved rhubarb and Irish coffee ice cream or strawberry dessert with almond biscuits and vanilla ice cream. Finely balanced sauces are the highlights here.

In the Munkebjerg Hotel, Munkebjergvej 125. ✆ **76-42-85-00.** Reservations required. 4-course fixed-price menu 535DKK ($89); 8-course fixed-price menu 735DKK ($123). AE, DC, MC, V. Daily 6:30–9:30pm. From Vejle's center, drive 7km (4½ miles) south, following the signs to Vejle Sid and the Munkebjerg Hotel.

VEJLE AFTER DARK

At the **Casino Munkebjerg Vejle,** Munkebjergvej 125 (✆ **76-43-50-00**), you can play roulette, blackjack, the slot machines, and—if you're willing to learn—"Viking poker." A photo ID is required to gain entrance and there is an admission

Discovering a Viking Past

In the center of town, **Jelling Kirke** ⭐ (© **75-87-16-28**) was erected at the beginning of the 12th century, and is one of the oldest churches in Denmark. The church itself is interesting, but it's visited mainly because of its two well-preserved runic stones, which sit outside the door. You should look inside the church as well to see its restored 12th-century frescoes. Admission is free, and the church is open Monday through Friday 10am to 5pm, and Saturday 10am to 2pm. It's closed for visits on Sunday because of Mass. You can attend Mass then, but casual sightseeing in the church is discouraged when it's being used as a place of worship.

Both **Gorm the Old** (883–940) and his son, **Harald Bluetooth** (940–985), lived in Jelling and left behind two large burial mounds and two runic stones—one small, one large. The small stone bears the inscription "King Gorm made these sepulchral monuments to Thyra, his wife, the grace of Denmark." The large stone is inscribed "King Harald had these sepulchral monuments made to Gorm, his father, and Thyra, his mother, the Harald who conquered all Denmark and Norway and made the Danes Christians."

The latter part of the inscription has often been called Denmark's baptismal certificate, though this is something of an exaggeration. But King Harald and his people were undoubtedly converted to Christianity, even if it was a century before the country as a whole can be said to have become Christian.

The north's oldest depiction of Christ appears over this part of Harald's runic lettering. The Christlike figure appears with his arms spread

---

fee of 50DKK ($8.35). The major cultural venue for the city is the **Musik Theatret Vejle,** Vedelsgade 25–31 (© **79-43-20-20**), the setting for operas, musicals, shows, and theater. You can check with the tourist office (see "Visitor Information," above) to see if any events at the time of your visit appeal to you.

Also consider a visit to the complex **Torvehallerne,** Kirketorvet 10–16 (© **79-42-79-00**). A large, spacious palm garden, Væksthuset, forms the center of a complex that includes restaurants, a hotel, a cafe, a stage, and a pub. There is always something going on here—jazz, dancing under the palm trees, concerts, or theatrical performances. We can't predict what will be going on at the time of your visit, but it's always a lively place to drop in on at night.

Vejle is also a town rich in pub life, our favorites being **The Irish Cat Pub,** Nørregade 61 (© **75-72-38-00**), and **Seven Oaks,** an old English-style pub at Dæmningen 42G (© **75-72-07-77**). Another good choice is **Crazy Daisy** (a disco), Nørregade 65–67 (© **75-83-23-03**).

2 Jelling ⭐

11km (7 miles) NW of Vejle; 144km (90 miles) W of Copenhagen

This sleepy little village is historically important as the 10th-century seat of Danish kings Gorm the Old and Harald Bluetooth, Gorm's son. These two kings left behind two large burial mounds and two runic stones, known as the

out but without a cross. This may have been because the artist at the time wanted to depict Christ as a victorious Viking king—hence no cross. The significance of the other depiction on the stone isn't known. It shows a snake locked in deadly combat with a mythical animal. The stones, decorated in the typical Viking style, with interlacing leaf and creeper-work, were originally painted in bright colors.

Excavations of the two barrows began in 1820 when the north barrow was dug up. It revealed a burial chamber but no human remains, only a few objects and fragments, including a silver goblet, later dubbed the Jelling goblet. It's thought that grave robbers may have plundered the site over the years. In 1861 King Frederik VII, who had a keen interest in archaeology, excavated the south barrow, but it didn't even have a burial chamber. It is now believed that both Gorm and Thyra had been buried in the north mound and that the empty south barrow was merely a memorial mound.

In modern times, the area beneath the church was excavated, and archaeologists discovered the remains of three wooden churches. The oldest was King Harald's and was even bigger than the present Jelling Kirke, earning the nickname "the Cathedral of the Viking Age."

The discovery of a burial chamber beneath the choral arch revealed human bones, but they were in complete disorder, indicating that they had been moved. The skeletal remains are believed to be those of Gorm, which were probably moved over from the north mound when Harald became Christian. It has never been determined where Queen Thyra was reburied.

Jelling stones. They have provided crucial information about early Danish history. Although the village of Jelling enjoys idyllic surroundings, set against a backdrop of forest and lakes, it is visited mainly for its runic stones. In 1994 Jelling's Viking monuments were declared a World Heritage Site.

At the peak of the Viking era, a thousand years ago, Jelling was the Danish Royal Seat. Gorm is important in Danish history because the royal line began with him and proceeds unbroken to the present Danish monarch, Queen Margrethe. The line, though tortuous, is still intact.

ESSENTIALS

GETTING THERE By Train and Bus Jelling is a 20-minute train ride from Vejle on the run to Struer and Herning. Trains depart about once an hour Monday through Friday, less frequently on weekends. Connections are possible by bus no. 211 from Vejle's bus station.

By Car From Vejle, take Route A18 north. If you're using Fredericia as your gateway to Central Jutland, go to Vejle first, then continue into Jelling.

VISITOR INFORMATION Jelling Turistbureau, Gormsgade 23 (© 75-87-13-01; www.visitvejle.com), is open daily June to August, 10am to 5pm. At other times of the year, contact the tourist office at Vejle (see "Visitor Information," above).

WHERE TO STAY

Jelling Kro ⭐ *Value*   The most evocative and appealing hotel in town occupies the dignified yellow-fronted premises of what has functioned since 1780 as a *kro* (old-fashioned inn). Capped with a terra-cotta roof and positioned in the center of town, across from the country's most famous burial site, the hotel offers a well-recommended restaurant (see "Where to Dine," below). Each of the simple but clean rooms is slightly different from its neighbor, and most have a shared bathroom. If you opt to stay in this hotel, know in advance that you'll share it with good company. In 1842, just before an overnight visit from the Danish king, it was reclassified as 1 of only about 30 hotels in Denmark suitable then and thereafter for overnight visits from a Danish monarch.

Gormsgade 16, DK-7300 Jelling. ℂ 75-87-10-06. Fax 75-87-10-08. 6 units, all without bathroom. 495DKK ($83) double. Rates include breakfast. AE, MC, V. Bus: 214. **Amenities:** Restaurant. *In room:* TV, no phone.

WHERE TO DINE

Jelling Kro DANISH   The most appealing restaurant in Jelling is in the previously recommended hotel. The dining room is much more modern than the historic setting would imply. Menu items usually stress fish that's parceled out into several kinds of platters, served either as a starter or in a more elaborate form as a main course configured into a "symphony of fish." Although the composition of each platter changes according to availability, you can almost always expect an emphasis on marinated salmon and fresh shrimp. Other excellent dishes include cream of leek soup with bacon, tournedos of beef garnished with mushroom stew and potato dish of the day, or breast of chicken with white wine sauce.

Gormsgade 16. ℂ 75-87-10-06. Reservations recommended. Main courses 110DKK–175DKK ($18–$29); fixed-price menus 130DKK–150DKK ($22–$25). AE, MC, V. Sept–May Wed–Sun 5–9pm; June–Aug daily 5–9pm.

---

3 Billund ⭐ & Legoland ⭐⭐

228km (142 miles) W of Copenhagen; 59km (36½ miles) NE of Esbjerg; 27km (17 miles) W of Vejle

The "Disneyland of Denmark," Legoland, an amusement park less than a kilometer (about ½ mile) north of the small Central Jutland town of Billund, is the second most visited tourist attraction in the country, after Tivoli in Copenhagen. Since it opened in 1968, some 27 million visitors from around the world have arrived. It can be a lot of fun if you're traveling as a family. Adults exploring Denmark without children in tow might want to seek other diversions (unless of course, they are hardcore Lego aficionados).

ESSENTIALS

GETTING THERE   By Plane   Planes fly into **Billund Airport,** just across the road from Legoland—a 5-minute walk from the arrival lounge to the park. **SAS** (ℂ **800/221-2350** in North America, or 70-10-20-20 in Billund; www.scandinavian.net) has frequent daily flights from Copenhagen (26 flights a week from Copenhagen). **Air Mærsk** (ℂ **70-10-74-74;** www.maerskair.dk) has direct flights from London, Stockholm, Frankfurt, Brussels, and Amsterdam to Billund.

By Bus   There is no train service. Rail passengers get off at Vejle (see earlier), then take a bus marked LEGOLAND for the final lap of the journey. In summer, more buses run from Vejle. There is also bus service from Esbjerg (ℂ **75-16-26-00**).

By Car   After crossing the bridge linking Funen and Jutland, continue northwest toward Vejle on the E20, linking up with Route 18, which connects with Route 28 going west into Billund.

VISITOR INFORMATION   The **Legoland/Billund Turistbureau** (© 76-50-00-55; www.visitbillund.dk) lies on the grounds of Legoland itself. From mid-June to the end of August, it's open daily 10am to 9pm. May to mid-June and September, it's open daily 10am to 6pm. It's closed October to April.

LEGOLAND ☆☆

Legoland theme park is constructed from—what else?—plastic Lego blocks. The greatest attraction is Castleland, which opened in 1997. Home to the King's Castle, a faux-medieval fairytale castle, it offers an action adventure ride on one of two 212-seat "dragons" that fly around this re-created world. On the upper floor is the Knight's Barbecue, a restaurant decorated with suits of armor and shields.

Miniland is the second major attraction, with miniature models of famous buildings and monuments from around the world. The entire medieval town of Ribe is re-created, for example, as is Amalienborg Castle in Copenhagen. Other thematic attractions in the park include Legoredo Town, a re-creation of a western town with an Indian camp and a sheriff's office, plus Pirateland, where you can take a boat trip through caves. There's even a Lego Safari, where children steer small zebra-striped jeeps on a ride through a faux savanna. There are dozens of amusement rides, mostly for children, including merry-go-rounds and Ferris wheels. All the rides, including the miniature train and boat trips, are included in one admission price.

April 1 to June 19 and August 31 to October 25, hours are daily 10am to 8pm; June 20 to August 30, daily 10am to 9pm. Admission is 180DKK ($30) for those over 14, or 160DKK ($27) for ages 3 to 13 (free for children age 2 and under). For more information, call © **75-33-13-33.**

WHERE TO STAY

Hotel Legoland *Kids*   This is the only hotel associated with Jutland's most famous theme park, and as such, it does a thriving summer business renting overnight accommodations to families with children. During the winter, the clientele shifts to more of a business-oriented crowd that checks in as part of an ongoing schedule of corporate conventions. It was originally built in 1968, and it's permeated with a Legoland theme. There are lots of Disney-style Legoland sculptures in the lobby, and a chipper and perky multilingual staff that's often preoccupied with the care, feeding, and amusement of children. Like everything else in Legoland, a bit of this goes a long way, especially if you happen to be traveling without children. Rooms have less of an emphasis on the Legoland theme than you'll find in the public areas. Suites are larger, and contain minibars. Each accommodation comes with a private bathroom—some with tub and shower, others with just shower. In 2004, the hotel opened up an additional wing with 22 new "Kids House rooms," ideal for families.

Aastvej 10, DK-7190 Billund. © 75-33-12-44. Fax 75-35-31-79. 176 units. 1,425DKK–1,465DKK ($238–$245) double; 2,425DKK–2,630DKK ($405–$439) junior suite. AE, DC, MC, V. Free shuttle bus to the hotel from the airport at Billund. **Amenities:** Restaurant; bar; gym; 24-hr. room service; laundry service; dry cleaning; non-smoking rooms. *In room:* TV, dataport, minibar (in suites), hair dryer, trouser press, iron/ironing board.

WHERE TO DINE

Le Petit ☆ DANISH/INTERNATIONAL   The creation of this restaurant in 1998 was part of Legoland's realization that its pervasive kiddie theme might have grown a bit tired among the corporate convention crowd that dominates its client roster throughout the winter. Consequently, you might be relieved to discover a mostly adult crowd in this attractively formal venue within the resort's only hotel. The decor is urbane and postmodern, and cuisine draws its inspiration from big-city venues. Don't expect a wide variety of menu items, as there might be only three or four starters, main courses, and desserts. Examples include roe of salmon garnished with red onions and sour cream, *Bündnerfleisch* (air-dried beef) with Parma ham served with exotic lettuces and marinated artichokes, a savory ragout of halibut and shellfish in a saffron sauce with wild rice, tuna steak with fresh spinach in a pasta basket on a bed of tomato sauce, and a succulent version of tenderloin of lamb with *Rösti* potatoes with rosemary-flavored gravy and glazed onions. One particularly delicious dessert is a chocolate basket filled with berries of the season and served with a Grand Marnier–flavored parfait. A drink within the Concorde Bar is a welcome preface to a meal here.

In the Hotel Legoland, Aastvej 10. (C) **75-33-12-44.** Reservations recommended. Lunch 60DKK–145DKK ($10–$24); main courses 165DKK–200DKK ($28–$33). AE, DC, MC, V. Daily 6–10pm.

4 Ringkøbing (★

320km (200 miles) W of Copenhagen; 9km (5⅓ miles) E of the North Sea; 85km (53 miles) W of Silkeborg

This old market town, lying on the north side of the lagoon-like Ringkøbing Fjord, is the seat—albeit tiny, with only 9,000 inhabitants—of the regional government. Its oldest known municipal charter dates from 1443, but the earliest archaeological finds establish its origins some time around the mid–13th century. At that time there was no outlet from the western end of Liim Fjord to the North Sea, so Ringkøbing Fjord was the only natural harbor in the area. It became one of the most important harbor cities on the west coast of Denmark with trading links extending to Norway, Germany, and Holland.

In time, though, especially during the 17th century, the approach at Nymindegab began to fill with sand and move south. With the opening of the West Jutland trunk line in 1875, shipping for Ringkøbing stopped almost immediately, leaving the town to reinvent itself. It wasn't until a lock at Hvide Sande was constructed in 1931 that Ringkøbing was once again assured of a passage to the North Sea. However, its role as a port for ships was never to return to its former glory. It did, however, become the first small town in Denmark to provide free universal education.

That falloff in commerce is what has probably kept Ringkøbing looking as old-fashioned and splendid as it does today. The townspeople also have a lively, cooperative spirit. For example, they have a beachcombing event to clean the town's 11km (6¾ miles) of coastline to ensure that the blue flags (symbol of unpolluted waters) fly over their beaches in summer.

ESSENTIALS

GETTING THERE   By Train   Ringkøbing lies on the main DSB rail lines between Esbjerg (trip time: 1¼ hr.) and Struer (1 hr.).

By Car   From Silkeborg (see later in this chapter), continue west along Route 15 into Ringkøbing.

VISITOR INFORMATION   Ringkøbing Turistbureau, Torvet ((C) **97-32-00-31;** www.ringkobingfjord.dk), is open mid-June to August, Monday to Friday 9am to 5pm, Saturday 10am to 2pm. September to mid-June, it's open Monday to Friday 9:30am to 5pm and Saturday 10am to 1pm.

GETTING AROUND   By Bicycle   The surrounding scenic flatlands are ideal for cyclists. Bikes can be rented at **Børgensen Cykler,** Nørredige ((C) **97-32-36-01**). Bicycles rent for 50DKK–60DKK ($8.35–$10) per day.

SEEING THE SIGHTS

Ringkøbing's townscape takes its characteristic look from houses mostly built from 1700 to 1800. The dominant building style—dark red houses with white cornices and semihipped rooftops—developed in the late 18th century. Ringkøbing's leading citizens were its merchants, whose large houses lined the narrow streets, particularly Algade and Østergade. Some have remained in a well-preserved condition, notably the addresses of Nørregade 2 and Algade 4–6. Much effort still goes into preserving Ringkøbing's pleasant old-town atmosphere, and a walk through the town's narrow cobblestone streets brings its own reward.

If you're standing at the *Torvet* (marketplace) seeking a way to the harbor, the obvious choice is **Vester Strandgade.** This is an old street whose earliest homes date from the early 1800s. The street was always known for its merchants, including a plumber, butcher, baker, grocer, and shoemaker, as well as a bike shop and inn. You can still smell fresh bread from the local bakery and can stop for a delicious Danish pastry at a coffee shop.

At the harbor you'll see a facility dating from 1904. This was a bustling fishing harbor until Ringkøbing lost out to Hvide Sande to the south. Today, the harbor is used mainly by pleasure craft and fjord fishing boats. Fishers from the fjords land their fish here at the harbor and every day at 9:30am hold an auction in a red wooden building at the harbor's edge. Everything from salmon, trout, flounder, perch, and eel to sea trout is sold here to the highest bidder.

At the edge of the town center, **Alkjær Lukke** is a lovely park, idyllic for a picnic lunch. Ducks quacking in the pond tell you they want to be fed. In the airy beech wood the forest floor is covered with wood anemones, buttercups, and lilies of the valley. It's a nice place to stop and enjoy the silence.

The town's main attraction—other than the town itself—is **Ringkøbing Museum Østerport,** Herningvej 4 (© **97-32-16-15**). A few blocks east of the Torvet, this museum is a virtual attic of local history, including coins and ecclesiastical artifacts, ships' figureheads, and even pictures of stranded ships in the North Sea. Someone at the museum is likely to show you what a chastity belt from 1600 looked like. We find the most intriguing exhibits to be those devoted to Ludwig Mylius-Erichsen (1872–1907), who led an expedition to Greenland in 1906. Regrettably, he died on the return journey. July and August, the museum is open daily 11am to 5pm; September to June, Monday through Thursday 11am to 4pm, and Saturday and Sunday 1 to 4pm. It's closed Friday during off season. Admission costs 30DKK ($5) adults, 10DKK ($1.65) children 8 to 12, free for children 7 and under.

SHOPPING

Some of the town's most sophisticated ceramics are sold at **Keramikkens Hus,** Ndr. Ringvej 14 (© **97-33-14-01**).

One of the most intriguing shopping prospects is not in Ringkøbing itself, but directly south of the town at the hamlet of Stauning. Follow the secondary road along the east side of Ringkøbing Fjord until you come to the village where you'll see a sign indicating **Bousøgaard,** Bousøvej 6, Stauning (© **97-36-91-72**). This is an old thatched West Jutland farm with four wings. The attractive barn is an art gallery, the biggest in West Jutland, with oils, graphics, and sculptures by well-known Danish artists. There's also an on-site potter's workshop, where the old potter's craft is still practiced. Next to the workshop is a museum of Danish decorated pottery from the 1800s to about 1950. Hours are Monday to Saturday 11am to 5pm.

WHERE TO STAY

Hotel Fjordgården ★ *Kids*   The best hotel in Ringkøbing lies less than a half-kilometer (about ¼ mile) north of the town center, on sandy flatlands 8 kilometers (5 miles) from the coast. Built in 1967 in a sprawling, generously proportioned format with between one and two stories, white walls, and a prominent brown roof, it has the most comfortable accommodations—and better dining—than any other hotel in town. Rooms are good size with firm beds, small but spanking-clean bathrooms (with tub and shower), and big windows that grant views over the surrounding land and seascape. Many of the units are large enough to use as family rooms. The hotel boasts an indoor subtropical water land, with spa, sauna, children's pool, and water slide.

Vesterkær 28, DK-6950 Ringkøbing. ✆ 800/528-1234 in the U.S., or 97-32-14-00. Fax 97-32-47-60. www. hotelfjordgaarden.dk. 98 units. 1,225DKK ($205) double; 1,525DKK ($255) suite. AE, DC, MC, V. **Amenities:** Restaurant; bar; indoor heated pool; gym; spa; sauna; room service (7am–10pm); laundry service; dry cleaning; nonsmoking rooms; solarium. *In room:* TV, minibar, hair dryer, coffeemaker.

Hotel Ringkøbing   Set on a cobble-covered square in the heart of town, near a quartet of linden trees, this is the second-oldest hotel in Jutland, established in its present format in 1833. The hotel is cozy but somewhat kitschy. Rooms are banal, even a bit dowdy, thanks to overly frilly bedcovers and clumsy attempts at gussying up relatively plain spaces. Two are in a nearby annex, and all units contain a private bathroom with shower. On the premises are an English-style pub serving lots of suds and occasional live rock-'n'-roll sessions and a restaurant that looks like it hasn't been redecorated since the 1960s.

Torvet 18, DK-6950 Ringkøbing. ✆ 97-32-00-11. Fax 97-32-18-72. www.hotelringkobing.dk. 27 units. 795DKK–995DKK ($133–$166) double; 1,195DKK ($200) suite. Rates include breakfast. AE, MC, V. **Amenities:** Restaurant; bar; gym; laundry service; dry cleaning. *In room:* TV.

WHERE TO DINE

Restaurant Helten ★ DANISH/INTERNATIONAL   This is the showplace dining room of the only government-rated four-star hotel in Ringkøbing, and as such, you're likely to receive more internationally conscious culinary finesse, and more diligent service than elsewhere in town. Within a very modern dining room with a view of the dunes and the sea, you'll find a lunch venue centered around one of the most appealing buffets in town. Look for a savory collection of soups, salads, open-faced sandwiches, Danish cheeses, smoked meats and fish, seasonal berries, and pastries. Dinners are more elaborate. We highly recommend, when it's available, a platter of smoked *helten* (a small, herring-shaped fish that's the restaurant's namesake). Found only in the nearby fjord, and traditionally served salted or smoked, it's prized as one of the unusual delicacies of Denmark. Among the menu items we've enjoyed here is fried North Sea plaice with brown butter or else the fresh salmon cutlet with vegetables, pasta, and herb butter. Also delectable is the guinea fowl with mushroom fricassee.

In the Hotel Fjordgården, Vesterkær 28. ✆ 97-32-14-00. Reservations recommended. Dinner main courses 165DKK–215DKK ($28–$36); fixed-price dinner menus 235DKK–295DKK ($39–$49). AE, DC, MC, V. Mon–Fri 7am–10pm; Sat 7am–1:30pm; Sun 7am–9pm.

EXPLORING RINGKØBING FJORD ★

Long straight sandy beaches, nature reserves, drifting North Sea sands, and heather-covered dunes create a dramatic West Jutland landscape on the narrow isthmus running south from Ringkøbing along Route 181. To reach the road that takes you along the western side of the fjord, head directly east of

Ringkøbing along Route 15, turning south when you see the junction with Route 181, going to the small town of Hvide Sande.

HVIDE SANDE

Midway along the isthmus, Hvide Sande (whose name translates as "white sands") is a typical West Jutland fishing town, founded in 1931 when it grew up around the large lock and sluice between the North Sea and Ringkøbing Fjord. Today, with its splendid beach on the seaside, it's the fifth largest fishing port in Denmark. A path follows along the windswept dunes between the sea and Ringkøbing Fjord, with panoramic views in all directions.

The most intriguing attraction here is the picturesque fishing harbor, the heartbeat of the town. Catches of delicious fish are unloaded at the auction building here. The auction is held every Monday through Friday at 7am, and again at 10am if the catch is heavy. A small nod or a lifted eyebrow is caught immediately by the auctioneer, and the purchase is registered. When the fish is sold, the catch is taken by truck for processing at local plants or exported directly in large refrigerated vans.

While in the area, you can visit the **Vestkyst Aquarium** (also known as Fiskeriets Hus), Nørregade 2B (© **97-31-26-10**), a museum devoted to anything and everything to do with fishing. The museum has a saltwater aquarium with fish from both the North Sea and Ringkøbing Fjord. It also includes tanks for large fish such as piked dogfish, rays, and big gadoids. April to October, the fish are fed every Tuesday and Friday at 3:30pm. Displays also include fishing tackle, and children can go on a voyage in the wheelhouse of a real cutter. While below deck, visitors experience the cramped conditions under which fishermen live at sea. April to October, it's open daily 10am to 6pm; November to March, daily 10am to 4pm. Admission is 50DKK ($8.35) adults, 25DKK ($4.20) children under age 12.

Windsurfing on Ringkøbing Fjord

Ringkøbing Fjord is one of the most popular places for windsurfing in the north of Europe. The area has Denmark's excellent breezes, and the shallow fjord waters are ideal for beginners. When the wind blows from the west, it comes in directly from the North Sea. Having passed the dunes, it accelerates across the fjord, creating a strong and constant wind. A wind from the east brings heat and sun, which in turn ensures increasing winds in the afternoon, so that surfing is generally possible every day. The wind is strongest in March, April, September, and October.

The best conditions are found at Hvide Sande, the venue for international and national speed weeks. This is the largest center around the fjord, with Denmark's best shallow water area for speed and slalom surfing. The center has a well-stocked shop with a school providing windsurfing instruction, equipment for hire, and a cafeteria with wind gauge. You'll be kept up-to-date on weather forecasts. You can stop in at **Westwind Nord** (© **97-31-25-99**), where you can get an introductory 3-hour course for 400DKK ($67). They also rent gear. Only available in summer months.

At Hvide Sande you'll find information available at **Holmsland Klit Turist-forening,** on the premises of the **Vestkyst Aquarium,** Nørregade 2B (© **97-31-18-66**). The office is open year-round, Monday through Friday from 9am to 5pm. From June to August, it's also open Saturday noon to 5pm and Sunday 11am to 4pm.

Where to Dine in Hvide Sande

Restaurant Slusen SEAFOOD/DANISH   In a building from the 1940s, directly astride the harbor, this is the most appealing restaurant in Hvide Sande, thanks to well-conceived cuisine and a tactful staff. Menu items include fried filets of plaice or turbot, different preparations of herring and salmon, a succulent seafood platter, and filets of catfish with mustard sauce. Lobster is available, kept fresh in an on-site aquarium. The dessert specialty is a Grand Marnier soufflé served on a purée of fresh peaches. The helpings are generous, the food flavorful, the fish fresh and well prepared, and the price right. Not only that, but the staff assured us readers will have "great fun" here. What more could you ask?

Bredgade 3. © **97-31-27-27.** Reservations recommended. Main courses 163DKK–260DKK ($27–$43); fixed-price menu 258DKK ($43). AE, DC, MC, V. Daily 1–4pm and 5–10pm. Closed Jan–Mar Sun night and Mon.

TIPPERNE NATURE RESERVE ⊛

You can continue south to Nymindegab, the gateway to the isthmus, if you're coming from Esbjerg. In times gone by, Nymindegab was the home of a small fishing harbor. From here you can explore **Tipperne Nature Reserve.** A small road, signposted from Nymindegab, leads into this tiny peninsula jutting into Ringkøbing Fjord. The flats and water surrounding the peninsula are one of the most important bird sanctuaries in West Jutland. The area's bird life is protected to establish undisturbed breeding. Today it is a favorite stopover for migratory birds. During both spring and autumn, thousands of ducks, geese, and waders stop here to rest. In July and August, when migration is at its peak, the sandpiper, curlew, snipe, and golden plover are some of the many species to be seen here. In the winter season, the swan, Denmark's national bird, is one of the species finding shelter at Tipperne. April to August, the bird reserve is open to visitors Sunday 5 to 10am only. September to March, the reserve can be visited every Sunday 10am to noon. You should continue by car until you reach a building marked TIPPERHUSET. You're not allowed to stop until you reach the parking lot, but once there you can climb a viewing tower to observe the birds. A 1.5km (1 mile) nature path departs from the bird tower. All walking in the area is restricted to this one path.

5 Ry ⟨★⟩

256km (160 miles) W of Copenhagen; 24km (15 miles) SE of Silkeborg; 35km (22 miles) SW of Århus

In the heart of Jutland, the little old town of Ry makes a less commercialized center than Silkeborg (see below) for visiting the mid-Jutland Lake District, one of the most beautiful areas of Denmark. Ry lies in a rural setting of extensive forests and rolling hills, valleys, gorges, and lakes, all linked by the Gudenå (also spelled Gudenåen), the longest river in Denmark. The region is filled with numerous sites of historical interest, including old churches, abbey ruins, villages with thatched roofs, and a number of small museums. Other than a walk through the town of Ry itself, there aren't many notable sights in the historic center. Most visitors use Ry as a base, branching out to see attractions in its environs.

ESSENTIALS

GETTING THERE   By Train   Ry lies on the main rail route linking Silke-borg (trip time: 20 min.) and Århus (trip time: 30 min.). There's also a bus from Århus, but it takes twice as long.

By Car   From Silkeborg (see below), take Route 15, heading east, and follow-ing the signs to Århus. Veer right (south) when you reach the town of Låsby, fol-lowing the signs to Ry.

VISITOR INFORMATION   The **Ry Turistbureau,** Klostervej 3 (© **86-89-34-22;** www.visitry.dk), is open June 15 to August 31, Monday to Saturday 9am to 4:30pm. Off-season hours are Monday to Friday 9am to 4pm and Saturday 9am to noon.

GETTING AROUND   By Bicycle   For many Danes, the only way to see the lake district and its little hamlets is by bike. **Ry Cykel,** Skanderborgvej 19 (© **86-89-14-91**), will rent you a bike for the day for 60DKK ($10).

By Canoe   Instead of a bike, you might prefer to explore the river and the beautiful lakes in the area by canoe. Brochures about canoeing are available from the Ry Turistbureau (see above) or from **Ry Kanofart,** Kyhnsvej 20 (© **86-89-11-67**), which will rent you a canoe for 300DKK ($50) per day.

EXPLORING THE AREA

A 10-minute drive west of Ry via Route 445, **Himmelbjerget** ⋆ (Sky Moun-tain) is the most visited spot in the Lake District. You can also get here by tak-ing bus no. 104 from the train station at Ry. Himmelbjerget rises 147m (482 ft.) above sea level, the highest point in Denmark. In 1871, the Danish crown obtained the property and turned it over to the people of Denmark as a sight-seeing attraction.

Himmelbjerget towers majestically over the surrounding countryside, not only when viewed from the lake, but from the many footpaths in the woods. Two modern tourist boats, the *Viking* and the *Turisten,* run summer cruises between Ry and Himmelbjerget. For information and schedules, call © **86-82-88-21** in Ry. The one-way cost is 45DKK ($7.50) adults and 30DKK ($5) children.

Himmelbjerget Tower, rising 25m (82 ft.), was designed by the architect L. P. Fenger and erected in commemoration of King Frederik VII, who, on June 5, 1849, gave the Danish people a new constitution. From the tower you'll have the most panoramic view of the area. It's open daily May and June, 10am to 5pm; July, 10am to 9pm; August to September 15, 10am to 6pm. From Sep-tember 16 to October, it's open only on Saturday and Sunday from 10am to 5pm. Admission is 7.50DKK ($1.25).

Even more interesting than Ry is the old hamlet of **Gamle Ry** ⋆, directly west of Ry along Route 461. This is called the "village of kings and springs." The name "Rye" comes from *rydning,* Danish for "clearing." In the Middle Ages this was a spiritual center of Denmark because of its "holy springs." The village gets its royal associations through Frederik II, who built a mansion here in 1582.

From the center you can follow a sign directing you to Sct. Sørens spring in Rye Sønderskov (Rye Southwood). This is a wonderful walk through a subglacial stream trench, called Jammerdalen or "The Vale of Tears." The water of this spring, thought to have curative powers, attracted many pilgrims, launching Gamle Ry on its heyday of medieval glory. In gratitude, pilgrims contributed to the funding of a granite church on the nearby hill where the present Sct. Sørens Kirke is situated. After the Reformation, when the pilgrimages stopped, the church fell into disrepair. In 1912, a rich farmer had the old tower reconstructed. The original church was the scene of the election of Christian III as king of Denmark on July 4, 1534, leading to the collapse of the Catholic Church in Denmark.

From the church you go east past a mill to Galgebakken (The Gallows Hill), a protected nature reserve set in lovely heather-clad hills.

East of Gamle Ry, if you cross the Gudenå at Emborg Bridge, you will come to the ruins of the largest Cistercian abbey in Denmark, the **Øm Kloster** (monastery). In the 12th century, a group of Cistercian monks left the Vitskøl Kloster monastery in Himmerland and arrived at Øm, where they founded the Øm Kloster monastery in 1175. The Cistercians were skilled farmers and preferred sites in forests and remote areas, where their hard work turned barren land into exemplary farms. During the Reformation, the monastery ceased to exist and the lands were taken over by the king. The monastery itself was pulled down. However, excavations in modern times have revealed one of the best-preserved ground plans of a medieval monastery to date. For information, call ℂ **86-89-81-94.** There is a little museum here open April, May, September, and October, Tuesday to Sunday 10am to 4pm; June to August, Tuesday to Sunday 10am to 5pm. The cloister is always closed on Monday. Admission is 35DKK ($5.85) adults, 15DKK ($2.50) children 7 to 12, free for children 6 and under. This minor museum has a historical medical exhibition, an herb garden, and a collection of skeletons discovered in the area. The plants in the herb garden date back to the days when the monastery flourished here.

You can take Route 461 south from Gamle Ry until you see the turnoff east to the hamlet of Emborg. This takes you to **Mossø,** the largest lake in Jutland. To the west of the lake are the Højlund Forest and the Sukkertoppen Hill, rising 108m (354 ft.).

The longest watercourse in Denmark, the Gudenå, also passes through Mossø en route from Tinnet Krat to Randers Fjord. Closer to the river are valley terraces created by water that melted after the Ice Age. The sandy surfaces are covered with heather and coniferous plantations, but make for poor farmland.

Mossø is the habitat of many types of birds. The sanctuary at Emborg Odde is a breeding site for a colony of black-headed gulls, which are extremely aggressive, thus providing protection from predators. The black-necked grebe takes advantage of this and breeds among the gulls. In the late summer, grebes can be seen along the edges of the reed banks, feeding on small animals.

Because of its size and varying depths, Mossø has always housed a wide variety of fish—some 20 species—the most numerous being perch, roach, and ruff, along with pikeperch, eel, and lake trout. Fishing licenses, going for 30DKK ($5) daily, are available from the Ry Turistbureau (see above).

WHERE TO STAY

Gamle Rye Kro ★ *Finds*   The most historic (but not the most luxurious) hotel in Ry lies in the satellite town of Gamle (Old) Ry. The place looks like a large white farmhouse, set 180m (591 ft.) north of the village church and the town market square. It has a history stretching back 400 years, to the time when pilgrims heading for the nearby (now ruined) monastery extolled the healing powers of local springs. Some rooms have TV and telephone. Don't expect your accommodations—or even the public rooms—to drip with a sense of antique nostalgia, as much of the inn's historic charm was erased during its renovations in the early 1990s. Overall, however, there's a sense of hospitality from the youthful and entrepreneurial staff, and a restaurant with worthwhile, albeit conservative, Danish cooking (see "Where to Dine," below).

Ryesgade 8, DK-8680 Ry. ℂ **86-89-80-42.** Fax 86-89-85-46. 20 rooms. 735DKK ($123) double. AE, DC, MC, V. From Ry, drive 5km (3 miles) southwest, following the signs to Gamle Ry. **Amenities:** Restaurant; indoor heated pool; fitness rooms; laundry service; dry cleaning; solarium. *In room:* TV, phone in some units.

Hotel Himmelbjerget ⭐ *Kids* Set at a higher altitude than any other hotel in Denmark, this charming, rustic, old-fashioned venue has changed little, despite subtle modernizations, since it was built in 1922. It lies 7km (4⅓ miles) northwest of the center of Ry, on a rocky plateau of its own, within a 10-minute walk of the Himmelbjerget Tower. Rooms retain some of their old-time paneling and accessories, and in many cases have terraces or balconies overlooking the nearby tower or the fields, lakes, and forests. Each has a writing table and twin beds that can be separated or moved together. On the premises are a bar and an appealing restaurant that serves generous portions of conservative, time-tested Danish recipes (see "Where to Dine," below). On-site is a children's cafeteria with direct access to a playground. The hotel's name, incidentally, translates from the Danish as "Heaven Mountain."

Ny Himmelbjergvej 20, DK-8680 Ry. ℂ **86-89-80-45.** Fax 86-89-87-93. www.hotel-himmelbjerget.dk. 18 units, none with bathroom. 559DKK ($93) double. Rates include breakfast. AE, DC, MC, V. Bus: 411. **Amenities:** Restaurant; cafeteria; bar; laundry service; dry cleaning; kids playground.

Nørre Vissing Kro ⭐ Set 11km (6¾ miles) northwest of Ry, amid rolling farmlands dotted with stately trees, this century-old inn has received many awards for the excellence of its cuisine. (See "Where to Dine," below.) It also maintains artfully decorated and stylish rooms, each with a small tiled bathroom with shower. Each has a scattering of rustic antiques that were in most cases acquired within Jutland. There are very few amenities per se, but the staff is very hip, and the owners are charming.

Låsbyvej 122, Nørre Vissing, DK-8660 Skanderborg. ℂ **86-94-37-16.** Fax 86-94-37-57. 16 units. 795DKK ($133) double. Rates include breakfast. DC, MC, V. Drive north from Ry, following the signs from Låsby. At Låsby, turn southwest, following the signs to Nørre Vissing. **Amenities:** Restaurant; bar; room service; nonsmoking rooms. *In room:* TV.

Ry Park Hotel Set in the center of Ry, this is one of the oldest *and* newest hotels in town. Originally built in 1888, it was radically reconfigured into a more streamlined and comfortable venue a century later. About 20 rooms are in a comfortable annex across the road. We find the accommodations in the annex more sterile and prefer to stay in the main building. All accommodations contain a private bathroom with tub or shower. The hotel is frequently reserved almost exclusively for participants in corporate conventions. The hotel's staff often can arrange fishing, canoeing, kayaking, bicycling, and yachting excursions.

Kyhnsvej 2, DK-8680 Ry. ℂ **86-89-19-11.** Fax 86-89-12-57. www.ryparkhotel.dk. 76 units. 950DKK–1,250DKK ($159–$209) double. AE, DC, MC, V. **Amenities:** Restaurant; bar; indoor heated pool; sauna; room service (7am–10pm); laundry service; dry cleaning; nonsmoking rooms. *In room:* TV, hair dryer, iron/ironing board, safe.

WHERE TO DINE

Gamle Rye Kro ⭐ *Finds* DANISH This is the most appealing component of one of the oldest inns in the region, thanks to generous portions of traditional Danish food and a cozy, albeit much-renovated, overly modernized interior design. Menu items include all the traditional Danish staples, such as *frikadeller* (meatballs), platters with several different preparations of herring, cream of mushroom soup, smoked salmon with chive-flavored cream sauce, roasted pork with red cabbage and onions, Dover sole meunière, and filet of plaice stuffed with asparagus and baby shrimp. Fried eel is even available on occasion. The cookery is always reliable in the best grandmotherly tradition.

Ryesgade 8. ℂ **86-89-80-42**. Reservations recommended. Main courses 70DKK–250DKK ($12–$42). AE, DC, MC, V. Daily noon–10pm. From Ry, drive 5km (3 miles) southwest, following the signs to Gamle Ry.

Nørre Vissing Kro ★★★ FRENCH/ITALIAN/DANISH   This is one of the most sophisticated and urbane restaurants in Jutland, with a string of awards for its culinary excellence and flair. Most of the dinner guests combine their meal with an overnight stay (see above). Luncheons, however, tend to include greater numbers of guests en route to somewhere else, and tend to be lighter and less elaborate. The dining room is a spacious, all-blue affair dotted with country antiques and artfully chosen accessories. Menu items change with the seasons. A well-conceived meal, however, might include foie gras with cherry sauce served on a bed of sautéed summer cabbage, poached lobster with a spinach flan and orange sauce, a medley of French and Italian cheeses, and a layer cake stuffed with summer berries marinated in rum, served with strawberry sorbet. There is a robust quality to the cuisine, yet each dish is imbued with a subtle texture that only a master chef—one who knows how to turn simple, natural produce into a gastronomic experience of unmistakable quality—can achieve.

Låsbyvej 122, Nørre Vissing, Skanderborg. ℂ **86-94-37-16**. Reservations recommended. Main courses 85DKK–230DKK ($14–$38); fixed-price menus 250DKK–895DKK ($42–$149). AE, DC, MC, V. Daily noon–3pm and 6–9pm. Drive north from Ry, following the signs from Låsby. At Låsby, turn southwest, following the signs to Nørre Vissing.

Restaurant Himmelbjerget DANISH   At a higher altitude than any other in Denmark, this is an appealingly old-fashioned restaurant where white napery, high ceilings, and old-world service are still offered. Menu items include most traditional Danish specialties, including marinated salmon with mustard and dill sauce and fresh-baked bread, filet of beef with onions and red wine sauce, filet of veal with fresh vegetables and mushroom sauce, cold potato soup with bacon and chives, brisket of beef with horseradish sauce, or tenderloin of beef with fried onions. Any of these might be followed with selections from a carefully arranged platter of Danish cheeses. The recipes seemingly haven't changed in a century— and that's exactly what the locals like to depend on when they come here.

Ny Himmelbjergvej 20. ℂ **86-89-80-45**. Reservations recommended. Main courses 140DKK–200DKK ($23–$33). AE, DC, MC, V. Daily 10am–10pm. Bus: 411 from Ry.

6 Silkeborg

43km (27 miles) W of Århus; 279km (174 miles) W of Copenhagen; 37km (23 miles) S of Viborg

In the heart of the Danish lake district, the small city of Silkeborg is surrounded by large forests, beautiful lakes, and the Gudenå River, the longest in Denmark. This provincial town lies on the shores of Lake Longsø, and its two major sights are the Kunstmuseum and the Silkeborg Museum. In 1845, Michael Drewsen, whose statue is seen in the town square, built a paper mill here on the east side of the river. With this he thus founded the town, and the mill and other industries grew until, today, Silkeborg has a population of some 35,000 citizens.

ESSENTIALS

GETTING THERE   From Århus, follow Route 15 west to Silkeborg. If you aren't driving, there's frequent train service from Copenhagen via Fredericia.

VISITOR INFORMATION   The **Silkeborg Turistbureau** is at Godthåbsvej 4
(© **86-82-19-11;** www.silkeborg.com). It's open June 15 to August, Monday to
Friday 9am to 5pm, Saturday and Sunday 10am to 2pm; September, October,
and April to June 14, Monday to Friday 9am to 4pm, Saturday 10am to 1pm;
November to March, Monday to Friday 10am to 3pm, Saturday 10am to 1pm.

GETTING AROUND   Numerous bus routes service the city; all local buses
depart from the bus stop on Fredensgade. There's no number to call for information. Tickets cost 15DKK ($2.50) per individual ride, or 18DKK ($3) if you
need a transfer.

SEEING THE SIGHTS

The most intriguing way to see Sky Mountain and the surrounding countryside
is aboard the paddle steamer *Hjejlen.* It has operated since 1861, and sails frequently in the summer. For schedules and more information, call **Hjejlen Co.
Ltd.,** Havnen (© **86-82-07-66**). A round-trip ticket costs 117DKK ($20) for
adults, half-price for children. Departures from Silkeborg Harbor are daily at
10am and 2pm from mid-June until mid-August.

AQUA Ferskvands Akvarium og Museum *Kids*   This freshwater aquarium
and museum on the south side of town offers visitors an intriguing journey
underwater. AQUA is a "converse aquarium," designed so that visitors feel as
though they're underwater. Come and see otters hunting and at play, or watch
the diving ducks, lurking pikes, and other fish and plants in their natural surroundings. You can have lunch in the park or pay a visit to the AQUA Café.

Vejsøvej 55. © **89-21-21-89.** Admission 75DKK ($13) adults, 45DKK ($7.50) children. June–Aug daily
10am–6pm; off season Mon–Fri 10am–4pm, Sat–Sun 10am–5pm.

Silkeborg Kunstmuseum   This museum offers unique exhibitions, including Asger Jorn's paintings and ceramics. The museum also displays paintings by
members of the COBRA School (**Co**penhagen, **Br**ussels, and **A**msterdam,
where the artists originated). Much of their work was produced between 1948
and 1951. Special exhibitions are also staged. The facade of the building features
a large ceramic relief by Jean Dubuffet.

Gudenåvej 9. © **86-82-53-88.** Admission 40DKK ($6.70) adults, free for children under 16. Apr–Oct
Tues–Sun 10am–5pm; Nov–Mar Tues–Fri noon–4pm, Sat–Sun 10am–5pm. Bus: 10.

Silkeborg Museum   This 18th-century manor by the Gudenå River, directly
east of Torvet, houses the 2,200-year-old **Tollund Man** ★★★, discovered in a
peat bog in 1950. His face is the least spoiled found to date. His body was so
well preserved, in fact, that scientists were able to determine that his last meal
was flax, barley, and oats. His head capped by fur, the Tollund Man was strangled by a plaited leather string, probably as part of a ritual sacrifice. Equally well
preserved is the **Elling Woman,** who was found near the same spot. Scientists
estimate that she was about 25 years old when she died in 210 B.C.

The museum also has a special exhibition of old Danish glass, a clog maker's
workshop, a collection of stone implements, antique jewelry, and artifacts from
the ruins of Silkeborg Castle. In the handicraft and Iron Age markets, artisans
use ancient techniques to create iron, jewelry, and various crafts.

Hovedgaardsvej 7. © **86-82-14-99.** Admission 40DKK ($6.70) adults, 10DKK ($1.65) children 6–14, free for
children under 6. May to mid-Oct daily 10am–5pm; mid-Oct to Apr Wed and Sat–Sun noon–4pm. Bus: 10.

NEARBY ATTRACTIONS

Jysk Automobilmuseum (Jutland Car Museum) ★   Near Silkeborg at
Gjern, this is the only automobile museum in Jutland, featuring 140 vintage cars

dating from 1900 to 1948. Sixty-eight different makes are represented, among them the V12 Auburn, V12 Cadillac, 1947 Crosley, famous Renault Taxis de la Marne, Kissel, Hotchkiss, Jordan, Vivinus, Rolls-Royce, and Maserati. A local mechanic, Aagi Louring, who collected and restored only Danish cars, motorcycles, trucks, and fire engines, established the museum in 1967. Today, although the collection is still privately owned, it has expanded its collections into the international cornucopia you'll see today. Mr. Louring, something of a local celebrity, still makes it a point to drop in on the collection at regular intervals.

Skovvejen, Gjern. ⓒ **86-87-50-50**. www.jyskautomobilmuseum.dk. Admission 65DKK ($11) adults, 25DKK ($4.20) children. Apr 1–May 15 and Sept 16–Oct 31 Sat–Sun and holidays 10am–5pm; May 16–Sept 15 daily 10am–5pm. Closed Nov 1–Mar. Bus: "Randers" from Silkeborg. Located 16km (10 miles) northeast of Silkeborg, it's accessible from Silkeborg by following the road signs to the town of Hammel, then turning off when you see the signs for Gjern and the Jysk Automobilmuseum.

SHOPPING

The main market is held at Torvet (town square) on Saturday mornings, starting around 7am. It's always best to go before noon. A smaller market begins about the same time every Wednesday at Nørretorv. Among specialty stores, **Bon Sac,** Søndergade 2C (ⓒ **86-82-60-55**), has an intriguing collection of fashionable leather goods. **Inspiration,** Østergade 5 (ⓒ **86-82-50-11**), offers a large collection of gift items for the home.

WHERE TO STAY

The Silkeborg Turistbureau (see above) can book you into nearby **private homes.**

MODERATE

Gl. Skovridergaard ⋆ This historic and luxurious property is devoted to conventions and conferences more than virtually any other hotel in the region, and as such, rooms (especially during the peak of convention season in winter) might not be available. But when rooms are available (usually midsummer) a stay here can be extremely pleasant and comfortable. All the accommodations contain private bathrooms, some with tub, others with shower. Set within a well-maintained park, the hotel originated in the 1700s, when the manager of the surrounding game reserve and forest built a well-appointed home for himself. In the mid-1980s, under the ownership of Silkeborg's largest bank (which books at least 30% of all convention space for its own managers and staff members), it was expanded into the convention center and hotel you'll see today.

Rooms are larger than you might expect, and filled with comfortable furnishings. Cafe tables are set up on the hotel's verdant lawns during mild weather, and the hotel's **restaurant** offers well-prepared, carefully choreographed meals. The restaurant merits special mention because of its ability to cater with aplomb to small or large groups. Lunches are almost always configured as a buffet; dinners are sit-down, internationally inspired meals served by a staff at artfully decorated tables.

Marienlundsvej 36, DK-8600 Silkeborg. ⓒ **87-22-55-00**. Fax 87-22-55-11. www.glskov.dk. 68 units. 1,150DKK–1,240DKK ($192–$207) double; 1,330DKK ($222) suite. Rates include buffet breakfast. AE, DC, MC, V. From Silkeborg, drive less than a kilometer (½ mile) south of town, following the signs to Horsens. **Amenities:** Restaurant; bar; sauna; room service (7am–10pm); babysitting; laundry service; dry cleaning; nonsmoking rooms. In room: TV, minibar (some units), coffeemaker, hair dryer, iron/ironing board (in some).

Hotel Dania ⋆ On Silkeborg's main square, within a 5-minute walk of the railway station, this is the oldest hotel in town. Established in 1848, it underwent a radical upgrade and renovation in 1997. Antiques fill the corridors and reception lounge, but the guest rooms have been renovated in functional, modern style. Each unit contains a neatly kept bathroom with a tub/shower combination. Outdoor dining on the square is popular in the summer, and the **Underhuset** restaurant serves typical Danish food along with Scandinavian and French dishes. The hotel's dining room is physically one of the longest restaurants in Denmark.

Torvet 5, DK-8600 Silkeborg. © **86-82-01-11.** Fax 86-80-20-04. www.hoteldania.dk. 49 units. 940DKK–1,265DKK ($157–$211) double; 1,640DKK–1,995DKK ($274–$333) suite. Rates include breakfast. AE, DC, MC, V. Free parking. Bus: 3. **Amenities:** Restaurant; bar; limited room service; babysitting; laundry service; dry cleaning; nonsmoking rooms. *In room:* TV, minibar, hair dryer, trouser press, safe.

Radisson SAS Hotel ★★ In a historic 150-year-old paper factory, this is the best hotel to open in the area. It lies right by the harbor, a short walk to attractions, shops, and restaurants. Both the doubles and the suites are furnished with traditional styling and contain state-of-the-art bathrooms with tub/shower combinations. When it's snowing outside, the lobby bar with its fireplace is the best place to be in Silkeborg. During fair weather, the restaurant, with its spacious terrace offering panoramic views of the Remstrup River, is a favorite spot.

Papirfabrikken 12, DK-8600 Silkeborg. © **88-82-22-22.** Fax 88-82-22-23. www.radissonsas.com. 86 units. 895DKK–1,095DKK ($149–$183) double; 1,045DKK–1,275DKK ($175–$213) suite. Rates include continental breakfast. AE, DC, MC, V. **Amenities:** Restaurant; bar; Jacuzzi (in suites); sauna; 24-hr. room service; laundry service; dry cleaning; nonsmoking rooms; rooms for those with limited mobility. *In room:* A/C, TV, dataport, minibar, fridge, hair dryer, iron/ironing board.

Scandic Hotel Silkeborg *(Kids* Launched in 1990, the largest hotel in Silkeborg lies 2.5km (1½ miles) west of the town center in a residential neighborhood surrounded by fields and forests. Rooms are well furnished and generally comfortable, although a bit cramped. Each includes a private tiled bathroom with shower. The hotel dining room, **Guldanden** (Golden Duck), is a glamorous spot serving Danish and international cuisine.

Udgårdsvej 2, DK-8600 Silkeborg. © **86-80-35-33.** Fax 86-80-35-06. www.scandic-hotels.com. 117 units. 790DKK–1,190DKK ($132–$199) double; 1,500DKK–1,700DKK ($251–$284) suite. AE, DC, MC, V. Bus: 3 from rail station. **Amenities:** Restaurant; bar; indoor heated pool; gym; sauna; children's playroom; laundry service; dry cleaning; nonsmoking rooms; rooms for those with limited mobility; solarium. *In room:* TV, minibar, coffeemaker (in some), trouser press, iron/ironing board (in some).

INEXPENSIVE

Hotel Silkeborgsøerne Set on a panoramic hillside 14km (8½ miles) west of Silkeborg, on the north shore of the region's largest lake (Lake Julsø), this lowrise, angular, and modern hotel was built in 1971 and radically renovated in 1996. It's the holiday home of north European urbanites who value the natural beauty of the many nearby lakes and forests. Overall, the venue is extremely simple, with staff and owners who live close to nature and the changing seasons. Rooms are small but sunny, with sliding glass doors that lead onto private verandas. Each comes with a private bathroom with tub or tub/shower combination. Main courses in the modern, big-windowed dining room cost from 100DKK to 180DKK ($17–$30), and usually follow the tenets of traditional Danish cuisine.

Himmelbjergvej 106, Laven DK-8600 Silkeborg. © **86-84-12-01.** Fax 86-84-17-40. 10 units. 775DKK ($129) double. MC, V. From Silkeborg, follow Rte. 15 and the signs to Århus, then veer south, following the signs to Laven. **Amenities:** Restaurant; room service (7am–10pm). *In room:* TV.

Kongensbro Kro ★★ Although a tavern stood on this site from 1663, it was little more than a ruin when members of the Andersen family bought and rebuilt it in 1949. The family's matriarch, Else, authored five Danish-language cookbooks during her active years here, and became something of a legend throughout Denmark. Today the charming and well-kept inn is directed by her son, Øle, and his hardworking staff. Accommodations are pleasant and cozy, and all contain private bathrooms with tub or shower.

Meals are served daily noon to 3pm and 6 to 9pm. A two-course fixed-price menu is available at lunch and dinner for 196DKK to 219DKK ($33–$37), although most serious gastronomes opt for a la carte meals. Delectable menu items include the best *frikadeller* in Jutland, served with red cabbage. Or you might opt for the alluring quail, which is quite scrumptious in its port-wine sauce. Perhaps the finest thing on the menu is the Danish trout, often served in puff pastry with a creamy dill sauce. The inn lies between Ans and Århus, about a 10-minute drive north of Silkeborg.

Gamle Kongevej 70, DK-8643 Ans By. ℂ 86-87-01-77. Fax 86-87-92-17. www.kongensbro-kro.dk. 15 units. 960DKK ($160) double. Rates include breakfast. AE, DC, MC, V. Closed Dec 23–24 and Dec 31–Jan 15. **Amenities:** Restaurant; room service (7am–10pm); laundry service; dry cleaning; 1 nonsmoking room. *In room:* TV.

Svostrup Kro ✦ *Finds*   This is one of the least-modernized inns around Silkeborg. It has more of its original architectural features than many of its competitors. On farmland between the Gudenå River and the Gjern hills, it was built in the 1600s as a bargeman's inn and designated by the Danish monarchy in 1834 as one of the inns suitable for a visit from the Danish king. Because of its authenticity and its hardworking, tactful staff, it's sought out by aficionados of old Danish inns, who appreciate its antique paneling and an interior that evokes the Denmark of long ago. Rooms contain appealing antique (or at least old) furnishings, with charmingly dowdy touches. The restaurant is open 7am to 11pm every day. Many of the food items include old-fashioned Danish cuisine such as herring platters with new potatoes, or fried steak with onions. Others are more modern, such as venison steak braised with red wine, and served with caramelized apples, nuts, celery, mushrooms, and a confit of baby onions.

Svostrupvej 58, Svostrup, DK-8600 Silkeborg. ℂ 86-87-70-04. Fax 86-87-70-47. 15 units. 795DKK ($133) double; 995DKK ($166) suite. Rates include breakfast. AE, DC, MC, V. Bus: 313 from Silkeborg. From Silkeborg, drive 10km (6¼ miles) north, following the signs to Randers and then the signs to Svostrup. *In room:* No phone.

WHERE TO DINE

Piaf ✦ *Finds* MEDITERRANEAN   The most exotic and deliberately counter-culture restaurant in town occupies a solid, 80-year-old brick building in the historic core. It was named after the uncanny resemblance of its owner, Anni Danielsen (who's known for her fondness for black dresses), to the late French chanteuse, Edith Piaf. Artwork within the restaurant is offset with brick walls, potted plants, poster-image testimonials to the late Gallic sparrow, and deliberately mismatched tables, plates, ashtrays, and accessories. Lunch platters tend to be light, airy, and flavorful; dinners more substantial with excellently chosen ingredients—always fresh and flavorful—deftly handled by a skilled kitchen staff. Both are inspired by the tenets of Spanish, Greek, Provençal, and Italian cuisine. Look for heaping platters of paella, bouillabaisse, roasted lamb with rosemary, carpaccio, and sliced veal. What's the only item you're likely not to find on the menu? Pork, since it reminds most of the clients of the cuisine served in Denmark during their childhood, and which is consequently something avoided within this consciously exotic setting.

Nygade 31. ℂ 86-81-12-55. Reservations recommended. Fixed-price menus 278DKK–588DKK ($46–$98). DC, MC, V. Mon–Sat 6–11pm.

Spiesehuset Christian VIII ★★ DANISH/FRENCH   The best restaurant in Silkeborg, this establishment was founded in 1992 in what was originally a private house built in the late 1700s. It seats only 30 people in a dining room painted in what the owners describe as the color of heaven (cerulean blue), accented with modern paintings. Delectable choices include lobster ravioli, carpaccio of marinated sole and salmon with saffron sauce, filet of beef with truffle sauce, medallions of veal stuffed with a purée of wild duck and herbs, and tender rack of Danish lamb with garlic sauce. Service is attentive and professional.

Christian VIII Vej 54. ℰ **86-82-25-62.** Reservations required. Main courses 165DKK–255DKK ($28–$43). AE, DC, MC, V. Mon–Sat 4–10pm.

SILKEBORG AFTER DARK

Rather historic is the **Underhuset Pub,** part of the dining and drinking facilities within the also-recommended Hotel Dania, Torvet 5 (ℰ **86-82-01-11**). And for a bout of dancing with the Danes of Silkeborg, check out the laser lights and electronic pulsations at the **Chaplin Disco,** Nygade 18B (ℰ **86-82-12-73**). Here, beginning around 10:30pm Wednesday through Saturday, a cover charge of 40DKK ($6.70) will get you into a site where locals—usually under 45 years old—dance till they drop.

7 Århus

159km (99 miles) NE of Fanø; 175km (109 miles) W of Copenhagen

Jutland's capital and the second-largest city in Denmark, Århus is a cultural center—a university town with a lovely port. Aside from enjoying the city's many restaurants, hotels, and nighttime amusements, you can use Århus as a good base for excursions to Silkeborg, Ebeltoft, and the manors and castles to the north.

To some, Århus is the "capital of the west," since Copenhagen is so far to the east. On the east coast of Central Jutland, it lies on a wide bay whose waters are sheltered by the Helgenæs peninsula. Its economic growth today is based on communications, the food industry, electronics, textiles, iron and steel, and Danish design, as well as the harbor which is now the second most important in Denmark, rivaled only by Copenhagen.

Originally Århus was a Viking settlement, founded as early as the 10th century; its original name, Aros, meaning estuary, comes from its position at the mouth of a river, Århus Å. The town experienced rapid growth and by 948 it had its own bishop. A church was built here in 1060, and a cathedral was started at the dawn of the 13th century. This prosperity came to a temporary end in the late Middle Ages when the town was devastated by the bubonic plague. The Reformation of 1536 also slowed the growth of Århus. But the coming of the railway in the 19th century renewed prosperity, which continues to this day.

ESSENTIALS

GETTING THERE   By Plane   Århus Airport is in Tirstrup, 43km (27 miles) northeast of the city. **SAS** (ℰ **800/221-2350** in North America, or 70-10-20-00 in Århus; www.aar.dk) operates some 12 flights a day from Copenhagen, Monday to Friday, and about six on Saturday and Sunday. SAS also operates an afternoon flight most days between Århus and London. An airport bus runs between the train depot at Århus and the airport, meeting all major flights. The cost of a one-way ticket is 70DKK ($12).

By Train   About five or six trains a day travel between Århus and Copenhagen (trip time: 4½ hr.). Some 20 trains a day connect Aalborg with Århus (1 hr., 40 min.). From Frederikshavn, the North Jutland port and ferry-arrival point from Norway, some 20 trains a day run to Århus (3 hr.).

By Bus   Two buses daily make the run to Århus from Copenhagen (4 hr.).

By Car   From the east, cross Funen on the E20 express highway, heading north at the junction with the E45. From the north German border, drive all the way along the E45. From Frederikshavn and Aalborg in the north, head south along the E45.

VISITOR INFORMATION   The tourist office, **Tourist Århus,** is in the Rådhuset, Park Allé (℃ **89-40-67-00;** www.visitaarhus.com). It's open mid-June to mid-September, Monday to Friday 9:30am to 6pm, Saturday 9:30am to 5pm. Off-season hours are Monday to Friday 9am to 4pm and Saturday 10am to 1pm.

GETTING AROUND   A regular bus ticket, valid for one ride, can be purchased on the rear platform of all city buses for 17DKK ($2.85). You can buy a **tourist ticket** for 50DKK ($8.35) at the tourist office or at newsstands (kiosks) throughout the city center. The 24-hour ticket covers an unlimited number of rides within the central city and includes a 2½-hour guided tour of Århus.

SEEING THE SIGHTS

For the best introduction to Århus, head for the town hall's tourist office, where a 2½-hour **sightseeing tour** leaves daily at 10am June 24 to August 31, costing 50DKK ($8.35) per person (free with the Århus Pass; see above).

In addition to the more major museums listed below, you can also visit two museums on the grounds of Århus University, Nordre Ringgade. They include **Steno Museet,** C. F. Møllers Allé (℃ **89-42-39-75;** www.stenomuseet.dk.; bus: 1, 2, 3, or 4), which displays exhibits documenting natural science and medicine. You'll see beautiful 19th-century astronomical telescopes, a 1920s surgical room, and some of the first computers made in Denmark in the 1950s. Posters, models, and do-it-yourself experiments, including tests of Galileo's demonstrations of gravity and of electromagnetism, are also on display. In addition, you can walk through an herbal garden with some 250 historical medicinal herbs. There is also a planetarium with shows daily at 11am, 1pm, and 2pm, as well as 8pm on Wednesday. Hours are Tuesday to Sunday 10am to 4pm. October to March it's also open 7 to 10pm. Admission is 40DKK ($6.70) adults and 15DKK ($2.50) children. To see a planetarium show costs another 40DKK ($6.70) adults, 20DKK ($3.35) children. A combination ticket for museum and planetarium is 60DKK ($10) adults, 30DKK ($5) children.

Also at the university is a **Naturhistorisk Museum,** Block 210, Universitetsparken (℃ **86-12-97-77;** www.naturhistoriskmuseum.dk; bus: 2 or 3),

---

Value The Århus Pass

The **Århus Pass** allows unlimited travel by public transportation and free admission to many museums and attractions. It also includes a 2½-hour guided tour. A 2-day pass costs 121DKK ($20) for adults and 61DKK ($10) for children; 1-week passes are 171DKK ($29) and 83DKK ($14). The Århus Pass is sold at the tourist office, many hotels, camping grounds, and kiosks throughout the city.

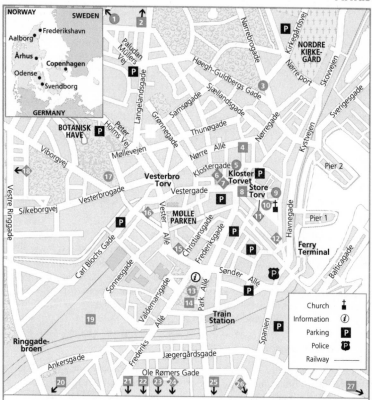

Århus

ATTRACTIONS ●

Århus Domkirke
  (Cathedral of St. Clemens) **9**
Århus Kunstmuseum **1**
Besættelsesmuseet **27**
Den Gamle By **6**
Det Danske Brandvaernsmuseum **5**
Forhistorisk Museum-Moesgård **13**
Marselisborg Slot **15**
Naturhistorisk Museum **2**
Rådhuset (Town Hall) **23**
Steno Museet **3**
Vikingemuseet **10**
Vor Frue Kirke **8**
Womens Museum in Denmark **12**

ACCOMMODATIONS ■

Best Western Ritz Hotel **14**
Comfort Hotel Atlantic **27**
Hotel Guldsmeden **4**
Hotel Kong Christian den X **21**
Hotel La Tour **2**
Hotel Marselis **22**
Hotel Mercur **25**
Hotel Philip **12**
Hotel Royal **8**
Radisson SAS
  Scandinavia Hotel Århus **19**
Scandic Plaza **20**

DINING ◆

Den Gremme Ælleng
  (The Ugly Duckling) **15**
Hotel Philip Restaurant **12**
Kroen I Krogen **24**
Ministeriet **7**
Prins Ferdinand **18**
Restaurant de 4 Arstider
  (Four Seasons) **16**
Restaurant Margueritten **5**
Restaurant Skovmøllen **26**
Teater Bodega **11**

filled with mounted animals from all over the world. Some of them are displayed in engaging dioramas. The collection of Danish animals, especially birds, is unique within Denmark. Skeletons, minerals, and a display devoted to the evolution of life are some of the other exhibits. It's open daily 10am to 4pm (to 5pm July–Aug). It's closed on Mondays November to March. Admission is 40DKK ($6.70) adults, free for children under 6.

Århus Domkirke (Cathedral of St. Clemens)   This late-Gothic red-brick, copper-roofed cathedral, crowned by a 96m (315-ft.) spire, begun in the early 13th century and completed in the 15th, is the longest cathedral in Denmark, practically as deep as its spire is tall. Of chief interest here are the Renaissance pulpit, 15th-century triptych, and 18th-century pipe organ. (After the cathedral, we suggest a visit to the nearby medievalesque **arcade** at Vestergade 3, with half-timbered buildings, rock garden, aviary, and antique interiors.)

Bispetorvet. ℂ **86-12-38-45.** Free admission. May–Sept Mon–Sat 9:30am–4pm; Oct–Apr Mon–Sat 10am–3pm. Bus: 3, 11, 54, or 56.

Århus Kunstmuseum   One of the oldest and best collections of Danish paintings is assembled here, as well as sculpture and drawings dating from 1750 to the present day. The Romantics, the Realists, the Impressionists—they are all here. Modern works from Denmark and abroad—including Germany and the United States—are featured as well. Special exhibitions are often staged here. The museum is south of the university. On Sunday there are free guided tours at 3pm. The location is close to the bus station.

Aros Allé 2, Århus C. ℂ **87-30-66-00.** www.aros.dk. Admission 60DKK ($10) adults, free for children. Tues–Sun 10am–5pm (Wed to 10pm).

Besættelsesmuseet   This museum illustrates dramatic events as well as everyday life in Århus during the Nazi takeover of the city, from 1940 until liberation in 1945. The museum is housed in the old city hall, off Domkirkepladsen. This was the Gestapo headquarters during the war. In the basement of the building, this Occupation Museum details a most troubled time, depicting Allied air raids on Århus, weapons, documents, World War II photo displays, guns, and even instruments of torture. The museum also describes sabotage carried out by the local resistance movement. An interesting display documents Allied, Nazi, and Danish propaganda.

Mathilde Fibigers Have 2. ℂ **86-18-42-77.** www.besaettelsesmuseet.dk. Admission 20DKK ($3.35) adults, free for children under 12. June–Aug Tues, Thurs, and Sat–Sun 11am–4pm; off season Sat–Sun 11am–4pm. Bus: 3 or 7.

Den Gamle By ★★   Århus's top attraction, Den Gamle By displays more than 75 buildings representing Danish urban life from the 16th to the 19th centuries re-created in a botanical garden. The open-air museum differs from similar attractions near Copenhagen and Odense, where the emphasis is on rural life. Visitors walk through the authentic-looking workshops of bookbinders, carpenters, hatters, and other craftspeople. There are also a pharmacy, a school, and an old-fashioned post office. A popular attraction is the Burgomaster's House, a wealthy merchant's antiques-stuffed, half-timbered home, built at the end of the 16th century. Be sure to see the textile collection and the Old Elsinore Theater, erected in the early 19th century. The museum also houses a collection of china, clocks, delftware, and silverware. Summer music programs are staged, and there are a restaurant, tea garden, bakery, and beer cellar.

Viborgvej 2. ℂ **86-12-31-88**. Admission 60DKK ($10) adults, 25DKK ($4.20) children. Sept–Oct and Apr–May daily 10am–5pm; Nov–Dec and Feb–Mar daily 10am–4pm; Jan daily 11am–3pm; June–Aug daily 9am–6pm. Bus: 3, 14, or 25.

Det Danske Brandværnsmuseum   This is the largest firefighting museum in Europe, with some 100 fire engines from the 19th century to the present day. There are examples of both horse-drawn and engine-driven vehicles. Children delight in the playroom, where they can have a hands-on experience with real firefighting equipment. The location is 5km (3 miles) west of the historic core of Århus and just off Viby Ringvej.

Tomasgervej 25. ℂ **86-25-41-44**. Admission 50DKK ($8.35) adults, 20DKK ($3.35) children. Apr–Oct daily 10am–5pm; Nov–Mar Tues–Sun 10am–5pm. Bus: 12 or 18.

Forhistorisk Museum-Moesgård   The former Århus Museum is now an archaeological and ethnographic museum in a country setting about 8km (5 miles) from town, at Moesgård Manor. It owns the incredibly well-preserved 2,000-year-old Grauballe man, who had lain since the Iron Age in a bog in central Jutland. Outside in the park and woods is an open-air museum that displays prehistoric reconstructions and a prehistoric trodden path. If you're driving from the center, follow the signs to Odder and the Moesgård Manor.

Moesgård Manor. Moesgård Allé 20, Højbjerg. ℂ **89-42-11-00**. www.moesmus.dk. Admission 45DKK ($7.50) adults, free for children under 16. Apr–Sept daily 10am–5pm; Oct–Mar Tues–Sun 10am–4pm. Bus: 6 from railway station. Positioned 9km (5½ miles) south of Århus's center.

Rådhuset (Town Hall)   A crowning architectural achievement in the center of Århus, the Rådhuset was built between 1936 and 1941 to commemorate the 500th anniversary of the Århus charter. It's been the subject of controversy ever since. Arne Jacobsen was one of the designers of the modern marble-plated structure, with lots of airy space and plenty of glass. It can be seen only on a guided tour. An elevator (and 346 steps) runs to the top of the 59m (194-ft.) tower, where a carillon occasionally rings. *Note:* The guided tour at 11am includes the tower. The elevator and stairs are open three times a day: 11am, noon, and 2pm.

Rådhuspladsen. ℂ **89-40-20-00**. Admission to tower 5DKK (85¢ guided tour 10DKK ($1.65). Guided tours Mon–Fri 11am. Tower 11am, noon, and 2pm. Closed Sept–June 23. Bus: 3, 4, 5, or 14.

Vikingemuseet   In the basement of the Unibank, close to the cathedral of Århus, original and reproductions of Viking objects can be seen. These objects were unearthed in an excavation on this site in 1963 and 1964. Remains of the town's Viking walls can be seen. Behind the museum, you'll find reconstructions of Viking houses—that is, a stave church and one of the small pit houses found during the excavation at the site. Objects illustrate how life went on in this bustling merchant city from its foundation in about A.D. 900 until around 1400.

St. Clemens Torv 6. ℂ **89-42-11-00**. Admission 45DKK ($7.50). Mon–Wed and Fri 10am–4pm; Thurs 10am–5:30pm. Bus: 3, 11, 54, or 56.

Von Frue Kirke   "The Church of Our Lady" lies to the northwest of Århus Domkirke. It was built between the 13th and 15th centuries but was originally part of a Dominican priory. The original Århus Cathedral was erected on this site in 1060. Today's church, built of red brick, has a largely whitewashed interior. It's mainly a Gothic building with frescoes and a significant altarpiece from the workshop of Claus Berg, painted in 1520. The altarpiece depicts a scene from the Passion, in a stunningly expressive style that is often compared to the work of Pieter Bruegel the Elder. Restoration work was begun here in the 1950s, and the crypt of the original Romanesque church from 1060 was uncovered under the chancel. Its early date makes it the oldest vaulted building in all Scandinavia. This vaulted crypt is now virtually "a church within a church." In addition, a chapter house, which once was a hospital for the elderly in the Reformation era, has been dedicated as a church and incorporated into the general structure. So "Our Lady" is actually three churches in one. Wall paintings from the Middle Ages adorn the walls of the chapter house. Because of all these multiple layers beneath the surface, Von Frue Kirke is often likened to a Russian matryoshka doll.

Frue Kirkeplads. (C) 86-12-12-43. Free admission. Sept–Apr Mon–Fri 10am–2pm, Sat 10am–noon; May–Aug Mon–Fri 10am–4pm, Sat 10am–noon. Bus: 7, 10, or 17.

Women's Museum in Denmark This museum is devoted to women, their history and culture, their everyday life, their art, and even work done by their own hands. The museum has collected objects and documents, photos, slides, and biographies to document the lives and heritage of women and to record their changing roles over the centuries. The museum documents the legacy of both famous and forgotten women. Three or four special exhibitions devoted to women are staged here annually.

Domkirkeplads 5. (C) 86-13-61-44. www.womensmuseum.dk. Admission 30DKK ($5) adults, free for children. June 1–Sept 15 daily 10am–5pm; off season Tues–Sun 10am–4pm. Bus: 3 or 7.

NEARBY ATTRACTIONS

The summer residence of Denmark's royal family, **Marselisborg Slot** ⋆, at Kongevejen 100, less than 2.5km (1½ miles) south of Århus's center (bus: 1, 18, or 19), is one of the most famous and symbolic buildings in Denmark. If you visit at noon on days Her Majesty and family are in residence, you can see the changing of the guard. It's announced on the local news and in the newspapers when Her Majesty is here. The royal family has used this white manor house since 1902.

It is not possible to visit the interior of the palace, but the castle grounds, even the Queen's rose garden, are open to the public admission-free 9am to 5pm when the castle is not occupied.

The setting is a large forest belt stretching for some 10km (6¼ miles) along the coast. The entire area is ideal for hikes, as nature trails have been cut through the forests. Bikers also like the terrain. Less than 1.5km (1 mile) from the royal palace on the main road south lies **Dyrehaven** (deer park), a protected forest area where you can see fallow deer, and even sika. The more elusive wild roe deer also live here, as well as wild pigs, although you're unlikely to spot the latter.

THE MANOR HOUSES OF EAST JUTLAND

Clausholm ⋆⋆ Seventeenth-century Clausholm is a splendid baroque palace, one of the earliest in Denmark. It was commissioned by Frederik IV's chancellor, whose adolescent daughter, Anna Sophie, eloped with the king. When Frederik died, his son by his first marriage banished the queen to Clausholm, where she lived with her court until her death in 1743.

The rooms are basically unaltered, but few of the original furnishings remain. The salons and ballroom feature elaborate stucco ceilings and decorated panels, and an excellent collection of Danish rococo and Empire furnishings has replaced the original pieces. The Queen's Chapel, where Anna Sophie and her court worshipped, is unchanged and contains the oldest organ in Denmark. In 1976 the Italian baroque gardens were reopened, complete with a symmetrically designed fountain system.

Clausholm is about 13km (8 miles) southeast of Randers and 31km (19 miles) north of Århus.

Voldum, Hadsten. © 86-49-16-55. www.clausholm.dk. Admission (including guided tour) 70DKK ($12) adults, free for children under 14. Castle (open only in July) daily 11am–4pm. Park (May–Sept) daily 11am–4pm. Bus: 221 from Randers.

The Museums at Gammel Estrup ✶   Positioned 21km (13 miles) from Randers and 39km (24 miles) from Århus, this is a compound of buildings that includes the **Jutland Manor House Museum,** complete with a great Hall, a chapel, and richly decorated stucco ceilings; and the **Danish Agricultural Museum,** which celebrates the role of Danish farming over the past thousand years. The entire compound dates from the 14th century, but the structures you see were extensively rebuilt and remodeled in the early 1600s. Expect a glimpse into medieval fortifications, baronial furnishings, the changing nature of tools and machines used during Danish plantings and harvests, and an enormous sense of pride in Denmark and its traditions.

Jyllands Herregårdsmuseum, Randersvej 2, Auning. © 86-48-30-01. www.gl-estrup.dk. Admission 70DKK ($12) adults, 60DKK ($10) students and seniors, free for children under 14. Agricultural Museum Jan–Mar and Nov–Dec Tues–Sun 10am–3pm; Apr–June and Sept–Oct daily 10am–5pm; July–Aug daily 10am–6pm. Manor House Museum Apr–June and Sept–Oct daily noon–4:30pm; Jul–Aug daily noon–4:30pm. Bus: 119. From Randers, take Rte. 16 east to Auning.

Rosenholm Slot ✶   On an islet 21km (13 miles) north of Århus and less than a kilometer (½ mile) north of Hornslet, this Renaissance manor with a moat has been the Rosenkrantz family home for 4 centuries. The four-winged castle, encircled by about 14 hectares (35 acres) of parkland, houses a Great Hall, as well as a large collection of Flemish woven and gilded leather tapestries, old paintings, Spanish furniture, a vaulted gallery walk, and pigskin-bound folios.

Hornslet. © 86-99-40-10. Admission 60DKK ($10) adults, free for children under 12. June 1–19 Sat–Sun 11am–4pm; June 20–Aug 31 daily 11am–4pm. Closed Sept–May. Bus: 119 or 121 from Århus.

SHOPPING

Århus is the biggest shopping venue in Jutland, with some 400 specialty stores, each of them tightly clustered within an area of about 1¼ sq. km (½ sq. mile). The centerpiece of this district is the Strøget, whose terminus is the Store Torv, dominated by the Århus Domkirke. You might try a large-scale department store first. One of the best is **Salling,** Søndergade 27 (© 86-12-18-00), with some 30 specialty boutiques, all under one roof. A wide range of articles for the whole family is sold here, including body-care items, clothing, gifts, toys, music, and sports equipment. **Magasin du Nord,** Immervad 2–8 (© 86-12-33-00), is the largest department store in Scandinavia, in business for more than 125 years. The staff will assist foreign visitors with tax-free purchases.

"The greatest silversmith the world has ever seen" is the name often used to describe **Georg Jensen,** Søndergade 1 (© 86-12-01-00). A tradition since 1866, Georg Jensen is known for style and quality, producing unique silver and gold jewelry, elegant clocks and watches, and stainless steel cutlery, among other items. A leading goldsmith, **Hingelberg,** Store Torv 3 (© 86-13-13-00), is the licensed Cartier outlet, and offers a wide selection of top-quality designer jewelry.

Galleri Bo Bendixen, Store Torv 14 (© 86-12-67-50), offers the brilliant, colored, top-quality designs of Bo Bendixen, the famous Danish graphic artist. The shop also sells a wide range of gifts and garments for children and adults. **Volden 4 Kunsthåndværk,** Volden 4 (© 86-13-21-76), specializes in top-quality applied art, and glass made by some of the leading artisans of the country. Silver, copper, and brass ornaments are for sale, as are exclusive bronze candlesticks.

Bülow Duus Glassblowers, Studsgade 14 (© 86-12-72-86), is a working glass-blowing shop open to the public. At an attractive old house in the heart of the city, you can watch the fascinating work of glass blowing. Drinking glasses, candlesticks, bowls, and other items are for sale. For traditional Danish pottery, head for **Favlhuset,** Møllestien 53 (© **86-13-06-32**).

If you haven't found what you're looking for after all that, head for **Inspiration Buus,** Ryesgade 2 (© **86-12-67-00**), which sells top-quality gifts, kitchenware, tableware, and toiletry articles, much of it of Danish design.

WHERE TO STAY

Low-cost accommodations in this lively university city are limited. Those on a modest budget should check with the tourist office in the Rådhuset (© **89-40-67-00**) for bookings in **private homes.**

Depending on the day of the week or the time of the year you check in, rooms in many of the hotels labeled inexpensive aren't inexpensive at all, but more moderate in price.

EXPENSIVE

Hotel Marselis ★   This is the most isolated and nature-conscious of the grand modern hotels of Århus, thanks to a long, narrow layout that rambles along a grass-covered bluff, a few steps from the sea, about 5km (3 miles) south of the city center. Built of earth-colored bricks in 1967, it plays up its views over the water and an interior decor that's the most nautical of all the hotels in the area. Rooms are smaller and less imaginatively decorated than those in, for example, the SAS Radisson, but overall, the setting is soothing and well maintained. Each unit is equipped with a full bathroom with tub and shower. Corporate conventions sometimes come here, but less often than the hotel would really like.

The **Restaurant Marselis** and its bar, the **Café Nautilus,** provide food, piano music, drink, and a log-burning fireplace. A less formal dining and drinking venue, open only during mild weather, is the **Beach Café,** whose tables are arranged on a sunny terrace. This is one of the few modern hotels in Århus with its own swimming pool, an indoor affair with big windows overlooking the sea.

Strandvejen 25, DK-8000 Århus C. © **86-14-44-11.** Fax 86-11-70-46. www.marselis.dk. 101 units. 850DKK–1,590DKK ($142–$266) suite. Rates include breakfast. AE, DC, MC, V. Bus: 6. **Amenities:** Restaurant; bar; indoor heated pool; gym; sauna; 24-hr. room service; laundry service; dry cleaning; solarium. *In room:* TV, dataport, minibar, hair dryer.

Hotel Philip ★★★ *Finds*   This discovery offers the finest accommodations in Århus and some of the best lodgings in Central Jutland, a 5-minute walk from the bus station. The hotel is owned by Marc Rieper, a former player on the Danish national football team, who headed the ball at the crossbar in the crucial moment against Brazil during the world championships in 1998. Opening onto a canal, the building housing this boutique hotel has been vastly renovated, each accommodation turned into a luxury suite. The six regular suites have been lavishly decorated in a French and Italian style, and the two remaining suites on the top floor are even more luxuriously equipped in a romantic style. Jutlanders on their honeymoon often book this pair of suites. All the suites are spacious, containing Oriental carpets and works of art. Each bedroom contains a king-size bed, and all the units come with a first-class bathroom with tub and shower. The service is the best in Århus—for example, you're greeted with fresh flowers. Even if not a guest, consider a meal at the Hotel Philip's new **restaurant.** See "Where to Dine," below.

Åboulevarden 28, DK-8000 Århus. © **87-32-14-44.** Fax 86-12-69-55. www.hotelphilip.dk. 8 units. 1,495DKK ($250) suite. Rates include breakfast. DC, MC, V. **Amenities:** Restaurant; cafe; bar; room service (7am–10pm); laundry service; dry cleaning; nonsmoking rooms. *In room:* TV, dataport, minibar, hair dryer, iron/ironing board, safe.

Hotel Royal ★★   This is the most glamorous accommodation in town, attracting such greats of yesterday as Marian Anderson and Arthur Rubenstein. The gilt date on its neo-baroque facade commemorates the hotel's establishment in 1838. There have been numerous additions and upgrades since. The Royal stands close to the city's symbol, its cathedral. A vintage elevator takes you to the guest rooms, many of them quite spacious. They're modernized, with good-size bathrooms containing tub/shower combinations. Beds are refurbished, with strong, durable mattresses, and accommodations are fitted with high-quality furniture, carpeting, and fabrics. The ground floor houses the Royal Scandinavian Casino and night club, offering such games of chance as international roulette, black jack, and seven-card stud poker.

Stove Torv 4, DK-8000 Århus. ✆ **86-12-00-11.** Fax 86-76-04-04. www.hotelroyal.dk. 102 units. 1,695DKK–1,895DKK ($283–$316) double; 3,000DKK ($501) suite. Rates include breakfast. AE, DC, MC, V. Parking 150DKK ($25). Bus: 56 or 58. **Amenities:** Restaurant; bar; sauna; room service (7am–10pm); babysitting; laundry service; dry cleaning; nonsmoking rooms; casino. *In room:* TV, dataport, minibar, hair dryer.

Radisson SAS Scandinavia Hotel Århus ★★★   This is one of the most modern and dynamic modern hotels in Denmark, and a city showplace that municipal authorities show off to visiting dignitaries. It was built in 1995 above the largest convention facilities in Jutland, and is the most popular convention hotel in the region. Bedrooms occupy floors 4 to 11 of a glass-and-stone-sheathed tower that's visible throughout the city. Lower floors contain check-in, dining, drinking, and convention facilities. Bedrooms are outfitted in plush upholstery with bright colors. Each has a tasteful decor that's different from its immediate neighbor, incorporating Scandinavian, English, Japanese, or Chinese themes. Each has a well-kept bathroom with a tub/shower combination, and large-windowed views over the city.

Margrethepladsen 1, DK-8000 Århus C. ✆ **800/333-3333** in the U.S., or 86-12-86-65. Fax 86-12-86-75. www.radissonsas.com. 234 units. 1,405DKK–1,860DKK ($235–$311) double; from 1,495DKK ($250) suite. Rates include breakfast. AE, DC, MC, V. Bus: 1, 2, 6, or 16. **Amenities:** Restaurant; bar; fitness center; sauna; 24-hr. room service; massage; babysitting; laundry service; dry cleaning; nonsmoking rooms; rooms for those with limited mobility. *In room:* TV, dataport, minibar, hair dryer, trouser press, safe.

Scandic Plaza   This dignified and traditional hotel is convenient to the Town Hall and city center attractions. Completely renovated and vastly improved several years ago, it is part of an original hotel that opened in 1930. The hotel is now first-class, with tastefully decorated guest rooms, good beds, and modern bathrooms with tub/shower combinations.

Banegårdspladsen 14, DK-8100 Århus C. ✆ **87-32-01-00.** Fax 87-32-01-99. www.scandic-hotels.com. 162 units. 820DKK–1,595DKK ($137–$266) double; 2,095DKK ($350) suite. Rates include breakfast. DC, MC, V. Bus: 3, 17, 56, or 58. **Amenities:** Restaurant; bar; fitness center; Jacuzzi; sauna; room service (7:30am–10:30pm); laundry service; dry cleaning; nonsmoking rooms. *In room:* TV, dataport, minibar, hair dryer, iron/ironing board, safe.

MODERATE

Best Western Ritz Hotel *Value*   Opposite the central station and the airport bus terminal, this hotel is one of the best values in the city, and perhaps the most convenient. It's close to the music hall, restaurants, theaters, and the best shopping. Facing the Town Hall, the hotel offers small to medium-size rooms, many of which have been renovated, and well-kept bathrooms with small showers (a few contain tubs). A well-known local chef, Rene Rohde Knudsen, has taken over the hotel, and operates a fine **restaurant** decorated in the Art Deco style of the 1930s. The hotel takes its name from a large painting in the restaurant that depicts the elegant Ritz in Paris. There is also an on-site cafeteria.

Banegardsplads 12, DK-8000 Århus. ℭ **800/528-1234** in the U.S., or 86-13-44-44. Fax 86-13-45-87. www. bestwestern.com. 67 units. Mon–Thurs 965DKK ($161) double; Fri–Sun 795DKK ($133) double. Rates include breakfast. AE, DISC, MC, V. Free parking. Bus: 3, 17, 56, or 58. **Amenities:** Restaurant; cafeteria; laundry service; dry cleaning. *In room:* TV, hair dryer.

Comfort Hotel Atlantic   A favorite of commercial travelers, the Atlantic was built in 1964 and fully renovated again in 2002. One of the city's tallest buildings, it rises 11 floors. Rooms are comfortably streamlined in a Nordic modern style, each with a balcony. Bathrooms are a bit small but well maintained, and all have tubs and showers. Ask for a room with a sea view if it's available. Breakfast is the only meal served, but many eateries are close at hand. The staff grants access to nearby health club and tennis courts.

Europlads 12–14, DK-8000 Århus. ℭ 86-13-11-11. Fax 86-13-23-43. www.choicehotels.dk. 102 units. 1,295DKK ($216) double; 1,495DKK ($250) suite. Rates include breakfast. AE, DC, MC, V. Bus: 3. **Amenities:** Breakfast lounge; bar; laundry service; dry cleaning; nonsmoking rooms. *In room:* TV, dataport, minibar, hair dryer, safe.

Hotel Kong Christian den X ⭐   This hotel, in the suburbs about 3km (1¾ miles) south of the commercial center, caters mostly to business travelers. Upscale and respectable, with an angular, big-windowed design that its detractors have compared to the departure terminal of an airport, it opened in 1987. Once you get used to the glistening modernity of the place, however, you'll discover a well-organized hotel with a polite, hardworking staff. Rooms are comfortable, well furnished, and quiet. Bathrooms are well maintained though a bit small—some with tub, others with showers. There's a big-windowed modern-looking restaurant that's often the venue for mealtime gatherings of participants in corporate conventions; it offers artfully laid-out breakfast buffets.

Christian X's Vej 70, Postbox 2262. DK-8100 Århus (Viby J). ℭ 86-11-61-11. Fax 86-11-74-00. www.christian dx.dk. 80 units. 1,050DKK–1,320DKK ($175–$220) double. AE, DC, MC, V. Bus: 11. **Amenities:** Restaurant; bar; wading pool for children; gym; sauna; room service (7am–10pm); laundry service; dry cleaning; nonsmoking rooms; rooms for those with limited mobility; solarium. *In room:* TV, dataport, minibar, hair dryer.

INEXPENSIVE

Hotel Guldsmeden *Value*   This affordable choice lies in a former town house from the 1800s that was completely renovated and turned into a cozy little place. We like to stop off here in the summer, when the garden is at its peak, and enjoy breakfast on the terrace outdoors. It's probably the best and healthiest breakfast in town—all organic, with fresh fruit, muesli, and the like. The bedrooms are small to midsize, and each is furnished tastefully, most often cheerfully, in soothing shades. Some of the rooms contain a small bathroom with shower; in units without bathrooms, corridor facilities suffice.

Guldsmedgade 40. ℭ 86-13-45-50. Fax 86-13-76-76. 27 units, 20 with bathroom. 745DKK ($124) double without bathroom; 945DKK ($158) double with bathroom; 1,095DKK–1,295DKK ($183–$216) suite. Rates include buffet breakfast. AE, DC, MC, V. **Amenities:** Breakfast room; lounge. *In room:* TV.

Hotel La Tour *Kids*   Since its construction in 1956, and its rebuilding in 1986, this hotel has followed a conscious policy of downgrading (yes, downgrading) its accommodations and facilities from a once lofty status to a middle-brow formula. The result is a hotel that's far from being the best in town—viewed, we imagine, as a great success by the management—that attracts hundreds of foreign visitors. The hotel, housed in an unimaginative two-story building, is 3.5km (2¼ miles) north of Århus center. It offers clean, simple bedrooms with small bathrooms containing tub/shower combinations. There are a patio-style restaurant serving competently prepared Danish and international food, a bar, and a children's playroom (open May–Sept only).

Randersvej 139, DK-8200 Århus. © **86-16-78-88.** Fax 86-16-79-95. www.latour.dk. 101 units. 920DKK ($154) double; 1,250DKK ($209) suite. Rates include breakfast. AE, DC, MC, V. Bus: 2, 3, or 11. **Amenities:** Restaurant; bar; room service (7am–10pm); laundry service; dry cleaning. *In room:* TV, minibar, hair dryer, safe.

Hotel Mercur   This is one of the most appealing and ultramodern hotels in town, 4km (2½ miles) south of the center and less than a kilometer (½ mile) from the park that surrounds Queen Margrethe's summer house (Marselisborg Slot). Overall, it's warmer and cozier than some of its most visible competitors, such as the Kong Christian den X. Rooms are masculine looking and conservatively contemporary with views that encompass panoramas over the town and the seacoast. Some have narrow, rarely used balconies, and each unit is equipped with a small bathroom with shower. There are a restaurant, the **Mercur,** and a bar on the premises, both of which are appealing and warmly decorated. There are two bowling alleys in the hotel's cellar, and a larger bowling alley complex a few blocks away. There's also a shopping mall, Viby Centret, with about 50 shops, on Skanderborgvej, a short walk from the hotel. The hotel is not associated with the France-based low-budget hotel chain Mercure.

Viby Torv, DK-8260 Århus, Viby J. © **86-14-14-11.** Fax 86-14-46-41. www.hotel-mercur.dk. 90 units. Mon–Thurs 650DKK–925DKK ($109–$154) double, 780DKK–925DKK ($130–$154) suite; Fri–Sun 500DKK–660DKK ($84–$110) double, 625DKK–740DKK ($104–$124) suite. Rates include breakfast. AE, DC, MC, V. Bus: 5, 15, or 25. **Amenities:** Restaurant; bar; dry cleaning; nonsmoking rooms. *In room:* TV.

WHERE TO DINE
EXPENSIVE

Hotel Philip Restaurant ⋆⋆ DANISH/FRENCH   In the most exclusive hotel in Århus, a delightful restaurant has opened, giving you a romantic atmosphere and quality food prepared with the best and freshest of ingredients—an unbeatable combination. Tables are placed on beautiful hardwood floors, and elegantly set tables are lit by brass candleholders. It's dim and romantic. The ceiling is adorned with a metal tapestry in the Art Nouveau style, and the walls are painted dark but brightened with summery yellow ornaments.

The front part of the restaurant, as can be viewed from the street, is decorated as an elegant cafe, with the luxurious dining found in the rear. Inventiveness goes hand in hand with solid technique. The kitchen also takes full advantage of the region's riches, with seafood predominating. One specialty is cannelloni stuffed with Serrano ham, seafood, and Danish cheese, and served with truffles and baby potatoes. The menu, however, is seasonally adjusted.

Åboulevarden 28. © **87-32-14-44.** Reservations required. Main courses 160DKK–200DKK ($27–$33). DC, MC, V. Mon–Sat noon–10:30pm.

Prins Ferdinand ⋆⋆ DANISH/INTERNATIONAL   On the edge of Århus's historic center in a former tea salon, this is one of the city's finest restaurants. It was established in 1988 by Per Brun and his wife, Lotte Norrig, who create a version of modern Danish cuisine that has won favor with the region's business community. In two pink-toned dining rooms laden with flickering candles and flowers, you can order a platter of fresh smoked salmon served with tartare of salmon and pepper-cream sauce, turbot with Russian caviar and a drizzle of olive oil, sea devil with lobster prepared Thai style with lemon grass, or boneless pigeon stuffed with fresh goose liver served with a raspberry sauce. A dessert specialty is pears cooked with elderberries and served with vanilla ice cream, nougat, and almonds. The restaurant's array of dessert cheeses, the most unusual array in Jutland, includes artisan creations produced by small farmers.

Viborgvej 2. ⓒ **86-12-52-05.** Reservations recommended. Main courses 140DKK–175DKK ($23–$29) at lunch, 160DKK–250DKK ($27–$42) at dinner; fixed-price menus 175DKK–235DKK ($29–$39) at lunch, 375DKK–545DKK ($63–$91) at dinner. AE, DC, MC, V. Tues–Sat 11am–3pm and 6–9pm. Bus: 3.

MODERATE

Kroen i Krogen DANISH   "The inn in the corner" has built a loyal clientele since it was established across from the railway station in 1934. It's got a good, conventional Danish menu and one of the most unusual interiors in town—the walls are decorated with about two dozen panels depicting local artist Michael Fisker's interpretation of the history of Århus from the 14th to the mid–20th centuries. They were painted shortly after World War II on the back of canvas coffee sacks because conventional art supplies weren't available.

You can order something as straightforward and simple as grilled sausages with black bread—a worthy foil for a glass of beer—or the house specialty, *kroens Anretning*, a platter with two kinds of herring, a fish filet, a handful of shrimp, and a small steak with fried onions. Other items include a savory orange-marinated salmon, perfectly grilled rib-eye steak, and hazelnut cake. Between April and September, there are at least 50 additional seats on an outdoor terrace.

Banegårdspladsen 4. ⓒ **86-12-11-76.** Main courses 198DKK ($33); fixed-price menus 100DKK–245DKK ($17–$41). DC, MC, V. Mon–Sat 11:30am–9pm.

Restaurant Margueritten ⭑ DANISH/FRENCH/ITALIAN   One of the town's better restaurants was carved out of what used to be stables for horses that pulled the carriages through Århus. It's a cozy place for lunch, and an ideal venue for a romantic dinner under old beamed ceilings. Old Danish stripped furniture enhances the ambience, and in summer a beautiful little garden in the rear is open. This isn't grandmother-type cooking, as the fare is as modern as tomorrow, but it always uses the freshest regional produce. Chefs offer such dishes as guinea fowl with a stuffing of tiger shrimp; the distinctive flavor comes from the marinade of yogurt and tandoori spices. Some of the best dishes we found on the menu included filet of wild pork with a balsamic chocolate sauce (yes, you read that right), medallion of beef in a cognac sauce with mixed vegetables, and a tangy breast of duck with a raspberry sauce and fresh plums which have been marinated in port. The English-speaking waitstaff is polite and helpful.

Guldsmedgade 20. ⓒ **86-19-60-33.** Reservations required. 1-course fixed-price menu 159DKK ($27), 2 courses 179DKK ($30), 3 courses 209DKK ($35). Mon–Sat 11:30am–11pm.

INEXPENSIVE

Den Gremme Ælleng (The Ugly Duckling) DANISH BUFFET   This cost-conscious member of a chain whose restaurants are scattered throughout Denmark offers a self-service Danish buffet. At lunchtime, dishes include at least 10 different preparations of herring, Nordic meatballs, and a varied salad bar. In the late afternoon a different array is laid out. These usually include such hot dishes as casseroles, meats, and vegetables, plus Danish cheeses and a salad bar.

Østergade 12. ⓒ **86-13-99-63.** Reservations recommended. Main courses 99DKK–129DKK ($17–$22); buffet dinner 100DKK ($17). MC, V. Daily 5:30–10:30pm. Bus: 2, 6, or 17.

Ministeriet DANISH/MEDITERRANEAN   This small and cozy inn with a courtyard is in the old Klostertorv across from Frue Kloster Abbey. You'll invariably stumble upon the charming old place if you're out sightseeing. It's a cafe-style place serving very good food, with lots of fish such as plaice, offered at reasonable prices. The atmosphere is informal, often attracting young people. The chefs offer various menus depending on the season, using fresh Danish produce whenever available. There's a strong Mediterranean influence here.

Klostertorvet 5. (℃) **86-17-11-88.** Reservations required. Main courses lunch 45DKK–108DKK ($7.50–$18); fixed-price dinner menus 130DKK–195DKK ($22–$33). AE, DC, MC, V. Mon–Sat 9:30am–1pm; Sun 10am–6pm. Bus: 1, 2, 6, or 9.

Restaurant Skovmøllen ★ *Finds* DANISH/INTERNATIONAL Since it was constructed of straw, wood, and stone more than 300 years ago, this building has functioned as a farmhouse, a gristmill, and a simple cafe. It's set beside the Giber River, 10km (6¼ miles) south of Århus, close to the Mosegaard Museum of Danish Prehistory. Beneath a beamed ceiling and frequent reminders of old-time Denmark, you can order typically Danish platters at lunchtime, and straightforward, not particularly esoteric dishes that are just a bit more cosmopolitan at night. Lunches might include meatballs, *smørrebrød* (open-face sandwich), herring platters, or roasted pork with onions and braised cabbage. Dinners are more elaborate, featuring shrimp cocktails, steak with french fries, stuffed filets of plaice with new potatoes, and salmon chops with garlic-flavored butter sauce. The place is always dependable, the cookery always reliable, but its main allure is that it's a charming, country-flavored getaway from the city center.

Skovmøllenvej 51. (℃) **86-27-12-14.** Reservations recommended. Main courses 48DKK–200DKK ($8–$33); fixed-price menus 148DKK–298DKK ($25–$50). MC, V. June–Aug Tues–Sun noon–6pm; Sept–May Fri–Sun noon–5pm. From downtown Århus, take bus no. 6.

Teater Bodega DANISH Originally established at a different address in 1907, Teater Bodega in 1951 moved across the street from both the Århus Dramatic Theater and the Århus Cathedral. It tries to provide an amusing dining ambience for theater and art lovers. The walls are covered with illustrations of theatrical costumes along with other thespian memorabilia. The food is solid and flavorful in the Danish country style. Various kinds of Danish hash, including *biksemad,* are served along with regular or large portions of Danish roast beef. There are also English and French beef, fried plaice, and flounder.

Skolegade 7. (℃) **86-12-19-17.** Reservations recommended. Main courses 89DKK–179DKK ($15–$30); lunch *smørrebrød* 45DKK–85DKK ($7.50–$14); 3-course fixed-price lunch or dinner 238DKK ($40). DC, MC, V. Mon–Sat 11am–11:30pm. Bus: 6.

ÅRHUS AFTER DARK

The city of Århus has the richest and most varied cultural life in Jutland. Its chief attraction, and a major venue for cultural events, is the Musikhuset Århus (see below). The Århus Symphony Orchestra and the Danish National Opera perform here frequently, among other attractions. For a look at what's happening here and in other venues, pick up a copy of the monthly booklet *What's On in Århus,* at the tourist office (see "Visitor Information," earlier in this chapter).

CULTURAL ÅRHUS

You'll have to speak Danish to enjoy most productions at the **Århus Theater,** Bispetorv (℃ **89-33-26-22**), which has five stages with a total of 1,200 seats. It was designed by Hack Kampmann and opened in 1900. Local actors and visiting stars entertain in a wide repertoire early September to mid-June.

Svalegangen, Rosenkrantzgade 21 (℃ **86-13-88-66**), presents an up-to-date repertoire, the latest in Danish drama, music, cabaret, modern dance, and guest artists. The company stages about 40 productions annually. **Entré Scenen,** Grønnegade 93B (℃ **86-20-15-36**), is an experimental feature of Århus's dramatic life. A varied range of performances, often by foreign artists, appeals to a wide spectrum of ages here. Guest opera and dance theater productions are also staged at **Gellerupscenen,** Gudrunsvej 78 (℃ **86-25-03-66**).

Opened in 1982, **Musikhuset Århus,** Thomas Jensens Allé (© **89-40-90-00**), is the home of the Århus Symphony Orchestra and the Danish National Opera. Tickets for most events range from 50DKK to 1,000DKK ($8.35–$167). Programs are presented on the great stage, the small stage, and the cabaret stage, as well as in the amphitheater and on the foyer stages, where free performances are presented year-round. The foyer, open daily 11am to 9pm, is the site of the box office, an information desk, a cafe/restaurant, and souvenir shops.

DANCE CLUBS

The most popular, charming, and fun dance club in town is **Train,** Toldbodgade 6 (© **26-12-58-00**), where a crowd that's under 35 or 40-ish dances on any of three floors of what used to be a warehouse down beside the waterfront. The top floors feature disco music from the '70s and '80s; the middle and lower levels are devoted to an English-style pub and louder, more jarring techno. The site is also a venue, at irregular intervals, for live concerts. There's sometimes, but not always, a cover charge that can range from 40DKK to 70DKK ($6.70–$12), depending on what's on that night.

BARHOPPING

Århus abounds in bars and taverns, most of which charge no cover unless there's live music on special nights. The oldest hostelry in town, **Thorups Kælder,** Store Torv 3 (© **86-12-04-14**), was founded by Cistercian monks in the 13th century. Here you can quench your thirst in historic surroundings. You'll find us at our favorite bar and cafe, **Café Under Masken,** Bispegade 3 (© **86-18-22-66**), next door to the Royal Hotel. This is the creation of a well-known local artist, Hans Krull, who designed the iron sculptures adorning the gateway to the hotel. If Salvador Dali were alive and could see the decor, he would call it surreal. Krull and some of his patrons apparently picked up the flotsam and jetsam of the world for decor. The only Aussie bar in Århus, **The Billabong Bar,** Skolegade 26 (© **86-13-27-15**), is a typical Outback-style bar, its raw edge adding to its charm. There's live music every weekend, and sports fans gather here to watch major events on TV, all the time sipping Australian beverages. **Tyngen,** Mejlgade 53 (© **86-19-22-55**), is the venue for rock, techno, and the like.

Bryggeriet Sct. Clemens ★, Kannikegade 10–12 (© **86-13-80-00**), is a combined brewery and public house which offers freshly tapped, frothy draft beer brewed in coppers in the cellar, matured, and served in glasses. The bartender's special is a 1-liter *kwak glas* (a round-bottomed glass held upright on a wooden stand). Regardless of which beer you select, this glass is designed for massive consumption. In addition to the pub, you can also order various Danish dishes here if you decide to stick around and dine.

Gays and lesbians gather to dance and enjoy the cafe at **Pan Club,** Jægergårdsgade 42 (© **86-13-43-80**). The cafe is open Friday and Saturday 10pm to 6am; the disco is open Friday and Saturday 11pm to 5am. Cover is 15DKK ($2.50) before 11pm, 60DKK ($10) after 11pm.

AN AMUSEMENT PARK

Tivoli-Friheden, Skobrynet (© **86-14-73-00;** bus: 4), is a pale imitation of the Tivoli in Copenhagen; the scale is much smaller here, but there is some of the same sense of fantasy. Set in a forest about 3.5km (2 miles) south of Århus, it's bright and modern, appealing to families and couples from the city and the surrounding communities. Entertainment includes an open-air theater, art shows, concerts, clowns, rides, and a scattering of restaurants. The park is open only mid-April to mid-August. Although the park opens every day at noon, the rides and attractions don't open until 2pm. Everything closes down at 11pm. Admission is 55DKK ($9.20) adults, 35DKK ($5.85) children.

THE TOWN'S ONLY CASINO

Hotel Royal Casino, Stove Torv 4 (© **86-12-00-11**), is one of only four in Jutland and one of a handful in the entire country. Blackjack—also French roulette on weekends—plus other games of chance are offered daily 3pm to 4am. Admission is 50DKK ($8.35). No jeans and no sports shoes are allowed; a jacket is preferred, although a tie isn't necessary.

8 Ebeltoft ⭐

96km (60 miles) E of Silkeborg; 53km (33 miles) NE of Århus; 335km (209 miles) W of Copenhagen

A well-preserved town of half-timbered buildings, Ebeltoft (which means "apple orchard") is the capital of the Mols hill country. This is a village of cobblestone streets, hidden-away lanes, old inns, and ruddy-faced fishermen, who still carry on the profession of their ancestors.

Ebeltoft's Viking Age wooden boats have given way today to yachts and modern ferries. Life at Ebeltoft developed around its harbor and the beautiful bay of Ebeltoft Vig.

The thriving port was prosperous in the Middle Ages, enjoying trade with Germany and Sweden as well as Copenhagen. However, in 1659 the Swedish army invaded, sacking the port and setting fire to its merchant fleet. Ebeltoft never really recovered until tourists—ironically the Swedes—began to arrive in the 1960s. Because it slumbered for so long, Ebeltoft retained its old look of timber-framed brick buildings topped with red-tile roofs.

ESSENTIALS

GETTING THERE   By Train and Bus   There's no direct train service to Ebeltoft. From Copenhagen, take the train (via Fredericia) to Århus; at Århus Central Station, board bus no. 123 for Ebeltoft.

By Car   From Silkeborg head east on Route 15 through Århus and continue around the coast, then follow Route 21 south to Ebeltoft.

VISITOR INFORMATION   Contact the **Ebeltoft Turistbureau,** Strandvejen 2 (© **86-34-14-00;** www.ebeltoftturist.dk), open June 15 to August, Monday to Saturday 10am to 6pm and Sunday 11am to 4pm; and September to June 14, Monday to Friday 9am to 4pm and Saturday 10am to 1pm.

GETTING AROUND   By Bicycle   Bikes can be rented at **L&P Cykler,** Nørre Allé 5 (© **86-34-47-77**), open Monday to Friday 8am to 5:30pm, Saturday 8am to noon. Rental fees cost around 60DKK ($10) per day.

SEEING THE SIGHTS

Det Gamle Rådhus   The Town Hall looks like something erected just for kindergarten children to play in—a 1789 building, blackened half-timbering, a red-brick with timbered facade, and a bell tower. Its museum houses an ethnographic collection from Thailand and artifacts from the town's history. It's in the town center north of Strandvejen.

Torvet. © **86-34-55-99.** Admission 25DKK ($4.20) adults, 5DKK (85¢) children. Apr–Aug daily 10am–5pm; Sept–Oct Tues–Sun 11am–3pm; Nov–Mar Sat–Sun 11am–3pm.

Farvergårdeb   Dating from 1772, the oldest part of this dyeworks goes back to 1683. Exhibits include the living quarters with original furniture, the dye facilities with a pressing room, a dye room with boilers, a printing room, and a stable wing with a coach house dating from the early 18th century. It's located directly west of Torvet in the town center.

Adelgade 13–15. (C) **86-34-13-82**. Admission 25DKK ($4.20) adults, 5DKK (85¢) children. June 1–Aug 31 daily 11am–5pm. Closed Sept–May.

Fregatten Jylland   The *Jylland* is the oldest man-of-war in Denmark (1860) and the world's longest wooden ship at 71m (233 ft.). The frigate is moored in the harbor.

Strandvejen 4. (C) **86-34-10-99**. Admission 60DKK ($10) adults, 20DKK ($3.35) children. Jan 2–Mar 21 and Oct 25–Dec 30 daily 10am–4pm; Mar 22–June 13 and Aug 23–Oct 24 daily 10am–5pm; June 14–Aug 22 daily 10am–7pm.

Glasmuseet Ebeltoft   At Ebeltoft harbor stands one of Denmark's most important glass museums, housed in a building that was once a customs and excise house. It displays both decorative and functional glass, ranging from the symbol-laden works of Swedish glass guru Bertil Vallien to the luminous gold pavilions of Japanese artist Kyohei Fujita. The artists exhibited decide which of their pieces they want to represent their work; this has resulted in a large permanent exhibition. May to September young glass students work with blowing irons and modern "syrupy" blobs of glass in the museum garden.

Strandvejen 8. (C) **86-34-17-99**. Fax 86-34-60-60. www.glasmuseet.dk. Admission 40DKK ($6.70) adults, 10DKK ($1.65) children. Jan–June and Aug–Dec daily 10am–5pm; July daily 10am–7pm. Closed Dec 24–25, Dec 31, and Jan 1.

Vindmølleparken   Five kilometers (3 miles) south of Ebeltoft, adjacent to the ferryboat terminal, 16 windmills sit on a curved spit of land open to gusts of wind from the Baltic to generate electricity for some 600 families. To see it, drive south of town, following the signs toward the hamlet of Øer, or the signs pointing to the ferryboat to Zealand. If you phone in advance, in some rare instances a free, 30-minute guided tour during open hours can be arranged by the city council.

Færgehavnen. (C) **89-52-11-11**. Free admission. Mon–Fri 10am–4pm.

SHOPPING

Since the mid-1980s, Ebeltoft has become Denmark's "glass kingdom." There are no fewer than six local glassworks producing and selling blown-glass items. At several of the studios, it's possible to see the workshops where glass bowls, vases, wine glasses, and beautiful dishes are created in the glowing furnace. You can visit various workshops and purchase glass at such outlets as **Glasværkstedet,** Skindergade 5 ((C) **86-34-08-89**); **Glaspusteriet,** Studsgade 14 ((C) **86-12-72-85**); and **Ebeltoft Glas,** Nedergade 19 ((C) **86-34-35-66**).

WHERE TO STAY

Hotel Ebeltoft Strand   This centrally located two-story hotel was constructed in 1978. Each comfortable, well-furnished guest room has a balcony or terrace that overlooks Ebeltoft Bay. All units are also equipped with well-kept bathrooms with tub/shower combinations. The hotel has a restaurant, bar, open fireplace, and playground. It's about a 5-minute drive from the ferry and a 15-minute drive from Tirstrup Airport.

Nordre Strandvej 3, DK-8400 Ebeltoft. (C) **86-34-33-00**. Fax 86-34-46-36. www.ebeltoftstrand.dk. 72 units. 1,195DKK ($200) double. Rates include buffet breakfast. AE, DC, MC, V. Free parking. Bus: 123 from Århus. **Amenities:** Restaurant; bar; indoor heated pool; 24-hr. room service; laundry service; dry cleaning; nonsmoking rooms; rooms for those with limited mobility. *In room:* TV, dataport, minibar, hair dryer, safe.

Hotel Hvide Hus An elegant establishment built in 1963, Hvide Hus has kept abreast of the times and today provides well-furnished rooms with terraces, refrigerators, and medium-size bathrooms with tub and shower. If you're a guest, its **restaurant,** offering an array of Danish and international dishes nightly 5 to 10pm, is worth a look.

Strandgårdshøj 1, DK-8400 Ebeltoft. © **86-34-14-66.** Fax 86-34-49-69. www.hhh-hotel.dk. 98 units. 1,025DKK–1,225DKK ($171–$205) double; from 1,425DKK ($238) suite. Rates include breakfast. AE, DC, MC, V. Closed Dec 18–Jan 4. Bus: 123 from Århus. **Amenities:** Restaurant; bar; indoor heated pool; sauna; room service (7am–9pm); nonsmoking rooms. *In room:* TV, dataport, minibar, hair dryer, trouser press.

Molskroen ✦ *(Finds* This hotel was vastly upgraded in 1998, and its prices rose dramatically, too. Nevertheless, it's one of the better places to stay in the area. Many rooms have terraces overlooking Mols Hills, and a fine white sandy beach is only 100m (328 ft.) away. The *kro* is in the center of an area of summer houses mostly built in the 1920s and 1930s. The medium-sized guest rooms are now sleek, functional, and most comfortable, with freshly tiled bathrooms equipped with tub/shower combinations. Ten of the bedrooms are found in the annex, a red-brick building with a tiled roof. Accommodations here are every bit as good in the main building. Nine of these annex accommodations are individually furnished junior suites set on two floors, with four beds in each room, making them suitable for families.

Hovegaden 16, Femmøller Strand, DK-8400 Ebeltoft. © **86-36-22-00.** Fax 86-36-23-00. www.molskroen.dk. 18 units. 1,280DKK–1,680DKK ($214–$281) double; 3,200DKK ($534) suite. Rates include breakfast. AE, DC, V. Free parking. Closed Dec 24–Jan 8. Bus: 123 from Århus. **Amenities:** Restaurant; bar; room service (7am–10pm); babysitting; laundry service; dry cleaning; 1 room for those with limited mobility. *In room:* TV, fax, dataport, minibar, hair dryer, safe.

WHERE TO DINE

Harriet ✦ DANISH/FRENCH/ITALIAN Our favorite restaurant in Ebeltoft presents a sophisticated, carefully choreographed cuisine. it occupies what was originally built in the heart of town as a general store in 1775. Lunches tend to include stable and relatively conservative platters, the most popular of which include salmon fish cakes with salad and fresh bread, and plates piled high with an assortment of various preparations of herring. Dinners are more elaborate, with menus that change frequently, according to the season, but which might include veal roasted with a ragout of locally picked forest mushrooms, veal cutlets in wine sauce, or filets of plaice served with a lemon-butter sauce. Any of these can be preceded with such exotica as Mediterranean-inspired carpaccio Piemontese with truffle oil, or hot pecorino cheese drizzled with hot maple syrup.

Adelgade 62. © **86-34-44-66.** Reservations recommended. Main courses 169DKK–102DKK ($28–$17); 2-course meal 215DKK ($36). Daily 11:30am–10pm. AE, DC, MC, V.

Restaurant "Mellem Jyder" ✦ DANISH The oldest and most historically evocative restaurant in Ebeltoft occupies a half-timbered building (ca. 1610), a few steps from the old Town Hall. Inside, you can order a roster of conservative and ultratraditional Danish dishes whose authenticity seems to go well with the antique setting. Menu items include roasted or marinated salmon with dill sauce; filet of sole meunière, or in some cases, fried and served with parsley and butter sauce; roasted pork with cabbage, fresh salad, french fries, and béarnaise sauce; and an old-fashioned hash dish known as *biksemal*. On afternoons, a beer garden in back—like you might expect in neighboring Germany—is popular during mild weather.

Juulsbakke 3. © **86-34-11-23.** Reservations recommended. Main courses 95DKK–170DKK ($16–$28); fixed-price menu noon–6pm 120DKK ($20), after 6pm 195DKK ($33). MC, V. Wed–Sun noon–8pm.

EBELTOFT AFTER DARK

The best place to gather in the evening is **Den Skæve Bar,** Overgade 23 (© **86-34-37-97**), an English-style pub in a building dating from 1683. This is often the venue for live music, including folk, rock, blues, and jazz.

9 Randers

37km (23 miles) N of Århus; 322km (200 miles) W of Copenhagen; 64km (40 miles) S of Aalborg

The sixth largest town in Denmark, with 60,000 inhabitants, Randers was founded at the point where Denmark's longest river, the Gudenå, becomes a natural fjord for the traffic between the northern and southern parts of Denmark.

As early as 1080, a royal mint was established here. It enjoyed prosperity in the medieval era when several churches and monasteries were founded in the area. At the apex of its prestige, in the 14th century, Valdemar IV constructed a royal castle near the town. A Franciscan monastery enjoyed influence here until it was forced to dissolve in 1530, becoming a royal palace.

By the 17th century the town's influence had diminished. Foreign occupation, a massive conflagration in 1672, and the Black Death contributed to the town's demise. Disputes with Prussia over Schleswig-Holstein to the south led to more hostilities in the 19th century. Its troubles with Germany were climaxed with the Nazi occupation in 1940 when Nazi troops rode into town to occupy Randers until the closing days of World War II.

Today Randers has rebounded from a troubled past. It is a town of industry, including woodcarvers, shoemakers, silversmiths, and bell foundry workers. Vehicle manufacture is also important to the local economy. But it's no dreary industrial town. There are a number of period brick and half-timbered houses here along with several attractions.

ESSENTIALS

GETTING THERE   By Train   Trains run hourly between Copenhagen and Randers. There are frequent rail links with Aalborg and Århus.

By Bus   Bus no. 118 runs between Århus and Randers (trip time: 50 min.); tickets can be purchased once you board.

By Car   Head north from Århus along the E45.

VISITOR INFORMATION   Randers Turistbureau, Erhvervenes Hus, Tørvebryggen 12 (© **86-42-44-77;** www.visitranders.com), is open June 16 to August 31, Monday through Friday 9am to 6pm, Saturday 9am to 3pm. September to March, hours are Monday to Friday 9:30am to 4:30pm and Saturday 9am to noon. April 1 to June 15, hours are Monday to Friday 9am to 5pm, Saturday 9am to noon.

GETTING AROUND   By Bicycle   Bike rentals are available at **Jørgen Schmidt Cykler,** Kirkegade 7 (© **86-41-29-03**). The cost is 60DKK ($10) per day, plus a deposit of 300DKK ($50). Hours are Monday through Friday 9:30am to 5:30pm, Saturday 9:30am to 2pm.

SEEING THE SIGHTS

As you stroll through the medieval streets and lanes of Randers, you'll see several well-preserved half-timbered houses from the 16th and 17th centuries that were originally built by prosperous merchants.

Armed with a map from the tourist office, walk from here along Denmark's first pedestrians-only street, **Houmeden.** The half-timbered houses on the north side date from around 1560. You come out at **Rådhustorvet** (Town Hall Square), the center of Randers. On the western side of the square is the oldest stone house in Randers, dating from 1468. The Rådhus (Town Hall) on the east side of the square was built in 1778 to the designs of Christian Mørup. A belfry crowns the hipped roof. On a plinth in front of the Rådhus is the seated figure of Niels Ebbesen, who killed the Duke of Holstein in 1340 when he attempted to gain control of Denmark.

Heading east behind the Town Hall, continue down Rosengade and Nygade. On the corner is **Fideikommishuset,** constructed in 1833 by Joseph Carl Wulff, a prominent Jew. This was a large Jewish quarter until the 19th century. Nygade 4 is the oldest half-timbered house in Randers, from 1550.

Turn right onto Østervold, which more or less follows the line of the old moat that used to run along the ramparts. At the northern end of Nørestræde and Østervold is one of the oldest school buildings in Randers, from 1861.

The town's most interesting church is the **Sankt Mortens Kirke,** Kirketorvet (© **86-42-29-21**), built as the church for the Holy Ghost monastery from around 1500. It is one of Denmark's most attractive town churches, noted for its beautifully carved doors to the main entrance. Inside this Gothic brick building is a choir with three sides facing east; it sits lower than the three-aisled nave. The interior of the church has rich trappings, mainly from the 17th and 18th centuries, including a lovely font, magnificent altar, baroque pulpit, and organ case. Admission is free, and the church can be visited Monday to Friday 10am to 4pm and Saturday 10am to 1pm. Sunday is reserved for mass.

Kulturhuset, Stemannsgade 2 (© **86-42-86-55**), lies on the east side of Randers, a 10-minute walk from Town Hall Square. Consisting of both an old and a new building, it is the museum of local history and culture. Fleming Lassen designed the newer section with two interior courtyards in 1964. On the main floor is a Historical and Cultural Museum, including a trio of burghers' rooms decorated in part with paintings by Rembrandt and Ostade. There are both a prehistory section and exhibitions devoted to ecclesiastical art. There is also a display of antique weapons and old glass. Upstairs is the art museum, housing mainly 20th-century Danish paintings, including works by Asger Jorn and Ejler Bille. The museum is open Tuesday to Sunday 11am to 5pm, charging 25DKK ($4.20) adults, 15DKK ($2.50) seniors, free for children.

A final attraction, **Randers Regnskov,** Tørvebryggen 11 (© **86-40-69-33**), is a rainforest—a tropical, zoological exhibition center where you can venture out on a "safari" through a terrain featuring impressive rocks and cliffs, colorful butterflies, and playful otters. This permanent exhibition of a rainforest's flora and fauna is found in two glass domes built next to the Gudenå River. May to August it's open daily 10am to 6pm. Off-season hours are Monday to Friday 10am to 4pm, Saturday and Sunday 10am to 5pm. Admission is 90DKK ($15) adults, 80DKK ($13) seniors, 50DKK ($8.35) children.

NEARBY ATTRACTIONS

Near the town of Hobro is the site of **Fyrkat** ☆, Fyrkatvej no. 37B (© **98-51-19-27**), a 10th-century Viking ring fortress. It is, however, somewhat smaller than the more famous Trelleborg fortress in southern Zealand (see chapter 6).

The ring fortress, or so it is believed, was constructed by Harald Bluetooth, the Viking king, around A.D. 980. Over time, its memory faded into history. As late as the 1950s it was still a farmer's field. Archaeologists from the national museum in Copenhagen began an excavation of the site, learning that it had been a community of some 1,000 souls, including Viking soldiers, women, and children. There was evidence that the fortress had been burned and probably abandoned. It is presumed that it enjoyed only a short life span.

As you walk along grass-covered ramparts, you can trace its symmetrical design. Like similar Viking constructions, the fortress was divided into four parts, opening onto a main courtyard, the center of life and bustling market activities. All structures, of course, are gone, but a Viking house of oak timbers has been constructed on-site to show the type of building that once stood here.

The field also contains some period farmhouses, including a 2-century-old water mill and a half-timbered *kro* where you can order lunch.

The E45 motorway, 27km (17 miles) northwest of Randers, reaches Hobro. You can also go by the hourly IC train to Hobro, a 20-minute ride from Randers. Fyrkat is 3km (1¾ miles) south of Hobro center on the Fyrkatvej. You can take a taxi from the Hobro train station for about 100DKK ($17). There's no public transportation. Admission is 55DKK ($9.20) adults, 20DKK ($3.35) children. March to May and September to October it's open daily 10am to 4pm; June to August daily 10am to 5pm. Guides in period clothing give demonstrations of Viking activities, including spinning and bronze casting.

To the north of the fortress, **Vikingegården Fyrkat** has opened to supplement the fortress site. This is a farmstead similar to one that might have provided food to the Vikings. Eight buildings on-site have been duplicated authentically.

SHOPPING

Randers's busiest and most prestigious shopping street is the all-pedestrian Bredegade. You'll find everything you need to dress yourself and your friends, and everything you need to decorate your home. Two premier stores for the acquisition of handicrafts, gift items, garden accessories, and housewares include **Inspiration,** Torvegade 1 (© 86-42-94-44), and **Axel W. Nielsen,** Bredegade 17 (© 86-42-33-77). At Nielsen's, check out the inventory of mostly blue-and-white, hand-painted Danish tiles as well.

WHERE TO STAY

Hvidsten Kro on the outskirts is the most atmospheric place to stay (see "Where to Dine," below).

Hotel Gudenå   Built in an angular, four-story format in 1962, this simple modern hotel sits close to the harbor, in the town center, and functions as an old standby for sales representatives in the maritime trades who are in town on business. Rooms are compact but clean and comfortable, with contemporary, durable furniture. All accommodations are furnished with a neatly tiled private bathroom with shower. Other than breakfast, no meals are served, and although someone on staff can bring you a drink, there's no actual bar.

Østervold 42, 8900 Randers. © 86-40-44-11. Fax 86-40-44-82. www.hotel-gudenaa.dk. 18 units. 695DKK ($116) double. Rates include breakfast. MC, V. **Amenities:** Restaurant (breakfast); bar; room service (7am–9pm); nonsmoking rooms. *In room:* TV.

Hotel Krojylland   One of Randers's most stately looking buildings sits near the center, and sports a neoclassically inspired late-19th-century facade. Thanks to an ongoing series of renovations, the most recent of which were in 2003, the clean, well-maintained rooms are more modern than the building's exterior might have you think. Each bedroom comes with a small private bathroom with tub or shower. There are very few amenities. There's a nearby health club, but you must pay a fee to use their facilities. Other than breakfast, no meals are served.

Vestergade 51–53, DK-8900 Randers. ✆ **86-41-43-33.** Fax 86-41-43-95. 33 units. 700DKK–945DKK ($117–$158) double. AE, DC, MC, V. Rates include breakfast. **Amenities:** Restaurant; bar; room service (6am–midnight); laundry service; dry cleaning; solarium. *In room:* TV, dataport, minibar.

Hotel Randers ★★   This is the best and most prestigious hotel in town, with a distinguished pedigree: It is the oldest hotel in Denmark outside Copenhagen. Inside, you'll find a smooth, seamless, discreetly upscale decor that might remind you of such bastions of bourgeois respectability as the Hotel d'Angleterre in Copenhagen. Built in 1856, and set behind a grand neoclassical facade in the center of town, it's the venue that civic planners tend to trot out whenever there's an impending visit from the Danish queen or an important dignitary from virtually anywhere. Inside, you'll find a series of richly decorated public areas. Rooms are decorated individually and are most comfortable, coming with mid-size private bathrooms with tub and shower.

Torvegade 11, DK-8900 Randers. ✆ **86-42-34-22.** Fax 86-40-15-86. www.hotel-randers.dk. 79 units. Mon–Thurs 995DKK–1,125DKK ($166–$188) double, 1,650DKK ($276) suite; Fri–Sun 770DKK–835DKK ($129–$139) double, 1,095DKK ($183) suite. Rates include buffet breakfast. AE, DC, MC, V. **Amenities:** Restaurant; bar; 24-hr. room service; laundry service; dry cleaning; nonsmoking rooms. *In room:* TV, dataport, hair dryer.

WHERE TO DINE

Niels Ebbesen's Spiesehus DANISH   The Germans named one of the premier restaurants in town in honor of Randers's most famous military hero, a 14th-century local son who helped liberate the area from oppression. Local legend claims that if the structure's uppermost window is ever closed, the building will burn to the ground. Consequently, out of respect for that fable, expect to see one of the gable windows wide open even during the coldest weather. Inside, there are four dining rooms on two floors, lots of art and antiques, and a hard-working staff. Menu items arrive well prepared and in generous portions. Examples include hot shrimp with feta cheese and garlic; smoked and marinated salmon; filets of plaice cooked in butter sauce; spicy spare ribs; and many forms of grilled steaks, fish, chicken, and all-vegetarian dishes.

Storegade 13. ✆ **86-43-32-26.** Reservations recommended. Main courses 89DKK–210DKK ($15–$35). DC, MC, V. Daily 11:30am–10pm.

Restaurant Gauttuin ★ DANISH/CONTINENTAL   This is the most respectable and prestigious dining room in town, and a highly visible rendezvous point for civic leaders and prominent guests from out of town. Service is discreet and very, very polite. Menu items might include cold tomato soup with garlic and pimento, prawns fried in chile paste and served with fresh herbs and arugula, tenderloin of veal with a gravy concocted from foie gras and fresh coriander, and salmon baked with potatoes and served with a spinach-flavored cream sauce. The chef manages to steer a course between gourmet exclusiveness and middle-of-the-road compromise for those who don't like their cuisine "too experimental."

In the Hotel Randers, Torvegade 11. ✆ **86-42-34-22.** Reservations recommended. Main courses 75DKK–238DKK ($13–$40). AE, DC, MC, V. Daily 5:30–10pm.

Restaurant Slotskroen DANISH/FRENCH/ITALIAN   Although the building that contains it was constructed more than 25 years ago, its conservative decor and the fact that it is very close to the site of Randers's ruined castle somehow makes it seem older than it really is. Within any of four dining rooms, you can order a medley of dishes that are a bit more adventurous than what's offered at equivalently priced restaurants nearby. Lunches are relatively simple, with an emphasis on clients in a hurry who prefer lighter-than-usual dishes such as a platter of herring with all the traditional fixings, or something a bit more unusual, such as a spicy saltimbocca. Dinners are more leisurely and more theatrical, stressing such dishes as a symphony of fresh fish with saffron sauce and new Danish potatoes, rack of Danish lamb with onion sauce, and an elegant version of mignons of veal with a red wine glaze. In general, the cuisine is top notch here, and the chefs show a lot of skill.

Slotscentret Slotsgade 1. © 86-43-56-64. Reservations recommended. Main courses 96DKK–185DKK ($16–$31) at lunch, 218DKK–230DKK ($36–$38) at dinner; fixed-price 3-course lunch menu 245DKK ($41); fixed-price dinner menus 265DKK–420DKK ($44–$70). AE, DC, MC, V. Mon–Fri noon–midnight; Sat 6pm–midnight.

NEARBY DINING

Hvidsten Kro ★★ DANISH   This thatched farmhouse has been a country inn since 1634, making it the oldest in Denmark. The evocative furnishings include copper, brass, ceramics, samovars, deeply recessed windows, old sea chests, and walls painted with primitive murals. Waitresses wear floor-length, cotton-checked kitchen aprons. For a stopover for the night, or a home-cooked farm-style meal, there's no better choice in the area. The cookery is pretty much what it was a century ago. One of the reasons for the fame of this place is its five-course "Gundruns Recipe," a meal that is gargantuan, with plenty of Danish specialties. Take your biggest appetite here if you order that. It's possible, too, to order only a half of this meal, including herring, a bacon omelet, and a Danish *dansk koldt bord,* which is like a mini-smörgåsbord. Nevertheless, this cheaper meal still contains plenty of food.

Rooms in the guesthouse out back are bright and clean, although small. Only four doubles are rented, each containing hot and cold running water. The cost is 500DKK ($84) a night.

Marlagevej 450, Hvidsten, DK-8981 Spentrup. © 86-47-70-22. Fax 86-47-74-22. Reservations required in summer. Main courses 70DKK–175DKK ($12–$29); fixed-price menus 95DKK–190DKK ($16–$32). Rates include breakfast. DC, MC, V. Daily 11:30am–7:30pm. Closed Sept–June Mon. Bus: 235 from Randers. By car: Rte. 507 north to Spentrup.

RANDERS AFTER DARK

Bar Kahytten, in the Hotel Randers, Torvegade 11 (© 86-42-34-22), is an appropriate venue for a business rendezvous or for a weekend tryst. Positioned on the ground floor of the previously recommended hotel, it's outfitted in a woodsy, carefully paneled, old-fashioned, nautically inspired style that pays tribute to 19th-century Danish seafaring traditions. It's open daily 5:30pm to 12:30 or 1am, depending on business.

10 Viborg

298km (186 miles) W of Copenhagen; 58km (36 miles) W of Randers; 66km (41 miles) NW of Århus

"Viborg is like a mother to Jutland," wrote a historian some 4 centuries ago. That could still be true today. It's been called "Jutland in a nutshell," and a "cocktail of all good things from sea to sea on the Jutland peninsula." To the west of Viborg is rolling countryside, dominated by pine forests. The east side of town offers hilly, fertile farmland, with the Nørreå River meandering through the valley.

South of town lies a deep lake, Hald Sø, at the foot of Dollerup Bakker, an area dominated by Denmark's largest oak forest and ancient beech woods. Viborg itself doesn't open onto the sea, however, even though Limfjord tries to reach Viborg with its salty tongue, Hjarbæk Fjord. The hamlet of Hjarbæk, to the north of town, is Viborg's link with the sea today, and Hjarbæk is also home to a unique fleet of skiffs—the brown-sailed fjord boats.

A stroll through the town will give you a sense of its history, which was launched in the Middle Ages, although settlements here may date from as far back as 700. Once the town was called Wibjerg; *wi* is the old Viking word for *sacred,* and it is believed that the site of present-day Viborg was once a pagan center of worship. By 1065 Viborg was the see of a bishop. At that time it was also the capital of Jutland. Today it's a lively town of commerce and industry.

ESSENTIALS

GETTING THERE   By Train   Trains from Århus (see earlier in this chapter) arrive during the day on the hour, less frequently on Saturday and Sunday (trip time: 70 min.).

By Car   From Randers, our last stopover, follow Route 16 directly west into Viborg.

VISITOR INFORMATION   Viborg Turistbureau, Nytorv 9 (© **87-25-30-75**; www.viborg.dk), is open in summer Monday to Friday 9am to 5pm, Saturday 9:30am to 12:30pm. Off-season hours are Monday to Friday 9am to 4pm and Saturday 9am to 2pm.

SEEING THE SIGHTS

The narrow, steep, and winding streets of the historic core reveal Viborg's medieval origins. Viborg is pedestrian-friendly, and motorists had best park outside and cover the inner city on foot. The city's main attraction is **Viborg Domkirke,** Sct. Mogens Gade (© **87-25-52-50**), a round-arched Romanesque structure, constructed in 1876 in a style similar to the original great church that stood here in the 12th century. Even before that, a wooden structure was built on this site in the Viking era. The ravages of time and many fires left their mark on the church, although there are still traces of its first stone crypt from 1130.

The crypt is worth examining in detail. In the leather-clad coffin of one of the crypt chapels lies the embalmed body of the alchemist Valdemar Daa, described so movingly by Hans Christian Andersen in his story *The Wind Tells of Valdemar Daa and His Daughters.*

The cathedral's most distinctive features are its twin towers with their pyramidal roofs. The interior is known for the Biblical wall paintings of Joakim Skovgaard, created between 1901 and 1906.

The black stone in the floor in front of the altar marks the grave of the murdered Danish king Erik Glipping, who received no less than 50 sword and dagger thrusts through his body when spending the night in Finderup, just southwest of Viborg, in 1286. Hours are Monday through Saturday 11am to 4pm and Sunday noon to 4pm; admission is free.

Skovgaard Museet, Domkirkestræde 2–4 (© **86-62-39-75**), fronts the cathedral. The museum is housed in the old town hall or Rådhus, a baroque structure designed by Claus Stallknecht of Hamburg, Germany. He came to Viborg to help rebuild the city after the last major fire in 1726. The museum here today is devoted to the paintings, sketches, and sculptures of Joakim Skovgaard (1856–1933), known mainly for his work in Viborg Domkirke (see above). The museum owns his preliminary sketches for his frescoes for the cathedral. You can also see works by some of his fellow artists and friends, including Johan Thomas Lundbye, Niels Larsen Stevns, and Thorvald B. Bindesbøll. Works by 20th-century artists can also be viewed. The museum is open May to

September, daily 10am to 12:30pm and 1:30 to 5pm. Off-season hours are daily 1:30 to 5pm. Admission is 30DKK ($5) adults, free for children.

A final museum, **Viborg Stiftsmuseum,** Hjultorvet 9 (✆ **87-25-26-10**), is housed in a building that was once the headquarters of the local health society, with statues of some of the society's pioneers. The museum relates the history of the city going back to the Ice Age, although exhibitions range up to modern times as well. There are also artifacts discovered in the area that date back to the Stone Age, the Iron Age, and, of course, the Viking era. An intriguing section of the museum displays commercial art as interpreted by the artists of the 1500s and 1600s. The museum is open May to August, Tuesday to Sunday 11am to 5pm. Off-season hours are Tuesday to Friday 1 to 4pm and Saturday and Sunday 11am to 5pm. Admission is 25DKK ($4.20) adults, free for children under 15.

SHOPPING

Most of the shopping outlets in Viborg line either side of the pedestrians-only Sct. Mathiasgade. Two of the most appealing include **Inspiration,** Sct. Mathiasgade 54–56 (✆ **86-62-59-00**); and **Bahne,** Vestergade 14 (✆ **86-62-63-55**). Both sell the kinds of housewares, gift items, and kitchen equipment that make you want to ship a box or two loaded with gadgets and art objects back home.

WHERE TO STAY

Restaurant Jagtstuen on the outskirts of town (see "Where to Dine," below) also rents rooms.

Golf Hotel Viborg ⊛ *Kids*   Few other hotels in the region convey as much of a sense of spaciousness, thanks to a sprawling interior and a location on a peninsula jutting into a freshwater lake. Set less than a kilometer (½ mile) east of the town center, the hotel was built in the mid-1980s as a getaway site for over-stressed urbanites, many of which spend part of their day on the links at the nearby Viborg Golf Club. Residents pay 175DKK to 200DKK ($29–$33) for greens fees—about 30% less than nonresidents. Much of the floor space here is devoted to state-of-the-art conference rooms. Rooms are stylish and modern, with big windows and such elegant touches as leather-upholstered armchairs, Oriental carpets, and whimsical works of art. Each unit comes with an immaculately maintained private bathroom with shower.

Randersvej, DK-8800 Viborg. ✆ **800/780-7234** in U.S. and Canada, or 86-61-02-22. Fax 86-61-31-71. www.golf-hotel-viborg.dk. 133 units. 1,095DKK ($183) double; 1,495DKK ($250) suite. Rates include breakfast. AE, DC, MC, V. **Amenities:** 2 restaurants; indoor heated pool; Jacuzzi; sauna; children's playroom; room service (7am–10pm); babysitting; laundry service; dry cleaning; nonsmoking rooms; solarium. *In room:* A/C, TV, dataport, minibar, hair dryer, trouser press.

Kongenshus Hotel   This hotel enjoys a location in the rolling foothills and scenic backdrop of Mindepark, southwest of Viborg. In 1953 it was built as an imitation of a Danish manor house, and paid for by a consortium of local farmers and ecologists who wanted to protect the grass- and heather-covered heath, to keep it the way most of Jutland looked in the 1700s. Rooms contain angular modern furniture. There's a good Danish **restaurant.** If you opt for a stay here, expect a genteel setting where the natural beauty of the surrounding heath is the main allure, and a roster of fellow guests who might tend to devote many hours to hiking over its surfaces. Fixed-price menus cost 435DKK to 585DKK ($73–$98).

Skivevej 142, Daugbjerg, DK-8800 Viborg. ✆ **97-54-81-25**. www.kongenshus.dk. 9 units, 3 with bathroom. 485DKK ($81) double without bathroom; 585DKK ($98) double with bathroom. MC, V. From Viborg, drive 19km (12 miles) along the Viborgvej, heading southwest of town, following the signs to Holstebro and Daugbjerg. **Amenities:** Restaurahnt (Danish). *In room:* No phone.

Palads Hotel ✿ Its facade is more grand than that of any other hotel in Viborg, and memorable because of its neoclassical detailing and touches of Art Nouveau. Inside, you'll find a gracefully modern, high-ceilinged collection of public areas that convey a light and airy feeling thanks to contemporary Scandinavian design and pale Nordic colors. Rooms contain comfortable but simple furnishings; some bedrooms have private bathrooms with tub, others with shower. A total of 26 units have a private shower. For an unusual way to spend 5 minutes or so, step outside the hotel. Here, sunk into the masonry of the sidewalk, you'll find a Danish interpretation of the handprints in the concrete near Los Angeles's Grauman's Chinese Theater. Look for the handprints of actors and actresses you might never have heard of (Max Hansen, Paul Hagen, Ghita Nørby, and Fritz Helmuth), each of whom is a household name throughout Denmark.

Sct. Mathias Gade 5, DK-8800 Viborg. ☎ 86-62-37-00. Fax 86-62-40-46. www.hotelpalads.dk. 102 units. 895DKK–1,195DKK ($149–$200) double; from 1,295DKK ($216) suite. AE, DC, MC, V. **Amenities:** Breakfast room; nearby indoor heated pool free to guests; gym; Jacuzzi; sauna; laundry service; dry cleaning; non-smoking rooms; rooms for those with limited mobility. In room: TV, dataport, kitchenette (in some), minibar, hair dryer, trouser press, iron/ironing board.

WHERE TO DINE

Arthur's ✿ DANISH/INTERNATIONAL The most charming small-scale restaurant in Viborg is set within the town's most central shopping district, adjacent to a thoroughfare that's usually reserved just for pedestrians. It contains a cafe in front and a more substantial-looking restaurant in back. Lunches tend to be relatively light, and include salads, open-faced sandwiches, pastas, omelets, burgers, and marinated or smoked fish. Menu items at dinner are offbeat and idiosyncratic, often based on ideas gathered by the staff during their holidays abroad. Examples include a terrine of guinea fowl seasoned with cognac and port; filet of veal with braised celery, new potatoes, and mushroom sauce; and French-style chocolate cake with orange sauce and a medley of fresh berries. The cookery is soundly based on classical principles, with a little imagination thrown in for good measure. Many dishes show considerable technical skills.

Vestergade 4. ☎ 86-62-21-26. Reservations recommended. Lunch platters 38DKK–125DKK ($6.35–$21); dinner main courses 160DKK–189DKK ($27–$32). MC, V. Mon–Sat 11am–10:30pm.

Brugger Bauer DANISH A temperance brewery that specialized in nonalcoholic beer was established on the main street of Viborg as early as 1840. All of that changed in 1872, when it was bought by a Hungarian-born entrepreneur named Bauer—who was nicknamed *Brugger Bauer,* or "Bauer the Brewer." He immediately changed the establishment's reliance on alcohol-free beer and began brewing the real thing in custom-built underground cellars. Today, those cellars house one of Viborg's busiest and most atmospheric restaurants, outfitted with tables, chairs, a tactful staff, and very good cuisine. A premier main-course specialty is a "beerbones" platter, consisting of pork filet boiled in beer, then fried with dill and served with sweetened and fried Danish potatoes. Also popular are salmon steak with lobster sauce and boiled white potatoes, and a traditional, all-Danish version of fried beefsteak with fried onions and potatoes.

Sct. Mathiasgade 61. ☎ 86-61-44-88. Reservations recommended. Main courses 49DKK–88DKK ($8.20–$15) at lunch; 138DKK–200DKK ($23–$33) at dinner. MC, V. Mon–Sat 11am–11pm; Sun 2–10pm.

Den Gyldne Okse DANISH Although its food is less imaginative than you might have hoped, the setting of this 400-year-old Danish *kro,* a few steps from Viborg's town hall, evokes 17th-century Danish mercantile days. Both the outside and the inside feature rich half-timbering and the patina left by many generations of cigarette smoke, spilled beer, and the noise and animation of hundreds of diners and drinkers. Lunches are lighter, quicker, and less formal than dinners, and might include a selection of sandwiches, salads, and simple platters such as salmon cakes with herb sauce and fresh-baked rye bread. Dinners are a bit more elaborate, with a limited number of steaks served with pepper sauce, béarnaise, or fresh mushrooms. Fish dishes include salmon, shrimp, and sole. No one will mind if you drop in just for a beer and a snack, but if you want a full-blown meal, the hardworking but bemused staff will think that's just fine too. The food is good and reliable, without being sensational in any way.

Store Sct. Peders Stræde. ✆ 86-62-27-44. Reservations recommended. Main courses 59DKK–90DKK ($9.85–$15) at lunch, 160DKK–210DKK ($27–$35) at dinner. DC, MC, V. Mon–Sat 11am–3pm and 5–10pm (last order).

Restaurant Jagtstuen DANISH/INTERNATIONAL Located in a contemplative and isolated rustic location, the solid and symmetrical building you'll see today dates from 1906. It was enlarged in the 1930s, and fully "winterized" in the 1960s. If you ask, owners Hanne and Frode Hansen will point out some of their prized historic mementos, including the body (but not the engine) of an American tank used during the invasion of Normandy (it occupies a prominent spot in their garden). Menu items are artfully prepared and include such delicious-tasting dishes as breast of wild duckling with port wine and game sauce, medallions of venison with black currant sauce, and fish hauled in directly from Denmark's western coast. These might include filets of plaice with parsley and butter, or catfish with lime sauce.

Upstairs, the family maintains seven simple, cozy rooms, only one of which has a bathroom. With breakfast included, doubles with bathroom cost 545DKK ($91).

In the Rindsholm Kro, Gammel Århusvej 323, DK-8800 Viborg. ✆ 86-63-90-44. Fax 86-63-97-44. Reservations recommended. Main courses 88DKK–210DKK ($15–$35). AE, DC, MC, V. Daily 4–8:30pm (last order). From Viborg's center, drive 5.5km (3½ miles) southeast, following the A26 hwy. and the signs to Århus.

VIBORG AFTER DARK

If there is a major cultural or musical event, it will no doubt take place at **Kongres-og Musikjhus,** Tingvej (✆ **86-62-62-65**), the town's cultural center. The tourist office (see "Visitor Information," above) has complete details of any events staged here.

You can rock and roll in Viborg's shadows at the bar within the previously recommended **Brugger Bauer,** St. Mathiasgade 61 (✆ **86-61-44-88**), or head to one of its most visible competitors, **Messing Jens,** Sct. Mathiasgade 48 (✆ **86-62-02-73**). Old, historic, and loaded with the patina of many generations of clients, it's a good choice for some beers and maybe a dance or two to recorded music. More closely geared to dancing than either of the two sites mentioned above is the **Crazy Daisy,** Grauene 20 (✆ **86-61-51-33**), the largest disco in town. Although you can get a drink here virtually any day of the week after 11pm, it's most popular every Thursday, Friday, and Saturday when it gets down as Viborg's premier disco.

11

North Jutland

Separated from the rest of Jutland (and also the mainland of Europe) by the Limfjord, North Jutland is a land unto itself. It's a landscape of North Sea beaches, coastal hamlets, fishing harbors, and wild heaths. It has only one large city, Aalborg, which lies at the narrow point of Limfjord, plus a number of midsize towns, notably Frederikshavn and Hjørring. Any of these would be a suitable base for exploration, but for scenic beauty we'd choose Skagen, at the northernmost boundary of Denmark, which has long attracted some of Denmark's leading artists and artisans.

Because of bridges linking Funen with Zealand and Jutland, you can drive to North Jutland from Copenhagen in 4½ hours.

"Why do we live here in such a rugged environment?" asked a painter in Skagen, who answered his own question: "The real Denmark is a winter day at the North Sea with the wind blowing back your hair and making your skin salty, a trip in the autumn forest to gather mushrooms, or a romantic stroll in the newly leafed beech forest."

The first visitors arrived in North Jutland some 4,000 years ago in a land created by the Ice Age some 10,000 years earlier. Many places in Vendsyssel (the name of the province) still bear traces from the Stone Age, the Iron Age, and certainly the Viking Age. You can see history at many ancient monuments and relics of antiquity on display in the area.

In 1859, Hans Christian Andersen said it best: "If you are a Painter then

follow us here, here are Subjects for you to paint, here is Scenery for Writing." In the 19th century, the Skagen painters—the Danish equivalent of the French Impressionists—were attracted to North Jutland for its intense light, the region's natural surroundings, the sea, and the people. Many of their paintings can be seen at the Skagens Museum. Some of their homes have been turned into museums.

After a long slumber, the towns of North Jutland are more alive than ever. Young people, who used to head for the bright lights of Copenhagen, often remain in the area of their birth, bringing new energy to its once dull towns and hamlets.

In Hjørring the main street has been renovated, and in some old back alleys, shops, cafes, and crafts stores have opened. In Hirtshals both town and harbor have been spruced up and linked by a new external sculptural staircase. Frederikshavn has worked creatively with street spaces and has brought life and light to previously rundown streets. And then there are monuments, many of them erected in memory of the members of the Resistance who struggled against Nazi oppression during World War II. Other monuments commemorate lifeboat-men who died while rescuing shipwrecked sailors. Almost everywhere there are reminders that the North Sea is something with which one must live daily. Many monuments note that the sea gives life but can brutally claim it as well.

Moments **A Breath of Fresh Air**

The air in North Jutland is among the purest in Europe. Locals are fond of pointing out that the nearest factory chimney is 800km (500 miles) to the west in Scotland.

---

1 Mariager ★

58km (36 miles) N of Århus; 341km (213 miles) NW of Copenhagen

Aalborg-bound motorists with time should stop over at Mariager. In a charming setting overlooking Mariager Fjord, the town has quaint cobblestone streets and half-timbered, red-roofed buildings.

Mariager was only a small fishing hamlet at the ferry crossing on the way between Randers and Aalborg before the foundation of Bridgettine Abbey in 1410. The abbey led to a flourishing trade and commerce in the area, and the town became a popular resort for the worshipping nobles. However, with the coming of the Reformation in 1536, the tide turned. When Mariager was granted its city charter in 1592, only 500 inhabitants remained. Many of the old buildings constructed in Mariager's heyday remain, however. Industrialization did not come until 1960, and by that time the town had become preservation-minded, as a walk through its cobbled streets will reveal.

ESSENTIALS

GETTING THERE **By Train and Bus** There are no direct trains to Mariager. Trains run from Aalborg to Hobro, east of Mariager, every 30 minutes, and from Århus to Hobro hourly. Take the bus from Hobro. Buses to Mariager run hourly from Hadsun, Hobro, or Randers. The ride on all three takes about a half-hour.

By Car From Randers, take the E45 north, then head east at the junction of Route 555.

VISITOR INFORMATION The **Mariager Tourist Association,** Torvet 1B (© 98-54-13-77; www.mariagerturist.dk), is open June 15 to August, Monday to Friday 9am to 5pm, Saturday 9am to 2pm. Off-season hours are Monday to Friday 9am to 4pm, Saturday 9am to noon.

SEEING THE SIGHTS

Mariager is connected to the Baltic via the Mariager Fjord, a deep but narrow saltwater inlet favored by sailors and yacht enthusiasts because of its smooth surface. You can sail aboard a small-scale cruise ship, the *Svanen,* as it circumnavigates the western recesses of the fjord. About four times a day, the ship touches down at such fjordside towns as Mariager, Hadsun, and Hobro, taking 2½ hours for a complete circuit that's priced at 90DKK ($15) per person. You can get off at any of five villages en route, and wait for the next boat to pick you up and carry you on to the next town. There's a cafeteria onboard, and a sun deck where guests can improve their suntans during the short Nordic summer. The tourist office in Mariager (see "Visitor Information," above) is the best source of advice about schedules and itineraries.

Although it's the old town itself that is the most alluring attraction, you may want to call on the abbey church, **Mariager Kirke Klostervej** (© 98-54-15-95), which was constructed in the 15th century as part of a nunnery. It was

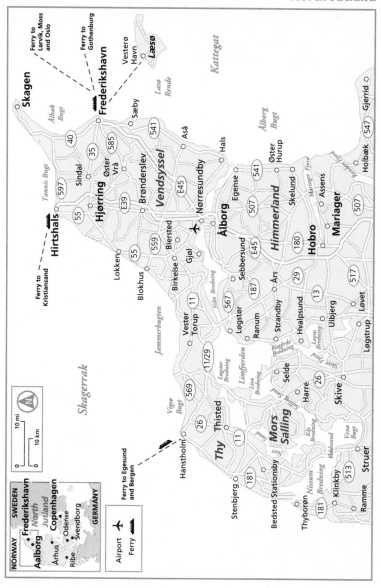

given to the town as its parish church following the Reformation. Although it has been largely reconstructed over the years, it's still a fine and lofty building with a magnificent carved altarpiece depicting the Last Supper and the Crucifixion, surrounded by 11 of the apostles. A memorial tablet to the last abbess can be seen in the south transept. Hours are Monday through Saturday 8am to 3:30pm; admission is free.

One of the most beautiful buildings in Mariager is the old merchant's house, now the **Mariager Museum,** Kirkegard 4B. In the museum you can see an attractive collection of domestic utensils and tools. The museum also contains relics from the ancient history of both Mariager and the surrounding district. Of special interest is a reconstruction of the abbey and its church, an exhibit established in 1981 in connection with the 500th anniversary of the church. It's open May 15 to September 15, daily 1 to 5pm. Admission is 15DKK ($2.50) adults; free for children.

Danmarks Saltcenter, Haven (© **98-54-18-16**), opened in 1998. It's the only science center in the country devoted to salt. Lying on the harbor at Mariager, close to the water, it traces the methods for extracting salt since the Middle Ages. Called white gold, salt was formed some 250 million years ago—as you learn at the museum. You can go exploring in the tunnels of the salt mine and experience what it was like to work in a mountain salt mine a century ago. You can watch a foreman at the salt works boil the salts in a boiling hut as they did in the Middle Ages. The salt garden is planted with plants that obviously can tolerate salt, and this is the setting for the museum's Salt Café, where, naturally, dishes connected with salt are served. There are also many activities for children, including, among others, shallow pools in the outdoor water playground. Tickets are 75DKK ($13) adults, 55DKK ($9.20) children 3 to 11, and free for age 2 and under. Hours are June 19 to August 8, daily 10am to 6pm; January 3 to June 18 and August 9 to December 23, Monday to Friday 10am to 4pm, Saturday and Sunday 10am to 5pm. Closed December 24 to January 2.

WHERE TO STAY

If you can't find a hotel room, the **Mariager Tourist Association** (see above) will help book you into a private home or boardinghouse.

Hotel Postgården ✿   The most authentically historic hotel in Mariager has extended hospitality to travelers since it was established in 1710 in the heart of town, near the main square and Town Hall. It was restored in 1982 and has been upgraded many times since. The building's facade and public areas, especially its pub and restaurant, are authentically historic and old-time. But about two-thirds of the rooms have been stripped of their historic charm and upgraded to a modern international look that's comfortable and cozy. If you really insist on antique decor, request room no. 305 (one that the hotel usually assigns to anyone claiming to be a honeymooner); or, to a lesser extent, room nos. 201, 203, or 307. Some of the bedrooms contain tubs, but most of them offer showers.

Torvet 6A, DK-9550 Mariager. © **98-54-10-12.** Fax 98-54-24-64. 14 units. 750DKK ($125) double. Rates include breakfast. AE, DC, MC, V. **Amenities:** Restaurant; bar; sauna. *In room:* TV.

Motel Landgangen   Set beside the river, a 5-minute walk north of the abbey, this is not a dreary motel, even though its white exterior and simple architecture date from the late 1960s. Rooms are cozy and inviting, well kept and neat, including the bathrooms, which contain either shower or tub. The place is even better known for its restaurant, which features Danish specialties and comfy furniture with a view of the water. It's open in summer daily noon to 8pm, and off season Friday through Sunday noon to 8pm.

Oxendalen 1, DK-9550 Mariager. © **98-54-11-22.** 6 units. 550DKK ($92) double. Rates include breakfast. AE, DC, MC, V. **Amenities:** Restaurant; bar. *In room:* TV.

⎛*Tips* **Getting to North Jutland**

For rail and bus information to any town in North Jutland, call © **70-13-14-15.**

WHERE TO DINE

Restaurant Postgården DANISH/FRENCH   Many diners appreciate this restaurant for its old-time decor and the sense of intimacy created by its small but bustling dining rooms. During mild weather, tables are set up outside. There's nothing particularly avant-garde about the food served here. Luncheon favorites include such tried-and-true favorites as *smørrebrød* (open-faced sandwiches) piled high with baby shrimp or Danish ham, and platters of herring or roasted pork with red cabbage and new potatoes. Dinners are more elaborate and might feature such good-tasting dishes as bacon-wrapped salmon with fettuccini in a saffron sauce or else lemon sole with crab in a lime-laced white wine sauce with dill potatoes. A special treat is the marinated leg of duck with sautéed cabbage and mushrooms served in a sweet pepper sauce with a potato soufflé.

In the Hotel Postgården, Torvet 6A. ℂ **98-54-10-12.** Reservations recommended. Main courses 82DKK–130DKK ($14–$22) at lunch, 128DKK–195DKK ($21–$33) at dinner; fixed-price menus 148DKK–298DKK ($25–$50). AE, DC, MC, V. Daily 11am–11pm.

MARIAGER AFTER DARK

One of the town's most consistently popular pubs is in the **Hotel Postgården,** Torvet 6A (ℂ **98-54-10-12**). Within a room sheathed with old-fashioned paneling, near a bar with antique-looking beer pulls, you're likely to find an animated crowd of office workers and after-dinner refugees from the confines of their homes, with lots of options for meeting and making new friends. Open daily 11am to 11pm, it serves platters of food, including herring, that taste good with the Carlsberg, and which cost 30DKK to 55DKK ($5–$9.20).

2 Aalborg ⭐

132km (82 miles) NW of Ebeltoft, 383km (238 miles) W of Copenhagen

The largest city in northern Jutland, Aalborg (Ålborg) is known worldwide for its *aquavit.* Although essentially a shipping town and commercial center, Aalborg makes a good base for sightseers, with its many hotels and attractions, more than 300 restaurants, and diverse nightlife.

History is a living reality in Aalborg. The city was founded 1,000 years ago when the Viking fleets assembled in these parts before setting off on their predatory expeditions. The city's historic atmosphere has been preserved in its old streets and alleys. Near the Church of Our Lady are many beautifully restored and reconstructed houses, some of which date from the 16th century.

Denmark's largest forest, **Rold,** where robber bandits once roamed, is just outside town. **Rebild National Park** is the site of the annual American Fourth of July celebration.

Not far from Aalborg, on the west coast of northern Jutland, some of the finest beaches in northern Europe stretch from Slettestrand to Skagen. The resort towns of **Blokhus** and **Løkken** are especially popular with Danes, Germans, and Swedes.

ESSENTIALS

GETTING THERE   By Plane   You can fly from Copenhagen to Aalborg; the airport (ℂ **98-17-11-44;** www.aal.dk) is 6.5km (4 miles) from the city center.

By Train   There is frequent train service from Copenhagen by way of Fredericia to Århus; there you can connect with a train to Aalborg, a 90-minute ride.

By Bus   Aalborg's bus station is the transportation center for northern Jutland and is served from all directions. For all bus information in northern Jutland, call **Nordjyllands Trafikselskab** (ℂ **98-11-11-11**).

By Car   From Ebeltoft, follow Route 21 north until you reach the junction with Route 16. Drive west on Route 16 until you come to E45, which runs north to Aalborg.

VISITOR INFORMATION   The **Aalborg Tourist Bureau** is at Østerågade 8 (© **99-30-60-90;** www.visitaalborg.dk). It's open June to August, Monday through Friday 9am to 6pm, Saturday 10am to 1pm; September to June, Monday through Friday 9am to 4:30pm, Saturday 10am to 1pm.

GETTING AROUND   For bus information, call © **98-11-11-11.** Most buses depart from Østerågade and Nytorv in the city center. A typical fare costs 15DKK ($2.50), although you can buy a 24-hour tourist pass for 96DKK ($16) to ride on all the city buses for a day. Information about bus routes is available from the *Aalborg Guide,* which is distributed free by the tourist office.

SPECIAL EVENTS   The **Aalborg Carnival** on May 27 is one of the major events of spring in Jutland. Streets are filled with festive figures in colorful costumes strutting in a parade. Up to 100,000 people participate in this annual event, marking the victory of spring over winter's darkness. The whole city seems to explode in joy. There's also the **Aalborg Jazz and Blues Festival** August 12 to 15. Jazz fills the whole city at dozens of clubs, although most activity centers on C. W. Obels Plads. Every year on the 4th of July, Danes and Danish Americans meet to celebrate America's **Independence Day** in the lovely hills of Rebild.

SEEING THE SIGHTS

You can hire an English-speaking taxi driver who will take you to the city's highlights. The maximum number of passengers allowed is four; the average tour lasts a half-hour, and costs 450DKK ($75) for the group. For more details, ask at the tourist bureau.

Aalborg Marinemuseum   This museum of marine exhibits is next to the harbor, Vestre Bådehavn. You can see the *Springeren,* a 23m (75-ft.) submarine; *Søbjørnen,* the world's fastest torpedo boat; or the inspection ship *Ingolf,* which was on active duty in the waters around Greenland until 1990. Various exhibits depict life at sea, the port of Aalborg, and activities at the Aalborg shipyard. At the Café Ubåden (submarine), you can order food and drink. There's also a playground on-site.

Vester Fjordvej 81. © **98-11-78-03.** Admission 65DKK ($11) adults, 30DKK ($5) children 6–14, free for children under 6. May–Aug daily 10am–6pm; off season daily 10am–4pm. Bus: 1, 4, 40, or 46.

Aalborgtårnet   This tower rises 100m (328 ft.) above sea level, offering a perfect view—reachable by stair or elevator—of the city and the fjord.

Søndre Skovvej, at Skovbakken. © **98-77-05-11.** Admission 25DKK ($4.20) adults, 15DKK ($2.50) children. Apr–July daily 10am–5pm; July daily 10am–7pm; Aug daily 10am–5pm. Closed Sept–Mar. Bus: 8 or 10.

Aalborg Zoologiske Have ⊛   Set 4km (2½ miles) south of Aalborg, this is the second largest zoo in Scandinavia, where some 800 animal specimens from all over the world wander freely in surroundings designed to mirror an open African range. Apes and beasts of prey are kept under minimal supervision. There's a good bistro, and snack bars here and there. The zoo is in Mølleparken, a large park with a lookout where you can see most of Aalborg and the Isle of Egholm. Look for Roda Reilinger's sculpture *Noah's Ark* near the lookout.

Mølleparkvej 63. © **96-31-29-29.** www.aalborg-zoo.dk. Admission 80DKK ($13) adults, 45DKK ($7.50) children, free for children under 3. Jan–Feb and Nov–Dec daily 10am–2pm; Mar daily 10am–3pm; Apr and Sept–Oct daily 10am–4pm; May–Aug daily 9am–6pm. Last ticket is sold 1 hr. before closing. Bus: 1.

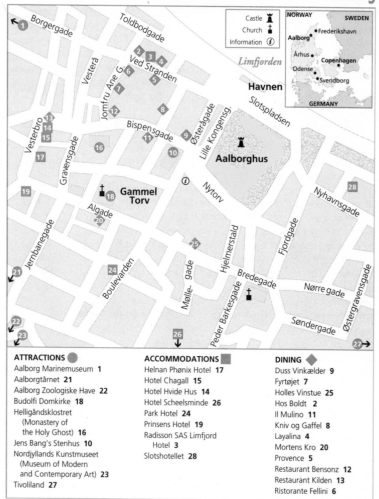

Castle ♜
Church ⛪
Information ⓘ

NORWAY   SWEDEN
Aalborg • Frederikshavn
Århus • Copenhagen
Odense •
• Svendborg
GERMANY

Limfjorden

Havnen

Slotspladsen

Borgergade

Toldbodgade

Ved Stranden

Vesterå

Jomfru Ane G.

Østerågade

Lille Kongensg.

Aalborghus

Vesterbro

Bispensgade

Gravensgade

ⓘ   Gammel
Torv

Nytorv

Nyhavnsgade

Algade

Jernbanegade

Hjelmerstald

Fjordgade

Boulevarden

Mølle- gade

Bredegade

Nørre gade

Østergravensgade

Peder Barkesgade

Søndergade

ATTRACTIONS ●
Aalborg Marinemuseum **1**
Aalborgtårnet **21**
Aalborg Zoologiske Have **22**
Budolfi Domkirke **18**
Helligåndsklostret
  (Monastery of
  the Holy Ghost) **16**
Jens Bang's Stenhus **10**
Nordjyllands Kunstmuseet
  (Museum of Modern
  and Contemporary Art) **23**
Tivoliland **27**

ACCOMMODATIONS ■
Helnan Phønix Hotel **17**
Hotel Chagall **15**
Hotel Hvide Hus **14**
Hotel Scheelsminde **26**
Park Hotel **24**
Prinsens Hotel **19**
Radisson SAS Limfjord
  Hotel **3**
Slotshotellet **28**

DINING ◆
Duss Vinkælder **9**
Fyrtøjet **7**
Holles Vinstue **25**
Hos Boldt **2**
Il Mulino **11**
Kniv og Gaffel **8**
Layalina **4**
Mortens Kro **20**
Provence **5**
Restaurant Bensonz **12**
Restaurant Kilden **13**
Ristorante Fellini **6**

Budolfi Domkirke   This elaborately decorated and whitewashed cathedral is dedicated to St. Botolph, patron saint of sailors. The baroque spire of the church is Aalborg's major landmark. The church you see today is the result of 800 years of rebuilding and expansion. On the south wall is a fresco depicting St. Catherine of Alexandria and some grotesque small centaurs. Look for the altarpiece from 1689 and the pulpit from 1692—both carved by Lauridtz Jensen. The marble font from 1727 was a gift to the church. Note too the gallery in the north aisle with its illustrations of the Ten Commandments. A similar gallery in the south aisle illustrates the suffering of Christ and also bears the names of a number of prominent Aalborg citizens from around the mid–17th century. A carillon sounds daily every hour 9am to 10pm.

Algade. ⓒ **98-12-46-70.** Free admission. Mon–Fri 9am–2pm. Bus: 3, 5, 10, or 11.

Helligåndsklostret (Monastery of the Holy Ghost) This vine-covered monastery is the oldest social-welfare institution in Denmark, as well as the oldest building in Aalborg. Built near the heart of town in 1431 and designed with step-shaped gables, it contains a well-preserved rectory, a series of vaulted storage cellars—some of which occasionally functioned as prisons—a whitewashed collection of cloisters, and a chapter house whose walls in some areas are decorated with 16th-century frescoes. The complex can be visited only as part of a guided tour.

C. W. Obels Plads (call the tourist office for information). Guided tour 40DKK ($6.70) adults, 10DKK ($1.65) children. Guided tour late June to mid-Aug Mon–Fri 1:30pm. Bus: 1.

Jens Bang's Stenhus ★ This six-floor mansion, built in 1624 in a glittering Renaissance style, once belonged to a wealthy merchant, Jens Bang. It's the finest example of Renaissance domestic architecture in the north of Europe. Bang was gifted but also argumentative and obstinate. He deliberately made his house rich with ornamentation and ostentation as a "challenge" to the other good citizens of the town. It was rumored that he revenged himself on his many enemies by caricaturing them in the many grotesque carvings on the facade of the house. In spite of his wealth, he was never made a member of the town council, and to this day his image is depicted on the south facade sticking his tongue out at the Town Hall. The historic wine cellar, Duus Vinkjaelder, is the meeting place of the Guild of Christian IV. On the ground floor is an old apothecary shop. The mansion itself is still privately owned and is not open to the public.

Østerågade 9. Bus: 3, 5, 10, or 11.

Nordjyllands Kunstmuseet (Museum of Modern and Contemporary Art) This building is a prime example of modern Scandinavian architecture. Built from 1968 to 1972, it was designed by Elissa and Alvar Aalto and Jean-Jacques Baruël as a showplace for 20th-century Danish and international art. It has changing exhibits, sculpture gardens, two auditoriums, a children's museum, an outdoor amphitheater, and a restaurant, the Museumscafeen.

Kong Christians Allé 50. ✆ 98-13-80-88. Admission 40DKK ($6.70) adults, free for children. Tues–Sun 10am–5pm. Bus: 15 or 16.

NEARBY ATTRACTIONS

Less than 4km (2½ miles) north of Aalborg, you'll find the remains of the Viking settlement of Nørresundby. It's the site of more than 700 cremation graves, and contains the charred remains of more than 150 Viking boats and ships that were ceremonially burned as part of the cremations. Set within a park, the excavations are open to the public 24 hours a day, year-round. Further details about the excavations, however, are on view within the **Lindholm Høje Museet,** Vendilavej 11 (✆ **96-31-04-10;** bus: 2). The museum is open Easter to mid-October, daily 10am to 5pm. Mid-October to Easter, it's open Tuesday through Sunday 10am to 4pm. Admission costs 30DKK ($5) adults, 15DKK ($2.50) children 5 to 11, free for children 4 and under.

Most of the graves are marked with stones placed in the form of a triangle, an oval, or a ship. The deceased person was usually cremated. North of the burial ground lay the associated village, where the finds include the remains of houses, fences, wells, and fire pits. The area was subject to drifting sand. About A.D. 1000, the whole burial ground became covered with sand, which meant that the stone markings and even a newly ploughed field were preserved until this day. A site museum contains archaeological finds from the excavations and illustrates how the inhabitants of Lindholm Høje lived at home and when trading abroad.

Voergård Slot ✴, Flauenskjold (© **98-86-71-08**), a Renaissance-era castle 35km (22 miles) north of Aalborg, is filled with sculpture, Louis XVI furniture, a banqueting hall, a grand salon, and paintings by Goya and Rubens. Admission costs 60DKK ($10) adults, 20DKK ($3.35) children. Take the E45 from Aalborg, cutting east on Route 559 to Droningland, and then follow the signs to Voergård Slot. May 1 to June 13 and August 21 to October 17, it's open Saturday 2 to 5pm, Sunday 10am to 5pm; July 10 to 18, daily 10am to 5pm.

Americans who are in Jutland for the Fourth of July should make a beeline to the **Rebild National Park,** 29km (18 miles) south of Aalborg. On these heather dunes, Danes, Danish Americans, and Americans celebrate America's Independence Day. The program often features opera singers, folk dancers, choirs, and glee clubs, together with well-known speakers.

A 1-hour drive from Aalborg takes you to the resort town of **Blokhus** and the broad white beaches of the North Sea coast. Not far from here is a 50-hectare (124-acre) amusement park, **Fårup Sommerland & Waterpark** (© **98-88-16-00;** www.faarupsommerland.dk; bus: 200). Admission: May 5–June 17 DKK 135 ($23); June 18–Sept 4 DKK 160 ($27). Seniors DKK75 ($13) May 5–June 17; DKK90 ($15) June 18–Sept 4. After 4pm: May 5–June 17 DKK 75 ($13); June 18–Sept 4 DKK90 ($15). Expect lots of noise, lots of families, and lots of emphasis on good, clean fun in a style that might remind you of a small-scale version of Disneyland. It's open mid-May to August, daily 10am to 7pm.

FOR FAMILY FUN

Tivoliland *(Kids*, Karolinelundsvej (© **98-12-33-15**), is an amusement park for the entire family, with lots of snap and sparkle, although a pale imitation of the more famous one in Copenhagen. A tradition since 1946 in the center of Aalborg, it's one of the most attended attractions in the north of Jutland. In addition to rides, there are beautiful gardens with thousands of flowers and fantastic fountains. You've seen it all before, but it's still an amusing and delightful way to spend an evening, as you can take everything from a flying carpet ride to a spin on Scandinavia's only boomerang roller coaster (with screws and loops both forward and backward). China Town is one of the most visited attractions, containing such attractions as the China dragon and the fun house. Other attractions include a Gravity Tower rising 55 meters (180 feet) with a free-fall experience, plus a Hall of Mirrors, a labyrinth showing you amazing dimensions of yourself. An open-air stage, restaurants, a pizzeria, dancing areas, and singalongs—it all makes for one big evening. The attraction is open May to June, daily noon to 9pm; July to September 6, daily 10am to 10pm. Admission is 50DKK ($8.35) adults, 25DKK ($4.20) children. However, you'll pay separately for the various attractions, with tickets ranging from 15DKK to 45DKK ($2.50–$7.50). An unlimited ticket for all rides, good for 1 day only, costs 200DKK ($33).

SHOPPING

This North Jutland city abounds in specialty stores. For the best collection of gold and silver jewelry, patronize **Aalborg Guld & Solvhus,** Gravensgade 8 (© **98-16-57-11**). The best and most sophisticated handicrafts—many quite amusing—are sold at **Lange Handicrafts,** Hjelmerstald 15 (© **98-13-82-68**). To watch a glass blower in action, and perhaps make some purchases, go to **Lene Højlund,** Nørregade 6 (© **98-13-01-20**).

The largest shopping center in North Jutland lies about 6.5km (4 miles) south of Aalborg's center. The **Aalborg Storcenter,** Hobrovej 452 (© **98-18-23-10;**

bus: 11, 14, or 16), contains at least 50 specialty shops and kiosks, as well as the all-inclusive **Bilka Department Store** (© 98-79-70-00).

Aalborg also has some other department stores that bring a vast array of Danish merchandise together under one roof, including **Salling,** Nytorv 8 (© **98-16-00-00;** bus: 1, 11, or 14), with 30 specialty shops. It has the city's largest selection of fashion, plus lots of other good stuff, including books and toys. A major competitor is **Magasin,** Nytorv 24 (© **98-13-30-00;** bus: 1, 11, or 14). **Gavlhuset,** Algade 9 (© **98-12-18-22;** bus: 16 or 18), has a little bit of everything—Indian silver, "dancing beans," old Kilim carpets, masks from around the globe, knitted goods, "gods" in bronze, exotic spices, wooden toys in bright colors, and even African woodcarvings. To look at and perhaps purchase some of the city's best contemporary art, head for **Galerie Wolfsen,** Tiendeladen 6 (© **98-13-75-66**).

WHERE TO STAY

The **Aalborg Tourist Bureau** (see above) can book a room for you in a private Danish home—double or single, with access to a shower. Bed linen is included in the price, and all rooms are situated within the city limits and reached by bus. In July and August, the peak tourist months, Helnan Phønix slashes its rates and becomes a moderately priced choice, because it's primarily a business hotel, and for them, high tourist season is their low season. Although many rooms at the Limsfordhotellet are labeled expensive, the hotel also rents dozens of more affordable accommodations as well.

EXPENSIVE

Helnan Phønix Hotel ✪   This is the oldest, largest, most historic, and most prestigious hotel in Aalborg, lying close to the bus station. It originated in 1783 on the main street of town as the private home of the Danish brigadier general assigned to protect Aalborg from assault by foreign powers. In 1853, it was converted into a hotel. Today, it appears deceptively small from Aalborg's main street, and very imposing if you see its modern wings from the back. Bedrooms are tastefully and elegantly appointed with dark wood furnishings. Some of the rooms have exposed ceiling beams, and all of them are equipped with neatly tiled bathrooms with tubs and showers.

The hotel's restaurant, **Brigadieren,** serves a sophisticated Danish and international cuisine.

Vesterbro 77, DK-9000 Aalborg. © **98-12-00-11.** Fax 98-10-10-20. www.helnan.dk. 244 units. Summer 955DKK ($159) double, 2,500DKK ($418) suite; winter 1,180DKK ($197) double, 2,500DKK ($418) suite. AE, DC, MC, V. **Amenities:** Restaurant; bar; gym; Jacuzzi; sauna; room service (7am–10pm); massage; laundry service; dry cleaning; nonsmoking rooms; solarium. *In room:* TV, dataport, minibar, hair dryer, safe.

Hotel Hvide Hus ✪   The first-rate "White House Hotel" is in Kilde Park, about a 12-minute walk from the heart of Aalborg and close to the bus station. Many international businesspeople now stay here instead of at the traditional Helnan Phønix Hotel. In cooperation with well-known galleries, the hotel is decorated with works by some of Denmark's leading painters. The guest rooms are well furnished in fresh Scandinavian modern style; all have private balconies with a view of Aalborg. Each unit is also equipped with a well-maintained bathroom with a tub/shower combination. This hotel is a member of Best Western hotels. The restaurant **Kilden** and the bar **Pejsebar** are both on the 15th floor and offer city views.

Vesterbro 2, DK-9000 Aalborg. © **800/780-7234** in the U.S. and Canada, or 98-13-84-00. Fax 98-13-51-22. www.hotelhvidehus.dk. 200 units. 1,275DKK–1,430DKK ($213–$239) double; 2,275DKK ($380) suite. Rates include buffet breakfast. AE, DC, MC, V. Free parking. **Amenities:** Restaurant; bar; room service (7am–11pm); massage; babysitting; laundry service; dry cleaning; nonsmoking rooms. *In room:* TV, minibar, hair dryer, trouser press.

Radisson SAS Limfjord Hotel ★ *Finds* This is the most avant-garde hotel in town—a five-story yellow-brick structure with huge expanses of glass in a streamlined Danish modern layout. In the center of town, a 3-minute walk east of the cathedral, the hotel opens onto the famous Limsjorden Canal. It's near Jomfru Anegade, a street packed with bars and restaurants. The public rooms are sparsely furnished with modern, streamlined furniture. Many of the comfortable guest rooms overlook the harbor. The medium-size rooms have good-size tile bathrooms with tub/shower combinations. Everything is maintained in state-of-the-art condition. The suites have Jacuzzis.

Ved Stranden 14–16, DK-9000 Aalborg. ✆ 800-333-3333 in the U.S., or 98-16-43-33. Fax 98-16-17-47. www.radissonsas.com. 188 units. 950DKK–1,395DKK ($159–$233) double; 2,750DKK ($459) suite. Rates include breakfast. AE, DC, MC, V. Parking 75DKK ($13). Bus: 1, 4, 40, or 46. **Amenities:** Restaurant; bar; fitness center; sauna; room service (7am–10pm); laundry service; dry cleaning; nonsmoking rooms; rooms for those with limited mobility; casino. *In room:* TV, dataport, minibar, hair dryer, trouser press.

Slotshotellet ★ Stylish and comfortable, this tasteful and well-designed hotel opened in 1986. Located a few blocks from the town center within view of the harbor, the hotel lies adjacent to the most important waterway in Aalborg, the Limsjorden Canal, and is about a 2-minute walk east of the cathedral. There are a cafe and a bar, and the rooms are comfortable, functionally furnished, and well maintained. Bathrooms, although a bit small and without enough storage space, are well maintained, and each has a shower.

Rendsburggade 5, DK-9100 Aalborg. ✆ 98-10-14-00. Fax 98-11-65-70. www.slotshotellet.dk. 155 units. 1,253DKK ($209) double; 1,589DKK ($265) suite. Rates include breakfast. AE, DC, MC, V. Bus: 1, 3, 5, or 7. **Amenities:** Breakfast lounge; bar; gym; sauna; breakfast-only room service; laundry service; dry cleaning; nonsmoking rooms; solarium. *In room:* TV, dataport, minibar.

MODERATE

Check into the Chagall on any Friday, Saturday, and Sunday night, and you'll find you're staying at an inexpensive hotel instead of a moderate one. Prinsen (see below) also rents a number of inexpensive rooms, although most of its accommodations are moderate. Likewise, the Park also rents a number of inexpensive rooms in addition to some pricey selections.

Hotel Chagall Originally built in the 1950s in a prominent position in the heart of town, this hotel was upgraded and redesigned in 1988 into the simple but well-managed hotel you'll see today. Other than a cafe-style area serving breakfast, there are no restaurants and bars, and very few amenities other than the well-maintained contemporary-looking rooms. Many contain reproductions of paintings by Marc Chagall, the hotel's namesake. Each room comes with a private bathroom—some with shower, others with tub.

Vesterbro 36–38, Postboks 1856, DK-9000 Aalborg. ✆ 98-12-69-33. Fax 98-13-10-34. www.hotel-chagall. dk. 71 units. 935DKK–1,080DKK ($156–$180) double; 1,385DKK ($231) suite. Rates include breakfast. AE, DC, MC, V. **Amenities:** Breakfast lounge; fitness room; gym; Jacuzzi; sauna; laundry service; dry cleaning; nonsmoking rooms; solarium. *In room:* TV, dataport (in some), minibar.

Hotel Scheelsminde ★ *Finds* One of the most popular hotels in the area lies 4km (2½ miles) south of Aalborg's center, in what was originally a manor house constructed in 1808. Many of the accommodations are in a modern addition, although the restaurant is housed in the original core. All accommodations contain private bathrooms, some with tub, others with shower. In classic surroundings, you can escape the noise of Aalborg and wander at leisure through the hotel's large private grounds. Reservations are strongly advised during peak season because of the hotel's popularity.

Scheelsmindevej 35, DK-9100 Aalborg. ✆ **98-18-32-33**. Fax 98-18-33-34. 96 units. 895DKK–1,095DKK ($149–$183) double. Rates include breakfast. AE, DC, MC, V. Bus: 5 or 8. **Amenities:** Restaurant; bar; indoor heated pool; gym; sauna; room service (6:30am–midnight); laundry service; dry cleaning; nonsmoking rooms; 1 room for those with limited mobility. *In room:* TV, dataport (in some), minibar, hair dryer.

Park Hotel   The original 18th-century atmosphere has been preserved but the hotel has been carefully modernized throughout the years. Rooms are a bit small, but clean and comfortable, with good beds and private tiled bathrooms—some with shower, others with tubs. The hotel also has a restaurant serving both Scandinavian and international food, but the major restaurant-filled street of Aalborg is just a 5-minute walk from the Park.

J. F. Kennedys Plads 41, DK-9100 Aalborg. ✆ **98-12-31-33**. Fax 98-13-31-66. www.park-hotel-aalborg.dk. 81 units. 915DKK–1,020DKK ($153–$170) double; 1,320DKK ($220) suite. Rates include buffet breakfast. AE, DC, MC, V. **Amenities:** Restaurant; bar; room service (7am–10pm); laundry service; dry cleaning; nonsmoking rooms; rooms for those with limited mobility. *In room:* TV, hair dryer.

Prinsen Hotel *(Value)*   Opposite the railroad station, this 1906 landmark is constantly updated and renovated. In spite of its age, rooms are decorated in a light, modern, Nordic style. The hotel is very well maintained, and the staff is welcoming. Guests gather in an inviting bar before going into the main restaurant, **Gallay,** where both Danish specialties and international dishes are served.

Prinsensgade 14–16, DK-9000 Aalborg. ✆ **98-13-37-33**. Fax 98-16-52-82. www.prinsen-hotel.dk. 40 units. 645DKK ($108) double. Rates include buffet breakfast. AE, DC, MC, V. Closed Dec 23–Jan 1. Bus: 1, 3, or 5. **Amenities:** Breakfast lounge; bar; Jacuzzi; sauna; laundry service; dry cleaning; nonsmoking rooms; solarium. *In room:* TV, dataport, hair dryer.

WHERE TO DINE

Jomfru Anegade is the most famous restaurant-filled street in Jutland. If you can't find good food here, you didn't try. It's got something for most palates and most pocketbooks.

EXPENSIVE

Hos Boldt *(★)* DANISH/FRENCH   One of Aalborg's most likable restaurants was established in 1992 in a 19th-century building that had been a simple tavern for many years. The family-run business consists of two deliberately old-fashioned dining rooms filled with antique furniture and candles. Menu items change with the availability of the ingredients but might include such perfectly prepared dishes as steamed turbot with julienne of leeks, consommé of veal with herbs and quail eggs, lobster bisque, a platter with various preparations of salmon, snails in herb-flavored cream sauce, rack of Danish lamb in rosemary-flavored wine sauce, and sea bass cooked in salt crust.

Ved Stranden 7. ✆ **98-16-17-77**. Reservations recommended. Main courses 186DKK–218DKK ($31–$36); fixed-price menus 268DKK–400DKK ($45–$67). AE, DC, MC, V. Mon–Sat 5pm–midnight. Bus: 1, 4, 40, or 46.

Mortens Kro *(★) (Finds)* FRENCH/DANISH   This artful restaurant is the domain of Morten Nealsen, the most gifted chef in Aalborg. It surfaces as the best place to dine in the city. In new quarters, it offers classic dining chairs and luxurious sofas. The chef wanted a "New York look but with a Parisian ambience," the latter evoked by the champagne bar. The rustic brickwork and glass and steel form a backdrop for fine dining. DJs entertain during the weekends. The only culinary option here is a fixed-price, six-course *menu gastronomique.*

Your meal might include filets of red snapper with an apricot-flavored curry sauce, chicken with truffles, filet of turbot with a lime-flavored mousseline and fresh spinach, and breast of duckling with pepper sauce. Dessert might include a Napoleon layered with pulverized raspberries and blueberries. This is really a top-rate restaurant with a lot of flair. The results are achieved with well-rehearsed rules of cooking technique, and the classic schooling of French cuisine has been beautifully blended with Danish flavors.

Mølleå 4-6, Mølleå Arkaden. ℭ **98-12-48-60**. Reservations recommended. Fixed-price menu 278DKK–498DKK ($46–$83). DC, MC, V. Mon–Sat 5:30–10pm. Bus: 3, 5, 10, or 11.

MODERATE

Il Mulino ✷ ITALIAN   Set on the second floor of an inner-city building that was originally erected as a warehouse in 1737, this is an authentic and completely engaging Italian restaurant with a cuisine that includes specialties from throughout the Italian peninsula. Its pastas, which are made and rolled out fresh every day, are among the best in town. Seasoned with flair, they're likely to include small macaroni with Gorgonzola sauce and smoked salmon or spaghetti flavored with fresh herbs and served with a lobster sauce. Among recent offerings we endorse are the grilled quail flavored with spices and served with a spicy tomato sauce and black olives, and the grilled veal cutlets drizzled with truffle oil and served with a zucchini-laced sauce.

Bispensgade 31. ℭ **98-12-39-99**. Reservations recommended. Main courses 175DKK–195DKK ($29–$33); fixed-price menu 289DKK–379DKK ($48–$63); vegetarian platter 85DKK ($14). AE, DC, MC, V. Tues–Fri 11:30am–3:30pm and 5:30pm–midnight, Sat 5:30pm–midnight. Bus: 1.

Kniv og Gaffel ✷✷ FRENCH/DANISH   This is a romantic choice for dining, housed in the oldest preserved citizen's house, dating from 1552, in Aalborg. The street takes its name from Maren Turis, a woman who lived here in the 16th century and was accused of witchcraft, tried, but found not guilty. Those terrifying memories are long erased today—you'll experience only lots of atmosphere, and wonderful food served by candlelight. Its old oak tables fill up every night, and the wooden floors are buckled and slanted with age. The house specialty is thick steaks, the best in Aalborg, although you can order an array of other dishes as well, each prepared with first-rate ingredients plucked from the markets that very morning. On our most recent rounds, we enjoyed fresh Norwegian salmon baked with mushrooms and served with a béarnaise sauce. The chicken breast platter is delectably cooked here with homemade basil and tomato sauce and served with a garden salad and baked potato.

Maren Turis Gade 10. ℭ **98-16-69-72**. Reservations recommended. Main courses 42DKK–160DKK ($7–$27). MC, V. Mon–Wed noon–10pm; Thurs–Sat noon–11pm; Sun 5–11pm. Bus: 1, 3, or 5.

Provence ✷ DANISH/FRENCH   This is Aalborg's foremost purveyor of Danish cuisine that's influenced in almost every case by the culinary traditions of France. Across from the Limsfordhotellet in the center of town, it offers a cozy, small-scale brown-and-white interior that's illuminated by a stained-glass skylight. The only complaint ever expressed is that its younger staff is not as well trained as those at some of its competitors. Your meal might begin with fresh oysters, a lobster cocktail, fish, or lobster soup. Main courses include a filet of Dutch sole with a salmon soufflé and fresh spinach, fired sea bass with leek sauce, or tournedos served either in its own juices or layered with foie gras. Any entree might be followed with a selection of cheeses from a trolley, or perhaps a chocolate mousse. Even if the service isn't always faultless, the cuisine itself usually is. The food remains classical and is always reliable.

Ved Stranden 11. ℭ **98-13-51-33.** Reservations recommended. Main courses 119DKK–189DKK ($20–$32); fixed-price menu 60DKK ($10) at lunch, 100DKK ($17) at dinner. AE, DC, MC, V. Sun–Thurs noon–10pm; Fri–Sat noon–11:30pm. Bus: 2, 12, or 13.

Restaurant Benzons DANISH/FRENCH The inviting decor, attentive service, and good cuisine make this pair of restaurants the very best on a street crammed with places to eat. The same kitchen prepares the tempting specialties served in the downstairs bistro and in the more formal upstairs restaurant. The menu, prices, and hours are the same in both. Choices include the best chunky lobster soup in the region, served with sour cream; sautéed Skagen shrimp; a delectable fish pâté; and a perfectly cooked roast breast of duck with Madeira sauce or Dijon-style beef. There's dining on the outdoor terrace in summer.

Jomfru Anegade 8. ℭ **98-16-34-44.** Reservations required. Main courses 59DKK–128DKK ($9.85–$21); fixed-price menu 59DKK ($9.85) at lunch, 59DKK–128DKK ($9.85–$21) at dinner. AE, DC, MC, V. Daily 11:30am–11:30pm.

Restaurant Kilden ✿ DANISH/INTERNATIONAL Set on the second-highest (15th) floor of the Hotel Hvide Hus, in the center of town near the bus station, this is a contemporary, stylish, and strongly recommended restaurant that attracts crowds of office workers to its attractively priced luncheon buffet, and both local residents and hotel guests to its smoothly choreographed evening meals. Some of its allure derives from the views that sweep over the nearby municipal park (the Kilden Park, after which the restaurant is named) and the seacoast. Menu items change with the season, but are likely to include lobster soup, pepper steak, sliced tenderloin of pork with mustard sauce, medallions of veal with truffle sauce, venison with cognac sauce, and roasted rack of lamb with garlic sauce. These are all elegant dishes, beautifully prepared by a skilled chef, using the freshest ingredients possible.

In the Hotel Hvide Hus, Vesterbro 2. ℭ **98-13-84-00.** Reservations recommended. Main courses 138DKK–168DKK ($23–$28); fixed-price menus 235DKK–355DKK ($39–$59). AE, DC, MC, V. Daily 6–10pm.

Ristorante Fellini SOUTHERN ITALIAN Your best opportunity for a change of pace from too constant a diet of Danish food will be within this hard-working restaurant in the center of Aalborg. Here, staff members from Campania (the region around Naples) will offer succulent Mediterranean dishes wherein the warmth and style of southern Italy will be presented at their very best. Menu items include choices from a display of fish and marinated-vegetable antipasti; spaghetti *con vongole* (with clams); and risotto *alla pescatore* (with shellfish and fish), an array of fresh shellfish that mingles that day's catch from the North and Baltic seas with Italian verve. There's also a particularly succulent version of lamb roasted with herbs and potatoes in a style perfected over the centuries by cooks in the highlands of Italy's south-central regions.

Vestergade 13. ℭ **98-11-34-55.** Main courses 139DKK–189DKK ($23–$32); 3-course fixed-price menu 259DKK ($43). AE, DC, MC, V. Daily 11:30am–11pm. Bus: 1 or 2.

INEXPENSIVE

Duss Vinkjaelder DANISH This old-world 1624 cellar lies beneath one of the most famous private Renaissance mansions (Jens Bang's Stonehouse), a 2-minute walk east of the cathedral. It features a selection of beer and wine (ever had Rainwater Madeira?), but it's a bit skimpy on the food. It's more of a snack restaurant and a wine bar than a full-fledged restaurant. However, you can order a plate of Danish *biksemad* (hash), a burger, or perhaps some pâté.

Østerågade 9. ℭ **98-12-50-56.** Snacks 30DKK–138DKK ($5–$23); wine by the glass 32DKK ($5.35). MC, V. Mon–Fri 11am–midnight; Sat 10am–2am.

Fyrtøjet DANISH/INTERNATIONAL   A cozy, small restaurant in the center of town, Fyrtøjet serves competent and filling fare—though it's not especially exciting. We suggest a Danish specialty, the *almueplatte* (peasant's plate), with marinated herring, curry salad, two warm rissoles, cold potato salad and chives, and deep-fried Camembert cheese with black-currant jam. Other main dishes include stuffed plaice with shrimp, pepper steak, and breast of duck. In the summertime, enjoy your meal at outdoor tables.

Jomfru Anegade 17. (©) **98-13-73-77.** Reservations recommended. Main courses 100DKK–190DKK ($17–$32). AE, DC, MC, V. Mon–Sat 11:30am–11pm; Sun noon–11pm. Bus: 1, 3, 5, or 15.

Holles Vinstue DANISH   A 4-minute walk west of Nytorv, this is a popular wine bar and restaurant, with an inviting atmosphere. Owners sell wine by the glass or bottle. Until 3pm you can fill up on some of the best *smørrebrød* in town. Or you can ask for more substantial meals, with many dishes designed to stand off the cold winds from the north. Sample a Wiener schnitzel, various omelets, and fish filets, or else some "granny" stews or hashes. Much of the cookery is designed to appeal to the old Norsemen of the North Sea instead of food "trendies."

Algade 57. (©) **98-13-84-88.** Main courses 45DKK–85DKK ($7.50–$14); *smørrebrød* from 25DKK ($4.20). Mon–Fri 11am–8pm; Sat 11am–4pm. Bus: 1, 3, or 5.

Layalina LEBANESE   *Layalina* means "our pleasant nights" in Arabic. Its owners are Lebanese, and they have decorated the restaurant warmly with handmade Middle Eastern artifacts. Exotic dishes (at least by Danish standards) such as shish kebab and hummus are served in an atmosphere of genuine Middle Eastern hospitality. The house special is three brochettes with lamb, meatballs, and spicy sausage. Although a true Lebanese might find fault with the cookery here, it comes as a wonderful change of pace for most of us after too many nights of unvarying Danish cuisine.

Ved. Stranden 7–9. (©) **98-11-60-56.** Main courses 50DKK–179DKK ($8.35–$30); 2-course fixed-price menu 99DKK ($17). MC, V. Mon–Thurs and Sun 5–10pm; Fri–Sat 5–11pm. Bus: 1, 4, 40, or 46.

AALBORG AFTER DARK

Hot summer days and long, mild evenings are ideal for open-air concerts of various kinds. Each year Aalborg hosts several major rock concerts in Mølle Park, with up to 16,000 attending. There are also rock concerts in Skovdalen, behind Nordjyllands Kunstmuseum, all through the summer. Kilden Park is also a setting for summer concerts. Information about these summer concerts becomes available at the tourist office (see "Visitor Information," earlier in this chapter) beginning in April.

The home of the Aalborg Symphony Orchestra is **Aalborg Kongres og Kultur Center,** Europa Plads 4 (© **99-35-55-55;** bus: 15), north of Kilden Park. Opera and ballet performances are also presented here. The tourist office (see earlier) keeps complete data on all cultural events staged here.

DANCE CLUBS

Young people often gravitate to **Musik Keller,** in the basement of the previously recommended restaurant Provence, Ved Straden 11 (© **98-13-51-33**). Neither the wildest nor the most conservative club in town, it's a bit staid by New York standards, although its DJ plays the most recent music arriving from London, Los Angeles, and elsewhere. There's never any live music, however. Admission is free, and the Keller is open Friday and Saturday 9:30pm to 6am.

Rendez-Vous, Jomfru Anegade 5 (© **98-16-88-80**), offers drinking facilities on its street level, and a dance floor upstairs, attracting university students and folks under 40. Or else head for **Cube,** Jomfru Anegade 10 (© **98-10-33-10**), a bar and dance club that's open every Friday and Saturday 11pm to 6am.

A CASINO

On the site of the Radisson SAS Limfjord Hotel, **Casino Aalborg,** Ved Stranden 14–16 (© **98-10-15-50**), offers such games of chance as American roulette, blackjack, stud poker, and the inevitable slot machines. It's open daily 7pm to 4am, charging 50DKK ($8.35) for entrance. No one under age 18 is allowed.

3 Frederikshavn

64km (40 miles) NE of Aalborg; 381km (238 miles) NW of Copenhagen; 40km (25 miles) S of Skagen

For many, this coastal town in Eastern Jutland is their final stop in Denmark. From here, ferry connections are possible to either Norway or Sweden (see "Getting There," below). But the town of some 26,000 people, the largest in Jutland north of Aalborg, is not just an international ferry port.

A relatively young town, it has a number of attractions but few historic sites. At first glance, however, you'll think the whole town is one vast supermarket, filled with Swedes or Norwegians on shopping expeditions. Danish food products are cheaper here than they are back in Sweden or Norway.

A strong maritime aura permeates the town. There are seven municipal harbors alone where the ferries leave or arrive from Norway and Sweden. Just north of Frederikshavn lies the fishing hamlet of Standby, where most of the famous "Frederikshavner plaice" are landed.

In the Middle Ages the fishing settlement here was called Fladstrand. During the Thirty Years' War the site became a defense entrenchment. In time a powder tower surrounded by a wall was erected. But it wasn't until as late as 1818 that Fladstrand was granted its municipal charter and the new name of Frederikshavn. In addition to tourists, ferry passengers, and shoppers from other Scandinavian countries, Frederikshavn also depends on fishing to spark its economy, and is the site of such industries as iron foundries, shipbuilding, and engineering.

ESSENTIALS

GETTING THERE   By Train   Trains leave from Aalborg hourly during the day.

By Bus   Frequent buses run between Aalborg and Frederikshavn.

By Car   Head north from Aalborg along the E45 to Frederikshavn.

By Ferry   Stena Line (© **96-20-02-00**), one of Europe's largest and most reliable ferryboat operators, runs the two most popular routes in and out of town. Passengers from Norway have the option, with or without their cars, of a daily, 9-hour ferryboat transit between Frederikshavn and Oslo. Depending on the season, pedestrians pay between 140DKK and 300DKK ($23–$50) each, and transport of a car with its driver costs from 230DKK to 750DKK ($38–$125), depending on the season and the size of the car. Be warned in advance that southbound boats originating in Oslo depart after dark, and consequently, all passengers are required to rent an overnight cabin for the 9-hour transit. Cabins, each suitable for two passengers, rent for between 380DKK and 1,560DKK ($63–$261) each. Stena also maintains five ferryboats a day between the Swedish port of Gothenburg and Frederikshavn. Transit time is between 2 and 3 hours, depending on the boat, all of which are capable of transporting cars. Pedestrians pay between 125DKK and 170DKK ($21–$28) each way. Transport

Frederikshavn

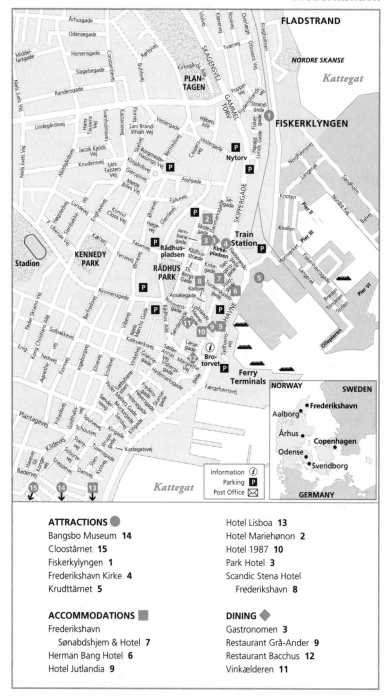

ATTRACTIONS ●
Bangsbo Museum **14**
Cloostårnet **15**
Fiskerkylyngen **1**
Frederikshavn Kirke **4**
Krudttärnet **5**

ACCOMMODATIONS ■
Frederikshavn
   Sønabdshjem & Hotel **7**
Herman Bang Hotel **6**
Hotel Jutlandia **9**

Hotel Lisboa **13**
Hotel Mariehønon **2**
Hotel 1987 **10**
Park Hotel **3**
Scandic Stena Hotel
   Frederikshavn **8**

DINING ◆
Gastronomen **3**
Restaurant Grå-Ander **9**
Restaurant Bacchus **12**
Vinkælderen **11**

of a car with its driver, depending on the speed of the boat and the season, costs between 650DKK and 980DKK ($109–$164). If you're traveling with a car during the midsummer crush between mid-June and August, advance reservations are advised. Stena also operates three catamaran crossings every day that are much faster than the ferries.

VISITOR INFORMATION   The **Frederikshavn Turistbureau,** Skandiatorv 1 (© **98-42-32-66;** www.frederikshavn-tourist.dk), near the ferry dock, is open January 2 to June 18 and September 1 to December 30, Monday to Friday 9am to 4pm, Saturday 11am to 2pm; June 19 to 30 and August 16 to 31, daily 8:30am to 5pm; July 1 to August 15, Monday to Saturday 8:30am to 7pm, Sunday 8:30am to 5pm.

SEEING THE SIGHTS

Although most of Frederikshavn is modern, the oldest part of town, **Fiskerky-lyngen,** lies to the north of the fishing harbor. Here you'll encounter a number of 17th-century houses, each well preserved. You can also see a former military fortification, **Norde Skanse** (North Entrenchment), which was constructed by the troops of Wallenstein during the Thirty Years' War.

Attractions are minor, but could easily occupy your time while you're waiting for a boat departure. If you're rushed, visit only the **Bangsbro Museum** (see below). Otherwise, some of the following sights are of minor interest.

Opposite the railway station rises Frederikshavn's most famous symbol, **Frederikshavn Kirke,** Kirkepladsen (© **98-42-05-99**). Most of this church dates from 1690, although it was significantly rebuilt in 1892. Inside you can see its major attraction, an altarpiece painted by Michael Ancher, the Skagen artist. The cemetery at the church contains graves of both Allied and German soldiers killed in World War II. Admission is free, and the church is open Tuesday through Saturday 9am to noon.

You can climb the whitewashed gun tower, **Krudttårnet,** at Havnepladsen (© **98-43-19-19**), a remnant of the famed citadel that stood here in the 1600s. The tower actually stood at another place in Frederikshavn, but when the shipyards had to be expanded it was moved here instead of being torn down. The former gunpowder magazine, built of stone in 1688, has been turned into a Museum of Military History, displaying weapons from the 17th to the 19th centuries. It's open daily June to mid-September 10:30am to 5pm, charging 15DKK ($2.50) adults, 3DKK (50¢) children, free for children under 4.

Another tower worth a visit is **Cloostårnet** (Cloos Tower; © **98-48-60-69;** bus: 210 or 225), lying 4km (2½ miles) southwest of town at an altitude of 165m (541 ft.) above sea level. This observation tower rises 58m (190 ft.), offering panoramic views over the sea and the countryside of Vendsyssel. An elevator will take you to the top, and in fair weather you can see most of the surrounding district. Admission is 15DKK ($2.50) adults or 5DKK (85¢) children. Hours are May to mid-June, Wednesday through Monday 1 to 5pm, Saturday and Sunday 10am to 5pm; mid-June to mid-August, daily 10am to 5pm; mid-August to August 31, Wednesday through Monday 1 to 5pm. It's closed the rest of the year.

Bangsbro Museum ⚐   One of the premier open-air museums of the region, this place is in a wooded area beside the Deer Park, 3km (1¾ miles) south of the town center, and contains a cluster of 18th-century buildings near the remnants of a 14th-century manor house. Of special interest is an old barn built in 1580, one of the oldest in Denmark, which houses antique farm equipment and implements. The main house has a collection of handicrafts made from human hair, a display of relics from World War II, and a nautical section including ship models, figureheads, and other mementos. An early ship, *Ellingå*, similar to the vessels used by the Vikings, is in one of the buildings. It's the reconstructed remains of a Viking-style merchant ship excavated 5km (3 miles) north of Frederikshavn.

Dronning Margrethesvej 6. © **98-42-31-11**. Admission 35DKK ($5.85) adults, 5DKK (85¢) children. June–Oct daily 10:30am–5pm; Nov–May Tues–Sun 10:30am–5pm.

SHOPPING

Frederikshavn is an active shopping town, with boutiques and emporiums that line both sides of the **Gågade,** one of the longest all-pedestrian streets in Denmark.

One of the most intriguing shopping possibilities, **Dot Keramik** is at Skagensvej 270, Nielstrup, Standby (© **98-48-14-10**), 7km (4⅓ miles) north of Frederikshavn. Here you'll find a wide display of hand-thrown ceramics, plus an array of applied art, gift articles, and intriguing decorations. At **Birgitte Munch,** Daanmarksgade 42C (© **98-43-80-66**), you can see the town's most talented goldsmith producing jewelry according to the best traditions of workmanship. A wide range of high-quality, locally designed jewelry is on sale.

WHERE TO STAY

In case you miss the boat and need a room, the Frederikshavn Turistbureau (see above) will book you into a private home if you'd prefer that to a hotel.

EXPENSIVE

Radisson SAS Jutlandia Hotel ★★ This is the largest and the best-rated hotel in town, and as such, it's the site where members of the Danish royal family have stayed during several of their visits. It's also the closest hotel to the spot where the boats from Gothenburg stop. The lobby, a study in high-ceilinged, 1960s-style architecture, outfitted in cool grays and violets, is one of the best examples of Scandinavian design in town. Rooms are carpeted, but in most cases, they're not excessively large. Luxury-category rooms, however, are very comfortable, outfitted with well-upholstered furniture. Bathrooms are first-rate with tub/shower combinations. One exceptional accommodation is the Thai Suite, the largest in the building, outfitted in carved teakwood furniture. Don't expect the amenities of a resort here, as it caters to business travelers who aren't necessarily interested in swimming pools and sports facilities.

Postboks 89, Havnepladsen, DK-9900 Frederikshavn. © **800-333-3333** in U.S. or Canada, or 98-42-42-00. Fax 98-42-38-72. www.radissonsas.com. 95 units. 1,150DKK ($192) double; 2,450DKK ($409) suite. Rates include breakfast. AE, DC, MC, V. **Amenities:** Restaurant; bar; sauna; room service (7am–1am); babysitting; laundry service; dry cleaning; nonsmoking rooms; rooms for those with limited mobility. *In room:* TV, dataport, minibar, hair dryer.

Scandic Stena Hotel Frederikshavn ★ *Kids* In the center of town, near the pedestrian shopping area and not far from the harbor, this 1987 hotel, one of the largest hotels in Denmark outside of Copenhagen, is not as fancy or as highly rated as the Jutlandia. Rooms are well furnished and well maintained. Some can be converted into three- or four-bed accommodations, so the Stena has long been a favorite with families. All the accommodations come with tiled private bathrooms with tub or shower. Good food is served in the hotel's premier dining room, Det Gulge Pakhus, or you can dine more informally in the Brasserie Søhesten. The hotel's primary attraction is its Aqualand, complete with water flume, foaming waterfalls, summery wavelets, and gentle whirls.

Tordenskjoldsgade 14, DK-9900 Frederikshavn. © **98-43-32-33**. Fax 98-43-33-11. www.scandic-hotels.com. 215 units. 1,154DKK ($193) double; 1,775DKK–2,295DKK ($296–$383) suite. AE, DC, MC, V. **Amenities:** 2 restaurants; bar; nightclub; indoor heated pool; gym; sauna; children's playroom; 24-hr. room service;

massage; laundry service; dry cleaning; nonsmoking rooms; rooms for those with limited mobility. *In room:* A/C, TV, dataport, minibar (some units), hair dryer, trouser press, iron/ironing board.

MODERATE

Frederikshavn Sømandshjem & Hotel *(Kids)*   In the center of town, near the shopping area and close to the harbor, this old-fashioned hotel was founded in 1880 as the Seamen's Mission. However, restored in 1998, it offers some of the best lodgings for your kroner in town. Many of its functionally furnished bedrooms can be converted into three- or four-bed rooms suitable for families. The restaurant serves good Danish food of the meat-and-potatoes (with gravy) variety.

Tordenskjoldsgade 15B, DK-9900 Frederikshavn. *C* **98-42-09-77.** Fax 98-43-18-99. 47 units. 725DKK–895DKK ($121–$149). Rates include breakfast. AE, DC, MC, V. **Amenities:** Restaurant; laundry service; dry cleaning; nonsmoking rooms. *In room:* TV, hair dryer.

Herman Bang Hotel   This inn in the center of Frederikshavn provides a decent stopover at a reasonable price. It has long sheltered passengers staying overnight and waiting to catch ferries to either Sweden or Norway. Rooms are comfortable and clean, but functionally furnished and rather plain, each with a small bathroom with shower. The free car park at the rear is convenient for ferry departures. Other than a breakfast room, facilities are at a minimum.

Tordenskjoldsgade 1, DK-9900 Frederikshavn. *C* **98-42-21-07.** Fax 98-42-21-66. 73 units, 27 with bathroom. 495DKK–595DKK ($83–$99) double without bathroom; 695DKK–795DKK ($116–$133) double with bathroom. Rates include breakfast. AE, DC, MC, V. **Amenities:** Breakfast room. *In room:* TV, hair dryer, iron/ironing board.

Hotel Lisboa   Outfitted in a blue-and-white color scheme, and with polished stone floors of the type you might expect in a hotel in Portugal, this hotel was named in honor of a holiday that its founders had taken in Lisbon just before the hotel's construction in 1958. In 1978, it was enlarged with an annex. With good views of the sand dunes and the beach, it appeals to a nature-loving, escapist crowd year-round. Rooms are simple, spartan, and uncomplicated, with straightforward-looking furniture. Each accommodation comes with a small bathroom with shower. Public areas and the restaurant are outfitted with the blue-and-white abstract paintings of Danish artist Peder Meinert.

Søndergade 248, DK-9900 Frederikshavn. *C* **98-42-21-33.** Fax 98-43-80-11. www.lisboa.dk. 32 units. 750DKK–850DKK ($125–$142) double. MC, V. From Frederikshavn, take bus nos. 1, 2, 3, or 4. **Amenities:** Restaurant; bar. *In room:* TV, hair dryer.

Hotel 1987   This hotel was configured from a 130-year-old marine warehouse in 1987—hence its name. Today, only the symmetrical yellow facade and massive interior beams and trusses remain from the original construction. Rooms are comfortable, cozy, and snug, each equipped with a small, shower-only bathroom. The staff is helpful, and although the hotel only serves breakfast, it's not far from the bars and restaurants of the rest of the town.

Damsgaards Plads 8E, DK-9900 Frederikshavn. *C* **98-43-19-87.** Fax 98-43-19-42. www.hotel1987.dk. 28 units. 600DKK–750DKK ($100–$125) double. Rates include breakfast. AE, DC, MC, V. **Amenities:** Breakfast room. *In room:* TV, minibar.

Park Hotel *(star)*   An atmospheric choice with a certain charm, this hotel was built in 1880 in a combination Old French and Old English style. Many of the handsomely furnished traditional rooms have marble bathrooms. Only the suites have tubs in the bathrooms; the doubles contain only showers. The Park is known for its gourmet restaurant, **Gastronomen,** which serves an international cuisine (see "Where to Dine," below).

Jernbanegade 7, DK-9900 Frederikshavn. (©) **98-42-22-55.** Fax 98-42-20-36. 30 units, 20 with bathroom. 590DKK ($99) double without bathroom; 990DKK ($165) double with bathroom; 1,490DKK ($249) suite. Rates include breakfast. AE, DC, MC, V. **Amenities:** Restaurant; bar; 24-hr. room service; laundry service; dry cleaning; nonsmoking rooms. *In room:* TV, minibar, hair dryer, iron/ironing board, safe.

INEXPENSIVE

Hotel Mariehønon   This hotel is among the most convenient in town, only 5 minutes from the ferry terminal and 3 minutes from the train depot. Most of its guests are passengers waiting overnight to catch ferries to Oslo or Gothenburg. A family-run hotel, Mariehønon offers rooms that are basic, functionally although comfortably furnished, and well maintained, some coming with a small bathroom with shower. It's known for providing a good night's sleep at a reasonable rate. There's no restaurant, but there are several places to eat nearby.

Scoolagade 2, DK-9900 Frederikshavn. (©) **98-42-01-22.** Fax 98-43-40-99. 32 units, 18 with bathroom. 390DKK–525DKK ($65–$88) double without bathroom; 490DKK–725DKK ($82–$121) double with bathroom. Rates include buffet breakfast. AE, DC, MC, V. **Amenities:** Breakfast lounge. *In room:* TV.

WHERE TO DINE
EXPENSIVE

Gastronomen ★★   FRENCH   Long known for its cuisine, this gourmet restaurant has an engaging appeal and infectious charm. The food is several notches above that of a typical French bistro, relying on quality ingredients served in formal, traditional surroundings. The menu lists an exciting assemblage of food, often served in perfect combinations, such as the Norwegian lobster with asparagus, or the grilled filet of beef in a velvety smooth tarragon sauce. As a nouvelle dish, the grilled tenderloin of veal appears with chanterelles and a raspberry sauce. Old Danish tradition is followed with the fried plaice with white potatoes and parsley, but you can try more daring innovations as well, like the light and tasty watercress soup with champagne. Marinated salmon with freshly chopped herbs is always welcome, and the fish of the day is usually your safest bet. For your grand finale, opt for the walnut nougat cake served with rhubarb purée or some other concoction of the day, or else settle for a dish of sorbet or perhaps a selection of cheese.

In the Park Hotel, Jernbanegade 7. (©) **98-42-22-55.** Reservations required. Main courses 158DKK–198DKK ($26–$33); 2-course fixed-price menu 258DKK ($43), 3-course fixed-price menu 328DKK ($55). AE, DC, MC, V. Mon–Sat 7am–10pm.

Restaurant Grå-Ander (The Gray Duck) ★★ *Finds*   FRENCH   This is one of the best-recommended dining rooms in Frederikshavn, with a reputation that the managers of the Hotel Jutlandia work hard to maintain. There's room inside for only 34 diners, who enjoy their meal in a dining room with windows overlooking the blue-gray expanse of the sea. Menu items are based on inspirations from France, and include duck liver pâté with apple salad, skewered and grilled scallops with fresh spinach and pepper sauce, and chicken breast layered with duck liver and served with sautéed mushrooms. Two dishes to rave about include lemon sole in a ragout of mussels and curried cream, and quail with foie gras and a red-wine flambé. Dessert might be a raspberry Napoleon with a honey parfait and chocolate sauce. The staff is justifiably proud of their food and the service they provide, which are both excellent. There are many luxury ingredients on the menu but prices are not as daunting as you might fear.

In the Hotel Jutlandia, Havnepladsen. (©) **98-42-42-00.** Reservations recommended. Main courses 190DKK–390DKK ($32–$65) at lunch, 580DKK–900DKK ($97–$150) at dinner. AE, DC, MC, V. Tues–Sat 6–10pm.

MODERATE

Restaurant Bacchus MEXICAN/ITALIAN   Set near the harbor within a simple building dating from the 1850s, this is an unassuming, unpretentious bistro. Although there's a well-chosen wine list, it's a lot less comprehensive than you might assume from the restaurant's name. Within an old-fashioned dining room with only 40 seats, you can order such standard fare as pizza, succulent pastas, burritos, and a spicy chili con carne.

Lodsgade 8A. ℃ 98-43-29-00. Reservations recommended. Main courses 90DKK–150DKK ($15–$25); fixed-price dinner menu 69DKK–199DKK ($12–$33). AE, DC, MC, V. Mon–Sat 5–10pm.

INEXPENSIVE

Vinkaelderen DANISH   Lying midway between the harbor and the center of town, this restaurant is recognized by its red-brick facade, bull's-eye glass windows, and multiple carriage lamps. Originally established after World War II, it has a warmly rustic coziness enhanced by the racks of European wines on the walls. Fresh fish and Danish beef dishes are specialties. The fixed-price menu is served day and night. This place is for those who want filling and flavorful fare at a reasonable price—but don't expect "fireworks" for the palate.

Havnegade 8. ℃ 98-42-02-70. Main courses 75DKK–200DKK ($13–$33); fixed-price menu 135DKK ($23). AE, DC, MC, V. Daily 10am–11pm.

FREDERIKSHAVN AFTER DARK

In Frederikshavn, nightlife simmers away in quiet, not particularly demonstrative ways, most visibly at the **John Bull Pub,** Havnepladsen (℃ **98-42-42-00**), a clone of an English pub adjacent to the Jutlandia Hotel. More Danish, and more suited to wine drinkers, is the **Vinkaelderen,** Havnegade (℃ **98-42-02-70**), where a roster of wines from throughout the world is sold by the glass, within a setting whose decor was inspired by old-time Danish models of long ago.

4 Laesø ⭐

201km (125 miles) NW of Copenhagen; 28km (17½ miles) SE of Frederikshavn

In the northern Kattegat, just 90 minutes east across the water from Frederikshavn (see earlier), lies an island that time seems to have forgotten. With a long seafaring tradition, little Laesø is today a holiday island, patronized mainly by the Danes themselves and also the Swedes who come here for "a taste of Denmark."

The history of Laesø goes back around 5,000 years when the island first appeared from the depths of the sea. By the Middle Ages islanders earned their living mainly from fishing and salt flats. The island is characterized by its salt marshes, woodland, heaths, and meadows. With a population of about 2,500 inhabitants, Laesø's total landmass is only about 117 sq. km (45 sq. miles). Even today two-thirds of the island consists of uncultivated land.

In the northern tier in the Højsande area, dunes reach a height of some 30m (98 ft.). The southern part of Laesø is characterized by low-lying meadows along the coastline, and is a favorite abode of seabirds that live here from May to September. One of the most dramatic parts of the island is the eastern section, Danzigmand Dune, which is protected by the government almost like a nature reserve. The dunes here take their name from the *Danzig*, a ship that was once stranded here. The flat, sandy beaches of the island attract many bathers (but generally not the type that favors the beaches of Florida). The two major ports of the island are Vesterøhavn and also Østerbyhavn, farther east.

The island's capital (and a good town to use as a base) is the small town of Byrum in the center. In this area you'll see lots of Danish farmhouses with roofs covered in seaweed instead of the typical Danish thatching. The islanders couldn't find reeds for their roofs so they turned to plentiful seaweed, which proved to be a worthy substitute.

The ethic in Laesø involves urban escapism. Many residents fleeing Copenhagen and other urban centers like to go to retreats like this that don't indulge too heavily in mass tourism, and where the old ways of life persist. There are quite a few Swedes who live on the island as well. Locals zealously protect the wonderful natural environment they've inherited.

The traditional island is quite famous and often photographed. There is a legend that claims Queen Margrethe I was rescued from a shipwreck off the coast in the 1300s. She gave her rescuers a beautiful dress, which so impressed them it was made into the national costume of Laesø. By the turn of the 20th century, most national costumes had disappeared from Denmark. However, the dress style given by Margrethe lasted until right after the Nazi occupation. Today it's worn only on special occasions.

ESSENTIALS

GETTING THERE   By Ferry   Four modern ferries sail several times a day from the port of Frederikshavn on the east coast of Jutland to the port of Vesterøhavn on the west coast of Laesø (trip time: 1½ hr.); round-trip fare is 170DKK ($28) adults, 90DKK ($15) children; 840DKK ($140) round-trip fare to transport a car and two passengers. For information about schedules and booking, call Færgeselskabet Laesø I/S (© **98-49-90-22**).

VISITOR INFORMATION   The **Laesø Turistbureau,** Vesterø Havnegade 17 (© **98-49-92-42**), is open January to March, Monday to Friday 9am to 2pm; April 1 to June 11, Monday to Friday 9am to 4pm, Saturday 9am to noon.

GETTING AROUND   By Bus   There's only one bus route on the island; the locals are serviced by a gray bus and a yellow bus (no numbers). Each goes in opposite directions along the same route daily, connecting the capital, Byrum, with the ports of Vesterbrøhavn and Østerbyhavn.

By Bicycle   With its flat terrain, Laesø is ideal for bikers, who can arrange rentals from **Jarvis Cykel Service,** Vesterø Havnegade 29 (© **98-49-94-44**), in Vesterøhavn. Rentals cost from 40DKK to 70DKK ($6.70–$12) a day.

EXPLORING THE ISLAND

The main attraction, frankly, is the unspoiled island itself, with its natural beauty and sandy beaches, although there are a few specific attractions as well.

Museumsgården, Museumsvej 3 (© **98-49-15-29**), at Byrum, is housed in what was one of Laesø's old seaweed farms, and the main building still has a seaweed roof. One of the last of the island's old stub mills is also on-site, and it is still in working order when wind conditions are right. Parts of the wood construction of the building itself reveal its origin: wreck timber from ships stranded on the shores of Laesø. The oldest part of the building dates back to the 17th century. It's open April 5 to September 10, daily 10am to 5pm; September 11 to November 10, Tuesday to Sunday 11am to 3pm. It is closed November 11 to April 4. Admission is 25DKK ($4.20) adults, 10DKK ($1.65) children.

In another part of the island, at **Vesterøhavn,** you can visit **Søfartsmuseet,** Vesterø Havnegard 5 (© **98-49-94-47**). Here you can inspect the second biggest find of 17th-century coins in Denmark, part of a great silver treasure buried in 1670 but later excavated. Other exhibitions illustrate the living conditions of the inhabitants of Laesø. Here visitors are informed about the history of the fisheries, the sailors, the local lifesaving service, and violent storms and shipwrecks. It's open June 16 to August, daily 10am to 4pm; off season, daily 11am to 3pm. Closed November to March. Admission is 25DKK ($4.20) adults, 10DKK ($1.65) children.

OUTDOOR ACTIVITIES

Many Danes come here to play golf at the **Laesø Seaside Golf Klub** (© **98-49-92-42**), midway between Østerbyhavn and Vesterøhavn. In 1998 it expanded from a 9-hole to an 18-hole course. It costs 250DKK ($42) to play, unless you have some special discount from a hotel where you are a guest. Because of the damage to the dunes and sea grasses, no electric golf carts are allowed. You can, however, rent a set of clubs for 100DKK ($17).

Some urbanites who crave the enforced isolation, the roaring winds, and the scrubby Baltic landscape of Laesø believe that the best way to enjoy them is on horseback. The island's best-recommended riding stable is **Krogbaekgaard,** Storhavevej 8, DK-9940 Laesø (© **98-49-15-05**). The 16 horses they shelter and protect include sturdy Icelandic ponies. An island tour that lasts 4 to 5 hours is 600DKK ($100) for adults, 500DKK ($84) for children, including lunch. Shorter, hour-long tours are 140DKK ($23) for adults, 120DKK ($20) for children. Advance reservations are vital. Your experience will include ample exposure to the island's rugged beaches, crashing surf, salt marshes, and bird life.

WHERE TO STAY

The tourist office (see "Visitor Information," above) will book you into private homes on the island.

Carlsen's Hotel   This is one of the most frequently recommended hotels on the island, and it has welcomed mariners and tourists since 1855. Today, it occupies a prime location a few steps uphill from the harbor. The mostly nautical-theme rooms are cozy, ultrasimple, and clean—the kind of retreat you might favor if you're escaping from urban cares and want to simplify your life. There's a restaurant, **Carlsen's** (see "Where to Dine," below), the **Krostue** bar—whose allure is raffish and salty enough to please any yachting enthusiast—and a dance club (see "Laesø After Dark," below).

Havnebakken 8, DK-9940 Vesterøhavn, Laesø. © **98-49-90-13**. Fax 98-49-90-72. 13 units, none with bathroom. 450DKK ($75) double. AE, MC, V. **Amenities:** Restaurant; bar; dance club. In room: No phone.

Hotel Nygaard ★ (Finds)   Set within 180m (591 ft.) north of the hamlet of Byrum, this top-notch hotel was originally built around 1700 as the core of a farm estate, and later functioned as the island's major purveyor of general merchandise and supplies. Public areas are more elegant than those within any other hotel on the island, and are replete with gentrified reminders of the agrarian Denmark of long ago. Rooms are clean, well maintained, and comfy, and each comes with a private tiled bathroom with tub or shower. Guests pay 100DKK ($17) for all-day play on the island's only golf course (nonresidents pay 250DKK/$42). There are no real distractions at this hotel, other than long walks along the sandy lanes or seacoasts of the island.

Østerbyvejen 4, DK-9940 Byrum, Laesø. © **98-49-16-66**. Fax 98-49-16-68. 18 units, 900DKK ($150) double. Rates include breakfast. DC, MC, V. **Amenities:** Restaurant; breakfast-only room service. In room: TV.

WHERE TO DINE

The cuisine here relies heavily on nature's bounty. Islanders call the local lobster "red gold," and fresh fish forms a large part of the diet. But you can also enjoy heather-fed lamb, some of the best this side of Scotland.

The Dining Room at Carlsen's Hotel ⚓ DANISH/SEAFOOD   You might be confused if you arrive here in midsummer, because of the way management expands its premises to two separate dining areas at opposite ends of the hotel. Most of the year, however, it occupies a single big-windowed room with nautical memorabilia and a view over the harbor. Menu items include all the traditional Danish specialties, including a medley of both fried and marinated herring, sautéed filets of sole and plaice, succulent North Atlantic lobsters (when they're available), freshly made salads, homemade soups, veal, tender steaks, chicken, and a dessert list of homemade cakes and pastries.

Havnebakken 8m, Vesterøhavn. ✆ **98-49-90-13.** Main courses 60DKK–200DKK ($10–$33). AE, DC, MC, V. Daily 8am–9:30pm.

Restaurant Bakken DANISH   This thriving restaurant has an outdoor garden that draws lots of requests for seating during clement weather. Originally built in the early 1950s, it's charming, conservative, and old-fashioned, specializing in traditional Danish food that includes lots of fish. Menu items feature different preparations of shrimp, marinated or baked salmon, and filets of sole and/or plaice; red mullet is oftentimes served with a simple parsley and butter sauce, and in some instances, citrus sauce, as a means of bringing out the innate flavors of the fish. When it's available, there's North Atlantic lobster as well. If you don't like fish, the standard beef, veal, chicken, and pork dishes are offered, usually prepared with braised cabbage, potatoes, onions, and herbs.

Hovedgaden 89. Byrum. ✆ **98-49-11-20.** Main courses 55DKK–245DKK ($9.20–$41). AE, DC, MC, V. Daily 10am–9pm.

Restaurant DeliKATEn DANISH   Respectable and tidy, this restaurant occupies the space that's created by the steep-sloping eaves of the second floor of a clapboard house directly beside the harbor of Vesterøhavn. Despite the fact that the building looks antique, it was actually constructed in the mid-1990s. Menu items include grilled halibut with butter, lemon, and parsley sauces; sautéed plaice stuffed with shrimp and seasonal asparagus; and three different types of beefsteak that the restaurant identifies, respectively, as French, English, and Danish. Only the staff here will be able to articulate the difference. The unusual use of capital letters within the restaurant's name (DeliKATEn) derives from its ownership by a local entrepreneur whose name is Kate Larsen.

Havn, Vesterøhavn. ✆ **98-49-99-01.** Reservations recommended. Main courses 90DKK–170DKK ($15–$28). AE, MC, V. Apr–May daily 4–8pm; June–Aug daily 6–10pm; Sept to mid-Dec daily 4–8pm. Closed Dec 15–Mar 30.

LAESØ AFTER DARK

The Pearl Disco/the Sailorpub is in Carlsen's Hotel, Havenbakken 8, Vesterøhavn (✆ **98-49-90-13**). A night on the town in sleepy Laesø might involve a chat with a stranger, a drink in the Sailorpub (aka "Krostue"), and, if it's open, a bout of dance music in the Pearl Disco. The pub is likely to be open anytime you feel like having a drink—9am to 2am daily—while the disco operates mostly when students and nature lovers from the European mainland are in residence, usually June to mid-September, Monday through Saturday 10pm to 3am. The rest of the year, it's open only on Saturday (same hours). In summer, there's likely to be live rock 'n' roll 2 nights a week. In winter, however, it rocks and rolls only about once a month, usually in conjunction with dinner dances that are widely publicized on billboards, lampposts, and newspaper articles around the island. A cover is imposed, except during one of the once-per-month dinner dances in winter, when the all-inclusive price is likely to be around 100DKK to 149DKK ($17–$25) per person, not including drinks.

5 Skagen ★★

104km (65 miles) NE of Aalborg; 485km (303 miles) W of Copenhagen

Skagen is the "Land's End" of Denmark—the northernmost tip of Jutland on its eastern coast. It has been compared to a "bony finger" pointing into the North Sea. Pronounced *skane,* Skagen is the second-biggest fishing port in Denmark. A thriving artists' colony has done much to enliven the town.

This town of 13,000 people who live here year-round is set against a back-drop of dramatic scenery—moors covered with heather, undulating stretches of dunes, and some of the best—but not the warmest—sandy beaches in Europe.

This small, windswept town is known for its artists and craftspeople. For cen-turies it remained unspoiled and isolated. But in the 19th century, artists—attracted to the desolation of the place—began to arrive in increasing numbers. With the coming of the railway in 1890, with a link connecting Skagen with Frederikshavn, tourists began to discover the area as well.

ESSENTIALS

GETTING THERE **By Car** Take E45 northeast to Frederikshavn. From there, head north on Route 40 to Skagen.

By Train Several trains a day run from Copenhagen to Århus, where you con-nect with another train to Frederikshavn. From Frederikshavn there are 12 daily trains to Skagen.

VISITOR INFORMATION The **Skagen Turistbureau** is at Skt. Laurentivej 22 (© **98-44-13-77;** www.skagen-tourist.dk). It's open June 26 to August 1, Monday to Saturday 9am to 6pm, Sunday 10am to 4pm; June 1 to 25 and August 2 to 31, Monday to Saturday 9am to 5pm, Sunday 10am to 2pm; Sep-tember 1 to May 31, Monday to Friday 9am to 4pm, Saturday 10am to 1pm.

SEEING THE SIGHTS

Since it opened in 1907, **Skagen Havn** (Skagen Harbor) ★ has been one of the major attractions of town. It's seen at its best when the boats come back to land their catches (times vary). For early risers, the fish auction "at the rack of the morning" is a popular attraction. Mid-May to mid-October, the oldest part of the harbor is a haven for the boating crowds centered around one of the mari-nas. Many yachting people in Jutland use Skagen as their favorite harbor haven.

Gammel Skagen (Old Town) ★ lies 2.5km (1½ miles) from Skagen Havn. Signs point the way. Originally Gammel Skagen was the fishing hamlet—that is, until Skagen Havn opened in 1907. Today, Gammel Skagen is a little resort town with large beach hotels that are mainly timeshares.

An attraction worth exploring is **Rådjerg Mile,** a migrating dune moving at the rate of about 11m (36 ft.) annually. Located 16km (10 miles) south of town, it can be reached via Kandestederne. This dune was formed on the west coast in the 16th century during the great sand drift that characterized the landscape until the 20th century. The dune continues to move yearly, eastward toward the forest.

Den Tilsandede Kirke   This church buried in sand dunes 1.5km (1 mile) south of town is an amusing curiosity. The only part that's visible is the upper two-thirds of the tower. When Hans Christian Andersen visited in 1859, he called the church "The Pompeii of Skagen." The sand didn't exactly surprise a congregation at worship. The only things hidden under the dunes are the remnants of a wall and the old floor and perhaps the baptismal font. By 1775, the church had fallen into disrepair and was used by fewer and fewer members. By 1795 it was closed down, and in 1810 it was partly demolished, the stones sold to people in the area as building materials for their private houses. Today red stakes in the ground indicate the placing and extent of the nave and vestry.

ⓒ **98-44-43-71.** Admission 10DKK ($1.65) adults, 5DKK (85¢) children. June–Sept 1 daily 11am–5pm; winter Sat–Sun 11am–5pm.

Drachmanns Hus   Built in 1828, the house was home to poet and artist Holger Drachmann until his death in 1908. Now a museum, it's filled with mementos of the artist.

Han Baghsvej 21. ⓒ **98-44-51-88.** Admission 25DKK ($4.20) adults, free for children. June 1–14 Sat–Sun 11am–3pm; June 15–Aug 15 daily 10am–5pm; Aug 16–Sept 15 daily 11am–3pm; Sept 16–Oct 16 Sat–Sun 11am–3pm; closed Oct 17–May.

Michael & Ana Ancher Hus ⁂   If you visit the Skagens Museum (see below), you will see work by talented artists Michael and Ana Ancher, who originally purchased this house back in 1884. After their daughter, Helga, died in the 1960s, it was converted into a museum of their work. It's preserved rather like it was in the lifetime of these artists.

Markvej 2–4. ⓒ **98-44-30-09.** Admission 50DKK ($8.35) adults, free for children. Feb–Apr and Oct–Nov Sat 11am–3pm; May–Sept daily 10am–5pm. Closed Dec–Jan.

Skagen By- & Egnsmuseum   This worthwhile open-air museum is in a compound where the homes of both rich and poor fishers were moved to create the aura of how people lived in this area from 1830 to 1880. Today there's a maritime museum devoted to shipwrecks, with photographs of vessels in distress. There's also a fisheries exhibition. You can also see a lifesaving station, and an original Dutch windmill. The museum is a 15-minute stroll from the train depot.

Fortidsminderne, P. K. Nielsensvej. ⓒ **98-44-47-60.** Admission 30DKK ($5) adults, 5DKK (85¢) children 7–14, free for children under 7. Mar–Apr Mon–Fri 10am–4pm; May–Sept daily 10am–5pm; Oct–Nov Mon–Fri 10am–4pm. Closed Dec–Feb.

Skagens Museum ⁂ *Finds*   This is the most important attraction in the town. It houses the works of many local artists who have painted in the area, and is especially rich in the works of artists from the 1930s. You'll see paintings by P. S. Krøyer (1851–1909), Michael Ancher (1849–1909), and Anna Ancher (1859–1935), among others.

Brøndumsvej 4. ⓒ **98-44-64-44.** Admission 60DKK ($10) adults, free for children under 15. May–Sept daily 10am–5pm; Apr and Oct Tues–Sun 11am–4pm; Nov–Mar Wed–Fri 1–4pm, Sat 11am–4pm, Sun 11am–3pm.

SHOPPING

Since so many artists live in Skagen, many visitors purchase art here. The best gallery is **Galerie Skagen,** Trondsvej 16 (ⓒ **98-44-44-25**), which also has a tasteful collection of handicrafts. The most sophisticated collection of pottery is found at **Skagen Potteri,** Sct. Laurentivej 27 (ⓒ **98-44-69-29**). Stunningly designed modern jewelry is sold at **Smykkekunstner,** Sct. Laurentivej 48

(© **98-44-11-08**), in Gammel Skagen. Some of Jutland's finest glass pieces—often works of art—are on display and for sale at **Skagen Glasvaerksted,** Sct. Laurentivej 95 (© **98-44-60-50**).

WHERE TO STAY

Color Hotel Skagen ★ *Finds*   Southwest of Skagen, beside the only road leading into town from the rest of Jutland, this sprawling, one-story hotel lies 2km (1¼ miles) from the sea. There, alone on sandy flatlands, it possesses an almost otherworldly sense of isolation. Unlike many of its competitors, which cater to families with children, this place appeals mostly to couples. Built in 1969, the hotel has an appealing formal restaurant. The spacious, attractively furnished guest rooms have hardwood floors, padded armchairs, and big windows. Each unit also contains neatly kept bathrooms with tub/shower combinations. Of the accommodations, 45 are listed as apartments, which are rented only for 3 days at a time except during midsummer, when they are rented per week.

Gammel Landevej 39, DK-9990 Skagen. © **98-44-22-33**. Fax 98-44-21-34. www.skagenhotel.dk. 153 units. 895DKK–1,295DKK ($149–$216) double; 1,695DKK–2,295DKK ($283–$383) suite; 6,500DKK–9,900DKK ($1,086–$1,653) apt per week. AE, DC, MC, V. From Skagen, drive 2km (1¼ miles) southwest of town along Rte. 40. **Amenities:** Restaurant; bar; outdoor heated pool; fitness center; sauna; 24-hr. room service; non-smoking rooms; rooms for those with limited mobility. *In room:* TV, dataport, hair dryer, safe.

Finns Hotel Pension   Originally built in 1909 in a style that the owner refers to as "a Norwegian wood house," this old-fashioned Danish homestead is designed like houses that Scandinavian immigrants made popular during the 19th century in American states such as Minnesota. In a residential neighborhood of Skagen, a 10- to 15-minute walk northeast of center and a 3-minute walk from the beach, it's furnished with old furniture and antiques. Many rooms have beamed ceilings and a charming but vaguely claustrophobic allure. Our only warning involves a rigidity on the part of the hardworking managers and staff, who establish very clear-cut rules for new arrivals, who aren't noted for their flexibility, and who maintain an aggressive "take it or leave it" approach to their unique hotel. If you give advance notice, they'll prepare a three-course evening meal, which is served only to residents, for a price of around 250DKK ($42) per person. If you agree to this, on pain of severe reproach, don't be late for dinner.

Østre Strandvej 63, DK-9990 Skagen. © **98-45-01-55**. Fax 98-45-05-55. 6 units, 3 with bathroom. 925DKK ($154) double with bathroom, 775DKK ($129) double without bathroom. Rates include breakfast. MC, V. Closed Jan–Mar. **Amenities:** Dining room. *In room:* No phone.

Strandhotellet/Strandhuset ★   Our favorite hotel in Skagen lies close to Gammel Skagen. It consists of two well-crafted buildings, the older of which (Strandhotellet) was built in 1912 as a holiday home, and the younger of which (Strandhuset) was constructed with a prominent hip roof in the early 1990s. The suites with kitchens tend to be focused within the Strandhuset. Rooms are evocative of the lodgings within an elegant and tasteful private home. Only the suites have tub/shower combinations; regular doubles have a shower. Breakfast is presented within a semicircular greenhouse-style extension jutting out from one end of the house.

Jeckelsvej, Gammel Skagen, DK-9990 Skagen. © **98-44-34-99**. Fax 98-44-59-19. 14 units, 6 suites with kitchenette. 1,000DKK–1,175DKK ($167–$196) double; 1,118DKK–1,405DKK ($187–$235) junior suite; 1,265DKK–1,925DKK ($211–$321) senior suite. AE, DC, MC, V. 4km (2½ miles) south of Skagen center. **Amenities:** Restaurant (summer only); bar; room service (7am–10pm). *In room:* TV, hair dryer, iron/ironing board.

WHERE TO DINE

Skagen Fiske Restaurant ✸ FISH   One of the best-known fish restaurants in Jutland occupies the red-sided premises of a gable-roofed building that was erected directly beside the harborfront in 1907. You'll enter a bar on the establishment's street level, where the floor is composed of the actual beachfront—nothing more than sand. Climb to the nautically decorated dining room one floor above street level for meals. Lunches usually include flavorful platters that might contain fish cakes, Norwegian lobster, peel-your-own-shrimp, three different preparations of herring, or grilled filets of sole with lemon sauce. Dinners are more elaborate, consisting of whatever fish has been hauled in that day by local fishermen, prepared any way you specify, with virtually any sauce that's reasonably available. Frankly, the only drawback to this place involves its short, summer-only season.

Fiskehuskai 13. ⓒ **98-44-35-44.** Reservations recommended. Lunch platters 58DKK–73DKK ($9.70–$12); dinner main courses 255DKK–288DKK ($43–$48). AE, DC, MC, V. Mid-May to Aug daily 6–10:30pm.

6 Hirtshals

322km (200 miles) NW of Copenhagen; 48km (30 miles) SW of Skagen; 41km (25½ miles) NW of Frederikshavn

West of Skagen, this is a small town of some 7,000 hearty souls, many of whom are connected with its commercial fishing harbor or the ferry terminal business with connections leaving from here to Moss, Oslo, and Kristiansand. As such, there are always plenty of Norwegians coming and going through the town. In fact, the entire main street of town seems to have gone supermarket crazy, and Norwegians pile off the ferries and dash to the markets before doing anything else. Why? Danish meats and groceries are relatively cheap compared to the prices back in their increasingly expensive homeland.

After a century of effort, locals were granted the right to construct a harbor at the end of World War I, but it wasn't until 1930 that it became fully operational. The main reason to visit is to see a bustling North Sea port, although there's one major attraction—the Nordsømuseet (see below).

ESSENTIALS

GETTING THERE   By Train   Hirtshals has good rail links with Hjørring to the south. Trains run throughout the day from Hjørring to Hirtshals, with the last departure nightly at 10:45pm (trip time: 20 min.). Once at Hjørring, you can connect with all the main major trains running across Denmark. Either Aalborg or Frederikshavn can be your linkup with the Danish rail system.

By Bus   Buses arrive from both Skagen and Hjørring at the rate of six per day mid-June to mid-August only.

By Car   From Skagen (see above), take Route 40 south to the junction with Route 597 heading west into Hirtshals. From Hjørring, follow the E39 directly north to Hirtshals.

By Ferry   Color Line (ⓒ **99-56-19-77**) runs three or four ferries a day between Hirtshals and Kristiansand on the southern coast of Norway (trip time: 4½ hr.). Fares depend on the season and the day of the week, and range from 180DKK to 420DKK ($30–$70) for a pedestrian without a car, and from 660DKK to 1,650DKK ($110–$276) for a car with up to five passengers, each way.

Color Line also makes one transit per day (except Sun in midwinter, when there's no service) between Hirtshals and Oslo. Departing from Hirtshals at

9:45pm, and arriving 9 hours later in Oslo, it costs 360DKK to 840DKK ($60–$140) for a pedestrian without a car, round-trip, and 1,320DKK to 3,300DKK ($220–$551) round-trip for transport of a car with up to five persons inside. On this long overnight run, rental of a cabin is required. These cost from 100DKK to 930DKK ($17–$155) per person, double occupancy, depending on the category of cabin and the season you travel.

VISITOR INFORMATION   **Hirtshals Turistbureau,** less than a kilometer (about ½ mile) south of the ferry harbor at Nørregade 40 (© **98-94-22-20;** www.toppenafdanmark.dk), is open September 1 to June 14, Monday through Thursday 9:30am to 3:30pm, Friday 9am to 4pm, Saturday 9am to 3pm; June 15 to August 31, Monday through Friday 9am to 4pm, Saturday 9am to 7pm.

SEEING THE SIGHTS

If the weather's fair, you can head for **Tornby Strand,** 5km (3 miles) south of town. Completely unspoiled, this is a beautiful stretch of beach set against a backdrop of North Sea sand dunes. Even if the day is chilly, you might do as the Danes do and go for a hike along this beach, breathing in the bracing North Sea air. You can also hike through the coastal forest in back of the stretch of beach. To reach Tornby Strand, take Route 55 from Hirtshals.

A minor attraction, **Hirtshals Museum,** Soph. Thomsensgade 6 (© **99-56-58-85**), is set up in a typical fisher's cottage, built of granite in 1880. The interior, through authentic furnishings from the era, duplicates what a building of this type would have looked like around 1915. The museum is open year-round Monday through Thursday 10am to 4pm, Friday 10am to 1pm. It's closed Saturday and Sunday. Admission is 20DKK ($3.35) adults, free for children 12 and under.

Nordsømuseet ★★   Even if you're rushing to catch a ferry to Norway, try to budget some time for the Nordsømuseet. The exciting news here is the opening in May 1998 of the largest aquarium in Europe. The main attraction of this Oceanarium is the giant aquarium itself, containing some 4.5 million liters of seawater. Visitors can gaze upon an 8m-high (26-ft.) column of water or view the "ocean" through an aquarium window, the thickest in the world. The aquarium is two stories high. A fire in 2003 destroyed part of the museum but final restoration is supposed to be complete early in 2005.

The large aquarium has been designed to house schools of fish of the North Sea. Through the huge windows viewers can watch fascinating schools of herring, mackerel, garfish, and horse mackerel, and see them react as predatory fish approach. Among other large creatures, several species of North Sea sharks can be viewed. Each day divers feed the shoal fish and the sharks and describe life in the aquarium to visitors.

Of course, the original museum is still intact. It's devoted to modern Danish sea fishing, detailing man's exploitation of the North Sea—for better or worse. Displays of the daily lives of fishermen, equipment, and vessels are placed alongside exhibits depicting the resources of the North Sea. Seals are common along the coast of Denmark, but you seldom spot them. However, in the on-site seal pool, you can observe the animals at close range—above as well as underwater. Feeding times for the seals are daily at 11am and again at 3pm.

Willemoesvej. © 98-94-44-44. Admission 60DKK ($10) adults, 30DKK ($5) children 3–11, free for children under 3. June–Aug daily 10am–10pm; Sept–May daily 10am–5pm.

WHERE TO STAY

Hotel Hirtshals   Built in 1989 in a position immediately adjacent to the town's harbor, this is a basic hotel that's clean and unpretentious. The clean and cozy rooms often have high peaked ceilings, and each comes with a small bathroom with shower. Most have views of the harbor. There are few (if any) amenities and extra facilities. However, there's a sunny restaurant, **Hirtshals Kro,** that serves well-conceived meals every day noon to 3pm and 6 to 9:30pm. Menu items, served within a marine blue and white setting with big windows that evoke the inside of a greenhouse, are Danish and, to a lesser extent, international. The restaurant, but not the hotel, is closed January and February.

Havnegade 2, DK-9850 Hirtshals. ② **98-94-20-77.** Fax 98-94-21-07. 18 units. 695DKK–795DKK ($116–$133) double. Rates include breakfast. AE, DC, MC, V. **Amenities:** Restaurant; bar. *In room:* TV.

Hotel Strandlyst   Although it was built as a holiday hotel around 1900, very little of the original design remained after this hotel was radically rebuilt in 1965. Today, you'll see a red-brick building set on grassy flatlands, a 3-minute walk from a sandy beach. Inside, within both the public areas and the rooms, you'll find stripped-down, efficient-looking furnishing in a laminated-wood style that's generic to Scandinavia. There are few amenities and grace notes associated with this hotel, but in light of the nearness of the beach, very few of its sun-and-sand–worshipping clients really seem to mind. There's a simple **restaurant** that serves fixed-price menus at both lunch and dinner for 50DKK to 170DKK ($8.35–$28).

Strandvejen 20, Tornby DK-9850 Hirtshals. ② **98-97-70-76.** 47 units, 28 with bathroom. 320DKK ($53) double without bathroom; 400DKK–490DKK ($67–$82) double with bathroom. AE, DC, MC, V. From Hirtshals, drive 5km (3 miles) south of town along Hwy. 55, following the signs to Hjørring. **Amenities:** Restaurant; bar. *In room:* No phone.

Skaga Hotel ★★   This is the most luxurious and upscale hotel in Hirtshals, with a government four-star rating that makes it one of the most stylish and luxurious beach hotels in Jutland. Built of russet-colored bricks and large expanses of glass in 1989, it lies less than a kilometer (½ mile) north of the center of town, amid sandy scrublands within a 2-minute walk from the beach. Most of its big windows furnish views of either the North Sea or the sand dunes that lead up to it. Rooms contain wall-to-wall carpeting, writing desks, comfortable beds, at least one chair or sofa upholstered in leather, and a simple and contemporary design in monochromatic colors. All accommodations contain immaculately kept bathrooms with tub/shower combinations.

Willemoesvej 1, DK-9850 Hirtshals. ② **98-94-55-00.** 108 units. 995DKK ($166) double. Rates include buffet breakfast. AE, DC, MC, V. **Amenities:** Restaurant; bar; indoor heated pool; gym; Jacuzzi; sauna; room service (7am–9pm); laundry service; dry cleaning; nonsmoking rooms; solarium. *In room:* TV, dataport, minibar, hair dryer, iron/ironing board.

WHERE TO DINE

Fiskehus ★ *(Finds* DANISH/SEAFOOD   A meal here involves a pleasant degree of surprise, as the menu features what the Ude family's patriarch, a local fisherman, hauls in that morning from the nearby sea. The setting is a century-old, stone-sided house that's beside the sea in the heart of town. No more than 30 diners at a time are fed the freshest seafood in Jutland within an artfully simple setting with no pretensions whatsoever. The menu changes daily but will usually include fried plaice, an assorted fish platter, halibut and herring, tournedos of beef, pepper steak, and, when the chef feels inspired, a spicy version of fish stew. Everything here is small-scale, personalized, and in very direct contact with the sea and its many moods.

Jørrengade 9 ② **98-94-41-44.** Reservations recommended. Main courses 100DKK–250DKK ($17–$42); fixed-price menus 100DKK–200DKK ($17–$33). MC, V. Easter–Nov daily 11am–11pm; Dec–Easter Thurs–Sun 11am–10pm.

HIRTSHALS AFTER DARK

It's fashionable among young people in Hirtshals to downgrade the town's limited roster of bars and pubs, and to migrate to nearby Hjørring for nightlife options. But if you want to stay in sleepy Hirtshals, consider a drink at **Haley's,** Søndergade 7 (② **98-92-10-06**), where local fishermen gather to warm themselves after a bout at sea, and to drink *aquavit,* whiskey, or beer in a cozy maritime setting. Open Monday through Saturday 3 to 11pm.

Appendix:
Denmark in Depth

The Danes may live in a small country, but they usually extend an enthusiastic welcome to visitors. The British novelist Evelyn Waugh called the Danes "the most exhilarating people of Europe." Few Danes would dispute this—and neither would we.

Made up mostly of islands, Denmark is a heavily industrialized nation, known for its manufactured products as well as its arts and crafts. However, it also boasts a quarter of a million farmers.

1 Denmark Today

Denmark has been called a bridge because it links northern Europe with the Scandinavian Peninsula. In 2000 that became literally true, as the Øresund Bridge opened across the sound, connecting the island of Zealand, on which Copenhagen sits, with southern Sweden, at the city of Malmö, for the first time in history.

The smallest of the Scandinavian countries (about half the size of Maine), its total land mass equals about 41,400 sq. km (15,985 sq. miles), most of which is on the peninsula of Jutland, which borders Germany. The major islands are Zealand, Funen, and Bornholm. Denmark has adequate space for its population of 5.5 million people, but its population density is much greater than that of the other Scandinavian countries. About 1.4 million Danes live in the capital city, Copenhagen, on the island of Zealand.

About 98% of all native-born Danes belong to the Danish Lutheran Church, the state church, although church attendance is actually low. The second-largest group is Catholics (30,000), and there are about 6,500 Jews.

Only 4.5% of the population is made up of immigrants, including refugees identified as Palestinians, Somalis, Bangladeshis, Kurds, and Iraqis, among others.

Fun Fact **Did You Know?**

- Denmark is a nation of nearly 500 islands.
- The reigning queen, Margrethe II, designs postage stamps, as well as opera and ballet sets.
- Second only to the Bible, the writings of Hans Christian (H. C.) Andersen are the most widely translated literary works in the world.
- Some historians argue that the fairy tale writer Andersen wasn't the son of a poor cobbler but the child of the 19th-century Danish king, Christian VIII.
- Denmark has the highest proportion of female clerics per capita.
- The country has a celebration honoring America's Fourth of July.
- Chilly Denmark used to grow grapes for winemaking in the Middle Ages.
- Danes pay the highest taxes on earth.

Vietnamese immigrants seem to be accepted, but Muslim and Arab immigrants tend to experience hostility.

Technically, Denmark is a parliamentary democracy and constitutional monarchy. Its territories include the Faroe Islands (an autonomous area under the Danish Crown) and Greenland (which was granted regional autonomy in 1985). The sovereign is Queen Margrethe II, who ascended the throne in 1972; her husband is a Frenchman, Prince Henrik. Margrethe is the first woman sovereign in Denmark in 6 centuries. Real power is vested in the unicameral parliament (the *Folketing*), which citizens over the age of 23 elect every 4 years. The royal family's primary function is ceremonial.

Although it has been a NATO member since 1949, Denmark does not permit nuclear weapons to be deployed on its soil. Denmark became the first NATO country to grant women the right to serve in frontline units. It's also an active member of the European Union (but not part of the euro zone, having voted in Sept 2000 to retain the Danish kroner), and enjoys harmonious relations with its Scandinavian neighbors and other European countries.

Denmark enjoys one of the world's highest standards of living plus a comprehensive social welfare system, which is funded through extremely high taxes. Danes enjoy 7½-hour workdays, cradle-to-grave security, state-funded hospitals and schools, and a month-long vacation every year. During their vacations, Danes tend to travel extensively. By and large the Danes are extremely well educated; they have pioneered the establishment of adult education centers (for those ages 18–35), a movement that has spread to other countries of Europe.

No country in the European Union has less poverty or a fairer distribution of wealth than Denmark. Both the poor and the rich get richer, and in most cases young people have little trouble finding employment.

Although a progressive, modern, and liberal state (it was the first country to recognize same-sex marriages), Denmark has its share of problems. Drug use among young people is a growing concern, and the young are increasingly rejecting the institution of marriage, with common-law relationships becoming the norm. Also, the divorce rate is rising.

The "melancholy Dane" aspect of their character (if there is one) is reflected in a relatively high suicide rate. Otherwise, their general health is excellent—a Danish girl born today has a life expectancy of 78 years; a Danish boy, 72 years.

Culturally, Denmark is an avid producer and consumer of art and culture. Some 12,000 books a year are published in Denmark. There are 42 newspapers, and the theater and film industries are thriving in spite of cutbacks in government funding.

Denmark in the late '90s built bridges to the world. On June 14, 1998, Queen Margrethe II cut a ribbon before driving across the Great Belt Bridge, a span that links the island of Zealand (on which Copenhagen sits) with the island of Funen. Because Funen is linked by bridge to Jutland (part of mainland Europe), and with Malmö across the Øresund Sound, Copenhageners can now drive to Germany or Sweden without having to rely on ferries.

Impressions

If I were a dictator, I would not occupy Denmark for fear of being laughed to death.

—John Steinbeck

2 History 101

Composed of a flat and sandy peninsula and a cluster of islands, Denmark is tiny. But despite its small size, its strategic position at the mouth of the Baltic has made Denmark one of the most coveted terrains in the world. Consequently, Denmark's struggles to secure its sovereignty and independence from the larger, stronger military forces that surround it on every side have repeatedly shaped Danish history. And although modern Danes are somewhat embarrassed when confronted with their country's militaristic past, Denmark used to be known as a fiercely aggressive nation, jockeying for territory, prestige, and strategic advantage with other such empire-building nations as England, Austria, and the precursors of modern-day Germany.

PREHISTORIC DENMARK & THE ROMANS

The mystery that surrounds early Denmark stems from the fact that the Romans and their legions never managed to transform it into a colony. Consequently, while former Roman provinces like France and Germany were depicted by numerous historians, including Julius Caesar himself, little was ever recorded about ancient Denmark. There is evidence of early trade. Amber found only in the Baltic has been identified within Egyptian jewelry, and some historians cite Danish trade with the Eastern Mediterranean, in which the Danes exchanged fur and slaves for bronze utensils and gold jewelry.

Concentrations of bones from various grave sites, and stone implements that archaeologists estimate at 80,000 years old, have been unearthed in regions of Jutland, but despite those discoveries, Denmark has never produced the wealth of archaeological finds that are commonplace, say, in Greece, Italy, or Egypt. Part of the

Dateline

- 810 The reign of the first recorded Danish king, Godfred, ends.
- 811 The southern boundary of the Danish kingdom is established at the banks of the Eider River, where it remains for almost a thousand years.
- 800–950 Vikings emerge to plunder the monasteries and settlements of England, France, and Russia.
- 940–985 Harald Bluetooth brings Christianity to Denmark.
- 1013–43 The crowns of Denmark and England are united.
- 1104 The foundation is laid for a Danish national church that's distinctly different from that within German lands to the south.
- 1397 The Union of Kalmar, under the leadership of Queen Margaret, unites Denmark, Norway, and Sweden. Meanwhile, high percentages of Danes are allowed to work their own farmland, forming the basis of Denmark's eventual strength as an agrarian nation.
- 1471 Sweden abandons the union; Denmark and Norway remain united under Christian I (1426–81).
- 1530 Lutheran preachers bring the Reformation to Denmark.
- 1536 After a siege of Copenhagen, most of the lands and assets owned by the Catholic Church are seized by the Danish crown.
- 1577–1648 The long reign of Christian IV brings prosperity but ends in a losing war with Sweden.
- 1675–79 The Skane War is fought, and Denmark loses large territories to Sweden, including the "château country" of southern Sweden.
- 1801–07 England, in a black chapter of its foreign policy, bombards Copenhagen and confiscates the ships of Denmark's navy as a means of ensuring that the Danes don't cooperate with Napoleon.
- 1813 The national treasury of Denmark, faced with punitive clauses in the treaty at the end of the Napoleonic Wars, goes bankrupt.
- 1810–30 The golden age of Danish literature, as defined by the creation of

continues

reason might stem from the great ice sheets that made much of Denmark uninhabitable for thousands of years.

Later, as the ice sheets receded northward, hunter-gatherers eked out a modest living. Their communal grave sites and the stone dolmens that mark their entrances show proficiency at erecting stone lintels and markers.

Ironically, the high acid and iron content within Denmark's peat bogs has had the macabre effect of preserving the bodies of at least 160 unfortunates, all of whom died violently, in some cases many thousands of years ago, and all of whom appear to have been unceremoniously dumped into bogs. Among the most famous of these is the well-preserved, 2,000-year-old body of the Grauballe Man, who was probably strangled to death, and whose body was discovered in the 1950s in a Jutland peat bog. His body revealed some clues about what life was like in prehistoric Denmark: A wool cap covered his head, stubble on his chin and cheeks indicated that the fashion at the time involved shaving, and the remains in his stomach showed that his last meal consisted mostly of barley.

As for literary references, other than a few cryptic comments that appear within such early English sagas as *Beowulf,* and the cryptic descriptions by the medieval Scandinavian historian Saxo Grammaticus of a long line of (otherwise undocumented) early medieval Danish warlords, there isn't a lot of documentation about post-Roman Denmark. Historians conclude that Denmark was a land of frequent migrations, frequent annihilations of one tribal unit by another, and frequent changeovers of the racial texture of the peninsula as one tribe of people was either annihilated or ousted by others.

VIKINGS TERRORIZE EUROPE

Denmark developed a reputation for violence as the Vikings ravaged

works by Søren Kierkegaard and Hans Christian Andersen.

- 1849 Simultaneous with revolutions that break out across Europe, liberal reforms are activated in the form of a new Danish constitution.
- 1866 Denmark loses Schleswig-Holstein to Prussia.
- 1890s Many liberal reforms in education and health insurance act as precursors of the liberal social policies of Denmark in the 20th century.
- 1914 Denmark struggles to maintain neutrality in World War I.
- 1915 A new constitution gives Denmark universal suffrage.
- 1916 Denmark sells Virgin Islands to the U.S. for $25 million.
- 1926–40 Economic depression causes great suffering in Denmark.
- 1940–45 Denmark is invaded and occupied by Nazi Germany.
- 1949 Over some protests, Denmark joins NATO.
- 1953 A new constitution provides for a single-chamber parliament.
- 1972 Denmark joins the European Economic Community; Margrethe, daughter of Frederik IX, becomes queen of Denmark.
- 1982 Poul Schluter becomes the first Conservative prime minister since 1894.
- 1989 Denmark leads the world in certain social policies: the first NATO country to allow women in front-line military units and the first country to recognize same-sex marriages.
- 1992 Denmark votes against the Maastricht Treaty, which establishes the framework for the European Economic Union.
- 1993 Denmark votes to support the Maastricht Treaty and then presides over the European Union for the first half of the year.
- 1996 Copenhagen is designated the "Cultural Capital of Europe"; the "Copenhagen '96" festival attracts artists and performers from all over the world, with more than 25,000 performances staged.
- 1998 By a narrow margin, Denmark votes to enlarge its ties with the European Union.

regions of central and southern Europe.

So ironically, the country with one of the most peaceful reputations in Europe today was originally a hell-raising land that, along with such other Viking areas as Norway and Sweden, was associated with terror for the rest of Europe. Lustfully pagan and undeterred by the belief that Christian churches and monasteries were sanctified, they exacted rich plunder from whatever monastery or convent they happened to judge as weak enough to be attractive.

Their longboats were especially feared: Measuring about 18m (59 ft.) from the dragon-shaped prow to stern, longboats were powered by 30 oars and a sail. They were still light enough, however, that their crews could drag them across land, thereby "hopping" from rivers to lakes, across sandbars, and across isthmuses that would otherwise have been unnavigable. It's no small wonder that the Danes would eventually become proficient as both mariners and traders.

Through rape and intermarriage, the Vikings mingled bloodlines with future English, French, Germans, and Russians. Despite the mayhem they unleashed on conquered lands, Vikings brought with them regimented rituals; for example, unlike most European peoples at the time, they bathed every Sunday, regardless of temperature or weather.

The most distinct threat to Danish territoriality came from Charlemagne, whose Frankish empire covered what is today France and Germany. If Charlemagne hadn't focused most of his territorial ambitions on richer, more fertile lands in central Europe and Spain, it's likely that what's known today as Denmark would have become a vassal state of the Franks. As it was, the Franks only took a slight imperial interest in Jutland. Godfred, the first recorded Danish king, died in 810 after spending most of his reign battling the Franks.

Godfred's successor, Hemming, signed a treaty with the Franks marking the Eider River, an east–west stream that flanks southern Jutland, as the southern boundary of his sovereignty. That boundary functioned more or less as the Danish border until 1864.

Two famous kings emerged from Denmark during the 10th century, Gorm the Old (883–940) and his son, Harald Bluetooth (940–85). Their reigns resulted in the unification of Denmark with power centralized at Jelling in Jutland. Harald, through the hard work of a core of Christian missionaries trained in Frankish territories to the south (especially in Hamburg), also introduced Christianity, which eventually became the country's predominant religion. As part of his attempt to obliterate Denmark's pagan past, he transformed his father's tomb, which honored a roster of pagan gods and spirits, into a site of Christian worship.

Harald eventually extended Danish influence as far as neighboring Norway. The links he established between Denmark and Norway weren't severed, at least politically, until the 1800s. Harald's son, Sweyn I, succeeded in conquering England in 1013, more than 50 years before the Norman invasion in 1066. The Normans, ironically, were also of Danish origin, through invasions several centuries before.

Under Sweyn's son, Canute II (994–1035), England, Denmark, and part of Sweden came under the rule of one crown. After Canute's death, however, the Danish kingdom was reduced to only Denmark. Canute's nephew, Sweyn II,

2000 Danes vote not to join the euro zone; Øresund Bridge links the island of Zealand (Copenhagen) with Sweden.

2004 Crown Prince Frederik takes a bride, HRH Crown Princess Mary.

ruled the Danish kingdom, and upon his death his five sons governed Denmark successfully. In 1104, the foundation was laid for a Danish national church that was distinct from the ecclesiastical administration in Hamburg.

THE BALTIC: A DANISH "LAKE"

The few remaining links between Denmark and the Frankish Holy Roman Empire were severed under Archbishop Eskil (1100–82) and King Valdemar I (1131–82). During a celebration at Ringsted in 1190, the Danish church and state were united, partly because of the influence of Archbishop Absalon (1128–1201), a soldier and statesman who is honored today as the patron saint of Copenhagen. Inspired by monarchical ideas, Absalon became a fierce and militaristic guardian of Danish independence. The hostilities became a religious confrontation, pitting the Christian Danes against the pagans to the south, as well as a territorial conflict. Absalon's most dramatic disfigurement of a pagan god occurred on the now-German island of Rügen around 1147, when he chopped the four-headed wooden figure (Svantevit) into little pieces and distributed them as firewood among his Danish (nominally Christian) soldiers.

In 1169, Denmark began what would evolve into a long series of conquests that increased its sphere of influence within city-states along the Baltic, including the ports of Estonia (which was conquered by the Danes in 1219), Latvia, eastern Germany, Poland, Sweden, and Russia. Part of Denmark's military and mercantile success derived from the general weakness of the German states to the south; part of it was because of a population explosion within Denmark, which increased the pressure for colonization.

Valdemar II (1170–1241) strengthened Denmark's control over the Baltic and came close to transforming it into a Danish lake. Grateful for their help, he ennobled many of his illegitimate sons and empowered many of his military cohorts with aristocratic titles and rewarded them with land.

The result was a weakening of the monarchy in favor of an increasingly voracious group of nobles, whose private agendas conflicted with those of the king. Valdemar's son, Eric IV (also known as Eric Ploughpenny; 1216–50), argued with church bishops and with his brothers over royal prerogatives, and was assassinated by his younger brother, Duke Abel of Schleswig, who proclaimed himself king of Denmark in 1250.

Civil wars ensued, and three of the four successive kings were killed in battle. Eric VI (1274–1319) also waged wars with Norway and Sweden, which led to Denmark's debilitation and the mortgaging of large parcels of the kingdom to pay for unsuccessful military campaigns.

Between 1332 and 1340, Denmark had no king and was ruled by an uneasy coalition of nobles. Valdemar IV Atterdag (1320–75) retained his grip on the Danish throne only by signing the peace treaty of Stralsund in 1370 with the towns of the Hanseatic League (a federation of free towns in northern Germany and adjoining countries formed around 1241 for economic advancement and

---

"Denmark"

It was during the early Middle Ages that the name "Denmark" was introduced to the consciousness of northern Europe. The name was inspired by the word for a primitive stone and earth barricade, known as the *Dannevirk* or *Danewerk,* which was erected in an ultimately futile attempt to shut out invaders from the south.

mutual protection). Its enactment did a lot to improve the fortunes of the city-states of the Hanseatic League, as it granted them enviable commercial privileges. The resulting prosperity of the Hanseatic League led to architectural enhancements, whose effects were visible all around the Baltic.

A UNITED SCANDINAVIA

Valdemar IV died in 1375, leaving Denmark without a male heir. Finally, Olaf (1375–87), the infant son of Valdemar's daughter Margaret through her marriage with King Haakon VI Magnusson (1339–80) of Norway, came to the throne. (Through a complicated chain of bloodlines, the infant Olaf was the nominal heir to all of Norway, Denmark, and Sweden.)

During Olaf's infancy, Margaret ruled the country as regent. When both her husband, Haakon, and 12-year-old Olaf died, she was acknowledged as queen of Norway and Denmark. A patroness of the arts and a savvy administrator of the national treasury, she was eventually granted wide political leeway in Sweden.

Although the three nations had already been combined under the stewardship of Margaret, they were merged into a united Scandinavia in 1397 as The Union of Kalmar. One of the largest political unions since the collapse of the Roman Empire, it extended from Iceland and the fledging communities in Greenland as far east as the western coast of Finland. It included the entire Danish archipelago as well as the Faroe, Shetland, and Orkney islands.

Acknowledging her advanced age and the need for a male figurehead at the reigns of power, Margaret arranged for her nephew, Eric of Pomerania (1382–1459), to be crowned king of all three countries as Eric VII. Margaret, however, firmly committed to the superiority of Denmark within the trio, continued to rule behind the scenes until her death in 1412. (A contemporary historian said of Margaret's comportment at public events, "All the nobility of Denmark were seized by fear of the wisdom and strength of this lady.") Despite later attempts to expand the Scandinavian union to northeastern Germany, the concept of a united Scandinavia was never as far-reaching or powerful as it was under Margaret. There were many 19th- and 20th-century visionaries who had hoped for the eventual unification of "the three separate nations of the Scandinavian north."

Margaret's designated heir, Eric VII, was childless. He was dethroned in 1439 and replaced by his nephew Christopher of Bavaria. His reign lasted only about 9 years, after which Sweden pressed for autonomy. It elected Karl Knutson (Charles VIII) as its Stockholm-based king in 1471. Denmark and the relatively weak Norway shared King Christian I (1426–81). Although Christian I lost control of Sweden, he did gain sovereignty over Schleswig and Holstein, ancient territories to the south of modern-day Denmark. But it was a troubled and culturally ambiguous acquisition that would vex the patience of both Denmark and the German states for centuries, as its citizens waffled in their allegiances.

Throughout the rest of the 15th century, the Danish church accumulated great wealth, and the merchant class profited from increases in agricultural production. By around 1500, about 12,000 Danes were estimated to own their own farms; about 18,000 Danes operated farms on land leased by the Danish king, and some 30,000 Danes maintained lease lands belonging to either Danish nobles or the increasingly wealthy (tax-exempt) Catholic church. Denmark became an exporter of foodstuffs, especially beef and grain, and livestock, especially horses.

The early 15th century marked a fundamental change in the definition of nobility. Prior to that, any Dane could become a noble by contributing a fully equipped private army, invariably composed of feudal-style serfs and vassals, to the king's war efforts. In exchange for this, he would be granted an exemption from all taxes generated by his estates. After around 1400, however, only nobles who could prove at least three generations of aristocratic lineage could define themselves as noble, with all the attendant privileges that such a title implied. With no new blood coming into the pool of Danish aristocrats, the number of noble families decreased from 264 to 140 between 1450 and 1650. Shakespeare borrowed the names of two of those families, the Rosenkrans and the Gyldenstjernes, for his drama about the mythical Danish prince, Hamlet.

The 16th century also saw changes in Danish religious practice as critiques of Catholicism began to gain currency across Europe. One of Denmark's most devoted Reformation-era theologians was Paul Helgesen, a staunch opponent of the corruption of Denmark's church. He was appointed to a position of academic prominence within the University of Copenhagen in 1519 and was a particularly vocal critic of the idea of buying salvation through the sale of indulgences. Ironically, Martin Luther's break with the Catholic Church in 1521, from a base in nearby Germany, transformed the reputation of Paul Helgesen into something of an archconservative defender of Danish Catholicism.

THE 16TH CENTURY

Christian II (1481–1559) ascended the throne in 1513. Sympathetic to the common man during his regency over the throne of Norway, he was mistrusted by conservative nobles. Their distrust was exacerbated by his commitment to seeking financial and military advice from commoners. He went so far as to turn over control of the kingdom's finances to his mistress's mother, Sigbrit Villoms, the frugal and canny widow of a Dutch burgher. A former alchemist, who claimed to have a telepathic hold over the king, she contributed to a reign alternating between bouts of genius and bouts of blood-soaked madness. Despite the massacre of more than 600 Danish and Swedish nobles in the "bloodbath of Stockholm" in 1520 and other violent atrocities, many Renaissance-style reforms were activated under Christian II's reign, without which Denmark might have erupted into full-fledged revolution.

Christian II recaptured Sweden in 1520 but was defeated by the Swedish warrior-king Gustavus Vasa a year later. Christian was deposed in 1522, whereupon he fled to the Netherlands. In the spring of 1532, he returned to Denmark, where he was incarcerated until his death, first in Sønderborg Castle and then in Kalundborg castle.

His successor, Frederik I (1471–1533), signed a charter granting the nobility many privileges. Under his regime, the Franciscans, an order of Roman Catholic monks, were expelled from their conspicuously wealthy houses of worship, and Lutheran ministers were granted the freedom to roam throughout Denmark preaching. Upon Frederik's death, the Reformation took earnest hold within Denmark. Conflicts between Lutherans and Catholics erupted in a civil war, with Catholic power centered in Copenhagen and with Lutherans mainly based on the islands of Funen and Jutland. The war ended in 1536 with the surrender of Copenhagen. In the process, vast Catholic-owned estates were forfeited to the Danish crown.

The Danish Lutheran Church was founded in 1536 during the reign of Christian III (1534–59). Before the end of the 1570s, Protestantism was firmly entrenched within Denmark. A Danish church organized in accordance with German Lutheran models ousted virtually every trace of Catholicism. Disciples of Martin Luther were brought in to organize the new Reformed Church of Denmark, which soon took on patriotic and nationalistic overtones, as hymn books, liturgies, and sermons were eventually conducted exclusively in vernacular Danish. As for the monarchy, its finances were vastly improved at the end of the Reformation thanks to its confiscation of the vast wealth formerly controlled by the Catholic Church.

WARS WITH SWEDEN

Much of the 17th century in Denmark was consumed with an ongoing series of wars with its archenemy, Sweden. Despite that, the reign of the Danish king Christian IV (1577–1648) was one of relative prosperity. The Danes worked hard, investing time and money in the development of their "overseas territory," Norway. That territory's capital, Christiania (now known as Oslo), was named after their king.

Sweden was understandably concerned about Denmark's control of the entrance to the Baltic, the sea on which Sweden and many members of the Hanseatic League depended. Denmark, thanks to its control of the narrow straits near Copenhagen, its ownership of such Baltic islands as Ösel and Gotland, and, in the Atlantic, its control of Iceland and the Faroe Islands, could be accused of being far more imperial than its size, and present-day pacifism, would imply.

Denmark continued to meddle in German and English politics throughout the 1600s, notably in the Thirty Years War that ripped apart the principalities of Germany.

Tensions between Denmark and Sweden also intensified during this period and were exacerbated by Sweden's emperor Charles V, who argued that Sweden held the right of succession to the Danish throne.

Sweden invaded Jutland and quickly defeated the Danes. Military scholars attribute the victory to Sweden's reliance on well-trained Swedish peasants who filled the ranks of the Swedish army. The Danes, in contrast, relied on paid, and less committed, mercenaries. By the Treaty of Christianople, Denmark was forced to cede to Sweden many of its former possessions, including scattered communities in Norway and the Baltic island of Gotland. Simultaneous with the loss of its territories in southern Sweden was the completion of two of Denmark's most-photographed castles: Frederiksborg in Hillerød and Rosenborg in Copenhagen, both finished under the regime of Christian IV.

Danish king Frederik III (1609–70) tried to regain the lost territories when Sweden went to war with Poland, but Charles X defeated him. Frederik ended up giving Sweden additional territory, including the island of Bornholm. Charles X attacked Denmark in an attempt to take control of the whole country, but this time Denmark won, regaining its lost territories. Sweden ended the war after the death of Charles X in 1660.

The Skane War (1675–79) was an ill-advised military campaign started by the Danish king Christian V (1646–99). Its outcome included Denmark's loss of Skane, a valuable territory in southern Sweden, which, because of its architectural appeal, is known today as Sweden's "château country." After the signing of the peace treaty that ended the war, Denmark managed to retain its claim on the island of Bornholm and on cities in northern Norway, such as Trondheim.

Frederik IV (1671–1730), Christian V's successor, resumed the war with Sweden in 1699. Named the Great Northern War, it raged, more or less inconclusively, from 1699 to 1730. Southern Sweden was not recovered, but part of Schleswig-Holstein (northern Germany) was ceded to Denmark by the German states.

During the 18th century, Denmark achieved many democratic reforms. Thanks to its navy and its seasoned core of merchant vessels, it also gained control of a group of islands in the West Indies (now the U.S. Virgin Islands) as well as the barren, snowy expanse of Greenland. Agriculture and trade prospered, and Copenhagen developed into a quietly prosperous but formidable guardian of the western entrance of the Baltic Sea.

THE 19TH CENTURY & THE NAPOLEONIC WARS

At the start of the Napoleonic wars, with France squarely opposed to most of the other nations of Europe, Denmark was engaged in a booming business of selling grain to both England and France. Despite the sweeping changes in the map of Europe engendered by Napoleon's military campaigns, Denmark strongly defended its right to remain neutral, and, as such, worked hard to ensure free passage of ships from other neutral nations within the Baltic.

This refusal to take sides, combined with the rich contracts that Danish merchants were able to acquire transporting supplies between hostile parties, infuriated England—the sworn enemy of Napoleon's France. In 1801, fearing that Denmark's formidable navy might be persuaded to cooperate with the French, England destroyed part of the Danish fleet in a battle at sea.

In 1807, as the threat of Napoleon's conquest of Europe became more and more of a reality, in one of the most arrogant acts of coercion in 19th-century history, England ordered the Danes to transfer their navy to British rule within 8 days or be bombarded. When the Danes refused, English warships opened fire on Copenhagen and destroyed the city's cathedral, its university, and hundreds of homes. England's treatment of Denmark forced the youthful king Frederik VI (1808–39) to ally Denmark with France and the policies of Napoleon. Later, after all of Napoleon's European allies abandoned him, Denmark remained loyal.

This led to a series of humiliating disasters for Denmark, especially when Napoleon was roundly defeated by an alliance of European countries in 1814. Because of England's embargoes on Denmark and the destruction of many Danish ships, Denmark lost control over its overseas colony of Norway, and its trade came to an almost complete standstill after the loss of its navy.

At a treaty that was signed at Kiel the same year, Denmark was forced to yield Norway to Sweden and Heligoland to England. The only remaining gems in Denmark's once-mighty empire included Greenland, Iceland, and the Faroe Islands.

Without a navy and crippled by huge debts and a loss of much of its prestige, Denmark sank into poverty. In 1813, the national treasury went bankrupt. Several years later, especially between 1818 and 1824, the price of grain virtually collapsed, which culminated in many farm failures and a massive exodus from Denmark to the New World. The country's precarious financial and military position also put a virtual end to any hope of liberal reforms.

Following the Napoleonic wars, the rulers Frederik VI and his successor, Christian VIII, formed very conservative governments. In 1848, as revolts and revolutions broke out across Europe, the Danes demanded a more liberal constitution. Representatives elected under a new constitution that was signed on June 5, 1849, tempered the absolute rule of the Danish monarchs.

The liberal reforms inaugurated in 1849 eventually applied to a smaller, more compact nation. In 1850, after a 2-year revolution, Schleswig-Holstein seceded from Denmark and allied itself with its German-speaking neighbor to the south, Prussia. After several years of indecisive referendums, military interventions, and the politicking of such other European nations as Austria, Schleswig-Holstein was ceded to Prussia in 1866 under the Treaty of Prague.

On July 28, 1866, a new constitution was adopted, but it was more conservative than the earlier one (1849), and granted more power to those who paid the highest taxes—in other words, the landowners.

Throughout the rest of the 19th century, Denmark's conservatives struggled against reform-minded liberals. Conservatives pledged to build up trade incentives and military fortifications around Copenhagen. In the event of war, liberals argued, most of the Danish countryside would be sacrificed to the invaders, and only Copenhagen would be defended.

Members of the left favored social reforms, a downsizing of the Danish army, and an official allegiance to political neutrality. Despite opposition, a process of liberalization continued apace with the changes wrought by the Industrial Revolution. In 1891, a system of old-age pensions was introduced; in 1892 came an early form of health insurance; and in 1899, funds were allocated for the acquisition of farmland by individuals who qualified for assistance from the Danish government.

WORLD WAR I & ECONOMIC CHAOS

When World War I broke out, Denmark found itself on a razor's edge and struggled to remain neutral, but its position astride the shipping lanes favored by both England and Germany made this especially perilous. On August 14, 1914, Germany laid mines in the sea channels of southern Denmark and then strongly implied that Denmark would be well advised to lay other mines in the channels leading toward Copenhagen. Fearing that if they didn't comply, Germany would lay the mines anyway and then commandeer parcels of Danish soil for installation of German naval bases, Denmark began laying mines.

Danish king Christian X had the unfortunate task of phoning his cousin, the king of England, about the situation. England agreed not to interpret Denmark's action as a direct act of hostility. Consequently, all the waters around Denmark were peppered with high-powered explosives, a situation that had a disastrous effect on Danish trade and the Danish treasury. Later, German U-boats sank at least 30% of Denmark's merchant fleet.

Eventually, through cooperation and joint commitments with Sweden and Norway, Denmark managed to retain its fragile hold on wartime neutrality, but at a high price in terms of unemployment, higher taxes, and endless neuroses and self-doubts.

Partly in reaction to the traumas of their untenable situation, the Danes signed a new constitution on June 5, 1915, establishing a two-chamber parliament and granting equal voting rights to men and women. In 1916, a law was passed that compelled industries to insure their workers against accidents. Also in 1916, a financially strapped Denmark concluded a treaty with the United States, selling the Danish West Indies (later known as the U.S. Virgin Islands) for $25 million.

In 1919, a land reform act resulted in the breakup of many large estates, with lands passing into the hands of greater numbers of farmers.

Because Germany was defeated in World War I, many people felt that all of Schleswig should be returned to Denmark and that the details should be hammered out during the Versailles Conference. But in an act that was later interpreted as remarkably callous, Denmark, because of its official neutrality during World War I, was not invited to the conference, despite the extreme losses its navy and merchant marine had suffered. Under pressure, the conventioneers eventually agreed to return North Schleswig, but not South Schleswig or Holstein, to Denmark.

A new treaty was drawn up between Iceland and Denmark in 1918. Although they functioned as separate, sovereign states, the two countries were united under one king, with Iceland under Denmark's protection. Danish ships were appointed as the official inspectors of Icelandic fisheries, and plans were laid for Iceland's eventual independence.

Denmark participated in the creation of the League of Nations and joined it in 1920. A crisis arose when Norway claimed jurisdiction over the territory of Greenland. However, in April 1933, the Permanent Court of International Justice granted Denmark sovereignty over Greenland, nullifying Norway's claim.

Although the Great Depression didn't begin in the United States until October 1929, Denmark was plunged into high levels of unemployment (30%) as early as 1926. Poor harvests and a 1926 tariff imposed on Danish grain by Germany, one of Denmark's largest trading partners, contributed to Denmark's fiscal woes. By 1932, a fiscal collapse of the Danish government seemed imminent. Fueled by the uncertainty, Danish branches of both the Fascist and the Nazi Parties had been established by the mid-1930s, although they remained relatively small. Part of their lack of success derived from the Danish government's policy of forbidding the civilian use of any kind of uniform in public, with the exception of the Boy Scouts. As a result, no mass demonstrations in the style of what the Germans later developed into the Third Reich ever took place on Danish soil.

THE COMING OF HITLER & NAZI OCCUPATION

In May of 1939, Hitler asked Denmark to sign a nonaggression pact. Denmark accepted it; Norway and Sweden did not, and as such, any semblance of a united Scandinavian front collapsed. The pact specified that Denmark and Germany would not go to war with each other for 10 years, and that Denmark would not give aid or assistance to any nation with which Germany was at war. When war broke out in 1939, Denmark declared its neutrality. Denmark's ties with Iceland were severed, and the United States and Great Britain occupied Greenland and the Faroe Islands, respectively.

Despite the nonaggression pact, Nazi forces invaded and occupied Denmark in 1940. In 1943, Hitler sent General Hermann von Hanneken to impose martial law on Denmark and commandeered two Danish destroyers. Danish resistance continued against the German occupying forces, often in the form of sabotage of German-controlled industries and military installations. In many cases, Danish sailors scuttled their own ships to prevent them from falling under Nazi control. Danish Jews and homosexuals were arrested and sent to concentration camps beginning in 1942, but most, aided by the brave Danish people, were able to escape to Sweden. Danish civil servants tended to remain at their posts, as a means of ensuring an orderly administration of the country during terrible times.

In September 1944, many members of the Danish police, suspected (often correctly) of helping the Danish resistance, were imprisoned. The same year, a general strike among the Danes crippled Copenhagen, until the Germans accepted an uneasy compromise, and the Nazi troops became less visible in the capital.

On March 21, 1945, the Gestapo's headquarters (in what had been the Danish headquarters for Shell Oil) were demolished during an Allied air raid, sending most of the Gestapo's archives up in flames, much to the regret of later historians. Later, the Gestapo's Danish strongholds in Odense and Århus were also bombarded.

Beginning in February 1945, as the defeat of Germany appeared imminent, thousands of refugees from Germany poured across the border, seeking safety in Denmark. When Germany surrendered in 1945, British troops occupied most of Denmark. The island of Bornholm, however, was occupied by Soviet troops, who bombed parts of the island in a successful effort to dislodge the occupying Nazi forces. After the war, Denmark joined the United Nations.

POST-WAR DENMARK

After 1945, the Liberal Party under Knud Kristensen assumed control of Denmark. In 1947, Kristensen resigned. The Social Democratic Party, who governed under Frederik IX, then governed the country. The economy remained sluggish until 1948.

In 1949, Denmark joined NATO. In 1953, the Scandinavian Council was formed, composed of Denmark, Norway, Sweden, and Iceland; the council lasted until 1961. Also in 1953, Denmark adopted a new constitution, providing for a single-chamber parliament.

In 1972, Denmark became the sole Nordic member of the EEC. That same year, Queen Margrethe, born in 1940 (the year of the Nazi invasion), became queen of Denmark upon the death of her father, Frederik IX.

In 1982, Denmark seemed to abandon its long-cherished liberalism when it elected Poul Schluter, its first conservative prime minister since 1894. However, by 1989 Denmark was leading the world in the development of a liberal social agenda. It became the first NATO country to allow women to join frontline military units. Later, it became the first country to recognize marriages between partners of the same sex.

The early 1990s were dominated by Denmark's continuing debate over its role (or lack thereof) in the European Union. In 1992, Denmark rejected the Maastricht Treaty, which had established a framework for the European Economic Union. However, in a 1993 referendum Denmark reversed its position (by a close vote), voting to support the Maastricht Treaty and its own limited involvement in it. Denmark presided over the European Union for the first part of that year.

In 1993 Denmark also observed the 50th anniversary of the virtual overnight rescue of 8,000 of its Jewish citizens, who were smuggled out of the country in 1943 into neutral Sweden. That same year the Tivoli Gardens celebrated its 150th year, and *The Little Mermaid* statue, inspired by the famous character from H. C. Andersen's fairy tales, turned 80.

In 1996, Copenhagen was named the "Cultural Capital of Europe." Following in the footsteps of other European cities (including Athens, Florence, Paris, and Madrid), Copenhagen celebrated with a year of festivities. A massive campaign of restorations and new construction revitalized the city.

In May 1998, Denmark held a referendum on extending its ties and connections with the European Union. In a tight race that was close to call, Danes, Greenlanders, and Faroese voted for enlargement of their position within EU. But the margin was extremely narrow, indicating how divided Danes remain on this important issue.

Denmark had a royal wedding on May 14, 2004. His royal highness, Crown Prince Frederik, married Mary Elizabeth Donaldson. She is now HRH Crown Princess of Denmark. The wedding took place in the Copenhagen Cathedral. Copenhagen is now her address, but the Crown Princess of Denmark was born in the Australian state of Tasmania, the daughter of two educators.

3 Danish Cuisine: From *Smørrebrød* to *Rødgrød med Fløde*

Danish food is the best in Scandinavia—in fact, it's among the best in Europe.

Breakfast is usually big and hearty, just right for a day of sightseeing. It usually consists of homemade breads, Danish cheeses, and often a boiled egg or salami. In most establishments you can order bacon and eggs, two items that are well stocked here. However, you may prefer a simple continental breakfast of Danish *wienerbrød* (pastry) and coffee. The "danish" is moist, airy, and rich.

The favorite dish at midday is the ubiquitous *smørrebrød* (open-faced sandwiches)—a national institution. Literally, this means "bread and butter," but the Danes stack this sandwich as if it were the Leaning Tower of Pisa—and then throw in a slice of curled cucumber and bits of parsley or perhaps sliced peaches or a mushroom for added color.

Two of these sandwiches can make a more-than-filling lunch. They're everywhere—from the grandest dining rooms to the lowliest pushcart. Many restaurants offer a wide selection; guests look over a checklist and then mark the ones they want. Some are made with sliced pork (perhaps a prune on top), roast beef with béarnaise sauce and crispy fried bits of onion, or liver paste adorned with an olive or cucumber slice and gelatin made with strong beef stock.

Smørrebrød is often served as an hors d'oeuvre. The most popular, most tempting, and usually most expensive of these delicacies is prepared with tiny Danish shrimp, on which a lemon slice and caviar often perch, perhaps even with fresh dill. The "ugly duckling" of the *smørrebrød* family is anything with a cold sunny-side-up egg on top of it.

For dinner, the Danes tend to keep farmers' hours: 6:30pm is common, although restaurants remain open much later. Many main-course dishes are familiar to North Americans, but they're prepared with a distinct flourish in Denmark—for example, *lever med løg* (liver and fried onion), *bøf* (beef, in a thousand different ways), *lammesteg* (roast lamb), or that old reliable staple, *flæskesteg med rødkål* (roast pork with red cabbage).

Danish chefs are really noted for their fresh fish dishes. The tiny Danish shrimp, *rejer,* are splendid; herring and kippers are also greeted with much enthusiasm. Top-notch fish dishes include *rodspætte* (plaice), *laks* (salmon), *makrel* (mackerel), and *kogt torsk* (boiled cod).

Danish cheese may be consumed at any meal and then eaten again on a late-night *smørrebrød* at Tivoli. Danish bleu is already familiar to most people. For something softer and milder, try Havarti.

Danish specialties that are worth sampling include *frikadeller,* the Danish meatballs or rissoles (prepared in various ways); a Danish omelet with a rasher of bacon covered with chopped chives and served in a skillet; and Danish hamburger patties topped with fried onions and coated with a rich brown gravy.

Two great desserts are Danish apple Charlotte, best when decorated with whipped cream, dried breadcrumbs, and chopped almonds; and *rødgrød med fløde*—basically a jellied fruit-studded juice, served with thick cream.

As for drinks, Carlsberg and Tuborg beer are Denmark's national beverages. A bottle of Pilsener costs about half the price of a stronger export beer with the fancy label. Value-conscious Danes rely on the low-priced *fadøl* (draft beer); visitors on a modest budget might want to do the same.

You may gravitate more toward *aquavit* (schnapps, to the British), which comes from the city of Aalborg in northern Jutland. The Danes, who usually drink it at mealtime, follow it with a beer chaser. Made from a distilling process using potatoes, aquavit should only be served icy cold.

For those with a daintier taste, the world-famous Danish liqueur, Cherry Herring, is a delightful drink; made from cherries, as the name implies, it can be consumed anytime except with meals.

Index

FROMMER'S® NATIONAL PARK GUIDES

Algonquin Provincial Park
Banff & Jasper
Family Vacations in the National
  Parks

Grand Canyon
National Parks of the American
  West
Rocky Mountain

Yellowstone & Grand Teton
Yosemite & Sequoia/Kings
  Canyon
Zion & Bryce Canyon

FROMMER'S® MEMORABLE WALKS

Chicago
London

New York
Paris

San Francisco

FROMMER'S® WITH KIDS GUIDES

Chicago
Las Vegas
New York City

Ottawa
San Francisco
Toronto

Vancouver
Walt Disney World® & Orlando
Washington, D.C.

SUZY GERSHMAN'S BORN TO SHOP GUIDES

Born to Shop: France
Born to Shop: Hong Kong,
  Shanghai & Beijing

Born to Shop: Italy
Born to Shop: London

Born to Shop: New York
Born to Shop: Paris

FROMMER'S® IRREVERENT GUIDES

Amsterdam
Boston
Chicago
Las Vegas
London

Los Angeles
Manhattan
New Orleans
Paris
Rome

San Francisco
Seattle & Portland
Vancouver
Walt Disney World®
Washington, D.C.

FROMMER'S® BEST-LOVED DRIVING TOURS

Austria
Britain
California
France

Germany
Ireland
Italy
New England

Northern Italy
Scotland
Spain
Tuscany & Umbria

THE UNOFFICIAL GUIDES®

Beyond Disney
California with Kids
Central Italy
Chicago
Cruises
Disneyland®
England
Florida
Florida with Kids
Inside Disney

Hawaii
Las Vegas
London
Maui
Mexico's Best Beach Resorts
Mini Las Vegas
Mini Mickey
New Orleans
New York City
Paris

San Francisco
Skiing & Snowboarding in the
  West
South Florida including Miami &
  the Keys
Walt Disney World®
Walt Disney World® for
  Grown-ups
Walt Disney World® with Kids
Washington, D.C.

SPECIAL-INTEREST TITLES

Athens Past & Present
Cities Ranked & Rated
Frommer's Best Day Trips from London
Frommer's Best RV & Tent Campgrounds
  in the U.S.A.
Frommer's Caribbean Hideaways
Frommer's China: The 50 Most Memorable Trips
Frommer's Exploring America by RV
Frommer's Gay & Lesbian Europe
Frommer's NYC Free & Dirt Cheap

Frommer's Road Atlas Europe
Frommer's Road Atlas France
Frommer's Road Atlas Ireland
Frommer's Wonderful Weekends from
  New York City
The New York Times' Guide to Unforgettable
  Weekends
Retirement Places Rated
Rome Past & Present

Travel Tip: He who finds the best hotel deal has more to spend on facials involving knobbly vegetables.

Hello, the Roaming Gnome here. I've been nabbed from the garden and taken round the world. The people who took me are so terribly clever. They find the best offerings on Travelocity. For very little cha-ching. And that means I get to be pampered and exfoliated till I'm pink as a bunny's doodah.

travelocity®

1-888-TRAVELOCITY / travelocity.com / America Online Keyword: Travel

Travel Tip: Make sure there's customer service for any change of plans — involving friendly natives, for example.

One can plan and plan, but if you don't book with the right people you can't seize le moment and canoodle with the poodle named Pansy. I, for one, am all for fraternizing with the locals. Better yet, if I need to extend my stay and my gnome nappers are willing, it can all be arranged through the 800 number at, oh look, how convenient, the lovely company coat of arms.

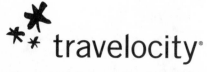

1-888-TRAVELOCITY / travelocity.com / America Online Keyword: Travel